Oman
& the United
Arab Emirates

Lou Callan
Gordon Robison

LONELY PLANET PUBLICATIONS
Melbourne • Oakland • London • Paris

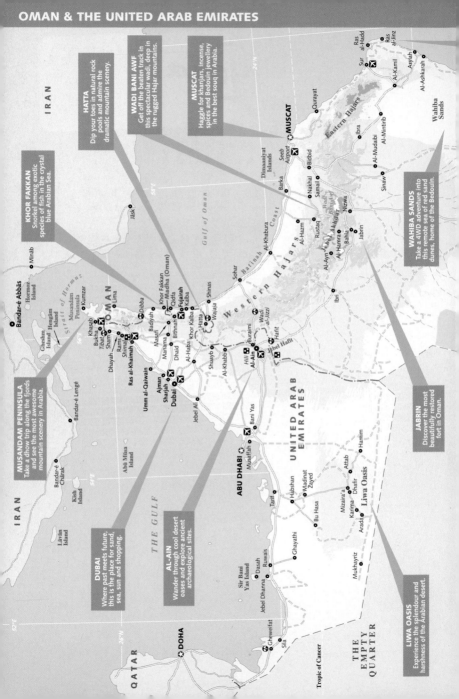

OMAN & THE UNITED ARAB EMIRATES

HATTA
Dip your toes in natural rock pools and admire the dramatic mountain scenery.

WADI BANI AWF
Get off the beaten track in this spectacular wadi, deep in the rugged Hajar mountains.

MUSCAT
Haggle for khanjars, incense, spices and Bedouin jewellery in the best souq in Arabia.

KHOR FAKKAN
Snorkel among exotic species of fish in the crystal blue Arabian Sea.

MUSANDAM PENINSULA
Take a dhow trip along the fjords and see the most awesome mountain scenery in Arabia.

WAHIBA SANDS
Take a 4WD adventure into this remote sea of red sand dunes, home of the Bedouin.

JABRIN
Discover the most beautifully restored fort in Oman.

DUBAI
Where past meets future, this is the place for sand, sea, sun and shopping.

AL-AIN
Wander through cool desert oases and explore ancient archaeological sites.

LIWA OASIS
Experience the splendour and harshness of the Arabian desert.

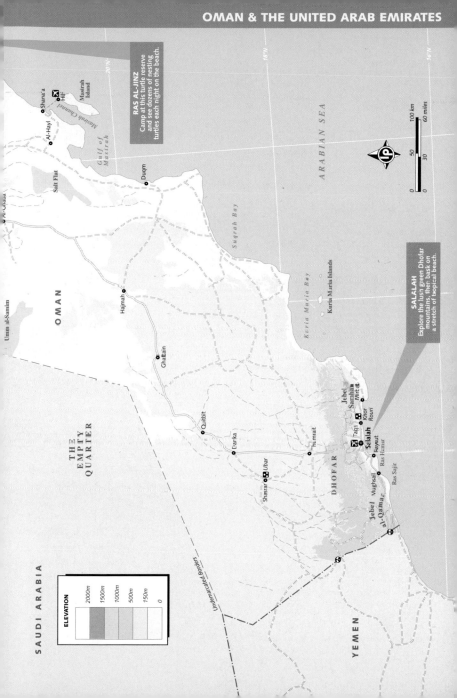

RAS AL-JINZ
Camp at this turtle reserve and see dozens of nesting turtles each night on the beach.

SALALAH
Explore the lush green Dhofar mountains, then bask on a stretch of tropical beach.

ARABIAN SEA

OMAN

SAUDI ARABIA

THE EMPTY QUARTER

YEMEN

DHOFAR

Gulf of Masirah

Suqrah Bay

Kuria Muria Bay

Kuria Muria Islands

Masirah Island

Masirah Channel

Umm al-Samim

Al-Ghaba

Shana'a
Hilf
Al-Hayl
Salt Flat
Duqm
Hajmah
Ghaftain
Qitbit
Tharka
Thumrait
Shasrar
Ubar
Taqa
Khor Rouri
Jebel Samhan Mtns
Salalah
Fayout
Ras Hamar
Wughsail
Jebel al-Qamar
Ras Sajir

Undemarcated Borders

ELEVATION

2000m
1500m
1000m
500m
150m
0

100 km
60 miles

0 30 50

20°N

18°N

16°N

Oman & the United Arab Emirates
1st edition – July 2000

Published by
Lonely Planet Publications Pty Ltd ABN 36 005 607 983
90 Maribyrnong St, Footscray, Victoria 3011, Australia

Lonely Planet Offices
Australia Locked Bag 1, Footscray, Victoria 3011
USA 150 Linden St, Oakland, CA 94607
UK 10a Spring Place, London NW5 3BH
France 1 rue du Dahomey, 75011 Paris

Photographs
Many of the images in this guide are available for licensing from
Lonely Planet Images.
W www.lonelyplanetimages.com

Front cover photograph
Wahiba Sands, Oman (Christine Osborne)

ISBN 1 86450 130 8

Contents – Text

GETTING THERE & AWAY 109

GETTING AROUND 111

MUSCAT 114

NORTH-WEST OMAN 134

NORTH-EAST OMAN 153

SOUTHERN OMAN 161

MUSANDAM PENINSULA 172

THE UNITED ARAB EMIRATES

THE NORTHERN EMIRATES
264

THE EAST COAST
286

LANGUAGE
296

GLOSSARY
304

INDEX
315

Contents – Maps

OMAN

UNITED ARAB EMIRATES

MAPS

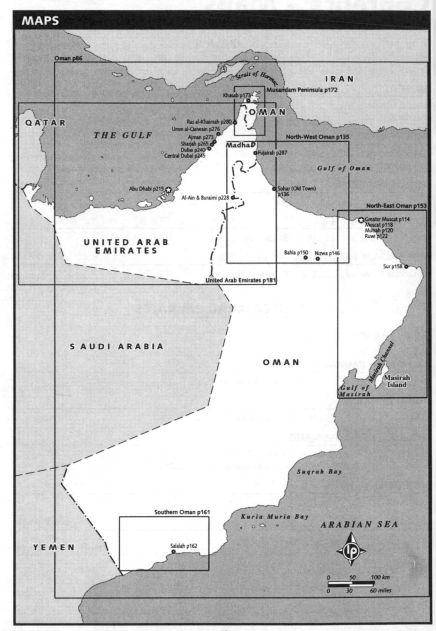

The Authors

Lou Callan

After completing a degree in languages, Lou wandered from publishing pillar to printing post while completing further study in publishing and editing. After lots of long lunches and strenuous book launch parties as Publicity Manager at Oxford University Press Australia, she found work as a contributing editor on *Australian Bookseller & Publisher*. With an affinity for languages and an itchiness for travel, Lou fell into the job of phrasebooks editor at Lonely Planet in 1994. In 1998, after a brief stint as guidebook editor, she packed up and followed her husband Tony to the red dunes of Al-Ain in the UAE for a couple of very hot years. As a natural progression, Lou found herself writing this book along with LP's *Dubai City Guide*. She also updated the Oman & UAE chapters of *Middle East* (3rd edition).

Gordon Robison

Gordon Robison was raised in Vermont and Maine in northeastern USA. He began to travel extensively while still a student and began writing for Lonely Planet in 1988. For LP, Gordon wrote both editions of *Arab Gulf States*, and has co-authored or contributed material to *Middle East*, *USA* and *West Asia on a shoestring*.

From 1988 to 1994 Gordon was a freelance journalist based in Cairo where he reported regularly for the American ABC Radio News. Since 1996 he has lived in Atlanta, where he is a producer with CNN International. Gordon is married to Dona Stewart. They have two children: Halle, who frequently accompanies her father on LP research trips, and Mallory, who doesn't know it yet, but will.

FROM LOU CALLAN

For their invaluable help during the research of this book and for putting up with all my questions and phone calls, I'd like to thank the following people: David Whitfield in Muscat; Egbert van Meggelen at Abu Dhabi National Hotels Company; Abdullah Mohammed al-Amry at the Oman embassy in Abu Dhabi; Ali bin Amer Al Kiyumi at the Ministry of Regional Municipalities & Environment in Muscat; Tarig Awad al-Jabry, Mohammed Rafi-Uz-Zaman and Mansour Ahmed Abood at Al-Ain Municipality; Alistair MacKenzie and Tim Binks at Explorer Publishing in Dubai; Peter Ochs and Christopher Beale in Muscat; Naji Alaeddine and Loay M Shadid. Lonely Planet's Melbourne staff also did a wonderful job turning this pile of words into a book. Thanks to

Isabelle Young and Anna Judd for their work on the manuscript and maps, and to Michelle Glynn for holding my hand throughout the whole process.

Extra special thanks go to Tony Cleaver, my tireless travel companion and darling husband, whose help with this book was indispensable (not to mention his help in digging our 4WD out of a few rough patches).

This Book

This book was based on the Oman and United Arab Emirates chapters of the 2nd edition of Lonely Planet's *Arab Gulf States*, which was researched and written by Gordon Robison. This new guide to Oman and the UAE was researched and written by Lou Callan.

From the Publisher

This first edition of Oman & the United Arab Emirates was edited and proofed in Lonely Planet's Melbourne office by Isabelle Young, with assistance from John Hinman, Dan Goldberg, Anne Mulvaney and Adam Ford. Anna Judd was the coordinating designer responsible for maps and layout. The illustrations were drawn by Ann Jeffree, Trudi Canavan and Verity Campbell, and the cover was designed by Vicki Beale. Katie Butterworth produced the climate charts and Quentin Frayne put together the Language chapter.

Acknowledgments

Many thanks to the following travellers who used *Arab Gulf States* and wrote to us with helpful hints, useful advice and interesting anecdotes about travelling in Oman and the UAE:

AF Gastaldo, AF Siraa, Abbas Farmand, Alain Morel, Alan Toms, Amy Furtado, Andrew Moss, Andrew Thorburn, Andy Hurst, Anja Nolte, Annie Graham, Ben Samuel, Bert Ververer, Brian Yates, Caroline Williams, Chris Lane, Chris Watts, DF Inglis, Dan Gamber, David Rubin, Dr JV Leonard, Dr Jacques De Ridder, Dr Michael Haisch, Dr Richard Beal, EE Atkins, Eric Hohmann, Ewen Donnelly, GH Peters, Georg Nikolaus Garlichs, George Joachim, George Moore, Gokhan Gungor, Graham Egerton, Harry Bonning, Harry Clark, Hope Rodefer, Ilja van Roon, Irmgard Dommel, J Saint, James Wallace, Jason Mountney, Javad Faharzadeh, Jens Baranowski, Jill Stockbridge, Joachim Behrmann, John Jacobs, John Pitman, Kay McDivitt, Kevin Troy, Klaus & Marion Hempfing, Linda Johnson, Lisa Martin, Luigi Vallero, M Carson, Manuel Wedemeyer, Maria Tarrant, Mark Hunt, Maryam Chabastari, Matt Birch, Matthew A Hadlock, Matty Cameron, Maureen Roult, Michael John Brown, Mirjam Coumans, Nicky McLean, Norman Sheppard, P Jerrett, Patric Colquhoun, Patricia Bulat, Paul Sechi, Peter Gray, Pia Kokkarinen, Rainer Sittenthaler, Ralph Lawson, Reinhard Fay, Ritchie Anderson, Robert Maitland, Robert Read, Roger Brand, Ruud Verkerk, Sandie Gustus, Sarah Dewes, Shailendra Shukla, Shona Fisher, Sruart Hales, Steve Rothman, Tamsin Turner, Tim Jessop, Tim Pritchard, Toby Hartnell, Tony Revel, Tony Troughear, Valkan Farkas, Virgil Williams, Warren J Iliff and William Kendrick.

Foreword

ABOUT LONELY PLANET GUIDEBOOKS

The story begins with a classic travel adventure: Tony and Maureen Wheeler's 1972 journey across Europe and Asia to Australia. Useful information about the overland trail did not exist at that time, so Tony and Maureen published the first Lonely Planet guidebook to meet a growing need.

From a kitchen table, then from a tiny office in Melbourne (Australia), Lonely Planet has become the largest independent travel publisher in the world, an international company with offices in Melbourne, Oakland (USA), London (UK) and Paris (France).

Today Lonely Planet guidebooks cover the globe. There is an ever-growing list of books and there's information in a variety of forms and media. Some things haven't changed. The main aim is still to help make it possible for adventurous travellers to get out there – to explore and better understand the world.

At Lonely Planet we believe travellers can make a positive contribution to the countries they visit – if they respect their host communities and spend their money wisely. Since 1986 a percentage of the income from each book has been donated to aid projects and human rights campaigns.

Updates Lonely Planet thoroughly updates each guidebook as often as possible. This usually means there are around two years between editions, although for more unusual or more stable destinations the gap can be longer. Check the imprint page (following the colour map at the beginning of the book) for publication dates.

Between editions up-to-date information is available in two free newsletters – the paper *Planet Talk* and email *Comet* (to subscribe, contact any Lonely Planet office) – and on our Web site at www.lonelyplanet.com. The *Upgrades* section of the Web site covers a number of important and volatile destinations and is regularly updated by Lonely Planet authors. *Scoop* covers news and current affairs relevant to travellers. And, lastly, the *Thorn Tree* bulletin board and *Postcards* section of the site carry unverified, but fascinating, reports from travellers.

Correspondence The process of creating new editions begins with the letters, postcards and emails received from travellers. This correspondence often includes suggestions, criticisms and comments about the current editions. Interesting excerpts are immediately passed on via newsletters and the Web site, and everything goes to our authors to be verified when they're researching on the road. We're keen to get more feedback from organisations or individuals who represent communities visited by travellers.

Lonely Planet gathers information for everyone who's curious about the planet – and especially for those who explore it first-hand. Through guidebooks, phrasebooks, activity guides, maps, literature, newsletters, image library, TV series and Web site we act as an information exchange for a worldwide community of travellers.

Research Authors aim to gather sufficient practical information to enable travellers to make informed choices and to make the mechanics of a journey run smoothly. They also research historical and cultural background to help enrich the travel experience and allow travellers to understand and respond appropriately to cultural and environmental issues.

Authors don't stay in every hotel because that would mean spending a couple of months in each medium-sized city and, no, they don't eat at every restaurant because that would mean stretching belts beyond capacity. They do visit hotels and restaurants to check standards and prices, but feedback based on readers' direct experiences can be very helpful.

Many of our authors work undercover, others aren't so secretive. None of them accept freebies in exchange for positive write-ups. And none of our guidebooks contain any advertising.

Production Authors submit their raw manuscripts and maps to offices in Australia, USA, UK or France. Editors and cartographers – all experienced travellers themselves – then begin the process of assembling the pieces. When the book finally hits the shops, some things are already out of date, we start getting feedback from readers and the process begins again ...

WARNING & REQUEST

Things change – prices go up, schedules change, good places go bad and bad places go bankrupt – nothing stays the same. So, if you find things better or worse, recently opened or long since closed, please tell us and help make the next edition even more accurate and useful. We genuinely value all the feedback we receive. A well-travelled team reads and acknowledges every letter, postcard and email and ensures that every morsel of information finds its way to the appropriate authors, editors and cartographers for verification.

Everyone who writes to us will find their name in the next edition of the appropriate guidebook. They will also receive the latest issue of *Planet Talk*, our quarterly printed newsletter, or *Comet*, our monthly email newsletter. Subscriptions to both newsletters are free. The very best contributions will be rewarded with a free guidebook.

Excerpts from your correspondence may appear in new editions of Lonely Planet guidebooks, the Lonely Planet Web site, *Planet Talk* or *Comet*, so please let us know if you *don't* want your letter published or your name acknowledged.

Send all correspondence to the Lonely Planet office closest to you:

Australia: Locked Bag 1, Footscray, Victoria 3011
USA: 150 Linden St, Oakland, CA 94607
UK: 10A Spring Place, London NW5 3BH
France: 1 rue du Dahomey, 75011 Paris

Or email us at: talk2us@lonelyplanet.com.au

For news, views and updates see our Web site: www.lonelyplanet.com

HOW TO USE A LONELY PLANET GUIDEBOOK

The best way to use a Lonely Planet guidebook is any way you choose. At Lonely Planet we believe the most memorable travel experiences are often those that are unexpected, and the finest discoveries are those you make yourself. Guidebooks are not intended to be used as if they provide a detailed set of infallible instructions!

Contents All Lonely Planet guidebooks follow roughly the same format. The Facts about the Destination chapters or sections give background information ranging from history to weather. Facts for the Visitor gives practical information on issues like visas and health. Getting There & Away gives a brief starting point for researching travel to and from the destination. Getting Around gives an overview of the transport options when you arrive.

The peculiar demands of each destination determine how subsequent chapters are broken up, but some things remain constant. We always start with background, then proceed to sights, places to stay, places to eat, entertainment, getting there and away, and getting around information – in that order.

Heading Hierarchy Lonely Planet headings are used in a strict hierarchical structure that can be visualised as a set of Russian dolls. Each heading (and its following text) is encompassed by any preceding heading that is higher on the hierarchical ladder.

Entry Points We do not assume guidebooks will be read from beginning to end, but that people will dip into them. The traditional entry points are the list of contents and the index. In addition, however, some books have a complete list of maps and an index map illustrating map coverage.

There may also be a colour map that shows highlights. These highlights are dealt with in greater detail in the Facts for the Visitor chapter, along with planning questions and suggested itineraries. Each chapter covering a geographical region usually begins with a locator map and another list of highlights. Once you find something of interest in a list of highlights, turn to the index.

Maps Maps play a crucial role in Lonely Planet guidebooks and include a huge amount of information. A legend is printed on the back page. We seek to have complete consistency between maps and text, and to have every important place in the text captured on a map. Map key numbers usually start in the top left corner.

Although inclusion in a guidebook usually implies a recommendation we cannot list every good place. Exclusion does not necessarily imply criticism. In fact there are a number of reasons why we might exclude a place – sometimes it is simply inappropriate to encourage an influx of travellers.

Introduction

The Arabian peninsula has always evoked romantic notions of deserts, ancient cultures and the Bedouin eking out a harsh existence in a rugged and hostile landscape. If you want to see date palm oases, loping camels, burning frankincense, black-shrouded women, bustling market places, Arabian horses in flight across a sea of dunes, you won't be disappointed. But Oman and the UAE have a lot more to offer the visitor and most people will be surprised at the range of attractions. Best of all, compared with Egypt and much of the rest of the Mediterranean Middle East, Oman (especially) and the UAE remain appealingly untrodden.

Although just about everyone knows Dubai as a stopover (and duty-free haven) on long-haul routes between Europe/North America and Asia or Africa, few people realise how accessible Oman is. Muscat is just a short hop from Dubai and a cross-border agreement means you can pass between the two countries without needing a second visa. It is hard to imagine now that for the

first half of the 20th century Oman was virtually closed to outsiders. Fortunately, all this is no longer the case and in the last decade or so, the country has opened its arms wide to tourism.

The UAE, too, has opened up to tourism in a way that would have been unimaginable a few decades ago. Sun, sea and sand package tours are fiercely promoted by local and overseas travel agents, and are especially popular with visitors from Europe and the CIS. Because of the time frame that most of these packages are squeezed into, many visitors only stay a few days, and few people venture beyond the main cities except for perhaps a camel ride or a drive in the desert. However, the great number of attractions that both Oman and the UAE have to offer warrant more than just a two- or three-day stopover.

In the UAE, for example, you can see archaeological sites dating back to the 3rd and 4th millenniums BC. Evidence of the 7th century AD Islamic conquests can also be

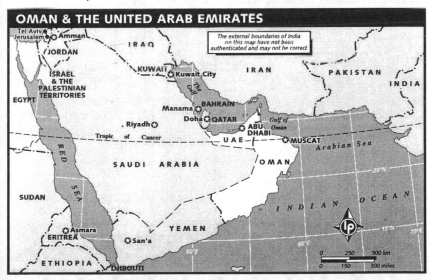

OMAN & THE UNITED ARAB EMIRATES

13

seen. Oman's greatest architectural heritage are its hundreds of forts, many of which have been painstakingly restored.

Don't think that barren and desolate are the only words to describe the landscape. Oman and the northern part of the UAE are home to one of the most mountainous regions of Arabia. Dramatic rocky peaks preside over fairy-tale villages, waterholes and caves. To appreciate these stunning landscapes, there are plenty of challenging and not-so-challenging off-road expeditions. Rockclimbing and mountain trekking are not activities usually associated with Oman or the UAE, but these pastimes are becoming more popular.

The coastlines of the Musandam peninsula (an enclave of Oman jutting into the Strait of Hormuz) and the east coast of the UAE offer some of the best diving in the world. There are also miles and miles of white sands and crystal clear waters in Oman and the UAE – perfect for swimming, snorkelling, camping or just enjoying the view.

And if you want to romp in sand dunes you've definitely come to the right place. Liwa oasis in southern UAE and the Wahiba

Sands in Oman have some of the most spectacular dunes in the region, and can be explored by camel or 4WD. Spending a night under the stars in the desert and enjoying a traditional feast will give you a feel for how the Bedouin, nomadic desert dwellers of this region, have lived for thousands of years.

Although the original inhabitants of the region are the Bedouin, Oman and UAE have also been the stomping ground of many different cultures over the centuries. Conquering civilisations from Persia, Yemen and Greece have all taken their place in the region at various times in history. Oman's colonisation of Zanzibar has given it strong ties with the people and culture of East Africa. These diverse cultural influences have continued into the modern era. The discovery of oil in the 1960s and the subsequent luxury of being able to bring in foreign labour has meant the arrival of workers from far and wide – Europe, Africa, India, America, Philippines and Pakistan, to name just a few. Needless to say, all these nationalities have had an influence on the culture of the region, in particular on traditional dance and music, food, handicrafts, pastimes and dress.

Facts about the Region

HISTORY

Although the early histories of Oman and the United Arab Emirates (UAE) are similar, their histories from the Islamic era (7th century AD) onwards are surprisingly different. The early history of the two countries is covered in this section; for the history from the Islamic era onwards, see the History sections of the individual country chapters.

Beginnings

It is not known exactly when the region that now covers Oman and the UAE was first settled but archaeological finds dating back to the 4th millennium BC have been discovered around Jebel Hafit, near Al-Ain/Buraimi on the border between Oman and the UAE. The sophisticated structure of the tombs found here indicates that their builders were part of a well-organised society. There is evidence that crops such as wheat, dates, melons and barley were grown at this time as the climate of the Gulf region during this period was much more temperate than it is today.

Around 3000 BC, at the beginning of the Bronze Age, a distinct culture arose near Abu Dhabi in present-day UAE. This culture, called Umm al-Nar after the small island where it was first discovered, thrived for only a few hundred years. Little is known about the Umm al-Nar culture except that archaeological finds such as pottery, beads and daggers link it with civilisations in the Indus Valley (in the subcontinent) and Baluchistan (part of present-day Pakistan and Afghanistan). It is likely that the people of Umm al-Nar relied on fishing for their livelihood, and it seems fairly certain that the culture extended well into the interior and down the coast of what is now Oman. Evidence of the domestication of the camel has also been discovered at Umm al-Nar.

There were also settlements at Badiyah (near Fujairah) and at Rams (near Ras al-Khaimah), both in present-day UAE, during the second half of the 3rd millennium BC.

Beehive-shaped tombs, also from this period, have been found near Ibri in north-western Oman. Findings at these settlements show that their inhabitants had sophisticated cultures, and their wealth was based on trade. Most of the cities of ancient Arabia derived their sometimes considerable wealth from trade – they lay on the main trade routes linking Mesopotamia with the Indus Valley. Due to the demands of trade and export, the Gulf region also became a centre for shipbuilding.

The Magan Empire

Archaeological evidence suggests that an empire called Magan, covering much of present-day northern Oman and the UAE, was an important influence. The Magan appeared in the 3rd millennium BC. Texts dating from the time of King Sargon of Akkad, who reigned over a large area from the Mediterranean to the western Gulf, mention trading with the Magan as early as 2370 BC. The wealth of the Magan empire was based on exploiting the rich veins of copper found in the hills around Sohar on the Batinah Coast of Oman. It came to dominate the ancient world's copper trade, supplying the precious metal to the powerful kingdoms of Elam (in present-day southern Iran) and Sumer (present-day southern Iraq) for weapons. The empire also traded wood and spices from the east coast of Africa and India. Magan was originally part of the Akkadian empire (based near Sumer) but it broke away from Akkad's control in the middle of the 3rd millennium BC establishing itself as an independent power.

Magan's copper mines were based near the towns of Lasail and Arja in present-day Oman and are thought to have produced between 48 and 60 tonnes of copper ore per year until the Middle Ages when the trade finally petered out and the region's economy declined.

Archaeological remains on the north-eastern outskirts of the city of Dubai in the UAE suggest that the Magan empire stretched at least as far as the Gulf. Pearling was a major activity in the Dubai area, and it is likely that the trade in pearls to Mesopotamia was an important source of wealth.

The Magan empire went into a decline in the 2nd millennium BC, possibly as a result of the increasing desertification of the area. The growing importance of iron in making weapons and tools may have also contributed to its decline.

The Frankincense Trade

In ancient times, southern Arabia was the source of two very important commodities: myrrh and frankincense. The trade in incense guaranteed prosperity for southern Arabia until well into the 6th century AD. Myrrh and frankincense are the resins of certain types of trees that grow only on the southern coast of Arabia and northern coast of the Horn of Africa, and the area that now makes up much of Yemen and southern Oman was the source of most of the world's frankincense.

Sea and land trading routes developed, first using donkeys and mules and later camels. The frankincense route ran from the Dhofar region (in southern Oman) and Wadi Hadhramawt (Yemen), through present-day UAE, to the Levant and Europe.

Settlements along the main trading routes became wealthy and powerful. The people of what is now the UAE derived much of their wealth from their location on the main frankincense routes. Ruins from one such settlement can be seen at the village of Shimal, near Ras al-Khaimah on the north-western coast, in the form of a set of 4th-century AD fortifications on a hilltop overlooking the sea.

The frankincense trade not only made southern and eastern Arabia wealthy but it brought its inhabitants into contact with merchants from the Levant, Persia, India and the Mediterranean. While the frankincense trade was at its peak around the 1st century AD, the Greeks turned their interest to the region that is now the northern part of the UAE and became a major cultural influence. Ruins from the 1st century AD, showing strong Hellenistic influences, have been found at Meleiha, about 50km from Sharjah. At Ad-Dour, in the emirate of Umm al-Qaiwain, pottery from Rhodes has been found, and at Tell Abraq, also in Umm al-Qaiwain, there are remains of a 1st-century AD Hellenistic temple.

Frankincense

Dhofar, Oman's southernmost region, is one of the few places in the world where the trees that are the source of frankincense grow. Frankincense is an aromatic gum which is obtained by making incisions in the trunks of trees of certain species of the *Boswellia* genus. These trees grow only in southern Oman, the Wadi Hadhramawt in Yemen and northern Somalia.

The gum has a natural oil content, which means that it burns well. It also has medicinal qualities. This combination and its relative scarcity made it one of the ancient world's most sought after substances. (The frankincense and myrrh offered as gifts to the infant Jesus were, at the time, far more valuable than the gold.) Frankincense became crucial to the religious rites of almost every people in the known world. The temples of Egypt, Jerusalem and Rome were all major customers. Pliny, writing in the 1st century AD, claimed that control of the frankincense trade had made the people of southern Arabia the richest on earth.

At the height of the trade in the 1st century AD, some 3000 tonnes of frankincense was moving each year, mostly by sea, from southern Arabia to Greece and Rome. The trade was centred on Sumhuram, which the Greeks called Moscha and which is now known as Khor Rouri. Today its ruins are a short drive from Salalah, the capital of Dhofar and the second-largest city in present-day Oman. Though it declined after the 3rd century AD, the incense trade kept southern Arabia relatively wealthy well into the 6th century.

Persian Influence

It was not only the Greeks who were enticed to the region by the successful frankincense trade. Control of this rich trade in Arabia was something the Persians also desired. From around 560 BC to about AD 200 the northern parts of the region came under the control of various Persian dynasties. Around 563 BC present-day northern Oman and, possibly, part of present-day UAE, were incorporated into the Achaemenid Persian empire. Later, both Oman and the UAE were dominated by the Sassanian empire of Persia. This empire first appeared in Oman in AD 226.

Not long after gaining control of Oman in the 3rd century AD, the Sassanian invaders were driven out of most of their coastal settlements by migrating tribes, known as the Azd, who came from the Hadhramawt region in present-day Yemen. The Azd are thought to have moved to the coastal regions of Oman when the great dam at Ma'rib in Yemen collapsed. The resulting scarcity of water forced the tribes northwards. The Azd pushed the Persians as far as Sohar then set up their base at Qalhat on the Batinah Coast. The Persians and the Arabs lived together in Oman until the 6th century AD when Islamic tribes forced the Persians out of Oman altogether.

In the 6th century AD, or possibly earlier, the Sassanians settled in what is now the emirate of Ras al-Khaimah in northern UAE and at Al-Qusais and Jumeira in what is now Dubai. The two Sassanian sites in the UAE show that the Persians here were also destroyed by Islamic tribes from the interior, namely the Umayyads, in the 7th century.

The Coming of Islam

The birth of the Prophet Mohammed marked the end of one era and the beginning of another. Mohammed received his first revelation in AD 610 and began to preach publicly three years later. It was only after he and a small band of followers fled Mecca (in what is now Saudi Arabia) for Medina in 622 that Islam became an established faith. From Medina the new religion spread out across the peninsula with remarkable speed between 622 and 632, and within a century Muslim armies had conquered an enormous empire stretching from Spain to India, including Arabia.

In 635, at the dawn of the Islamic era, Dibba (on the east coast of present-day UAE, at the southern edge of Oman's Musandam peninsula) was the site of the battle which traditionally marks the completion of the Islamic conquest of the Arabian peninsula. Tombstones from this battle can still be seen at Dibba.

The histories of Oman and the UAE from the Islamic era onwards are continued in the history sections of the individual country chapters.

GEOLOGY

The Arabian peninsula is thought originally to have been part of a larger landmass that included Africa. A split in this ancient continent created the Afro-Arabian rift system that stretches from the Dead Sea through Jordan and the Red Sea, becoming Africa's Great Rift Valley. As Arabia moved away from Africa, part of this process involved tilting of the peninsula, with the western side rising and the eastern edge dropping in elevation, a process that led to the formation of the Gulf.

Geologists divide this region into two distinct parts: shield and shelf. The shield consists of the volcanic and folded, compressed sedimentary rocks that make up the mountainous areas of the region's north. These mountains consist of layers and layers of rock, formed by the oldest prehistoric ocean floors. The shelf is made up of the lower-lying areas that slope gently away from the shield to the waters of the Gulf and the Arabian Sea. The rocks beneath the sands of the Arabian shelf are mostly sedimentary.

The Hajar mountains which stretch across northern Oman and into the north-eastern areas of the UAE once sat on the ocean floor. They were formed around 70 million years ago when two tectonic plates crashed into one another. One was forced upwards, the other downwards. The edge of the upwards plate created the mountains. Proof that the mountains once rested on the ocean floor lies in the discovery of marine fossils in the foothills of the Hajars, particularly at Fossil Valley near Al-Ain, on the border between Oman and the UAE.

The mountains in the Musandam peninsula in the Strait of Hormuz are 100 to 200 million years old. They were formed by a gradual uplifting, over a much longer period of time than the Hajars. The rocks of Musandam are mainly limestone from the Jurassic era whereas the valleys are of sandstone from the earlier Triassic era. A significant proportion of the Musandam mountains are submerged under water. The valley dividing the Hajars from Musandam is called the Dibba Fault.

Hundreds of millions of years ago, as the shelf was being formed, the Gulf extended much farther west. It was in the waters and, later, marshes of this area that plants, animals and other organic matter died, sank to the bottom and eventually were covered with rock and compressed to form oil.

CLIMATE

From April to October much of the region experiences daytime highs of around 40°C almost daily. In most of the UAE and the north of Oman the humidity during summer is stifling.

The inland desert areas do not have the high humidity of the coastal regions, although it's usually a couple of degrees hotter inland. In the mountainous regions the climate is more temperate. During summer it is often a few degrees cooler than the coast, and in winter it can be quite chilly at night.

Southern Oman catches the monsoon which makes the Dhofar mountains and the low-lying areas around them very lush and green during August and September.

For more details, including climate charts, see the individual country chapters.

ECOLOGY & ENVIRONMENT

Oil and natural gas aside, the Gulf is an area with few natural resources and a fragile ecosystem. The UAE and Oman have been the leaders in the region as regards commitment and action to protect the environment. There are environmental public awareness campaigns as well as a number of government agencies committed to ensuring protection of the environment and of endangered species.

There was a tendency a generation ago, during the region's first rush of wealth, to see the desert as a gigantic rubbish tip. On one level this made sense – for centuries the Bedouin had left their garbage behind them to be consumed by the desert. But that way of life presupposed a society based on very small communities of people who continually moved around and were in harmony with their surroundings. There has been an effort by both governments to make their people more aware that the desert is a fragile resource.

Water is a valuable resource in the desert and it is becoming more scarce. Although Oman still has plenty of underground water reserves and run-off from mountains, most of the water consumed in the UAE comes from desalination plants. With an average annual rainfall of just 100mm, experts estimate that there will be a serious shortage in the next 10 years. Campaigns to encourage people to save water, and to be more careful about how they use it, are now common throughout Oman and the UAE.

The waters of the Gulf are also being treated with greater care today than they were a generation ago. The fishing industry is regulated throughout the area and as is the case with the oil industry all over the world, safety standards are much higher now than they were in the 1960s.

For more details, see National Parks & Reserves in the Facts about Oman chapter, and Ecology & Environment in the Facts about the UAE chapter.

FLORA & FAUNA
Flora

The varied terrain of the region – mountains, deserts, coastal salt flats, gravel plains, dry river beds – makes for an equally wide variety of plants. Many towns at the foothills of the mountainous regions of Oman such as Nizwa, Samail and Ibra, the Buraimi oasis and the east coast towns of the UAE have acres of natural date palm groves which have been supplemented by plantations of

Date Palms

The ubiquitous date palm has always held a vital place in the life of inhabitants of the Arabian peninsula. For centuries dates were one of the staple foods of the Bedouin, along with fish, camel meat and camel milk. There are around 80 different kinds of dates in the region. The reason dates are such a good foodstuff is that they are roughly 70% sugar. This stops the rot and makes the date edible for longer than other tropical fruits.

Dates are harvested by hand in mid- to late summer when they turn from a yellow colour to light brown. The harvester climbs the trunk with the help of a thick rope that wraps around the top of the legs and the trunk of the tree. He then leans back against the rope and hacks away at the cluster of dates with a long, curved knife. The dates are then spread on a mat on the ground to ripen further in the sun. After a few days to a week they take on their wrinkly appearance and are taken to the souq to sell. Al-Ain souq in the UAE or Nizwa souq in Oman are good places to see the various types of dates piled up for sale. Most forts in the region have a date storage room with channels for collecting the date syrup.

Apart from traditionally providing a major foodstuff, the date palm is used to make all kinds of useful items. Its trunk was used to make columns and ceilings for houses while its fronds were used to make roofs and walls (called *areesh*). Date palms provided the only shade in desert oases. Livestock were fed with its seeds and it was burned as fuel. The palm frond was, and still is, used to make bags, mats, boats (called *shasha*), shelters, brooms and fans.

banana palms, papaya trees, lime trees and coconut palms.

The flat-topped, scraggly-looking tree which you see in most wadis (seasonal river beds) is the hardy acacia tree. In the foothills of the Hajars around Al-Ain and Buraimi in the east of the UAE, in the mountainous north of the UAE and in the Musandam peninsula of Oman, you will also see the *ghaf*, a large tree that looks a bit like a weeping willow. It survives well because its roots stretch down for about 80m, allowing it to tap into deep water reserves. You will recognise the ghaf by its lower foliage which is usually trimmed flat by grazing camels and goats.

In the cooler months, wildflowers add a welcome splash of colour. Near the coast you may see the yellow and dark-red desert hyacinth. The *qafas* is a yellow-flowering shrub which you'll find in some wadis during spring.

The Dhofar mountains in the south of Oman are home to the frankincense tree, *Boswellia sacra*. Frankincense trees grow about 4m high and are rather gnarled and dry in appearance. It is from the sap of these trees that frankincense is derived.

The desert areas of the interior of Oman and most of the southern regions of the UAE are home to wild grasses and the occasional date palm oasis. Generally, though, they are rather bleak and featureless and only a naturalist with some experience of desert flora could find much to enthuse over.

Fauna

You're unlikely to see anything more exciting than camels and goats on your travels in Oman and the UAE. Although the desert teems with animals, many are nocturnal and all are hard to spot.

A number of species have evolved to meet the demands of desert life, including the sand cat, the sand fox and the desert hare. All of these animals have unusually large ears compared to their non-desert-dwelling relatives, and tufts of hair on their feet. The large ears, full of blood vessels, allow the animals to lose heat, while the hair on their feet enables them to cross dunes and other areas of loose sand with ease. (The tufts act like snow shoes so that the animal doesn't sink into the sand too much, and walking across the sand does not use up too much energy; they also protect the animal's tender footpads from the heat of the ground.)

Ship of the Desert

The camel, referred to as *ata Allah* (the gift of God) by the Bedouin is well adapted to life in the desert: it's able to survive without water for long periods of time, it can digest just about anything, from cardboard boxes to old shoes, and it has enormous stamina. The Arabian camel has one hump. When food and water are scarce the camel draws its energy from the supply of fat and oils which is stored in the hump.

The Bedouin owe much to the camel. As well as providing transport, the camel was a source of milk and meat. Its wool was used for weaving rugs, bags and tents, its manure was used for fuel and its skin for water and milk containers.

Today in Oman and the UAE you are considered to be preserving the tradition and pride of the country if you own and breed camels and there are plenty of camel owners in the region. The government provides subsidies to camel owners and breeders, and there is even a Directorate General of Camels' Affairs within the Omani government. Camel racing is a popular sport in the region, and winners of camel races receive large sums of money.

One of the best camel markets in the region is in Buraimi on the Oman-UAE border. A non-racing yearling camel goes for about Dh1000 (US$270) while a full-grown male fetches around Dh5000. A good, pure-bred racing camel can be worth as much as US$1 million.

The camels you see in the deserts along the roadside are always owned by somebody. There are no wild camels in the region, although there may be a few who have strayed too far from the farm.

As any early morning visit to the fish markets will show, the waters of the Gulf and the Arabian Sea teem with fish life. Diners will be most familiar with the *hamour*, a species of groper, but the area is also home to an extraordinary range of tropical fish and several species of sharks. The Gulf of Oman is home to dolphins, as well as a number of whale species from December to March when they come to breed.

Several species of turtles, notably the endangered green turtle and hawksbill turtle, nest along the east coast of Oman. Ras al-Jinz, the stretch of coast with the most dense population of nesting turtles, is now protected by the government, and you need a permit to visit the turtle nesting sites. For more details, see that section in the North-West Oman chapter.

The UAE and Oman provide a stopover for thousands of species of migrating birds on the path between Europe, Asia and Africa, and studies show that the variety of bird life is increasing each year, possibly because of the increase in green areas such as parks, golf courses and hotel grounds. In the UAE over 400 species have been recorded so far, 80 of which breed locally. These include the crab plover, the socotra cormorant, the purple sunbird, the European bee-eater and a variety of predatory birds. It's not hard to see why this region has become the most popular destination in Arabia for bird-watchers.

Endangered Species

Most of the region's indigenous species are endangered. Over the last 50 years or so, species that were once plentiful throughout Arabia, such as the houbara bustard (sort of a wild desert chicken), sand cats, Gordon's wildcat and the caracal lynx have been hunted nearly to extinction. Although the hunting of endangered species has been banned in most of the region and endangered species such as the Arabian oryx are protected, poaching still occurs. The process of educating the population to no longer hunt the animals they have hunted for centuries is a slow one.

The Arabian oryx has long been on the Arabian peninsula's endangered species list, and was brought to the brink of extinction in the late 1970s and early 1980s. The Omani government has an extensive program to revive oryx herds and there is also a breeding reservation in the emirate of Sharjah in the UAE. The oryx remains endangered but is no longer in imminent danger of extinction. Oman also runs a breeding centre for Arabian tahr (a kind of wild goat) and has been instrumental in helping to protect Arabian gazelles, Arabian wolves, striped hyenas, Arabian leopards and the sooty falcon, a species of grey falcon which nests in Oman every year in April and May. The Nubian ibex, a member of the goat family and larger than the tahr, is also protected. It's mainly found in the southern region of Oman.

National Parks & Reserves

Under Sultan Qaboos, Oman has one of the most environment and conservation-aware governments in the region, and there are a number of nature reserves and conservation centres scattered around the country. These include the Arabian Oryx Sanctuary and the Ras al-Jinz turtle sanctuary. The UAE has a few breeding centres and nature reserves, including the Breeding Centre for Endangered Species in Sharjah and Sir Bani Yas Island off the south-western coast of Abu Dhabi. However, with a few exceptions, these places are generally not open to the public. See the individual country chapters for more details.

GOVERNMENT & POLITICS

Both Oman and the UAE are monarchies. Rulers in the region require the support of their family and the public, in particular the powerful ruling families. They are accessible to any and all of their subjects in ways that would be unthinkable almost anywhere else in the world. They regularly sit in a *majlis* (literally 'meeting place' or 'reception room'), when any citizen can come and present a petition or discuss a problem. This means that rulers are not as detached from their citizens as many in the West imagine.

Access, however, should not be confused with activism. Politics, in the Western sense of the term, is essentially nonexistent in Oman and the UAE. TV and newspaper accounts of meetings of the cabinet or the local consultative council never impart any of the substance of whatever discussions may have taken place, and sometimes they do not even mention what decisions, if any, were actually made. As for publicly criticising a governmental decision or action, as is common in the West, it just doesn't happen.

ARTS

Traditional music and dance is one of the most recognised art forms of the region. Practically every event, religious or secular, and collective emotion can be expressed through it.

For details about the region's arts and crafts, including silver jewellery, *khanjars* (Omani daggers), palm frond weaving and textiles, see the special section 'Shopping' at the end of Regional Facts for the Visitor chapter.

Music

Traditional music of the region is almost always performed as a group effort, by members of the same tribe or clan. Over time the tribal chants and rhythms of the Bedouin absorbed characteristics from the music and song of the many other cultures that had an influence on the region. The dominant influence comes from East Africa with which Oman has a long trading history. The many Persians who settled in the UAE and northern Oman have also had a marked influence on the music of the region.

Although you may still come across traditional Bedouin music, either on the radio or television or being performed during festivals, most of the music currently produced is Arabic pop – formulaic pop songs which mostly tell the story of lost or unrequited love. Sweeping string sounds in this modern form of Arabic music give the songs a very Middle Eastern feel. You will hear this music being pumped out of car stereos or local television and radio stations.

Musical Instruments Percussion instruments include the *alrahmani* (bass drum) and *alkassir* (treble drum), both made of goatskin, as well as the *daf* which is like a tambourine. The *buq* is a large shell that is played by blowing. The *burghoum*, a wind instrument, is made from an oryx or deer horn and originated in Zanzibar, and the *mimzar* is a reed instrument made of wood which looks and sounds like an oboe.

The six-stringed *tambura* is probably the best known instrument. It is African in origin and is like a harp in structure. The strings are stretched between a wooden base and a bow-shaped neck. The base is covered with camel skin and the strings are plucked with sheep horns. It has a deep and resonant sound, similar to that of a violin.

The bagpipes have become a feature of music played at festivals and celebrations such as National days – an indication of the extent of British influence in the region. A regional variation of the bagpipes is also used in Oman and UAE. The sack part is made from a goat skin, and there are two pipes which protrude from where the front legs of the goat would have been. The instrument looks very strange indeed as it retains its goat shape. It produces a much rougher, shriller sound than Scottish bagpipes.

Although the *oud* is common to much of the Middle East, this Arabic musical instrument is considered one of the traditional instruments of the region. Like a cross between a guitar and a bazouki to look at, the 10- or sometimes 12-stringed oud has a delicate and lilting sound, much like a harpsichord or mandolin. The oud is believed to be descended from the *barbat*, an ancient Persian instrument which was similar in design.

Dance & Song

Traditional dances and song are inspired by the environment – the sea, desert and mountains. Sometimes they have religious themes, but they can also be homages to family unity, war and victory. Contact with other cultures through the region's trading history has brought many other influences to the art form. East African rhythms and percussion are a prominent feature of music of the region.

Although traditional dance is alive and well in Oman, displays in the UAE are generally confined to special events and celebrations such as weddings. It is unlikely that you will come across a spontaneous music recital in the UAE as you might in Oman.

One of the most popular dances is the Liwa which is performed to a rapid tempo and loud drum beat. It was brought to the region by East African slaves and is traditionally sung in Swahili. The Ayyalah is a typical Bedouin dance. These dances traditionally praise courage and strength. The Ayyalah is performed throughout the Gulf but Oman and the UAE have their own variation. In this variation, which is performed to a simple drum beat, anywhere between 25 and 200 men stand with their arms linked in two rows facing each other. They wave walking sticks or swords in front of them and sway back and forth, the two rows taking it in turn to sing. Basically it is a war dance and the words expound the virtues of courage and bravery in battle. At the beginning of the dance both rows are the aggressors but as the dance progresses one of the rows becomes submissive and gives in to defeat by lowering their heads as if in surrender.

The Na'ashat is danced by young girls who must have long hair to perform it properly. In this dance the girls stand in a row with their right hands on their chests and toss their heads from side to side, while swaying back and forth. The movement is done to the slow beat of drum.

SOCIETY & CONDUCT
Traditional Culture

In the more remote areas of the region, especially in Oman, life appears not to be too far removed from the way it was before the discovery of oil brought money and modernity. People grow their own vegetables, slaughter their own goats and fetch water from a well. Some build their own houses. The only modern amenity which has found its way to all

[Continued on page 27]

TRADITIONAL ARCHITECTURE

The traditional architecture of the region was influenced by the demands of the environment, the teachings of Islam and the social structure of the town. There were four categories of buildings – religious (mosques), residential, defence (forts and watchtowers) and commercial (souqs).

They used the materials that were readily available locally. In the coastal regions this was usually coral which was quarried from offshore reefs and cut into stone for building. Sometimes this shell rock was combined with gypsum. The Shaikh Saeed House in Dubai and the heritage buildings in Sharjah, both in the UAE, are examples of constructions using a mixture of coral and gypsum.

In inland areas of Oman and the UAE houses were built of mud, wood and palm fronds. There are examples of these constructions in the Buraimi oasis on the border of Oman and the UAE, as well as in villages of the interior of Oman such as Al-Hamra, Bahla and Al-Kamil. In the mountainous regions of Oman, such as the Musandam peninsula and the Jebel Akhdar, houses were built from stone slabs and boulders.

Mosques

A mosque is fundamentally a simple structure, made up of a few basic elements. The most visible of these is the minaret, the tower from which the call to prayer is issued five times a day. Most mosques have at least one minaret, which can be plain or ornate. The first minarets were not built until the early 8th century, some 70 years after the Prophet's death. The idea for the minarets may have originated from the bell towers that Muslim armies found attached to some of the churches they converted into mosques during the early years of Islam.

Right: Mosques come in shapes and sizes, from his tiny Omani mosque at Kalbuh (between Muscat and Mutrah) to Sharjah's King Faisal Mosque, said to be able to accommodate 3000 worshippers.

DAVID PETHERBRIDGE

VERITY CAMPBELL

A mosque must also have a *mihrab*, a niche in the wall facing Mecca which indicates the *qibla*, the direction believers must face while praying. Like minarets, mihrabs can be simple or elaborate, and they are thought to have been introduced into Islamic architecture around the beginning of the 8th century.

The *minbar* (also pronounced 'mimbar') dates from the Prophet's lifetime. The minbar is a pulpit, traditionally reached by three steps.

In addition, a mosque needs to have a water supply so that worshippers can perform the ablutions that are required before they can go in to pray.

The Jumeira Mosque in Dubai conforms to what is known as the Anatolia structure, identified by a massive central dome. Other mosques in the region are modelled on the style from Iran and Central Asia, which have more domes covering different areas of the mosque. One stunning example is the Iranian Mosque in Dubai. The multi-domed Jami al-Hamoda Mosque in Jalan Bani Bu Ali in Oman and the Grand Mosque in Dubai are both variations on the Anatolia structure. Other mosques are small and simple in style. Above all they simply serve their most basic of purposes – to provide a place for the faithful to pray.

TONY WHEELER

CHRIS MELLOR

Top Left: All mosques have a *mihrab*, a niche indicating the direction of Mecca.

Bottom: Minarets (such as these in Dubai) are perhaps the most distinctive architectural feature of any Muslim town, and you'll see a wide range of styles throughout Oman and the UAE.

Wind Towers

Called *barjeel* in Arabic, wind towers are the region's unique form of non-electrical air-conditioning. Traditional wind towers rise 5m or 6m above a house. They are usually built of wood or stone but can also be made from canvas. The tower is open on all four sides and hence catches even small breezes. These are channelled down around a central shaft and into the room below. In the process the air speeds up and is cooled. The cooler air already in the tower shaft pulls in, and subsequently cools, the hotter air outside through simple convection.

The towers work amazingly well. Sitting beneath a wind tower on a humid, 40°C day you will notice a distinct drop in temperature and a consistent breeze even when the air outside feels heavy and still.

In the UAE a handful of wind towers still exist, sometimes in people's homes and sometimes carefully preserved or reconstructed at museums. The Bastakia area in Dubai is home to about a dozen wind tower houses. In Sharjah a set of massive wind towers are used to cool the modern Central Market building. In Oman, however, they are less common.

Air Flow

Central Shaft

VERITY CAMPBELL

CHRIS MELLOR

Barasti

Middle: Wind towers are a traditional feature of buildings in Oman and the UAE but are rarely seen now except in heritage areas and museums. The design of many modern houses includes a tower structure but the traditional function of a wind tower, namely to cool the house, has long been overtaken by air-con units.

The term *barasti* describes both the traditional Gulf method of building a palm-leaf house and the completed house itself. Throughout much of the Gulf barasti houses were common until the 1950s. This was because they were relatively easy to build and maintain since, unlike the mud-brick houses you find in the oases around Al-Ain and Buraimi and many of the villages in the interior of Oman, they do not require water for their construction. The circulation of air through the reed also made barasti houses much cooler than mud-brick structures during the summer.

Barastis consist of a skeleton of wooden poles made from the trunk of a date palm onto which palm leaves *(areesh)* are woven to form a strong structure through which air can still circulate. They were extremely common throughout coastal areas of the region in the centuries before the oil boom but are now almost nonexistent. The few surviving examples include fishermen's shacks in Sur in Oman and the east coast of the UAE, but you are most likely to see them sitting in the courtyards of museums. For a detailed description of how a barasti is constructed see Geoffrey Bibby's book *Looking for Dilmun*.

Courtyard Houses

Many traditional houses in the region are built around a central courtyard. The courtyard, known as *al-housh* in Arabic, was considered the heart and lungs of a house. It provided light and fresh air, and a garden could be cultivated here. It was also a place for entertainment and somewhere for children to play. If a family owned livestock this is where the animals lived.

All the rooms of the house surrounded the courtyard and all doors and windows opened onto it, except those of the guest rooms which opened onto the outside of the house. On one or more sides was a verandah which provided shade and was usually the place where the women would weave their mats or sew their clothes. The verandah also served to keep sun out of the rooms during the day.

Courtyard houses are surrounded by a high wall with no windows. Many of the rooms had few windows, and almost all of them had shutters. This was to keep the rooms cool in the hot months but also to afford the family a certain degree of privacy. Most houses were built with this degree of privacy to protect the *hareem* (women of the household) from the eyes of men outside. Most traditional houses also had rooms (usually a *majlis* or reception room) which were solely for the hareem – men were not allowed to enter.

For a fine example of a well-restored courtyard house visit the Heritage House in the Al-Ahmadiya district of Dubai.

Below: The gates into courtyard houses are usually colourful and decorated with traditional motifs, such as this doorway to a courtyard house in Barka, Oman.

ISABELLE YOUNG

[Continued from page 22]

parts of the region is electricity. In the remote areas of the Musandam peninsula this only happened as recently as 1992.

Boat building is still practised in Ajman and Umm al-Qaiwain in the UAE, and in Sur and parts of the Batinah Coast in Oman. Date cultivation is an important part of life though it is no longer as necessary to survival as it was. Pearling was once the livelihood of many coastal inhabitants but now you'll have to visit a museum to learn about it.

The UAE and Oman have been very active over the last few years in trying to revive and preserve many of the traditions that have diminished in the wake of modernity, wealth and the influx of foreigners. Heritage villages displaying traditional barasti houses and village life have sprung up at Dubai, Badiyah, Hatta and Fujairah in the UAE. The Bait al-Zubair in Muscat has been set up as a showcase of traditional village life. The Muscat and Khareef festivals in Oman and the Dubai Shopping Festival always include displays of traditional song and dance as well as food and crafts. The aim of these festivals is not just to attract and entertain tourists, they also aim to educate young nationals about their culture and heritage.

There is now a new generation of Emiratis and Omanis who have grown up in a very different world from that of their parents. Modern amenities, cars, free education, travel, free housing and, in some cases, in the UAE especially, incomes without work mean that many people lead what would be considered by most an enviable life.

Those who work spend most of their spare time with family or socialising with friends in their homes. Others have diverse business interests which keep the money rolling in and ensure a very comfortable existence. Many of the wealthier families spend three or four months of the year (usually in summer) in Europe. Young men and women are beginning to have girlfriends and boyfriends although, as you can imagine, these relationships are very much clandestine ones. Islam is still a very fundamental part of life here.

Weddings

Traditionally, weddings are a very lavish affair. It would not be unreasonable for a family to spend over US$100,000 on the celebration, and since the bill is the responsibility of the groom, it often takes years of saving before a man can afford to marry.

Traditionally, the bride is not seen for 40 days before her wedding. During this time she stays at home with the other women of the household (*hareem*) and prepares for the wedding day. These preparations involve an assortment of ablutions and rituals. She is anointed with traditional perfumes from head to toe, her skin is rubbed with cleansing and conditioning oils and creams, her hands and feet are decorated with henna and her hair is washed and treated with oils. Also during this time the groom gives her all kinds of presents for her *addabia* (trousseau). These gifts include jewellery, perfumes and silk.

The wedding festivities last for about a week before the bride and groom actually experience normal married life. During that week, music, singing, dancing and eating form the bulk of the entertainment. The feasts occur night after night, with men and women celebrating separately. Everyone is welcome to attend the wedding festivals, even strangers, but the bride must remain unseen, except by the hareem, until the wedding night.

Dos & Don'ts

Dress Oman and the UAE, although more liberal than most other Gulf countries, are still very conservative in comparison with the West, and the majority of men and women in the region wear traditional dress.

See the Women Travellers section in the Regional Facts for the Visitor chapter for advice for women travellers on what to wear. Men should never appear barechested in public, except when at the beach or at a swimming pool. People in cities are used to seeing Westerners in shorts and they are seen as something comical rather than offensive. If you do wear shorts they should be relatively long – all the way to the knee if possible – but don't wear them into someone's home. Just look around you – how many local men wear shorts?

Western men should not wear dishdashas because traditional dress has become an unofficial national uniform throughout the region, visually setting nationals of the region apart from the foreign population. People may think that you are making fun of them if you adopt Arabian dress.

Alcohol With alcohol legally available in Oman and in all of the emirates except Sharjah, the usual warnings about drinking and driving are as pertinent here as at home. Apart from the obvious safety hazards, if you are caught there will be, at the very least, a steep fine to pay and you may wind up spending a month or more in jail.

Photography It is impolite to photograph people without asking their permission and you should avoid pointing your camera at police stations, police officers, airports, palaces, embassies and consulates.

Social Etiquette Although many Emiratis and Omanis are used to the habits of a wide variety of foreigners, and are particularly forgiving of Westerners and their faux pas, etiquette is still very important. You will generate more respect for yourself if you remember a few basic rules and rituals.

- Always stand when someone enters the room. When you enter a room yourself, shake hands with everyone. Men should not offer to shake hands with an Arab woman unless the woman takes the lead by extending her hand first. Western women will occasionally find that a man may not extend his hand to shake hers, or he will cover his hand with his dishdasha first and extend his fist. This is because some stricter Muslims will not touch a woman who is not of his family.
- Do not sit in such a way that the soles of your feet are pointing at someone else and do not eat or offer things with your left hand.
- Many Omanis and Emiratis prefer to begin meetings with what, in the West, would be con-

sidered an excessive amount of small talk. In such situations you may cause offence if you try to move directly to business.

- If you are in a frustrating situation, be patient, friendly and sensitive. Never lose your temper. A confrontational attitude doesn't go well with the Arab personality and loss of face is a sensitive issue. If you have a problem with someone, be firm, calm and persistent instead.
- You'll notice that people do not use the term 'thank you' as much as in the West. This is be-

Bedouin Hospitality

Bedouin hospitality towards strangers is legendary. These traditions have not been lost on the new generation of Omanis and Emiratis and invitations into people's homes for tea and coffee are common. Unlike many in the West who are reluctant to share themselves too much, or to make the effort to get to know strangers, the Bedouin are welcoming, friendly and helpful. You may find yourself invited to *fudell*, especially in rural areas. This is an invitation to share food with someone, often it means you are invited to take food off their plate.

You'll also find that people will be very willing to help if you are in any kind of trouble. And they won't leave you until the problem is sorted out. If you are looking lost, people will stop and offer their assistance. Once a couple of young Emiratis drove 25 minutes out of their way to guide me back to a main road when I was lost on an off-road jaunt. They could have just pointed me in the right direction.

Lou Callan

A traditional reception room or *majlis*.

cause one is expected to repay significant favours by actions – words alone are not enough. For a service that is paid for or expected, such as a bell-boy bringing luggage to a room, thanks are not considered necessary.

Forms of Address Throughout the Arab world it is common to attach forms of address to people's given, as opposed to their family, names. Just as Arabs refer to each other as 'Mr Mohammed' or 'Mr Abdullah', they will generally refer to you as 'Mr John', 'Miss Simone' or 'Mrs Susan'. Often women will be referred to by their husband's name, for instance 'Mrs Tony'.

In the UAE the term 'sheikh' (or shaikh) applies *only* to members of the ruling family. The rulers themselves carry the formal title of 'emir' (literally, 'prince'), but are usually referred to as 'sheikhs'. The feminine form of sheikh is 'sheikha' (or shaikha). It applies to all female members of the ruling family. In Oman, the term sheikh is not used.

Coffee & Tea It is considered impolite to refuse an offer of coffee or tea. If you are the host it is considered equally impolite to fail to make such an offer. Throughout the region you may be offered Arabic coffee (sometimes called Bedouin coffee or *qahwa*), and this involves a certain ritual all its own. After finishing your coffee hold out the cup in your right hand for more. If you have had enough, rock the cup gently back and forth to indicate that you're through. (At all other times act as though the coffee boy is invisible.) It is generally considered impolite to drink more than three cups, though if the conversation drags on for an extended period of time the coffee and tea may be passed around again.

RELIGION

Islam is the dominant religion of both Oman and the UAE. As with any religion embraced by about one billion people, Islam has produced many sects, movements and offshoots. Most Emiratis are Sunni Muslims subscribing to the Maliki or Hanbali schools of Islamic law. Many of the latter are Wahhabis, though UAE Wahhabis are not nearly as strict and puritanical as the Wahhabis of

Saudi Arabia. There are also smaller communities of Ibadi and Shi'ite Muslims. The Shi'ite are probably descended from merchants and workers who crossed to the Trucial Coast from Persia in the late 19th or early 20th century.

Most Omanis (about 75%) are Ibadis, a sect of Islam that is practised nowhere else in the world. Ibadis are a moderate faction of the Khariji sect which was one of the earliest fundamentalist movements in Islam.

Other religions are tolerated and there are a number of Christian churches and Hindu temples throughout both countries. Note that non-Muslims are not permitted to enter mosques in either Oman or the UAE.

Principles of Islam

Muslims believe the religion preached in Arabia by the Prophet Mohammed to be God's final revelation to humanity. For them the Quran (the Muslim holy book; meaning 'the recitation' in Arabic) is God's words revealed through the Prophet. It supplements and completes the earlier revelations around which the Christian and Jewish faiths were built, and corrects human misinterpretations of those earlier revelations. For example, Muslims believe that Jesus was a prophet second only to Mohammed in importance but that his followers later introduced into Christianity the heretical idea that Jesus was the son of God. Adam, Abraham, Moses and a number of other Christian and Jewish holy men are regarded as prophets by Muslims. Mohammed, however, was the 'Seal of the Prophets' – the last one who has, or will, come.

The essence of Islam is the belief that there is only one God and that it is the people's duty to believe in and serve God in the manner laid out in the Quran. In Arabic, *islam* means submission and a Muslim is one who submits to God's will.

To be a Muslim, you need to observe the five pillars of the faith:

Shahadah This is the profession of faith, the basic tenet of Islam: 'There is no God but God, and Mohammed is the messenger of God'. '*La il-laha illa Allah Mohammed rasul Allah.*' It is commonly heard as part of the call to prayer and at other events such as births and deaths.

Salat This is the obligation of prayer, performed ideally five or six times a day at dawn, noon, mid-afternoon, sunset and at twilight. Muslims can pray anywhere but most prefer to pray together in a mosque. Prayers are performed facing the direction of the Qaaba in Mecca, and before praying, ritual ablutions are carried out.

Zakat This refers to alms-giving. Muslims must give a portion of their income to help those poorer than themselves. How this has operated in practice has varied over the centuries: either it was seen as an individual duty or the state collected zakat as a form of income tax to be redistributed through mosques or religious charities.

Sawm The month of Ramadan commemorates the revelation of the Quran to Mohammed and is a demonstration of a Muslim's renewal of faith. During this time, they are asked not to let anything pass their lips during daylight hours and to abstain from sex. Young children, travellers and those whose health will not permit it are exempt from the fast, though those who are able to do so are supposed to make up the days they missed at a later time.

Haj All Muslims who are able to do so are required to make the pilgrimage to Mecca at least once during their lifetime. However, the pilgrimage must be performed during a specific few days in the first and second weeks of the Muslim month of Dhul Hijja. Visiting Mecca and performing the prescribed rituals at any other time of the year is considered spiritually desirable, but it is not the same as haj.

Beyond the five pillars of Islam there are many other duties incumbent on Muslims. In the West the best known and least understood of these is *jihad*. This word is usually translated into English as 'holy war', but literally means 'striving in the way of the faith'. Exactly what this means has been a subject of keen debate among Muslim scholars for the last 1400 years. Some scholars have tended to see jihad in spiritual, as opposed to martial, terms.

Muslims are forbidden to eat or drink anything containing pork or alcohol. Nor can they consume the blood or meat of an animal that has died of natural causes (as opposed to having been slaughtered in the prescribed manner – see the boxed text 'Meat & Islam'

under Food in the Regional Facts for the Visitor chapter for more information).

Muslim women may not marry non-Muslim men, though Muslim men are permitted to marry Christian or Jewish women (but not, for example, Hindus or Buddhists).

Sunnis & Shi'ites In the early days of Islam, a major schism occurred that divided the Muslim world into two broad camps: the Sunnis and the Shi'ites.

When Mohammed died, in 632, he left no clear instructions either designating a successor as leader of the Muslim community or setting up a system by which subsequent leaders could be chosen. Some felt that leadership of the community should remain with the Prophet's family, and supported the claim of Ali bin Abi Taleb, Mohammed's cousin and son-in-law and one of the first converts to Islam, to become the *caliph*, or leader. But the rest of the community chose Abu Bakr, the Prophet's closest companion, as leader, and Ali was passed over in two subsequent leadership contests.

This split the Muslim community into two competing factions. Those who took Ali's side in these disputes became known as the *shiat Ali*, or 'partisans of Ali'. Shi'ites believed that a descendant of the Prophet through Ali's line should lead the Muslims. Because Shi'ites have rarely held temporal power their doctrine came to emphasise the spiritual position of their leaders, the *imams*. Sunni belief, on the other hand, essentially holds that any Muslim who rules with justice and according to the Sharia'a (Islamic law) deserves the support of the Muslim community as a whole.

Wahhabis Wahhabism takes its name from Mohammed bin Abdul Wahhab (1703–92), a preacher and judge who, after seeing an ever-increasing lack of respect for Islam among the Bedouin tribes of central Arabia, preached a return to Islam's origins and traditions as interpreted by the Hanbali school of Islamic jurisprudence. This meant strict adherence to the Quran and the Hadith (accounts of the Prophet's words and actions).

Wahhabism is a rather austere form of the Islamic religion. Wahhabis reject concepts such as sainthood and forbid the observance of holidays such as the Prophet's birthday. Even the term Wahhabi makes strict followers of the sect uncomfortable because it appears to exalt Mohammed bin Abdul Wahhab over the Prophet. Strict Wahhabis prefer the term *muwahidin*, which translates as 'unitarian' because they profess only the unity of God.

Ibadis The Ibadis are one of the Muslim world's few remaining Khariji sects, and are a product of Islam's earliest fundamentalist movement. In 657 Ali, the Prophet's cousin and son-in-law and fourth caliph, agreed to peace talks with his main rival for the leadership of the Muslim community. The Kharijis (seceders) were originally followers of Ali (Shi'ites) but broke with him over a point of principle. They believed that by agreeing to discuss the leadership question he had compromised on a matter of faith. This compromise, they held, rendered him unworthy of both their loyalty and the leadership itself.

Various Khariji sects developed over the next 200 years, all generally adhering to the principle that Muslims should follow the adult male who was best able to lead the community while upholding the law. If the leader failed to uphold the law he could be replaced almost instantly. Most Kharijis also rejected out of hand the idea that any person could have an hereditary claim on the leadership of the Muslim community. The leader, or imam, was to be chosen by the community as a whole.

Ibadis take their name from Abdullah bin Ibad al-Murri al-Tamimi, a theologian who was probably from Najd, in modern Saudi Arabia, but who did most of his important teaching while living in Basra (in present-day southern Iraq) during the late 7th century. His teachings seem to have caught on in Oman partly because politically they touched the right chords at a time when the Omani tribes were rebelling against the Damascus-based Umayyad caliphate. A hereditary Ibadi imamate emerged in Oman from the mid-8th to the late-9th century, when it was suppressed by the Abbasid empire that had replaced the Umayyads as the predominant power in the Muslim world.

Islamic Law

The Arabic word Sharia'a is usually translated as 'Islamic Law'. This is misleading. The Sharia'a is not a legal code in the Western sense of the term. It refers to the general body of Islamic legal thought. At the base of this lies the Quran itself, which Muslims believe to be the actual speech of God, revealed to humankind through Mohammed. Where the Quran does not provide guidance on a particular subject Muslim scholars turn to the Sunnah, a body of works recording the sayings and doings of the Prophet and, to a lesser extent, his companions as reported by a string of scholarly authorities.

There are four main Sunni and two principal Shi'ite schools of Islamic jurisprudence. The orthodox Sunni schools of jurisprudence are the Shafi'i, Hanbali, Hanafi and Maliki. All but the first of these schools, or rites as they are sometimes known, are found widely in the Gulf though Hanbalis are probably the most numerous. This owes much to the fact that Wahhabism, the predominant Islamic sect in Saudi Arabia and Qatar, follows the Hanbali school. Hanbali Islam is generally regarded as the sternest of the four orthodox Sunni rites. The largest schools of Shi'ite jurisprudence are the Jafari and the Akhbari. Ibadi Islam, the variety practised in Oman, has its own separate school of jurisprudence.

The Quran and Sunnah together make up the Sharia'a. In some instances the Sharia'a is quite specific, such as in the areas of inheritance law and the punishments for certain offences. In many other cases it acts as a series of guidelines. Islam does not recognise a distinction between the secular and religious lives of believers. Thus, a learned scholar or judge can with enough research and if necessary, through use of analogy, determine the proper 'Islamic' position on or approach to any problem.

LANGUAGE

Arabic is the official language of Oman and the UAE. English is spoken throughout the region, although if you venture into rural areas you will find that English is not as widespread, especially in Oman. Due to the large number of expats in the UAE espe-cially it would be useful to know a little of the Persian language, Farsi. Some basic words of Urdu and Malayalam (the language of Kerala in India) may also come in handy.

For an Arabic grammatical primer and basic vocabulary list, see the Language chapter at the end of this book.

Is that 'Sheikh' or 'Shaikh'?

The transliteration of Arabic words is a very inexact science, partly because Arabic contains several letters which have no real English equivalent in sound. Although we have tried to standardise the spellings of Arabic words in this book as far as possible, you will undoubtedly see a great variety of spellings of words and place names on local road signs, street signs and maps. Wherever possible we have tried to stick with local usage (ie, what you will actually see on street signs or locally produced maps). There is bound, however, to be some variation. So keep in mind that 'beit', 'bait' and 'bayt' are the same word, as are 'sheikh' and 'shaikh'. Flexibility, after all, is the hallmark of a good traveller.

Regional Facts for the Visitor

PLANNING
When to Go

The best time to visit Oman and the UAE is in the tourist season from November to February, when the climate is the most comfortable. If possible, avoid travelling to Oman and the UAE from late April to early October, when daily temperatures can soar to well over 40°C and humidity levels on the coast are high. If for some reason you decide to go in high summer (July/August), you'll find that hotel rates are heavily discounted,

Suggested Itineraries

Many people make the UAE and, to a lesser extent, Oman, a stopover on a longer trip from Europe to Asia or Australia/New Zealand or vice versa. It is possible to cover the major cities of Muscat and Dubai in just two or three days each, but it's well worth taking the extra time to go out of the cities to explore the country areas. Even if you only have a couple of days, take a day trip from Dubai to Al-Ain or Fujairah. If you are in Muscat, make a short excursion to Nizwa or Sur.

The recent introduction of a dual visa which allows visitors to travel between Oman and the UAE on the one visa means that planning a holiday to both countries has become much more simple. See Visas & Documents in this chapter for more details.

The following suggestions should give you a rough idea of the best way to spend your time in the region:

One Week
Make Dubai your base. Take a day to explore the main sights of Dubai then a day trip to Al-Ain and an overnight trip to the East Coast (Fujairah or Khor Fakkan). Then fly or go by bus to Muscat. Spend one day in Muscat then do an overnight trip to Nizwa from where you can explore Jabrin, Bahla, Tanuf and Al-Hamra.

Two Weeks
We suggest one week in each country. See the country Facts for the Visitor chapters for the best way to spend your time.

Three Weeks
This is the perfect amount of time to spend in the region. Due to Oman's size, you would be better off spending the most part of your three weeks in Oman. One week in the UAE will give you time to see the most interesting places, while two weeks in Oman will allow you to explore some of the mountain villages and wadis, as well as going as far as Salalah in the south. See the country Facts for the Visitor chapters for more detailed suggested itineraries for the individual countries.

One Month
To get the most out of your trip you should try to spend the greater part of your time in Oman. Ten days in the UAE should be sufficient, and will leave you three weeks to get the most out of Oman. See the country Facts for the Visitor chapters for more detailed suggested itineraries.

sometimes by up to 75%. However, you'll have to put up with temperatures of 45° to 48°C, and many locally based tour operators close down in July and August.

The monsoon *(khareef)* season in the south of Oman lasts from June to September, and while you probably do not want to be in Salalah during the rains, it is definitely worth a visit in October when everything in Dhofar is still lush and green.

Public Holidays & Special Events Most public holidays last only a day or two and shouldn't seriously disrupt any travel plans. The exception is the month of Ramadan – for dates, see Public Holidays & Special Events later in this chapter. During Ramadan, shops and government institutions have shorter opening hours, and you cannot eat, drink or smoke in public during daylight hours. Alcohol is prohibited which means that bars shut down completely for the month and restaurants do not serve alcohol (although in Dubai you'll find that many hotel restaurants still serve alcohol with meals, they just don't shout about it). On the plus side, however, most hotels offer 50% or more discount on their room rates during Ramadan and you'll find there are relatively few tourists around. If you want to avoid Ramadan you will need to plan carefully as it will overlap with at least part of the November to February tourist season from now until 2005.

There are some special events in the UAE, such as the Dubai Shopping Festival in March/April, that you might want to bear in mind when you are planning your trip, either because they are of interest to you or to avoid the crowds. See Public Holidays & Special Events later in this chapter.

What Kind of Trip

If you are planning to visit both Oman and the UAE, you'll need to be aware of the current visa regulations, which make crossing between the two countries by different methods something of a hassle (for example, if you want to travel in by land and out by air or vice versa). See Visas & Documents later in this chapter for more details.

One way to avoid this would be to go on a package tour. Package tours, of course, have their drawbacks but they do tend to make it easy for you to cover a lot of territory in a short amount of time without having to worry about the best route over the border.

Although the long-distance taxi systems in both Oman and the UAE are very thorough and cheap, hiring a car will give you greater independence and freedom to travel in your own time. It will also give you the opportunity to be adventurous and to get to some of the more interesting sights off the beaten track. Almost everything covered in this book can be reached using a regular car. You will also save money on expensive day or overnight tours with the tour companies. However, if you want to see something of the desert and the mountains you should consider booking a half-day, full-day or overnight 4WD trip. These are available from most of the region's major cities.

It is possible to hire a 4WD and explore the wadis and deserts on your own but at Dh750/OR75 (US$200 per day) or more, this ends up being very expensive. If there are a few of you, however, and this option becomes affordable, then you should definitely do it.

What to Bring

You should be able to buy most things you might need in any of the region's bigger cities, although it is a good idea to have some basics with you. A good hat, sunglasses and sunscreen are essential, as it is always sunny here. A comfortable pair of sandals is preferable to lace-up walking shoes as even in winter the daytime temperatures are in the mid to high 20s. A sweater or fleece is probably a good idea for chilly winter nights in the mountains and inland desert areas. Even in autumn and spring it can get quite chilly at night in the upper reaches of the Hajar mountains in Oman. It's best to bring your own camping gear as you won't find any hire places. Alternatively you can buy camping equipment at department stores in the major cities.

Moneybelts are not really necessary in the region as crime is very low and locals are probably carrying around much larger amounts of cash than you anyway. Headscarves for women are not really necessary in any situation but if you feel more comfortable wearing one in the more conservative country areas then it can certainly do no harm. Pharmacies in the major towns and cities here are just as well stocked as anywhere in the West.

Voracious readers of anything other than spy novels should note that there are few really good bookshops, and books tend to be very expensive. Also, most Western works on the history and politics of the Middle East are unavailable in the region.

RESPONSIBLE TOURISM

Although tourism in Oman and the UAE has not reached the heights it has in other Middle Eastern countries, it does have an effect on the environment and the people within it. There are a number of things you can do to be a more responsible tourist. A British organisation called Tourism Concern (☎ 020-7753 333), Stapleton House, 177-281 Holloway Rd, London N7 8NN, has come up with some guidelines for travellers who wish to minimise the negative impact they may have on countries they visit. Check out its Web site at www.gn.apc.org/tourismconcern. We have adapted some of its suggestions to be pertinent to visitors to Oman and the UAE:

- Preserve natural resources. Try not to waste water. Switch off lights and, unless it is the height of summer, air-con when you go out.
- Ask before taking photographs of people, especially women. Don't worry if you don't speak Arabic; a smile and gesture will be understood and appreciated.
- Remember that Oman and the UAE are Muslim countries. Wearing tight-fitting and revealing clothes causes offence to most people.
- Similarly, public displays of affection between members of the opposite sex are inappropriate.
- Learning something about the region's history and culture helps you to understand its people and their traditions, and helps prevent misunderstandings and frustration.

Being a responsible tourist also means being aware of the effect of various activities on the environment. Driving in wadis or over sand dunes in a 4WD make for a popular day excursion for visitors but they are potentially damaging to the environment. Here are some guidelines for minimising your impact on the environment:

- Stick to the tracks to avoid damaging the all-too-rare vegetation that is such an important part of the fragile desert ecosystem.
- Driving in wadis should be avoided as far as possible to ensure that they are not polluted with oil and grease. Some wadis are important sources of irrigation and drinking water.
- When diving or snorkelling, do not touch or remove any marine life, especially coral.
- If you plan to camp out remember to take your own wood – don't take branches or uproot shrubs. Even plants that look dead are often not.

VISAS & DOCUMENTS
Passport

Your passport should be valid for at least six months beyond the date you plan to leave the region. Make sure there is ample room in your passport for any visas you may need, and take a dozen or so extra passport photos.

Visas

Most visitors need a visa to enter Oman or the UAE. The only visitors who do not need a visa for Oman are citizens of another Gulf country. For the UAE, you do not need a visa if you are a national of another Gulf country or a British national with the right of abode in the UK. For full details on the types of visas available and how to go about getting them, see the Visas sections of the individual country Facts for the Visitor chapters.

Visa Sponsorship For some visas to Oman and all visas to the UAE, you will need a sponsor. This can be a hotel, a tour company or a friend who is a resident in the country. The sponsor has to vouch for your good behaviour while in the country and take responsibility for your departure. In the UAE and Oman, hotels and tour companies will charge you a fee for this service, although it is usually less expensive in Oman.

STOP PRESS: Joint Visa

Early in 2000, the governments of Oman and the UAE introduced a cross-border accord whereby tourists with a visa for one country could cross freely into the other country, without needing another visa. Unfortunately this idea seems to have been passed over, and there is still much confusion among officials about it.

In any case, because both countries have relaxed their tourist visa regulations, you are likely to be able to cross at border posts. Check with both countries' embassies before you depart for the latest information about border crossings and visas. See also the boxed text 'STOP PRESS: Visas for Oman' in the Oman Facts for the Visitor chapter, and the boxed text 'STOP PRESS: Visas for the UAE' in the UAE Facts for the Visitor chapter for information about tourist visas for both countries. The information in these boxed texts overrides references to tourist visas in the Visas section of this and the Oman and the UAE Facts for the Visitor chapters.

Processing can take anything from a few days to a few weeks.

Collecting Visas Most visas for Oman and the UAE are issued for pick-up (rather than stamped in your passport) at Muscat's Seeb airport or at Dubai, Sharjah or Abu Dhabi airports, although at the time of writing more and more UAE visas issued from embassies abroad were being stamped into passports. Be sure to have some proof (a fax or telex with a visa number) that you have a visa waiting for you at your destination or you may not be allowed to board the plane.

Travel Insurance

A travel insurance policy to cover theft, loss and medical problems is a good idea. A wide variety of policies are available, so check the small print before you commit yourself. Check that the policy covers ambulances or an emergency flight home.

Driving Licence & Permits

Most Western driving licences are accepted in Oman and the UAE as long as you are resident of the country in which the licence was issued. A few car rental companies insist on an International Driving Permit (IDP) so getting one of these before you leave might be a good idea. Remember that an IDP is only valid when carried in conjunction with your licence from home.

If you are intending to take up residence in either country, you will need to get a local licence if you want to drive. In the UAE, most Western nationals can just swap their own driving licence for a local one. Expats from other countries have to sit a test. In Oman, any expat with a driving licence can swap it for a local one.

Note that if you are a foreign resident of Oman you will need a road permit from the Royal Oman Police to enter or leave the country by land (see Other Documents/Road Permits in the Oman Facts for the Visitor chapter for more details). This does not apply if you are visiting Oman on a tourist visa.

Hostel Card

Only the UAE has youth hostels. You will need an HI card to stay in a hostel: foreigners can purchase cards on the spot at any of the UAE's youth hostels for Dh75.

Student, Youth & Seniors Cards

These are of little use in Oman and the UAE. They are not recognised and you will not be given any discounts by flashing one around. Children who look under 12 are given discounts on admission fees to most museums, amusement parks and beach clubs.

Copies

It's a good idea to photocopy all important documents (such as your passport data page, insurance information, air tickets, employment documents, professional qualifications etc) before you leave home. Leave a copy with someone back home and take a copy with you, separate from the originals. Leave copies of your travellers cheques and credit card numbers in the same place.

Consider storing details of your vital travel documents in Lonely Planet's free online Travel Vault in case you lose the photocopies or can't be bothered with them. Your password-protected Travel Vault is accessible online anywhere in the world – create it at www.ekno.lonelyplanet.com.

CUSTOMS

Video tapes are a particularly sensitive subject throughout the region and customs officers are likely to take them from you at the airport. They will be viewed by censors from the information or interior ministry and returned to you in a few days, though you will probably have to trek back out to the airport to get them. The importation of pornography is strictly prohibited, and there are the usual restrictions on firearms and drugs. You can bring reading matter like women's magazines into the region (although the ones on sale in Oman and the UAE are censored with a black marker), but anything considered as anti-Muslim literature will be confiscated.

Note that the import of alcohol into the emirate of Sharjah in the UAE is forbidden, and you can only bring alcohol into Oman if you arrive by air. See Customs in the country Facts for the Visitor chapters for details of restrictions and duty-free allowances.

EMBASSIES & CONSULATES

It's important to realise what your own embassy – the embassy of the country of which you are a citizen – can and can't do to help you if you get into trouble. Generally speaking, it won't be much help in emergencies if the trouble you're in is remotely your own fault. Remember that you are bound by the laws of the country you are in. Your embassy will not be sympathetic if you end up in jail after committing a crime locally, even if such actions are legal in your own country.

In genuine emergencies you might get some assistance, but only if other channels have been exhausted. For example, if you

need to get home urgently, a free ticket home is exceedingly unlikely – the embassy would expect you to have insurance. If you have all your money and documents stolen, it might assist with getting a new passport, but a loan for onward travel is out of the question.

Some embassies used to keep letters for travellers or have a small reading room with home newspapers, but these days the mail-holding service has usually been stopped and even newspapers tend to be out of date.

Refer to each country's Facts for the Visitor chapter for listings of Oman and UAE embassies and consulates around the world.

MONEY

For information on exchange rates, costs and currency, turn to the individual country Facts for the Visitor chapters.

Exchanging Money

In Oman and the UAE, you can change money at banks, commercial moneychangers or Thomas Cook and American Express (AmEx offices). Large and most medium-sized hotels will also change money although the exchange rate is not going to be as good. Moneychangers offer reasonable rates that are generally better than most banks, may not charge commission and generally have longer opening hours than the banks. The major international currencies, currencies of countries with large expat communities in the region (such as India and Sri Lanka) and currencies of most neighbouring countries are all recognised and easily changed.

Changing money in the smaller towns and more remote rural areas can be difficult so you might want to ensure you have plenty of cash before leaving the city.

Cash US dollars or UK pounds are the most popular currency with moneychangers, but French francs and German deutschmarks are also readily accepted. All major currencies are accepted at the larger exchange centres and banks. If you are changing more than US$250 it might pay to do a little shopping around the banks and moneychangers for the best rates and lowest commissions.

Travellers Cheques Most banks change travellers cheques but they take a commission, usually around 1%. You just have to weigh this up with the commission charged by moneychangers. One problem with moneychangers is that some of them either will not take travellers cheques or will take only one type. Some places will only exchange travellers cheques if you can produce your original purchase receipt. If you don't have the receipt try asking for the manager. It's a good idea to carry either AmEx or Thomas Cook cheques as these are the most widely recognised brands.

ATMs These are widespread, though not all of them are tied into the big international systems, especially in Oman. The exception is the British Bank of the Middle East, some of whose machines accept cards on the Plus and Cirrus systems. National Bank of Oman's ATMs are tied into the Global Access network. Machines at Emirates Bank International and Abu Dhabi Commercial Bank in the UAE are also on Global Access, as well as Cirrus, Plus and, sometimes, Switch.

You will need a personal identification number (PIN) to operate the machines. If you don't have one, you'll need to get one from your card issuer several weeks before travelling. It also pays to find out what sort of commissions are charged by both your bank or card issuer and the local bank whose machine you will be using.

Credit Cards These are widely accepted at hotels (even the cheaper ones), travel agents, larger restaurants and car hire places in Oman and the UAE. The most popular card appears to be Visa but MasterCard and AmEx are also accepted at most places. Keep in mind that if you use AmEx you may incur a merchant fee of 5%.

International Transfers You can transfer money from banks in the region to an overseas account without any problem. You don't need to hold an account with the bank if you are handing over cash. If you are sending money to another GCC country or to India, the fee charged is Dh30 in the UAE or OR2 in Oman. If the money is going farther afield it will cost you between Dh60 or OR5 and Dh100 or OR10, depending on the bank.

Security
Oman and the UAE are very safe places and carrying cash around is not the issue it is in some other tourist destinations. Even though crime is relatively rare you should habitually exercise the same caution with your personal belongings as you would at home.

Costs
It is safe to say that you will find it hard to get around on much less than US$35 to US$40 per day. The lack of real budget accommodation is the main drawback. In Oman, where there are no youth hostels, you will find that you need to spend more than this unless you have a free place to sleep. However, eating cheap is rarely a problem in the region and transport costs range from very cheap to reasonable. Public transport within cities costs less than US$1; minibus and long-distance taxis cost around US$8 per 100km. You can get away with paying as little as US$22 per day including insurance to hire a car at the smaller rental car companies. Admission to most museums and tourist sites is free, or you may pay a token amount.

Tipping & Bargaining
Tips are not generally expected although tipping is becoming more common. Note, however, that the service charge added to most hotel and restaurant bills is not an automatic gratuity that goes to the waiters. It usually goes into the till, and is simply the restaurant's way of making the prices on the menu look 20% cheaper than they really are. Waiters in the region tend to be paid appallingly low wages, so if the service is good a small tip (about 10% is fair), while not required, is definitely in order. This applies to most restaurants, although unless you really wanted to, you generally would not leave a tip in a shwarma joint or one of the biryani cafes.

As for bargaining, well, this is the Middle East. You can bargain over hotel rates, plane tickets, taxi fares or even with moneychangers over the exchange rate. Some prices are fixed: menu prices, taxi rides in metered taxis, bus or minibus fares and the prices in grocery stores. Just about everything else is negotiable. Even in shopping centres you can, ask for a discount or for their 'best price'.

In Oman and the UAE, 25 to 30% off the first quote is more or less the norm. This will vary from place to place and product to product. Shopkeepers in the cities tend to offer only a small discount off the marked price. The country souqs (markets) are the places where you can really get a bargain. Hang in there, be firm and be prepared to spend some time at it and you'll find that prices will come down by about 50%.

POST & COMMUNICATIONS
Post
The postal systems in Oman and the UAE are generally very good. Even from the more remote parts of the region you should have no trouble sending mail home. Mail generally takes about a week to Europe or the USA and eight to 10 days to Australia. Incoming mail can be something of a lottery. Poste restante is only available in Muscat in Oman, although AmEx in both Oman and the UAE will hold clients' mail.

Telephone & Fax
The telephone systems throughout the region are excellent, and there are telephone offices in most towns, however small. Both Oman and the UAE have efficient phonecard systems that make calling home relatively easy without either going to an office and booking a call or carrying around a small mountain of change. As you might expect, phonecards issued in Oman cannot be used on phones in the UAE and vice versa.

Home country direct services are available in the UAE but not in Oman.

Fax machines are now widespread in the region, and even the smallest hotels often have them. You can send faxes from the local telephone office.

Email & Internet Access
Internet cafes have sprung up in the major cities in the region and private Internet access is available through the national telecommunications companies. See the individual city entries for details of Internet cafes. Most four- and five-star hotels have business centres with Internet access for guests.

The Internet is heavily censored in the UAE and Oman, and if you try to look up anything that is censored, they'll know it!

INTERNET RESOURCES
The World Wide Web is a rich resource for travellers. You can research your trip, hunt down bargain air fares, book hotels, check on weather conditions or chat with locals and other travellers about the best places to visit (or avoid!).

One good place to start your Web explorations is the Lonely Planet Web site (www.lonelyplanet.com). Here you'll find succinct summaries on travelling to most places on earth, postcards from other travellers and the Thorn Tree bulletin board, where you can ask questions before you go or dispense advice when you get back. You can also find travel news and updates to many of our most popular guidebooks, and the subWWWay section links you to the most useful travel resources elsewhere on the Web.

For details of sites specific to Oman and the UAE, see Internet Resources in the relevant country's Facts for the Visitor chapter.

BOOKS
In this section we've listed publications containing general information about the region and the Gulf. For books specifically about Oman or the UAE refer to Books in the relevant country's Facts for the Visitor chapter. Be aware that you are unlikely to find some of the more political books mentioned here in bookshops in Oman or the UAE.

Note that bookshops and libraries search by title or author so we have not included publisher details here unless particularly relevant.

Lonely Planet

Lonely Planet's *Middle East* (covering all the Arab Gulf countries, as well as Libya, Egypt, Israel and the Palestinian Territories, Jordan, Syria, Turkey, Iran and Iraq) includes chapters on Oman and the UAE, and there's a language section in Farsi, spoken by many expats in Oman and the UAE. Lonely Planet also publishes a city guide to Dubai.

Guidebooks

Lots of locally produced 'guidebooks' are actually commercial directories consisting of little more than advertising interspersed with lists of telephone numbers. Most of these are aimed exclusively at upmarket business travellers. The only guidebook covering just Oman and the UAE is the Insight Guide to *Oman & the UAE*.

Travel

For an intimate view of life on the Trucial Coast (present-day UAE) before oil was discovered, read Thesiger's classic *Arabian Sands*, originally published in 1959. It also details the explorer's epic crossing of the Empty Quarter by camel in 1946. *Thesiger* by Michael Asher is the quintessential book on the explorer. *Crossing the Sands*, released in 1999, the year Thesiger turned 89, is an account of the five years the explorer spent living with the Bedouin in Arabia, including Oman and the UAE.

History & Politics

Most books covering the history of the Gulf tend to be either heavy academic works or propagandist in tone. Books on the broader history of the Middle East pass only fleetingly over the Gulf. An exception is Peter Mansfield's *The Arabs*, which is also one of the better books with that particular catch-all title. In addition to a broad-brush history of the Middle East, Mansfield comments on the individual countries in the region.

Daniel Yergin's *The Prize: the Epic Quest for Oil, Money, and Power*, a history of the oil industry, is essential reading for anyone headed to the Gulf, though its scope is worldwide rather than strictly Middle Eastern.

Among the best general histories of the Middle East is Albert Hourani's *A History of the Arab Peoples* (1997). There's not a lot of information specifically on the Gulf, but as a general introduction to the region's history and philosophy you could hardly do better.

People & Society

Possibly the best single overview of life, business and culture in the Gulf is *The Merchants* by Michael Field. While ostensibly focusing on the rise of nine of the Gulf's prominent merchant families, it is really a book about Arabian society, how it works and how it has changed since the discovery of oil. You may find this one difficult to find but if you can get a hold of it, it's well worth reading.

Peter Theroux gives a witty, candid portrait of culture and politics in the Middle East in his book *Sandstorms – Days and Nights in Arabia*.

Don't They Know it's Friday by Jerry Williams is a very useful how-to-do-business-with-the-Arabs sort of book, written by an expat who has lived and worked all over the Gulf and now runs courses for Westerners doing business with Arabs. It's very interesting and straightforward and should be compulsory reading for those intending to live and work in the Gulf. Also in the same vein is *The Economist Business Traveller's Guides – Arabian Peninsula*, if you can find it.

Women

Women's role in society in the Middle East is a topic often discussed, and often misunderstood, in the West. Over the last few years a number of books addressing the subject have come out, helping to take the perception of women and their role in the Muslim world beyond old stereotypes.

Fatima Mernissi, a Moroccan scholar, and Nawal El-Saadawi, an Egyptian physician and novelist, are probably the female Arab writers best known to Western readers. Mernissi's *Beyond the Veil – Male/Female Dynamics in Modern Muslim Society* and *Two Women in One* make a good starting point for exploring of the subject of women in the Muslim world. Also by Mernissi are *The Veil and the Male Elite: A Feminist Interpretation of Women's Rights in Islam*, looking at the role of the male elite's interests in the denial of rights to women in Islam, and *The Forgotten Queens of Islam*.

Another in this genre of literature is *Nine Parts of Desire – The Hidden World of Islamic Women* by Geraldine Brooks, although with the crushing criticisms it contains of Islam's treatment of women it is unlikely you will find this book in any bookshop in the region.

On an academic level the work of the Norwegian scholar Unni Wikan has been ground breaking. Her book *Behind the Veil in Arabia – Women in Oman* isn't easy to find but it is well worth the effort. Wikan's focus is primarily on rural society.

Islam

You cannot hope to understand this region of the world without some understanding of Islam and its history. If you are looking for a relatively short book on Islamic beliefs and practices that is aimed at the general reader, one of the best is *Mohammedanism – An Historical Survey* by HAR Gibb.

If, on the other hand, you want to immerse yourself in the minutiae of Islamic history, culture and civilisation, the best work on the subject in English is Marshall GS Hodgson's *The Venture of Islam*. Even if you have no intention of wading through three volumes of Hodgson (totalling some 1500 pages), the first 100 pages of volume one (the introduction and prologue) are required reading for anyone headed for the Middle East.

The Quran itself is notoriously difficult to translate. Pious Muslims insist that it cannot be translated, only rendered or interpreted, into other languages. AJ Arberry's *The Koran Interpreted* is generally considered to be the best version available in English.

Those interested in Islamic literature should try another of Arberry's works, *Aspects of Islamic Civilization* (published in 1967) or James Kritzeck's *Anthology of Islamic Literature*.

Islam & the West The idea that the West is locked in some sort of struggle with the Islamic world (for which, usually, read the Arab Middle East, Iran and Iraq) has captured the imagination of many scholars, journalists and politicians in both the West and the Middle East in recent years. This struggle is usually seen as taking place on a variety of levels – security, immigration and economics to name but a few – and there is a growing cottage industry in books on the subject.

Noteworthy contributions in this genre include *Islam and the West* and *Cultures in Conflict: Christians, Muslims, and Jews in the Age of Discovery*, both by the respected US scholar Bernard Lewis. *The Failure of Political Islam* by Olivier Roy is a well-written discussion of the perceived shortcomings of Islam as a political force.

NEWSPAPERS & MAGAZINES

Both Oman and the UAE have local English-language newspapers. The best are *Gulf News* and *Khaleej Times* which both come out of Dubai in the UAE but are also available in Muscat (Oman). They provide fairly comprehensive coverage of regional events, though they will not tell you a lot about the Gulf itself. The English-language newspapers in Oman are OK but don't cover much ground.

Foreign publications such as the *International Herald Tribune*, the *Financial Times*, *The Daily Telegraph*, *The Independent*, *Le Monde* and the major German papers are all widely available in Oman and the UAE. These arrive between one and three days late, depending on the country of origin.

RADIO & TV

Both Oman and the UAE have English-language radio stations. BBC broadcasts can be received on various short-wave (SW) frequencies, including 12.095MHz, 11.760MHz, 9.410MHz, 15.070MHz and 15.575MHz, throughout the day. Some rental cars come equipped with short-wave radios.

Oman and the UAE also have English-language TV stations; SOTV (Sultanate of

Oman TV) is the best station in the region. These stations broadcast 24 hours a day and in the evening they carry a mix of old US, British and Australian programs (subtitled).

Most hotels, including small ones, have satellite TV. This usually consists of the standard four-channel package from Hong Kong-based Star TV: a music video channel, a sports channel, a movie channel, and BBC World Television or CNN for news. There are often one or two Indian or Pakistani services (Zee TV and/or PTV) and sometimes one or more of the Arabic satellite services (MBC, Dubai Satellite Channel, Nilesat, ART).

VIDEO SYSTEMS

Oman and the UAE use the PAL video system which is used in most of Western Europe, Australia and New Zealand. This has limited compatibility with the SECAM system in use in France and is not compatible with the NTSC systems in use in the USA. Videos sent out from the USA will not work on the region's TVs unless the set and video player are both multisystem units that accept the NTSC system. It's easy to buy multisystem VCRs from electronics shops in the major cities of the region.

PHOTOGRAPHY & VIDEO

The basic rules in Oman and the UAE are simple – do not photograph anything even vaguely military in nature (this always includes airports and border crossings) and don't point your camera at palaces, police stations or police officers, embassies and consulates. Authorities tend to be more sensitive about this in the UAE than in Oman. It's discourteous to photograph people without their permission, and you should never photograph women without asking their permission.

If you are taking photographs during the day, it's best to use a daylight filter on your lens. The glare is very strong and photos usually come out overexposed. Try reducing your aperture if you don't have a daylight filter. Winter is slightly less hazy and the glare is not quite as bad as in summer.

TIME

The UAE and Oman are in the same time zone, four hours ahead of GMT/UTC. Daylight saving is not observed. When it's noon in Oman or the UAE, the time elsewhere is:

city	time
Paris, Rome	9 am
London	8 am
New York	3 am
Los Angeles	midnight
Perth, Hong Kong	4 pm
Sydney	6 pm
Auckland	8 pm

ELECTRICITY

The voltage is 220 AC, 50 Hz. British-style three-pin wall sockets are used, even though most appliances are sold with two-pin plugs. Adaptors are available in most small grocery stores and supermarkets.

WEIGHTS & MEASURES

The metric system is in use throughout the region, although in the UAE petrol is sold by the imperial gallon. See the conversion chart at the back of this book if you are not familiar with the metric system.

LAUNDRY

There are no laundrettes in the region but all cities and most larger towns have small laundry shops. These places generally take about 24 hours to wash and iron your laundry, and their prices are usually very reasonable (OR1 or OR2 per item or Dh10 for a medium-sized load). Dry-cleaning services are also offered in most cities.

TOILETS

Most public toilets in the region's cities are Western-style and are generally clean. You'll find them in shopping centres (at the smaller ones you may have to ask a shopkeeper for the key as they are usually just for staff), hotels, public gardens, museums and some of the forts in Oman. Public toilets in souqs, bus stations or on the street are usually just for men.

Most restaurants and petrol stations on the main highways and in smaller towns and villages will have a toilet out the back but be aware that they are just holes in the ground and are generally in a pretty poor state. Toilet paper is usually not provided in these toilets, so take a supply with you.

HEALTH

Travel health depends on your predeparture preparations, your daily health care while travelling and how you handle any medical problem that does develop. While there *are* potential dangers, in reality the most a traveller will experience is an upset stomach.

Throughout the region the quality of health care is very high. When Oman and the UAE began to prosper, their rulers invested huge sums of money in hospitals, clinics and long-term health programs. The result is that these countries which only a generation or two ago were frequently overtaken by epidemics (which the Bedouin traditionally used as a way of marking time – for example, a child would be said to have been born 'in the year after the year of measles') now enjoy a standard of health care which equals that of the richest countries in the West.

Emergency medical care at government hospitals is free; the cost of nonurgent care varies considerably depending on whether you attend a private or government clinic. For details see the Health sections in the country Facts for the Visitor chapters.

Predeparture Planning

Immunisations Plan ahead for getting your vaccinations: some require more than one injection, while some vaccinations should not be given together. Note that some vaccinations should not be given during pregnancy or in people with allergies – check with your doctor. It is recommended you seek medical advice at least six weeks before you travel.

It's a good idea to have a record of your vaccinations, which your doctor or a public health department will be able to provide you with.

Discuss your individual requirements with your doctor, but following is a list of vaccinations you should consider for a trip to Oman or the UAE. For details about the diseases themselves, see the relevant entries later in this section.

Note that if you are coming from a yellow fever-infected area (sub-Saharan Africa and parts of South America), you will need to show proof of vaccination against yellow fever as a condition of entry to Oman (but not the UAE).

Diphtheria & Tetanus Vaccinations for these two diseases are usually combined and are recommended for everyone. After an initial course of three injections (usually given in childhood), boosters are necessary every 10 years.

Polio Everyone should keep up to date with this vaccination, which is normally given in childhood. A booster every 10 years maintains immunity.

Hepatitis A Hepatitis A vaccine provides long-term immunity (possibly more than 10 years) after an initial injection and a booster at six to 12 months.

Alternatively, an injection of gamma globulin can provide short-term protection against hepatitis A – two to six months, depending on the dose given. It is not a vaccine, but is ready-made antibody collected from blood donations. It is reasonably effective and, unlike the vaccine, it is protective immediately, but because it is a blood product, there are current concerns about its long-term safety.

Hepatitis A vaccine is also available in a combined form with hepatitis B vaccine. Three injections over a six-month period are required, the first two providing substantial protection against hepatitis A.

Typhoid Vaccination against typhoid may be a good idea if you are travelling for more than a couple of weeks in Oman and the UAE. It is available either as an injection or as capsules to be taken orally.

Hepatitis B Travellers who should consider vaccination against hepatitis B include those on a long trip, as well as those visiting countries where there are high levels of hepatitis B infection, where blood transfusions may not be adequately screened or where sexual contact or needle sharing is a possibility. Vaccination involves three injections, with a booster at 12 months. More rapid courses are available if necessary.

Rabies Vaccination should be considered by those who will spend a month or longer in a country where rabies is common, especially if they are cycling, handling animals, caving or travelling to remote areas, and for children (who may not report a bite). Pretravel rabies vaccination involves having three injections over 21 to 28 days. If someone who has been vaccinated is bitten or scratched by an animal, they will require two booster injections of vaccine; those not vaccinated require more.

Malaria Medication Discuss with your doctor, but you should consider taking malaria medication if you are venturing out to rural areas in Oman or the northern emirates of the UAE.

Antimalarial drugs do not prevent you from being infected but kill the malaria parasites during a stage in their development and significantly reduce your risk of becoming very ill or dying. Expert advice on medication should be sought, as there are many factors to consider, including the area to be visited, the risk of exposure to malaria-carrying mosquitoes, the side effects of medication, your medical history, your age and whether you are pregnant.

Health Insurance Make sure that you have adequate health insurance. See Travel Insurance under Visas & Documents earlier in this chapter for details.

Travel Health Guides There are a number of books on travel health, including:

Travellers' Health, Dr Richard Dawood, Oxford University Press, 1995. Comprehensive, easy to read, authoritative and highly recommended, although it's rather large to lug around.
Travel with Children, Maureen Wheeler, Lonely Planet Publications, 1995. Includes advice on travel health for younger children.

There are several excellent travel health sites on the Internet. From the Lonely Planet homepage there are links at www .lonelyplanet.com/weblinks/wlprep.htm#he al to the World Health Organization (WHO) and the US Centers for Disease Control & Prevention.

Other Preparations Make sure you're healthy before you start travelling. If you

---

Medical Kit Check List

Following is a list of items you could consider including in your medical kit – consult your pharmacist for brands available in your country. Although you will be able to find most common items in pharmacies throughout Oman and the UAE, it's handy to have some basics with you. If you are planning on going off-roading, you should definitely take a well-stocked medical kit with you.

☐ **Aspirin or paracetamol (acetaminophen in the USA)** – for pain or fever
☐ **Antihistamine** – for allergies, eg, hay fever; to ease the itch from insect bites or stings; and to prevent motion sickness
☐ **Cold and flu tablets, throat lozenges and nasal decongestant**
☐ **Loperamide or diphenoxylate** – blockers for diarrhoea
☐ **Prochlorperazine or metaclopramide** – for nausea and vomiting
☐ **Rehydration mixture** – to prevent dehydration, which may occur, for example, during bouts of diarrhoea; particularly important when travelling with children
☐ **Insect repellent, sunscreen, lip balm and eye drops**
☐ **Calamine lotion, sting relief spray or aloe vera** – to ease irritation from sunburn and insect bites or stings
☐ **Antifungal cream or powder** – for fungal skin infections and thrush
☐ **Antiseptic (such as povidone-iodine)** – for cuts and grazes
☐ **Bandages, Band-Aids (plasters) and other wound dressings**
☐ **Water purification tablets or iodine**
☐ **Scissors, tweezers and a thermometer** – note that mercury thermometers are prohibited by airlines

---

are going on a long trip make sure your teeth are OK. If you wear glasses take a spare pair and your prescription.

If you require a particular medication take an adequate supply, as your brand may not be available locally. Take the prescription or, better still, part of the packaging showing the generic rather than the brand name, as it will make getting replacements easier. It's a good idea to have a prescription or doctor's letter with you to show you legally use the medication, to avoid any problems.

Basic Rules

Care in what you eat and drink is the most important health rule. Although you are unlikely to suffer any stomach upsets in Oman or the UAE, you may find some of the following advice useful.

Food In general, the standard of hygiene in restaurants in Oman and the UAE, even the smaller ones, is quite good. Take note of the cleanliness of a place when you walk in. If it's clean and flies are few and far between, the kitchen and the food prepared in it are likely to be clean as well. The only food you should consider actively avoiding is shwarmas from street stands. The skewered meat that sits on these grills out in the open attracts flies and dirt. In the UAE, the Health Department is making moves to get rid of them. You can still get shwarmas from cafes where the meat is cooked indoors. Also, if you are eating at some of the smaller Arab, Indian or Pakistani restaurants, you may want to avoid raw salads. If you are buying food from the market get there early. It's just common sense to buy food as fresh as possible. Avoid buying meat from these markets; the risk of disease is too high. It's better to buy packaged meat from Europe, Australia or Saudi Arabia available from supermarkets.

Dairy products in the region are manufactured to Western standards, though in more remote places you might want to check the 'use by' date and see whether the products have been stored properly.

Water Although the water in Oman and the UAE is safe to drink, it tastes awful as most of it comes from the desalination plants. Most people drink bottled water which is readily available from shops everywhere and from vending machines in the cities.

In this hot climate make sure you drink enough – don't rely on feeling thirsty to in-

dicate when you should drink. Not needing to urinate or very dark yellow urine are danger signs. Always carry a water bottle with you on long trips. Excessive sweating can lead to loss of salt and therefore muscle cramping. Salt tablets are not a good idea as a preventative, but in places where salt is not used much, adding salt to food can help.

Nutrition Make sure your diet is well balanced. Eggs, beans, lentils (*dahl* in the region's numerous Indian restaurants) and nuts are all safe ways to get protein. Fruit you can peel (such as bananas, oranges or mandarins) is safe and a good source of vitamins. Try to eat plenty of grains (including rice) and bread. Remember that although food is generally safer if it is cooked well, overcooked food loses much of its nutritional value. If your diet isn't well balanced or if your food intake is insufficient, you may want to consider taking vitamin and iron supplements.

Medical Problems & Treatment

Self-diagnosis and treatment of medical problems can be risky, so wherever possible seek qualified help. You can take some comfort from the fact that the standard of medical care throughout the region is among the highest in the world. An embassy, consulate or five-star hotel can usually recommend a local doctor or clinic.

Although we give treatment dosages in this section, they are for emergency use only. Correct diagnosis is vital. In this section we have used the generic names for medications because these should be understood anywhere – check with a pharmacist for brands available locally.

Environmental Hazards

Sunburn This is a problem year-round in Oman and the UAE. You can get sunburnt surprisingly quickly here, even through cloud. Use a sunscreen and take extra care to cover areas which don't normally see the sun, such as your feet. A hat provides added protection and should be considered a necessity in this part of the world. You should also use zinc cream or some other barrier cream for your nose and lips. Calamine lotion, aloe vera or an insect sting relief spray are good for mild sunburn. Protect your eyes with good-quality sunglasses.

Prickly Heat Prickly heat is an itchy rash caused by excessive perspiration trapped under the skin. It usually strikes people who have just arrived in a hot climate. Keeping cool, bathing often, drying the skin and using a mild talcum or prickly heat powder or resorting to air-conditioning may help.

Heat Exhaustion Dehydration or salt deficiency can cause heat exhaustion. However, life in the Gulf is now so universally air-conditioned that this is less of a problem than you might think. Still, it pays to take time to acclimatise to high temperatures and make sure you get sufficient liquids, especially if you are out and about in the heat of the day.

Salt deficiency is characterised by fatigue, lethargy, headaches, giddiness and muscle cramps: salt tablets may help, but adding extra salt to your food is better. Vomiting or diarrhoea can deplete your liquid and salt levels.

Heatstroke This serious, and sometimes fatal, condition can occur if the body's heat-regulating mechanism breaks down and the body temperature rises to dangerous levels. Long, continuous periods of exposure to high temperatures and insufficient fluids can leave you vulnerable to heatstroke. You should avoid excessive alcohol or strenuous activity when you first arrive in a hot climate.

The symptoms are feeling unwell, not sweating very much or at all and a high body temperature (39° to 41°C). Where sweating has ceased the skin becomes flushed and red. Severe, throbbing headaches and lack of co-ordination will also occur, and the sufferer may be confused or aggressive. Eventually the casualty will become delirious or convulse. Hospitalisation is essential, but meanwhile get the casualty out of the sun, remove their clothing, cover them with a wet sheet or towel and then fan continually. Give them fluids to drink if they are conscious.

Jet Lag Jet lag is experienced when a person travels by air across more than three time zones (each time zone usually represents a one-hour time difference). It occurs because many of the functions of the human body (such as temperature, pulse rate and emptying of the bladder and bowels) are regulated by internal 24-hour cycles. When we travel long distances rapidly, our bodies take time to adjust to the 'new time' of our destination, and we may experience fatigue, disorientation, insomnia, anxiety, impaired concentration and loss of appetite. These effects will usually be gone within three days of arrival, but to minimise the impact of jet lag:

• Rest for a couple of days prior to departure.
• Try to select flight schedules that minimise sleep deprivation; arriving late in the day means you can go to sleep soon after you arrive. For very long flights, try to organise a stopover.
• Avoid excessive eating (which bloats the stomach) and alcohol (which causes dehydration) during the flight. Instead, drink plenty of noncarbonated, nonalcoholic drinks such as fruit juice or water.
• Avoid smoking.
• Make yourself comfortable by wearing loose-fitting clothes and perhaps bringing an eye mask and earplugs to help you sleep.
• Try to sleep at the appropriate time for the time zone you are travelling to.

Infectious Diseases

Diarrhoea Simple things like a change of water, food or climate can all cause a mild bout of diarrhoea, but a few rushed toilet trips with no other symptoms is not indicative of a major problem.

Dehydration is the main danger with any diarrhoea, particularly in children or the elderly, as dehydration can occur quite quickly. Under all circumstances *fluid replacement* (at least equal to the volume being lost) is the most important thing to remember. Weak black tea with a little sugar, soda water, or soft drinks allowed to go flat and diluted 50% with clean water are all good. With severe diarrhoea a rehydrating solution is preferable to replace minerals and salts lost. Commercially available oral rehydration salts (ORS) are very useful; add them to boiled or bottled water. In an emergency you can make up a solution of six teaspoons of sugar and a half-teaspoon of salt to 1L of boiled or bottled water.

You need to drink at least the same volume of fluid that you are losing in diarrhoea and vomiting. How much urine you are passing is the best guide to whether you are drinking enough – if you're passing small amounts of concentrated (dark) urine, you need to drink more. Keep drinking small amounts often. Stick to a bland diet as you recover.

Antidiarrhoeals or 'blockers' such as Lomotil, Imodium and other brand names can be used to bring relief from the symptoms, although they do not actually cure the problem. Only use these drugs if absolutely necessary, for example if you must travel. These drugs should not be used in children under 12 years or if you have a high fever or are severely dehydrated.

When to See a Doctor Although most cases of travellers diarrhoea clear up on their own, in some situations you will need to seek medical help. Avoid antidiarrhoeals and see a doctor if:

- You have diarrhoea with blood or mucus (dysentery).
- You have a fever of 38°C or over.
- If the diarrhoea is severe (frequent and/or large quantities) or the diarrhoea does not improve after 48 hours.
- If you have persistent diarrhoea (it doesn't clear up after a week or so).

If for some reason you can't get medical help (for example you are in a remote area), the recommended drugs for bacterial diarrhoea (the most likely cause of severe diarrhoea in travellers) are norfloxacin 400mg twice daily for three days or ciprofloxacin 500mg twice daily for five days. These are not recommended for children or pregnant women. The drug of choice for children would be a five-day course of co-trimoxazole with dosage dependent on weight. Ampicillin or amoxycillin may be given in pregnancy, but medical care is necessary.

Persistent Diarrhoea Although relatively rare in travellers to Oman and the UAE, two causes of persistent diarrhoea to be aware of are giardiasis and amoebic dysentery. Symptoms of giardiasis include stomach cramps, nausea, a bloated stomach, watery, foul-smelling diarrhoea and frequent gas. The symptoms may disappear for a few days and then return; this can go on for several weeks.

With amoebic dysentery you get a gradual onset of low-grade diarrhoea, often with blood and mucus. Fever, cramping abdominal pain and vomiting are less likely than in other types of diarrhoea. Amoebic dysentery will persist until treated and can recur and cause other health problems.

You should seek medical advice if you think you have giardiasis or amoebic dysentery but where this is not possible, tinidazole (Fasigyn) or metronidazole (Flagyl) are the recommended drugs. Treatment is a 2g single dose of tinidazole or 250mg of metronidazole three times daily for five to 10 days.

Fungal Infections Fungal infections occur more commonly in hot weather and are usually found on the scalp, between the toes (athlete's foot) or fingers, in the groin and on the body (ringworm). You get ringworm (which is a fungal infection, not a worm) from infected animals or other people. Moisture encourages these infections.

To prevent fungal infections wear loose, comfortable clothes, avoid artificial fibres, wash frequently and dry yourself carefully. If you do get an infection, wash the infected area at least daily with a disinfectant or medicated soap and water, and rinse and dry well. Apply an antifungal cream or powder. Try to expose the infected area to air or sunlight as much as possible and wash all towels and underwear in hot water, change them often and let them dry in the sun.

Hepatitis Hepatitis is a general term for inflammation of the liver. Hepatitis is no longer common in the Gulf but it is not unheard of.

There are several different viruses that cause hepatitis, and they differ in the way that they are transmitted. The symptoms are similar in all forms of the illness, and include fever, chills, headache, fatigue, feelings of weakness and aches and pains, followed by loss of appetite, nausea, vomiting, abdominal pain, dark urine, light-coloured faeces, jaundiced (yellow) skin and yellowing of the whites of the eyes. People who have had hepatitis should avoid alcohol for some time after the illness, as the liver needs time to recover.

Hepatitis A is transmitted by contaminated food and drinking water. You should seek medical advice, but there is not much you can do apart from resting, drinking lots of fluids, eating lightly and avoiding fatty foods. Hepatitis E is transmitted in the same way as hepatitis A; it can be particularly serious in pregnant women.

There are almost 300 million chronic carriers of **hepatitis B** in the world. In some areas of the Gulf up to 20% of the population carry the hepatitis B virus. It is spread through contact with infected blood, blood products or body fluids, for example through sexual contact, unsterilised needles and blood transfusions, or contact with blood via small breaks in the skin. Other risk situations include having a shave, tattoo or body piercing with contaminated equipment. The symptoms of hepatitis B may be more severe than type A and the disease can lead to long-term problems such as chronic liver damage, liver cancer or a long-term carrier state. Hepatitis C and D are spread in the same way as hepatitis B and can also lead to long-term complications.

There are vaccines against hepatitis A and B, but there are currently no vaccines against the other types of hepatitis. Following the basic rules about food and water (hepatitis A and E) and avoiding risk situations (hepatitis B, C and D) are important preventative measures.

HIV & AIDS Infection with the human immunodeficiency virus (HIV) leads to acquired immune deficiency syndrome (AIDS), which is a fatal disease. Any exposure to blood, blood products or body fluids may put the individual at risk. The disease is often transmitted through sexual contact or dirty needles – vaccinations, acupuncture, tattooing and body piercing can be potentially as dangerous as intravenous drug use. HIV/AIDS can also be spread through infected blood transfusions; blood is said to be screened for AIDS in Gulf countries, but most Gulf countries also play down the incidence of AIDS locally. Public education campaigns tend to present the disease as something dangerous but also essentially as a foreign problem. Note that you need an HIV test to get a residency visa in both Oman and the UAE.

If you do need an injection, you can be sure that procedures and hygiene in Oman and the UAE are first class. If you are worried though, ask to see the syringe unwrapped in front of you, or take a needle and syringe pack with you.

Fear of HIV infection should never stop you from seeking treatment for serious medical conditions.

Intestinal Worms These parasites are most common in rural, tropical areas and are uncommon in Oman and the UAE. The different worms have different ways of infecting people. Some may be ingested on food such as undercooked meat (eg, tapeworms) and some enter through your skin (eg, hookworms). Infestations may not show up for some time, and although they are generally not serious, if left untreated some can cause severe health problems later. Consider having a stool test when you return home to check for these and determine the appropriate treatment.

Sexually Transmitted Infections HIV and hepatitis B can be transmitted through sexual intercourse – for more details, see the relevant sections earlier in this chapter. Other sexually transmitted infections (STIs) include gonorrhoea, herpes and syphilis. Common symptoms include blisters or rashes around the genitals and discharge or pain when urinating. In some STIs, such as wart virus or chlamydia, symptoms may be less marked or not observed at all, especially in women. Syphilis symptoms eventually disappear completely but the disease continues and can cause severe problems in later years. While abstinence from sexual contact is the only 100% effective prevention, using condoms is also effective. Many STIs can be treated with appropriate antibiotics. There is currently no cure for HIV/AIDS.

Malaria

This serious disease is spread by mosquito bites. Malaria has virtually been eradicated in much of the Gulf but is still a problem in Oman and rural areas of the northern emirates of the UAE. In recent years there have been reports of the disease in both the northern and southern coastal areas of Oman and in the mountainous regions of northern UAE. For up-to-date information on the risks, check with your doctor or a specialist travel health clinic, or contact the Omani and UAE embassy in your home country.

If you are travelling in risk areas it is extremely important to avoid mosquito bites and to take tablets to prevent this disease. Symptoms range from fever, chills and sweating, headache, diarrhoea and abdominal pains to a vague feeling of ill-health. Seek medical help immediately if malaria is suspected. Without treatment malaria can rapidly become more serious and can be fatal.

If medical care is not available, malaria tablets can be used for treatment. You need to use a malaria tablet which is different from the one you were taking when you contracted malaria. The standard treatment dose of mefloquine is two 250mg tablets and a further two six hours later. For Fansidar, it's a single dose of three tablets. If you were previously taking mefloquine and cannot obtain Fansidar, then other alternatives are Malarone (atovaquone-proguanil; four tablets once daily for three days), halofantrine (three doses of two 250mg tablets every six hours) or quinine sulphate (600mg every six hours). There is a greater risk of side effects with these dosages than in normal use if used with mefloquine, so medical advice is preferable. Be aware also that halofantrine is no longer recommended by the WHO as emergency stand-by treatment, because of side effects, and should only be used if no other drugs are available.

The best preventative is to avoid getting bitten by mosquitoes:

- Wear light-coloured clothing.
- Wear long trousers and long-sleeved shirts.
- Use DEET-containing mosquito repellents on exposed areas (prolonged overuse of DEET may be harmful, especially to children, but its use is considered preferable to being bitten by disease-transmitting mosquitoes).
- Avoid perfumes or aftershave.
- Use a mosquito net impregnated with mosquito repellent (permethrin) – it may be worth taking your own.
- Impregnating clothes with permethrin effectively deters mosquitoes and other insects.

Cuts, Bites & Stings

See Less Common Diseases later in this chapter for details of rabies, which is passed through animal bites.

Cuts & Scratches Wash well and treat any cut with an antiseptic such as povidone-iodine. Skin punctures can easily become infected in hot climates and may be difficult to heal. Where possible avoid bandages and Band-aids, which can keep wounds wet. Coral cuts are notoriously slow to heal, as the coral injects a weak venom into the wound. If coral cuts are not cleaned properly, small pieces of coral can become embedded in the wound. Avoid coral cuts by wearing shoes when walking on reefs (or better still, don't walk on reefs), and clean any cut thoroughly.

Bites & Stings Bee and wasp stings are usually painful rather than dangerous, unless you are allergic to bee (and ant) stings, which is a medical emergency.

Calamine lotion or a sting relief spray will give relief or ice packs will reduce the pain and swelling. There are some spiders with dangerous bites but antivenoms are usually available.

Sandfly Bites Avoid sandfly bites by covering up and applying insect repellent, especially between late afternoon and dawn. Sandflies can transmit leishmaniasis, a group of parasitic diseases sometimes seen in travellers.

Scorpions Scorpion stings are a serious cause of illness and occasional deaths in Oman and the UAE. Shake shoes, clothing and towels before use. Inspect bedding and don't put hands or feet in crevices in dwellings where they may be lurking. A sting usually produces redness and swelling of the skin, but there may be no visible reaction. Pain is common, and tingling or numbness may occur. At this stage, cold compresses on the bite, and pain relief, such as paracetamol are called for. If the skin sensations start to spread from the sting site (eg along the limb) then immediate medical attention is required.

Snakes There are a variety of snake species that live in the mountains and wadis of the region. Most are not dangerous and it's likely that you will not spot a single one on your travels. You should be wary of the poisonous horned viper though. It is a rather small, pale-coloured snake with a diamond-shaped head.

To minimise your chances of being bitten always wear boots, socks and long trousers when walking through undergrowth where snakes may be present. Don't put your hands into holes and crevices, and be careful when collecting firewood.

Snake bites do not cause instantaneous death and antivenins are usually available. Keep the victim calm and still, wrap the bitten limb tightly, as you would for a sprained ankle, and attach a splint to immobilise it. Then seek medical help, if possible with the dead snake for identification. Don't attempt to catch the snake if there is even a remote possibility of anyone being bitten again. The use of tourniquets and sucking out the poison have now been comprehensively discredited.

Jellyfish These are a common problem in the waters around Oman and the UAE. Get local advice on risk areas and avoid contact with these sea creatures which have stinging tentacles. Stings from most jellyfish are simply rather painful. Dousing in vinegar will deactivate any stingers which have not 'fired'. Calamine lotion, antihistamines and simple painkillers may reduce the reaction and relieve the pain.

Less Common Diseases

The following diseases pose a small risk to travellers, and so are only mentioned in passing. Seek medical advice if you think you may have any of these diseases.

Cholera This diarrhoeal disease is now quite rare in the Gulf. If you think you may have cholera, remember that *fluid replacement is the most important treatment* as the biggest risk is dehydration.

Leishmaniasis This is a group of parasitic diseases transmitted by sandflies, which are found in Oman and the UAE, as well as other parts of the world. Cutaneous leishmaniasis affects the skin tissue causing ulceration and disfigurement, and visceral leishmaniasis affects the internal organs. Avoiding sandfly bites by using insect repellent is the best precaution.

Meningococcal Meningitis This very serious disease attacks the brain and can be fatal. It has appeared in the Gulf several times in recent years, although vaccination is not recommended for most travellers to Oman and the UAE. Check for reports of current epidemics.

The first symptoms are a scattered, blotchy rash (sometimes), fever, severe headache, sensitivity to light and neck stiffness which prevents forward bending of the head. Death can occur within a few hours, so it is vital to get medical help urgently.

Rabies Rabies is found in many countries, including Oman and the UAE, and is caused by a bite or scratch by an infected animal. Dogs, cats and rodents are common carriers, although you won't see many dogs in Oman and the UAE in keeping with the Muslim belief that the dog is an unclean animal.

Any bite, scratch or even lick from a warm-blooded, furry animal should be cleaned immediately and thoroughly. Scrub with soap and running water, and then clean with an alcohol solution. If there is any possibility that the animal is infected, medical help should be sought immediately. Even if the animal is not rabid all bites should be treated seriously as they can become infected or can result in tetanus. A rabies vaccination is now available and should be considered if you are in a high-risk category – eg, if you intend to explore caves in Oman (bat bites can be dangerous) or work with animals.

Tetanus This disease is caused by a germ which lives in soil and in the faeces of horses and other animals. It enters the body via breaks in the skin. The first symptom may be discomfort in swallowing, or stiffening of the jaw and neck; this is followed by painful convulsions of the jaw and whole body. The disease can be fatal. It can be prevented by vaccination.

Tuberculosis (TB) There is a worldwide resurgence of tuberculosis and there are high rates of infection in locals in Oman and the UAE. It is a bacterial infection which is usually transmitted from person to person by coughing but may be transmitted through consumption of unpasteurised milk or milk products. Milk that has been boiled is safe to drink, and the souring of milk to make yoghurt or cheese also kills the bacilli. You are unlikely to come across unpasteurised milk except in remote rural areas.

Travellers are usually not at great risk, as close household contact with the infected person is required before the disease is passed on. The usual site of the disease is the lungs, although often other organs may be involved. Most infected people never develop any symptoms. In those who do, especially infants, symptoms may arise within weeks of the infection occurring and may be severe. In most, however, the disease lies dormant for many years until, for some reason, the infected person becomes physically run-down. Symptoms include fever, weight loss, night sweats and coughing.

Typhoid Typhoid fever is a dangerous gut infection which can be acquired through ingesting contaminated water and food. Get medical help urgently if you think you may have typhoid. Early symptoms are a headache, body aches and fever. There may also be vomiting, abdominal pain, diarrhoea or constipation.

In the second week the high fever and slow pulse continue and a few pink spots may appear on the body; trembling, delirium, weakness, weight loss and dehydration may occur. Complications such as pneumonia, perforated bowel or meningitis may occur.

Women's Health

Gynaecological Problems Antibiotic use, synthetic underwear, sweating and contraceptive pills can lead to fungal vaginal infections, especially when travelling in hot climates. Fungal infections are characterised by a rash, itch and discharge. Nystatin, miconazole or clotrimazole pessaries or vaginal cream are the usual treatment but if you are in a remote area without access to treatment, you could try a vinegar or lemon-juice douche or natural yoghurt. Maintaining good personal hygiene and wearing loose-fitting clothes and cotton underwear may help prevent these infections.

Sexually transmitted infections are a major cause of vaginal problems. Symptoms include a smelly discharge, painful intercourse and sometimes a burning sensation when urinating. Medical attention should be sought and male sexual partners must also be treated. Remember that in addition to these diseases, HIV or hepatitis B may also be acquired during exposure. Besides abstinence, the best thing is to practise safe sex using condoms.

Pregnancy If you are planning to travel to Oman and the UAE while you're pregnant, discuss this with your doctor. Some vaccinations used to prevent serious diseases are not advisable during pregnancy, and some diseases you may be at risk for while travelling (such as malaria) are much more serious in pregnancy and may increase the risk of a stillborn child.

Timing is important: most miscarriages occur during the first three months of pregnancy, and can occasionally lead to severe bleeding. The last three months should also be spent within reasonable distance of good medical care.

On the road, you'll need to take additional care to prevent illness and pay particular attention to your diet and nutrition.

WOMEN TRAVELLERS

Travel in Oman and the UAE can be hard work for women, especially unaccompanied women. Half-truths and stereotypes exist on both sides – many Westerners assume that all local women are repressed, veiled victims and there is a large section of the male community in Oman and the UAE that thinks all Western women are promiscuous and 'easy'.

There are several reasons for this. Traditionally, in conservative Muslim families, wives and daughters stay out of sight of other men – in the house, behind the veil and in special 'family' areas of restaurants. This is one reason why women travellers are regarded with such amazement and curiosity. In traditional society, the role of the woman is specifically defined: she is wife and mother. This is one reason why women travellers are often asked 'Where is your husband' or 'Are you married' and, if the answer is yes, 'How many children?'.

Conservative Muslim men, by the same token, have little contact with women outside their own family. This is why a Western woman's questions may be answered to her male companion rather than directly to her. Because many men have little contact with women other than members of their own family, their views of 'other' women, including Western women, tend to come from popular culture and the media.

This is not to say that all people in Oman and the UAE are conservative. You'll find that in the major cities of the region, people

Changing Roles

The young Emirati or Omani woman with her lime-green platform shoes, confidently strolling through a modern shopping centre and chatting on her mobile phone, is an enormous contrast to the older veiled or masked woman, selling her handicrafts in souqs throughout Oman and the UAE. The modernisation of Oman and the UAE has dragged many women with it and most of them have grasped the opportunities given to them to seek a broader role in society. Attitudes towards the traditional role of women are gradually shifting in the region, and women now have a strong presence in public life.

The number of women in the workforce, in both private and government sectors, has increased enormously over the past two decades. In the public service in the UAE, women now account for over 40% of employees, while in Oman they make up just over 30%. Apart from the traditionally female-dominated professions, such as teaching and nursing, local women can be found in the media, military, travel and tourism industry and police force.

It may surprise you to hear that in the UAE female students outnumber male students in universities by three to one. This means that more women than men are now demanding and obtaining a variety of jobs at graduate level. In 1995 the UAE government made a great effort to encourage all nationals seeking work to register with the Ministry of the Interior. Of those who registered, 61% were women. In Oman, women account for almost half of the tertiary students.

This doesn't mean that the traditional role of women has been abandoned. Woman as carer, mother and nurturer is still very much in place, and the family is still considered the most important unit in society. Traditional handicrafts such as weaving are still practised and encouraged. The task at hand for Emirati and Omani women is to strike a comfortable balance.

are used to seeing Western women, and Western attitudes towards women are common. Unlike in nearby Saudi, women in the UAE and Oman can drive cars, eat in restaurants alone or with men to whom they are not married or related, shop in stores where men are also present etc.

On the plus side, serious physical harassment of women is rare. However, most women travellers will probably experience regular harassment in the form of unwanted male attention, intent stares and being beeped at by men in passing cars. This is more likely to occur in the UAE. In towns and rural areas in the UAE, although not so much in Oman, you may find that men cruise up to you if you are out walking on your own or in your car, and beep or gesture at you. If you find this particularly threatening or you are just fed up with the hassle, take down the number plate and report it to the police.

It is refreshing to know that in Dubai, at least, something positive is being done about harassment of women. Under the directive of Sheikh Mohammed, the Crown Prince of Dubai, any man found harassing women in public is arrested and has his picture published on page two of the *Gulf News*. Very embarrassing!

You don't have to act timid and vulnerable – maintaining your self-confidence and a sense of humour are vital. If a person or a situation is becoming troublesome head for a busy place, preferably where a lot of other foreigners and a few policemen are gathered (a shopping mall or the lobby of a big hotel, for example).

What to Wear

Women in Oman and the UAE dress very conservatively, even in relatively liberal Dubai – just look around you! The amount of hassle you get, especially if you are on your own or with other women travellers, is directly related to how you are dressed. Don't wear tight or revealing clothes as this is just going to make your life difficult. Your best bet is to wear baggy tops and loose cotton trousers or a long skirt. You'll find this is a good idea anyway to protect your skin from the sun. Although local women mostly cover their heads, Western women are not generally expected to wear a headscarf. Be especially careful to dress conservatively if you are travelling outside the main cities.

You can wear what you like on private beaches or in hotel swimming pools but at public beaches or pools, you'll probably feel very uncomfortable wearing anything less than a one-piece swimming costume and probably a sarong too. If local women go in the water (for example, at waterholes or hot springs in country areas), they go in fully clothed.

Around Town

In small towns and rural areas women, especially Western women, who enter small restaurants and coffeehouses will invariably suffer the embarrassment of men staring intently at them. At the less touristy coffeehouses women travellers will often get the feeling that they are just not meant to be there. Our advice is that if the staring makes you uncomfortable, don't go in. Alternatively, if you don't have a choice (ie, if it's the only place to eat in town), sit where you can face the wall and have your back to the starers. What you don't see won't bother you. (Better yet, travel with a male companion who can stare back threateningly.) In the small Indian and Pakistani restaurants you (and any male companion) will often be ushered into the 'family room'. You don't *have* to sit here but the room is there to save you from being stared at, and can be a real godsend.

Try to avoid the really cheap hotels, especially in Dubai, as they are renowned for accommodating prostitutes from the CIS and Africa and you could run the risk of being mistaken for one. In fact, many budget hotels in the UAE will not rent rooms to single women. In Oman, the cheapest places are not really 'cheap' and are perfectly OK for single women travellers.

You'll find that you'll often be required to take the front seat in buses or be asked to sit next to other women. This is so that women

Tips for Women Travellers

- Wear a wedding ring. Local men generally seem to have more respect for a married woman. You could also carry a picture of a child for when you get asked the inevitable 'Any children?'
- If you are travelling with a man, it is better to say you're married rather than 'just friends'.
- Avoid direct eye contact with a local man unless you know him well. Wearing dark sunglasses can help.
- Try not to react to an obnoxious comment from a man; act as if you didn't hear it.
- Be very careful about behaving in a flirtatious or suggestive manner, however unintentional – it could create unimaginable problems for you.
- If you need help for any reason (directions etc), consider asking a woman first, if possible.
- Be extra careful with your dress and actions in rural areas. In the major cities of the region people are used to seeing Western women but it's different once you're out of the cities, although people are generally more polite.

don't have to sit next to a man they are unrelated to or don't know. It's best to sit in the back seat of taxis and avoid making chitchat, as this friendliness on your part could be misconstrued.

In banks, telephone offices, post offices and libraries there are usually separate sections or windows for women – great when there's a queue!

Note that single women are not permitted to enter or leave Oman by land unless they are travelling on a public transport bus. See Visas & Documents/Other Documents in the Oman Facts for the Visitor chapter for more information on this restriction.

GAY & LESBIAN TRAVELLERS

Officially, homosexuality is illegal in Oman and the UAE and can attract a jail sentence of up to two years. Unofficially, prosecu-

tion is unlikely if you are reasonably discreet. We have had a number of letters from gay travellers who have had no trouble travelling in the region, and have met other gays there. The only trouble is likely to come from homophobic Westerners. Men walking hand in hand is quite common here and not seen as indicative of sexual orientation as it often is in the West. It's less common to see women walking hand in hand.

DISABLED TRAVELLERS

Although you may see car parks around the major cities with areas marked for disabled drivers, it seems that services and facilities end here in most places. Unfortunately, ramps in car parks and into most buildings in the cities are few and far between. Things are slightly better in the UAE than in Oman, and most major shopping centres have wheelchair access while the newly renovated Dubai airport has facilities for the disabled, including low check-in counters. In Dubai, Dubai Transport (☎ 04-208 0808) has a number of taxis that can take wheelchairs but this is the only service of this kind in the UAE. Most five-star hotels in the region have rooms equipped for disabled guests.

If you are going to the UAE, try contacting North Tours in Dubai (☎ 04-398 6173, fax 398 8355), run by a disabled man. North Tours can arrange cruises, desert safaris, mountain tours, whatever you like. It can also book hotels that have facilities for disabled guests and it can sponsor visas.

Organisations

For more information, try contacting the Association for the Disabled in Oman (☎/fax 597657, PO Box 331, Muscat 113, Sultanate of Oman). At the time of writing there were no official associations or societies for the disabled in the UAE although a pressure group in Dubai was calling for an Association for Disabled Persons to be set up. Its aims are to develop a disabled-friendly environment and transport system, promote tourism for the disabled and ensure a wide range of rehabilitation services.

SENIOR TRAVELLERS

For a region that traditionally respects its elders, it is surprising to find that there are no discounts available to senior travellers for such things as admission fees and public transport. If you are not as mobile as you might be, one good thing is that all hotels have elevators, even the cheapest ones, so you won't have to contend with endless flights of stairs.

TRAVEL WITH CHILDREN

In Oman and the UAE the family is acknowledged as the most important unit in daily life. Consequently, travellers with children will find themselves well looked after. Entertaining the kids is a breeze, and Oman and the UAE are relatively healthy places to take children – just watch out for sunburn and the heat, if your children are not used to it. There are nappy-changing facilities in most shopping centre toilets. High chairs are available at most restaurants although eating out with the kids is not very common among local families. One thing is for sure, breast-feeding in public is definitely out of the question. Lonely Planet's *Travel with Children* is full of tips and ideas for those on the move with the clan.

DANGERS & ANNOYANCES

In general you should find Oman and the UAE to be very safe places to travel in. Muggers are all but unknown and you can feel perfectly safe walking the streets at night alone (although this is never recommended for women alone). As a region it has largely been spared the high-profile political unrest associated with some other parts of the Middle East.

Although theft is practically unknown in most parts of the region, pickpockets have been known to operate around the Deira souq area of Dubai, so take care. In any case, it's common sense to exercise the same sort of caution with your personal safety and belongings as you would anywhere.

The main danger is bad drivers. They abound here, so if you are planning to drive, be alert on the roads and don't expect people

to drive as considerately as you may be used to. The UAE has a particularly bad reputation for reckless driving. People tend to cut in front of you, turn without indicating, race each other on freeways, and take up three parking spaces. They have a tendency to wander across lanes at roundabouts and to try to turn out of them from inside lanes. Don't be surprised if a car stops dead on the road in front of you so the driver can chat to a friend or watch a nearby spectacle. Eternal vigilance is the price of avoiding fender-benders. If you are on foot, be very careful crossing the road. Pedestrian crossings mean nothing to drivers here and they will not slow down, let alone stop, for you.

LEGAL MATTERS

Involvement with drugs in either country will usually get you a jail sentence and deportment. Those attempting to bring in very large amounts of narcotics could receive the death sentence. Jail sentences for being involved in drugs just by association are also likely. That means that even if you are in the same room where there are drugs, but you are not partaking, you could still be in as much trouble as those who are. Theft and writing a bad cheque are also taken pretty seriously and usually involve jail and deportation. Drink driving is another misdemeanour that is taken pretty seriously.

If you are arrested for any reason you will be allowed to make a phone call. Get in touch with your embassy/consulate first if you are on a visit visa, or your sponsor if you are a resident.

If you are involved in a road traffic accident, it's a case of guilty until proven innocent. In the UAE this means you may be held under police guard (even if you are in hospital) until an investigation reveals whose fault the accident was.

BUSINESS HOURS

The weekend is Thursday and Friday. Some embassies, consulates and private businesses open on Thursday mornings and shops generally close on Friday morning only, reopening Friday evening. Banks are usually only open in the morning, Saturday to Wednesday, and sometimes Thursday as well. A few companies and embassies, particularly in the UAE, have recently gone to a Friday/Saturday weekend, but this remains the exception rather than the rule. During the month of Ramadan, government offices keep shorter hours.

Businesses (except banks – see earlier) are generally open 7.30 or 8 am to 1 pm and 4 or 4.30 to 7 or 8 pm. Note that most smaller shops, souqs and small cafes, but not restaurants, close for a few hours in the afternoon; most shopping centres in the UAE (though not in Oman) stay open all day. During Ramadan, shops tend not to open until 6 or 7 pm but stay open late (11 pm or midnight). See Business Hours in the individual country Facts for the Visitor chapters for more specific information.

Ramadan

This month, during which Muslims fast from dawn until dusk, is observed more strictly in Oman and the UAE (and elsewhere in the Gulf) than in many other parts of the Muslim world. The sale of alcohol is banned so bars, pubs and discos close up for the month. Everyone, regardless of their religion, is required to observe the fast in public. That not only means no eating and drinking but no smoking as well. Although it is unlikely you will be arrested for breaking these rules, as you would be in Saudi Arabia, you may be stopped by the police and told to get rid of your sandwich or put your cigarette out.

In spite of these restrictions, Ramadan is an exciting time to be here. The breaking of the fast each evening (*iftar* in Arabic) is a big event and the streets tend to come alive after dark. Tents are set up in public areas and food and coffee is served throughout most of the night. Sheesha pipes are brought out at night in the UAE but they are banned in Muscat during Ramadan.

Few restaurants are open during the daytime. Some hotels will still serve breakfast and lunch to guests but most of the time eating during the day means room service or self-catering. Non-Muslims offered coffee or tea when meeting a Muslim during the daytime in Ramadan should initially refuse politely. If your host insists, and repeats the offer several times, you should accept as long as it does not look as though your doing so is going to anger anyone else in the room who may be fasting.

PUBLIC HOLIDAYS & SPECIAL EVENTS

Most of the holidays observed are Islamic religious celebrations. The only secular holiday observed by both countries is New Year's Day (1 January), although both countries celebrate their national days. Note that if a public holiday falls on a weekend, the holiday is usually taken at the beginning of the next working week.

Because the Islamic or Hejira (meaning 'flight' as in the flight of Mohammed from Mecca in AD 622) calendar is 11 days shorter than the Gregorian (Western) calendar, Islamic holidays fall approximately 11 days earlier each year. This is not a fixed rule, however, as the exact dates of Islamic holidays depend upon the sighting of the moon at a particular stage of its cycle. This is why definitive dates for Islamic holidays are not announced until a day or two before they occur. The table of Islamic holidays in this section is an approximation of dates for the next few years.

Lailat al-Mi'raj is the celebration of the Ascension of Prophet Mohammed. Eid al-Fitr is a three-day celebration marking the end of Ramadan, the month of fasting, and Eid al-Adha is a four-day celebration that occurs after the main pilgrimage to Mecca (*haj*).

In the UAE, the death of a minister, a member of the royal family or the head of state of another Arab country is marked by a three-day mourning period. Government institutions and some private companies will close. In Oman these mourning holidays generally only occur if someone important in the Oman government dies. These extra-

Table of Islamic Holidays

Hejira Year	New Year	Prophet's Birthday	Ramadan	Eid al-Fitr	Eid al-Adha	Lailat al-Mi'raj
1421	06.04.00	14.06.00	27.11.00	27.12.00	06.03.01	04.11.00
1422	26.03.01	03.06.01	16.11.01	16.12.01	23.02.02	24.10.01
1423	15.03.02	23.05.02	05.11.02	05.12.02	12.02.03	13.10.01
1424	04.03.03	12.05.03	25.10.03	24.11.03	01.02.04	02.10.01
1425	22.02.04	01.05.04	14.10.04	13.11.04	21.01.05	10.09.04
1426	11.02.05	20.04.05	03.10.05	02.11.05	10.01.06	30.08.05

ordinary holidays are announced in the newspaper on the day they occur.

ACTIVITIES

This section gives an overview of activities available in Oman and the UAE; for details of activities specific to each country, see Activities in the individual country Facts for the Visitor chapters.

Off-Road Safaris

Expeditions to the desert and mountain wadis in 4WD vehicles are a long-established pastime among both locals and expatriates. They involve zooming around the dunes or mountains in a 4WD, with stops for food and merriment. There are dozens of possibilities for off-road jaunts that take in amazing desert and mountain scenery, waterholes, ruins, archaeological sites and villages. Driving over the dunes is exhilarating and sometimes frightening. It is quite easy to tip over and roll down the side of a dune if the driver is not experienced. Bear in mind, however, that 'wadi-bashing', as it is known by local expats, is potentially damaging to the environment – see Responsible Tourism earlier in this chapter for guidelines on minimising your impact on the environment.

Unless you have your own 4WD or can borrow one, the cost of hiring is prohibitive for many travellers (around US$200 per day). The alternative is to book a trip with any one of the tour companies in the major cities of the region. These trips can be for half a day, a whole day or overnight with some camping in the desert and maybe a spot of camel riding as well. See Organised Tours in the individual country Getting Around chapters for details of tours and tour companies.

It's not a good idea to go driving into the dunes unless you know what you are doing, or are accompanied by an experienced desert driver. Even if you are experienced you should go with another vehicle in case you get seriously stuck in the sand and need help getting out. Here are some basic safety tips for driving in the desert:

- Always let someone know where you are going and how long you expect to be.
- Deflate your tyres by one-third to a half.
- Always engage low 4WD.
- Descend the slope of a dune diagonally, unless it is particularly steep, in which case you should descend straight down.
- Always carry a spade, at least two flat pieces of wood (to stick under the tyres if you get stuck), a tow rope, a tyre pump, a jack and spare petrol and water (for you and the car).

Desert Driver's Manual by Jim Stabler is a handy publication with some vital tips on desert driving. It is not specifically focused on this region but the theory is the same for desert driving anywhere. Another book widely available in the region, which covers a variety of terrains, is *The Off-Roader's Manual* by Jehanbaz Ali Khan which is published by Motivate in Dubai.

Water Sports

Diving and snorkelling are popular along the Gulf of Oman which is home to coral reefs and abundant marine life, including

Safety Guidelines for Diving

Before embarking on a scuba diving, skin diving or snorkelling trip, careful consideration should be given to a safe, as well as an enjoyable, experience. You should:

- Possess a current diving certification card from a recognised scuba diving instructional agency (if scuba diving).
- Be sure you are healthy and feel comfortable diving.
- Obtain reliable information about physical and environmental conditions at the dive site (eg from a reputable local dive operation).
- Be aware of local laws, regulations and etiquette about marine life and the environment.
- Dive only at sites within your realm of experience; if available, engage the services of a competent, professionally trained dive instructor or dive master.
- Be aware that underwater conditions vary significantly from one region, or even site, to another. Seasonal changes can significantly alter any site and dive conditions. These differences influence the way divers dress for a dive and what diving techniques they use.
- Ask about the environmental characteristics that can affect your diving and how local trained divers deal with these considerations.

various colourful tropical fish, reef sharks, turtles, stingrays and dolphins. Oman's Musandam peninsula is renowned for having some of the best diving in the world – and being one of the best-kept secrets – but it is strictly for more experienced divers.

Jet-skiing and water-skiing are popular activities at many of the larger hotels and beach clubs in the coastal areas, though you usually have to pay an exorbitant entry fee to use the premises and must pay hire fees on top of this.

COURSES
Language Courses

Language courses available are almost exclusively for learning English. If you want to learn Arabic, there are a few cultural centres offering Arabic classes in the major cities of the region. You can also learn a number of other languages, such as French and German, through the relevant country's embassy or cultural centre. See the individual city entries for details on language courses, and keep an eye on the local English-language newspapers.

Diving Courses

There are several diving companies in the region that offer accredited PADI diving courses. See Activities in the country Facts for the Visitor chapters for details.

WORK

Labour laws throughout the region are strict, especially in Oman where the process of Omanisation (replacing expatriates with Omanis wherever possible) is in full swing. Unless you arrive with a contract in hand, it's probably a waste of time – as well as being illegal – to look for a job. If you want to work in Oman or the UAE, you will have to apply for a job from your home country.

Labour laws in the UAE are designed to stop people from job-hopping. If you obtain your residence visa through an employer and then quit the job because you've found something better, you may find yourself under a six-month ban from working in the UAE. You will most likely receive the ban if your employer is unhappy about the fact that you've resigned after they have undertaken the expense and hassle of organising your residence visa. You can call the Ministry of Labour Helpline for advice on ☎ 0904 0044 if you have any work-related problems.

In Oman you are only permitted to leave your job and work for another employer if your sponsor supplies a no-objection letter of release. If they do not, you will have to leave the country for the duration of your work visa (two years) before finding work with a new sponsor.

In Oman nonworking husbands and wives are always sponsored by the working spouse's employer. This is because the working spouse is not permitted to sponsor anyone else. In the UAE, husbands/wives and children are often sponsored by the working spouse, as long as their salary is above Dh3500 per month.

In the UAE, people on a residence visa who are sponsored by a working spouse (who is in turn sponsored by an employer) are not officially permitted to work. This rule is often broken, however, and it is possible to find work in the public or private sector. If you are in this situation, remember that your spouse, and not the company you work for, is still your sponsor. One effect of this is that you may only be able to apply for a visit visa to another Arabian peninsula country with a consent letter from your spouse. In some cases you will need to be accompanied by your spouse who has company sponsorship. Similarly, if you want to apply for a driving licence you will also need a consent letter from your spouse.

ACCOMMODATION
Camping

There are only two formal camping grounds in the region and both are in Oman. In spite of this, camping is a popular activity and you are allowed to set up camp on beaches, mountains and in the desert in both Oman and the UAE.

Choose your camp site carefully to avoid intruding on someone's land or otherwise causing offence. Do not, for example, camp in the shadow of a village, especially if you plan to drink alcohol. This might offend members of the local population.

There are also certain practical and safety aspects to camping in the region. Although wadis are great places to camp, do not camp in narrow parts of wadis. Rain in another part of the mountains can cause sudden flash floods. Try to find a spot that is in the wide part of a wadi bed, on higher ground.

If you plan to camp in the desert there are a few things you should be aware of. The first is to have more than one vehicle if at all possible and always to let someone know what your plans are so they can raise the alarm if necessary. There have been a number of tragic incidents in the past when people have not followed this basic advice. Anyone planning to make an overnight trip of this sort should pick up *Staying Alive in the Desert* by KEM Melville.

Hostels

Only the UAE has youth hostels. It is an HI member and hostel cards are required. If you don't have one, you can buy a yearly membership at any of the hostels for Dh75.

Hotels

There are very few truly horrible hotels in the region. Even rooms in the cheapest places will have air-conditioning and hot water (look for the hot water switch somewhere in the room, sometimes labelled), and minifridges are standard. The worst hotels listed in this book may seem quite decent if you have recently arrived from Egypt or India. The flip side of this is that no place in the region is really cheap – apart from the youth hostels you are not generally going to find a bed for less than US$20 a night. Most major cities in teh region have ample midrange hotels (US$30 to US$50) and are awash in four- and five-star accommodation. In Oman, however, accommodation options are very limited outside Muscat.

During Ramadan and in the off season (late May to the beginning of September) most hotels drop their rates by about 50%, and sometimes by up to 75%.

FOOD

The Gulf has never been known for its cuisine, although traditional Omani cuisine is more inspiring than that of the UAE. The traditional food of the region consists of fresh fish, dried fish, dates, camel meat and camel milk. Not terribly mouthwatering, you may say, and you'd be right. Although there are a few restaurants offering traditional food, as a rule, whenever you see Arab or Arabian food advertised, you can assume that the place is offering a Lebanese menu.

If you want to eat cheaply, this usually means eating at one of the many Indian or Pakistani 'biryani cafes'. In the major cities it is also possible to get cheap South-East Asian food – Thai, Filipino and Chinese being the most common. However, this food often tastes suspiciously like the national cuisine of the chef, who is usually Indian. You'll generally be able to find cheap snack food in most town centres, especially around transport hubs and souqs.

In the major cities, you'll find the usual collection of Western-style fast-food outlets which, surprisingly, are around the same price or more expensive than in the West. For those with more money to spend, almost anything from fish and chips to burritos to sushi is available in the larger cities. Most of the more exotic restaurants are attached to five-star hotels, with prices to match.

Snacks & Takeaways

In most budget hotels it is perfectly acceptable to have takeaway food delivered to your room or for you to bring back takeaway to eat in your room. Street food consists mainly of *shwarma*, which is lamb or chicken carved from a huge rotating spit and served in pita bread (flat Arabic bread), often with lettuce, tomatoes, chips and garlic or chilli sauce. In many places you can also find *fuul* (pronounced 'fool'), mashed and stewed fava beans, usually eaten for breakfast, and *falafel*, a mixture of chickpeas and herbs deep-fried into a small patty and served in pita bread like a shwarma. Roasted chickens are widely available and usually come with salad and plenty of garlic sauce.

In general, the small Indian 'cafes' or 'coffee shops' serve only tea and coffee, sandwiches, fresh fruit juices and snacks such as samosas and *pakora* (bite-size pieces of vegetable dipped in chickpea-flour batter and deep-fried).

The term 'sandwich' covers a variety of snacks. If you ask for a chicken or mutton sandwich, you're usually asking for a shwarma. Sometimes, you'll get the meat in a European-style roll or you may even get a chicken or mutton burger with chips. If you want to be sure of what you're getting, just look around at what other people are eating, or ask to be shown the bread.

Omelette sandwiches make a great snack or breakfast. One- or two-egg omelettes are wrapped in Indian paratha bread with tomato, cucumber, onion and chilli. If you want the less oily Arabic bread instead, just ask for it. The staff in these places are not afraid to make a sandwich out of anything – you can also have a *kima* sandwich, fuul sandwich, *moutabel* sandwich or even a samosa sandwich if you want.

Traditional Food

Although the cuisine from this region is not as rich in variety and ingredients as in other parts of the Middle East, there are a few dishes that are particular to the region. Most dishes contain rice, fish or meat as well as a variety of spices, including cardamom, cloves, turmeric and saffron. Some of these include:

Machboos consists of meat and onions, seasoned with spices, salt and dried limes (called *loomi*) and cooked in a large pot for a couple of hours until very tender. The meat is then removed and rice is added to the rest of the ingredients. When the rice is cooked, the meat is returned to the pot and it is cooked for another hour or two.

Harees is a dish eaten mainly during Ramadan. Small pieces of meat are boiled in water with wheat, then mashed. The ingredients are then left to cook slowly over hot charcoal for about six hours. The end result is kind of like a meat porridge. It's an acquired taste but once you like it, you'll love it.

Balaleet is sweet vermicelli dish which is made from eggs, onions, cinnamon, sugar and oil. It is usually eaten at breakfast time.

Lebanese

The Arabic food of the region is largely borrowed from Lebanese cuisine. Lebanese meals are built around a wide selection of appetisers, or *mezze*. *Humous*, a paste made from chickpeas with lemon juice, garlic and tahina, is the standard dish whose quality is

Meat & Islam

All meat consumed by Muslims must be *halal*, meaning religiously suitable or permitted. The animal must be killed by having its throat cut and the blood drained out. This is why red meat in the supermarkets that is produced in the Gulf is very pale in colour. If you are a red meat eater you might find it a little bland here.

Pork is not eaten by Muslims. It is *haram*, which means it is forbidden by Islam. Dishes containing pork generally only appear on the menus of top-end restaurants. These dishes are usually identified by an asterisk.

the acid test of any Lebanese restaurant. Other specialities include *arayes* (mince meat with spices spread inside Arabic bread then fried), *fatayer* (baked pockets of pastry filled with mince meat, cheese or spinach) and fried *kibbe*, balls of spiced ground meat filled with pine nuts.

Also look out for *tabouleh*, a salad of parsley, onions, tomatoes and soaked bulghar wheat dressed with oil and lemon juice, and *fattoush*, a salad of lettuce, tomato, cucumber, croutons made from Arabic bread, and a lemon, garlic and olive oil dressing. Any decent Lebanese restaurant should also place a selection of vegetables (lettuce, tomatoes, onions, mint) on the table as a free appetiser.

Main dishes consist of grilled chicken, lamb or beef. Be sure to try *shish tawouk*, a skewer of mildly spiced chicken grilled over open coals.

The best known Lebanese dessert is *baklava*, made from filo pastry and nuts, often pistachios, soaked in honey in a myriad different interpretations, all delicious. You'll find Lebanese bakeries all over the cities but very few or none at all in the small towns and villages.

Indian/Pakistani

Apart from street food, the cheapest meals in Oman and the UAE are almost always found in small Indian or Pakistani restaurants. The menu at these places tends to be very limited, usually *biryani* dishes (chicken, mutton or fish cooked in a pile of mildly spiced rice), chicken and/or mutton *tikka* (basted with spices and roasted in a tandoor oven), *kima* (minced meat with peas and tomato served with salad and paratha), *dahl* (lentils) and a variety of Indian breads, including *dosa*, *roti*, chapatti and tandoor or naan. *Puri baji* is a delicious snack dish of curried vegetables and flaky bread, usually served with a coconut dipping sauce, sometimes only available for breakfast.

Indo-Pakistani restaurants have also adopted a number of Arabic staples into their menus such as *moutabel* (eggplant and sesame seed dip) and fuul, eaten with either flat Arabic bread or an Indian bread.

Iranian

You'll find plenty of places serving Iranian food in Dubai especially, but also in the rest of the UAE and the Musandam peninsula in Oman. The Iranians are big on *berenj* (spicy rice dishes which are usually topped with nuts and raisins) and *koresh* (tasty meat stews with vegetables). Kebabs are also a staple of Iranian cuisine, served in many different ways. *Chelow kebab* is a grilled kebab served on top of rice, *chelow kebab barg* is a thinner than usual kebab, *chelow kebab makhsous* is a thicker than usual kebab, *bakhtari kebab* is served with grilled capsicum and a *lari kebab* is marinated and cooked in yoghurt.

An Iranian-style biryani is called *Istanboli polow* and consists of rice with haricot beans and chicken or mutton on top. Other Iranian dishes include *baghleh polow* (rice with dill, broad beans and chicken or mutton) and *zereshk polow* (rice mixed with barberry and chicken).

Iranian food is usually served with a plate of lettuce, cabbage, tomato and onion and a minty yoghurt dipping sauce. *Naan* (a type of bread) is baked in different ways, but the most common variation in the UAE is *lavash*, which is thin, square and somewhat elastic.

Vegetarian

Although vegetarianism is not a concept that is widely recognised in Oman or the UAE, vegetarians should have no trouble dining out, and there are even some dedicated vegetarian restaurants in Dubai. Although the Indian restaurants, especially the South Indian ones, are the obvious choice, vegetarians can still enjoy plenty of dishes from any Lebanese restaurant, for example, felafel, humous, *labneh* (a yoghurt dip), tabouleh, spinach and cheese pastries and salads. Generally the ultracheap biryani cafes are a bit of a dead loss if you are looking for a vegetarian main meal.

Self-Catering

Those interested in self-catering will find plenty of Western-style supermarkets and small grocery stores in the major cities. In the smaller towns you'll find that the grocery stores are very sparsely stocked. A few of them might sell a small selection of fruit and vegetables but these are not always the best quality. We don't recommend you buy meat from the open markets, however. It's probably better to buy wrapped and refrigerated meat from the supermarket, where hungry flies don't hover.

For Arabic breads and sweets there are a number of bakeries in the major cities. Western-style bread from the supermarkets is usually sweetened as well as being stale most of the time.

DRINKS
Nonalcoholic Drinks

There are very few traditional regional drinks, though if you want to try camel's milk you can often find it in supermarkets. *Laban*, a heavy, and often salty, buttermilk is a local speciality.

In the Mutrah souq in Muscat you can get a delicious rosewater milk from the kiosks. In most coffeehouses and traditional cafes in the region you can also get a glass of sweet, warm ginger milk, which is delicious.

Western soft drinks, mineral water and fruit juice are the standard fare. There are plenty of juice stands serving freshly squeezed fruit juice, usually mango or orange, with loads of added sugar. Water is bottled locally from mineral springs in the region. The standard price for a small bottle of water is Dh1 (UAE) or 100 baisa (Oman). There are also lots of drink vending machines on the streets so you won't die of thirst if you're tramping around in high temperatures.

Coffee & Tea

Arabic coffee or *qahwa* is usually unsweetened and is served in small handleless cups.

Coffeehouses

Arabic coffeehouses are places where menfolk go to drink qahwa (coffee) or sweet Arabic tea, smoke *sheesha* and talk. Although women are allowed to go into coffeehouses, it's very unlikely you will see a local woman here as traditionally it's a man's domain. Although women are welcome in the traditional coffeehouses mentioned in this book, they might feel uncomfortable in some of the less touristy places. Some of the very small coffeehouses in town are quite obviously for men only.

A sheesha (also called hubbly bubbly) is a long-stemmed, glass-bottomed smoking implement about two feet high. They are common in much of the Middle East but the ones used in this region are most similar to those found in Lebanon and Egypt. They have curved glass bases and long, stainless steel stems. The long, bendable hose that extends from the base is often colourfully decorated. Sheesha are usually packed with apple-flavoured tobacco but you can also ask for something different, such as strawberry, coffee, liquorice or 'tropical'.

This traditional pastime has almost been completely banned in Muscat and the emirate of Sharjah in the UAE. The governments in these cases believe it to be detrimental to health and destructive of family life as it lures men away from the home.

The coffee is flavoured with cardamom which gives it a green, or sometimes greenish-brown, colour. The version served in the cities is fairly tame but should you ever find yourself out in the desert with Bedouins be prepared for an extremely bitter taste.

In cities it is most likely that you will be offered Turkish coffee. This will usually be served *mazboot*, or with medium sugar, unless you specify otherwise. If you only want a little sugar ask to have the coffee *areeha*. *Khafeef* means with a lot of sugar and *saada* with no sugar at all. Those unfamiliar with Turkish coffee should be aware that it is very thick and strong. Even if you drink regular coffee black you will probably want to have at least some sugar in your Turkish coffee. Turkish coffee is served in small cups similar to those used for espresso. You will find a layer of grounds, possibly quite thick, in the bottom of the cup, so don't be tempted to drain your cup.

For a real pick-me-up, try a cup of *chai* (tea) from any of the Indian cafes or restaurants. For 50 fils or 100 baisa you get a cup of Lipton's with a good dash of Rainbow milk (sweetened milk) and loads of sugar.

Arabic tea is served black and very sweet, often with a mint leaf floating on top. Like coffee it is served in small glass cups that hold only a few sips. *Zatar* is a tea made of various strong herbs such as thyme and marjoram. It too is served with lots of sugar.

Alcoholic Drinks

For religious reasons there are no local alcoholic drinks. Where alcohol is available it has been imported from the West. In the UAE, alcohol is only available in restaurants that are attached to hotels. In Muscat there are a few independent restaurants that serve alcohol too (we've indicated which ones).

Only non-Muslim residents with an alcohol licence are permitted to buy alcohol to take away from a few licensed retailers. Omanis and Emiratis, being Muslims, are not given alcohol licences but you do see them drinking in bars.

SHOPPING

Dubai, and the rest of the UAE to a lesser extent, has a well-deserved reputation as a shopper's paradise. You'll find shopping malls and souqs in all the major towns and cities, with a mind-boggling range of goods for sale from designer clothes to traditional arts and crafts. Although Oman doesn't have the glitzy shopping malls that the UAE excels in, at least outside Muscat, every town and village has a souq of some sort, and it's one of the best places in the Gulf to buy traditional crafts and souvenirs.

Although there are regional and local specialities (see Shopping in the Oman and UAE Facts for the Visitor chapters for more information on what to look out for, and where), the following section is intended to give you some idea of what you might look out for.

Although prices are fixed in a few places (mainly the Women's Craft Centre in Abu Dhabi and the Omani Heritage Gallery in Muscat), elsewhere it's always worth asking for a discount, or their best price, before you agree to buy, especially in the smaller souqs. See Tipping & Bargaining in the Regional Facts for the Visitor chapter for more details.

Silver

Oman is the best place to buy silver (Bedouin) jewellery, as the selection is better and prices are lower. In the UAE, a few shops in Al-Ain, Abu Dhabi and Dubai sell silver jewellery, but most of it comes from Oman anyway.

Traditional jewellery ranges from bracelets and rings to huge belts and chest pieces. It is often very intricately designed. Thin layers of

---

A Scarcity of Traditional Handicrafts

With Oman and the UAE developing at such a rapid rate, and mass-produced items such as buckets and mats so cheap and easy to obtain, traditional crafts in the region have taken a beating, and it can be hard to find a good range of traditional crafts on sale. You'll probably see the best selection in museums. However, initiatives such as the Omani Heritage Gallery (see Shopping in the Muscat chapter) and the government-run Women's Craft Centre in Abu Dhabi (see the Abu Dhabi chapter) provide recognition and financial support for artisans, and increased tourism has helped to encourage local craftspeople. In Oman, and occasionally in the UAE, you can find a small section with local crafts in most souqs.

Many of the tourist-oriented items on sale throughout Oman and the UAE are actually made outside the region, generally in Egypt, Syria, Iran, India or Pakistan. This is true of most of the textiles, wooden and brass items and carpets and rugs. If you are looking for something specifically Omani or Emirati, as opposed to something vaguely Middle Eastern or Oriental, it's best to check before you buy.

Top: The Central Market in Sharjah, with its distinctive wind-tower design. (Photo by Christine Osborne)

CHRIS MELLOR

CHRIS MELLOR

CHRIS MELLOR

CHRIS MELLOR

PHILIP GAME

The souq is the heart and soul of an Arab town. Vibrant and colourful, it's a great place for people-watching – and shopping. You'll find the best fresh produce here, especially fruit and vegetables (top), and fish straight from the waters of the Gulf (middle right). Although the influx of mass-produced goods threatens to overwhelm the souq, traditional handicrafts still survive, including copper coffeepots (middle left), pottery (bottom left) and woven *areesh* (palm leaf) goods (bottom right).

CHRIS MELLOR

CHRISTINE OSBORNE

RUSSELL MOUNTFORD

CHRIS MELLOR

CHRIS MELLOR

Sharjah and Dubai are the best places outside Iran to buy Persian carpets (top left), while Dubai's renowned Gold Souq is obviously *the* place to buy anything and everything that glitters. Check out the Mutrah or Salalah souqs for Omani daggers or *khanjars* (middle right) and colourful textiles, such as this bright Dhofari material (top right). Most souqs in the region also sell *sheesha* pipes (bottom), which make a quintessentially Middle Eastern souvenir – if you can get it home in one piece!

gold or bronze, coloured glass and old coins are sometimes used to decorate the basic silverwork.

If you are looking for 'antique' jewellery, you will probably be disappointed. Most of this stuff was made as wedding jewellery, and as it is considered an insult for a bride to be given used jewellery to wear on her wedding day, the tradition has long been that a woman's jewellery is melted down and sold for its weight after her death. Because of this, very little of the jewellery you will see on sale is more than 50 to 60 years old.

A particularly common Omani necklace design has a pendant in the shape of a rectangular box that opens at one end (a small paper containing verses from the Quran would normally have been inserted into the box) and is decorated with gold leaf laid on top of the silver.

Bracelets and anklets are also very common. They vary in design depending on which part of Oman they were made in. Nizwa bracelets are usually wide, flat bands decorated with studs, while bracelets from the Batinah Coast are narrower, rounded and open-ended. Interestingly, bracelets and anklets are usually worn in pairs by women and that's why you usually find two together that are the same. The design is slightly altered from pair to pair so that each pair is different.

Silver jewellery is generally sold by weight but often the shopkeeper has a fixed price for these items. The going rate is Dh1.8 per gram. For a simple studded-type bangle you will pay around Dh200 after bargaining. For larger and more ornate items such as brides' chest and head pieces you will probably be quoted around Dh1500. In the souqs in Oman, you should be able to get one or two nice pieces for OR30 to OR50. For more information on Omani silver jewellery read *Disappearing Treasures of Oman* by Avelyn Foster.

Gold

If there's one thing Dubai is famous for it's gold. Gold jewellery manufactured in Dubai, Bahrain, Saudi Arabia, India, Singapore and Italy finds its way here to be sold by the bucketload to Arab and Indian families. Most of the time this gold is destined for brides to wear on their wedding day or for women's dowries. There are also shopping centres filled entirely with gold shops in Abu Dhabi and Sharjah. Although there are gold shops in the modern shopping centres in Muscat, there are no gold souqs as such. Most tourists find the gold jewellery on offer a little too over-the-top or gaudy for their tastes, but it is still interesting to view the glittering array on offer. See the boxed text 'All That Glitters …' in the Dubai chapter.

Top: *Qiladahs* are triangular pendants, sometimes also worn as a head ornament. They are made in the Hand of Fatimah design (Fatimah was the Prophet's daughter), and are worn to ward off the evil eye.

TRUDI CANAVAN

Khanjars

One of the most distinctive components of Omani traditional men's dress is the curved dagger or *khanjar*, also spelled *khanja*. They are worn on important occasions and in rural areas they are still sometimes worn every day. Traditionally the handles of these daggers were made from rhino horn, although today they are almost always made from plastic or wood. Keep an open mind if a shopkeeper tells you that the handle is made from rhino horn – if they are asking less than OR800, the khanjar handle is most likely *not* made from rhino horn. In any case, do you really want to help promote the illegal slaughter in East Africa of an endangered species? As a rule anything under OR50 tends to be pretty nasty but you probably don't want to invest more than OR115 (about US$300) in a khanjar. If you don't want the display box, make this clear during the bargaining and get a few riyals knocked off the price.

Khanjars come in two basic designs: regular khanjars are identified by two rings where a belt is attached. *Sayidi* khanjars have five rings. A generation or two ago these were a sign that the wearer was a member of the ruling Al-Busaid family, but today anyone can wear either style. Regular khanjars are decorated entirely, or nearly entirely, using thin silver thread. The intricacy of the thread pattern, and the skill with which it is executed, are among the main determinants of value. Sayidi khanjars are often covered entirely in silver sheet with little or no thread used.

The most important things to look for in assessing a khanjar's quality are weight and the workmanship on the scabbard. A khanjar is a substantial item and ought to feel like one when you pick it up. Few khanjars are more than 20 to 40 years old, and quality, not age, should be your main criterion. Don't be surprised to see very new-looking blades in the scabbards of fairly old daggers. Unless you are actually planning to use the dagger this is not something you need to be concerned about. Some khanjars have a second knife inserted in a small scabbard attached to the back of the main scabbard.

Although khanjars are not part of the UAE traditional dress, you can still buy them in souvenir shops in Dubai's Gold Souq and in Sharjah's Central Market and Al-Arsah Souq. They are also available in major shopping centres in Abu Dhabi and Dubai. Generally you don't pay any more for khanjars in the UAE than you do in Oman.

CHRIS MELLOR

Bottom: A good-quality khanjar should feel heavy and have detailed workmanship on the scabbard. As they are expensive items to buy it's worth taking time to look at as many as possible before you decide to buy.

Kohl Boxes

Men's kohl boxes (right) are thin silver cylinders connected by a small chain to a silver applicator rod that looks like a big toothpick. The women's model (below) is smaller and wider with a flat bottom and a smaller applicator. Men's boxes usually have screw-off tops connected to the chain, while women's have tops that simply pull off. Traditionally, a man wore his kohl box on his belt, whereas a woman usually wore hers tucked into her clothing.

Kohl boxes are usually the cheapest silver pieces available at OR8/Dh80 to OR20/Dh200. You may also see kohl containers made from plastic bottles covered in beads. These come from the Dhofar region of Oman and tend to be cheaper than the silver ones. Expect to pay about OR2 or OR3 for the small ones, especially if you buy them in Salalah.

BOTH ILLUSTRATIONS BY VERITY CAMPBELL

Prayer Holders

Called '*aud saleeb* in Arabic, these are small to medium-sized cylinders into which wood or a piece of paper containing verses from the Quran or incantations against evil spirits are placed. The larger ones, which may be 20 to 25cm in length, were sometimes used to carry messages between VIPs. Most of the prayer holders you see in the souqs and shopping centres are made in India or Pakistan, and they are not always silver. They make a nice, affordable Arabic-style souvenir.

Gunpowder Horns

Relics of an era when every man carried a rifle, silver gunpowder horns (*tilaheeq*) are crescent-shaped items with a removable top. They range from 10 to 25cm in length and usually have a leather strap attached which was used to sling the kohl box around the neck or from a belt. As with khanjars you should look for solidity and workmanship when picking out a powder horn. The top should come on and off cleanly and should not be flimsy. The mechanism for releasing the powder out through the spout at the narrow end should work, at least on the newer ones.

A cheaper silver gunpowder horn will probably cost between OR20/Dh200 and OR30/Dh300, and a good one will be nearly as much as a cheapish khanjar dagger, around OR50 (especially for the ones that have some gold leaf worked into the decoration).

Top: Kohl, powdered antimony sulphide, is traditionally used by women and men to blacken the area around the eyes, to enhance beauty and protect the eyes. The powder is kept in beautifully decorated vessels such as these.

Copper & Brass

Copper coffeepots (*dalla* in Arabic) are ubiquitous in the souqs, and make a good souvenir. They cost from Dh50/OR5 for small ones (about 8cm high) to Dh500/OR50 for large ones (about 50cm high). Antique dallas cost from Dh300/OR30 to Dh1000/OR100, depending upon their condition. Decorated metal food platters are used for special occasions such as wedding banquets. One about 60cm in diameter will cost about Dh150/OR15. These are not strictly speaking an Emirati or Omani souvenir as they are used all over the Middle East, northern Africa and the subcontinent. They do look good mounted on a wall though.

Usually made from brass or copper, rosewater shakers are traditionally brought out after a formal meal in an Arab home and offered to guests. The rosewater is then sprinkled on the hands or head. The shakers have round bases that taper off into a thin stem with holes in the top where the rosewater comes out. You should be able to pick up a small one for around Dh25/OR2.5.

Another affordable souvenir is a brass incense burner. These heavy objects are usually a round shape with holes in the top for the incense fumes to escape. You can also buy more valuable silver incense burners from upmarket shopping centres in the region.

Omani Dowry Chests

Called *mendoos* in Arabic, these chests were traditionally given to a girl by her father when she was betrothed. From then until the wedding the task at hand was to fill it with all kinds of valuables and household items – clothes, jewellery, sheets, crockery, rugs and embroidery. They are usually made from teak and are decorated with metal (usually brass and copper) in the form of stud patterns. Dowry chests were also made elsewhere in the Gulf and in India but the design of Omani chests imitated that of Portuguese seaman's chests. All chests have a hinged lid, some have drawers at the bottom or the sides, some have brass handles, some have legs and some sit flat on the ground. A true antique could cost up to OR1000/Dh10,000. Chests are still made, however, and you could pay around OR100/Dh1000 for one of these beautiful items.

ANN JEFFREE

Left: How can you resist an exquisitely decorated chest such as this? It's an essential item for any living room or bedroom but getting it home could be a challenge.

Quran Holders

You will see Quran holders in almost every souq and souvenir shop in the region. They are generally made in India. If you're wondering what you could use them for once you get them home, they make a nice magazine rack or door stop. They are made from two, flat carved pieces of wood that fold out nicely into an x-shape to sit on the floor. You shouldn't pay more than Dh20/OR2 for one of these.

Sheesha

Sheeshas are a typical Middle Eastern-looking souvenir but they are not very practical to transport. Large sheeshas with a hose cost from Dh120/OR12 to Dh150/OR15. Some are as little as Dh60/OR6 but these ones might not work very well. The ones that work the best and last the longest are those with stainless steel stems. Always check that air flows well through a sheesha before you buy. If you intend to smoke your sheesha there are a number of accessories you'll need but they cost only a few dirhams each. You can buy sheesha from most major shopping centres and from local grocery stores (not supermarkets though).

Areesh (Palm Leaf) Items

For centuries the Bedouin have used date palm fronds (areesh) to weave various household items. Palm leaf roofs reinforced with date palm trunks were used in traditional houses, from simple barasti huts to big forts. The cone-shaped mat used to cover food is called a *surood* while the large, round floor mat on which food is placed is called a *semma*. A *jefeer* is a shopping basket and a *mehaffa* is a hand fan.

Weaving

Weaving was one of the main traditional activities of women in the region. In country areas, especially in Oman, you will still see women at work in groups, enjoying social contact at the same time. In the past, goat and camel hair were used but now you also find items made from imported cotton and sheep's wool. Traditionally, natural dyes were used but artificially dyed items are now the norm. Some of the things to buy include camel rugs and ropes, cushion covers, carry bags, blankets and bedspreads, and wall hangings.

Textiles & Talli Work

Most souqs and shopping malls have a large area in which textiles, mostly from the subcontinent, are sold, as well as ready-made garments, scarves and saris. The material sold is usually polyester or silk. It's very hard to find much choice if you're looking for cotton, linen or wool. Bold, floral designs are the most common, and these are what women like to use for their kandouras which are worn under the black abaya.

Prices are very reasonable: cotton fabrics, depending on the weave, cost anywhere from 30 fils to Dh5 per metre (30 to 500 baisa). Silk costs around Dh8/OR800 baisa per metre and linen about Dh7/OR700 baisa per metre.

Talli is the interweaving of different coloured cotton threads with silver or gold threads to make decorative ankle, wrist and neck bands which are worn by women at special events such as weddings.

Pottery

Most of the pottery you will see is made in the mountainous areas of the region where the sand is more suitable for making clay. You can find pottery in Fanjar and Bahla in Oman and in Ras al-Khaimah, Fujairah and Dibba in the UAE. Traditional pots of various shapes and sizes had different uses in traditional society. The one used to preserve dates is called a *khir*. Milk was stored in a *birnah* and a *hibb* kept water cold. Pots were also used as cooking vessels.

Pottery incense burners (left) are widely available and make attractive, affordable souvenirs.

ANN JEFFREE

Perfume & Incense

You'll find perfume shops in all the shopping centres of the major cities. Shopkeepers will want to daub you senseless with various perfumes but a word of warning – the Arabic perfumes *(attar)* are oil-based and once on your clothes they can leave a stain. You can buy perfumes in bottles ranging from 12 to 36ml. It is sold by the *tolah* (12ml or 12g) and prices vary, depending on the perfume. The cheapest is about Dh10/OR1 per tolah while the most expensive is an incredible Dh1500/OR150 per tolah. This expensive stuff is made from agar wood from Malaysia, and can be overpowering when you smell it in the perfume shop. When it settles down, it's a lovely, spicy fragrance and one drop is enough to last the whole day.

The perfume shops also sell an enormous range of incense. It can be in the form of compressed powder, crystals, rock or wood. Frankincense (*luban* in Arabic) is probably the most common form of incense (for more details see the boxed text 'Frankincense' in the History section of Facts about the Region). The quality varies – frankincense from Japan is not as valuable as the stuff from Iran or Dhofar in southern Oman. The cheaper stuff is about Dh15/OR1.5 per kilo and the more expensive stuff is about Dh50/OR5. The wooden incense (called *somok* in Arabic) is the nicest and most valuable of all the incenses. Like the expensive perfumes, it comes from agar wood in Malaysia. When burned it gives off a sweet, log fire smell. Agar wood ranges in price, depending on quality, from Dh10/OR1 per tolah to Dh30/OR3.

Left: Pottery incense burners come in a variety of shapes and sizes, all with an attractive rough finish and often colourfully decorated.

Carpets

Dubai and Sharjah in the UAE are among the best places outside Iran to buy Persian carpets. Kilims from Turkey and Afghan rugs are also widely available as well as Turkoman and Kashmiri rugs. Buying carpets without getting ripped off takes skill and patience. Do not feel embarrassed or obliged to buy just because the shop attendant has unrolled 40 carpets for you; this is part of the ritual. The best way to get a good price is to visit several stores, ask a lot of questions and bargain hard over a long period of time (preferably two or three visits). For more guidance on buying carpets, see the boxed text 'The Art of Buying Carpets' in the Sharjah section of the Northern Emirates chapter.

Electronics

The UAE is the cheapest place in the Middle East to buy electrical goods. If it plugs into the wall, you can buy it here but the selection tends to be limited. Most shops stock the same three or four varieties at pretty much the same prices. Shop assistants don't tend to be very knowledgeable about their stock so it helps to have an idea of what you want before setting off on a shopping expedition. It is also a good idea, and accepted practice in the UAE, to plug your new gadget in at the shop to make sure that it works properly.

Computer hardware is also very cheap in the region, especially in Dubai, and the latest products are available. Software is still pirated in the region, even though this is now officially illegal, and is very cheap. It's difficult to find, however, as shopkeepers face big fines for peddling this stuff. Ask the shopkeepers quietly if you can see the 'copies'.

Spices & Nuts

Most markets in Oman and the UAE will have a tantalisingly aromatic section devoted to herbs and spices. You can get every herb or spice you can think of here, as well a whole lot more you have never heard of or seen before, and they are generally cheaper than the packaged stuff you find in the West. You'll also see mounds of greenish powder – henna, used to dye hair and for the elaborate reddish-brown patterns that traditionally adorn women's hands and feet (see also the boxed text 'Henna' in the Dubai chapter). Nuts are another excellent buy, and you'll see roasted and salted, spicy or plain varieties of cashews, almonds, peanuts and pistachios in most markets.

Kitsch

If you're looking for the ultimate kitsch souvenir, it has to be the tacky mosque clock. This costs Dh20/OR2, and if it doesn't get you out of bed in the morning, then you must be dead. You can also buy a variety of souvenirs with a sample of different coloured sands from each of the emirates encased within. These vary in price depending on the size but a small one will cost you about Dh20/OR2. Camels of all shapes, sizes and forms, made of brass or silver, are another popular souvenir shop item.

Getting There & Away

AIR
Airports & Airlines
Dubai international airport in the UAE is the main travel hub in the region. In Oman, Muscat's Seeb airport is the main international airport. You can fly to Dubai from a wide range of destinations in Europe, the USA, the Middle East, the subcontinent and Australia. Flying to Muscat from most destinations outside the subcontinent, the Middle East or Europe means going via Dubai or Abu Dhabi (in the UAE). These are just generally drop-off stops involving a wait of only an hour or so, although in some cases you may have to get a connecting flight to Muscat from Dubai.

The regionally based carriers are Gulf Air (based in Bahrain, and co-owned by Bahrain, Qatar, Oman and Abu Dhabi), Emirates Airlines (owned by, and based in, Dubai) and Oman Air. The safety records of all three

> ### Warning
>
> The information in this chapter is particularly vulnerable to change: Prices for international travel are volatile, schedules change, routes are introduced and cancelled, special deals come and go, and rules and visa requirements are amended. Price structures and regulations can be complicated. You should check directly with the airline or a travel agent to make sure you understand how a fare or ticket works. In addition, the travel industry is highly competitive and there are many lurks and perks.
>
> The upshot of this is that you should get opinions, quotes and advice from as many airlines and travel agents as possible before you part with your hard-earned cash. The details given in this chapter should be regarded as pointers and are not a substitute for your own careful, up-to-date research.

carriers are excellent. All of the major European, Asian and Middle Eastern airlines serve Dubai, and some also serve Abu Dhabi. A few serve Muscat direct.

Buying Tickets
An air ticket alone can gouge a great slice out of anyone's budget, but you can reduce the cost by finding discounted fares. Stiff competition has resulted in widespread discounting – good news for travellers! The only people likely to be paying full fare these days are travellers flying in 1st or business class. Passengers flying in economy can usually manage some sort of discount. But unless you buy carefully and flexibly, it is still possible to end up paying exorbitant amounts for a journey. Your best bet for cheap plane tickets to or from Oman or the UAE is to buy them in countries like Egypt, India or Pakistan, which send masses of workers to the region.

For long-term travel there are plenty of discount tickets which are valid for 12 months, allowing multiple stopovers with open dates. For short-term travel cheaper fares are available by travelling midweek, staying at least one Saturday night or taking advantage of short-lived promotional offers.

When you're looking for bargain air fares, go to a travel agent rather than directly to the airline. From time to time, airlines do have promotional fares and special offers, but generally they only sell fares at the official listed price. One exception to this rule is the expanding number of 'no-frills' carriers operating in the United States and north-west Europe, which mostly sell direct to travellers. Unlike the 'full service' airlines, no-frills carriers often make one-way tickets available at around half the return fare, meaning that it is easy to put together a return ticket when you fly to one place but leave from another.

The other exception is booking on the Internet. Many airlines, full-service and no-frills, offer some excellent fares to Web surfers. They may sell seats by auction or simply cut prices to reflect the reduced cost of electronic selling. Many travel agents around the world have Web sites, which can make the Internet a quick and easy way to compare prices – a good start for when you're ready to start negotiating with your favourite travel agency. Online ticket sales work well if you are doing a simple one-way or return trip on specified dates. However, online superfast fare generators are no substitute for a travel agent who knows all about special deals, has strategies for avoiding layovers and can offer advice on everything from which airline has the best vegetarian food to the best travel insurance to bundle with your ticket.

The days when some travel agents would routinely fleece travellers by running off with their money are, happily, almost over. Paying by credit card generally offers protection, as most card issuers provide refunds if you can prove you didn't get what you paid for. Similar protection can be obtained by buying a ticket from a bonded agent, such as one covered by the Air Transport Operators Licence (ATOL) scheme in the UK. Agents who only accept cash should hand over the tickets straight away and not tell you to 'come back tomorrow'. After you've made a booking or paid your deposit, call the airline and confirm that the booking was made. It's generally not advisable to send money (even cheques) through the post unless the agent is very well established – some travellers have reported being ripped off by fly-by-night mail-order ticket agents.

You may decide to pay more than the rock-bottom fare by opting for the safety of a better known travel agent. Firms such as STA Travel, which has offices worldwide, Council Travel in the USA and Usit Campus (formerly Campus Travel) in the UK are not going to disappear overnight and they do offer good prices to most destinations.

If you purchase a ticket and later want to make changes to your route or get a refund, you need to contact the original travel agent. Airlines only issue refunds to the purchaser of a ticket – usually the travel agent who bought the ticket on your behalf. Many travellers change their routes halfway through their trips, so think carefully before you buy a ticket which is not easily refunded.

Within Oman & the UAE There are many more travel agencies in the region than the local market can support, and your best bet is to check several different places in a particular city. Some recommended travel agencies are listed in the Information sections of the Muscat, Abu Dhabi and Dubai chapters. Among the international airlines there is a low season (December to March) and a high season (April to August) which, luckily, do not coincide with the high and low tourist seasons in Oman and the UAE. Special fares are available at different times all through the year.

Expect to get similar prices everywhere – travel agencies are usually controlled either by the local government or by a cartel organised by the airlines and/or the agents themselves. It is almost unheard of to find an agency significantly undercutting everyone else in town but it is not at all uncommon to find a few who are quoting markedly higher prices than the norm. Getting quotes from four to six places guarantees that you do not wind up paying too much.

Round-the-World Tickets & Stopovers

The cheapest way to visit the region is often to stop over there when travelling between Europe and Asia, or to include it in a Round-the-World (RTW) ticket. As Dubai is a major transport hub, it is the most common stop on RTW tickets.

RTW tickets are often real bargains. They are usually put together by a combination of two airlines and permit you to fly anywhere you want on their route systems so long as you do not backtrack. There may be restrictions on how many stops you are permitted and usually the tickets are valid for 90 days to a year. An alternative type of RTW ticket is one put together by a travel agent using a combination of discounted tickets.

Air Travel Glossary

Cancellation Penalties If you have to cancel or change a discounted ticket, there are often heavy penalties involved; insurance can sometimes be taken out against these penalties. Some airlines impose penalties on regular tickets as well, particularly against 'no-show' passengers.

Courier Fares Businesses often need to send urgent documents or freight securely and quickly. Courier companies hire people to accompany the package through customs and, in return, offer a discount ticket which is sometimes a phenomenal bargain. However, you may have to surrender all your baggage allowance and take only carry-on luggage.

Full Fares Airlines traditionally offer 1st class (coded F), business class (coded J) and economy class (coded Y) tickets. These days there are so many promotional and discounted fares available that few passengers pay full economy fare.

Lost Tickets If you lose your airline ticket an airline will usually treat it like a travellers cheque and, after inquiries, issue you with another one. Legally, however, an airline is entitled to treat it like cash and if you lose it then it's gone forever. Take good care of your tickets.

Onward Tickets An entry requirement for many countries is that you have a ticket out of the country. If you're unsure of your next move, the easiest solution is to buy the cheapest onward ticket to a neighbouring country or a ticket from a reliable airline which can later be refunded if you do not use it.

Open-Jaw Tickets These are return tickets where you fly out to one place but return from another. If available, this can save you backtracking to your arrival point.

Overbooking Since every flight has some passengers who fail to show up, airlines often book more passengers than they have seats. Usually excess passengers make up for the no-shows, but occasionally somebody gets 'bumped' onto the next available flight. Guess who it is most likely to be? The passengers who check in late.

Promotional Fares These are officially discounted fares, available from travel agencies or direct from the airline.

Reconfirmation If you don't reconfirm your flight at least 72 hours prior to departure, the airline may delete your name from the passenger list. Ring to find out if your airline requires reconfirmation.

Restrictions Discounted tickets often have various restrictions on them – such as needing to be paid for in advance and incurring a penalty to be altered. Others are restrictions on the minimum and maximum period you must be away.

Round-the-World Tickets RTW tickets give you a limited period (usually a year) in which to circumnavigate the globe. You can go anywhere the carrying airlines go, as long as you don't backtrack. The number of stopovers or total number of separate flights is decided before you set off and they usually cost a bit more than a basic return flight.

Transferred Tickets Airline tickets cannot be transferred from one person to another. Travellers sometimes try to sell the return half of their ticket, but officials can ask you to prove that you are the person named on the ticket. On an international flight tickets are compared with passports.

Travel Periods Ticket prices vary with the time of year. There is a low (off-peak) season and a high (peak) season, and often a low-shoulder season and a high-shoulder season as well. Usually the fare depends on your outward flight – if you depart in the high season and return in the low season, you pay the high-season fare.

If you are flying with one of the regionally based carriers it is usually possible to stop over at little or no extra cost. Gulf Air, Emirates Airlines and Oman Air all offer stopover packages to Dubai and Muscat that include one or two nights' hotel accommodation, airport transfers and a short city tour, all for a fairly reasonable flat fee.

Travellers with Special Needs

Most international airlines can cater to people with special needs – travellers with disabilities, people with young children and even children travelling alone.

Travellers with special dietary preferences (vegetarian, kosher etc) can request appropriate meals with advance notice. If you are travelling in a wheelchair, most international airports can provide an escort from the check-in desk to the plane where needed, and ramps, lifts, toilets and phones are generally available.

Airlines usually allow babies up to two years of age to fly for 10% of the adult fare, although a few may allow them free of charge. Reputable international airlines usually provide nappies (diapers), tissues, talcum and all the other paraphernalia needed to keep babies clean, dry and half-happy. For children between the ages of two and 12, the fare on international flights is usually 50% of the regular fare or 67% of a discounted fare.

The UK & Continental Europe

Airline ticket discounters are known as bucket shops in the UK. Despite the somewhat disreputable name, there is nothing under-the-counter about them. Discount air travel is big business in London. Advertisements for many travel agents appear in the travel pages of the weekend broadsheets, such as the *Independent* on Saturday and the *Sunday Times*. Look out for the free magazines, such as *TNT*, which are widely available in London – start by looking outside the main railway and underground stations around town.

For students or travellers under 26, a popular travel agency in the UK is STA Travel (☎ 020-7361 6161), which has an office at 86 Old Brompton Rd, London SW7 3LQ, and other offices in London and Manchester. Visit its Web site at www.sta travel.co.uk. This agency sells tickets to all travellers but caters especially to young people and students. Other recommended travel agencies include: Trailfinders (☎ 020-7938 3939), 194 Kensington High St, London W8 7RG; Bridge the World (☎ 020-7734 7447), 4 Regent Place, London W1R 5FB; and Flightbookers (☎ 020-7757 2000), 177-178 Tottenham Court Rd, London W1P 9LF.

Although London is the travel discount capital of Europe, there are several other cities in which you will find a range of good deals. Across Europe many travel agencies have ties with STA Travel. Outlets in major cities include: Voyages Wasteels (☎ 08 03 88 70 04 – this number can only be dialled from within France, fax 01-43 25 46 25), 11 rue Dupuytren, 756006 Paris; STA Travel (☎ 030-3 11 09 50, fax 3 13 09 48), Goethestrasse 73, 10625 Berlin; Passaggi (☎ 06-474 09 23, fax 482 74 36), Stazione Termini FS, Galleria Di Tesla, Rome; and ISYTS (☎ 01-322 1267, fax 323 3767), 11 Nikis St, Upper Floor, Syntagma Square, Athens.

All of the major European carriers fly between their home city and Dubai or Abu Dhabi, usually several times a week. Only British Airways, Lufthansa, SwissAir and Gulf Air fly direct to Muscat from Europe. Emirates Airlines has three flights daily between London and Dubai, one flight between London and Abu Dhabi and several flights a week between Dubai and a handful of other European cities (Paris, Frankfurt, Rome and Athens are the most common destinations). There are also charter flights to Muscat and Salalah in Oman. Most of these originate in Britain, Germany or, in a few cases, Switzerland and they tend to only happen in the high tourist season (December to February). As tourism picks up around the region it may soon become much easier to make your way to Oman at a reasonable cost.

From London to Dubai you will pay around UK£265 on Turkish Airlines via Istanbul and Qatar Airways via Doha. The cheapest nonstop flight at the time of writing was with Royal Brunei for UK£390. If you're lucky enough to strike a British Airways special offer you'll pay about the same, but regular tickets on BA cost about UK£1250. Emirates Airlines charges about UK£465 return to Dubai or Abu Dhabi.

Return fares from the UAE to Paris, London or Frankfurt range from Dh3300 to Dh3680. During summer and Christmas when many expats return home, airlines lock horns and fares to/from London and major Western European cities can be as low as Dh2000 return. At other times the cheapest return fare to London may be with Cyprus Air via Larnaca for Dh2100. A return ticket to Athens costs Dh2000 with Olympic Airways or Dh1300 one way. A return ticket to Europe from Muscat costs from OR200 to OR285, depending on the airline and the season.

Middle East

Although Cairo, Istanbul, Tel Aviv and Dubai are the main cities visited by travellers in the Middle East, they are not necessarily the best places to look for good travel deals. Usually the best travel deal you will manage in the Middle East is an airline's official excursion fare. Some travel agencies will knock down the price by up to 10% if you're persistent, but they may then tie you into fixed dates or flying with a less popular airline. In Istanbul, the Overseas Travel Agency (☎ 216-513 4175), Alemdar Caddesi 16, Sultanahmet, is a recommended travel agency.

Every international airport in Oman and the UAE has at least one flight a week to Cairo. All other cities in the Gulf, as well as Beirut, Damascus and Amman are also easy to reach from the UAE and Oman. To the other Gulf States, cheap 'weekend fares' are often available. Restrictions vary, but these usually allow outbound travel on a Wednesday or Thursday with the return on Friday or Saturday.

Following is a table of sample one-way/ return fares from Dubai and Muscat to give you an idea of what you should expect to pay. These were the best fares available at the time of writing and they will vary from month to month, airline to airline and travel agent to travel agent. Fares from the UAE are considerably cheaper than those from Muscat, but if you decide to fly from Dubai, you'll have to weigh up these fares with the cost of the flight between Muscat and Dubai. See the respective Getting There & Away chapters for details about flying between the UAE and Oman.

to	from Dubai (Dh)	from Muscat (OR)
Amman	830/1560	142/164
Bahrain	640/490	106/86
Beirut	1220/1810	148/225
Cairo	1010/1550	114/171
Damascus	1350/1800	149/193
Dhahran	480/670	81/114
Doha	470/360	91/75
Jeddah	1250/1620	159/204
Kuwait	910/1190	111/148
Riyadh	630/880	93/130
San'a	1235/1660	246/169
Tehran	700/1240	164/165

The USA & Canada

Discount travel agents in the USA and Canada are known as consolidators (although you won't see a sign on the door saying 'consolidator'). San Francisco is the ticket consolidator capital of America, although some good deals can be found in Los Angeles, New York and other big cities. Consolidators can be found through the *Yellow Pages* or the major daily newspapers. The *New York Times*, the *Los Angeles Times*, the *Chicago Tribune* and the *San Francisco Examiner* all produce weekly travel sections in which you will find a number of travel agency ads.

Council Travel, America's largest student travel organisation, has around 60 offices in the USA; its head office (☎ 800-226 8624) is at 205 E 42 St, New York, NY 10017. Call it for the office nearest you or visit its

Web site at www.ciee.org. STA Travel (☎ 800-777 0112) has offices in Boston, Chicago, Miami, New York, Philadelphia, San Francisco and other major cities. Call the toll-free 800 number for office locations or visit its Web site at www.statravel.com.

Air fares tend to be about 10% higher in Canada than in the USA. The *Globe & Mail*, the *Toronto Star*, the *Montreal Gazette* and the *Vancouver Sun* carry travel agents ads and are a good place to look for cheap fares. Travel CUTS (☎ 800-667 2887) is Canada's national student travel agency and has offices in all major cities. Its Web address is www.travelcuts.com.

Coming from the US to Dubai, you'll pay just over US$2100 return on KLM, Lufthansa or United (via London). From New York to Dubai on Northwest (via Amsterdam), American (via London) or Lufthansa it costs US$1690 return. The best deal from Vancouver direct to Dubai is on Canadian Air, British Airways or Air Canada for US$2300 return. One-way fares on all these flights are generally about US$500 cheaper. There are no direct flights from the UAE to Canada.

The only airline flying nonstop to New York from Dubai is Malaysian Airlines for Dh4380, but there are usually special offers on this fare. All other flights go via Europe and fares tend to be between Dh4500 and Dh5000. The cheapest tickets to New York at the time of writing were with Kuwait Air for Dh3280 and Czech Airlines via Prague for Dh3500. To west coast USA or Vancouver it costs Dh3950 with Cathay Pacific (via Hong Kong), Singapore Airlines (via Singapore) or Eva Air (via Taipei).

If you are headed for Oman and you are coming from outside Europe, you will usually have to arrange a connecting flight from Dubai or Abu Dhabi with Gulf Air, Emirates Airlines or Oman Air.

Australia & New Zealand

The *Age* in Melbourne, the *Sydney Morning Herald* and the *New Zealand Herald* all have travel sections that have travel agent ads. Two well-known agents for cheap fares are STA Travel and Flight Centre. STA Travel (☎ 03-9349 2411) has its main office at 224 Faraday St, Carlton, Vic 3053, and offices in all major cities and on many university campuses. Call ☎ 1300 360 960 Australia-wide for the location of your nearest branch or visit its Web site at www.statravel.com.au. Flight Centre (☎ 131 600 Australia-wide) has a central office at 82 Elizabeth St, Sydney, NSW, and there are dozens of offices throughout Australia. Its Web address is www.flightcentre.com.au. In New Zealand, Flight Centre (☎ 09-309 6171) has a large central office in Auckland at National Bank Towers (corner Queen and Darby Sts) and many branches throughout the country. STA Travel (☎ 09-309 0458) has its main office at 10 High St, Auckland.

Gulf Air and Emirates Airlines both have regular return flights out of Melbourne, Sydney and Auckland, via Singapore, to Dubai and Abu Dhabi but not to Muscat. It is also possible to fly to the UAE with one of the large Asian carriers. From Melbourne or Sydney you'll pay from A$1649 to A$1849 to the UAE. Fares from Auckland are NZ$2527 to NZ$2775. A return air fare from Dubai to Melbourne via Singapore costs Dh4200 on Emirates Airlines. Singapore Airlines and Malaysian Airlines are usually a cheaper alternative to Australia or New Zealand. Prices vary, depending on the season, between Dh3600 and Dh4100.

If you're buying a ticket in Muscat you'll pay OR415 return (OR259 one way) to Sydney or Melbourne in the low season. In the high season it will cost you OR521 return but special fares are often available during this period.

South-East Asia

Although most Asian countries are now offering fairly competitive air fare deals, Bangkok, Singapore and Hong Kong are still the best places to shop around for discount tickets. Hong Kong's travel market can be unpredictable, but some excellent bargains are available if you are lucky.

From Dubai, Abu Dhabi and Muscat there are frequent services to Bangkok, Hong

Kong, Manila, Singapore and Seoul. It is often possible to book relatively cheap air/hotel packages to Thailand, Singapore and other popular Asian holiday destinations if you fly with Asia-based airlines. A return flight to Bangkok from Dubai on Thai Airways costs Dh2000. The best fare to Singapore is with Royal Brunei for Dh2000. To Hong Kong it costs Dh2550 on Cathay Pacific. Fares from Muscat to Bangkok on Thai Airways go via Karachi and are quite reasonable at OR176 return or OR151 one way. To or from Hong Kong it's OR167 one way and OR261 return.

The Subcontinent

Although you can get cheap tickets in Mumbai (Bombay) and Calcutta, Delhi is the centre of the real wheeling and dealing. In Delhi there are a number of discount travel agencies around Connaught Place, but as always, be careful before handing over your cash. If you use one of these discount agents, double-check with the airline to make sure that the booking has been made. STIC Travels (☎ 011-332 5559), an agent for STA Travel, has an office in Delhi in Room 6 at the Hotel Imperial in Janpath.

In Mumbai, STIC Travels (☎ 022-218 1431) is at 6 Maker Arcade, Cuffe Parade. Another travel agent in Mumbai which comes highly recommended is Transway International (☎ 022-262 6066), 2nd floor, Pantaky House, 8 Maruti Cross Lane, Fort. Most of the international airline offices in Mumbai are in or around Nariman Point.

The UAE and Oman probably have the best air links to Pakistan and India of any region in the world. There are daily flights to New Delhi, Mumbai, Calicut, Karachi, Lahore, Islamabad and Peshawar. All of the smaller international airports in the UAE also operate services to the subcontinent. Tickets tend to be fairly affordable because of the high volumes on the routes and because the distances are relatively short. To Karachi from the UAE it costs Dh900 return or Dh500 one way. Lahore is more expensive at Dh1580/900. An average fare to Mumbai and New Delhi is Dh1535 return and Dh940

one way. From Muscat to Mumbai or New Delhi on Gulf Air or Indian Airlines it costs OR172 return and OR103 one way.

Africa

Nairobi (Kenya) and Johannesburg (South Africa) are probably the best places in East Africa and South Africa to buy tickets. Some major airlines have offices in Nairobi, which is a good place to determine the standard fare before you make the rounds of the travel agencies. Getting several quotes is a good idea as prices are always changing. Flight Centres (☎ 02-210024) in Lakhamshi House, Biashara St, Nairobi, has been in business for many years. In Johannesburg the South African Student's Travel Services (☎ 011-716 3045) has an office at the University of the Witwatersrand. STA Travel (☎ 011-447 5551) has an office in Johannesburg on Tyrwhitt Ave in Rosebank.

There is frequent service on all of the main Gulf carriers to Nairobi and Johannesburg. Addis Ababa (Ethiopia) is also fairly easy to reach and Tanzania and Zanzibar, for historical reasons, have good air links with Oman. A return air fare from Dubai to Johannesburg costs Dh3630 with Emirates Airlines. Kenya Airways flies direct to Nairobi for Dh1570 return, which is cheaper than Gulf Air via Bahrain for Dh1700 return or Dh1250 one way. Gulf Air also flies to Khartoum (Sudan) for Dh2000 return and Dar es-Salaam (Tanzania) for Dh1950 return.

From Muscat to Nairobi it costs OR266 return (minimum stay six days, maximum stay two months), OR218 one way. A similar fare to Johannesburg with South African Airlines via Dubai is less of a bargain at OR450 return. Gulf Air flies direct between Zanzibar or Dar es-Salaam and Muscat for OR250 return.

LAND

This section covers travel between Oman and the UAE and the neighbouring countries of Saudi Arabia and Yemen, as well as transit through Saudi Arabia to various Middle Eastern destinations. For information on border crossings and land transport between

Oman and the UAE, see the individual country Getting There & Away chapters.

Border Crossings

Oman-Yemen There are three border crossings between Oman and Yemen. The Masyouna-Makinat Shihan crossing, 140km inland from the coast in southern Oman, is on the main truck route between Dubai and San'a. At this time it is the only border we recommend you pass through to get to Yemen. The other two – Habarut, 80km inland, and the one on the coast road – are less reliable because roads are bad and there is very little traffic, posing a potential danger to unescorted travellers.

It's not possible to pick up visas at the border posts. When applying for an Omani visa you need to tick the appropriate border crossing on the application form. Only the border crossings between Oman and the UAE are mentioned on this form, so if you are entering from Yemen you will have to write the Yemen-Oman border crossing you intend to pass through next to the 'Other' box on the form.

UAE-Saudi Arabia The border checkpoint between the UAE and Saudi Arabia is 18km west of the town of Sila in the western region of Abu Dhabi emirate. You will pass through customs here if you are catching a bus between the UAE and Jordan, Syria, Lebanon or Egypt. The bus company will arrange your Saudi transit visa. If you are coming into the UAE you should have your UAE visa already in your passport. Visas cannot be picked up at the border.

Jordan, Syria, Lebanon & Egypt

It is possible to cross the desert by bus to Syria, Jordan and Egypt from the UAE. Fares are very reasonable and usually include the cost of the transit visa for Saudi Arabia. Bus companies will arrange the Saudi transit visa only, so it's up to you to organise the visa to your destination country.

With Balawi Bus Services in Dubai (☎ 04-710 539) you can get to Jordan and back again for only Dh350/200 for adults/children. Buses run once a week on Thursday from the roundabout on Al-Khaleej Rd, just north of the Hyatt Regency Hotel (next to the Khansa Primary School), and the trip takes 38 hours. Buses to Egypt leave each Wednesday and return tickets cost Dh850/450 for adults/children.

To get to Syria and Lebanon you will have to arrange tickets through Alfajan (☎ 02-729 944) in Abu Dhabi. Buses to Syria leave twice a week and return tickets cost Dh400/200 for adults/children. To Lebanon they leave once a week and it costs Dh500/250. The trips to both places take nearly 48 hours.

You will need to contact these companies well in advance so that they can arrange your Saudi transit visa. These trips are pretty long and boring. Unless money is a real concern, you might be better off catching a plane for only a couple of hundred dirhams more, considering the fact that you will be spending money on food and drink during the bus journey as well.

Saudi Arabia

SAPTCO (Saudi Arabian Public Transport Company) runs a daily bus service direct from Damman, in the eastern region of the kingdom, to Abu Dhabi and on to Dubai. The trip takes 10 hours to Abu Dhabi, 12 hours to Dubai. The service originates in Damman and tickets cost SR170 (about US$40).

Yemen

It's possible to drive between Oman and Yemen. The border was, until 1992, closed off to tourists but has now been confirmed as open. This doesn't mean, however, that it is easy to get from Oman to San'a. There is no public transport and getting there involves driving yourself in your own car or hitching a ride. Of course, with the volatile nature of the political scene in Yemen, there are security issues to think about as well.

To get to the border at Masyouna (in Oman) you will have to get to Thumrait, 80km north-west of Salalah. You can catch a microbus to there from Salalah for OR1.

From Thumrait you can hitch or drive another 82km west to the village of Muday. From here it's 39km to Qafa. The border crossing is another 68km from here. Catching a lift all the way from Thumrait should not be difficult as there are plenty of trucks on this route. If you are driving yourself you must pay for an armed guard (US$10) once you get to Makinat Shihan, the Yemeni border post, as you can't drive alone in this region of Yemen. If you have come this far by picking up rides but want your own car, you can arrange a car for around US$50 to the nearest town.

SEA

There are passenger services between Sharjah and Dubai in the UAE and the port of Bandar Abbas in Iran. The trip to/from Sharjah takes 12 hours and costs Dh160 one way. You can take a hydrofoil for Dh215/205 for 1st/economy class which takes four hours. To/from Port Rashid in Dubai it costs Dh215/175 for 1st/2nd-class passage one way, and Dh375/295 return. For more details contact Oasis Freight Co (☎ 06-559 6325) in Sharjah. If you are taking this ferry from Iran to Dubai, make sure that the hotel organising your visa deposits it at Sharjah port or Port Rashid for pick up.

There is a passenger and car ferry between Jebel Ali, just south of Dubai, and Umm Qasr port in Iraq every Saturday. Passengers taking cars must return on the Jebel Ali ship with their cars. Bookings are handled by Al-Majid Travel Agency in Dubai (☎ 04-221 1176). One-way/return fares are Dh830/1280 in economy and Dh1065/1640 in 1st class, including meals and port taxes. The trip takes one-and-a-half days. GCC residents (including expat residents, but not tourists) can get a visa on arrival in Iraq for US$100 but they must submit to a blood test.

At the time of writing, there were no sea services of interest to travellers to/from Oman.

Getting Around the Region

This chapter briefly outlines the various ways in which you can travel within the region. For specific details, including details of travelling between the two countries, see the Oman and UAE Getting There & Away and Getting Around chapters.

AIR

There are no internal flights within the UAE but, given that distances are not great, this is not a problem. Within Oman, Oman Air has a well-established network of internal flights. The most useful flights for travellers are between Muscat and Salalah in the south, which saves a long, tedious bus journey, and between Muscat and Khasab on the Musandam peninsula.

BUS

In Oman, there is an efficient system of intercity buses run by the national bus company, Oman National Transport Company (ONTC). Services are frequent, cheap and comfortable and this is a great way to get around the country if you are on a budget. Safety standards are high as buses are given a limited life span. At the time of writing a brand-new fleet of ONTC buses were hitting the highways of Oman. There are also some private bus services between Muscat and Salalah.

There are no intercity bus services between the emirates in the UAE but Dubai Transport runs a minibus service to the other emirates, although for administrative reasons there is currently no service back to Dubai – see Microbus/Minibus later in this section for more details.

LONG-DISTANCE TAXI

As elsewhere in the Middle East, long-distance taxis (also called shared taxis or service taxis) are a cheap and convenient way of getting around the country, provided time is not an important factor. Both Oman and the UAE have comprehensive systems of long-

Fares Fair

As in so many other Middle Eastern countries, a pernicious taxi fare system operates in Oman and the UAE. If you bargain you will inevitably pay two or three times what you ought to, but the only way to pay the proper fare is to know it before you get into the taxi and not to raise the subject of money at all – just hand the driver the proper sum at your destination.

distance taxis. Long-distance taxis usually carry from four (Oman) to seven (UAE) passengers, sometimes more. There's usually a long-distance taxi depot in the centre of most major towns, often near the main bus station, or on the outskirts of the town, and they congregate at main junctions. In the UAE, taxis wait until they are full before leaving. In Oman, taxis don't generally wait to fill up before they leave, the rationale being that they will most likely fill up along the route.

If you don't want to wait for the taxi to fill up you can take it 'engaged' if you pay for all the seats in it. This generally still works out as a cheap way of travelling and it is quicker and more comfortable than taking the taxi shared. On some less popular routes you'll always have to pay the engaged rate as you will not be able to find enough people to fill the taxi. If it is late at night or you are asking the driver to travel a very long distance, he may demand a premium over the simple seats-times-the-usual-fare formula. Remember, engaged rates are for the vehicle, not per person. When taking an engaged taxi always have an idea of how much you should be paying for the ride. As everywhere, there are some unscrupulous taxi drivers who will bump up the price.

MICROBUS/MINIBUS

Minibuses and microbuses are generally more comfortable than long-distance taxis,

Women Travellers

Women travellers should have no problem using the microbuses or long-distance shared taxis. If you are not accompanied by a man, you'll generally be expected to sit in the front, next to the driver. Otherwise, sit next to another woman. It can be considered offensive for men to sit next to women they don't know, so if you are travelling with a male companion, you will be expected to sit on the inside of your companion. Be aware, however, that a foreign woman, especially a foreign woman unaccompanied by a man, remains an unusual sight in provincial towns in Oman (especially) and the UAE. In the UAE, it's probably best to avoid travelling alone in a long-distance taxi, especially at night – see the boxed text in the UAE Getting Around chapter for more details.

and are roughly the same price. Oman has a comprehensive system of microbuses within and between towns. In the UAE, there are minibuses from Dubai to the other emirates and between Abu Dhabi city and other parts of the emirate. Microbuses and minibuses generally use the same depots as long-distance taxis, and they have the same system of waiting until they fill up before leaving, although microbuses are likely to leave before they are full in Oman. You can take microbuses engaged in Oman, although you can't do this with the minibuses in the UAE.

CAR

Most of the main roads in the region are high-quality two- or four-lane highways. Most other roads, if they are not blacktop, are at least graded tracks that are still suitable for saloon cars. 4WDs are only necessary for desert, wadi and mountain drives.

Rental

Renting a car in Oman or the UAE is relatively straightforward. Technically, drivers need an International Driving Permit if they want to rent a car, but in practice Western dri-

ving licences are almost always accepted. If a particular place asks for an International Driving Permit, and you don't have one there will probably be another car rental company next door which will settle for your home driving licence. See the Oman and UAE Getting Around chapters for more information regarding costs and local regulations.

Road Rules

Vehicles drive on the right-hand side of the road. In both Oman and the UAE, seat belt use is mandatory for passengers in the front seat of cars. This rule is much more strictly enforced in Oman where the fine for not wearing one is OR10.

Speed limits are posted on all roads and highways. The speed limit on main highways is 120km/h, although it is usually 100km/h on smaller roads. In cities, towns and villages the speed limit is 60km/h. In Oman, and sometimes in the UAE, drivers are not stopped for speeding. Instead, speed cameras take a photo and speeders are notified by post. You must pay any traffic fines before a passport, residence permit, new car registration or any other government document can be issued. Car rental companies usually make renters sign a statement to the effect that they are aware of this policy.

If your car is particularly dirty you may be stopped by the police and told to clean it. In Oman you could also cop a fine of OR50, though it is unlikely. This is why car washes do a roaring trade on Friday night when people are returning with filthy cars from their jaunts into the mountains and deserts.

Unfortunately bad drivers are all too common in Oman and the UAE and this is a major factor to take into consideration if you are planning to drive here. See Dangers & Annoyances in regional Facts for the Visitor for more information.

Lastly, if you have an accident do not move your car until the police get there to make a report. You should report all accidents, however small, to the police. Moving your car could distort the outcome of the report and you may find yourself the guilty party, even if the accident wasn't your fault.

The police report is needed if there is to be an insurance claim. This rule applies everywhere in the region except if you are in Dubai, where you should move your car out of the way if it is causing a traffic jam – you are liable to a fine if you do not.

BOAT

Various boat cruises are available from the UAE to destinations in the region, including Iran, Oman and the other Gulf States – see the UAE Getting Around chapter for more details. You can hire a dhow for short trips along the coast in Oman and the UAE, in the Musandam peninsula in Oman or across to islands but this isn't a major way of getting around in either country.

BICYCLE

Long-distance bicycling is a hot and sweaty affair, but it's not impossible to do here. It's also a cheap, environmentally sound and potentially fun way to get around. If you do decide to take the challenge, bear in mind that the heat is a major factor and always take plenty of water with you. Also bear in mind that bikes used in the region tend to be old clunkers ridden by labourers. Having any repairs made on an expensive touring or mountain bike is likely to be difficult if not impossible, so take *lots* of spare parts and know how to repair the bike yourself.

Bicycles can travel by air. You can take them to pieces and put them in a bike bag or box, but it's much easier simply to wheel your bike to the check-in desk, where it should be treated as a piece of baggage. You may have to remove the pedals and turn the handlebars sideways so that it takes up less space in the aircraft's hold; check all this with the airline well in advance, preferably before you pay for your ticket.

If you are riding on main roads, be aware that the standard of safety among drivers here is pretty low, and that people are not used to sharing the road with cyclists. Always watch out for, and yield to, drivers to avoid any accidents.

Mountain biking has become more popular with expats and some tour companies offer mountain adventures – see Activities in the Oman Facts for the Visitor chapter for details.

HITCHING

Hitching is never entirely safe in any country in the world, and we don't recommend it. Travellers who decide to hitch should understand that they are taking a small but potentially serious risk. People who do choose to hitch will be safer if they travel in pairs and let someone know where they are planning to go.

Hitching is legal in Oman and the UAE and it is also extremely common, especially among Indian and Pakistani expats. If you are a Westerner trying to hitch a ride you may attract the attention of the police. A Westerner hitching would be regarded as unusual and therefore suspicious. We recommend that women do not hitchhike at all in this part of the world.

The most common way of signalling that you want a ride is to extend your right hand, palm down. You shouldn't have any trouble finding a ride. Most people are very friendly and would love to give you a ride. Some drivers may expect you to pay the equivalent bus or shared taxi fare, so be sure of whether, and how much, money is expected before you get in the vehicle.

ORGANISED TOURS

Tourism authorities in Oman and the UAE will develop joint marketing and promotion operations once the single visa for travel in both countries is introduced. This means you will be able to arrange tours which cover both countries once you arrive in either the UAE or Oman. At the moment, tours covering both countries have to be arranged outside the region. Most of the international tour companies offer package tours to just one country or the other, although a few offer trips to both. See the country Getting There & Away chapters for details of package tours arranged outside the region.

Full-day, half-day and overnight tours can be booked locally. To visit some places, for instance those only accessible by 4WD, taking a tour may actually be the most cost-effective and hassle-free way to travel. However, the problem for independent travellers is that much of the region's nascent tourism industry remains geared towards groups. If you cannot scare up at least four people you will have to pay a hefty supplement. The good thing is that tour companies are not locked into set tours. They will cater a tour depending on what you want to do, although these tend to be more expensive.

As a rule you are going to pay around US$30 or more in local currency for a half-day tour of whatever city you are in. Full-day tours to some places two or three hours away by road (an Al-Ain tour booked from Dubai in the UAE or a Nizwa tour booked from Muscat in Oman, for example) cost US$40 to US$50 in local currency. More elaborate packages, involving 4WD trips into the desert, lunch on a dhow or camping out in a Bedouin tent, run anywhere from around US$90 to US$150. Really elaborate tours can reach the US$200 to US$300 level, even for a two-day, one-night trip.

See Organised Tours in the Oman and UAE Getting Around chapters for more details of the kinds of tours available.

Facts about Oman

Once known as the hermit of the Middle East, Oman has now emerged from its shell. Recent efforts to build up the tourist infrastructure and to promote the sultanate's attractions to overseas visitors are bringing an ever-increasing number of visitors to the country. However, Oman has taken a cautious approach to the development of the tourist industry. Along with Yemen, Oman remains one of the most traditional countries in the Arabian peninsula.

In contrast to the vast desert wasteland of Saudi Arabia or the tiny city-states of the Gulf, Oman is a land of dramatic mountains and long, unspoiled beaches. Its capital, Muscat, does not have the nouveau-riche feel that typifies many cities in the Gulf region. Oman's development since the ascension of Sultan Qaboos bin Said is all the more striking both because the country's oil reserves are so limited and because under the previous sultan, Said bin Taimur, the country was almost hermetically sealed off from the outside world. Said banned anything that smacked of Western influence – even sunglasses were not allowed!

Said's xenophobic rule, however, was very much the exception in Omani history. During the 17th, 18th and 19th centuries Oman was an imperial power which vied first with Portugal and later with Britain for influence in the Gulf, the Indian Ocean and along the coasts of India and East Africa.

This chapter covers information specific to Oman. For a general introduction to the history, geology and culture of the region, see Facts about the Region.

HISTORY

The early history of Oman up to the Islamic era in the mid-7th century is covered in the Facts about the Region chapter.

Oman & Ibadi Islam

Omanis pride themselves on being among the earliest converts to Islam, and the north-ern part of what is now Oman became important during the first generations of the Islamic era in the 7th century AD. During this period, Sohar, on the Batinah Coast, was the area's most important settlement. The Prophet sent envoys to the rulers of Sohar, who accepted Islam as did many of their subjects. Among the envoys was Khalid bin al-Waleed, who was to become one of early Islam's greatest generals.

Shortly after their conversion to Islam, the Omani tribes came under the rule of the Umayyads, an Islamic dynasty. The Omanis adopted the doctrines of Ibadi Islam (for more details about the Ibadi doctrine, see Religion in the Facts about the Region chapter) in the late 7th or early 8th century AD. Ibadi Islam in its earliest and strictest form was opposed to the idea of the Muslim community being ruled by a hereditary leader, which was to have repercussions throughout Oman's history.

Around AD 746, Talib al-Haqq led the Omani Ibadis in a revolt against the Umayyads. Although the uprising originated in a relatively remote and isolated part of the Islamic world, it proved to be remarkably successful. The Umayyads had already been weakened by years of internal strife, and the Ibadis swept out of Oman into the rest of Arabia, conquering Medina by 748. Their triumph was short-lived. Within months the Umayyads reconquered Medina, but shortly after their decaying dynasty was overthrown, this time by the Abbasids, who went on to build their new capital at Baghdad in present-day Iraq.

In contrast to other parts of the region, the Arabisation of Oman had begun several centuries before the time of the Prophet. Around the beginning of the Christian era a number of Arab tribes migrated from the western regions of southern Arabia (present-day Yemen) to what is now south-western Oman. The coming of Islam in the 7th and 8th centuries helped to accelerate the spread

OMAN

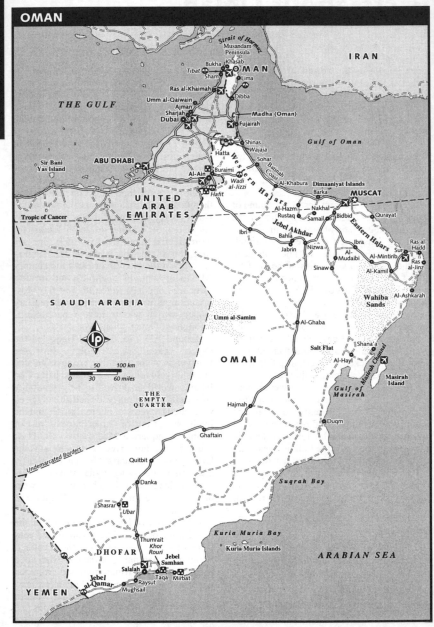

OMAN

IRAN

Strait of Hormuz
Musandam
Peninsula
Khasab
Tibat
Bukha
OMAN
Sham
Lima
Ras al-Khaimah
Dibba
THE GULF
Umm al-Qaiwain
Ajman
Madha (Oman)
Sharjah
Dubai
Fujairah
Shinas
Wajaja
Gulf of Oman
Hatta
Sohar
Western Hajars
ABU DHABI
Batinah Coast
Sir Bani
Yas Island
Al-Khabura
Dimaaniyat Islands
Buraimi
Al-Ain
Wadi
al-Jizzi
Barka
MUSCAT
Hafit
Al-Hazm
Nakhal
Tropic of Cancer
Rustaq
Samail
Bidbid
Qurayat
UNITED
ARAB
EMIRATES
Jebel Akhdar
Ibri
Bahla
Ibra
Ras al-
Hadd
Jabrin
Nizwa
Al-
Mudaibi
Al-Mintrib
Sur
Ras
al-Jinz
Al-Kamil
Sinaw
SAUDI ARABIA
Wahiba
Sands
Al-Ashkarah
Umm al-Samim
Al-Ghaba
Salt Flat
Shana'a
Al-Hayl
OMAN
Gulf of
Masirah
Masirah
Island
THE
EMPTY
QUARTER
Hajmah
Duqm
Ghaftain
Undemarcated Borders
Quitbit
Suqrah Bay
Danka
Shasrar
Ubar
Kuria Muria Bay
Thumrait
Khor
Rouri
Kuria Muria Islands
ARABIAN SEA
DHOFAR
Jebel
Samhan
Salalah
Taqa
Mirbat
Jebel
al-Qamar
Raysut
YEMEN
Mughsail

0   50   100 km
0   30   60 miles

of Arabic as the primary language of communication, and within a few generations Oman was predominantly Arabic-speaking.

The Omani Ibadis elected their first imam (prayer leader) in AD 749, and a hereditary imamate emerged, which represented a break with strict Ibadi doctrine, lasting into the late 9th century. The Abbasids managed to suppress the imamate, but Oman itself managed to remain relatively free of Abbasid control. It also remained loyal to the Ibadi strain of Islam which is still dominant in the country today. As the Islamic empire grew, Arabia became increasingly marginal, and it was Oman's remoteness from the rest of the Islamic world that allowed the Ibadis to survive as a sect long after they had been suppressed in other parts of the Muslim world.

Trade & Naval Power

A recurrent theme of Omani history is the split between the country's coastal and inland areas. In the 9th century Nizwa became the capital, indicating that the interior had political sway over the coasts. But by the 10th century the balance had shifted and Sohar, on the Batinah Coast, was the largest city. The coastal regions have nearly always had the upper hand, both politically and economically, ever since. The coast's trade-derived wealth was formidable.

Until the Portuguese arrived in the region early in the 16th century, the Omanis had few naval power rivals in the area. Omani merchants were dealing with China and the Malay peninsula on a regular basis by the 9th century. Sohar was at its height as a trading centre during this period. In the 10th century the Arab geographer Al-Ishtaraki described Sohar as 'the most prosperous and wealthiest city in the entire region of Islam'.

Sohar was succeeded as the country's principal city by Qalhat (18km north-west of present-day Sur) which prospered until the 14th or 15th century. Although Qalhat was the main city in the country, the kings of the day lived in Hormuz, the island in the middle of the strait of the same name. The Kingdom of Hormuz, which included most of present-day UAE and northern Oman,

controlled the entrance to, and most of the trade in, the Gulf. Hormuz is still the geographical key to control of the Gulf.

The Portuguese Arrive

Portugal was the first European power to take an interest in the region. In 1498 the explorer Vasco da Gama visited Oman's northern coast, the Strait of Hormuz and the sheikhdom of Julfar (near the city of Ras al-Khaimah in present-day UAE). In 1506 the Portuguese returned to the Gulf. They quickly realised, as would the British some three centuries later, that control of the sea routes linking Lisbon (Portugal) to Bombay and Goa on the Indian coast, in other words control of the Gulf, was vital for any European power with imperial designs on India. They occupied Oman in 1507 and, predictably, made Hormuz their main base of operations. By 1515, they had occupied Julfar (near the present-day city of Ras al-Khaimah on the east coast of the UAE) and built a customs house through which they taxed the Gulf's flourishing trade with India and the Far East.

The Portuguese seem to have treated Oman as little more than a way-station on the route to India. Contrary to popular belief, Oman is not littered with Portuguese forts. Apart from the Muscat and Mutrah forts and five bronze cannons at Al-Hazm, there are few physical reminders of the 143 years during which they controlled Oman's coastline. This dearth of Portuguese ruins strongly implies that Lisbon's interest in the country did not extend much beyond the protection of its supply lines.

It was, however, the Portuguese who first brought Muscat to prominence. In 1622, they made it their main base in the region after being forced to abandon Hormuz in the face of attacks by hostile tribes from the land and the British and Dutch from the sea. Although the Portuguese built up and fortified Muscat they were not able to hold it. Under Nasser ibn Murshid, imam from 1624 to 1649, Sur and Qurayat were recaptured. In 1650, Nasser's successor Imam Sultan bin Saif of the Al-Ya'ruba dynasty expelled the

Portuguese from Muscat and Oman. Omani independence is usually dated from this victory, by which reckoning Oman is the oldest independent state in the Arab world.

Building an Empire

The recapture of Muscat marked the beginning of a great expansion of Omani power throughout the Gulf and the Indian Ocean. Almost immediately Omani merchants began to build up their influence along the East African coast. Politically, the Ibadi imamate, though still based in the agricultural area around Jebel Akhdar, controlled much of the country under a new line of imams descended from the Al-Ya'ruba clan.

Four years before the expulsion of the Portuguese the imamate signed its first treaty with the British who were then vying with the Portuguese for influence in the area. The Treaty of 1646, signed with the British East India Company, covered trading rights and allowed British merchants to practise their religion. It also established a separate judicial system for British subjects and employees of the company. The Dutch East India Company received similar rights in 1670 but was soon forced out of Oman.

Throughout all this, the Omanis retained their independence, which is a lot more than can be said for much of the rest of the Gulf over the next 300 years. Oman's growing empire in East Africa, where Omani and British merchants competed, gave the Omanis an economic power base that none of Arabia's sheikhs could match. Far from finding themselves under the heel of imperialism, by the end of the 18th century the Omanis were ruling their own far-flung empire.

In 1749, Ahmed bin Said, the first ruler of the present dynasty, the Al-Busaid, was elected imam. In 1786, with maritime trade becoming more and more important to the empire, the capital was formally moved from the interior to Muscat. It was around this time that the Al-Busaid adopted the title of sultan, which implied a secular authority that the religious title of imam did not.

Treaties providing for British protection of the sultanate were signed in 1798 and

Oman's Empire

The Omani empire reached its peak in the mid-19th century under Sultan Said bin Sultan (reigned 1804–56), who added the southern region of Oman, Dhofar, to his realm and pushed the sultanate's control far down the East African coast. Areas under Omani control included Mombasa (on the coast of present-day Kenya) and the island of Zanzibar, as well as trading posts further down the East African coast.

As well as its East African territories, Oman also controlled parts of what are now India and Pakistan. It was not until the British withdrew from India in 1947 that Oman surrendered its last colonial outpost at Gwadar, in what is now Pakistan, near that country's border with Iran.

Sultan Said bin Sultan commanded an army of 6500 men and a navy that included 15 ships. Traders under his flag sailed the globe. One ship, the *Sultana*, visited New York in 1840 (a portrait of the vessel's captain still hangs in New York's City Hall) and another of Said's vessels called at London in 1842.

When Said died, the empire was divided between two of his sons, one becoming the sultan of Zanzibar, and the other ruling over Oman. Although the rest of the empire suffered economically by this division, Zanzibar continued to prosper. The British took advantage of the empire's weakness and, in 1891 they made Zanzibar a British protectorate. Administration of the island was taken over by the British consulate and the sultan was stripped of all power, reduced to an honorary figure. The situation continued until the 1950s when an Arab Zanzibarian party was established and assumed the majority at a general election. The British withdrew from East Africa in 1957.

1800. These involved the British government, as opposed to the East India Company, and unlike the treaties Britain signed with the Gulf sheikhs later in the 19th century, they were neither imposed by force nor did they turn Oman into a protectorate; Oman was better able to defend itself than were the Gulf sheikhdoms. For their part the British were concerned mainly with protecting their own supply lines to India which were then being threatened by the French, who had just occupied Egypt.

The treaties marked the beginning of a special relationship between Britain and Oman which continues to this day. They were later supplemented by similar 'peace, friendship and navigation' treaties in 1891, 1939 and 1951.

When Sultan Said died in 1856, the empire was divided between two of his sons. One, Majid bin Said, became the sultan of Zanzibar, whose progeny ruled Said's African colonies well into the 20th century, while the other, Faisal bin Turki, became known as the sultan of Muscat and Oman (the coast and interior of today's sultanate were regarded as two separate realms at that time, ruled by one monarch).

Muscat & Oman

The split between Muscat and Oman had been signalled in the late 18th century when conservative tribes in the interior elected their own imam. There was a feeling that the sultan in Muscat had grown too liberal and they were dissatisfied with the re-introduction of a hereditary monarchy, an act that went against strict Ibadi tradition.

In the 19th century it became common for the positions of imam and sultan to be held by different men. The imam of Oman increasingly came to represent the political interests of the interior against those of the coast though, in keeping with Ibadi teachings, the post of imam was not always filled. Despite his title, the sultan's sphere of influence rarely extended very far inland. From 1868 to 1873 one sultan, Azzan ibn Qais, managed to claim both posts, but this was unusual. The result was that Muscat's control of the interior depended to a great extent on the tribes' opinion of the sultan of the day.

Following Sultan Said's death in 1856 and the subsequent division of the empire, Muscat was cut off from some of its most lucrative domains, causing the country to stagnate economically during the late 19th century. The British exacerbated this situation by pressing Sultan Faisal bin Turki to end the trade in slaves and arms for which Oman had long been known. This left the sultan a great deal poorer and lack of money made it even harder to control the interior. This episode also highlighted the extent of the British influence in the sultanate. Many of the sultan's advisers were British and the army itself (known as the Muscat and Oman Levies) was commanded by British officers.

In the early 20th century the imams began to hold more and more power in the interior, while the sultan's power diminished. When Muscat's Sultan Faisal bin Turki died in 1913 the tribes of the interior refused to recognise his son, Taimur bin Faisal, as imam. In 1915, with the sultan's control still tenuous and tensions running high, a group of tribes tried to take over Muscat but were pushed back by the British. Things remained unsettled until 1920 when the sultan and the imam signed a treaty at Seeb. Under the treaty, the sultan recognised the imam as a spiritual leader and allowed him limited jurisdiction over the interior without formally yielding his own claim to sovereignty. For the next 35 years the treaty was the main document governing relations between the rival leaders.

The treaty's weakness was that it avoided the one really important question: namely, who had ultimate authority over the inland areas. In 1938 a new sultan, Said bin Taimur, came to power. When he sought to extend his sovereignty into the interior in the early 1950s the British backed him, largely because they believed there might be oil there. To prospect for it, they needed the sultan to have effective control of the area and Oman's undefined borders with Saudi Arabia and the emirate of Abu Dhabi (part of present-day UAE) to be clearly demarcated.

The territorial dispute centred on the Buraimi oasis, which now straddles the border between Oman and UAE but was then under Saudi control. In 1952 Said, the British and the imam managed a rare show of unity in

Said bin Taimur

Said bin Taimur, who reigned from 1938 to 1970, was a fascinating figure, 'an arch-re-actionary of great personal charm', in the words of the British writer Peter Mansfield. Said was opposed to any sort of change and sought to isolate Oman from the modern world. Under his rule, a country which only a century earlier had rivalled the empire builders of Europe became a medieval anachronism.

Said personally issued all visas. He forbade travel inland by residents of the coast and vice versa. He opposed education, which he saw as a threat to his power. Most Omanis were not allowed to leave the country and the few who managed to get out were rarely allowed to return. He forbade the import of anything that he felt smacked of progress or the West, including eye glasses, radios and books.

What little contact Said had with the outside world came through his British advisers and Muscat's trading families. Said allowed them to establish commercial empires in Muscat based on hugely lucrative monopolies for the import of the few goods that he, grudgingly, regarded as crucial to his survival. In exchange, the trading families tacitly agreed to stay out of politics and not to import any 'Western' items. Two positive aspects of Said's rule were that he cleared Oman's then-large foreign debts and also brought some semblance of political stability to the country.

After he was overthrown in 1970 by his son, he spent the rest of his life in exile, living in a London hotel.

ejecting the Saudis from Buraimi. But the Saudis continued to lay claim to the area and, in 1954, Said concluded that the imam had taken the Saudis' side in the dispute. This brought to a head the entire question of sovereignty and the Seeb treaty. Said's forces occupied Ibri, cutting the imam off from Buraimi. Having been outflanked on the ground the imam, Ghalib bin Ali, sought to outflank Said politically by applying to the Arab League for recognition as ruler of an independent state.

In December 1955, Said responded by occupying the imamate's dual capitals of Nizwa and Rustaq. He then annexed the whole of the interior on the grounds that Ghalib had violated the Seeb treaty. The Arab League was generally sympathetic to Ghalib's membership application (an attitude which was probably more anti-British than pro-imamate) but was in no position to help him. The British, by contrast, were in a position to help Said, in return for securing oil concessions for British companies.

Ghalib was allowed to go into exile in his home village but his brother, Talib, escaped to Cairo and returned 18 months later to continue the civil war. The revolt was short-lived. With British help the sultan was back in control within three months, though the imam and his brother held out from a base near Jebel Akhdar until early 1959.

Under the rule of Sultan Said bin Taimur, trade stagnated in the country as a whole and most of the population relied on agriculture or fishing (both concentrated on the north coast) for their livelihood. A few merchants were allowed to establish lucrative trading monopolies, and through customs receipts, the merchants provided Said with most of the country's income of about UK£50,000 per year, a sum which had changed little since the turn of the 20th century.

Sultan Qaboos

In 1958 Said boarded himself up in his palace at Salalah, which he rarely left thereafter. The formation of a nationalist rebel group, the Dhofar Liberation Front (DLF), in 1962 did little to change this. The DLF's battle against the state, known as the Dhofar rebellion, began in 1965 and was far more serious than Said's earlier clashes with the imamate. Over time (and, after 1967, under South Yemeni influence) the DLF moved from a pan-Arabist toward a more doctrinaire Marxist ideology. In 1966 a dissident group of Dhofari soldiers almost succeeded in assassinating Said.

The combination of the ever-escalating rebellion and Said's refusal to spend any of the money he had begun to receive from oil exports in 1967 soon began to try even Britain's patience. In July 1970 Said was overthrown by his only son, Qaboos, in a bloodless palace coup. The British denied any involvement in or advance knowledge of the coup, but this is hard to believe as British officers effectively commanded the army at the time. Said spent the rest of his life living in exile in a London hotel.

Sultan Qaboos bin Said was 30 years old when he came to power. He had been educated abroad, including a stint at Sandhurst, the British military academy. Returning to Oman in 1964 he spent most of the next six years under house arrest in Salalah. On assuming power, Qaboos flew to Muscat where he promptly repealed his father's oppressive social restrictions, surrounded himself with foreign (mostly British) advisers and began to modernise Oman's semi-feudal economy.

In a speech delivered on his arrival in Muscat, Qaboos said he had seized power after watching 'with growing dismay and increasing anger the failure to use the new-found wealth of this country for the needs of its people'. He added that his government's 'first aim must be to remove unnecessary restrictions under which you, my people, now suffer, and to produce as rapidly as possible a happier and more secure future for all of you'.

There was a certain urgency in Qaboos' program to bring the country into the 20th century. Oman's oil revenues were, and still are, small and its resources limited. Qaboos saw the need to move quickly if the oil wealth was to have any significant effect on his people's lives. He pushed localisation of the workforce much harder than the rulers of the other Gulf countries. Oman, he knew, needed foreign aid and know-how, but it could hardly afford the luxury of the armies of foreign labourers who had built the infrastructure of states such as Kuwait.

Despite Qaboos' apparent desire to make a clean break with the past, the Dhofar re-bellion continued. In 1973, the sultan asked Iran for help in quelling the rebellion. As the rebels were receiving aid from Marxist South Yemen, the Shah of Iran, who was in the process of grinding down his own country's communist party, was only too happy to oblige. Qaboos also received assistance from several hundred British troops, including elite SAS units. By 1976 the rebels, never very great in number to begin with, had been reduced to a few bands operating out of South Yemen. The rebellion only ended, however, when Oman and South Yemen established diplomatic relations in 1982 and the Aden government cut off its assistance to the rebels.

In foreign affairs Qaboos has carved out a reputation for himself as a maverick. In spite of Oman's past military ties with the Shah he has managed to maintain friendly relations with post-revolutionary Iran. Oman was also one of only two Arab countries (the other was Sudan) which refused to break diplomatic ties with Egypt after it signed a peace treaty with Israel in 1979. In late 1993 the sultan became the first Gulf leader to welcome a representative of Israel to his country when Prime Minister Yitzhak Rabin paid a brief visit.

Oman's relationship with the West, in particular with the US and Britain, remains friendly and interested. During the Gulf War in 1991 Oman's air force bases were of vital importance to the allied forces.

In developing his country, the sultan has shown an acute desire to preserve as much as possible of Oman's traditional character. Old port cities like Muscat and Mutrah (now both part of Greater Muscat) have been modernised without being bulldozed out of existence. The construction of modern housing and office blocks around Greater Muscat has been confined to areas like Qurm and Ruwi, which had few, if any, inhabitants 25 years ago. This pattern has also been reflected in many provincial cities.

In his latest five-year plan, Qaboos has called for greater diversification of the economy to ensure security and jobs for Omanis. Further relaxation on issuing tourist visas

OMAN

means that tourism is high on the list of industries in Oman.

In 1998 Sultan Qaboos was awarded the International Peace Award in recognition of his insight and his role in maintaining peace and stability in the region.

GEOGRAPHY

Oman has the most diverse geography of the Arabian peninsula. Approximately 300,000 sq km in area, it occupies the south-eastern corner of the Arabian peninsula and boasts some 1700km of coastline. Its territory includes the Musandam peninsula, which overlooks the Strait of Hormuz and is separated from the rest of the country by the east coast of the UAE. Oman also controls a tiny enclave of territory entirely surrounded by the UAE in and around the village of Madha. There are also a number of islands in Oman, the most important of which is Masirah, chosen as the site of a military base due to its strategic position near both East Africa and the subcontinent.

The most populated area is along the northern coast although the largest city, after the capital, is Salalah in the far south on the Arabian Sea coast. The northern coastal strip, known as the Batinah Coast, is a sand and gravel plain separated from the rest of Arabia by the Hajar mountains on the southern side of which are the seemingly endless sands of the Empty Quarter (Rub al-Khali). The highest peak in the country is Jebel Akhdar (which translates as 'Green Mountain') at 2980m. Another, lower, range of mountains, the Dhofar mountains, rise behind the southern coastal plain.

Oman also has two large areas of salt flats. The smaller of the two is Umm al-Samim, at the 'elbow' where the country's desert border with Saudi Arabia makes a sharp turn. The other is a huge area of the coast opposite Masirah Island and just south of the Wahiba Sands, a huge expanse of spectacular sand dunes, home to Bedouin tribes.

One feature of the landscape in Oman, as well as the other Gulf countries, is the *wadi* (seasonal river bed). These cut through the countryside and most wadis in the moun-

tainous regions fill with water only after heavy rains in the winter months.

The mountainous areas of the interior and the Musandam peninsula in the north are strikingly beautiful and fiercely rugged while the southern coast is tropical in appearance with long stretches of white sandy beaches.

CLIMATE

Oman's varied geography makes for a wide range of climatic conditions. Coconuts are grown in the southern coastal areas while the highlands around Jebel Akhdar produce roses and grapes.

Muscat is hot and very humid from mid-March until October with an average temperature of 38°C in June. In the interior it can get up to 50°C but it is a drier heat. Throughout the whole country it's pleasantly warm from October to March and the temperature during December and January usually stays around 25°C. In winter the highest peaks of the Hajars have been known to receive light snowfall.

In the Salalah area, humid weather with temperatures approaching 30°C is common, even in December. The Salalah area gets drenched by the monsoon rains *(khareef)* every year from June to September when drizzle and mist are the norm.

If you are already in Oman and want weather information dial ☎ 1103 for a local forecast.

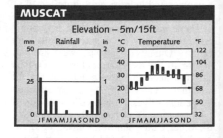

MUSCAT

Elevation – 5m/15ft

NATIONAL PARKS & RESERVES

Oman has one of the world's most rigorously 'green' governments. There are a number of nature preserves, known as National Protected Areas, scattered around the country. Not all of these nature reserves are open to the public. To visit those that are you will need a permit from the Directorate-General of Nature Reserves (☎ 602285, fax 602283) at the Ministry of Regional Municipalities & Environment in Muscat. Call them to find out which areas are currently open to tourists. The ministry is on the sea side of Ministries St in Al-Khuwair. It is the large white building that stands alone.

The Dimaaniyat Islands Nature Reserve, 16km off the coast between Muscat and Barka, consists of nine islands surrounded by coral reefs and diverse marine life. Hawksbill turtles, green turtles and migratory birds visit the islands each year to nest. The endangered sooty falcon also breeds here from May to October.

The Arabian Oryx Sanctuary in the Al-Wusta region in southern Oman is also a natural habitat for species such as the Nubian ibex, caracal, Arabian gazelle, sand cat and houbara bustard. Although the breeding of Arabian oryx (also called white oryx) has been successful, the constant poaching of the

animals has reduced their numbers greatly and still threatens to wipe them out. At the moment the only way to visit the sanctuary is with Heide Beale Tours (☎ 799928) at the Mercure al-Falaj hotel in Muscat.

As-Saleel Natural Park near Al-Kamil, in north-eastern Oman, is an alluvial plain of acacia woodland with diverse plant species, providing a good habitat for animals such as the Arabian gazelle and the rare Gordon's wildcat.

A coastal strip of 42km, running south from Ras al-Hadd at the north-eastern tip of Oman, is a protected breeding ground for turtles. A camping area has been set aside for visitors at Ras al-Jinz, about 20km south of Ras al Hadd (see Ras al-Jinz in the North-East Oman chapter).

The *khors* (inlets or creeks) around Salalah are protected, and are home to many bird and fish species as well as mangroves.

Useful Organisations

The Whale & Dolphin Group (☎ 595903) helps to rescue animals caught in nets and keeps a record of sightings. If you are interested in volunteering your services, contact Robert Baldwin to find out what you can do. Avid bird-watchers can contact the Oman Bird Group (☎ 695498).

The Historical Association of Oman (☎ 563074) collects artefacts for display and has lectures covering such topics as archaeology and natural history. Field trips are also arranged, some to other Gulf countries. Meetings are held once a week at various locations and membership costs OR10 per year or OR20 for a family.

GOVERNMENT & POLITICS

The government is very much a one-person show. Sultan Qaboos is the ultimate authority. National Day, for example, is celebrated each year on the sultan's birthday (18 November) and not on the anniversary of his assumption of power (23 July). The sultan is also prime minister, foreign minister and defence minister, and all laws and decrees are issued by him. There are a number of administrative bodies appointed by

---

Bird-watching in Oman

During October/November Muscat is the raptor capital of the world. This is the time to see a variety of birds of prey, including the steppe eagle, the greater spotted eagle, the long-legged buzzard and various species of kestrel.

In Salalah, the best time for bird-watching is during December and January when all kinds of waders and waterfowl – storks, flamingos, herons, gulls, terns – are attracted to the many *khors* (inlets) in and around the city. May is the best time to see migratory birds from Africa, including the European roller, Didric cuckoo and the grey-headed kingfisher.

There are three species of bee-eater that breed along the Batinah Coast in May. They are the blue-cheeked, the European and the little green bee-eater. By July these birds have usually dispersed to other parts of the Arabian peninsula.

the sultan which carry out the day-to-day governing. The Diwan of the Royal Court advises the sultan and provides a protocol of internal affairs. It is also the main liaison body between the sultan and the people.

There are eight administrative regions in Oman and these are broken up into 59 *wilayats* (districts). Each wilayat is governed by a *wali* (governor), who is responsible to the Ministry of the Interior.

The sultan married in 1976 but later divorced. He has no children and no designated heir. Speculation about the succession is not, however, one of Muscat's favourite parlour games. In Oman this simply is not done.

There's an oft-quoted remark by the sultan to the effect that the country is not yet ready for Western-style parliamentary democracy and that no purpose would be served by setting up a sham parliament. The implication is that, over a period of time, the country will move towards a less personalised system of government.

In January 1992, an elected consultative council, or Majlis ash-Shura (*majlis* means parliament, *shura* means 'mutual consultation'), convened for the first time, replacing an appointed state consultative council which had existed since 1981. Though a far cry from a Western parliament, the council is widely seen as a first step towards broader participation in government. It mainly comments on draft laws and other such topics as the sultan chooses to put in front of it.

A royal decree issued in 1996 re-established the systems of government that are in place and reconfirmed that Oman is a constitutional monarchy.

ECONOMY

In 1970, when development in much of the rest of the Gulf was already well under way, Oman still had only 10km of surfaced road (between Muscat and Mutrah in Greater Muscat). There were only three primary schools in the country and no secondary schools. There was one hospital which was run by US missionaries.

Though the economy is essentially oil-based, Oman's oil production is relatively modest by Gulf standards. As a result diversification of the economy is high on the list of economic goals. Vision 2020 is a government program that aims to achieve this diversification through support for small businesses, further education and initiating new industries. Reserves of natural gas are being tapped, and Oman's mining industry has been given the task of exploiting deposits of gold, copper, silver and coal.

Agriculture in the inland areas and fishing on the coast continue to be important sources of income for much of the population. A long-term goal of the government is to be self-sufficient in food production. The export market has been expanded through the manufacture of furniture, textiles, electrical goods and paper and metal products.

Employment of nationals is vital if Oman is to achieve the economic goals it has set for itself. The government has been more successful than any other in the region at 'localising' its economy, that is, replacing foreigners with Omanis wherever possible, a process called Omanisation. Many expats are relocating to other Gulf States where there is a higher dependence on foreign labour and professionals. It is far more common to see Omanis in service positions, such as working behind the reception desk at a hotel, or working manually, at a petrol station for example, than it is to see Emiratis doing similar jobs in the UAE.

POPULATION & PEOPLE

Oman's population is estimated to be about 2.1 million, of whom about 500,000 are expats. While Omanis are Arabs, the country's long trading history has led to a great deal of mingling and intermarriage of Omani Arabs with other ethnic groups, such as East Africans.

The Bedouin of the interior were basically a tribal people, often moving from place to place within a certain area. Tribal divisions are slowly being lost as moving around the country has become easier and there has been much intermarriage among the clans. One of the most traditional Bedouin groups are the Wahibas who inhabit the Wahiba

Sands in north-eastern Oman, although their numbers are very small now. The Jabalis are another group who inhabit the mountains of the Dhofar region in southern Oman and who migrate from the hills to the coast in winter (see the boxed text 'The Jabali' in the Southern Oman chapter).

There has been an Indian merchant community in Muscat for at least 200 years and, in the north, it is also common to find people who are at least partly of Persian or Baluchi ancestry. Other expats come from other Middle Eastern countries, in particular Palestine, Jordan and Syria, or from Western countries such as the UK, US, Australia and northern Europe.

EDUCATION

Before Sultan Qaboos came to power in 1970, only a few children (boys) were permitted to have a basic education, while secondary education was discouraged. Now, free primary and secondary education is one of the mainstays of Oman's modernisation program. Sultan Qaboos University on the outskirts of Muscat is the country's main tertiary education institution.

The sultan has recognised that to deny women an education is to deprive the country of 50% of its genius. Girls now make up almost half of the classroom populations, and there are now 13,000 women employees in the government sector holding a range of positions, including in the majlis ash-shura, the consultative council of the government.

The government has been working hard to eradicate illiteracy, which remains high among older people living in the interior.

ARTS

Oman's traditional arts, ie dance, music and crafts, remain a rich element of everyday life. In most villages and towns traditional crafts, including jewellery making, are still alive and well, although the availability of modern jewellery from Saudi, India and Kuwait has meant that fewer people buy traditional silver Bedouin jewellery any more, and therefore less is produced. Dance and music is very important to the identity

and comradeship of a community, evident in the spontaneous displays of song and dance which take place in villages all over the country, especially during festivals such as National Day and the holiday at the end of Ramadan. For more information on the music and dance of the region, see Arts in the Facts about the Region chapter.

Oman is well known for its traditional silver jewellery such as kohl boxes, necklaces and *khanjars* (ornate daggers worn by men) although Omani women tend to prefer gold jewellery now. For a complete rundown of traditional Omani handicrafts, including jewellery, weaving and pottery, see the special section 'Shopping' at the end of the Regional Facts for the Visitor chapter.

SOCIETY & CONDUCT
Traditional Culture

Despite the modern appearance of Muscat's western districts, much of the country, including parts of the capital area, remains intensely conservative and traditional. In these places life revolves around the family which is usually large (up to 15 children). Marriage outside the village or the clan is not common. In many rural villages water is still fetched from a well, fruit and vegetables for the household are grown in vegetable plots next to the house, families slaughter their own goats and chickens, clothes and crockery are washed in nearby streams and women are restricted to household duties.

There are still many nomadic (or Bedouin) tribes living in the interior, especially in the Wahiba Sands (the Wahibas), or tucked away in the mountains (the Jabali).

Family and community bonds are very strong. Omanis seem to be adept at assimilating what they want or need of modern life, and enjoying its benefits without letting the new technology adversely affect their own lives and values.

Every spring the sultan spends several weeks driving around the country on a 'meet the people tour'. This is covered extensively on Omani TV. A few minutes viewing one of the reports will show you the extent to which the day-to-day life of the average

Traditional Dress

Most Omanis wear traditional dress. In fact, by law all Omanis employed by the government (a not insignificant portion of the employed population) are required to wear traditional dress at work.

For men, traditional dress consists of a loose *dishdasha*, a floor-length shirt-dress. These are usually light purple though white, gold and other colours are sometimes seen. The tassel that hangs down from the neckline is called the *kashkusha* and is often dipped in perfume. A *wizar* is a piece of cloth worn under the dishdasha. It is wrapped around the waist like a sarong.

For everyday wear and informal occasions, Omani men also wear brimless, embroidered caps called *kumma*. For formal occasions and at work, the caps are replaced by a turban called a *massar*. In some coastal areas the massar is worn in preference to the kumma on informal occasions. How the massar is worn indicates the region the wearer is from. The Bedouin wrap it loosely and sometimes fasten it with a rope, while in Muscat it is tightly wrapped around the head with no loose ends.

On important occasions men traditionally wear a khanjar (dagger) on a belt round their waists. In rural areas, khanjars are still sometimes worn every day. See the special section 'Shopping' earlier in this book for more information about khanjars.

Women's dress is far more colourful than in the UAE and other Gulf countries. Colourfully printed dishdashas are wrapped with even more colourfully printed shawls and veils (*lihaff*). Under their *kandouras* (a long colourfully embroidered cloak which is a little like a kaftan), women wear baggy trousers (called *sirwal*) that come in tight at the ankle and are often decorated with gold and coloured thread woven together (called *talli*). On formal occasions women wear an *abaya* which is the long black cloak seen in the UAE and most Gulf countries.

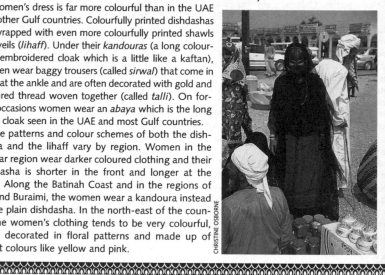
CHRISTINE OSBORNE

The patterns and colour schemes of both the dishdasha and the lihaff vary by region. Women in the Dhofar region wear darker coloured clothing and their dishdasha is shorter in the front and longer at the back. Along the Batinah Coast and in the regions of Ibri and Buraimi, the women wear a kandoura instead of the plain dishdasha. In the north-east of the country the women's clothing tends to be very colourful, often decorated in floral patterns and made up of bright colours like yellow and pink.

Omani living in a town in the interior or a fishing village on the coast is close to what it would have been centuries ago.

Dos & Don'ts

Apart from the usual dos and don'ts (see Traditional Culture in the Facts About the Region chapter), note that outsiders are not welcome in the Lewara quarter of Muscat's Mutrah district, where many of the capital's Shi'ite Muslims live. There are usually a couple of people sitting in the gateway which leads from Mutrah Corniche into the Lewara quarter, who will stop you.

Non-Muslims are not permitted to enter mosques in Oman.

CHRIS MELLOR

LOU CALLAN

CHRIS MELLOR

The stunningly retro Alam Palace (top left), elegant merchant's houses on the Corniche (top right) and fishermen unloading their catch at Mina Qaboos (bottom) are all part of Muscat's rich heritage as seat of the ruling Al-Busaid family and as trade centre and port.

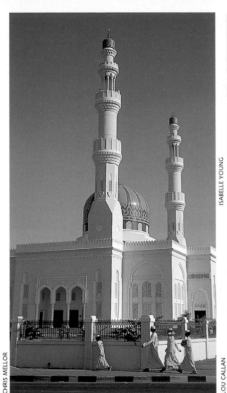

CHRIS MELLOR

ISABELLE YOUNG

LOU CALLAN

CHRISTINE OSBORNE

Outside the big cities, life in Oman goes on much as it has done for centuries (prayer time at Buraimi mosque, top left, and bargaining for livestock at Nizwa souq, middle right), albeit with some concessions to modernity (top right and bottom).

Facts for the Visitor

SUGGESTED ITINERARIES

Even if you only have a few days to a week in Oman, you should be able to cover most of the highlights in the north of the country.

One Week

This gives you time to see Muscat (three days), including a day trip to the Bimmah Sinkhole, and leaves you two days to take in Nakhal, Wadi Bani Awf, Rustaq and Al-Hazm, plus a day in Sohar.

Two Weeks

Extend your stay in Muscat to five days, including day trips to Yitti Beach and the Bimmah Sinkhole. Then do the Nakhal, Rustaq and Al-Hazm circuit, with an overnight camp in Wadi Bani Awf. Spend two nights in Nizwa, from where you can go to Bahla, Jabrin and the tombs at Al-Ayn. You've also got time to spend a night at Ras al-Jinz turtle reserve and a night in Sur, plus three nights in Salalah (take a flight)

Three Weeks

Same as for two weeks plus a night in Sohar. A third night in Nizwa or camping in the area would allow you to stop off in Samail and Izki and to explore some more of the surrounding villages. You could also include a two-day jaunt from Muscat to Mintirib, Wadi Bani Khalid, Al-Kamil, Jalan Bani Bu Hassan and Jalan Bani Bu Ali, staying overnight at the Al-Qabil Resthouse.

One Month

This gives you enough time to see everything talked about in the Oman chapters of this book without having to rush too much.

MAPS

The *Second Pictorial Map of Oman* has a red cover and is available from most hotel bookshops for OR3. It has a large country map as well as smaller maps of Muscat, Salalah, Sohar and Nizwa. Also recommended is the

Highlights

- Mutrah souq in Muscat, one of the best traditional markets in Arabia.

- The spectacular mountain landscapes of the Musandam peninsula, an enclave of Omani territory guarding the southern edge of the Strait of Hormuz.

- Jabrin fort, with the best restoration work of any fort in Oman; it provides an insight into what life was like behind the walls of a 17th century Omani fort.

- The strikingly beautiful Wadi Bani Awf, the perfect place to go camping or for a day trip out of Muscat.

- Nizwa souq, colourful and traditional, especially the goat market at the far end.

- Job's Tomb, a lovely drive out of Salalah through the Dhofar mountains, with great views back over the city.

Bartholomew *Map of the Sultanate of Oman*, although it can be hard to find. It has a light blue cover with a picture of the Seeb clock tower on one side and palm trees on the other. The National Survey Authority *Map of the Sultanate of Oman* is an excellent road map, but it is very large. This, too, is difficult to find. If you can't find it in the English-language bookshops, try the smaller Arabic bookshops. The *Apex Map of Oman* is widely available but it doesn't have as much detail on lesser roads and villages as the other maps mentioned in this section.

TOURIST OFFICES

There are no tourist offices as such in Oman. The National Tourism Office (☎ 799 500, fax 794 213) which is run by the Directorate General of Tourism in Muscat will gladly help with any information you may need over the phone. Otherwise, for any literature try one of the larger tour operators or hotels.

OMAN

VISAS & DOCUMENTS
Visas

Unless you are a citizen of another Gulf country or you are a tourist with a visit visa to the UAE, you need a visa to enter Oman. You must have at least six months validity on your passport before you can apply for a visa.

Costs vary according to your nationality and the type of visa. Processing the visa application usually takes about three working days. Express visas, issued the same day, are available for business travellers who have urgent business affairs in Oman. There is no problem getting a visa for Oman if your passport shows evidence of a visit to Israel.

Wherever you apply you need four photographs and must fill out an application. Be prepared to show an onward or return ticket.

Transit Visas Available to travellers of selected nationalities on arrival at Muscat's Seeb airport, these last 72 hours, cost OR25 and you need proof of an onward flight.

Single-Entry Visa A standard single-entry tourist visa, allowing a stay of three weeks, costs OR20 for British passport holders and OR7 for Australians. This visa allows you to enter Oman by land or air unless it specifically says something like 'By Air Only'. Note that hotel-sponsored visas are often only valid for entry by air. Although you are not bound to the entry point or points you declare on your visa application form, if you check Seeb airport only you may get a visa allowing entry and exit by air only.

Business Visas These are usually valid for between three months and one year (depending on your nationality). They allow a stay of three weeks at a time. They require a supporting letter from your employer. It is also a good idea to have a letter of invitation from any company you plan to visit.

Multi-Entry Visas These are available to American and British residents of GCC countries but are not yet available to tourists. They cost OR40, are valid for two years and allow a stay of up to one month.

STOP PRESS: Updated Visa Information for Oman

In a bid to encourage tourism, Oman further streamlined its visa regulations in July 2003. Visas are still required (except for citizens of other Gulf countries) but it is now possible for many foreign nationals (including those from the EU, the Americas, Australia and New Zealand) to obtain a single-entry visit visa upon arrival at all land, sea and air entry points. These visas cost OR6 and are valid for one month. Extensions of one month can be obtained at the Directorate General of Passports & Residency in Muscat or at police stations elsewhere in the country.

Multiple-entry visas are also available; these cost OR10 and allow the holder to stay three weeks with each visit.

Oman now also has a common visa facility with the Emirate of Dubai, such that if you arrive from Dubai with an entrance visa or stamp from Dubai you are not required to obtain a separate visa for Oman.

Resident expats in GCC countries can obtain visas at land and air terminals for OR3.

This information overrides other references to tourist visas in this chapter. See www.omantourism.gov.om/ for further information.

'On the Spot' Visas Resident expats in GCC countries can collect visas for Oman at land border posts or at the airport. You must have lived in the GCC for at least one year and you must also have six months validity left on your residence visa. These 'on the spot' visas are only issued to employees who have a company sponsorship. If you reside in the GCC under the sponsorship of your spouse and not a company, you will need a consent letter from your spouse to be able to pick up a visa at the border, according to immigration authorities. However, there have been cases where the Oman embassy has assured people they can collect visas at the border, unaccompanied by their spouses, but refuse when they arrive.

Sponsored Visas If you are not close to an Omani embassy it is also possible to obtain a visa through most of the country's three- to five-star hotels and tour operators. This process usually takes a week. The main drawback to this method is the expense.

The procedure for getting a visa through a hotel is simple. Fax the hotel, make a reservation and send them a copy of the data page of your passport. The hotel will charge you for this service and usually requires you to stay a minimum of three nights.

Hotel-sponsored visas do have other drawbacks in that they are set up for entry through Seeb airport in Muscat. If you decide you want to enter the country by land, when you get to the border post you will need to produce a fax copy or some written acknowledgment from your sponsor that your visa has been approved. If you go through one of the smaller border posts you may be denied entry because they do not have the technology to check on the authenticity of your visa with the immigration department in Muscat.

If you are entering the country by air you will need to have a fax of your visa or some other written proof before you will be allowed to board your flight to Muscat.

Visa Extensions One-week extensions are available on the standard three-week visit visa through your sponsor. If you don't have a sponsor or you want to extend for a longer period you will need a good reason why you need it. To get an extension, go to the Immigration & Passports Directorate (☎ 699785) in the Ministries area of Muscat.

Other Documents

For information about driving licences in Oman, see Visas & Documents in the Regional Facts for the Visitor chapter.

Site Permits Until about 1997, a permit from the Ministry of National Heritage & Culture in Muscat was needed to visit most archaeological sites, old forts etc. Now the

general rule seems to be that only groups of more than four or five people have to call ahead to make arrangements to visit a fort or an archaeological site.

Permits are definitely needed for conservation sites such as the green turtle nesting area at Ras al-Jinz. These are available from the Directorate-General of Nature Reserves in the Ministry of Regional Municipalities & Environment in Muscat (☎ 602285, fax 602283). It is a good idea to apply for these permits three working days before you plan to visit. The ministry is the large white building standing alone on the sea (north) side of Ministries St in Al-Khuwair in Muscat.

Road Permits If you have a tourist visa, you do not need a road permit to enter or leave Oman by land.

If you are a foreign resident of Oman you will need a road permit to enter or leave the country by land. This includes trips between the main part of Oman and the Musandam peninsula, since these require crossing through the UAE. Road permits are easily obtained in three to five days through your sponsor. The only problem is that permits are not issued to single women, which means that single women cannot drive to Dubai for the weekend, even if you are in a group of friends or with a single male friend. This is the only travel restriction on single and/or unaccompanied women in the sultanate.

EMBASSIES & CONSULATES
Oman Embassies
The contact details of Oman embassies in some key countries around the world are as follows:

France (☎ 01-47 23 01 63, fax 47 23 77 10) 50 Ave de Lena, 75116 Paris
Germany (☎ 228-35 70 31, fax 35 70 40) Lindenallee 11, D-53173 Bonn
Japan (☎ 03-3402 0749 or 3402 2122, fax 3404 1334) 2-28-11 Sendagaya, Shibuya-ku, Tokyo 151
Netherlands (☎ 70-361 5800, fax 360 7277) Koninginnegracht 27, 2514 AB Den Haag
UAE (☎ 02-463 333, fax 464 633) Saeed bin Tahnoon St, next to Immigration Department, Abu Dhabi (PO Box 2517, Abu Dhabi)

OMAN

UK (☎ 020-7225 0001, fax 7589 2505) 167
  Queen's Gate, London, SW7 5HE
USA (☎ 202-387 1980, fax 745 4933) 2535 Bel-
  mont Rd NW, Washington DC 20008

Oman does not have embassies in Canada,
Australia or New Zealand. Travellers from
Australia and New Zealand need to contact
the embassy in Japan to apply for visas.
Travellers in Canada should contact the em-
bassy in the USA.

Embassies & Consulates in Oman

Countries with embassies or consulates in
Oman include the following, all of which
are in Muscat. All are embassies except for
the Netherlands representation, which is a
consulate.

Bahrain (☎ 605074 or 605133, fax 605072) Al-
  Kharjiyah St, just off Way 3015, Shatti al-
  Qurm
France (☎ 681800, fax 681843) Jameat ad-
  Duwal al-Arabiyya St, Al-Khuwair
Germany (☎ 702164, fax 7735690) Near the Al-
  Nahdha Hospital on Al-Nahdha St, Ruwi
India (☎ 702957, fax 797547) Bank al-Markazi
  St, Ruwi
Iran (☎ 696944, fax 696888) Jameat ad-Duwal
  al-Arabiyya St, Al-Khuwair
Kuwait (☎ 699626 or 699627, fax 699628)
  Jameat ad-Duwal al-Arabiyya St, Al-Khuwair
Netherlands (☎ 603706 or 603719, fax 603397)
  Villa 1366, Way 3017, Shatti al-Qurm
New Zealand (☎ 794932, fax 706443) Mutrah
  High St, opposite Iehab Travels
Qatar (☎ 691152, fax 691156) Jameat ad-Duwal
  al-Arabiyya St, Al-Khuwair
Saudi Arabia (☎ 601744, fax 603540) Jameat
  ad-Duwal al-Arabiyya St, Al-Khuwair
UAE (☎ 600302, fax 602584) Jameat ad-Duwal
  al-Arabiyya St, Al-Khuwair
UK (☎ 693077, fax 693091) Jameat ad-Duwal al-
  Arabiyya St, Al-Khuwair
USA (☎ 698989, fax 604316) Jameat ad-Duwal
  al-Arabiyya St, Al-Khuwair
Yemen (☎ 600815, fax 609172) Bldg No 2981,
  Way 2840, Shatti al-Qurm, near Muscat Inter-
  Continental

There is no Australian representation in
Oman; the Australian government covers
Oman from its embassy in Riyadh, Saudi
Arabia (☎ 01-488 7788, PO Box 94400

Riyadh). The British embassy processes
visas and handles emergencies for Canadian citizens.

CUSTOMS

Non-Muslims arriving at Muscat's Seeb international airport can bring in one bottle of
alcohol. Those arriving by road are not permitted to import alcohol. Do not press your
luck on this or assume that you can talk
your way around it. Bags and cars are often
searched and alcohol will be confiscated at
the border.

The customs regulations allow travellers
to import a 'reasonable quantity' of cigars,
cigarettes and tobacco. There are no unusual regulations regarding things like cameras, computers or cassette players.

MONEY

For more general information on money
matters, including exchanging cash and
travellers cheques, see Money in the Regional Facts for the Visitor chapter.

Currency

The Omani riyal (OR) is divided into 1000
baisa (baiza). Notes come in denominations
of 100 and 200 baisa, and OR1/2, 1, 5, 10,
20 and 50. The 1/4-riyal note has been dis-
continued but you might still come across
it. Coins come in 5, 10, 25, 50 and 100 baisa
denominations, though the 25 and 50 baisa
coins are the only ones you are likely to see
on a regular basis. The notes have both English and Arabic script, but the numbers on
the coins appear only in Arabic characters.
A word of warning: the OR5 note and the
old OR1 are the same colour and look very
similar. It's easy to mistake them, so always check your change.

The good thing about travelling to Oman
from the UAE is that you can use up all
your UAE dirhams. They are accepted just
about everywhere in the country at a basic
rate of exchange of Dh10 = OR1. Unfortunately this doesn't work the other way
round, and even in Al-Ain, which is on the
border, your Omani currency may not be
accepted.

Exchange Rates

The riyal is a convertible currency and there are no restrictions on its import or export.

country	unit		Omani riyal
Australia	A$1	=	OR0.240
Canada	C$1	=	OR0.250
Europe	€1	=	OR0.430
France	FF1	=	OR0.065
Germany	DM1	=	OR0.570
Japan	¥1	=	OR0.003
New Zealand	NZ$1	=	OR0.210
UK	UK£1	=	OR0.630
USA	US$1	=	OR0.390

In Oman, the latest foreign exchange rates are available by phone 24 hours a day on ☎ 1106.

Costs

It is not possible to travel very cheaply in Oman. Budgets of OR15 per day in Muscat and OR20 to OR25 outside the capital, where cheap hotels are much rarer, are about as low as you are likely to achieve. Oman doesn't have the sort of low-budget accommodation you may find in parts of Asia, for instance. Hotel rates vary from OR18 to OR42 for mid-range accommodation, and from OR42 to over OR100 for five-star accommodation. Finding a free bed or camping can cut your daily expenses by one-half to two-thirds.

Once you've sorted out accommodation, many other aspects of daily life are quite cheap. A bus or microbus ticket from Muscat to any provincial city in the north of the country costs, at most, a couple of riyals, and you can get a bus ticket to Salalah in the south for as little as OR5 one way. You can fill your stomach for as little as 600 baisa at one of the country's innumerable cheap Indian restaurants. Admission to museums, forts and other places of interest is generally free.

Taxes

A 5% municipality tax and a 4% tourism tax are applied to all hotel and restaurant bills, as well as an 8% service charge. If prices are quoted 'net', it means that they include all taxes and service charges.

POST & COMMUNICATIONS
Postal Rates

Sending a postcard costs 50 baisa to other Gulf and Arab countries and 150 baisa to the rest of the world. Postage for letters weighing 20g or less is 80 baisa to other Gulf countries and 100 baisa to the rest of the Arab world. Postage on letters to everywhere else is 200 baisa for the first 10g, 350 baisa for 10 to 20g and OR1 for anything between 20g and 50g.

To other Arab countries a 0.5kg/1kg package costs OR1/2, and to most of the rest of the world it's OR2/4.

Parcel rates for up to 1kg are OR1 within Oman. Elsewhere surface/air rates for a 1kg parcel are: Gulf countries OR2/3, other Arab countries OR3/3, rest of world OR4/6. Sending a 5kg parcel costs OR3 domestically, OR10/15 within the Arab world and OR15/20 elsewhere.

Sending Mail

Post offices are open 7.30 am until 2 pm Saturday to Wednesday. They close at 11 am on Thursday and are closed all day Friday.

Receiving Mail

You can use the poste restante service at the main post office in Ruwi or the branch post office in Muscat to receive mail. Have your mail addressed to: [Your Name], Poste Restante, Ruwi Central Post Office, Ruwi, Sultanate of Oman, or to Poste Restante, Muscat Post Office, Muscat, Sultanate of Oman. American Express clients can also receive mail through the Muscat AmEx office (for contact details, see Information in the Muscat chapter).

Any parcels you receive while in the sultanate will incur a 250 baisa charge for presentation to customs. You may also be required to collect them from the post office and have them cleared through customs there. Parcels received poste restante incur an additional 50 baisa handling charge. The authorities are particularly sensitive about books and other printed matter (basically, they look for anything that could be deemed indecent or pornographic or critical of Islam or the Omani government) and the same goes for videos, which are likely to be held for inspection for several days.

Telephone, Fax & Telegraph

There are public telephone offices in both Muscat and Salalah, and in a few smaller cities and towns as well. These offer card phones, as well as fax, telex and telegraph services. Phonecards are available from most grocery stores and petrol stations. You won't have any trouble finding a payphone, even in the smallest towns, but whether they work or not is another matter.

Some useful numbers include:

Oman country code	☎ 968
Directory assistance (local)	☎ 198
International directory assistance	☎ 143
Talking clock	☎ 140
Weather information	☎ 1103

When calling Oman from outside the country, key in the country code, followed by the local six-digit number. There are no area or city codes in Oman.

Email & Internet Access

You'll find a few Internet cafes in Muscat but not many elsewhere. If you're staying at a four- or five-star hotel, you should be able to use their business centre. Private Internet access is available through Omantel, the national telecommunications company. See the individual city entries for details of Internet cafes.

INTERNET RESOURCES

By far the best, biggest and most informative site on Oman is www.oman.org. It is specifically set up for travellers, researchers and journalists and is linked with the Oman Studies Centre which has masses of information on culture and lifestyle, as well as a comprehensive bibliography. For basic facts and data go to www.omanet.com which is the official site of the Ministry of Information. Although it's not as directed towards the tourist there is good information on politics, economy, foreign affairs, commerce and media, as well as links to other sites on Oman.

Try www.oman-online.com for good introductory information on the sultanate and its culture as well as information for travellers, including what to see and where to stay (although the latter is limited to five-star hotels).

BOOKS

For general titles related to the Gulf and the Middle East, see Books in the Regional Facts for the Visitor chapter.

If you want good foreign-language novels bring them with you. Books in Oman are quite expensive – a paperback that in the USA sells for US$4.95 will cost OR6 (about US$15.60) or more in Muscat. Outside Muscat and Salalah there simply are no foreign-language bookshops.

Guidebooks

Oman – a Comprehensive Guide to the Sultanate of Oman by Joan Pickersgill is very thorough and includes interesting anecdotal information. However, it is published under the auspices of the Directorate-General of Tourism in Oman, so it does not tend to be very objective.

The *Maverick Guide to Oman* by Peter Ochs is an essential book if you plan to do some off-road exploring. It has detailed information on dozens of off-road sites. It also includes general information on the country for expats and travellers. *APEX Explorer's Guide to Oman* is another useful guide if you are planning to go off-roading. *Off-Road in Oman* by Heiner Klein & Rebecca Brickson covers a smaller selection of off-road sites.

Muscat Explorer is produced in Dubai by Explorer Publishing and has detailed information on sport, activities, shopping and restaurants. It's a particularly good reference for expats.

An Introductory Guide to Life in the Sultanate of Oman by the American Women's Group is a good reference for new expats, especially those with children. It includes details on activities and clubs, where to buy what, medical and emergency facilities, and things to do with children.

Somewhat more specialised titles include *Snorkelling and Diving in Oman* by Rod Salm & Robert Baldwin, *Birds of the Batinah of Oman* by RA & GE Honeywell and *Rock Climbing in Oman* by R A McDonald.

Travel
Oman has been well covered by a variety of travellers. *Travels in Oman – On the Track of the Early Explorers* by Philip Ward is a highly recommended read. It combines a modern travel narrative with the best of the 18th, 19th and early 20th century travellers' accounts of the country, but it is difficult to find.

Sultan in Oman by James Morris is a travelling journalist's account of a visit to Oman in the 1950s, though you should be aware that it is banned in Oman itself.

History & Politics
There are few good history books devoted specifically to Oman. *Oman and its Renaissance* by Sir Donald Hawley covers the first 25 years of Sultan Qaboos' rule, and charts the history of Oman from the end of the Ice Age until the present.

For an analysis of the foreign policy of the sultanate, read *Oman and the World: the Emergence of an Independent Foreign Policy* by Joseph A Kechichian.

To find out more about Oman's presence in East Africa read John Gray's *History of Zanzibar from the Middle Ages to 1856*.

General
There are a large number of coffee table books on Oman that can be found in the bookshops listed in the city sections of the following chapters. *Forts of Oman* by Walter Dinteman is a great souvenir. Photographic books include *A Day Above Oman* by John Nowell, *The Heritage of Oman: A Celebration in Photographs* by Ozzie Newcombe and Pauline Shelton, and *Oman – An Arabian Album* by Ronald Codrai, which is a collection of mid-20th century photographs.

Oman Silver by Ruth Hawley might be a good investment for travellers intending to visit Oman's jewellery souqs, particularly since most of the shopkeepers in Muscat's silver souq have well-thumbed copies. Another book worth looking at is *Disappearing Treasures of Oman* by Avelyn Foster.

NEWSPAPERS & MAGAZINES
The major Arabic-language newspapers are *Oman* and *Al Watan*. The *Times of Oman* and the *Oman Daily Observer* are the local English-language newspapers. They can be difficult to find outside Muscat. Foreign newspapers and magazines are available only in the bookshops in Muscat's five-star hotels and in a few other places frequented by the Western community (supermarkets in Qurm and the Family Bookshop chain, for example) and are usually about three days old. Outside Muscat you can forget about finding foreign papers except perhaps at the Salalah Holiday Inn and the Salalah Family Bookshop.

The widely available *Oman Today* is a magazine-cum-handbook published every two months. For OR1, it is an excellent publication with interesting articles and comprehensive listings of clubs, activities, restaurants and entertainment. It is mainly aimed at the expat community.

Adventure Oman is a glossy magazine with articles on caving, mountain biking, rock climbing and ecology. It also has general information for the visitor and listings of hotels, restaurants, car hire and tour companies. It is available for OR1.500 in hotel bookshops. Less thorough listings can be found in *What's On*, a monthly publication based in the UAE and available in the sultanate for OR1.200.

RADIO & TV
The Sultanate of Oman FM Service is the Muscat-based English-language radio station. It broadcasts on 90.4 FM every day from 7 am until 10 pm, with news bulletins at 7.30 am, and 2.30 and 6.30 pm. The fare is mostly classical music interspersed with light entertainment. Broadcasts in Arabic are

OMAN

made on 1242 AM in Muscat and 738 AM in Salalah.

The main source of information for the expat community is the seemingly omnipresent BBC World Service – see Radio & TV in the Regional Facts for the Visitor chapter for a list of short-wave frequencies for the BBC.

Sultanate of Oman Television (SOTV) began transmission from Muscat in November 1974. It now has a daily newscast in English at 8 pm and English-language movies two or three nights a week. It often has interesting programs focusing on Omani culture and traditions.

PHOTOGRAPHY & VIDEO

Apart from the usual provisos (see Photography & Video in Regional Facts for the Visitor) there are no special restrictions on taking photographs in Oman.

Omani labs are reliable and world standard. Getting a roll of 36 prints developed costs about OR2.200. You can get passport photos done in one day for OR1. All types of films are available in Muscat, but outside the capital you may have difficulty finding particular types of film (such as slide film). A regular 36-print colour film will cost you about OR1.500.

HEALTH

Since his ascension to power, Sultan Qaboos has made improving health care and hygiene standards in Oman one of his main priorities. The result is that Oman is one of the most squeaky-clean countries you could ever hope to visit. Even the smallest restaurants in the souq exhibit high standards of cleanliness, and the tap water is drinkable throughout the country.

If you are coming from a yellow fever infected area you will need proof of vaccination against yellow fever before you will be allowed in the country. Malaria, virtually endemic only 30 years ago, is no longer a huge problem but you may want to consider antimalarial medications, particularly if you plan to travel extensively in the south. Discuss this with your doctor before you leave.

Clinics and hospitals will be able to help you if you fall ill during your stay. Emergency treatment at government hospitals is generally free. Hospitals or clinics can be easily recognised by the red crescent sign. There is no emergency ambulance service in Oman. Ambulances are only used for transferral between hospitals. If you need to get to a hospital fast, you will have to rely on taxis, friends or a Good Samaritan. Some major hospitals are listed in the relevant city sections throughout this book.

See Health in the Regional Facts for the Visitor chapter for a more general discussion of health issues for travellers in the region.

TRAVEL WITH CHILDREN

Oman is an easy place to bring kids. There are plenty of activities and places for them. In Muscat, Funworld in Qurm has a number of rides of varying degrees of terror, including water rides, and is open 4 to 11 pm Saturday to Wednesday and 10 am to 11 pm Thursday, Friday and public holidays; admission is OR2. The Qurm Nature Reserve next door is a large park with a lake, waterbirds, shelters and plenty of shady trees to sit under for a picnic. It is open Saturday to Wednesday 3 to 11 pm; Thursday, Friday and public holidays 10 am to 1 am. Admission is free. The Children's Museum in Muscat is a must, for both kids and adults (see that entry in the Muscat chapter for more details).

Most shopping centres in Muscat have video game arcades and even nurseries for smaller children, so that parents can do their shopping unencumbered.

The week-long Muscat Festival, which starts in late January (the date varies from year to year) and the 45-day Khareef Festival in Salalah in July and August feature lots of outdoor entertainment and activities that kids will enjoy.

If you are planning on going hiking or doing any off-road exploration, the *Maverick Guide to Oman* and *Off-Road in Oman* both indicate hikes and activities that are ideal for children, as well as those that are too difficult.

BUSINESS HOURS

Businesses are open Saturday to Thursday 8 am to 1 pm and 4 to 7 or 7.30 pm, and are closed all day Friday. Most businesses are also closed on Thursday afternoons. Many of the shops in Muscat's Mutrah souq are open during the early evening hours on Friday. Shops in most of Muscat's shopping malls stay open until 9 or 9.30 pm most nights. Shops in Mutrah souq close at 8.30 pm. During Ramadan shops don't open until 7 pm but they stay open to about 10.30 pm or later.

Banks are open Saturday to Wednesday 8 am to noon (11 am Thursday). The money-changers in and around the Mutrah souq keep much the same hours as other businesses. Government offices are open Saturday to Wednesday 7.30 am until 2 pm; some are open until 1 pm on Thursday. Note that during Ramadan government offices are open 9 am to 1.30 pm.

PUBLIC HOLIDAYS & SPECIAL EVENTS

In addition to the main Islamic holidays (see Public Holidays & Special Events in the Regional Facts for the Visitor chapter), Oman observes National Day, which is celebrated on the sultan's birthday (18 November). You should be aware, however, that National Day and the sultan's birthday are somewhat fluid.

Sometimes the days around a public holiday are also declared as holidays. The exact dates and length of holidays are announced by royal proclamation in the newspaper a day or two before they occur. Since most government employees are required to spend National Day participating in the lavish official ceremonies marking the occasion, the entire country is usually given two or three days holiday a week or so after the actual event. For the visitor the main significance of this is that everything (and, be warned, this means *everything*) closes down again.

The National Day festival features all sorts of highly visible official celebrations. A few of these are usually open to the public – check the local newspapers or Radio Oman a few days before National Day for details of the celebrations you can attend. Most of the official functions are by invitation only, but these are usually broadcast live on TV.

The week-long Muscat Festival held after Eid al-Fitr features lots of activities and performances, traditional dancing, music and singing. Similar festivities take place during the Khareef Festival in Salalah which runs for 45 days from mid-July until the end of August. Check the local newspapers for details of events and daily programs.

ACTIVITIES

All the activities listed in this section are offered by most tour companies, so shop around. Some tour operators offer tailor-made tours for small groups (usually four to eight people). Although these packages can be relatively expensive, they are a great way to do some of the more unusual activities without the hassle or expense of hiring a your own 4WD or other equipment. Some recommended companies are listed in the Activities section of the Muscat chapter. For a complete listing of tour operators and what they offer, check out *Adventure Oman* or *What's On* magazines (see Newspapers & Magazines earlier in this chapter).

The widely available *Oman Today* has complete listings of the various sports clubs and societies in Oman.

Off-road Safaris

The variety of terrain in Oman makes mountain and desert motoring particularly worthwhile. It's a great way to see the country. See Activities in Regional Facts for the Visitor for more information on this favourite pastime, and Organised Tours in Getting Around for details of the sort of trips you can do and how much it will cost.

If you are planning to hire your own 4WD, the *Maverick Guide to Oman* and the *APEX Explorer's Guide to Oman* are essential reading.

Hiking, Climbing & Cycling

With the Hajar mountains reaching heights of 3000m and stretching for over 300km, rock climbing, hiking and caving are increasingly popular activities in Oman, especially with the expat community. A venture into the Hajars will reveal wadis and gorges, spurs, cliffs and remote villages.

Sunny Day Tours in Muscat (☎ 591244, fax 591478) can arrange caving, trekking and rock climbing trips. As all trips are individually arranged there are no fixed prices, but allow around US$100 per day per person. Mezoon Travel (☎ 796680) in Muscat also offers trekking and rock climbing tours. If you are feeling fit *Adventure Trekking in Oman* by Jerry Hadwin details a number of superb hikes of varying degrees of difficulty.

If you are interested in mountain biking, contact Ras al-Hamra Cycling Club on ☎ 678556. They organise weekly rides and in winter they host the occasional overnight ride.

Diving & Snorkelling

Oman has some excellent diving and snorkelling sites, and several centres offer diving and snorkelling trips. Most diving centres offer accredited PADI diving courses. It costs roughly OR120 for an open water course, including equipment hire and tuition. For more details, see the Diving entry in the Muscat, Southern Oman (Salalah) and Musandam Peninsula (Khasab) chapters.

Water Sports

Other water sports such as sailing or jet-skiing are becoming the recreational mainstay of five-star hotels and exclusive marinas. Most of these, such as the Hyatt Regency and the Inter-Continental in Muscat, have a beach of their own and sport small fleets of sailing boats, windsurfers and pedal boats.

Whale & Dolphin Watching Cruises

The waters off the north and south coasts of Oman provide ideal breeding grounds and habitats for a number of whale and dolphin species. Whales found here include the false killer whale, sperm whale and Indo-Pacific humpback. Dolphin species include the bottlenose and Risso's dolphin. You are not guaranteed a sighting but at the right time of year (December to March) you're likely to spot something.

Marina Bander al-Rowdha (☎ 737293) in Muscat offers a whale and dolphin watching cruise for OR3 per hour. In Salalah you can book a whale and dolphin watching cruise with Samharam Dive & Watersports Centre (☎ 235333) at the Salalah Holiday Inn. Prices vary greatly depending on the number of people and the length of the cruise.

LANGUAGE COURSES

The British Council in Muscat (☎ 600548, fax 698018) offers 10-week Arabic courses for beginners, usually two or three times a year. Polyglot Institute Oman (☎ 701261) in Muscat also has courses throughout the year for beginners.

ACCOMMODATION
Camping

The only formal camp sites in Oman are at the Oman Dive Centre in Muscat (see Places to Stay in the Muscat chapter) and at the Ras al-Jinz turtle reserve (see the Ras al-Jinz section in the North-East Oman chapter).

Hotels

Muscat has a range of hotels to suit most budgets, all of which are generally clean and comfortable. Outside of the capital most hotels are still fairly clean but you will find your choice of accommodation severely limited. Most of Oman's main provincial hotels have only one or two hotels. Even Salalah, the largest city in the country after Muscat has fewer than 10 places to stay.

In Muscat you can spend anything from OR7 to OR70 on a single room. In Salalah the selection levels out at around OR8 for a single and OR12 for a double.

FOOD

Traditional Omani food includes some mouth-watering national dishes and flavours. Eating cheaply in Oman almost always means eating Indian. Biryanis, shwarmas, felafel and kima are available just about everywhere for 200 to 600 baisa. See Food in the

Omani Food

Omani cooking is spicy (but not overly so), colourful and varies from region to region. Rice, an essential part of any meal, is served in a number of different ways, including *qabooli* (rice browned with spices such as cardamom, cinnamon, saffron and turmeric), *arsia*, a gooey mashed rice dish, eaten during festivals such as Eid, and *makbousa*, a saffron-flavoured rice cooked on top of spicy meat.

A famous festival delicacy in the interior is *shuwa*, a dish prepared by burying spiced meat (usually a goat carcass) and roasting it over a period of eight hours in an underground clay oven.

The Dhofar region of the south is famous for its *maqudeed* – pieces of dried, shredded meat (a bit like beef jerky).

One of the staples in an Omani kitchen is *rukhal*, a thin, round bread made from flour and water. It's usually served with honey, yoghurt or barbecued meat.

While in Oman you really should try the *halwa*. Although common in the rest of the Gulf, this sticky sweet is definitely superior in Oman. Made from sugar, water, eggs, ghee, nuts, cardamom and sometimes rosewater, it is delicious and highly addictive. The Sultan's late mother was reputedly a halwa fan. Whenever she travelled to London, she took bucket loads with her.

Regional Facts for the Visitor chapter for more details.

Muscat also has a number of upmarket Indian, Lebanese and Chinese restaurants, and the usual collection of Western-style fast-food establishments and chain restaurants. The big hotels offer the usual selection of international fare, but the food is very expensive and only average in quality. Buffets are popular at the big hotels and usually cost around OR6 (plus tax).

DRINKS

Small restaurants are likely to offer you a choice of little more than Coke, Pepsi or water. Larger restaurants have a wider variety of soft drinks as well as fruit juice, sometimes freshly squeezed with lots of added sugar. One of the local drinks is rosewater milk. It's a bit like liquefied Turkish delight and when it's served ice-cold it is very refreshing on a hot day.

Alcohol is generally only available at mid-range and top-end hotels. Some of the more upmarket restaurants also offer alcohol but the prices are usually very high. A pint of beer costs from OR1.500 to OR2, while even the most ordinary bottle of wine costs at least OR8. Restaurants don't always include a drinks list on their menus so it's worth asking if they serve alcohol.

Sweet Thing

Omani honey is no ordinary honey. This stuff, which you'll see for sale in bottles in the souqs for anything between OR10 and OR70, is the liquid gold of the region. Apiculture in Arabia goes back thousands of years.

Honey has always been used as a panacea but in Oman it was also used as a weapon against enemies. Boiling honey was poured from above the doors of a fort onto the unsuspecting attackers below. Look for the holes above fort doors.

The extraordinary thing is that there are more apiarists in Oman now than there were 10 years ago, and honey production has increased 10-fold. This increase has been facilitated mainly by more modern methods of beekeeping. Traditionally, honey is collected from wild beehives in the branches and trunks of trees, found in the upper reaches of the Hajar mountains. The higher the price tag, the more likely it is that the honey has been collected in the traditional way.

The honey ranges in colour from light golden to almost black. The light-coloured honey comes from date palm pollen, the deep golden honey comes from *sumar* tree blossom and the dark-brown honey comes from *sidr*, a mountain shrub.

OMAN

ENTERTAINMENT
Cinemas
Only Muscat and Salalah have cinemas. Most of the screenings are of Hindi movies but there is usually an English film showing every day.

Bars & Nightclubs
Although there are not nearly as many pubs and clubs in Oman as in the UAE, you'll still find plenty of this sort of action in Muscat, but considerably less in Salalah. Due to liquor licensing laws, all these venues are located at the major hotels. There will be the occasional lounge act, usually from the Philippines, and some of the more British-style bars have happy hours each day. Pubs and bars shut around midnight while nightclubs stay open until 2 or 3 am.

Coffeehouses
Unfortunately there are very few traditional coffeehouses in Oman where you can enjoy a coffee and sheesha. You may find a few sheesha cafes at the major shopping areas in Muscat. The government periodically bans the smoking of sheesha, on the grounds that it is detrimental to health.

SPECTATOR SPORTS
Camel Racing
This is a traditional sport in Oman, although it is not as popular as in other Gulf countries. Most racing events take place during National Day celebrations and other public holidays. Camel races in the interior are usually held early on Friday mornings, but not on a regular basis. There are signs along the main roads for camel racetracks, so if you are passing it might be worth swinging by to have a look. Even if races are not taking place you will probably be able to watch the camels training, but this usually finishes up by about 8 am. Races are announced in the major Arabic dailies, but not necessarily in the English-language newspapers. Alternatively, contact one of the tour companies listed under Organised Tours in the Oman

Getting Around chapter. They will be able to arrange a visit to a camel race for you.

Bull Fighting
Bull fighting, or bull butting as it is more descriptively called, is a common event in the smaller towns in Oman. It involves a gathering of up to 20 Brahmin bulls, that are then paired off to fight each other, one pair at a time. It doesn't involve any blood or injury. The best place to see bull butting is at Barka, 45km west of Muscat, on Fridays in winter from 4 pm to 6 pm. This is generally also the time you will see bull butting in other towns of the interior. For more information about this traditional sport, see the boxed text 'Bull Butting' in the Barka section of the North-West Oman chapter.

SHOPPING
Oman is unquestionably the best place in the Arabian peninsula to go souvenir shopping. You'll find a good selection of traditional silver Bedouin jewellery and khanjars, even in the small souqs in rural areas. Prices are very reasonable, as long as you put in some bargaining time, and the quality is very good (most of the time). Coffeepots, pottery and woven items such as camel bags, mats and cushion covers are other good buys. Khanjars are cheaper in Muscat than in Nizwa. Beautifully made new khanjars can be bought in Salalah around the textile and incense souq but these will set you back about OR100 to OR150.

See the special section 'Shopping' at the end of the Regional Facts for the Visitor chapter earlier in this book, as well as the shopping entries in the individual city sections of the relevant chapters, for the best places to buy these items and costs.

For non-tourist-oriented shopping, such as clothes, household goods, books etc, you should head for the modern shopping centres in Qurm commercial district in Muscat. You'll find lots of the major European and American brands and labels here. You won't find any such stores outside Muscat.

Getting There & Away

AIR

Seeb airport in Muscat is the main international airport in the country. Salalah in the south of Oman has an international airport, but the only direct flights are to Dubai during the high tourist season in July and August. All other flights go via Muscat, although baggage can be checked through all the way to your destination. There are domestic airports at Sur and Masirah Island, off the east coast of Oman, and at Khasab, in the Musandam peninsula.

The national carrier is Oman Air, which has direct flights to Cairo (Egypt), Colombo (Sri Lanka), Dhaka (Bangladesh), Doha (Qatar), Dubai (UAE), Mumbai, Tiruvananthipuram and Chennai (all in India), Kuwait and Karachi (Pakistan). Few of the major European, Asian or Middle Eastern airlines serve Muscat direct; you generally have to fly via Dubai or Abu Dhabi in the UAE. For more details on getting to Oman from Europe, North America and Australasia, see the regional Getting There & Away chapter.

Between Emirates Airlines, Gulf Air and Oman Air, there are daily flights between Muscat and Abu Dhabi or Dubai. There is very little difference between fares. A one way/return ticket to Abu Dhabi will cost you around OR46/62 and to Dubai it's OR44/52. During the Khareef Festival in July and August you can get a direct flight to Salalah from Dubai for around OR99/185 with Oman Air.

The international departure tax is OR3.

LAND

Note that foreign residents of Oman need a road permit to enter or leave the country by land. See Visas & Documents in the Oman Facts for the Visitor chapter for more details.

Oman has borders in the north with the UAE, west with Saudi Arabia and in the south with Yemen. It is possible to cross into the UAE or Yemen from Oman but there is no border crossing with Saudi Arabia. For details on crossing between Yemen and Oman, see the regional Getting There & Away chapter at the beginning of this book.

There are a number of border crossings between Oman and the UAE. The main crossing points into the UAE are at Al-Ain/Buraimi and Hatta. You can cross freely between Al-Ain and the Omani town of Buraimi without any border formalities. There is a border crossing on the road from Sohar to Buraimi at Wadi al-Jizzi, 53km from the UAE border at Buraimi. This means if you are in Oman and you want to visit Buraimi, you will need a UAE visa. Once you are past the border post at Wadi al-Jizzi, you can cross freely between Buraimi and Al-Ain. There's also a border crossing at Hafit, just south-east of Al-Ain, on the road between Ibri and Al-Ain.

The Wajaja crossing near Hatta in the UAE is on the road from Shinas (on the northern coast) to the border. There is also a border crossing at Khor Kalba (UAE) but it is in the mountains, reachable by 4WD only and manned by an old man who speaks no English.

You can cross into the UAE from the Musandam peninsula. The main crossing is at Tibat on the west coast, just north of Sham. (This crossing is often called the Sham crossing point, although the border is at Tibat.) There is also a border crossing at Dibba on the east coast, but at the time of research it was no longer possible to drive from Khasab to Dibba.

As long as you have your visa already, and it doesn't specify entry by air only (see Visas & Documents in the Oman Facts for the Visitor chapter) you shouldn't have any trouble at these border crossings. What you should ensure, though, is that if you plan to enter and exit Oman by land from the UAE, you should do it at the same border crossing. A number of travellers have had hassles when trying to go into Oman through Buraimi and back into the UAE through Hafit,

OMAN

for instance. Although the officials at the immigration department will tell you that this is no problem, what happens at the border post is another story. The recently introduced joint visa between Oman and the UAE should hopefully make crossing at land borders between the two countries much more simple, at least for tourists, although at the time of writing this only applied to the main land border crossing at Hatta. See Visas & Documents in the Oman Facts for the Visitor chapter for more details.

Oman National Transport Company (ONTC) operates a coach service twice daily from Muscat to Dubai, once a day to Abu Dhabi and three times a day to Buraimi (just across the border from Al-Ain in the UAE). See Getting There & Away in the Muscat chapter for more details.

ORGANISED TOURS

Most package tours to Oman are offered by European companies. Kuoni in Switzerland (☎ 01-277 44 44, fax 271 52 82, @ internet .travelshop@kuoni.ch) and Tauchreisen Roscher in Germany (☎ 02234-96 70 96, fax 96 70 97, @ tauchreisen-roscher@t-online .de) are two of the biggest tour operators for German-speaking tourists, which is why many tour companies in Oman advertise German-speaking guides and hotel brochures and restaurant menus are in German.

In Italy, Siesta (☎ 06-884 45 28, @ siesta .to@trave.it) have tours to Oman and UAE.

In the UK, Steppes East (☎ 01285-810267, fax 810693, @ sales@steppeseast .co.uk) in Wiltshire and Gane & Marshall Tours (☎ 020-8441 9592, fax 8441 7376) in London both have package tours to Oman.

To organise a tour from the US contact Maluku Adventures (☎ 415-731 2560, fax 731 2579, @ maluku@maluku.com in California, Border Discoveries (☎ 703-356 2826, fax 749 9569) in Virginia, or Cox & Kings (☎ toll free 1800-999 1758, or in New York on ☎ 212-935 3935).

Getting Around

AIR

Oman Air is the only domestic airline. Routes, fares and schedules are as follows:

from	to	fare (one way/return)	time; duration
Muscat	Salalah	OR27/50	daily; 1½ hours
Muscat	Sur	OR14/28	3 flights/week; 30 mins
Muscat	Khasab	OR20/40	4 flights/week; 1 hour
Sur	Masirah Island	OR12/24	3 flights/week; 50 mins

Oman Air flights can be booked through just about any travel agent. For Oman Air phone ☎ 707222 in Muscat or ☎ 295747 in Salalah. The central booking number is ☎ 519347.

BUS

Intercity buses are operated by the national bus company, Oman National Transport Company (ONTC), whose symbol is a leaping oryx. There are daily services to all main provincial towns. The main bus station is in Muscat on Al-Jaame St in Ruwi. Outside Muscat and Salalah there aren't any main stations but there are ONTC offices in some of the larger towns. An intercity bus may stop at the edge of town along the main highway or, in larger towns like Nizwa, Sohar and Ibri, it will make a pass through the town, stopping at bus stop signs (usually every couple of hundred metres) to pick up passengers before swinging back onto the highway. Tickets are available from the bus driver. There is no division of classes.

Complete timetables for all routes are posted at the Ruwi station. In provincial towns there is usually a small signboard with the timetables for the routes from that town posted at the stop. If you are travelling during Ramadan, remember that bus timetables change and services are often reduced so

check with the ONTC offices in the town or, if there isn't one, check with shopkeepers near the bus stops or phone ONTC in Ruwi (☎ 708522).

Reservations are accepted only for the express services to Salalah. It's generally a good idea to book these seats a day or two in advance. There are also a number of private bus companies operating a service between Muscat and Salalah. See Getting There & Away in the Muscat chapter for more details of services between Muscat and Salalah.

LONG-DISTANCE TAXI & MICROBUS

Oman has an extraordinarily comprehensive system of long-distance taxis and microbuses. These are orange and white and have an orange medallion painted on the driver's door. This medallion includes, usually in large letters, the name of the vehicle's home *wilayat* (administrative region) or, in the case of vehicles from Muscat, district. Unfortunately, it is written only in Arabic. If you can read Arabic look for the medallion first as it provides a guide to where the vehicle is headed. They congregate at main junctions and often, but not always, at a central spot in most towns. They also spend a lot of time cruising around looking for passengers.

Unlike shared taxis in other Middle Eastern cities, Oman's taxis and microbuses don't wait until they are full to leave, though how empty the driver will be willing to travel is a judgment call. For example, if you have arrived at a main road junction and want to cover the last 10km to 15km into a particular village the driver of a 14-passenger microbus may set off with only you in the vehicle, reasoning that he can pick up a lot of local business in the other villages he will have to pass through. Taxis, since most of them only carry four passengers, are more likely to wait around for extra passengers before setting off. This is a very cheap way to get around, provided you are in no particular hurry.

You can also, of course, take an 'engaged' (ie private) taxi by paying for all of the seats in it. Some sample fares to/from Muscat are listed in Getting There & Away in the Muscat chapter later in this book.

CAR

See Car in the Getting Around the Region chapter for details of road rules that are common to both Oman and the UAE. For information on licences and road permits, see Visas & Documents in the Regional Facts for the Visitor chapter.

Road Rules

Traffic laws are enforced fairly strictly in Oman, especially in Muscat. All of the crazy driving habits you may have acquired in the UAE, Saudi Arabia or Kuwait should be unlearned before you get behind the wheel in Oman unless you want to part with a lot of money in fines. In Oman, you won't be able to drive as fast as you please, not give way when you enter a roundabout or make liberal use of the horn. (Those blue-and-white signs next to traffic lights in Muscat do not mean 'no trumpet playing in the street', they mean 'no tooting your horn'.) Although drivers in Oman are not as bad as in other Gulf States, you should always be alert and keep a look-out for kamikaze drivers, especially in Muscat.

There are a few things you should know before you drive in Oman. Right turns are not allowed at red lights. When oncoming drivers flash their lights at you it doesn't necessarily mean that there's something wrong. It's more of an acknowledgment, and to make sure that you know they are there. Vehicles in front will flick their right indicator to let you know it's safe to pass; left indicator means it's not safe to pass.

If an oncoming car has its hazard lights on, it means that camels (or other animals) may be crossing the road ahead. Similarly, if you see camels crossing, or even close to the road (they can lurch out quite suddenly) you should put on your hazard lights to warn those behind and in front of you. As you can imagine, high-speed accidents involving camels are usually pretty serious. It is for this very reason that you should take great care if you are travelling between cities at night.

Many roads around the country pass through wadis which are marked by red and white posts on either side of the road. If water on the road reaches the red mark on the posts, it is unsafe to drive through and you'll have to wait until the water level drops.

Petrol

Petrol comes in two grades: super and regular. It costs 118 baisa per litre for super and 112 baisa for regular. You will have no trouble finding petrol stations in cities and towns or anywhere along the major routes in the north. If you are travelling to Salalah, fill up whenever you can. There are only a few petrol stations along this route. If you are going off road for any considerable distance, always carry petrol with you.

Rental

You will probably have to leave a credit card imprint with the rental company, even if you are planning to pay cash at the end of the day. If you are cited for speeding or any other traffic violation it will be charged to your credit card, possibly several weeks after you return the car.

Rates for small cars start at about OR12 per day plus OR2 to OR3 per day for insurance. You can plan on spending a total of about OR90 to OR100 to rent a medium-sized car for a week. If you rent from the larger chains like Avis or Thrifty you will probably pay OR2 to OR3 per day more. Rentals usually include a free 100km to 150km per day but beyond that you will probably be paying at least 70 baisa per km. This adds up pretty quickly considering how spread out the capital is, let alone driving anywhere else. Renting a 4WD will cost you about OR35 per day with 200 free km per day though you will probably be able to negotiate a discount on this rate if you are hiring for a week or more.

Note that some car rental companies charge an extra OR2 to OR4 if you pick up or drop off the car at Seeb airport in Muscat.

LOCAL TRANSPORT

Only Muscat has a local bus system. There are plenty of local taxis and 14-passenger microbuses throughout the country. You can flag down a taxi just about anywhere in the cities. Microbuses and shared taxis have fixed drop-off and pick-up points. Local taxis do not have meters, although there is a standard fare system, at least in Muscat and Salalah, for trips around town. See Getting Around in the relevant sections for fare details. In smaller areas it is difficult to distinguish between local and long-distance taxis and microbuses. Most drivers wear both hats and are willing to consider driving you wherever you want to go, for a price.

ORGANISED TOURS

There are many tour operators in Oman. *Adventure Oman* magazine has a complete listing of companies and what they offer. *Oman Today* also lists a number of companies in its back pages. All tour companies offer the standard activities: camel safaris, 4WD trips, camping, dhow cruises and city tours, so it's worth shopping around. If you want an English-speaking guide make sure you ask.

Bahwan Travel Agencies (☎ 797405) on Markaz Mutrah al-Tijari St in Ruwi and at the Muscat Inter-Continental Hotel is one of the main tour operators in the country. It offers a large selection of day trips around Muscat and the north of the country and also overnight desert camping safaris. As well as all the usual tours, they also offer a full-day tour to Nizwa, Tanuf, Bahla and Jabrin for OR70, and one to Nakhal, Rustaq and Al-Hazm for OR60. Full-day 4WD excursions to the Wahiba Sands are available for OR120. Note that these prices are per vehicle, ie for four people.

Zubair Travel (☎ 787563 or 708071) on Ruwi High St in Muscat has a number of full-day wadi-bashing trips for OR120 per vehicle. One trip goes to Nizwa souq, Wadi Nakher and Jebel Shams, the highest mountain in Oman. Another goes to Bimmah Sinkhole, east of Muscat, and the villages of Shab and Qalhat. Their half-day dolphin watching cruise costs US$65 per person.

In Nizwa, Al-Azri Tours (☎ 412368), opposite Nizwa fort, offers a number of tours including Nizwa town, Jebel Akhdar, Wadi Muaydin and the village of Birkat al-Mawz for OR65 per vehicle. They will tailor trips to the places you want to visit. They also have three- to five-day tours covering the entire northern region of Oman. Prices vary depending on whether you want to camp or stay in hotels. You can work on an average for these trips of OR50 per day per vehicle.

As well as all the usual tours, Sunny Day Tours (☎ 591244, fax 596816) in Muscat can offer tailor-made tours for any interest in any part of the country. They will arrange rock climbing, hiking or caving to suit different levels of experience. Specialist tours can also be arranged covering bird-watching, archaeology, wildlife photography, geology and fishing. You find them in the Technique building next to the Bowshar Hotel in Al-Ghubra, west of the ministries area, just off Sultan Qaboos St.

Heide Beale Tours (☎ 799928) offers tailor-made and specialised tours. It operates through Al-Nadha Tourism at Hotel Mercure al-Falaj in Ruwi. Heide and Chris Beale have lived and worked in Oman for 20 years and have a wealth of local knowledge and experience. They also specialise in packages for youth and educational groups.

National Travel & Tourism (☎ 566046, fax 566125) is on An-Nahdah St in Muscat at the Wutayyah roundabout or you could try Global Tours (☎ 695959, fax 695969). To get to Global Tours, turn right at the Al-Khuwair roundabout, then take the first right onto the service road, turn left just after the BMW garage, go straight through the next roundabout and it's in the building with the Chicken Tikka sign.

For tours based in and around Salalah, see Organised Tours in the Salalah section of the Southern Oman chapter. For tours in and around the Musandam peninsula, see Organised Tours in the Khasab section of the Musandam Peninsula chapter. For tours arranged outside Oman, see Organised Tours in the Oman Getting There & Away chapter.

Muscat

Muscat is a port the like of which cannot be found in the whole world where there is business and good things that cannot be found elsewhere.

So wrote the great Arab navigator Ahmed bin Majid al-Najdi in AD 1490. Five centuries later Muscat still enchants visitors in a way no other city in the Gulf can even begin to, perhaps because it does not have that slightly artificial feel that typifies so much of the rest of the region.

HISTORY

Muscat dates from at least the 1st century AD, and may have been where the 2nd-century geographer Ptolemy meant when he referred to a 'concealed harbour', a description which aptly fits the old section of Muscat if you approach it from the sea. Although Muscat was settled at this time it was neither large nor important. Even well into the Islamic era (from the 7th century onwards) it was eclipsed by Sohar and the island of Hormuz which, lying in the middle of the strait

of the same name, was by far the most important port in the area for many centuries.

Muscat began to grow during the 9th century when ships bound for India from ports in the Mediterranean started calling at the harbour to take on fresh water, but it first gained importance during the 14th and 15th centuries. However, at this time it was little more than a small trading post, albeit an important one. Muscat was an outpost of the powerful kings of Hormuz and, eventually, it became their entrepot. It was in this role that, inevitably, it attracted the attentions of the Portuguese who conquered the town in the 16th century.

In 1622, after they had been driven out of Hormuz, the Portuguese made Muscat their main stronghold in the area. It was around this time that the town walls (a refurbished version of which still stand) were built. But by then Lisbon's era in the Gulf was drawing to a close. Muscat was Portugal's last stronghold in the region and the Omani re-

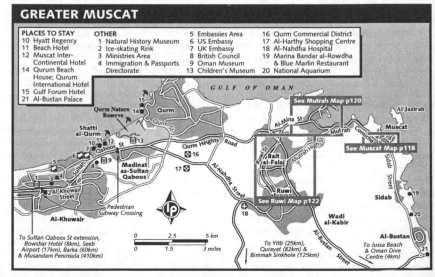

GREATER MUSCAT

PLACES TO STAY	OTHER	5 Embassies Area	16 Qurm Commercial District
10 Hyatt Regency	1 Natural History Museum	6 US Embassy	17 Al-Harthy Shopping Centre
11 Beach Hotel	2 Ice-skating Rink	7 UK Embassy	18 Al-Nahdha Hospital
12 Muscat Inter-Continental Hotel	3 Ministries Area	8 British Council	19 Marina Bandar al-Rowdha
14 Qurum Beach House; Qurum International Hotel	4 Immigration & Passports Directorate	9 Oman Museum	& Blue Marlin Restaurant
15 Gulf Forum Hotel		13 Children's Museum	20 National Aquarium
21 Al-Bustan Palace			

GULF OF OMAN

Qurm Nature Reserve
Qurm
See Mutrah Map p120
Al Jazirah
Al-Mina St
Mutrah
Muscat

Shatti al-Qurm
Qaboos St
Qurm Heights Road
See Muscat Map p118

Madinat as-Sultan Qaboos
Bait al-Falaj
Ruwi St
Mutrah High St
Sidab Street

Al-Khuwair Street
Al-Nahdha Street
Ruwi
See Ruwi Map p122
Sidab

Pedestrian Subway Crossing

Al-Khuwair
Wadi al-Kabir

To Sultan Qaboos St extension, Bowshar Hotel (8km), Seeb Airport (17km), Barka (60km) & Musandam Peninsula (410km)

0   2.5   5 km
0   1.5   3 miles

To Yitti (25km), Qurayat (82km) & Bimmah Sinkhole (125km)

Al-Bustan
To Jussa Beach & Oman Dive Centre (4km)

conquest of the town in 1650 effectively ended the Portuguese era in the Gulf.

Since the mid-18th century, Muscat has been the seat of the Al-Busaid dynasty, the current ruling family of Oman. It has seen the growth and, later, the partition of a maritime empire that once controlled much of the coast of East Africa. Despite the splendour of this history, the Omani capital languished in an almost medieval torpor for most of the 20th century. During the 1960s, as the economies of the other Gulf States roared ahead, life in Muscat and the rest of Oman seemed to slip further and further behind.

This all changed in the wake of the 1970 palace coup that brought Sultan Qaboos bin Said to power. The advantage that Muscat gained from a late start at modernisation and development was the opportunity to learn from the mistakes of others. The result is a capital which has retained much of its traditional architecture and beauty, while making great strides towards modernisation in a remarkably short time.

ORIENTATION

You will sometimes hear Muscat referred to as the 'three cities' or the 'capital region'. Greater Muscat covers a huge area from Seeb airport in the west to the sultan's palace in the east, a distance of about 50km. Many of the districts that make up Greater Muscat are separated by low hills and ridges, helping to compartmentalise the various areas of the capital.

The 'three cities' are Muscat, Mutrah and Ruwi. Muscat is the old port area and the site of the sultan's palace. It is a fascinating place to wander around and it has a couple of good museums, but it has few shops and no hotels. The real attraction is the traditional feel of the place. South of Muscat, but still part of Greater Muscat, lie the small villages of Sidab and Al-Bustan and, further south, the huge Al-Bustan Palace Hotel.

Mutrah, 3km north-west of Muscat, is the main trading and residential port. Its long, sweeping Corniche is one of the most beautiful spots in Arabia, and its souq one of the best. This is where the cheaper hotels and

the best views can be found. Behind the Corniche is a labyrinth of streets and alleys into which few tourists venture. The Mutrah area is also referred to as 'the Corniche'.

A few kilometres inland from Mutrah lies Ruwi. A generation ago this was an undeveloped valley; today it is the capital's modern commercial district. The Ruwi valley includes both the districts of Ruwi and Bait al-Falaj (which derives its name from the fort that now houses the Sultan's Armed Forces Museum and was once virtually the only building in the valley). Part of the area is also formally known as Mutrah al-Tijari, or Commercial Mutrah. However, the whole area is generally referred to simply as Ruwi.

Two roads connect the Ruwi valley to Mutrah. One is the highway, which sweeps around to the west to end on the Corniche at the roundabout by the Mina Hotel and the Mutrah bus station. The other road is Mutrah High St, which takes in the small district of Mutrah al-Khubra and ends at the gate to the inland side of the Mutrah souq. If you are travelling by car take the highway as Mutrah High St is narrow, often jammed and eventually dumps you into that maze of streets and alleys that is the inland portion of Mutrah. At the time of writing, however, there were plans to widen Mutrah High St to ease the traffic congestion. There is no direct link between Ruwi and Muscat, so you have to first drive to Mutrah.

Along the coast to the west of Mutrah are a number of new, mostly residential, districts. The main ones are Qurm (which includes some hotels, five or six big shopping malls and the Qurm Nature Reserve), Shatti al-Qurm where you'll find the Muscat Inter-Continental Hotel and most of the foreign embassies, Madinat as-Sultan Qaboos, an upmarket residential area, and Al-Khuwair, the site of the government ministries and a couple of museums. West of Al-Khuwair is Athaibah, and beyond that is Seeb, where the airport is. The Seeb clock tower roundabout several kilometres beyond the airport marks the outskirts of the capital region.

Except for an excursion to the museums and embassies of Madinat as-Sultan Qaboos and Al-Khuwair you are likely to spend most of your time in the capital in the Muscat-Mutrah-Ruwi area.

If you are out in the Qurm-Madinat as-Sultan Qaboos-Khuwair area on foot note that there are only two pedestrian passages across Sultan Qaboos St along this entire 15 or 20km stretch of road. One is the bridge over the highway at the exit near the Muscat Inter-Continental Hotel, the other is a pedestrian subway near the Ministry of National Heritage & Culture.

Maps

The best maps available are a series of four maps covering the Greater Muscat area produced by the National Survey Authority of Oman. You should be able to find them at hotels and bookshops. However, they are large and bulky to carry around.

The next best map of Greater Muscat is in the *Second Pictorial Tourist Map – Oman* published by the Directorate-General of Tourism. This is available for OR3 from hotel bookshops; look for a red cover. It includes a good road map of the country. The *Apex Map of Oman* by Apex Publishing has a map of Greater Muscat but it is not nearly as detailed. There are no decent maps of individual areas such as Mutrah, Muscat or Ruwi.

INFORMATION
Tourist Offices

There are no official tourist offices as such but the tourism board at the Directorate-General of Tourism (☎ 771 4923) in the ministries area of Al-Khuwair will gladly give you any information you need. However, it's probably easier to pick up brochures and maps from larger hotels and tour operators.

Money

Most of the big banks are in Ruwi along Markaz Mutrah al-Tijari St, and there's a branch of the Standard & Chartered Bank with an automated teller machine (ATM) on Bait al-Falaj St. There is a British Bank of the Middle East (BBME) ATM with Global Access on the Corniche in Mutrah, and

there's another branch of the BBME with an ATM in Muscat near the post office and the Al-Kebir Gate.

Moneychangers are concentrated mainly in and around the main souq in Mutrah and in Ruwi along Souq Ruwi St. They keep the same morning hours as banks and are also usually open from around 4 to 7 pm. Some are also open for an hour or two on Friday afternoon from 4.30 or 5 pm. There is an Oman & UAE Exchange Centre in the OC Centre in Ruwi by the main roundabout.

AmEx (☎ 701488) is represented by Zubair Travel on Ruwi St in Ruwi; it opens 8 am to 1 pm and 4 to 6.30 pm, daily except Friday. The office does not cash travellers cheques but it will hold mail and issue travellers cheques. Thomas Cook (☎ 706798) is represented by Bahwan Travel Agencies on Markaz Mutrah al-Tijari St in Ruwi and does cash travellers cheques.

Post

The main post office is at the northern end of Markaz Mutrah al-Tijari St in Ruwi. It is open 8 am to 2 pm and 4 to 6 pm Saturday to Wednesday. On Thursday, Friday and holidays it keeps a shorter 8 to 11 am schedule. There is a philatelic department on the upper floor.

There is a branch post office in Mutrah near the Mina Qaboos port services building, just off Al-Mina St about 150m inland from the Corniche. It's opposite the Bank of Muscat and is open 8 am to 2 pm and 4 to 6 pm Saturday to Wednesday. There's also a branch in Muscat in the BBME building, near the Al-Kebir Gate. It keeps the same hours as the Mutrah branch.

If you get mail sent to the AmEx office, it should be addressed to: American Express – client's mail, PO Box 833, 112 Ruwi, Oman.

Telephone & Fax

The telephone office is in Ruwi on Souq Ruwi St near the intersection with Street 37. There are international call cabins on the upper floor. You can also send faxes from a desk in the main lobby. The office is open

7.30 am to 10.30 pm daily. It gets very crowded at night; the quietest time is mid-afternoon. There are plenty of cardphones around town where you can make local or international calls.

Email & Internet Access

Cyberworld (☎ 566740) on the ground floor of the Al-Asfoor Plaza in Qurm commercial district charges OR2 per hour (OR1.500 for members) for Internet access. Membership is OR10 per year and the first four hours are free. Cheap snacks and drinks are also available. Opening times are 9 am to 9 pm Saturday to Wednesday. The Oman Chamber of Commerce & Industry on the corner of Al-Jaame and Markaz Mutrah al-Tijari Sts in Ruwi has a library (☎ 707674, ext 314) on the ground floor that offers public Internet access for OR1.500 per hour. There are only a couple of terminals, however. It is open 8.30 am to 1.30 pm Saturday to Wednesday.

Travel Agencies

The capital's greatest concentration of travel agents is in and around Markaz Mutrah al-Tijari St in Ruwi and on Al-Burj St in Bait al-Falaj. When booking flights to and from Muscat, your best bet is to go to the larger agencies dealing with multiple airlines. Two of the larger agencies are Bahwan Travel Agencies (☎ 704455) on Markaz Mutrah al-Tijari St and Mezoon Travel (☎ 796680) just off Al-Burj St.

Bookshops

Decent English-language bookshops are hard to find. The easiest place to look for books, maps, newspapers etc is in the bookstalls at Muscat's big hotels. The Family Bookshop chain has a store in Qurm at the Qurm Commercial Centre, across from the Sabco Commercial Centre, and another in Ruwi just across from the White Nile Hotel. Al-Oloum Bookshop in the Al-Harthy complex in Qurm stocks many of the same titles. There is a small bookshop on the Corniche in Mutrah that has a few tourist maps as well as a number of coffee-table books in English.

Libraries

The US Information Service (☎ 698989, ext 201) at the US embassy in Al-Khuwair has an Information Resource Centre with reference books, periodicals, journals, databases and CD-ROMs. Membership is free and opening times are 9 am to 4 pm Saturday to Wednesday. The British Council used to operate a library but it closed down due to lack of use. The French embassy on Jamcat ad-Duwal al-Arabiyya St in Al-Khuwair has a library (☎ 681874) and membership is free. It is open 4 to 7 pm Saturday to Monday and Wednesday, and 9 am to noon on Tuesday.

The Oman Chamber of Commerce & Industry (☎ 707674, ext 314) in Ruwi has a library with books in Arabic and English on subjects such as economics, law and accounting as well as trade directories. It is open 7.30 am to 1.30 pm Saturday to Wednesday, to noon on Thursday.

Cultural Centres

The British Council (☎ 600548, fax 698018) is on Al-Inshirah St in Al-Khuwair. It offers language courses in English and Arabic as well as computer courses and educational information for those wishing to study in Britain. It is open 9.30 am to 7 pm Saturday to Wednesday.

The US Information Service is in the US embassy and can be reached on the embassy's main number (☎ 698989 ext 201).

Left Luggage

There is a left luggage counter in the departures area of Seeb airport. It costs OR1 per day per item.

Medical Services

Large hotels generally have a doctor on call, and this should be your first stop if you get ill. You may or may not be charged for a consultation with a hotel doctor.

The Al-Nahdha Hospital on the outskirts of Ruwi (on the left as you head from Ruwi towards Al-Khuwair) is the main medical centre in the 'three cities' area.

There are several pharmacies around the Ruwi roundabout. The English-language newspapers have a list of pharmacies open for 24 hours each day.

Emergency

Dial ☎ 999 for the police, an ambulance or to report a fire.

MUSCAT
Jalali & Mirani Forts

Both forts took on more or less their present form in the 1580s during the Portuguese occupation of Muscat. Although these forts were built before the arrival of the Portuguese, alterations were so extensive that they are usually counted as among the few forts in Oman of Portuguese rather than Arab construction.

Both forts are still used by the police and/or military and are closed to the public. Fort Mirani is used as a museum for visiting heads of state and royalty. It's OK to photograph the forts. If you are walking around Fort Mirani, look across the harbour to the rocks underneath Fort Jalali where graffiti has been left by visiting ships over the years.

Alam Palace

The sultan's Muscat residence is a stunning example of modern Arabic architecture. Built in the 1970s, it is colourful and tasteful, without being ostentatious. It's on the waterfront between Jalali and Mirani forts and can be approached from Qasr al-Alam St. It's OK to go right up to the entrance gate and to take photos.

Omani-French Museum

This museum (☎ 736613), also called Beit Fransa ('French House'), is in a restored, early 20th century building inside Muscat's walls near the Al-Kebir Gate. It is laid around several courtyards, in a design typical of a two-storey Muscat house.

The museum is largely an extended celebration of the sultan's state visit to France in 1989 and then French president François Mitterrand's state visit to Muscat in 1992. Downstairs is a display on the history of the house, antique maps, photographic records of Mitterrand's visit and miniatures of Parisian landmarks. Upstairs is a history of relations between France and Oman from 1700 to 1913. The upper level also includes an interesting display on shipbuilding and scale models of different types of ocean-going vessels as well as displays of traditional dress and jewellery.

The house itself was built in 1896 by the sultan's niece and enlarged in 1906 when it became the office and residence of the French consul in Muscat. His office remains as it was on the upper level. Sultan Qaboos gave the building back to the French government in 1989, at which point it was converted into a museum. The museum's signs are in French, Arabic and English.

The museum is open 8.30 am to 1.30 pm Saturday to Wednesday. Admission is free. If you are coming into Muscat from Mutrah the museum is well signposted. Once you pass through the Al-Kebir Gate, the museum is about 50m further in and to your right.

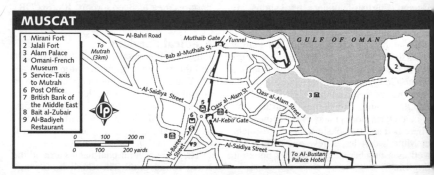

MUSCAT

1 Mirani Fort
2 Jalali Fort
3 Alam Palace
4 Omani-French Museum
5 Service-Taxis to Mutrah
6 Post Office
7 British Bank of the Middle East
8 Bait al-Zubair
9 Al-Badiyeh Restaurant

Bait al-Zubair

This place (☎ 736688), on Al-Saidiya St, is a museum and souvenir shop, with exhibits of Omani heritage in photographs and documents as well as displays of traditional handicrafts, weapons, furniture and cooking implements. There is a re-creation of an Omani mountain village, complete with *falaj* (irrigation system) and wadi (seasonal river), and a souq with typical merchandise for sale, although at rather inflated prices. It is open 4 to 8 pm on Saturday; 4 to 7 pm Monday and Wednesday; and 9 am to 12.30 pm Sunday, Tuesday and Thursday. The place is well signposted from the main road into Muscat.

National Aquarium

There is an aquarium at the Marine Sciences & Fisheries Centre (☎ 740063), next to Marina Bander al-Rowdha off Sidab St. At the time of writing, it was closed for renovation work and there was no indication of when it would be open to the public again.

MADINAT AS-SULTAN QABOOS
Oman Museum

The museum is small but well organised and is worth the trek to Madinat as-Sultan Qaboos, if you have the time. Displays on the ground floor cover the history, geography and geology of Oman from the 3rd millennium BC onwards, with an emphasis on trade routes and the country's trading history. There is also a display on shipbuilding detailing the designs of different types of ocean-going dhows. One section of this floor charts the growth of Muscat and there is a display on agriculture in the sultanate, including a section on falaj systems. The 1st floor has a small display on Islam, a fairly good display of Omani arts and crafts, a display of Omani weapons, and an excellent room on architecture in the sultanate, with an emphasis on forts.

The Oman Museum (☎ 600946) is open 8 am to 2 pm Saturday to Wednesday, 9 am to 1 pm on Thursday. Admission is free.

If you are driving, take the exit off Sultan Qaboos St marked for the Muscat Inter-Continental Hotel and the Children's Museum. If you are coming from the direction of Ruwi or Mutrah go around the roundabout at the exit and take Al-Ilam St across the bridge over Sultan Qaboos St then turn right on Al-Inshirah St. If you are approaching from the other direction (say, from the Natural History Museum or the embassies area) turn right on Al-Ilam St and then immediately right onto Al-Inshirah St.

Once you are on Al-Inshirah St take the fifth left onto Way 1595, after about 850m. Then go 400m and turn left onto Way 1526. After another 250m turn right onto Way 1530. From there, go 550m and turn right at a sign for the Oman Museum. It's the small, white building with an Omani flag on top, next to the much larger, brown building.

You can also reach the museum by taking bus No 23 to the Inter-Continental exit and walking from there. However, it's a long way and all uphill, so it's probably worth taking a taxi instead and asking it to wait. There are no microbuses or shared taxis to the museum.

Children's Museum

This museum (☎ 605368) in a large, dome structure near the Foreign Ministry off Sultan Qaboos St is well signposted, and is open 8 am to 2 pm Saturday to Wednesday, 9 am to 1 pm on Thursday. It is also open 4 to 8 pm on Monday evenings for families only. It is closed Friday; admission is free. The museum is a practical, science-oriented place with lots of hands-on displays.

Natural History Museum

The displays in this museum (☎ 605400) are very well done and will be of interest to everyone. It is housed within the Ministry of National Heritage & Culture on Al-Wazarat St in Al-Khuwair. (Al-Wazarat St runs parallel to Sultan Qaboos St on the sea side.) Look for a small green sign with a drawing of a lynx (the museum's symbol) indicating the exit. The museum is open 8 am to 2 pm Saturday to Wednesday, 9 am to 1 pm on Thursday. It is also open 4 to 7 pm Sunday and Friday.

OMAN

The first hall to the right as you enter the museum contains a region-by-region description of Oman's geography, geology, flora and fauna. There's also a whale hall, which has a display of marine skeletons and photographs and is dominated by the skeleton of a sperm whale which hangs overhead. There is a small botanical garden near the museum's parking lot. Everything at the museum is labelled in both English and Arabic.

To get there by public transport, take any bus going to Al-Khuwair or beyond and ask to be let off at the Ministry of National Heritage or the Natural History Museum.

MUTRAH
Corniche
If you only do one thing in Muscat, make it a walk along the Corniche, combined with a visit to the souq. The best time for a stroll along the Corniche is first thing in the morning or in the evening at or just after sunset. From the fish market and bus station at Mutrah's western end, the Corniche sweeps along the water's edge for about 1km to the incense burner statue in Al-Riyam Park at Mutrah's eastern end. As you walk along

here notice the Portuguese-influenced, whitewashed houses with their decorative balconies and facades. Set against the backdrop of bare, rugged hills, they are a striking sight. In the harbour you'll see dozens of dhows and small fishing boats bobbing on the water. You also might see the Sultan's huge white yacht docked in the port.

Up above the Corniche is **Mutrah Fort**, which was built from scratch by the Portuguese in the late 16th century. It is still used by the police and/or military and is generally closed to the public, although it is opened to foreign tour groups with special permission from time to time.

Fish Market
The fish market is at the northern end of the Corniche near the Mina and Corniche hotels. Meat, fruit and vegetables are also sold here, as well as fish. It's always lively but the best time to come is early in the morning. The market usually opens around 6.30 am.

Al-Riyam Park
At the eastern end of the Corniche, opposite the Al-Inshirah Restaurant, is Al-Riyam

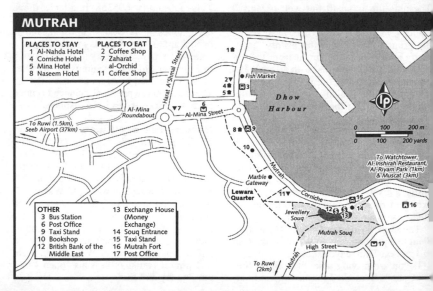

MUTRAH

PLACES TO STAY	PLACES TO EAT
1 Al-Nahda Hotel	2 Coffee Shop
4 Corniche Hotel	7 Zaharat
5 Mina Hotel	al-Orchid
8 Naseem Hotel	11 Coffee Shop

OTHER	13 Exchange House
3 Bus Station	(Money
6 Post Office	Exchange)
9 Taxi Stand	14 Souq Entrance
10 Bookshop	15 Taxi Stand
12 British Bank of the	16 Mutrah Fort
Middle East	17 Post Office

To Ruwi (1.5km), Seeb Airport (37km)

Al-Mina Roundabout

Harat A'Shmal Street

Al-Mina Street

Fish Market

Dhow Harbour

Marble Gateway

Lewara Quarter

Mutrah

Corniche

Jewellery Souq

Mutrah Souq

High Street

To Ruwi (2km)

To Watchtower, Al-Inshirah Restaurant, Al-Riyam Park (1km) & Muscat (3km)

0   100   200 m
0   100   200 yards

Mutrah Souq

The Mutrah souq is one of the most interesting souqs on the Arabian peninsula. The large number of shops and stalls, combined with its traditional layout and roof covering, make it a fascinating place to explore. Although visited by tourists, this souq is very much a place for Muscat residents to shop or just to hang out. It's open in the morning from 8 am to 1 pm and in the afternoon from 4 to 8 pm. The main entrance to the souq is on the Corniche. Be sure to stop for a rosewater milk or cup of sweet, milky tea at the teahouse on the left just inside the main entrance.

As with any good Arab souq the best thing to do is simply to wander at will and see what you find. The Mutrah souq is not really very big and you are in no danger of getting lost, though there may be moments when it doesn't feel that way.

Many visitors head for the dozen or so shops specialising in antique silver jewellery. To reach these turn up the first alley on your right (more or less opposite the teahouse) after entering the souq through the main entrance.

Another place worth wandering around is the spice souq. To reach this, head directly into the souq from the entrance on the Corniche and make a sharp turn (nearly a U-turn) to your left after about 100m when you reach a fountain with large mock-ups of Omani jewellery in it.

Other things to buy are fabrics, clothes, incense, perfumes, shoes, toys and plastic wares. There is also a lot of merchandise, antique and otherwise, from India and Thailand.

Park. It has seats and grassy areas as well as amusement rides for the kids, although it is popular with the local male adult population too, especially on Fridays. The park is dominated by a large incense burner statue on a hill, from where you get a great view. To get to the statue you can go through the park or you can walk up the service road that comes off the Corniche, just below the statue. You won't be able to drive a car up this service road, though, as it is usually blocked to traffic. The park is open 4 to 11 pm Saturday to Wednesday, 9 am to midnight Thursday, Friday and public holidays.

Watchtower

At the eastern end of the Corniche, above and behind the Al-Inshirah Restaurant, a restored watchtower looks out over Mutrah. The climb is steep, up about 100 stairs, but the view from the top is worth it. There are also a couple of cannons inside the watchtower. The tower's staircase can be reached by walking down past the restaurant's service entrance (on the right-hand side as you face the building).

RUWI
National Museum

You could easily miss the National Museum (☎ 701289), on An-Noor St near the intersection with Al-Burj St, but it is definitely worth a look. The museum is open 7.30 am to 2.30 pm Saturday to Wednesday. It is closed Thursday and Friday. Admission is free. Photography inside the museum is prohibited.

On the ground floor, the entry area contains what are best described as odds and ends – Omani-made pottery and several excellent examples of the ornately decorated wooden chests for which Oman is known (and which Arab craftspeople in the former Omani colonies along the East African coast still make).

The real exhibit area is on the upper floor. Much of the central area of this main hall is given over to cases displaying Omani silverwork of various kinds, making this a good place to visit before going souvenir-hunting. Other displays on the right side of the room show typical rooms in an Omani house, traditional costumes and weapons. A mural on the back wall shows trade routes throughout Oman's history and there are scale models of several different types of trading vessels.

On the left side of the room there is a display of different kinds of coffeepots (again,

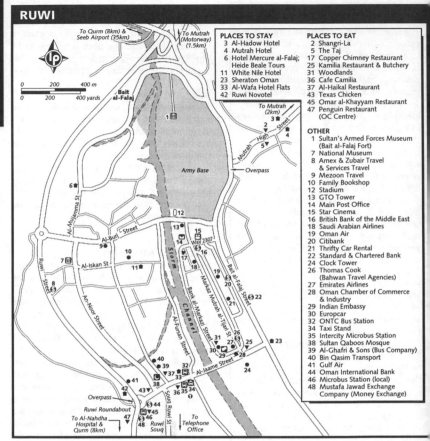

RUWI

To Qurm (8km) &
Seeb Airport (35km)

To Mutrah
(Motorway)
(1.5km)

Bait
al-Falaj

Army Base

Overpass

To Mutrah
(2km)

Mutrah High St

Storm

Channel

Al-Mujamma St

Al-Burj Street

Al-Iskan St

Ruwi St

An-Noor Street

Way 2307

Bank al-Falaj Street

Markaz Mutrah al-Tijari St

Bank al-Markazi Street

Al-Fursan Street

Al-Jaame Street

Souq Ruwi St

Overpass

Ruwi Roundabout
To Al-Nahdha
Hospital &
Qurm (8km)

To
Telephone
Office

To
Ruwi
Souq

PLACES TO STAY	
3	Al-Hadow Hotel
4	Mutrah Hotel
6	Hotel Mercure al-Falaj; Heide Beale Tours
11	White Nile Hotel
23	Sheraton Oman
33	Al-Wafa Hotel Flats
42	Ruwi Novotel

PLACES TO EAT	
2	Shangri-La
5	The Taj
17	Copper Chimney Restaurant
25	Kamilia Restaurant & Butchery
31	Woodlands
36	Cafe Camilia
37	Al-Haikal Restaurant
43	Texas Chicken
45	Omar al-Khayyam Restaurant
47	Penguin Restaurant (OC Centre)

OTHER	
1	Sultan's Armed Forces Museum (Bait al-Falaj Fort)
7	National Museum
8	Amex & Zubair Travel & Services Travel
9	Mezoon Travel
10	Family Bookshop
12	Stadium
13	GTO Tower
14	Main Post Office
15	Star Cinema
16	British Bank of the Middle East
18	Saudi Arabian Airlines
19	Oman Air
20	Citibank
21	Thrifty Car Rental
22	Standard & Chartered Bank
24	Clock Tower
26	Thomas Cook (Bahwan Travel Agencies)
27	Emirates Airlines
28	Oman Chamber of Commerce & Industry
29	Indian Embassy
30	Europcar
32	ONTC Bus Station
34	Taxi Stand
35	Intercity Microbus Station
38	Sultan Qaboos Mosque
39	Al-Ghafri & Sons (Bus Company)
40	Bin Qasim Transport
41	Gulf Air
44	Oman International Bank
46	Microbus Station (local)
48	Mustafa Jawad Exchange Company (Money Exchange)

a good place to look before you shop) along with guns and Chinese porcelain, some of which was once owned by the (Omani) sultan of Zanzibar. Next is a room devoted to the ruling Al-Busaid (also written Al-Bu Said) family, including jewellery and *khanjars* (Omani daggers) once owned by various members of the family. The final room on this side of the main hall is devoted to space travel and includes two small Omani flags carried to the moon and back by American astronauts. The staff here are very friendly and, even if they speak Arabic

only, will gladly show you around and explain the exhibits.

Sultan's Armed Forces Museum

This museum (☎ 312648) is open 7.30 am to 2 pm Saturday to Thursday. Admission is 500 baisa for adults, free for children under 18. You are usually required to go through the museum with a guide (even if you don't share a common language).

The museum, run by the Omani Army, is in the Bait al-Falaj Fort, which gives its name to the Bait al-Falaj district. The fort is one of the oldest buildings in Muscat. It was built in 1845 as a royal summer home, was restored extensively in the early 1900s, and served as the headquarters for the Omani Army from WWI until 1978.

The museum is divided into sections on pre-Islamic Oman, Oman and Islam, the Portuguese in Oman, the Al-Ya'ruba dynasty, the Al-Busaid dynasty, the establishment of the armed forces and the 'incident at Jabal Akhdar and Dhorfur (Dhofar) mutiny' (the insurrections which the current sultan had to put down during his early years on the throne).

The ground floor's exhibits provide an excellent outline of Omani history, while those on the upper level are more specifically military in nature. Leaving the fort's main door and turning left around the building you will pass a low stone enclosure on your right. This contains the fort's falaj. Beyond this is the remainder of the military exhibit – a re-creation of a field command post, a large collection of military vehicles and weapons and a Cadillac Fleetwood that once belonged to the sultan.

ACTIVITIES

You'll find details of all Muscat's sporting clubs and societies in *Oman Today*, *Adventure Oman* or *Muscat Explorer*, all of which are widely available in bookshops.

Beaches

Muscat's long coastline means there are plenty of beaches to choose from. You can either go to a public beach or you can use the beach facilities at one of the large hotels. Although expensive (free if you are staying in the hotel), hotel beaches are a good idea for unaccompanied women, as you are less likely to suffer from harassment here than at a public beach. Women with a male escort who simply do not like being stared at might want to consider forking out for the hotels too. On most beaches, women should be prepared for some extremely blatant staring by men. See Women Travellers in the Regional Facts for the Visitor chapter for advice on what to wear.

Public Beaches There is a good stretch of public beach with palm trees and *barasti* (palm-leaf shelters) for shade in Qurm, next to the Gulf Forum Hotel. The beach stretches from here to the Hyatt Regency Hotel and beyond to the embassies district in Al-Khuwair. Some embassies have blocked off sections of their beach frontage so if you want to take a long promenade along the beach, it's best to go no further than the Hyatt Regency.

Another popular public beach is the one at Jussa, south of the Al-Bustan Palace Hotel off the Qantab Rd. It is a popular picnic spot for Omani families, especially on public holidays.

Beach Clubs Many of the large hotels will let outsiders use their beach facilities for a fee. The Al-Bustan Palace Hotel has great facilities, although the entrance fee is pretty steep at OR6.300 (OR10.500 on Thursday and Friday). For this you get access to its pool, spa, sauna, gym and a large private beach. The complex also includes a restaurant, beachside cafe and two bars. Kayaks can be rented for OR3.150 per hour and windsurfers for OR4 per hour. Snorkelling equipment is OR2 per hour.

Getting onto the beach at the Muscat Inter-Continental is a bit cheaper at OR4 Saturday to Wednesday and OR5 Thursday and Friday (OR3 for children under 18 years), but both the facilities and the beach itself are a lot less impressive. Windsurfers cost OR5 per hour, and you can use the squash and tennis courts for free. Sheraton Qurm Resort, behind the Muscat Inter-Continental, is good value at OR3 per person for private beach, pool, gym and sauna.

A better alternative is to pay a day fee (OR3) at the Oman Dive Centre on Qantab Rd, near the Al-Bustan Palace Hotel (see the following Diving & Snorkelling section for more details), as Jason Mountney wrote to tell us:

For a day by the sea, a day membership to the Oman Dive Centre is a better bet than the hotel beach clubs. It is cheaper and the beach is much more attractive. There are also far fewer people there. During the week it is possible to be the only person there. You also escape the hotel's extortionate prices for food and drink (although the dive club's menu is hardly suited to the budget traveller).

Diving & Snorkelling

Oman Dive Centre (☎ 950261) in Jussa, south of the Al-Bustan Palace Hotel, charges OR19 for one dive with full equipment hire and OR9.500 for a half-day snorkelling trip. If you have your own equipment the price drops by about half. To reach the centre take the Qantab exit off the road from Al-Bustan to Ruwi then go right at the turn-off for Jussa and follow the signs to the dive centre.

Blu Zone Watersports (☎ 737293) at Marina Bander al-Rowdha charges OR10 for one dive and OR6 if you have your own equipment. The marina is on Sidab St and is signposted about halfway between Muscat and the Al-Bustan Palace Hotel.

Ocean Extreme Dive Centre at Al-Sawadi Forum Resort, about 60km west of Muscat, has a dive package that includes two dives and one night's stay at the resort with breakfast, lunch and dinner for OR48.

The Hyatt Regency's Boathouse offers a variety of scenic cruises and snorkelling trips ranging from 2½ to four hours in length for between OR15 and OR20. A snorkelling trip to the Dimaaniyat Islands Nature Reserve off the coast of Muscat costs OR25, including equipment hire. You can also camp overnight on an uninhabited island off the coast of Muscat for OR45 including camping gear, food and snorkelling and fishing equipment. See Places to Stay – Top End for the Hyatt Regency's contact details.

Ice Skating

Muscat's ice rink (☎ 696492) is on Al-Khuwair St, 2.5km west of the Khuwair roundabout. The rink is open 9 am to 10 pm Saturday to Wednesday, 8.15 am to 10 pm on Thursday and 9.30 am to 10 pm on Friday. There are general skating sessions, special women-only sessions (usually in the mornings) and an informal ice hockey league. Call the rink for an up-to-date schedule of sessions and times. Single-session admission is OR2.500 for adults and OR2 for children under 12 years. Skates can be hired for 500 baisa. Monthly memberships are OR30, inclusive of skate hire.

Note that if you are coming from Ruwi by bus you will be left on the wrong side of Sultan Qaboos St, but there is a pedestrian subway crossing here for you to get across the road.

ORGANISED TOURS

Half-day city tours are offered by all the tour companies. On average these cost OR22 for a car (usually four people) and take in Jalali and Mirani forts and the Alam Palace in Muscat, Mutrah souq and fish market, and one or two of the museums. Full-day tours are not as common but they can be arranged – just contact any of the tour companies listed in the Oman Getting Around chapter earlier in this book.

PLACES TO STAY

The prices quoted in this section include the 17% municipality tax, tourism tax and service charge. These are rack rates, so it's always worth asking for a discount.

PLACES TO STAY – BUDGET
Camping

There is only one place to camp in Muscat, and it's not exactly roughing it. The *Oman Dive Centre* (☎ 950261), in Jussa south of the Al-Bustan Palace Hotel, offers its beach to campers for OR3 per person plus the entrance fee to the centre, OR4. You must have your own tent. The beach has full amenities – toilets, showers, drinking water – and there is even a kiosk and a restaurant a stone's throw away. It's one of the cheapest accommodation options in Muscat.

Hotels – Mutrah

The cheap hotels along the Corniche offer the best views and atmosphere in the city.

The *Naseem Hotel* (☎ 712418, fax 711728) is by far the best hotel on the Corniche with large, clean, comfortable singles/doubles for OR10.900/15.300. The staff are friendly and helpful and you can get a decent breakfast downstairs with omelette, toast and coffee or tea for OR1.

Corniche Hotel (☎ *714636 or 714707, fax 714770*) has singles/doubles/triples for OR9.800/15.300/18. It has a few singles with balconies overlooking the Corniche and the port. However, the rooms at the back of the hotel are cramped and have uncomfortably small bathrooms.

Al-Nahda Hotel (☎ *712385 or 714196, fax 714994*) at the fish market end of the Corniche is cheap, but there may be nightly comings and goings. Rooms are OR8.700/12.800/14.600.

Mina Hotel (☎ *711828, fax 714981*), opposite the fish market, has surly staff and tiny rooms for OR12.500/15.600.

Hotels – Ruwi

Al-Hadow Hotel (☎/*fax 799329*), at the Ruwi end of Mutrah High St, has Muscat's cheapest beds at OR7/10. However, the building appears to be falling apart, and this place is probably best avoided if you are a woman travelling alone.

Mutrah Hotel (☎ *798401, fax 790953, Mutrah High St*), across the road from Al-Hadow Hotel, has rooms for OR10/13. At the time of writing the hotel was undergoing renovation which included a new bar and restaurant.

White Nile Hotel (☎ *708989, fax 750778, Al-Iskan St*) has small but clean rooms with bathrooms for OR13.200/22. The staff are helpful and friendly and the location is quiet. There is a small shopping area and plenty of places to eat across from the hotel.

PLACES TO STAY – MID-RANGE

Hotel Mercure al-Falaj (☎ *702311, fax 795853, Al-Mujamma St*) in Bait al-Falaj has rooms for OR42.120/49.120. It has a bar on the top floor that's worth visiting for its great views of Ruwi, especially at night. The health club here is reputed to be the best in Muscat, and there are separate gyms and pool for men and women.

Ruwi Novotel (☎ *704244, fax 704248, Ruwi St*) near the main roundabout is cen-

trally located but in a noisy area. Rooms are OR39.780/45.630, and it has a swimming pool and health club.

Al-Wafa Hotel Flats (☎ *786522 or 786540, fax 786534, Al-Jaame St*) is just behind the Ruwi bus station. One-bedroom and two-bedroom flats are a very reasonable OR20/25. Each flat has a bathroom, a kitchen with cooking facilities, and a sitting area. The two-bedroom flats have two bathrooms. The flats are clean and well maintained and the location is great, if noisy.

Qurum Beach House (☎ *564070, fax 560761, Way 1622*) just off Qurm St in Qurm is in a peaceful location across from the beach. The rooms at OR18/23 are clean, spacious and appealingly odd. The hotel also has a cheap bar which is popular with young Omani men. The bar has snacks and there is room service until midnight. Although it is almost as good value as most of the hotels on the Corniche in Mutrah, you don't get the view and the location is less convenient.

Qurum International Hotel (☎ *571700, fax 571414*), next door to the Qurm Beach Hotel, has large but bland rooms for OR17.250/23. There's a restaurant and bar, as well as a pool and a gym.

Beach Hotel (☎ *696601 or 696602, fax 696609*) in Shatti al-Qurm has rooms for OR40.250/51.175. The hotel is in a large white villa and you will pass it if you follow the signs for the Muscat Inter-Continental Hotel.

Bowshar Hotel (☎ *501105, fax 501124*) is in Al-Ghubra, just west of the ministries and embassies districts. Turn right at the Al-Ghubra roundabout from Sultan Qaboos St. Rooms are very reasonable at OR17.550/23.400 but the staff and service tend to be a bit lax.

Seeb Novotel Muscat (☎ *510300, fax 510055*), just off Sultan Qaboos St about 5km from the airport towards town, is the only hotel near the airport and it's correspondingly overpriced with rooms for OR41.400/49.450. If you want to be nearish the airport, the Bowshar Hotel is a much better option.

PLACES TO STAY – TOP END

Muscat's top-end hotels can all sponsor tourist or business visas.

Sheraton Oman (☎ 799899, fax 795791) on Bait al-Falaj St in Ruwi is conveniently located for business travellers. Singles/doubles cost OR66.700/75.900. It sits on the hill at the top of Al-Jaame St and commands an excellent view of Ruwi and Wadi al-Kebir. There is a nightclub (apparently more popular during the day) in the basement of the hotel. The Sheraton also has a beach club in Qurm for free use by guests. Shuttle buses go there daily.

Al-Bustan Palace Hotel (☎ 799666, fax 799600) is a long way from anything else in the Greater Muscat region and is more trouble than it's worth if you don't have a car. It is worth the drive, however, just for a look at the massive atrium lobby. Nestled away in its own cove south of Muscat, the hotel was built in the early 1980s as the venue for a Gulf Cooperation Council (GCC) summit meeting. The hotel is a small resort with an emphasis on water sports. Singles/doubles start at a whopping OR132.210/150.930. If you want to live like an emir you can always stay in the Grand Deluxe Suite for a mere OR842.400 per night.

Hyatt Regency (☎ 602888, fax 605282) in Al-Khuwair rivals the Al-Bustan for ostentation. Beautifully decorated rooms cost

SS John Barry Liberty

The Hyatt Regency was the brainchild of a Yemeni prince, who became a diplomatic refugee in Oman after conflicts in Yemen in 1994. As you enter the hotel you will see a cabinet to the left of the lobby displaying copies of silver coins retrieved from the wreck of the SS *John Barry Liberty* ship. The ship was carrying the coins from India to Saudi Arabia in 1944 when it was torpedoed by a German U-boat off the coast of Oman in 2600m of water. In 1994 the prince financed an expensive deep-sea salvage and the US$20 million worth of coins and silver became his.

OR93.600/105.300 or OR826.500 for the Crown Suite.

The *Muscat Inter-Continental Hotel* (☎ 600500, fax 600012) in Shatti al-Qurm is a self-contained mini-resort with its own beach but it's not as grand as the Al-Bustan Palace or Hyatt Regency. Rooms can be had for OR72.540/78.390 (more if you want a sea view).

Gulf Forum Hotel (☎ 560100, fax 560650) on Qurm St in Qurm is in a quiet part of town on a hill overlooking the beach to the west. Rooms are OR53.820/65.520. The hotel does not have a private beach but there is a stretch of public beach next door with plenty of palm trees.

PLACES TO EAT

Restaurants add 17% tax and service charge to the bill. All the mid-range and top-end hotels have one or more restaurants. These are usually Lebanese, continental or Italian. The Hotel Mercure al-Falaj in Ruwi has the capital's only Japanese restaurant. All these restaurants are expensive and the quality of the food isn't necessarily reflected in the price. And, of course, if you have alcohol with your meal the bill skyrockets.

Mutrah

The usual range of snacks are available from the *kiosks* at the bus station on the Corniche.

Zaharat al-Orchid coffee shop and restaurant, on the first roundabout inland from the Corniche on the way to Ruwi, has excellent shwarma and also offers cheap sandwiches, burgers and fresh juice. Oddly there are two restaurants with this name a few metres apart. The better of the two is the one further inland.

The *coffee shop* next to the Mina Hotel is a popular local gathering spot, particularly on cool evenings when both Omanis and travellers can be found munching shwarma or falafel and sipping tea or playing cards.

The semicircular building on the Corniche between the Naseem Hotel and the entrance to the souq with the words *Coffee Shop* emblazoned on it is a particularly good place for cheap, quick meals. Try the chickpea masala for 200 baisa.

Al-Bahr (meaning 'The Sea' in Arabic) upstairs at the Mina Hotel has a great view of Mutrah and offers continental and Indian cuisine. Main dishes are about OR3 and it's a popular spot with travellers. Although its card advertises the restaurant as licensed, it no longer serves alcohol.

Sindebad Restaurant (☎ 712385 or 714196) at the Al-Nahda Hotel has curries and biryanis for OR1. The restaurant is small and private, and is good for women travellers who want to enjoy cheap food but who don't want the stares as a side dish.

Al-Inshirah (☎ 711292), opposite the giant incense burner on the Corniche, has two restaurants. One is a seafood restaurant specialising in Thai dishes but, although delicious, it is expensive at OR3 to OR5 a dish. The other restaurant is an American steakhouse serving burgers (OR2.500), steak and fresh fish, although it was closed for renovation at the time of writing. There is a bar and the view of Mutrah at night is superb.

Muscat

The pickings here are pretty slim. Try the *Al-Badiyeh Restaurant* on Al-Bareed St, near the post office. The menu is mostly mid-priced Indian and there are a few Western-style dishes too. Most mains cost OR1 to OR2.

Blue Marlin Restaurant (☎ 737940) at the Marina Bander al-Rowdha is a continental-style fish restaurant, open for lunch and dinner. Mains cost around OR5 to OR7, including service charge, and alcohol is served. Booking is advisable at weekends. The marina is on Sidab St about 3km south-east of Muscat off the road to Al-Bustan Palace Hotel.

Ruwi

There are several good bets in Ruwi for snacks and more upmarket eating.

Cafe Camilia, across Al-Jaame St from the Ruwi bus station, is a good spot for a quick snack with sandwiches and shwarma for 200 baisa.

Texas Chicken (☎ 700175) on the corner of An-Noor and Al-Jaame Sts has good chicken and burgers and even better Chinese and Filipino noodle dishes for OR1.200.

Penguin Restaurant (☎ 701995) in the OC Centre at the Ruwi roundabout is part of a local fast-food chain serving rather disappointing burgers and fried chicken.

Kamilia Restaurant & Butchery on the corner of Al-Jaame and Markaz Mutrah al-Tijari Sts serves snacks such as shwarma and ice cream or you can have mains such as biryanis (OR1.500) and grilled dishes, including kebabs, for OR1.800, with soup and salad. Chinese main dishes cost OR1.200 to OR1.500. Outdoor tables are available during winter. The view of the parking lot is hardly romantic but the breeze is nice.

Omar al-Khayyam Restaurant (☎ 703035 or 707082), near the Oman International Bank at the Ruwi roundabout, is a bit more upmarket but still fairly cheap. It has good, fresh-tasting Chinese and Indian food, including a wide selection of Indian vegetarian dishes, most of which are about OR1.400 to OR2.

Al-Haikal Restaurant (☎ 708447), just around the corner from the Ruwi bus station, has delicious, spiced fried fillets of king fish with rice, salad and paratha (a type of Indian bread) for under OR1. There are a number of other grilled meats and fish dishes available and prices are listed on a board inside the restaurant. The fish is cooked in a giant wok just outside the restaurant. Let your nose lead you there.

Woodlands (☎ 700192) is an Indian restaurant off Bank al-Markazi St. It is the place to go if you want to have a drink with dinner and do not want to pay handsomely for the privilege. The food is pretty good and moderately priced with most main dishes at OR1.500 to OR2.200. Most of the food is fairly spicy.

Copper Chimney Restaurant (☎ 706192), just off Bank al-Markazi St in Ruwi, is a good choice if you need an upmarket restaurant for a business meeting. Dinner is fairly expensive at OR5 to OR7, but the food is great and the surroundings dignified.

Shangri-La (☎ 791095) at the Ruwi end of Mutrah High St, near the Mutrah Hotel, offers what may be the best Chinese food in Oman. Main dishes mostly cost OR3.500 and up, and the portions are large.

The Taj (☎ 796583), across the road from Shangri-La, comprises an Indian and a Chinese restaurant. The menu is similar and the prices are roughly the same as at Shangri-La.

Qurm

All the usual fast-food places can be found in the commercial area of Qurm. There are also a number of Indian and Lebanese restaurants with main meals for around OR1.800, as well as coffee shops serving Western-style sandwiches and pastries. Alcohol is not served at these restaurants.

Self-Catering

There are a number of Western-style supermarkets in Ruwi and the Qurm commercial district. There are also dozens of little grocery stores in Ruwi and Mutrah which sell basics. The cheapest place for fresh fish and vegetables is the fish market in Mutrah.

ENTERTAINMENT

Muscat is rather thin when it comes to entertainment. *Oman Today* and the UAE-based *What's On* magazine are your best sources of information on what is currently available.

Cafes & Coffeehouses

No visit to Muscat would be complete without a pit stop at the *teahouse* at the entrance to the Mutrah souq. Here you can get sweet tea for 100 baisa a cup, served as you sit on stone benches, just inside the entrance archway. It's a great place to sit and watch the world go by.

The atrium at the *Hyatt Regency hotel* in Al-Khuwair is a great place for a coffee and to admire the luxurious decor.

You will have to look hard to find coffeehouses that serve *sheesha* (also known as 'hubbly bubbly') as the government periodically bans the practice, saying it pollutes the environment and is detrimental to health. You could try the Qurm commercial district or the stretch of beach near the embassies area.

Bars & Nightclubs

All the five-star hotels and some of the smaller ones have bars. The cheaper places are probably best avoided by women on their own, as they tend to be almost exclusively frequented by men.

There is a *terrace bar* behind the Al-Inshirah restaurant at the eastern end of the Corniche where you can go for a quiet (and fairly cheap) drink.

The Muscat Inter-Continental Hotel, the Al-Bustan Palace Hotel, the Sheraton in Ruwi and the Gulf Forum Hotel all have clubs of one type or another usually with live acts, as well as one or two bars. *Copacabana* at the Hyatt Regency in Al-Khuwair seemed *the* place to be at the time of writing. The door charge is OR3 and the clientele is young and hip – in a Middle Eastern kind of way.

Cinema

Star Cinema (☎ 791641) shows both Western and Indian films (especially). Tickets are OR1 for the best seats. It is the unmistakable round building with flashing lights near the main post office in Ruwi.

SPECTATOR SPORTS

The Marina Bander al-Rowdha on Sidab St, between Muscat and the Al-Bustan Palace Hotel, hosts the President's Cup Muscat-Dubai Sailing Regatta every year in late February/March. For details of football matches around town see the daily newspapers.

SHOPPING

If you are planning to set off in the middle of the day, bear in mind that most shops close for a couple of hours in the afternoon, from about 1 pm to about 4 pm.

The Mutrah souq is a great place to wander around and soak in the atmosphere (see the boxed text 'Mutrah Souq' earlier in this chapter), although it has become a pretty pricey place to shop for Omani handicrafts.

The souq in Ruwi is a good place for shopping but it is not exactly a tourist attraction. Like the rest of Ruwi it is a modern creation and most of what you are likely to find is house and kitchen wares. There are gold jewellery shops on Souq Ruwi St.

Qurm commercial district is *the* place for shopping mall-type shopping and, oddly enough, it is also the best place to look for khanjars and silver jewellery. In the Sabco Commercial Centre is an area with dagger and jewellery shops called, appropriately, 'the Souq', which includes a government-run handicrafts centre with fixed prices. The government shop's khanjars go for about OR70 each. This, and the fact that most people shopping in Qurm are expats who have more time on their hands than the average tourist, has held down prices at the other shops in the area. Bear in mind that much of the jewellery and souvenirs here have come from Thailand and India though some shopkeepers would have you believe that it is all made in Oman. Qurm Commercial Centre also has a few handicrafts and silver shops.

The Omani Heritage Gallery (☎ 696974) is a nonprofit organisation, set up to encourage traditional handicrafts in rural areas and to put money back into the communities through sales. Prices are high but so is the quality of the work. You can get woven cushion covers (OR18) and camel bags (OR50 for a small one) made by Bedouin tribes from the Wahiba Sands, or little clay water pitchers for OR3 and glazed pottery incense burners from Dhofar for OR4.200. The Omani Heritage Gallery is on the ground floor of the Ash-Shatti Shopping Complex, opposite the Muscat Inter-Continental. It's open 9.30 am to 1 pm and 4 to 8 pm Saturday to Thursday.

If you are looking for more substantial things to buy for your home you should visit the Majlis Gallery (☎ 501057) in Athaibah, out past Al-Khuwair. It has antique furniture including coffee tables and cabinets made from antique doors from Oman and India. There are khanjars and rugs, paintings and ornaments, and many other items. It is open 9 am to 8 pm Saturday to Wednesday. To get there turn right at the Ghala-Athaibah roundabout on Sultan Qaboos St if you are

coming from Ruwi. The gallery is about 200m down on the left in villa number 57.

Duty-Free Shopping

Seeb airport duty-free is not the place to do your last-minute souvenir shopping. The handicrafts are hugely overpriced and the khanjars are not good quality. Domestic passengers can buy goods in the duty-free shop (but not alcohol).

GETTING THERE & AWAY
Air

Seeb international airport is 37km from Mutrah. Domestic and international flights use the same check-in and departure areas. The departure lounge offers duty-free shopping, a post office, bank, restaurant and bar.

For airport flight information call ☎ 519223 or 519456. See Air in the Oman Getting Around chapter for details of domestic flights out of Muscat. The addresses of some airline offices are as follows:

Air India (☎ 708639) Markaz Mutrah al-Tijari St, opposite Bahwan Travel Agencies, Ruwi
British Airways (☎ 568777) 3rd floor, Al-Harthy Shopping Centre, Qurm
EgyptAir (☎ 796134) Intersection of Bank al-Markazi and Markaz Mutrah al-Tijari Sts, Ruwi
Emirates Airlines (☎ 786600) intersection of Bank al-Markazi and Markaz Mutrah al-Tijari Sts, Ruwi
Gulf Air (☎ 703555) Musandam Bldg, Ruwi St, opposite Ruwi Novotel
KLM (☎ 566737) 1st floor, Al-Riid Bldg, opposite Sabco Centre, Qurm
Kuwait Airways (☎ 707119) Bahwan Travel Agencies, Markaz Mutrah al-Tijari St, Ruwi
Lufthansa (☎ 708986) Mezoon Travel, Al-Burj St, Bait al-Falaj
Oman Air (☎ 707222) just off Markaz Mutrah al-Tijari St, Ruwi
Royal Jordanian (☎ 796680) Mezoon Travel, Al-Burj St, Bait al-Falaj
Swissair (☎ 787416) Bank al-Markazi St, Ruwi
Thai Airways International (☎ 704455) Bahwan Travel Agencies, Markaz Mutrah al-Tijari St, Ruwi

Bus

The Ruwi bus station (☎ 708522) is the main depot for intercity and international buses in

OMAN

the sultanate. There is a waiting room at the bus station. Luggage can be stored in the cargo area (around the side of the ticket office). The information office is open from about 6 am to 8 pm but it closes between 1 and 2 pm.

Oman National Transport Company (ONTC) buses leave for Salalah daily at 7 am and 7 pm with an extra bus at 6 pm from mid-June through mid-September. They leave one hour later during Ramadan. The trip takes 12 hours, including a couple of rest stops. The fare is OR8 one way and OR16 return. There is also a 'family fare' of OR40 which includes return transportation for two adults and two children. From mid-June to mid-September the family fare can only be used on the day buses and it is not valid for travel during and for two days before and after Eid al-Fitr and Eid al-Adha. Any return reservation you make to or from Salalah should be reconfirmed directly with ONTC as soon as you arrive, especially if you are travelling on a weekend or a holiday. Booking a day or two early is not necessary but would be a good idea if you really want to travel on a particular bus.

There are also three private companies with bus services to Salalah. Abu Nawaf Road Transport (☎ 785252), just off An-Noor St round the corner from the Ruwi bus station, has buses daily at 3.30 pm for OR6 one way and OR11 return. Al-Ghafri & Sons (☎ 707896) has two buses daily at 6.30 and 4.30 pm for OR7, return OR13. Bin Qasim Transport (☎ 785059), next door to Al-Ghafri, has a daily bus at 3 pm for OR7 one way, OR13 return.

ONTC's coaches on the Salalah route are high-quality, relatively new, European-made vehicles with toilets on board. Al-Ghafri and the others use older, Egyptian-made buses, some of which have toilets. Have your passport handy in case there's an inspection at a checkpoint about midway through the trip.

The only international bus service is to the UAE. Buses leave Muscat for Dubai twice a day, at 7.30 am and 4.30 pm, from the Ruwi bus station. During Ramadan the late bus leaves at 5.30 pm. The trip takes six hours.

In Dubai the buses come and go from the Airline Centre on Al-Maktoum Rd in Deira. The fare is OR9 one way, OR16 return. There is also a daily service to Abu Dhabi via Al-Ain, departing Muscat at 7 am (OR6.700/13.300 one way/return). The family fare is OR30 return for two adults and two children. In Abu Dhabi the bus departs at 3 pm from the Madinat Zayed Shopping Centre on East Road.

If you are coming from or going to the UAE and intend to visit Al-Ain, consider taking the Buraimi bus. The fare is much cheaper at OR3.600 one way and there are three buses a day from both Muscat and Buraimi at 7 am, and 1 and 3 pm. The trip takes 4½ hours and goes via Sohar. The border post is 50km from Buraimi.

Taxi & Microbus

Greater Muscat has two long-distance taxi and microbus stands. One is in Ruwi across Al-Jaame St from the main bus station and the other is out at the Seeb clock tower (formally the Sahwa Tower) roundabout, 200m beyond the airport. Most of the taxis and microbuses out at the clock tower wait around in a parking lot on the far side of the clock tower as you approach it from Muscat. A shared taxi from Ruwi to the clock tower costs 500 baisa. Microbuses charge 300 baisa for the same trip. From Mutrah the taxi/microbus fare is 700/300 baisa.

There is a lot of traffic along main routes to places like Rustaq, Sohar, Nizwa and Ibri. Taxis and microbuses to Sur and Buraimi are harder to come by and drivers going to Salalah exist more in theory than in practice.

Some sample shared taxi/microbus fares from Muscat are as follows:

to	fare
Barka	OR1/300 baisa
Ibri	OR3/2
Nakhal	OR2/1
Nizwa	OR1.500/1
Rustaq	OR2/800 baisa
Samail	OR1/500 baisa
Sohar	OR2.500/1.700
Sur	OR3.500/3

There are no microbuses to Buraimi, but a taxi costs OR5 per person. To take any vehicle 'engaged' (ie, all by yourself) multiply the number of seats by the fares listed here and be prepared to bargain. The driver won't go below the seats-times-fare formula but he may insist on a premium, particularly if you want to travel after dark.

Car

There are several rental agencies in the area around the Ruwi roundabout as well as the usual desks in big hotels and at the airport. We were able to negotiate a fairly good rate for a long-term (10-day) rental with Europcar (☎ 700190) but it took quite a lot of haggling. There is an office at the airport and at the Seeb Novotel Muscat. Thrifty Car Rental (☎ 604248) was also competitive, though not as willing to bargain over the number of free kilometres. Avis Rent-a-Car (☎ 607235) has branches at the airport, Al-Bustan Palace Hotel, Muscat Inter-Continental and the Sheraton. You will find plenty of local agencies around Ruwi roundabout.

Most car rental agencies in Muscat charge an extra OR2 to OR4 if you pick up or drop off the car at the airport.

GETTING AROUND
To/From the Airport

To get a bus to the city centre go to the departures end of the terminal building and walk out of the airport car park. The bus stop is at the roundabout on Sultan Qaboos St.

Buses leave for Ruwi and Mutrah twice an hour from 6.44 am until 8.54 pm. On Friday buses leave the airport three times an hour from 7.02 am until 9.20 pm. The trip takes about 50 minutes and the fare is 200 baisa. Route 28 also passes the airport but it stops only at the Seeb airport roundabout on Sultan Qaboos St.

Bus Nos 23 and 24 leave for the airport from the Mutrah bus station at 20 and 50 minutes past the hour from 6.20 am to 9.50 pm daily, except Friday. On Friday and holidays there is an additional bus at five minutes past the hour, but the buses do not start running until 7.20 am.

Private taxis between the airport and the centre cost OR8 to/from Ruwi and Mutrah and OR6.5 to/from Qurm, Madinat as-Sultan Qaboos and Al-Khuwair. If you share a taxi you should pay 500 to 700 baisa.

A few of the intercity buses and the express buses from Salalah and Dubai also stop at the airport on their way into and out of Muscat.

Bus

ONTC's system of local buses covers Greater Muscat fairly thoroughly. Fares are either 100 or 200 baisa (300 baisa to Sultan Qaboos University), depending on the distance travelled. Destinations are displayed on the front of the buses in Arabic and English, but the bus numbers are only in Arabic numerals. The main bus station (☎ 708522) is on Al-Jaame St in Ruwi (the same place the intercity buses leave from) and there is a secondary station (☎ 714422) by the roundabout near the Mina Hotel in Mutrah. Generally, most buses run two or three times an hour from around 6.30 am until around 10 or 10.30 pm.

Bus Nos 2, 4, 23, 24, 28, 31 and 32 all run between the Mutrah and Ruwi stations for 100 baisa. Most buses go along Sultan Qaboos St: bus Nos 23, 24 and 28 go as far as Seeb, bus No 25 goes as far as Ghala roundabout past Al-Khuwair, and bus No 26 as far as Al-Bowshar roundabout. Printed schedules for each route are available in English at the Ruwi bus station but if you're not sure where a particular bus is going just ask the driver. Drivers are usually very helpful and will get you to where you want to go.

Taxi

Muscat's taxis, like all others in Oman, are orange and white. There is one rank on the Corniche, and another in Ruwi opposite the bus station. Drivers usually stand by their vehicle shouting the destination or cruise around the neighbourhood looking for the last couple of passengers when they are almost full.

Taxis are not metered. A taxi between Mutrah and Ruwi costs OR1 if you take it engaged (ie, not shared), or 200 baisa if shared. The same trip in a microbus costs 100 baisa. Mutrah to Muscat is OR1 engaged and Ruwi to Muscat is OR1.500 engaged. There are no shared taxis between Muscat and Ruwi. Mutrah to Qurm is OR3 engaged or 300 baisa shared, and Ruwi to Qurm OR2 engaged or 300 baisa shared.

If you are taking an engaged taxi to or from a hotel the fare goes right up. There seems to be a fixed fare system from/to hotels. If you take an engaged taxi from a hotel in Ruwi to a hotel in Mutrah you will be charged OR3; from a hotel in Ruwi to a hotel in Shatti al-Qurm will cost you a ridiculous OR4. This is exceedingly expensive and it's worth walking well away from a hotel and hailing a cab on the street.

Phone Taxi There are some taxi services that can be ordered by phone and pager. These are private companies but are generally not more expensive than taking an engaged taxi. They will give you a fare quote over the phone.

Al-Dar Taxi	☎ 700555 or 700777
Bid Bid Taxi	☎ 693377 or 693388
Habibi Taxis	☎ 9345901

Microbus

In Mutrah, local microbuses cruise the Corniche and congregate at the end near the Mina Hotel, while in Ruwi they park en masse in a lot across Al-Jaame St from the main bus station. Mutrah to Ruwi costs 100 baisa and Mutrah to Muscat 150 baisa. No microbus journey within Greater Muscat should cost more than 300 baisa, including trips to the airport. The only significant exception to this rule is trips to the main microbus station at the Seeb clock tower (beyond the airport), which is 500 baisa.

Microbuses do not wait until they are full to begin their journey and may even set off on a heavily travelled route (such as Mutrah to Ruwi) with only one or two people on board. Microbus drivers within the city generally go wherever the spirit moves them. Before you get into the bus simply ask the driver 'Ruwi?', 'Madinat Qaboos?', 'Khuwair?' or whatever. He may not have originally planned to go there but will now that he has a paying passenger.

Around Muscat

YITTI

About 25km from Ruwi, this is a popular **beach** on weekends with both locals and expats and can be easily reached without a 4WD. It's also a good place for kids to swim as the bay provides calm water. There is no shade, however, so take an umbrella and hats with you. To get there from Ruwi roundabout, head down Al-Jaame St towards the Sheraton Oman hotel and turn right at the next roundabout onto Souq Ruwi St. This is the Al-Hamriya turn-off. Head along Souq Ruwi St and you will see the sign for Yitti after about 1km. The road winds through shops and houses, up a steep hill and then along Wadi Qanu. After about 16km you will come to a junction. Turn left for Yitti (it's signposted), which is another 7.5km. A right turn will take you to the blacktop road that leads to Qurayat.

QURAYAT

If you have the time this charming coastal village is worth a peek. It's 82km east of Muscat by blacktop road. If you are travelling to the Bimmah Sinkhole (see the following section) you will pass through Qurayat so take a bit of time to explore the place. As you enter the village you will pass by a 150-year-old **fort**, which was not open to the public at the time of writing, and a bustling **souq** where you can buy Omani handicrafts, including some silver jewellery. Keep going as the road swings round to the right then to the left where it meets the coast. If you are there early in the morning you will see fishermen hard at work, otherwise the scene is likely to be of young boys playing soccer on the beach among the dozens of fishing boats. There is a watchtower about 50m from the beach that can be approached only at low tide.

BIMMAH SINKHOLE

This place, about 125km east of Muscat, is a must if you have your own 4WD or, if you don't, you should be able to arrange a tour without any trouble. The sinkhole, 40m wide and 20m deep, is a great place for a swim and a picnic, and you can camp here. The sinkhole sits on a flat area halfway between the coast and the Eastern Hajars. It was formed when underground water dissolved the limestone rock above, causing it to collapse. The crystal-clear blue-green water is a mixture of salt water from the sea and fresh water. Bring snorkelling gear if you have it to get a proper look at the marine life living here.

To get there take the blacktop road from Muscat to Qurayat. When you get to Qurayat turn right at the roundabout where there is a sign for Dagmar. After 6km you will see a dirt track off to the right where the sealed road ends. This road will lead you to Dibab. Just before you come into Dibab you should see a green sign that says, among other places, 'Bama 16km'. From this point you pass through Dibab (don't take the turn-off for Wadi Arbien just out of Dibab) and continue along the coastal plain for another 5.8km. At this point you will see a faint track off to the right which leads to the sinkhole, just 100m away. You won't be able to see the sinkhole until you are right next to it, but you will see some barasti shelters.

The road from Qurayat to Dibab is pretty rough in parts, especially on the descent into Dibab, and is impassable in a saloon car. It is an enjoyable 2½-hour drive to get there so, if you want to spend a decent amount of time at the sinkhole, you'll need a day for this trip.

A'RUSAYL

On the road from Muscat to Nizwa, about 10km past the Seeb clock tower and just before you reach the exit for A'Jifnain, you pass two small forts. Until the ascension of Sultan Qaboos the fort closer to Muscat marked the boundary between Muscat and Oman. The fort has undergone some limited restoration work and is worth a quick photo stop if the traffic on the highway is not too heavy.

A shared taxi/microbus from the Ruwi station in Muscat to A'Rusayl costs 600/300 baisa. Regular ONTC buses make the trip for 300 baisa. Any of these will drop you in the village, several kilometres from the fort, although you will pass the fort on your way into town.

FANJA

The town of Fanja is 75km from Mutrah and just off the highway from Muscat to Nizwa. The old part of the town is set well back from the road, above a wadi.

Fanja is well known as a good place to shop for locally made **pottery**, though you should be aware that most other things in the souq are from Iran, not Oman. Look for people selling pots out of the back of small trucks on the edge of the main souq area. Some of the larger plain pieces of pottery or the smaller painted ones, such as incense burners, cost just OR1 or OR3.

If you arrive by microbus this is probably the area where you will be dropped off. Microbus drivers charge 700 baisa for the trip to or from the Ruwi taxi and microbus stand. Long-distance taxis charge OR1 for the trip. Regular buses (600 baisa; one hour) bound for places further afield (such as Nizwa) stop in Fanja.

North-West Oman

This region of Oman is dense with mountain villages, towns, souqs, forts, wadis and mountain drives. Distances are not huge. If you only have a week or so in Oman, we suggest you base yourself in Muscat and explore the north-west before attempting to take in any other regions of Oman. The western Hajars offer visitors some of the most stunning scenery in the country, as well as an opportunity to see traditional village life.

BARKA

The small town of Barka, some 80km west of Muscat just off the coastal highway, makes an excellent day trip outside the capital. If you are passing by Barka on your way to or from Muscat it's worth pulling off the main highway for a quick visit.

The turn-off is well signposted on the main road from Muscat to Sohar. If you are taking a microbus it will probably drop you at this junction (where the shops sell excellent Omani *halwa*, an addictively delicious traditional sweet). You will have to pick up

---

Bull Butting

Barka is the best place to see the traditional Omani sport of bull butting. There is no bloodshed involved in this activity in which two bulls are pitted against each other. They just push and butt each other around the ring until one backs down and the other is declared the winner. It's very much a casual social gathering for the men and boys from Barka and surrounding villages. There is a notable absence of women from these events but this doesn't mean that women travellers are not welcome.

Bull butting takes place in Barka every second Friday in winter from 4 to 6 pm. To get to the bullring turn left at the T-junction in the centre of town. After about 2.5km you will see the shallow, concrete structure standing alone on your right.

---

another microbus to cover the extra few kilometres to the centre of Barka. In the centre there is a T-junction at which a number of banks and a few small restaurants can be found.

Fort

The fort is on the right as you approach the centre of town, just before the T-junction. As you enter the fort's main court look right. The door with spikes is approximately 300 years old. If you go through this door and up the stairs to the right, you'll find a small courtyard. The door on the left leads to what was the office of the *wali* (governor), which now displays several *khanjars* (Omani daggers) and other weapons as well as some jewellery. The door at the end of the office leads to a hall that served as a waiting room.

Other doors off the small courtyard lead to what was originally a bathroom and to the living quarters for the wali and his family, which occupy both this floor and the one above it. The master bedroom, on the upper level, has a display of china and porcelain which is worth seeing. The living area also includes a small prayer room, easily identified by the *mihrab* (niche indicating the direction of Mecca) in its west wall.

Below the prayer room and to the left is a large open courtyard with a well and a mosque. The only tower open to visitors is directly across the courtyard if you enter it from the prayer room. Inside the tower is a well, several rooms that were used to store weapons and ammunition, and an underground prison. A staircase in the centre of the tower leads to the top, from where you get a good view over the entire town.

It's open 7.30 am to 6 pm (2 pm on Friday) daily. Admission is free. Photography is permitted inside the fort but videos are not.

Bait Nua'man

This restored fortified house shows how the wealthier residents of the area lived several

NORTH-WEST OMAN

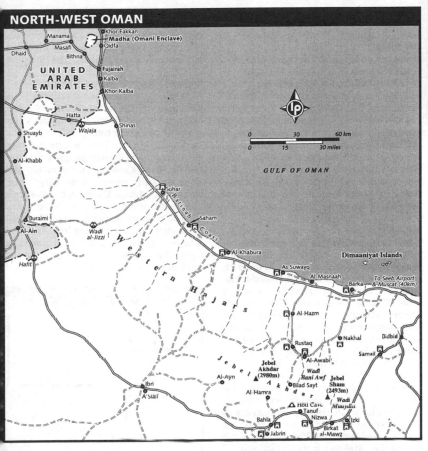

generations ago. To reach Bait Nua'man from the fort continue along the road that brought you into Barka from the main highway and go 4.8km past the fort. This will bring you to a left turn onto a blacktop road. Take this turn (if you reach a roundabout you've gone too far) and follow the road for 1.9km. Bait Nua'man will be on your right. It keeps irregular hours so just take a chance.

Getting There & Away

There are four buses per day between Barka and Ruwi (400 baisa, one hour express, 1½ hours regular). The express bus leaves Ruwi at 7 am. Regular buses leave at 1, 3 and 6 pm. The express bus from Barka to Ruwi leaves daily at 4.40 pm. Regular buses leave at 8.30 and 11.30 am, and 7.30 pm. The buses all come and go from the Barka turn-off on the Muscat-Sohar highway.

Taxis and microbuses can be found both around the T-junction in Barka and at the Barka turn-off on the Muscat-Sohar highway. A shared taxi from the Seeb clock tower to Barka costs OR1 per person and around OR8 engaged. Microbuses charge

OMAN

300 baisa per person for the trip from the Seeb clock tower.

SOHAR

Home port of the fictional Sinbad the sailor, Sohar is a place with a significant history. A thousand years ago it occupied three times its present area and was the largest town in the country. By those standards Sohar today is something of a disappointment. However, there is a lovely esplanade along the beach, and the fort and its small museum are worth seeing. If you have the time to combine Sohar with the sites further inland, it makes a good turn-around point for a two- or three-day swing out of Muscat via Barka, Nakhal and Rustaq and back.

History

Sohar's history stretches back to the 3rd millennium BC, when it was the seat of the Magan empire and at the centre of the Batinah Coast's copper trade with powerful empires further afield, including Sumer. It may be the 'Omana' mentioned by Pliny in the 1st century AD, and it is almost certainly the 'Emporium Persicum' ('Persian Market') near the Strait of Hormuz mentioned in a 5th-century Byzantine text. The city, by then, was extremely rich – the Prophet Mohammed was buried in a silk shroud from Sohar.

From the 7th to the 13th centuries AD Sohar was the most important port and trading centre in Oman, rising to prominence as the frankincense trade in the south of the country died out. The 10th-century Arab geographer Makdisi wrote glowingly of Sohar as a rich and beautiful city.

The city prospered during the Middle Ages and was incorporated into the Kingdom of Hormuz in the 14th century. In September 1507 the governor of Sohar surrendered the city to the Portuguese without a fight, as reinforcements from Hormuz – and the governor's wages – did not arrive. The Portuguese held the town more or less uninterruptedly until the early 17th century, making it a major part of their empire in the Gulf.

It was at Sohar in 1744 that Ahmed bin Said al-Busaid, then the town's governor, distinguished himself by his stand against the Persians who were threatening to take over Oman. His actions led to his election at Nizwa later that year as imam of all Oman. His descendants have ruled Oman ever since.

Orientation & Information

Confusingly, Sohar has two centres – the old centre on the waterfront near the fort, and a more modern business district a couple of kilometres inland, closer to the Muscat-Dubai highway. The post office and taxi stand are both in the new part, which is centred on Sohar's souq and the main hospital. To reach both centres take the 'City Centre' exit off the Muscat-Dubai highway. For the new centre turn right onto An-Nahdah St at the next roundabout you come to. Taxis and microbuses are in a parking lot to the left a little way up the road and the hospital on the right. The post office is 250m past the hospital along the same road.

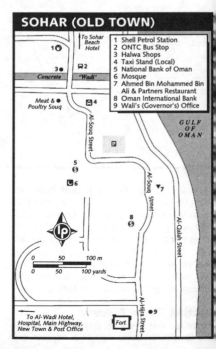

SOHAR (OLD TOWN)

1 Shell Petrol Station
2 ONTC Bus Stop
3 Halwa Shops
4 Taxi Stand (Local)
5 National Bank of Oman
6 Mosque
7 Ahmed Bin Mohammed Bin Ali & Partners Restaurant
8 Oman International Bank
9 Wali's (Governor's) Office

To Sohar Beach Hotel

Concrete

'Wadi'

Meat & Poultry Souq

Al-Souq Street

GULF OF OMAN

Al-Souq Street

Al-Qalah Street

0   50   100 m
0   50   100 yards

Al-Hijra Street

To Al-Wadi Hotel, Hospital, Main Highway, New Town & Post Office

Fort

If you keep straight on the road from the highway instead of taking the An-Nahdah St turn, you'll come to a second roundabout after 2.1km. Turn right and you will reach the fort and coast road. This is the old town.

Sohar Fort

Sohar Fort is a large, whitewashed, slightly irregular rectangle with a single tower rising from its courtyard. It is a dramatic sight after the earth-coloured forts that dominate the rest of Oman.

The first fort on the site is thought to have been built in the late 13th or early 14th century, though much of what you see today dates from the first half of the 17th century. The fort was extensively restored by the Omani government in 1992.

There's a small museum in the tower. On the ground floor there are displays on Oman's geology, geography and ancient history, including a good section on the ancient copper trade that was centred on the Batinah Coast. Also on this floor is the tomb of Sayyid Thuwaini bin Said bin Sultan al-Busaid, the ruler of Oman from 1856 to 1866.

The three rooms on the museum's 1st floor continue the story of Sohar's development as a trade centre from the centuries before Islam into the Middle Ages. Room seven includes information on the history of a number of Oman's important forts with an emphasis on the development of Sohar Fort itself. The 2nd floor, which is empty, provides access to the tower's roof from where you get a sweeping view across Sohar and the sea.

At the far end of the courtyard from the main entrance there are the excavated remains of the 13th-century houses on whose ruins the original fort was built.

The fort is open 7.30 am to 2.30 pm Saturday to Wednesday; 8 am to noon and 4 to 6 pm Thursday and Friday. Admission is free.

Souqs

Fishing remains one of Sohar's main industries and if you are around either at dawn or at dusk a visit to the fish souq in the old part of town, where the day's catch is on sale, can be fun. The fish souq is on the coast road, 2km west of the old town centre.

The **main souq**, which sells mainly food and produce, is in the new part of town just behind the taxi and microbus stand. Walk through the covered fruit and vegetable section of the main souq and you will come to the **women's souq**. The local women set up stalls here and sell perfumes, cheap jewellery, shampoo, henna, cooking spices and oils, all sorts of incense and incense burners.

The new **handicraft souq**, just being completed when we visited, is also worth a visit. It is between the old centre and the new, 1.8km from the An-Nahdah roundabout towards the old part of town. The souq features workshops producing and selling a variety of traditional Omani handicrafts, including silverwork, woven palm leaf items, pottery, textiles and talliwork, as well as incense and perfume, traditional medicines and traditional weaponry (this appears to be basically a gun shop and was the busiest part of the souq when we visited!). There is also a traditional coffeehouse/restaurant in the souq.

Places to Stay

There are just two hotels in Sohar. *Al-Wadi Hotel* (☎ 840058, fax 841997), just off the main highway about 10km west of Sohar's new centre, is the cheaper of the two at OR23.100/31.500 for singles/doubles. It has small beach-cabin-like rooms surrounding its swimming pool but is a bit of a disappointment, considering the price. Nevertheless, it remains a lot cheaper than the alternative, and the rooms were undergoing renovation the time of writing. To get there from Muscat, turn left at the second Sohar roundabout, the one with a mosque's dome on stilts for a centrepiece, and follow the signs.

Sohar Beach Hotel (☎ 841111, fax 843776) has rooms for OR33.930/40.950, as well as unnecessarily large chalets with living rooms for OR58.500. If you can afford the extra money this is one case where the more expensive hotel is definitely the better value for money. It is about 6km north of the old town on the coastal road. From the highway follow the big green signs.

Places to Eat

In the old town, there are a number of good cheap biryani restaurants within easy walking distance of the fort. *Ahmed bin Mohammed bin Ali & Partners Restaurant* on Al-Souq St has a few tables outside overlooking the coastal road and the sea.

Omar al-Khayyam (☎ 842606) in the new part of town, has good Indian and Chinese food for about OR1.500 for mains. It is in the main souq area – turn left at the taxi stand (it's signposted). For more upmarket dining and booze you will have to go to one of the hotels.

In the old town there are a number of very good Omani *halwa shops*. They are just to the west of the concrete wadi which cuts across the main road through the old town.

Getting There & Away

Bus There are three buses per day between the Sohar Hospital and Ruwi. They leave at 9 am, and 2.55 and 5 pm. The 2.55 pm bus is an express bus and takes 2¾ hours. The other buses are regular services and take four hours. The fare on either service is OR2.200. Buses from Ruwi to Sohar leave daily at 7 am (express) and at 1 and 3 pm (regular).

The daily express buses between Dubai and Muscat make a meal stop in Sohar at the Penguin Restaurant on the main highway about 2.5km towards Muscat from the main turn-off to Sohar (look for a small commercial complex that also includes a Shell petrol station and a Land Rover dealership). From there you can get a nonstop lift into Muscat (OR5) or to Dubai (OR4). Tickets can be purchased from the driver but it is better to phone ahead to the Ruwi bus station in Muscat (☎ 708522) to make a booking so the driver knows to look for you when he reaches Sohar. The Muscat-bound buses come through daily at approximately 10.30 am and 8.30 pm. The Dubai-bound buses arrive at around 9.30 or 10 am and 6.30 or 7 pm.

Taxi & Microbus Microbuses and taxis arrive and depart from a parking lot across the street from the hospital and 150m to the north of it. A few can also be found at the Sohar turn-off on the Muscat-Dubai highway. Microbuses charge OR1.500 to the Seeb clock tower, OR2 to Ruwi. Shared taxis charge OR2.500 to the clock tower and OR3 to Ruwi, or about OR15 engaged. There is no direct taxi or microbus service to Rustaq or Nakhal from Sohar. Expect to pay about OR15 one way to take a taxi engaged. Alternatively, you can take a Muscat-bound shared taxi or microbus as far south as one of the two road junctions leading to Rustaq and Nakhal and get another ride from there.

For OR30 the taxis will take you to Dubai (engaged only).

NAKHAL

Nakhal is a picturesque town dominated by one of Oman's more dramatic forts. Its other attraction is the hot spring at A'Thowarah.

Fort

As you enter the town the fort is 2km from the main highway, on the right, set on a small hill. After you enter the fort, go upstairs and turn left at a large carved door. This will take you to a small courtyard with a cannon. The wali's winter reception area is the small room to your left. Beyond this is the kitchen area and the fort's east tower, which provides a good view over the town.

Back near the wali's office a short flight of stairs leads up into the main part of the fortress passing several storerooms and the fort's prison. When you reach another staircase go up, heading straight rather than turning left. This leads to the living quarters of the wali and his family. An attempt has been made to restore the various rooms – bedrooms and a women's *majlis* (reception area) – to their original form. A U-turn at the top of the stairs leads into these living quarters and to the more strictly military part of the fort, from where a passageway leads back to where you started.

The fort is open 7 am to 5 pm daily. Admission is free.

A'Thowarah

This lush spring lies a few kilometres beyond the fort. It is a perfect place for a stroll or a picnic. Put your hand into the stream close to the point where it rises from the rocks – the water is surprisingly warm even in winter. Here you may see local children swimming, or women washing their clothes and dishes. Walk up the wadi a little way if you want to find a more private spot and to give the locals some space.

To reach A'Thowarah continue past the fort for another 2.5km on the blacktop road to its end. You will see signs. The narrow road winds through a residential area, date gardens and *falaj* (irrigation system). If there are any around you could get a taxi to the springs for 500 baisa but it makes a nice walk too, if you have the time and energy, but watch out for vehicles speeding along the narrow road, as there is no pedestrian track.

Getting There & Away

There is only one bus (OR1.500) per day between Muscat and Nakhal. The bus leaves the Ruwi station in Muscat daily at 6 pm arriving at 7.55 pm. The return trip leaves Nakhal every morning at 8 am, arriving in Ruwi at 10 am. The bus stop is at the junction on the main road from Barka. There is no place to stay in Nakhal, so you'll need to take a taxi or microbus at least one way.

You'll find microbuses and taxis at the junction with the main road. Microbuses charge OR1 for the trip to the Seeb clock tower and 300 baisa to/from the Barka roundabout on the Muscat-Sohar highway. Taxis charge about OR2 for the same trip. A short local run (such as between the main road and the town) is a couple of hundred baisa.

AL-AWABI

This village, on the road from Nakhal to Rustaq and Al-Hazm, is noteworthy only for its small **fort**. It's worth a quick look if you have your own car but it's not worth breaking your microbus journey here simply for a look at the fort, as it might take a while for you to find another bus or taxi and get moving again.

The fort has not been restored and different parts of it are in various stages of disrepair. The building is basically square in

---

The Falaj

The falaj is the main source of irrigation water in most of rural Oman. It consists of a network of narrow channels which crisscross agricultural plots, delivering water for irrigation and domestic use. The source of the water is a deep shaft, dug into the water table of the mountains. The water then runs through an underground tunnel for some kilometres until it surfaces in the small channel. Water flow depends on the gravity gradient along the tunnel.

The falaj has been used in agriculture since ancient times. It was brought to Oman by Persian settlers about 2000 years ago. For the ancient Omanis, the falaj provided a permanent and stable water supply in a region that was always under the threat of drought. This opened up for colonisation the arid plains at the foot of the Hajar mountains and guaranteed the survival of the Omanis.

---

design and has only one watchtower/bastion. The part of it that includes the door facing the road appears to be a later addition. The fort is not open to the public.

The fort is 2.4km off the Nakhal-Rustaq road. Coming from Nakhal take the first Al-Awabi turn-off (the second Al-Awabi turn-off if you are coming from Rustaq) and then just follow the road through the village.

WADI BANI AWF

This is one of the most stunning wadis in Oman, and an absolute must if you have a 4WD. If you don't, a number of tour companies do day trips here from Muscat. There is a lot to see and explore in this wadi and it is also suitable for camping. At the end of the road which winds around the mountains is the incredibly scenic mountain village of **Bilad Sayt**.

You will see the signposted turn-off for Wadi Bani Awf on the left, 43km from Nakhal towards Rustaq, 5km after Al-Awabi. *Village Resort Motel* (☎ 691445) is a couple of kilometres into the wadi from this turn off. Although it promises accommodation in an authentic Omani setting at the time of writing it looked very deserted and run-down; camp sites further on in the wadi are more attractive.

The first 10km is a lovely drive as the track winds through the wadi and the *jebel* (mountain) walls rise up high on either side. You have to skirt around giant boulders and through small creeks in the narrower parts. After this first 10km the track opens out to a wider area with a small creek and a ***camping spot*** on the left.

At 13.2km from the main road there is a T-junction. Turn left here. After a further 3km (ie at 16.2km from the main road), you will be at the opening of a gorge on the right, although it's blocked from view by large rocks. You are at the right spot if there is a track going off to the left. Park off the track and walk past the rocks into the gorge. Here you'll find **pools** and small **waterfalls**. The further you walk, the deeper the pools get and the more you will have to clamber over large rocks.

Back on the road, you'll reach the village of **Zammah** after another 5km. Just past this village you will see a sign for Bilad Sayt. Although the village is only 6km from here the road is very steep and it will take you about 40 minutes. You will need to use low gear 4WD for most of the drive. The views into the wadis and out across the mountains along the way are staggering. The road dips down into a wadi where there are few houses and then up the other side and round another mountain. Considering how difficult and steep the drive is in parts there's a lot of traffic on this road and you may find that you have to back up or squeeze over to the side to get past oncoming vehicles.

After 5km you will see a sign for the village of Hat but continue on the main track for Bilad Sayt. Look for the soccer pitch that has been smoothed out on a large rock ledge just below the road before you get to the village. Bilad Sayt comes into view after a few more bends. It is an extraordinary sight with its green terraces of various crops, date palm oasis and old stone and concrete houses built

right into a steep hill. Less than sensitive tour companies sometimes bring carloads of tourists through here but it's possible to enjoy the sight from a distance – you don't need to traipse through the narrow and private streets of the village for a closer look.

RUSTAQ

Some 175km south-west of Muscat by road, Rustaq (Rostaq) is best known today for its imposing **fort**, though for a time in the Middle Ages it was Oman's capital.

To enter the fort you go up a ramp, passing through the large open area between the inner and outer walls until you reach a second gate (note the niche above the light bulb at this second gate – it is from here that the hot oil would have been poured down on any attacking army). At the second gate, go up a flight of stairs and through an archway. At this point the first door on your left leads to the fort's prison. Inside, a low and narrow hole in one wall leads to what was once the women's section of the prison. Having made your way back out of the prison area head straight and then look down to the left to see the spring which rises inside the fort. This natural supply of fresh water would have helped the fort's defenders to withstand a siege. A nearby staircase leads down to a washing basin.

Once upstairs (moving anticlockwise around the court) the first room was a guard room while the second leads to a windowless 'final punishment' prison. The third room was another guard room; and the fourth a Quranic school, one room of which was a small mosque. Just off this room is a well with a stone-cut basin for the ablutions Muslims must perform before prayer. At the back of the school complex another staircase leads up to the lower of two roofs. Turn right, then walk straight to reach the library. The small room to the right of the library was reserved for the imam. The closet-sized room next to this was the prayer room of the imam's wife. A storeroom (which looks a lot like the library in its present state) at the rear of the roof level includes the entrance to an underground passage. Local legend has it that this used to connect Rustaq with the fort at Al-Hazm.

One of the fort's turrets is sometimes open to visitors. Try to get the guide to take you up. From here you get a superb view over the area.

The small **souq** near the entrance to the fort has a few antiques and souvenirs but the new souq on the main street, about 1.5km from the highway, far surpasses the old one. Here you can buy traditional Omani wooden chests, silver jewellery and khanjars, as well as meat, fish and vegetables. Prices are reasonable but you will have to bargain.

Getting There & Away

There is one bus a day from Muscat to Rustaq, leaving Ruwi at 6 pm. The bus back to Muscat from Rustaq departs at 7.05 am each day. It costs OR1.800 and takes three hours.

Microbuses can be found at the junction on the main road to Nakhal and the coast. Microbus fares from Rustaq include: Nakhal, 500 baisa; the junction with the coastal highway, 400 baisa; Sohar, OR1; and Mutrah/ Ruwi, OR1 (800 baisa to the Seeb clock tower). The fare to Muscat in a shared taxi is OR2.

AL-HAZM

The town of Al-Hazm is little more than a fort surrounded by a few houses off the road from Muscat to Rustaq, but it is well worth a stop if you have your own car.

The fort, which does not appear to be actively used by the local police but remains under their jurisdiction, is open 7.30 am to 2 pm daily. You will probably be given a (non-English speaking) police officer as a guide when you visit the fort.

Before you enter take a look at the falaj which flows underneath the fort. It is still in use, irrigating the gardens surrounding the fort.

The carved doors of the fort are interesting. The inscription on the left-hand door dates its construction to 1162 AH on the Islamic Hejira calendar (about 1750 AD). The inscription on the right identifies as the fort's builder Imam Sultan bin Saif II, a

member of the Al-Ya'ruba dynasty, who reigned from 1706 to 1719.

As you enter the fort move around to your right to see the well, which is about 25m deep. At the end of the corridor beyond the well is a room with a huge stone pillar in its centre. When you get to the centre of the fort the falaj comes into view again. An inscription to the right of it dates this part of the fort to 918 AH (1512 AD). The imam's tomb is just beyond the hole in the wall.

There is a small mosque upstairs and to the right, identified by a mihrab, or prayer niche. Another flight of stairs nearby leads to a room which may once have been used as a Quranic school. Nearby, another doorway leads to a room directly above the main gate which has holes through which callers were scrutinised and hot oil was poured onto the heads of unwelcome visitors. Climbing up through the bastions on the upper levels of the fort you will pass a set of antique cannons bearing the crest of the Portuguese monarchy. These cannons and the Muscat forts are virtually the only physical remnants of Oman's century and a half of Portuguese rule. You get a good view of the surrounding countryside from the top of the tower.

Getting There & Away

Al-Hazm is 20km north of Rustaq and 24.5km south of the Muscat-Dubai highway. Coming from the coast make a right turn at the Al-Hazm roundabout at a sign for Hazm. Follow this road for 1.5km and then turn left at a sign for 'Qal'at Al-Hazm'.

SAMAIL

Known as the Samail Gap, the wadi running through this town forms a natural break through the eastern and western Hajar mountains. The passage through here is the main artery of communication from the capital to the interior.

From the main Muscat-Nizwa road the town of Samail appears to be little more than a bus stop, one that people usually head straight past. But turning off the road is a great short side trip for those with the time to spare. The town is home to Oman's oldest mosque, Samail Fort, a halwa factory and a number of watchtowers.

Masjid Mazin bin Ghadouba

This is Oman's oldest mosque. It has been rebuilt and is constructed out of blocks of stone. The wooden window frames and coloured glass makes it an unusual building. To get there turn right off the main road through Samail at the sign for 'Sefalat Samail'. After 500m you'll come to a T-junction. Turn left and follow the narrow street through town, past the halwa factory on your right, for 1.5km. The mosque will be on your right, opposite a grocery store. Be careful driving along here, it's a narrow street and cars tend to tear along. If you continue along this road you will come out on the main road at the sign that says 'Luzugh 10km' from where you can get to the fort.

Fort

The fort is irregularly shaped. It has only one bastion, though there are also two **watchtowers** on the hilltops just above the fort itself. Although you may not be able to get into the fort, it is worth stopping for a look, and making the climb up to the watchtowers for a view out over the oasis.

To get to the fort turn off the Muscat-Nizwa road (a left turn if you are coming from Muscat) at the big green sign welcoming you to the Samail Wilayat. If you are coming from Nizwa you will not be able to see this sign, so look for a sign saying 'Samail 4km'. Follow the road for 10km through the villages of Al-Qrain and Al-Ulaiya, both of which also have forts that are visible from the main road, though neither one is restored. You will come to a sign saying 'Sefalat Samail'. Continue for another 4.4km until you reach a small junction with a sign saying 'Luzugh 10km', pointing in the direction you are travelling. At this point you should be able to see one of the watchtowers on the hill above you and to the left. About 250m beyond the sign turn left onto a dirt track between two yellowed walls. The fort will be on your left.

Getting There & Away

The Samail road junction is a stop on the bus route from Muscat to Nizwa (it appears in the printed timetables as 'Samail Hospital'). The fare to Samail is 900 baisa and the trip takes just over 1¼ hours express and just over 1½ hours regular. See the Nizwa Getting There & Away section for departure times from Nizwa.

Microbuses from the Seeb clock tower to Nizwa will drop you at the Samail road junction for 500 baisa. The shared taxi fare from the Seeb clock tower is OR1. From Nizwa to Samail the microbus/taxi fare is 700 baisa/OR1.500. From the junction to the fort the microbus fare is 200 to 300 baisa each way. Microbuses park around the junction. To get to the fort and the mosque, however, you will need to make a deal with a local taxi driver, as he will have to wait for you and bring you back to the main highway.

IZKI

If you have your own car and the time, it's worth making a diversion to this town off the road from Muscat to Nizwa. There are **ruins** of a large town, complete with citadel, forts and numerous watchtowers, sitting above a wadi to the east of the new town. The new town sits below the citadel and is interspersed with the ruins of mud houses. Some of the old houses are still inhabited. A drive through the narrow streets of the town with its date palms and falaj gives you a taste of traditional Oman.

The best approach to the old town is to take the turn-off for Izki from the Muscat-Nizwa highway and follow the road for exactly 4.8km. Turn right at this point onto a track just after a walled-in public park. The track will take you through a large cemetery, across the wadi and up to the ruins.

BIRKAT AL-MAWZ

This picturesque oasis village, 30km north of Nizwa and 140km south of Muscat, just off the main highway, is worth visiting if you have your own car but it's probably not worth the hassle of stopping if you are travelling by microbus. The **Bait al-Radidah** is just a short diversion off the main road. This two-storey fortified house has been recently restored. The main building is constructed from stones and clay and the tower is made of stones and gypsum. Inside the walls surrounding the house is a small mosque.

If you are coming from Muscat turn right at the second signposted turn-off for the town. The fortified house will be on your right after about 1km.

WADI MUAYDIN

From the village of Birkat al-Mawz you can take an off-road jaunt into the picturesque Wadi Muaydin. You will need a 4WD however. If you don't have one, most tour companies in Muscat operate trips to this wadi. Parts of the wadi are suitable for camping, and for the fit there is a **hiking trail** that will take you up to the highest plateau of the Hajars, Saiq Plateau on Jebel Akhdar.

The graded road to Wadi Muaydin is signposted off to the right at Birkat al-Mawz if you are coming from Muscat. If you are coming from the other direction, turn left into the town of Birkat al-Mawz and take the track to the left of Bait al-Radidah (see previous entry) to enter the wadi. The wide, open area about 3km to 5km into the wadi is the best place to *camp*. At 7.4km the road splits. The road to the right goes all the way to the plateau but it is a military area and you will not be able to pass without a permit. This can be hard to get but if you are keen to drive here contact the Administration Affairs Office at the Ministry of Defence in Muscat (☎ 618236).

If you take the left road you will only be able to drive for another 4.5km but from there you can hike up to the Saiq Plateau without a permit. The trail begins after about a 10-minute walk further into the wadi from where you left your car, and is marked with rocks painted white. Getting all the way to the top takes six hours. You could consider camping on the plateau, where there are several traditional mountain villages, but this means carrying all your gear with you. If you make it to the top, you will be rewarded with a spectacular view over the Hajars.

NIZWA

Only 45 years ago the British explorer Wilfred Thesiger was forced to keep well clear of Nizwa. As the seat of the imams who then ruled much of the country's interior it had a reputation for ferocious conservatism. Thesiger's Bedouin companions were convinced he would have little chance of emerging from the town alive. Today, visitors need have no such worries; Nizwa has rapidly emerged as one of Oman's major tourist centres. It is probably the country's most popular tourist destination after Muscat.

At 172km from Muscat, Nizwa is a fairly easy day trip from the capital but if you have the time to spare, it's worth pausing for a day or so to get the real feel of the place. In addition to its aesthetic charms Nizwa is also the centre for Oman's jewellery and craft industries. Most of the khanjars you see on sale in Muscat's Mutrah souq are manufactured here. Prowl the back alleys of the Nizwa souq and you may even find a group of Indians or Pakistanis hard at work making khanjars under the watchful eye of an Omani craftsman.

Orientation

Nizwa's main visual landmark is the large, blue-domed mosque which is on your left if you enter town from the direction of Muscat. The souq is the citadel-like construction on the south side of the parking lot. The fort's large round tower can be seen just behind the mosque. Past the mosque the main street swings around to the right into the town's modern commercial area.

Information

The post office is on the main street near the book roundabout. It is open 9 am to 2 pm Saturday to Wednesday and 8 to 11 am on Thursday. You can change money at any of the several banks in the city centre. There's no tourist office as such but you can get information on Nizwa and the surrounding area from Al-Azri Tours (☎ 412368), in the group of shops near the entrance to the fort.

[Continued on page 146]

FORTS IN OMAN

There are around 500 forts in Oman, ranging from simple defensive structures to massive complexes capable of housing an army. Every town or populated area was protected by a fort, which often doubled as the residence of the *wali* (governor). Today, many old forts are still used as the area police headquarters. Although you'll see forts in most parts of the country, the highest concentration is in strategically important areas, such as mountain passes (eg, Samail Gap between the Eastern and Western Hajars, the main communication route between Muscat and the interior) and the coastline.

To understand why there are so many defensive structures in Oman, you need to look to the history books. There's a long legacy of hostility between different tribes and clans in different parts of the country, and lucrative trade routes had to be protected from attack. Invasion and occupation of parts of Oman by outsiders such as the Portuguese and the Persians also had an influence on fort-building.

If you're expecting to see knee-high ruins, you'll be pleasantly surprised. Since 1976 the Ministry of National Heritage & Culture has undertaken a program of restoration and preservation of Oman's heritage, including its forts. To date, about 60 forts have been restored. As many of the skills needed to restore these buildings have been lost by the local Omani population, outside help has been brought in. In 1983, the ministry entered into an agreement with the Moroccan government to use the skills of Moroccan artisans. For the restoration of Jabrin fort, with its intricate internal decorations, the skills of an Italian team were used.

Although the Portuguese had an important influence on fort building in Oman, only three forts – Fort Jalali, Fort Mirani and Mutrah Fort in Muscat – are actually of Portuguese construction. Many forts (such as Bahla and Nakhal) date from the pre-Islamic era, although they have undergone modifications over time. The immense fort at Bahla, for example, declared a World Heritage Site by UNESCO and currently undergoing its latest restoration, is known to have undergone at least three previous major restorations in the 9th, 17th and 19th centuries.

The materials originally used to construct the forts were what was available locally – stone, mud and clay, mixed with straw or dung, and palm trunks for wooden structures. As a result, most of the old forts have a characteristic sandy colour. The most notable exception is the strikingly whitewashed fort at Sohar. Ceilings were traditionally constructed using palm trunks for beams, on top of which palm-leaf matting was laid, with a layer of mud or clay on top of this. The forts were solidly built, with walls usually around 2m thick for rooms, thicker (up to 3.5m) for 'fire' towers, in order both to withstand enemy attack and the reverberations of their own cannon fire.

Some forts are small and functional, such as Taqa, Bukha, Khasab and Barka, whereas others, such as Rustaq, Nakhal and Jabrin, are massive complexes with multiple rooms, the mosque and library, as well as underground cellars and storerooms – and a prison. Jabrin's exquisitely

Box: Detail from carve wooden shutter at Mirbat fort near Salala (Photo by David Petherbridge)

DAVID PETHERBRIDGE

DAVID PETHERBRIDGE

DAVID PETHERBRIDGE

Top: The huge fort at Nizwa, once the capital of Oman, was a classic example of fort architecture at the time of its construction. Its most striking feature is this massive, central round tower, built to withstand enemy mortar attack.

Middle: The variety of architectural styles on display, from these graceful arches in Samail fort to the precise angles of Sohar fort's white-washed tower, makes touring Oman's forts a fascinating experience.

Bottom: Nakhal fort, once vital in the defence of the route between the interior and the Batinah Coast, has a stunning oasis setting, with the rugged Hajar mountains rising above it.

CHRIS MELLOR

Top: Watchtowers, similar to this one at Qurayat near Muscat, were scattered throughout the country, usually perched on hills and coastal promontories. The watchtower guard was responsible for raising the alarm if the enemy was sighted.

Middle: The recent restoration of Al-Khandaq Fort, in Buraimi, has been impressively thorough throughout, down to the geometric decorations on the tower and surrounding the main entrance. Unusually for Oman, the square fort has only three corner towers.

Bottom: If you see only one fort in Oman, make it Jabrin. This restored 11th-century fort started life as a palace and was later modified as a fort. Features include exquisitely decorated ceilings and an inner courtyard overlooked by wooden balconies.

decorated ceilings and intricate architecture, including inner courtyards overlooked by screened windows, reflect its original design as a palace.

As you enter a fort, look out for the many features that indicate its principal function as a defensive structure. You will probably have come through the main entrance by way of a small trap-door in the main door – this was to prevent visitors carrying large weapons (such as rifles) from entering. The massive wooden entrance doors, studded with metal spikes, were to prevent enemies from battering their way in. Although the portcullises themselves are long gone, you can often see the stone grooves for them above entrances. Strategic parts of the fort, such as the towers, usually had a single access, via a twisting stair-way – again, to prevent the enemy from storming it. As you stand in the courtyard of a fort, look up – all around you'll see firing slits and windows angled down towards you. Above entrances, there are usually shutes for pouring boiling water, oil or date syrup on the enemy below. The view from most fort towers is spectacular – and perfect for spotting the enemy creeping up on you.

It was important for a fort to be self-sufficient in case of siege, and many forts have a well and their own falaj system, as well as underground cellars for storage. In most forts you'll see a date storeroom, with stone grooves for collecting the date syrup. Some forts even had secret passageways, for example there is said to be one between Al-Hazm and Ruslaq.

If you want to read more about Oman's forts, there is a lavish coffee-table book, *Forts of Oman*, by Walter Dinteman, published by the UAE-based Motivate Publishing.

Isabelle Young

Below: This is the view it would have greeted anybody trying to capture Nakhal Fort – small wonder it is still standing today!

CHRISTINE OSBORNE

[Continued from page 143]

Nizwa Fort

Visually, Nizwa's fort is hardly the most breathtaking set of battlements in Oman but it has an impressive history and a great view over the Nizwa area from the top of the watchtower. The fort was built in the mid-17th century by Sultan bin Saif, the first imam of the Al-Ya'ruba dynasty. For the next 300 years it was the primary seat of the imamate, serving as a combination palace, seat of government and prison.

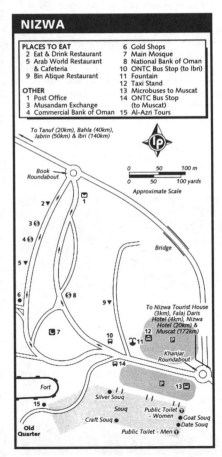

NIZWA

PLACES TO EAT
2 Eat & Drink Restaurant
5 Arab World Restaurant
  & Cafeteria
9 Bin Atique Restaurant

OTHER
1 Post Office
3 Musandam Exchange
4 Commercial Bank of Oman

6 Gold Shops
7 Main Mosque
8 National Bank of Oman
10 ONTC Bus Stop (to Ibri)
11 Fountain
12 Taxi Stand
13 Microbuses to Muscat
14 ONTC Bus Stop
   (to Muscat)
15 Al-Azri Tours

To Tanuf (20km), Bahla (40km),
Jabrin (50km) & Ibri (140km)

Book Roundabout

0   50   100 m
0   50   100 yards
Approximate Scale

Bridge

To Nizwa Tourist House
(3km), Falaj Daris
Hotel (4km), Nizwa
Hotel (20km) &
Muscat (172km)

Khanjar Roundabout

Fort

Old Quarter

Silver Souq
Souq
Craft Souq
Public Toilet - Women
Public Toilet - Men
Goat Souq
Date Souq

There is a large map of the fort by the main doorway. The fort is actually quite a large complex of buildings – much larger than it looks from the street. A small guidebook in English is sometimes available at the entrance for free. At the back there is a garden and falaj irrigation system.

Nizwa fort is open 7.30 am to 4 pm (until 5 pm from June to September) daily. Admission is free. Still photography is permitted inside the fort.

Old Town

From the fort's tower there is a good view of old Nizwa. About 100m from the fort's door is the small maze of narrow alleys, mudbrick homes and some craft workshops.

Nizwa Souq

Apart from the fort, Nizwa's main attraction is its souq. Despite having been purpose-built for tourists, including signs in English, the souq has a lot of colour and vitality. The bad news is that the souq's popularity with package tours has made it one of the worst places in the sultanate to shop for souvenirs. Everything in the silver souq is outrageously overpriced, especially the khanjars. Even worse, because most people visiting with groups have only an hour or so to spend here,

Goat Souq

The goat souq at the far end of Nizwa souq, behind the date souq, remains very traditional and is the main attraction of the market. Men, most wearing light purple *dishdashas* (traditional dress) and khanjars, and brightly cloaked women crowd around the showing area as goat after goat is paraded through. There is much shouting and yelling as people bid for the goats they want. Brahmin cows are also auctioned here. Goats go for OR25 to OR30 and cows for about OR120. The goat market takes place on Thursday and Friday only, and bidding starts at 8 am and continues to past midday, although it's best to get there early.

the merchants are often not interested in serious bargaining – there will always be another group along later. The result is that Nizwa-made jewellery and khanjars actually cost more here than they do in Muscat and much of what is on display in the souq is often either of poor quality or in poor condition. If you are intending to visit Bahla, 40km west of Nizwa, you will be able to pick up Bedouin silver jewellery at much better prices from the souq there.

The best thing to do is to avoid the silver souq altogether and spend your time wandering among the merchants buying and selling fish, meat, fruit and vegetables or household goods.

Organised Tours

Al-Azri Tours (☎ 412368), in the souq near the entrance to the fort, offers tours of Nizwa and further afield. For OR45 for one vehicle (ie, four people) you can get a tour of the town's fort and souq, and the villages of Tanuf and Bahla. Three- and five-day trips are also offered that will take you as far as Ras al-Jinz on the north-east coast or Sohar in the north-west and all the places of interest in between. They will also design a tour for you depending on where you want to go. You can expect to pay about OR50 per day per vehicle. You will have to pay for petrol on top of this, and if you cover more than 250km a day you will have to pay 70 baisas per km. They will also arrange camping equipment and/or accommodation in hotels or resthouses.

Places to Stay

Nizwa Tourist House (☎/fax 412402) is the cheapest place to stay. Rooms are large and comfortable, if a little sparse, and are the best value in town at OR14. Most rooms can sleep three people, or two adults and two children. It is on the main highway, 3km from the khanjar roundabout towards Muscat. Nizwa's other two hotels will both put a dent in your budget.

Falaj Daris Hotel (☎ 410500, fax 410430) is by far the better deal with singles/doubles for OR21.800/29.500. Decent-sized rooms

surround a small pool and the hotel also has a tiny gym that looks like it's never been used. The hotel is 1km past the Nizwa Tourist House towards Muscat. It's on the left if you are coming from the capital.

Nizwa Hotel (☎ 431616, fax 431619) is about 20km from the centre towards Muscat; rooms are OR37.950/43.700. There are conference and banqueting facilities too but it is a long way out of town and the other hotels are much better value.

Places to Eat

The restaurants and bars at the Falaj Daris and Nizwa hotels are the only places in Nizwa that serve alcohol.

For a quick snack there are plenty of shwarma stands and biryani cafes in town.

Bin Atique (☎ 410466) is the place to go for traditional Omani food in a traditional setting. It is on a side street that runs past the fountain opposite the souq. Look for the sign. They have rice, meat and fish dishes for 750 baisa to OR1. The restaurant is divided into partitions for privacy for families, and the meal is served on mats on the floor.

Arab World Restaurant & Cafeteria on the main street, near the Commercial Bank of Oman has meals for OR1 to OR2. Most of the items on the menu come with lots of side dishes. There is another restaurant with the same name a couple of kilometres outside the centre, on the road to Muscat.

Eat & Drink Restaurant tells it like it is and serves Indian and Chinese meals for 600 baisa to OR1. It's on the main street, the same side as the Arab World, just past the Musandam Exchange.

Getting There & Away

Bus ONTC operates six buses per day between Nizwa and Muscat (OR1.600, 2½ hours express, three hours regular). Express buses leave for Muscat at 7.45 am and 5.45 pm. Regular buses leave at 5.55 and 9.45 am, and at 1.55 and 3.55 pm. All Nizwa to Muscat buses travel via Samail and Fanja and also stop at Seeb airport.

There are three buses per day from Nizwa to Ibri (OR1, around two hours express, 3¼ hours regular). These leave Nizwa at 10.30 am and 5 pm (express) and at 7 pm (regular).

You can catch the southbound bus from Muscat to Salalah at the roundabout on the edge of Nizwa, where the highway from Muscat to Ibri meets the road coming up from Salalah. There is a sign marked 'Express bus stop' near the roundabout. The buses come through here at approximately 9 am and 9 pm every day. The fare from Nizwa to Salalah is OR7.200 one way and tickets can be purchased from the driver. You might want to telephone the Ruwi bus station in Muscat (☎ 708522) to reserve a seat in advance.

Taxi/Microbus Taxi/microbus fares from Nizwa to the Seeb clock tower in Muscat are OR1.500/1.300, to Ruwi add 500 baisa. An engaged taxi to Ruwi is OR15. Microbuses go to Samail for 700 baisa while shared taxis charge OR1.500 for the same trip. Ibri is 1.500 by microbus or OR2 by shared taxi (OR20 engaged). Other microbus destinations include Bahla (500 baisa) and Jabrin (700 baisa). An engaged taxi to Bahla or Jabrin costs OR10.

Car It's worth considering hiring a 4WD as Nizwa is a good starting point for day trips. Mohd bin Abdulla bin Mohd al-Jabri Rent-a-Car (☎ 412367 or mobile 934 9227) is good value compared with the cost of 4WD hire in Muscat but they only have one vehicle. We were given a quote of OR25 per day plus insurance. The office is on the left, 200m from the khanjar roundabout on the road to Muscat.

TANUF

This village, 20km west of Nizwa on the road to Bahla, is home to the spooky **ruins** of the old city. Take the first turn-off signposted to Tanuf if you are coming from Nizwa, the second turn-off if you are coming from Ibri. The road leads straight to the ruins which you will be able to see from the main highway. If you follow a track around behind the ruins you will go down into a wadi and a picnic area with bins and shel-

ters. A falaj runs along the top of the wadi and you will sometimes see people cooling themselves off here. If you have a 4WD you can continue along this track for about 8km, past a dam and on to the village of Al-Far. From here there are hiking trails into the mountains where you'll find a number of pools and waterfalls suitable for swimming.

HOTI CAVE

The Hoti cave system is an underground wadi that stretches for several kilometres through the Hajars. The cave is decorated with stalactites, stalagmites, columns and the occasional bat. Inexperienced cavers will be able to negotiate the drops, tunnels and chambers but will need to have good torches, ropes and, preferably, a hard hat. Plan on taking at least half a day if you want to go into the cave. If you just want to have a look around the entrance, it's only a short diversion off the main road from Nizwa to Bahla.

To get to the cave's most accessible entrance, turn right off the main road before you reach Bahla, 25km from Nizwa, onto the road to Al-Hamra. The turn-off is on the left about 8km from town if you are coming from Bahla. Look for a BP pump. After 4.5km take the turn-off for 'Qal'at al-Masalha'. Stick to the right-hand track at this turn-off. After another 300m make a sharp right. You will notice here a ridge on your left with Jebel Akhdar looming behind it. Follow this track along the wadi for exactly 4.5km. At this point you will see a faint track leading up to the top of a small, rocky hill on your left. If you have a 4WD you can drive to the top. If you have a saloon car, leave it at the bottom and walk up.

From the top of this hill you will see the large, gaping jaw of the cave entrance. You will have to walk from here to the cave. It takes about 30 minutes and you will see tracks leading the way. This walk is a bit too difficult for young children.

Once you get there you will see three holes leading down into the cave. The largest should have a rope attached but you can't be certain it will be there. The drop can be negotiated without a rope but be very careful,

AL-HAMRA

This village, in the foothills of the Hajars, is worth a quick look if you have the time to swing off the Nizwa-Bahla highway. From Al-Hamra you can get up to the plateau on Jebel Shams – see the boxed text 'Jebel Shams' below for more details. Take the same turn-off as for Hoti Cave (see the previous section) but instead of turning right at the sign for 'Qal'at al-Masalha' continue straight for another 10km.

What is interesting here are the huge two- and three-storey **mud-brick houses** built on a steep hill in the old part of town. They have palm-frond roofs and small windows set quite high off the ground, in the Yemeni style. Some of them are still inhabited. The most interesting of these is **Beit al-Safa** which is three storeys high and about 400 years old. The house is now used to store antiques and is not open to the public. It stands on its own, just off the road at the bottom of the hill. Follow the road up through the old quarter, then around to the left and down again. If you keep following this road along the falaj through the village you will come to a dead end.

About 1km from the beginning of town on the left as you head back towards the highway, there is a track that runs next to a garden and towards a wadi. Less than 1km along this track, sitting in the wadi is a rock standing alone, about 20 feet high. This rock is called **Hasat bin Sult** and is covered with engravings that date back to the 3rd millennium BC. The engravings tell the story of a couple who give birth to a deformed child. In a fit of distress and shame they kill the baby by dashing it against the rock. As a punishment for their sin, God froze the couple into the rock for all eternity. If you are having trouble finding it, just ask someone – everyone knows the rock.

BAHLA

Bahla, 40km west of Nizwa, is the **pottery** capital of Oman. Most pottery that you buy in Muscat or other towns in northern Oman will have come from here. The town's souq is about 1km along the road to the right (if you are coming from Nizwa) just past the fort. The souq is partially undercover and has a huge shady tree in the centre, making this one of the most attractive souqs in Oman.

Although you can find some good value antique jewellery, textiles, spices and nuts and, for some reason, an inordinate number of tin trunks, you won't find the pottery. To see the pottery you will need to go past the souq and turn right into the village. The potters are at work deep in the oasis among the palms and the falaj.

Bahla's huge **fort** has been listed by UNESCO as a World Heritage Site. At the time of writing the fort was undergoing extensive restoration work and was closed to the public. Parts of Bahla fort are thought to be

---

Jebel Shams

A spectacular site not to be missed is Oman's 'Grand Canyon' in the Jebel Akhdar range opposite Jebel Shams. From a plateau at a level of 2000m is a sheer drop of nearly 1000m. What a view! A walk along the edge is not for the faint-hearted. You can drive right up to the plateau, but you definitely need a 4WD for the 41km of steep rocky track.

Cheaper, and more fun, is to take a minibus or hitchhike (not easy) to Al-Hamra, 16km off the main road between Nizwa and Bahla. At the end of the paved road, before the village there is a gas station and some houses. My companion asked the attendant how to get up to Jebel Shams and minutes later a local presented himself and offered to drive us up in his huge old Toyota 4WD – for OR20. He was the owner of an adjacent shop and simply closed his business for our trip. Off and up the mountain we went at breathtaking speed giving lifts to an old man and a bee-keeper on the way, taking a break for our driver's prayer and stopping at his home for dates and coffee (the traditional Omani welcome) plus goat's milk with a hefty dose of hot spices.

Reinhard Fey

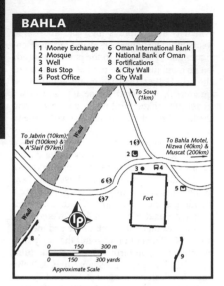

BAHLA

1 Money Exchange
2 Mosque
3 Well
4 Bus Stop
5 Post Office
6 Oman International Bank
7 National Bank of Oman
8 Fortifications
 & City Wall
9 City Wall

To Souq (1km)

To Jabrin (10km);
Ibri (100km) &
A'Slaif (97km)

To Bahla Motel,
Nizwa (40km) &
Muscat (200km)

Fort

0   150   300 m
0   150   300 yards
Approximate Scale

pre-Islamic in origin and when work on it is complete the site should be a major tourist attraction.

Between the road and the fort you can see a well, which is still in use. Behind the fort is a portion of Bahla's city wall. West of the town centre, there are more fortifications guarding the approach to the town across the adjacent wadi.

Places to Stay & Eat

The only hotel in the area is the circular *Bahla Motel* (☎ *420211, fax 420212*), 5.4km east of the centre on the road to Nizwa. They have large and rather run-down singles/doubles for OR15/20. You'll find a couple of Arab-Indian eateries along the main highway, about 200 metres or so towards the centre of town from the hotel. Here you'll be limited to the usual fare of biryani, omelette sandwiches and kima for around 500 baisa.

Getting There & Away

Buses for Bahla leave Muscat daily at 8 am, and 2.30 and 4 pm (3½ hours; OR2). The buses travel via Nizwa, leaving Nizwa for Bahla at 10.30 am, and 5 and 7 pm. The bus fare from Nizwa should be no more than 300 baisa. There is an ONTC office on the corner of the road leading to Bahla's souq.

Microbuses charge 500 baisa for the trip to Bahla from Nizwa. An 'engaged' taxi should cost around OR10.

JABRIN

If you only see one **fort** in Oman, make it this one. Jabrin is just over 50km from Nizwa on the Ibri road and can be visited on a day trip from Muscat, even using public transport (provided you get an early start). If you are stretching the trip out overnight you should plan to stay either in Nizwa or at the Bahla Motel as there is no hotel in Jabrin. As for Jabrin itself there really is no town to speak of – just a large and imposing fort standing on a plain, though there is a housing development nearby. It has been very well restored and decorated and its location commands the entire plain and surrounding hills for quite some distance around. Despite its imposing battlements, the fort was originally built as a palace. Its construction was ordered in 1671 by Imam Bal'arab bin Sultan al-Ya'ruba, who is buried there. The design was only later modified to fortify the building.

Many of the rooms inside the fort are labelled, most of them in English. It is a much more dramatic place than Nizwa and its restored state gives some sense of what it looked like in its prime. Various household items and furnishings are on display throughout the fort.

Entering through the main door brings you into a dramatic, high-walled courtyard through which the falaj containing the fort's water supply used to flow. A door to the right leads to the fort's kitchen area (through which the falaj also flowed) and to several storage rooms. If you go left out of the main courtyard, you'll get to two large, empty rooms that were the servants' quarters. From these a staircase to the left leads up to a prison (complete with manacles still hanging on the wall).

This second level of the fort includes the imam's majlis, or formal public meeting room, and a dining hall. In the majlis there are recesses built into the floor beside the windows to allow the fort's defenders to shoot at attackers from a standing position, and also to duck incoming fire.

The next level brings you to a series of small, open courtyards on the fort's roof around which are some living quarters and a school. These rooms are a peaceful spot to sit for a few minutes and admire the view. Another staircase takes you to the private living quarters of the imam and his family. The painted ceilings here are particularly impressive. Most of the rooms are filled with various sorts of household items as well as a smattering of weapons.

Stairs continue down from this level through more family rooms to the guard's quarters. On a narrow staircase, before you reach the guard's rooms, is another staircase leading to the imam's tomb. From there, a short walk through the fort's gunpowder store and another low passage brings you back to the main entrance.

The fort is open 8 am to 4 pm daily. Admission is free.

Getting There & Away

To reach the fort from Nizwa follow the Ibri road for 45.5km then turn at a sign for Jabrin. After another 4km the pavement ends at a small roundabout. Turn right, go 500m, and you will reach the fort.

Buses between Muscat and Ibri stop at the road junction for Jabrin. The trip from Muscat costs OR2.200 and takes four hours by express bus and five hours on a regular bus. Microbuses from Nizwa charge about 600 baisa, engaged taxis OR10.

A'SLAIF

A few kilometres east of the uninteresting city of Ibri is the very interesting village of A'Slaif. Although the village's residents now live in modern houses, above them looms a fascinating fortified town complete with falaj access shafts in its outer courtyard. The entrance to the main fortified area is through a large gap in the city wall to the right from where the road arrives at the com-

plex. A'Slaif is in a state of semi-ruin and there was no sign of restoration work in progress when we were there. Although you are free to wander through the old town, the area inside the walls is in quite bad shape.

To reach A'Slaif from Nizwa and Muscat turn left off the road to Ibri onto a dirt road at a sign for the village. Follow this dirt track for a few hundred metres and you will come to the old fortified town.

AL-AYN

If you have your own car you shouldn't miss a diversion to this quiet town to see the 3rd millennium BC **beehive tombs**. The 20 tombs are fairly well preserved and make a striking sight on top of a ridge with Jebel Misht rising in the background.

The turn-off for Al-Ayn is approximately halfway between Bahla and Ibri, about 110km from Nizwa. The tombs are 22km from the main road along a graded track, suitable for a saloon car. As the track winds through the village outskirts there are tombs on a small ridge in front and slightly to the left. Turn left onto another small track just before you come to the town centre. The town centre consists of a small mosque and two or three shops. If you follow this track to the left of a cultivated plot and past a black iron gate, you'll get to a wadi from where it's a short walk up the hill to the tombs.

IBRI

Although Ibri is a fairly large provincial city, there really isn't much to it. If you are driving into Oman from the UAE via Buraimi it is the first large Omani town you pass through after clearing customs. Ibri has a bustling souq, and there are shady date palm oases and falajes in the old town.

Ibri's lone hotel, the surprisingly good *Ibri Tourist Hotel* (☎ 491400, fax 491554), charges OR17.600/22 for singles/doubles. It is a few kilometres east of the main intersection on the main road towards Nizwa. Downstairs is the clean and comfortable *Ibri Tourist Restaurant*. Here you can get the standard fare of Arab-Indian restaurants as well as (not so tasty) burgers, fresh juice and French fries for less than OR1. The only other places to eat are a few small restaurants and shwarma stands dotted around town.

The main taxi and microbus stand is opposite the hotel. Taxis can also be found in the town centre, about 2km from the main highway.

There are three buses per day between Muscat and Ibri (OR3.200, 4½ hours express, 5¼ hours regular). Buses leave Ruwi at 8 am and 2.30 pm (express) and 4 pm (regular). From Ibri, buses leave at 5.30 am (express), 7.35 am (regular) and 3.30 pm (express). The main bus stop is at the roundabout in the centre, about 2km from the main road.

Microbuses charge OR2 to Seeb clock tower in Muscat. Shared taxis cost OR3 for the same trip. An engaged taxi to Ruwi costs OR20. A microbus or shared taxi to/from Nizwa should cost OR1.500.

BURAIMI

The long-disputed Buraimi oasis straddles the border between Oman and the emirate of Abu Dhabi in the UAE. The Omani town of Buraimi sits next to the town of Al-Ain in the UAE. The Omani portion of the oasis is effectively in a customs union with Abu Dhabi emirate. Buraimi and Al-Ain are covered in the Abu Dhabi Emirate chapter later in this book.

Approaching the oasis from the Omani side requires you to pass through out-going Omani customs 50km before Buraimi. Once through this checkpoint you can pass freely between the Omani town of Buraimi and the city of Al-Ain, in the UAE. You can also continue up the road to anywhere else in the UAE. Approaching the oasis from the UAE side does not involve a customs check or require any documentation beyond that ordinarily required to enter the UAE.

There are three buses per day between Buraimi and Muscat (4½ hours; OR3.600). Buses leave Muscat every day at 7 am, 1 and 3 pm. Buses from Buraimi to Muscat depart at the same times. Microbuses do not make the trip between Buraimi and Muscat but taxis do, at least in theory, for OR5.

MADHA

This is an enclave of Omani territory separated from the rest of the country by the UAE. This tiny area, which sits within the emirate of Fujairah, consists of a few villages spread out over a small patch of semi-desert. The Madha enclave is completely surrounded by UAE territory and if it were not for a sign on the road saying it's part of Oman you would not know the difference. There are no customs controls, just a sign saying you've crossed the border. However, your UAE car insurance is not valid once you cross into the enclave. Madha is covered in more detail in the UAE East Coast chapter.

North-East Oman

The north-east of Oman has plenty of attractions for the more adventurous traveller, especially if you have a 4WD. This area includes the wadis and mountains of the Eastern Hajars, which are less populated than the Western Hajars, the spectacular Wahiba Sands and Masirah Island, which is just emerging as a tourist destination. The main town in the region, Sur, remains the centre of traditional ship-building in Oman. Fewer tourists visit the north-east than the northwest, and there is not much choice of accommodation apart from government resthouses and camp sites. But if you decide to explore this region you will be rewarded with some fascinating insights into the country.

IBRA

This agricultural town, 175km from Muscat on the road to Sur, marks the western edge of the Sharqiya region which covers most of north-east Oman. Ibra is not particularly attractive, situated as it is on the dull flat plain between the Hajars and the Wahiba Sands. If you are on your way to Sur, it's not really worth getting out of the bus but if you have your own car you could make a pit stop here to explore the ruins of fortified houses and watchtowers in the old quarter. In the late 19th and early 20th centuries, Ibra was a prosperous and strategically important town; it had close trading links with East Africa through the ports of Sur and Al-Ashkarah on the east coast. The ruined houses are those of wealthy merchants.

Ruins

Turn right off the main highway at the BP petrol station. Turn immediately left, then follow the road as it veers around to the right past the white building with two cannons out the front, the office of the *wali* (governor). Now just take any road that heads towards the date plantation in the distance. You will cross a wide wadi and after about 2km you will come to a track that leads into an oasis

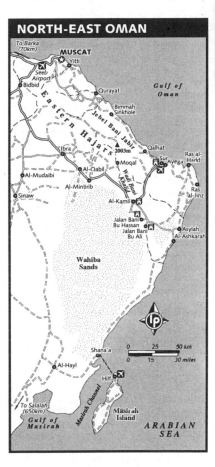

NORTH-EAST OMAN

of date palms, papaya and banana trees and coconut palms. The track veers around to the right at which point you will see the ruins of an old mosque on your left. You can park here and walk through some of the old quarter which is cool and shady.

The next track on the left after the mosque leads to a large fortified house, complete with two tiny cannons positioned defensively at windows near the top. The fort appears to be used as a storage area at present and the doorway is padlocked shut.

Women's Souq

Ibra is also famous for its busy souq that is for women only (buyers and sellers) on Wednesday mornings when a large variety of Omani handicrafts, Dhofari perfumes and frankincense are for sale. Many of the handicrafts are woven products such as camel bags, cushion covers and baskets made by women from the region. The souq is 3.2km from the highway along the road that veers to the right past the wali's office.

Places to Stay & Eat

Ibra Motel (☎ *471666, fax 471777*) is opposite the BP petrol station, just off the main highway. It has clean enough rooms with bathroom for OR10.400. This is the only other place to stay in the region besides the Al-Qabil Resthouse, 15km east of Ibra. Downstairs from the hotel is *Ibra Tourism Restaurant* where you can get the usual fare of omelette sandwiches, kima or biryani for 200 to 500 baisa.

Getting There & Away

The Muscat to Sur bus stops in Ibra three times a day in both directions. The fare is OR1.600 and it takes about 2¼ hours from Muscat.

AL-MINTIRIB

The main reason for travelling to this town, about 220km from Muscat on the road to Sur, is to get a closer look at the magnificent Wahiba Sands – see the boxed text for more details. Mintirib becomes a hive of activity most Fridays when many of the Bedouin visit the town's souq to buy camel feed and other supplies, and to chat.

There is not much choice of accommodation in this region unless you have camping equipment and a 4WD and can camp in the Sands. *Al-Qabil Resthouse* (☎ *481243, fax 481119*), 10km west of Al-Mintirib on the main highway, has good singles/doubles for OR13.100/17.500. There is a restaurant of-

---

Wahiba Sands

As you approach Al-Mintirib you will see in the distance the great orange mountains of sand rising out of the flat plain. The Wahiba Sands are a sea of rolling dunes that reach 200m in height – a true desert in all its romantic glory. The Sands are 200km long and 80km wide and are inhabited by Bedouin tribes who have survived in these harsh conditions for centuries. The Bedouin are nomadic and move from waterhole to waterhole with their camels and a few possessions.

If you have a 4WD you can enter the sands from Al-Mintirib. Continue past the fort and take any track that leads towards the sands. You will pass a few Bedouin dwellings, and children may come running out to greet you. Don't travel more than a couple of kilometres into the sands unless you are familiar with desert driving and are fully prepared. This means having a partner vehicle, food and water supplies and a 4WD kit in case the car breaks down or gets stuck. And always let someone else know where you are going and when to expect you back. There have been a few tragic incidents over the years because people have not followed these simple rules. See Activities in Regional Facts for the Visitor for a few recommended books on desert and off-road driving.

If you don't have a 4WD or you would prefer not to drive in the Sands, you can organise a day or overnight trip to the Wahiba Sands through any of the tour operators mentioned in Organised Tours in the Oman Getting Around chapter.

---

fering simple snacks like sandwiches, shwarma and humous for 600 baisa and basic meals for OR1.200. If you are planning to stay here on a weekend it's a good idea to book ahead.

The Muscat to Sur bus stops in Al-Mintirib three times a day in both directions. The fare is OR1.600 and it takes about 2½ hours from Muscat.

WADI BANI KHALID

If you are travelling to Sur from Muscat and have time for a diversion, this very scenic wadi is well worth the time – but you will need a 4WD. It hides waterholes, waterfalls and a cave at the village of Moqal. The turn-off from the main highway, 15km east of Al-Mintirib, is signposted. Follow the black-top road up the mountain and down the other side to a village. Just before a mosque on your right the road curves around to the left. After about a kilometre this road becomes gravel. (From this point it is 6.3km to the place where you will have to get out of your car and start walking.)

Continue along the gravel track past a new blue and white building with a flag on top. There will be a rock wall on your left and a wadi on your right. After a couple of kilometres the road climbs up and down a very steep hill and you will need to engage low 4WD. It then continues along a wadi floor and curves around some big rocks. You will arrive at a very pebbly part of the wadi bed and at some point soon you won't be able to drive any further. But you can ponder how on earth the saloon cars lining the wadi bed got this far.

From here it's about a 15-minute walk to the **waterhole**. Begin walking along the wadi bed, past a falaj. After a few minutes the creek opens out to a larger expanse of still water, but this is not the place to swim. There is often a lot of activity around here as villagers use this pool to wash clothes and water their donkeys. Continue walking up over some large rocks that rise above the wadi. You will pass a *barasti* (palm-leaf) shelter to the right on top of these large rocks. After a few minutes you will come to a very blue and clear waterhole. It is a welcome sight after the hot walk from the car and the water is beautifully refreshing. Cover up as much as possible if you go swimming; women should keep a T-shirt on and maybe wear a sarong as well.

You can continue walking along this wadi for about another 30 minutes to **Moqal cave**. You'll know you are there when you see concrete steps leading up to a ledge about 12m above the ground. Above here is the cave entrance. If you want to enter the cave, which is 450m long, you'll need hard hats and torches. Sometimes in winter the cave is inaccessible due to flooding.

AL-KAMIL

The small town of Al-Kamil, 60km south-west of Sur, is a good stopping place if you are on the lookout for traditional architecture in its pre-restoration state. There are a number of fascinating buildings in the town centre, including a **fort** with a simple square design and three tapered watchtowers. The only parts of the fort that have been restored are the main gateway on the eastern side and a portion of the north-eastern corner. The (new) lavishly carved door in the east wall is worth a look.

The town is full of other interesting mud-brick buildings. Of note is a large house about 150m east of the fort. The house includes a four-storey tower that lends it an almost Yemeni feel. Tall houses are common in Yemen but, forts aside, are unusual in Oman.

To reach the fort from the main road turn off the Muscat-Sur road at the second Al-Kamil exit if you are coming from Muscat (the first if you are coming from Sur) where the sign says 'Al-Ashkara'. There is also a sign parallel to the road that says 'Sur 60km', as opposed to the one further on that says 'Sur 61km'. From this turn go 650m and turn left onto a track at a pharmacy (which will be on your right). If you reach a roundabout you have gone too far.

The Muscat-Sur buses stop in Al-Kamil about 45 minutes before reaching Sur. The fare between Al-Kamil and the capital is OR2.500.

JALAN BANI BU HASSAN & JALAN BANI BU ALI

Both of these towns, but especially Jalan Bani Bu Hassan, are brimming with ruins of watchtowers, fortified houses, castles and palm plantations. If you are interested in the old architecture of Oman you should definitely take the time to visit these towns.

Jalan Bani Bu Hassan is 17km south-east of Al-Kamil on the road to Al-Ashkarah. Take the second turn-off for the town where there is a BP service station and a brown sign for the **castle**. Turn right after 1.5km. When you get to a watchtower roundabout turn right again and follow the signs to the castle. About 1km past the castle there is a five-storey Yemeni-style house.

Back to the main road, about 7km further along, is Jalan Bani Bu Ali. Here you will see what is probably the most unusual piece of architecture in the country. Tucked away in the old part of town is the **Jami al-Hamoda Mosque** with its 52 domes sitting amid dozens of palm trees. It is a very unusual building. The domes support a forest of pillars and a falaj running through the courtyard is used for ablutions.

To get to the mosque take the first turn-off for the town from the main road and drive to the fort which you will see from quite a distance. Drive behind the fort (which is closed to the public) and onto a wide dirt track between houses. Turn right at the next corner, head straight and you will see the mosque. It's about 300m from the fort.

MASIRAH ISLAND

There are lots of reasons for visiting this island: huge stretches of white sandy beaches, tonnes of marine life, coral reefs, shipwrecks, archaeological sites, old forts, oases and absolute serenity. However, until recently, this remote desert island was not considered a tourist destination, and was home to a small local population of about 8000 and an airforce base. But this notion is gradually changing with the construction of a resthouse in the island's only town, and regular flights each week from Sur with Oman Air.

The island is 80km long and 18km wide and sits about 20km off the east coast of Oman, just south of the Wahiba Sands. Beaches surround the island and the rest of the area is characterised by flat gravel plains and wadis with a central rocky area rising to 274m (Jebel Hamra). Fishing is the main livelihood here and there are a number of fish factories from where the daily catch is

Masirah's Wildlife

Bird-watchers consider Masirah Island a goldmine, with 331 species being recorded here, the highest species diversity of anywhere in Oman. The best time for bird-watching is September to November. If you are interested in knowing more, read *Birds of Masirah* by the Historical Association of Oman, *A New list of the Birds of Masirah Island* by TD Rogers or *Birds of Oman* by Michael Gallagher.

Shell collectors will find unusual and unique shells along the beaches. Books on the subject include *Seashells of Eastern Arabia* by Bosch, Dance, Moolenbeek and Oliver, and *Seashells of Southern Arabia* by Donald & Eloise Bosch, both published by Motivate.

Masirah is also home to the world's largest nesting population of loggerhead turtles. Each year, between June and August, 30,000 of them lay about three million eggs along the island's eastern coastline. As at Ras al-Jinz on the mainland, the turtles here are protected by the Ministry of Regional Municipalities & Environment.

taken to wholesale markets in Muscat and even as far as Dubai in the UAE.

The only town is Hilf, on the northern tip of the island. There are a few fishermen who live along the coast. In winter the population increases as fishermen from the mainland come to Masirah to harvest the waters. In summer when the fishing is poor, the island's population decreases as the Masirans head to the mainland to harvest dates.

Places to Stay & Eat

There is a hotel but the best way to enjoy the island is to camp on the beach and buy fresh fish, lobster or squid for dinner from the fishermen bringing in their daily catch. Ice is available from the fish factories nearby. There is no official camp site and no permit is necessary.

The **Masirah Hotel** (☎ 404 401, 404 035) in Hilf has only six rooms and booking ahead is advisable. At the time of writing there was no restaurant at the hotel, and the few shops in Hilf have limited supplies. You'll be able to get a biryani and the odd omelette sandwich but if you think you're likely to tire of this fare you should bring your own groceries.

Getting There & Away

There are two ways to get to Masirah Island. One is to fly with Oman Air from Sur (OR24 return, 50 minutes) but unless you have arranged to be met by someone with a car on the island, you will literally be stuck in the middle of nowhere. There are no taxis or car rental agencies on the island. The flight does provide some spectacular views as it soars across the Wahiba Sands, however.

The more viable way to get to and around the island is to drive (4WD is essential) and catch the ferry across from Shana'a. The trip takes about 1½ hours and costs OR15 one way. It leaves each day but at what time is anybody's guess. You'll find that it depends on the tides. From Muscat take the blacktop road to Sinaw, then a graded road that runs along the western edge of the Wahiba Sands to Al-Hayl from where you head east to Shana'a. The trip takes about five to six hours and you should take spare petrol and water with you.

RAS AL-JINZ

Ras al-Jinz (Ras al-Junayz) is the easternmost point of the Arabian peninsula. Up to 13,000 turtles come to nest on the beach here annually and the area is under the protection of the Ministry of Regional Municipalities & Environment. To get onto the beach or the camp site here you need a permit from the Directorate-General of Nature Reserves (☎ 602285, fax 602283) at the Ministry of Regional Municipalities & Environment in Muscat (see Other Documents/ Visas & Documents in the Oman Facts for the Visitor chapter). It costs OR1 per person.

The *camping area* is set back from the beach behind large rocks so campers' lights do not disturb the turtles. There are about eight shelters with barbeques and tables and

a toilet block (closed if there are not many campers). There is also a small grocery store at the entrance to the reserve. At night you are not allowed to go onto the beach by yourself. The park ranger will take you there sometime between 10 pm and midnight and show you the turtles.

Loggerhead, green, olive Ridley and hawksbill turtles nest here. Unfortunately the government has not banned fishermen from this beach as their livelihood depends on it. If you see a turtle caught in a fisherman's net, report it to the park ranger. If you see hatchling turtles caught up in nets at night, try to get them out and help them to the sea. If you find baby turtles during the day take them to the park ranger who will ensure they get to the sea in the safety of night.

Getting There & Away

Don't despair if you don't have your own car. Tour companies in Muscat can arrange overnight trips to Ras al-Jinz for small groups. If you have your own vehicle, there are two ways to get to Ras al-Jinz. One is to take the road from Muscat to Sur, then take the turn for Al-Ashkarah at Al-Kamil. There is a signposted turn-off for Ras al-Hadd onto a graded road 40km from Al-Kamil. For the more scenic coast road, continue past this turn-off for another 20km and take the turn for Asylah. Once you get to this sleepy little fishing town the blacktop road ends and a graded road continues north along the coast for 70km to Ras al-Jinz.

If you have a 4WD there is an alternative route via Sur. Take the road to Ayega from Sur. The blacktop road ends shortly after Ayega and a track goes along the coast for about 20km before it heads inland. Stick to the track and you will soon see signs for Ras al-Jinz.

SUR

Sur (Soor) has a lot going for it, starting with a nearly ideal location. It is a fairly quiet place but has several interesting things to see and an attractive coastline. Sur is only 150km down the coast from Muscat as the crow flies, though by road it is a bit over

OMAN

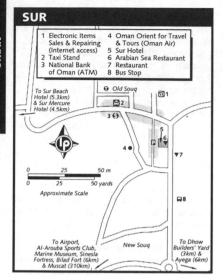

SUR

1 Electronic Items
  Sales & Repairing
  (Internet access)
2 Taxi Stand
3 National Bank
  of Oman (ATM)
4 Oman Orient for Travel
  & Tours (Oman Air)
5 Sur Hotel
6 Arabian Sea Restaurant
7 Restaurant
8 Bus Stop

To Sur Beach
Hotel (5.3km)
& Sur Mercure
Hotel (4.5km)

Old Souq

0   25   50 m
0   25   50 yards
Approximate Scale

To Airport,
Al-Arouba Sports Club,
Marine Museum, Sinesla
Fortress, Bilad Fort (6km)
& Muscat (310km)

New Souq

To Dhow
Builders' Yard
(3km) &
Ayega (6km)

twice that distance. That makes it too far for a day trip but you could combined it with a trip to Ras al-Jinz turtle reserve if you have a 4WD and two days up your sleeve.

History

Sur once played a major role in trade with India and East Africa. It was once a bustling port and the main shipbuilding centre in the country. The Portuguese benefited from Sur's prominence during the 16th century but it was recaptured in the 17th century by the first imam of the Ya'ruba dynasty, Nasser ibn Murshid. Zanzibar's split from Oman in the late 19th century, together with the arrival of the British India Steamer Navigation Company, reduced the demand for Omani-built ships, and Sur's shipping industry declined.

Orientation & Information

Sur's commercial centre, with the taxi stand and bus stop, the cheaper of the town's three hotels, the souq and a few restaurants, is a few kilometres north-east of the government buildings that make up its administrative and historical centre. The souq has

souvenirs, jewellery, *khanjars* (Omani daggers), perfume, incense and fabric shops. The post office is on the roundabout between the Sinesla Fortress and the main mosque. If you arrive from Muscat (or from the airport) you will pass the fortress on your left as you head into both the administrative and the commercial centres. The dhow builders' yard and ferry to Ayega are on the coast beyond the commercial centre as you approach it from Muscat.

Surprisingly, there is an Internet cafe, in the town's centre at a shop imaginatively called 'Electronic Items Sales & Repairing'. Access costs OR2 per hour.

Sinesla Fortress

Sur's main fort is relatively simple in construction: an almost square defensive wall with towers at the four corners on a hill overlooking the town. Look carefully and you will notice that the two watchtowers facing the sea are slightly taller than the two that face inland.

On the right through the main gate you will see a mosque noteworthy for having both indoor and outdoor prayer areas. The small building in the centre of the courtyard was a storeroom, the building to the left of the entrance was a prison. To the extreme left of the entrance you will find a wooden door at ground level – a cistern for water storage. Both of the towers facing the sea are open to visitors. The larger one has cannons. The smaller one was a lookout post and has no gun emplacements.

The fort is open 7.30 am to 6 pm daily. Admission is free.

Bilad Fort

The more impressive of Sur's two forts is just over 6km inland from the town centre on the road headed back toward Muscat. Although there are no explanatory signs the fort is well worth a visit. The fort is about 200 years old and its basic design – lots of open space, little in the way of accommodation – implies that it was constructed as a defensive centre rather than an administrative one.

Like many Omani forts Bilad is built around a single large courtyard, but the overall design of the fort is quite irregular. The two main towers are unlike anything else you will see in Oman, featuring extra high lookout posts above the main portion of the tower. In the courtyard itself the small building next to the well was a mosque. There is a *mihrab* (niche) carved into one of its outer walls, facing the direction of Mecca, providing guidance for the faithful too numerous to fit into the mosque itself. The rooms built into the outer wall of the far right corner from where you enter the fort were the governor's office and quarters.

Bilad Fort is open 7.30 am to 6 pm daily. To get to the fort, take the Muscat road from the centre. After 6km turn right just past a green sign with a white drawing of a fort (in Arabic the sign says 'Bilad Fort – Sur') with an arrow pointing to the right. (The turn-off is not signposted if you approach it from the direction of Muscat.) From the turn-off go 300m and you will see the fort directly in front of you.

Marine Museum

This is not your standard Omani museum. The marine museum is actually a project of the local youth club. It is, however, open to the public and is definitely worth a visit. The highlight of the small exhibit is a collection of photographs of Sur in 1905. These were taken by the French consul in Muscat during a visit to the town and they are a striking contrast with the Sur of today. The museum also has an exhibition on ships and shipbuilding and on life in coastal Oman. Another room contains traditional regional costumes, navigational charts, and photographs of some of the region's ancient sites, most of which can only be reached by 4WD. In the clubhouse adjacent to the museum there's a scale model of Sur and its surroundings.

The museum is inside the Al-Arouba Sports Club and is open from approximately 8 am to noon and 4 to 7 pm daily. Admission is free. The club is across the road from the side of Sinesla through which the fort's compound is entered and about 100m closer to

the centre. Look for a stone wall with sports figures painted on it.

Ayega

Just beyond the dhow yard (see the boxed text) is a small ferry that will carry you across the narrow sound to Ayega, a village where many of the dhow builders live. The two-storey sand-coloured building near the Ayega ferry landing is the house reserved for the sultan whenever he comes to visit. Some rather expensive and luxurious villas were being built here at the time of writing. The ferry crossing is free and takes about two minutes. There's a good beach for swimming a kilometre or so east of Ayega.

Places to Stay

There are only three hotels in Sur and all of them are overpriced.

Sur Hotel (☎ 440090, fax 443798) in the town's centre has noisy rooms for two people at OR17.250 without bath, OR28.250 with bath. The rooms are sparsely furnished but adequate. If you are sharing a bathroom you may want to check on its state before

OMAN

taking a room. Similarly, if you think you may be using the air-conditioner make sure it works.

Sur Beach Hotel (☎ 442031, fax 442228) has expensive singles/doubles for OR39.780/49.140. The hotel is 5.3km north of the centre. To get there turn right at the third roundabout after leaving the centre of town. As you come into Sur from Muscat there are signs for the hotel.

Sur Mercure Hotel (☎ 443777, fax 442626) opened in 1998 and is the most upmarket of the three. Its rooms cost OR42.120/50.310 and they are definitely better value than those at the Sur Beach Hotel. However, it doesn't have the beachfront location. To get there take the same road out of the centre for the Sur Beach Hotel but instead of turning right, continue straight. The hotel is just past the next roundabout.

Places to Eat

If you want alcohol with your meal you will have to go to the Sur Beach or the Mercure. The *Arabian Sea Restaurant (☎ 441474)*, on the ground floor of the same building as the Sur Hotel (the entrance faces the other side of the block), is a good enough place to eat. Most main dishes cost OR1 to OR1.500, though you can also get sandwiches for 200 to 500 baisa.

There's an Indo-Pakistani *restaurant* opposite, with tables out front, which has basic meals and the usual snacks and sandwiches.

Getting There & Away

Air The airport is south of the town centre on the Sur-Muscat road. For flight information ring ☎ 440423. Oman Air has three flights a week between Muscat and Sur on Saturday, Monday and Wednesday. The fare is OR14 single, OR28 return. The flight from Muscat continues on to Masirah Island. The fare from Sur to Masirah Island is OR12 one way, OR24 return.

Oman Air does not have an office in Sur, but tickets can be purchased, and return flights reconfirmed, through Oman Orient for Travel & Tours (☎ 440279), in the town centre.

Bus There are three buses per day between Muscat and Sur. The fare in either direction is OR3.400. Express buses (4¼ hours) leave Sur for Muscat daily at 6 am and 2.30 pm. On Friday and holidays the later bus departs at 4.30 pm. The regular bus (5½ hours) leaves every day at noon. From Muscat express buses leave Ruwi for Sur at 7.30 am and 2.30 pm. The regular bus departs at 4.30 pm.

Taxi Long-distance taxis for Muscat (OR3.500 shared or OR15 engaged to the Seeb clock tower roundabout) tout for passengers in the parking lot around the corner from the Sur Hotel. You will also find microbuses headed in the same direction for OR3 per person.

Southern Oman

The south of Oman is dominated by the province of Dhofar (population 300,000) and its capital Salalah, on the southern coast. Dhofar is the frankincense capital and you will see hundreds of these curly trees if you drive into the mountains. When young or not flowering they are mostly small, gnarled and less than impressive. The Dhofar mountains are very different from the Hajars in the north and make for some good exploring, especially during the monsoon (*khareef*) season from June to September.

There are marked differences between the Omanis of the south and those of the north. These tribal variations can be seen in the way people dress, the way they farm (you actually see cattle down here) and even their appearance. Many Dhofaris share their ancestry with Yemenis, and the region was once under Yemeni control. In ancient times, the people of this region enjoyed the riches of the area's precious yield of frankincense. For centuries Dhofar remained an autonomous state and it wasn't until the late 19th century that it fell under the governance of Muscat, along with the rest of Oman. In 1962, under the Marxist influence of what was then South Yemen, the Dhofar Nationalist Front was formed but the rebellion was soon quashed by the north.

Unless you have a very reliable vehicle and lots of stamina, the best way to get down south is to fly to Salalah from Muscat.

GHABA, GHAFTAIN & QUITBIT

The only reason you are likely to stop at these places is if you are travelling the 1047km to Salalah from Muscat by road and need a place to stay overnight, a bite to eat, petrol or your car fixed. Each town has a resthouse run by the same company that manages the Al-Qabil Resthouse on the road from Muscat to Sur. *Ghaba Resthouse* (*☎/fax 951385*) is 340km from Muscat and has 10 rooms for OR6/10 a single/double. *Ghaftain Resthouse* (*☎/fax 956872*) is

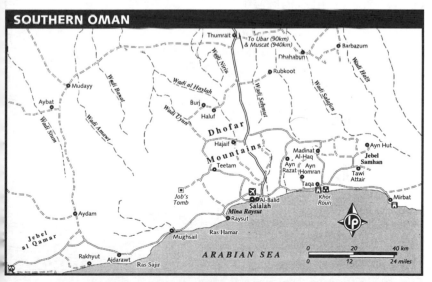

SOUTHERN OMAN

161

640km from Muscat and has rooms for OR10.900/15.300. Rooms cost the same at *Quitbit Resthouse* (☎/fax 951386), 767km from Muscat or 280km from Salalah.

Each resthouse has a restaurant, a towing service and vehicle workshops.

SALALAH

Salalah, Oman's second city, is the capital of the country's southern region and the birthplace of Sultan Qaboos. It's a striking change from Muscat. The southern region catches the monsoon, or khareef, and as a

result is cool, wet, green and misty from mid-June to mid-September just as the rest of Arabia is going through the worst of the summer heat. Salalah becomes extremely busy at this time with GCC tourists who come to enjoy the rain and get away from the extraordinary heat of the summer further north. If you plan to travel here during khareef you should book well in advance – six months in advance is not too early.

Salalah has a small museum but the real attraction of the area is its temperate climate (during the khareef), the striking mountain

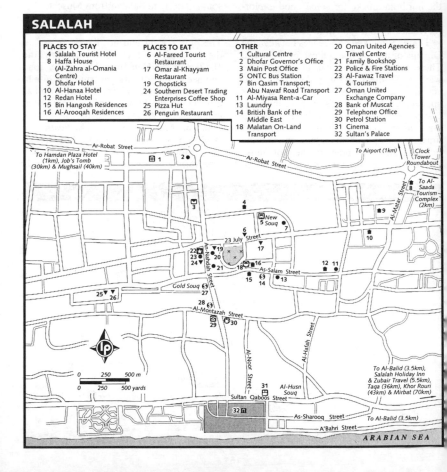

SALALAH

PLACES TO STAY
4 Salalah Tourist Hotel
8 Haffa House
   (Al-Zahra al-Omania
   Centre)
9 Dhofar Hotel
10 Al-Hanaa Hotel
12 Redan Hotel
15 Bin Hangosh Residences
16 Al-Arooqah Residences

PLACES TO EAT
6 Al-Fareed Tourist
   Restaurant
17 Omar al-Khayyam
   Restaurant
19 Chopsticks
24 Southern Desert Trading
   Enterprises Coffee Shop
25 Pizza Hut
26 Penguin Restaurant

OTHER
1 Cultural Centre
2 Dhofar Governor's Office
3 Main Post Office
5 ONTC Bus Station
7 Bin Qasim Transport;
   Abu Nawaf Road Transport
11 Al-Miyasa Rent-a-Car
13 Laundry
14 British Bank of the
   Middle East
18 Malatan On-Land
   Transport

20 Oman United Agencies
   Travel Centre
21 Family Bookshop
22 Police & Fire Stations
23 Al-Fawaz Travel
   & Tourism
27 Oman United
   Exchange Company
28 Bank of Muscat
29 Telephone Office
30 Petrol Station
31 Cinema
32 Sultan's Palace

Exploring Thesiger

The last of the region's great explorers, Sir Wilfred Thesiger made countless journeys through Arabia, North Africa, Iraq, Afghanistan, Kurdistan and Pakistan in the 1940s and '50s. He estimates that he has walked over 100,000 miles.

The most amazing journey of all, though, was his epic 1000km crossing of the Empty Quarter, Rub al-Khali, one of the harshest, driest and hottest spots on the planet. This lonely sea of dunes stretches from southern UAE to eastern Saudi Arabia and across to Oman. Thesiger and his four Bedouin companions from the Beit Kathir tribe of southern Oman travelled with a team of camels.

In his book, *Arabian Sands*, Thesiger writes of this legendary crossing of the Empty Quarter. He talks of the hardship and danger and the complete solitude that the desert imposes on any living creature that dares to be there. He had to rely heavily on the companionship of the Beit Kathir, so that the stark emptiness of the desert would not destroy him.

Although others have made this crossing since, vehicles were used instead of camels. It wasn't until early 1999 that three Canadian explorers successfully retraced Thesiger's steps and completed the crossing by camel from Salalah in southern Oman to Abu Dhabi in the UAE. They, too, were accompanied by the Beit Kathir and felt the utter loneliness and emptiness described by Thesiger.

scenery just after the monsoon and the beautiful beaches of white sand which stretch along the coast. It is also a good base for exploring the villages and archaeological sites of Oman's southern region.

Orientation

Salalah's centre is at the intersection of An-Nahdah and As-Salam Sts. The bus station and a number of hotels and restaurants are a 10- to 15-minute walk from this intersection. The gold souq is right around the corner. Most of the city's businesses are either along, or just off, one of these streets.

You can pick up a free map of Salalah at the Redan Hotel on As-Salam St. The Salalah Holiday Inn has a free map of the Dhofar region, available at the front desk (useful if you plan to do any touring of the area by car).

Information

Money There are several banks and a few exchange houses around the intersection of An-Nahdah and As-Salam Sts. The Oman United Exchange Company has been known to bargain a bit over the rate. As always in Oman, travellers cheques draw a less favourable rate than cash, although the difference is unlikely to work out to much more than 500 baisa or so per US$100. The British Bank of the Middle East's branch on As-Salam St has an ATM linked into the Global Access cash machine network.

If you arrive by bus and need cash immediately there is a branch of the Commercial Bank of Oman on 23 July St just south of the new souq.

AmEx is represented by Zubair Travel (☎ 235581 or 235582) in the lobby of the Salalah Holiday Inn. They cannot cash cheques for AmEx clients but they will hold mail. Mail should be addressed to: American Express – Client's Mail, c/o Zubair Travel – Salalah Branch Office, PO Box 809, Salalah, Postal Code 211, Oman. Their office is open 8 am to 1 pm and 4 to 6.30 pm Saturday to Thursday.

Post & Communications The main post office is on An-Nahdah St, next to the telephone company's administrative centre (the place with the big antenna), although you have to enter the building from the back. It is open 7.30 am to 1.30 pm Saturday to Wednesday and 9 to 11 am Thursday. It is closed on Friday.

The telephone office is at the intersection of An-Nahdah and Al-Montazah Sts. It's open 7.30 am to 11.30 pm daily. Fax and telex facilities are also available but these close down around 9 pm.

Bookshops Although the pickings are small, the best places to find foreign-language books, newspapers or magazines are the bookstalls at the Salalah Holiday Inn or at the Family Bookshop on An-Nahdah St near the intersection with As-Salam St.

Laundry A small shop on As-Salam St, about 500m east of the Redan Hotel, with only the word 'Laundry' in large letters on the sign offers in-today, out-tomorrow washing for most clothes for around 100 baisa per item. It is open 7.30 am to 1 pm and 3.30 to 11 pm daily. Another small laundry (similar prices) can be found further down As-Salam St across from the Redan Hotel.

Medical Services In an emergency, you could go to the Sultan Qaboos Hospital (☎ 211151). Four- and five-star hotels should be able to recommend a local doctor.

Museum

Salalah's museum (☎ 294549) is in the Cultural Centre on Ar-Robat St (access is from the back, via An-Nahdah St). There is no English lettering on the building, but it is the huge white building, west of the intersection of Ar-Robat and An-Nahdah Sts. The museum is on the left inside the entrance; the doors on the right lead to a theatre.

In the lobby there is an exhibition of Wilfred Thesiger's photographs of Salalah and other parts of Arabia in the 1940s and '50s. Most of the photos are from his book *Arabian Sands* (see the boxed text on the previous page). Immediately to the left, as you enter the main part of the museum from the lobby, are stones with inscriptions in the ancient script known as South Arabian. This exhibit blends into a display of the geology of the area, weapons and locally made pottery. The centre of the museum displays models of half a dozen different types of sailing ships and several display cases containing Omani jewellery. There is a very interesting display of 11th and 12th century Chinese coins found at Al-Balid, near Salalah. The same room also has displays of traditional wooden chests and scale models

of a Bedouin tent and a reed house similar to those once used by coastal dwellers. In the rooms on the right are displays of traditional clothing and basketry. There are also exhibits of shells and coral as well as whale bones found at Mirbat, east of Salalah.

The displays are labelled in both English and Arabic though the English explanations are much shorter.

The museum is open 8 am to 2 pm Saturday to Wednesday. Admission is free.

New Souq

There is nothing particularly special about this souq except that it is a good place to buy fruit and vegetable supplies if you are self-catering, and it's a lively place to wander round. Meat, fish, fruit, vegetables and, occasionally, livestock are on sale. Mixed in among these are a handful of stalls selling kohl boxes, pottery and other locally made handicrafts. The souq is also the home of the bus station and a few modern shops, most of which sell textiles.

Al-Husn Souq

This is the place to buy your genuine Dhofari frankincense. On Ash-Sharooq St, behind all the textile and shoe shops, you will find stalls selling all kinds of incenses and perfumes, as

---

Scents of Oman

When you pass an Omani woman (or man) on the street you will probably be overwhelmed by the intense perfume that wafts all around her. Arabic perfumes *(attar)* are very strong and spicy, unlike Western perfumes which tend to be flowery and light by comparison. Perfumes are still concocted in small workshops in larger towns and cities throughout Oman (and the UAE).

Incense is traditionally used to perfume a room. Men and women also traditionally use incense to keep their clothes smelling nice. Women place the incense burner on the ground in front of them then lift their many layers of clothes over the top, somehow managing not to catch fire.

well as ceramic, wooden and electric incense burners. Your sense of smell will be blitzed after you've sampled all the incenses and been daubed by a dozen or so perfumes.

There are also a number of silver shops selling beautifully made *khanjars* (Omani daggers), swords and jewellery. There are lots of Omani *halwa* (sweet) shops on the corner of Al-Hafah and Sultan Qaboos Sts. This is really good stuff and you are likely to become addicted.

Al-Balid
The ruins of Al-Balid, site of the ancient city of Zafar, lie about 4.5km east of the city centre on the coast, just west of the Salalah Holiday Inn. Zafar's heyday was in the 11th and 12th centuries AD when it was an active trading port. Coins from as far away as China have been found at the site (on display in Salalah's museum). The site is fenced in , and you need a permit to enter or to be taken with a guide. Even with this caution, parts of the site have been vandalised.

There is not much to see. The site is heavily overgrown and is likely to impress only serious students of archaeology. Near the mound that dominates the site are the remains of a large mosque.

To reach the site head east along Sultan Qaboos St from An-Nahdah St. It is on the right side (sea side) of the road about 4.5km from the centre.

Diving & Snorkelling
The Samharam Dive & Watersports Centre (☎ 235333) at the Salalah Holiday Inn is on the expensive side, but it's the only choice you have. One dive costs OR25.500 plus OR4 for wetsuit hire. A snorkelling trip is OR9 and a half-day boat trip to Ras Hamar (also called Donkeys Head) west of Salalah costs OR12 per person (with lunch).

Organised Tours
The prices listed in this section are per vehicle, ie, up to four people. Zubair Travel (☎ 235581 or 235582), in the lobby of the Salalah Holiday Inn, has a three-hour city tour for OR23. They also offer a half-day

tour to Job's Tomb and Mughsail blowholes for OR36. For the same price a tour goes east to Taqa and Mirbat. Al-Fawaz Travel & Tourism (☎ 294324, fax 294265) on An-Nahdah St offers the same half-day tours for OR40. They also have a tour to the 'Lost City of Ubar', 175km from Salalah, then to the edge of the great Empty Quarter and back for OR120 with lunch. Al-Miyasa Rent-a-Car (☎/fax 296521), on As-Salam St next door to the Redan Hotel, offers three different, slightly cheaper day tours.

Places to Stay – Budget
Salalah's cheapest (and shabbiest) rooms are at two small hotels on As-Salam St.

Al-Arooqah Residences (☎ 294538), the cheaper of the two, offers rooms with one bed for OR8; two beds for OR12, three beds for OR15 and four beds for OR18. Most rooms have private baths. The hotel is on an upper floor of the building beside which the Al-Ghafri buses to/from Muscat stop.

Bin Hangosh Residences (☎ 298079) across the street is a bit pricier at OR12 for a room for two people. Look for a 'Residences for Rent' sign on the left-hand side of the building. These two places are both very grotty and, unless you are on a very tight budget, you'll get much more value for money staying at one of the other budget hotels. Women travelling on their own should probably avoid this place and the Al Arooqah Residences.

The *Al-Hanaa Hotel (☎ 298305, fax 291894, 23 July St)*, near the corner of Al-Matar St, is very good value for money with bright, clean singles/doubles for OR10/15. These prices include tax and breakfast.

Salalah Tourist Hotel (☎ 295332, fax 295626), opposite the ONTC bus stop just north of 23 July St, is equally good value for money with large, comfortable rooms and friendly staff for OR10/15, also including tax and breakfast.

Places to Stay – Mid-Range
The following hotels all have restaurants serving breakfast, lunch and dinner for reasonable prices.

Redan Hotel (☎ 292266, fax 292255) on As-Salam St in the centre is the cheapest in this range. Singles/doubles are OR14/17. The location is good and the rooms are large and clean.

Dhofar Hotel (☎ 290484 or 292300, fax 294358) on Al-Matar St is more upmarket with rooms for OR18.720/23.400.

Haffa House (☎ 295444, fax 294873), in the Al-Zahra al-Omania Centre at the clock tower roundabout on the corner of Al-Matar and Ar-Robat Sts, charges OR19.800/22. The rooms are large and comfortable and there is a pool.

Places to Stay – Top End

Hamdan Plaza Hotel (☎ 211025, fax 211187), on the main road leading west out of the city, is a huge five-star place with very large rooms for OR32.200/40.250. At the time of writing they were constructing a new pool and health club. The hotel has a restaurant and coffee shop but no alcohol is served.

Salalah Holiday Inn (☎ 235333, fax 235137) on the coast, about 5.5km east of the centre, charges OR38.610/ 48.555. It has a pool, private beach, health club and two bars and an expensive seafood restaurant. This place is the hang-out for Western expats in Salalah.

The *Salalah Hilton* (☎ 211235, fax 210084, Ar-Robat St), about 4km west of the Hamdan Plaza Hotel, has recently opened. Rooms are OR39/51.

Al-Saada Tourism Complex (☎ 225250, fax 225251) has been designed with large families from the GCC in mind. The complex has its own cafeteria, children's playground, park and security guard. Three/four bedroom villas cost OR33/44. It's about 3.5km from the centre. To get there head east along Ar-Robat St from Haffa House. At the next roundabout turn left. There will be a sign for the complex on your right.

Places to Eat

At the bottom of the price scale you would be hard-pressed to do better than the *Southern Desert Trading Enterprises Coffee Shop* on An-Nahdah St. They have very good samosas for only 50 baisa apiece and also offer cheap sandwiches and other quick snacks. There is a *Pizza Hut* (☎ 297373) on As-Salam St, west of An-Nahdah St with the usual offerings. Nearby on the same street is *Penguin Restaurant* (☎ 225380) but the burgers here are pretty awful. There are also lots of Indian cafes along As-Salam St offering the usual fare.

Chopsticks (☎ 291400) Chinese restaurant has only passable food and the service is awful but at least it offers an affordable change from cheap Indian food and shwarma. Main dishes cost OR1 to OR2.

A better bet for Chinese and Indian food is *Omar al-Khayyam Restaurant* (☎ 293004, 23 July St). Entrees are about OR1 and mains OR1.500 to OR2. This is a popular place and is usually pretty full in the evenings.

Al-Fareed Tourist Restaurant, across the road from Omar al-Khayyam on 23 July St, has similar meals for roughly the same price. They also have buffet dinners most evenings with a mixture of Lebanese and Indian food.

For anything much fancier you'll probably have to head for the Salalah Holiday Inn which has a couple of restaurants serving the basic hotel menu of European dishes (steaks, sandwiches, pasta, omelettes etc) and Middle Eastern (usually Lebanese) food.

Lou Lou'A (☎ 211025) restaurant at the Hamdan Plaza Hotel has basic Western meals. The view over Salalah is great but the food is expensive.

Entertainment

What social life there is in Salalah centres on the Salalah Holiday Inn. For the latest information get a copy of *Oman Today* or just stop by the hotel when you are in town. Outsiders can join the hotel's health club on a monthly basis for OR30. Use of the pool for the day costs OR3 for nonguests. The hotel also has a nightclub with live entertainment, usually a lounge band and a belly dancer, and a disco at weekends.

There is a cinema next to Al-Husn Souq on Sultan Qaboos St that mostly shows Hindi movies, plus the occasional English film.

Shopping

As Dhofar is the frankincense capital of the world, Salalah is the place to buy the stuff. You can get gift packs of frankincense, ceramic burner and charcoal for OR1.500. Pottery incense burners cost OR1.500 to OR10 depending on the size. The OR10 ones would make excellent doorstops.

Among Dhofar's most distinctive souvenirs are the small, bead-covered plastic bottles used by women to carry kohl for decorating their eyes. These are a far cry from the silver kohl boxes used by both men and women in the northern part of the country, and also a lot more affordable. They can be purchased in the souqs for OR3 to OR5.

If you are looking for khanjars, the best place to go is Ash-Sharooq St behind the Al-Husn souq. The large khanjars here are beautifully crafted but they are expensive at OR100 to OR250. They are not antiques but they are beautifully made. In the city centre, several shops in the gold souq also have khanjars as well as a limited selection of old silver jewellery.

Getting There & Away

Air Salalah's small airport is served only by Oman Air (☎ 295747). Their office is on the 1st floor of the Haffa House building by the clock tower roundabout. There are two flights per day to Muscat The fare is OR27 one way and OR50 return.

Bus Buses to Muscat leave from the ONTC office (☎ 292733) in the new souq. The fare is OR8/16 one way/return, and buses leave from Salalah at 6 am and 7 pm every day. You can store luggage in the ONTC ticket office at the new souq.

Al-Ghafri & Sons (☎ 293574) also run buses to Muscat every day at 7 am and 4.45 pm. Departures are from the office (which is actually called Malatan On-Land Transport) just off As-Salam St. Bin Qasim Transport and Abu Nawaf Road Transport have offices near ONTC in the new souq.

Taxi & Microbus Salalah's taxis and microbuses hang out in front of the British Bank of the Middle East on As-Salam St in the centre. Taxis will generally only make intercity trips on an engaged basis (ie, not shared), which is invariably expensive (OR10 to Taqa, for example). Microbus destinations and fares from Salalah include Taqa (300 baisa), Mirbat (500 baisa), Mughsail (OR1), Thumrait (OR1) and Muscat (OR8).

Getting Around

To/From the Airport There are no buses to/from Salalah airport. The taxi fare between Salalah airport and anywhere in town is OR2.500. This price appears to be fixed and is the same whether you're going to the Salalah Holiday Inn about 6km away or Haffa House only 1km down the road from the airport.

Taxi & Microbus Local taxis and microbuses congregate on As-Salam St, with the long-distance taxis, although you don't see as many taxis and microbuses in Salalah as you do in other parts of the country. Generally, a microbus ride inside the city costs around 200 baisa and a taxi ride about 500 baisa. To go further (for example, to the Salalah Holiday Inn), OR1.500 should be sufficient.

Car Rental If you want to rent a car try Al-Miyasa Rent-a-Car (☎ 296521) on As-Salam St next door to the Redan Hotel. They offer small cars for OR14, including insurance and 200 free km per day. Additional kilometres are 50 baisa each, but you can probably bargain a couple of riyals off the daily rate, even if you only need the car for a day or two.

As for the larger agencies, Budget (☎ 235160) has a desk at the Salalah Holiday Inn, there is an Avis office at Zubair Travel (☎ 235581, also in the Salalah Holiday Inn) and Thrifty has an office in the Haffa House building. The rates at all of the larger agencies are the same as in Muscat. Thrifty and Budget also have offices at the airport but these seem to be hardly ever staffed.

OMAN

AROUND SALALAH

There are very good **beaches** all along the road to Mughsail once you're about 5km out of Salalah. The road runs along the beach and all the beaches are open to the public (but women travellers should remember to cover up). The water is generally calm but the wind can sometimes kick up a lot of sand. Overnight camping on the beach is not allowed. If you do not have a car and decide, for some reason, to forgo microbuses, you should not have too much trouble hitching rides, though they are often for only a few kilometres at a time. It's too hot and humid to cycle most of the time, and there is nowhere to hire a bike.

If you plan to drive through the **Dhofar mountains** during the khareef, take care. The low-lying mist that covers the entire region at this time of year means that you can't see more than a metre or so in front of you. There are a large number of accidents on the mountain roads due to people not understanding how to drive in these conditions.

During the khareef and in winter you'll see camps set up by the Jabalis, the 'mountain people' of Dhofar, in the foothills and plains. They come down from the upper reaches of the mountains with their animals and settle in tents or temporary shacks for the season.

JOB'S TOMB

In religious terms the mortuary known as Job's Tomb (and referred to in Arabic simply as Nabi Ayoub – Prophet Job) is probably the most important site in Dhofar. Regardless of your religious convictions, the tomb – situated on an isolated hilltop overlooking Salalah – is a must-see both for the beautiful drive up to its mountain site and for the excellent view over Salalah that the parking lot affords on a clear day.

The tomb is open more or less around the clock and admission is free. When you enter the enclosure a footpath from the gate goes past a mosque and through some trees to a small white building with a gold-coloured dome. This is the tomb. The tomb is open to everyone but mosque decorum must be

The Jabali

The 'mountain people' of Dhofar have lived in a world that, until recently, has remained largely isolated from the encroaching modernity of the rest of Oman. For generations they have inhabited the hills, caves and wadis of the Dhofar mountains, tending cattle and conforming to the tribal traditions that dictate their way of life.

Oman owes much to these mountain people who played an important role in the country's recent history. Due to their knowledge of the harsh mountain terrain and their ingrained ruggedness, the Jabali were recruited by the British SAS in the 1970s, at the request of Sultan Qaboos, to help fight the Marxist rebels who had risen up against the government in Dhofar.

The Jabali are gradually succumbing to the amenities that have found their way to the most remote parts of Oman. Most Jabali homes are now built from modern materials – concrete slabs and corrugated iron. It is unlikely you will find many of the original circular houses made from chunks of stone and wood. Jobs in nearby Salalah threaten to steal younger generations from their agricultural way of life. The tribal bedrock of these mountain clans is gradually being hacked away.

observed: shoes must be removed and women are expected to cover up. The guard will hand women a piece of material to cover their heads. Inside you will find a single, remarkably long grave set into the floor and covered in ornate shrouds embroidered with verses from the Quran.

Near the parking lot the *Prophet Ayoub Region Restaurant* offers scenery and food (in high season – just tea, coffee and soft drinks the rest of the time) from its spot on the hillside overlooking Salalah and the Arabian Sea.

The tomb is just over 30km from Salalah's centre. To reach it, take the main road, Ar-Robat St, west from the centre towards Mughsail and turn right at the sign for Ittin, just after the Hamdan Plaza Hotel. Follow this road for 22km and then turn left off the main road at a sign that says 'Al-Nabi Ayoub 1½km'. After 1.4km you will come to a fork in the road. Keeping right takes you to the restaurant, going left takes you to the parking lot outside the tomb enclosure. There is no public transport to or from the tomb.

MUGHSAIL

Mughsail (Mugsail), 45km west of Salalah, offers beautiful unspoilt beaches as well as some spectacular scenery, including several **frankincense** groves, on the drive out. Mughsail itself is a fishing community and you can often see the fishing boats pulled up on the shore while camels wander about on the beach. There are barasti shelters along the **beach**, which is popular with local families at the weekends.

There are some **blowholes** near the beach that spray sea froth high into the air. To get to these continue past the town for about 1km and take the turn-off for 'Kah'fal Marnaif'. Drive past the Al-Mughsail Beach Tourist Resthouse to a parking area at the bottom of some stairs. Follow the path around a bluff and you will come to the blowholes.

If you continue beyond Mughsail on the road towards the Yemeni border the landscape is even more spectacular as the road zigzags up and down the mountains.

Al-Mughsail Beach Tourist Resthouse (☎ 290641 or 298805), run by Dhofar Tourism, has one bedroom cabins on the beach for OR20. It had just opened at the time of writing but was already very popular with Omani and Emirati families on holiday, as well as camels who wander in from time to time. There's a roof-top restaurant and coffeehouse which has basic meals (and sheesha). This is a good place to spend an evening or to watch for dolphins during the day.

Microbuses charge OR1 in either direction between Salalah and Mughsail.

THUMRAIT

There is not much to the town of Thumrait, 80km inland from Salalah on the road to

---

Ubar

In early 1992 a group of US explorers announced that they had found the remains of Ubar, one of the great lost cities of Arabia. According to legend Ubar was a sort of Arabian cross between Atlantis, and Sodom and Gomorrah. Scholars are fairly certain that the place *did* exist, that it came to control the frankincense trade, and that, as a result, it grew incredibly wealthy. That is about all that is known for sure. The Quran says that God destroyed Ubar, causing it to sink beneath the sands, because the people were decadent and had turned away from religion.

Predictably some scholars have disputed the expedition's claim to have found Ubar. At the time of writing, excavations at the site were proceeding slowly and little had been turned up that was anywhere near old enough to date from Ubar's golden age. For an adventurous and romantic discussion of the lost city read *The Road to Ubar: Finding the Atlantis of the Sands* by Nicholas Clapp.

Reaching the site at the village of Shasrar requires a 4WD. Take the main highway north from Salalah to Thumrait. Slightly more than 10km beyond Thumrait turn left at a sign saying 'Shasrar 72km'. When you enter the village the site is to your right and the wali's office to your left. Go to the wali's office if the site is locked up. It might also be a good idea to stop by the Salalah museum before making the trip – the site is more likely to be open if the people at the museum let the people in Shasrar know you are coming.

Be warned: although archaeologists are very excited about Ubar the site has a reputation with tourists for being something of a disappointment. If you do not have a 4WD, you can do a day tour to Ubar – see Organised Tours in the Salalah section.

Muscat, but the contrasts in scenery make it worth the drive if you have the time and a car. The first half of the drive is spent climbing to and through the mountain plateau overlooking Salalah. The second half of the route takes you along the plateau itself and finally into the desert area beyond it. The plateau is strikingly green in the late summer and early autumn, just after the monsoon season, but rapidly reverts to desert once the rains are over. Microbuses charge OR1 for the trip from Salalah.

AYN RAZAT

This spring, approximately 25km north-east of Salalah, makes a pleasant stop for half an hour or so if you are making a tour of the sites east of Salalah. There is a well-kept **park** beyond which is the **stream**, deep enough in parts for a dip. There are also caves in the small mountain overlooking the park that you can clamber around.

To reach Ayn Razat head east out of Salalah towards Taqa and follow the signs to the spring. From the turn-off it is 7km to the park entrance.

TAQA

The village of Taqa, 36km east of Salalah, is worth a stop. There is a fort and, nearby, a cemetery where you can see the grave of Sultan Qaboos' mother, Maizoun bint Ahmed al-M'ashti, who died in August 1992.

The **fort** is easy to find – just follow the brown-and-white signs once you enter Taqa. Once inside you will find a cramped courtyard surrounded by rooms. Most of the rooms have signs in English indicating what they were once used for. The castle itself was used as the office of the local *wali* (governor) until 1984. The fort is open 7.30 am to 2.30 pm Saturday to Wednesday. Admission is free.

Between the castle and the road is the **Mosque of Shaikh al-Afif**. The graveyard is in front of the mosque. Stand facing the mosque and the graveyard and look all the way to your left. At the left-hand corner of the graveyard nearest the road you will see several particularly ornate graves each marked by two stones. Among these is a single grave with three stones – this is the **grave of Sultan Qaboos' mother**. Immediately to

the right of it is the grave of her brother. The next grave to the right is her father, the sultan's grandfather.

There is also a deserted house on top of a hill overlooking the castle. A climb to the top gives you a great view of the town.

Microbuses pick up and drop their charges on the town's main road a few hundred metres west of the turn for the castle. The fare from Salalah to Taqa is 300 baisa. Taxis will only make the trip from Salalah engaged (around OR10).

KHOR ROURI

The *khor* (inlet) itself is under the protection of the Directorate-General of Nature Reserves as it is home to many bird and plant species. Centuries ago Khor Rouri was an important port at the southern end of the frankincense route. It was then known as Sumhuram. From this small bay, boats and rafts took the frankincense to Qana, 640km down the coast in what is today Yemen, on the first stage of its journey to the bazaars of Damascus and the temples of Rome. Today, little remains of the city except the ruins of a palace-cum-fort which looks like rather nondescript rubble sitting atop a mound. The setting, however, is dramatic enough to make the site worth going out of your way for. The calm here is almost unearthly, but it's somehow easy to imagine a time 18 or 20 centuries ago when this quiet bay was one of the most important ports on earth.

The site is completely fenced in and trespassing is not allowed. If you want to get inside the fence and walk among the ruins you must go with a guide which means taking a tour with one of the companies in Salalah. The site is in slightly better condition than Al-Balid and individual rooms among the ruins are easier to make out, though it would take an archaeologist to find out what any given room was used for.

To reach the site take the road from Salalah towards Mirbat and turn at the Khor Rouri sign, about 7km beyond Taqa's centre. There is another turn-off further down the road, but the first turn (coming from Salalah) is the easier of the two to navigate. The site is 2.5km off the main road along a bumpy dirt track.

The microbus fare from Salalah should be 300 to 400 baisa, but you will have to walk from the main road.

TAWI ATTAIR

Tawi Attair is a sinkhole, about 100m wide and 200m deep, on the high plateau of Jebel Samhan. A cave system can be accessed from the sinkhole but only by experienced cavers. If you have your own car it's worth the drive both for the sinkhole and the striking views over the surrounding countryside, especially during the green months of the late summer.

It is 41km by road east of Salalah. To reach it, turn at the sign just west of Khor Rouri saying 'Tawi Attair 18km' and follow the blacktop road until you get to a junction just before a large police station. Take the turning to the left, marked 'Kisais Adeen'. Follow the blacktop road for 400m, when it becomes a gravel road. Continue on the gravel road for 400m and turn right onto a small track (opposite a yellow house). Continue on this track, past a water trough, to a group of sheds at the end of the track. From

here you have to continue on foot. The sinkhole is about 50m further along on your right. You can't miss it – it's enormous.

MIRBAT

The town of Mirbat (Mirbaat), just over 70km east of Salalah, is about as far east of Salalah as you can go without a 4WD. The town's small fort has a lonely, end-of-the-road feel about it as it overlooks both the town and the coastline trailing off back towards Salalah. Brown-and-white signs in English will point you towards the **fort** as you enter town. Note that it is not the first fort you will see. The one visible from a great distance as you approach Mirbat is a police fort that is still in use.

Mirbat's other noteworthy site is the **Bin Ali Tomb**, a small, photogenic mosque built in a style typical of Yemen's Hadhramawt region. The tomb is 1km off the main road. It is the larger of the two white tombs in the cemetery – the one closer to the parking area. You will see the tomb off to the right as you approach Mirbat from Salalah. There are also some good **beaches** about 6km west of Mirbat. Look for the picnic shelters.

Microbuses from Salalah charge 500 baisa for the trip.

Musandam Peninsula

Separated from the rest of Oman by the eastern part of the UAE, and guarding the southern side of the strategically important Strait of Hormuz, the entire Musandam peninsula was once a military zone and was largely off limits to tourists. Though the military is still a major presence throughout Musandam, the area is now open to visitors, and it is one of the highlights of the country. Musandam is a land of stark beauty. It is the least developed part of the Gulf's least developed country; an area of fjords, small villages and dramatic, mountain-hugging roads. Musandam remains one of Arabia's least accessible areas, but also one of its most memorable.

Public transport around Khasab exists more in theory than in practice and some of the region's settlements are accessible only

MUSANDAM PENINSULA

by boat. It is also very expensive, even by Omani standards. The good news is that the widely held belief that you cannot move about outside Khasab without a 4WD is not true. Most of the places covered in this chapter can be visited using a saloon car.

Apart from the road from Tibat, there are no blacktop roads around Musandam except in the town centres of Khasab, Bukha and the Omani portion of Dibba.

KHASAB

Musandam's capital is small but far from sleepy. The port bustles with activity, much

Getting In ... and Out

Musandam is much more accessible to tourists than it used to be. However, getting there and away still requires a certain amount of advance planning.

Khasab is accessible by road from the rest of Oman and from the UAE. However, bear in mind that getting here by road from the rest of Oman means passing through the UAE and re-entering Oman. Hopefully the new cross-border accord between Oman and the UAE will make this easier for travellers on a tourist visa, otherwise flying from Muscat is your best – and cheapest – option.

If you decide to drive to Musandam, note that foreign residents of Oman need a road permit to leave and re-enter Oman by land (tourist visa holders do not need road permits). A departure tax of Dh20 is payable on leaving the UAE by road.

If you are taking a hire car from Muscat, remember you will need to get permission from Muscat's car rental agencies to drive in the UAE. However, this is likely to send the cost of both the rental and the insurance through the ceiling.

See Getting There & Away in the Khasab section later in this chapter for more details on the various transport options.

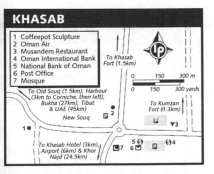

KHASAB

1 Coffeepot Sculpture
2 Oman Air
3 Musandem Restaurant
4 Oman International Bank
5 National Bank of Oman
6 Post Office
7 Mosque

To Khasab
Fort (1.5km)

0   150   300 m
0   150   300 yards

To Old Souq (1.5km), Harbour
(3km to Corniche, then left),
Bukha (27km), Tibat
& UAE (45km)

To Kumzan
Fort (1.3km)

New Souq

To Khasab Hotel (3km),
Airport (6km) & Khor
Najd (24.5km)

Changing money is also pretty much the same as it is anywhere else – that is to say it is a somewhat slow and bureaucratic process at banks, and quick (but with bad rates) at the hotel.

Khasab Fort

There is nothing especially remarkable about Khasab Fort. The design, though a bit odd, will be familiar to anyone who has already

of it involving the smuggling of American cigarettes to Iran, and its souq is filled with visitors from other parts of Musandam, from Iran and now an increasing number of tourists, predominantly expats from the UAE and Oman. The waterfront is a beautiful spot for a sunset stroll with its carefully restored fort framed by bare, rugged hills. Khasab is also a good base for exploring the region. Starting from here you can easily visit Bukha, Tawi and Khor Najd in a single day.

The bad news is that Khasab is something of a one-horse town commercially. There is one hotel and one tour operator and they charge predictably monopolistic prices.

Orientation & Information

For such a small place Khasab is surprisingly spread out. The town's commercial centre is the port and the old souq about 1km south-east of it. The old souq consists mainly of merchants who sell cigarettes to the Iranian smugglers who crowd the port every day, along with a couple of restaurants and small groceries and the Khasab Travel & Tours office. Another 1.5km to the east is the town's new souq. This consists of a few more restaurants and grocery stores, the post office, a couple of banks and the Oman Air office. Most of Khasab's houses are just north, or further east, of the new souq. The Khasab Hotel and the airport lie a short distance to the south of the new souq.

Although Khasab is remote, its telephone and postal systems are just as efficient as those found throughout the rest of Oman.

Smugglers' Port

What is interesting about Khasab port is not so much the main dhow jetty and customs administration building, but the little bay next to the main port where, on any given day, a hundred or so speedboats from Iran are anchored or pulled up on the shore. These Iranians are smugglers who make the short trip over from Bandar Abbas (about two hours using the souped-up boats and outboard motors needed to outrun the Iranian coastguard) to purchase goods that are expensive or hard to find at home. The Omani authorities charge them a couple of rlyals for the privilege of tying up in Khasab for the day and then let them go shopping in the souq. A quick walk through the souq will show you what the Iranians are in the market for. Maybe half of all the shops in the souq are bulk cigarette merchants. The Iranians buy enormous quantities of cigarettes ('Only American cigarettes', according to one boat captain), wrap the boxes up in plastic and, after dark, head back across the strait. You will occasionally see other goods being loaded onto the boats but cigarettes are the main business, and the smugglers are remarkably open about it. During the day they wander around Khasab chatting and getting in the odd bit of personal shopping. Every shop and restaurant in Khasab accepts Iranian rials without question and apart from tourism – an industry still in its infancy – it appears to be the town's economic mainstay.

looked at other forts in northern Oman. However, the setting of this fort is different. It is some distance from the modern port and souq, dominating the bit of coast that provides access to Khasab's older sections. None of the corner towers match each other or the large fifth tower in the centre of the fort's courtyard. Though the fort has been restored, little effort has gone into making it tourist-friendly beyond hanging *khanjars* (Omani daggers) in a few of the rooms.

To get to the fort, continue along the coast from the port area, past the turn-off for the centre and you'll see it on your right. If you are coming from the hotel go straight through the roundabout where the Oman Air office is. Follow the road as it winds through a residential area and you will eventually come out on the coast road, with the fort on your right. Its opening hours are a bit erratic. Try government office hours (7.30 am to 2.30 pm Saturday to Wednesday). Admission is free.

Kumzan Fort

Kumzan Fort is a ruin, but it is a good contrast to Khasab Fort. It was built by a local imam approximately 400 years ago and originally had 22 rooms inside its walls. Little remains of the fort today except for two of its towers.

To reach the fort go east from the roundabout by the Oman Air office (a right turn if you are coming from the Khasab Hotel, straight if you are coming from Khasab Fort and the port) in the new souq area and turn left onto a paved street after 300m. Follow this street for 1.3km as it winds through a residential area. The fort will be on your left.

Beaches

There is a small beach suitable for swimming just outside Khasab. Follow the road from the port towards Bukha. The beach is at a lay-by on the right about 2km from the port. As on public beaches everywhere in the region, women should cover up as much as possible.

Diving

Some of the best diving in the world is said to be at Musandam. There are coral reefs

and shipwrecks to explore and the area is relatively uncharted. The Ministry of Regional Municipalities & Environment permits only 20 divers in Musandam at a time (to protect the marine life). The conditions in the water off Musandam are suitable only for experienced divers with a minimum of a PADI Open Water Certificate and 50 logged dives. There are some very strong currents around. Trips can be arranged with Scuba International in Dubai (☎ 968-4 420 553). A standard package costs Dh400 (OR40) and includes two dives with tank and weights, overnight accommodation and meals. Khasab Travel & Tours (see Organised Tours, following) also do diving trips but you will need to book well ahead so that permits can be arranged.

Organised Tours

Khasab Travel & Tours (☎ 830464, fax 830364), in the old souq, offers a variety of trips around Musandam. A full-day tour by boat of the Sham fjords, including lunch and snorkelling stops, costs OR30 per person (OR12 for children under 12) for two to three people and OR25 per person for four plus. Their shorter half-day boat trip costs OR15 (OR8 for children). For OR60 a head for two to three people or OR40 for four plus, they will take you all the way to Kumzar (on the northern edge of the peninsula) and back. They also have a kayaking trip in the fjords that can be combined with a two-night camping trip and hiking for a whopping OR200 per person (minimum four people). You can also design your own 4WD tours into the mountains if you are prepared to pay OR80 per day for a 4WD and driver.

Places to Stay & Eat

The only hotel on the entire peninsula is the *Khasab Hotel* (☎ 830267, fax 830989). At OR20.475/33.930 for singles/doubles it is rather overpriced. The rooms are pretty basic and in need of some repairs. There's a swimming pool and restaurant and the hotel has Musandam's only bar. Do not expect any discount on the rack rate unless you are staying for five days or more. Because the hotel is small, calling ahead for reservations is a very good idea. To get there, head south from the new souq roundabout (a right turn if you are coming from the port area).

Khasab Travel & Tours have two *three-bedroom villas* near the hotel for OR40 per night. This is good value if there are a few of you, and you can do your own cooking.

Bukha Restaurant in the old souq has good biryanis for 600 baisa per serving. Roast chicken and kebabs are available in the evening and the place is popular with the Iranian cigarette smugglers – always a good sign. There are a number of other restaurants serving the same fare in the old souq area and one or two in the new souq area.

Shopping

There isn't an abundance of jewellery or handicrafts to buy in Khasab but you will find plenty of traditional walking sticks. These walking sticks are used by the Shihuh tribe who inhabit Musandam. They are unusual in that they are topped with a little axe blade. Apparently they were originally used for protection and defence. If any suspicious strangers came too close, the Shihuh would wave their walking sticks menacingly as a warning to back off. If the stranger kept coming the walking sticks could be used as weapons. The walking sticks you can buy here are usually made of shesham wood which comes from India. They should cost about OR1.5 to OR2.

Getting There & Away

Air Oman Air's office (☎ 830543) is at the new souq roundabout, between the Khasab Hotel and the port area. It is the first building to the left of the roundabout if you are coming from the port area. There is no sign, just an Oman Air sticker on the door. There are daily flights between Muscat and Khasab, some of which go via Dibba on the east coast. Fares are OR20 one way and OR40 return, a price you will find hard to beat by going overland unless you have your own car. Flights cruise at around 2800m providing passengers with a spectacular view of the peninsula. That alone is worth OR20.

Khasab airport is an air force base at which Oman Air is allowed to land a couple of times a week. This means that Khasab flights are subject to cancellation whenever the air force feels like it, such as during National Day when the air base simply shuts down for a couple of days. This, and the extremely small size of the planes used on the Khasab route, means you should reconfirm your flight back to Muscat as soon as possible after you arrive. The airport is on the southern edge of town, a few kilometres beyond the Khasab Hotel.

Car The only way into Musandam by car is from the west coast of the UAE. The blacktop road from Tibat, on the border with the UAE, to Khasab winds around the sheer mountain sides and along the Gulf, and is spectacular in parts.

There is a road (4WD only) from the east coast of the UAE that goes to Khasab via Rawdah Bowl but there is a military checkpoint about 45km from Dibba and, at the time of writing, it was not possible to pass through. Some years ago it was possible for tourists with visas to get through this way.

Taxi The 10-passenger 4WD pick-up trucks that serve as Musandam's shared taxi system gather in Khasab's old souq, near the port. The drivers say they travel to Bukha and Tibat for OR1 per passenger but there does not appear to be a lot of action. It's most likely you will have to take a vehicle engaged. The standard engaged rates are Bukha OR5, Tibat or Khor Najd OR10, Dibba OR25 and Muscat OR70.

Although it is only about 70km from Ras al-Khaimah to Khasab there isn't a regular long-distance taxi service. The Khasab pick-up drivers charge OR15 for an engaged trip to Ras al-Khaimah (about two hours if there are no hold-ups at the border). If you are travelling to Ras al-Khaimah (or Muscat) make sure the driver has his identity card and car papers as these will be needed to cross the border. If you want to go to the city of Ras al-Khaimah make sure the driver understands that, otherwise you may find yourself dumped just across the border at Tibat (also referred to as the Sham border post), which is part of the emirate of Ras al-Khaimah but a good 40km north of the city of the same name.

Getting from Ras al-Khaimah to Khasab by public transport is an entirely different story. Ras al-Khaimah's long-distance taxi drivers demand Dh200 for the trip to Khasab, though for Dh40 they will take you to the Tibat border crossing from where you can try to hitch a ride into Khasab.

If you are in Khasab and need a lift back to Muscat, try asking around in the bar at the Khasab Hotel.

Boat There are cruises from Dubai that stop at Khasab. See Boat in the UAE Getting There & Away chapter for more details.

Getting Around

To/From the Airport Khasab has possibly the only airport in the world that is completely devoid of taxis. The Khasab Hotel will meet your flight if you have a reservation there (confirm this when you make your reservation) and can also give you a lift to the airport when it is time to leave. Either of these services costs OR3. A lift into town from the airport should cost about OR2.

Taxi There are a few orange-and-white taxis that will take you around town for 200 to 300 baisa but these are usually permanently booked by locals. The only other form of public transport is open 4WD pick-up trucks with benches in the back. These are the local shared taxis, although it is rare to see one actually going anywhere with passengers in it. Mostly they just seem to hang around Khasab's old souq and wait for people who need engaged trips to other towns. Should one of these vehicles actually be moving, the driver will charge a couple of hundred baisa for a lift within the town.

Car There is no car rental company in Musandam. The Khasab Hotel can arrange rental with one of the locals for OR30 per day but you should be able to haggle this

outrageous fee down to OR25 or less, depending on demand. However, considering that there is no insurance cover or contract it may not be the best option.

TAWI

About 10km from Khasab port lies the village of Tawi, home to a handful of prehistoric **rock carvings** of boats, houses and warriors on horseback. These are easy to miss because there are only a few of them and they are at ground level by the track running through the village, but they are worth a quick diversion if time is not a major concern.

To reach the carvings turn off the Khasab-Bukha road at Quida onto a dirt track. Coming from Khasab the track is just beyond the sign for Quida but before you pass any houses. Follow this track up Wadi Quida for 2.3km. Notice the decorative remains of houses along the way to your left. There is also a graveyard. The carvings are on your left on two rocks on the ground at a point where the track bends sharply to the right just before a large white house. Across the track from the carvings is an ancient **well** that is still used by Tawi's residents.

AL-HARF

This small village roughly mid-way between Khasab and Bukha is noteworthy for two things. One is the remnants of traditional stone houses which can be seen from the road, and the second is the spectacular view. The drive from Khasab to Bukha involves crossing a mountain. Al-Harf is the village at the point where the road crests. Along the road are several places where you can pull over and admire the view. Legend has it that on a clear day you can make out the Iranian coast from Al-Harf. The villagers here are very friendly, and you'll probably get lots of waves and smiles from the children.

BUKHA

Bukha has two forts. The more interesting of the two is **Bukha Fort**, on the coast. If you are coming from Khasab the fort is the first thing you will arrive at. The other fort, which is in ruins, is on a hill a short distance

Building dhows is a dying art, but some are still built in the traditional way – by hand – in Sur.

Mirbat fort, near Salalah, guarded the town against invasion from the sea.

Yemeni-style tomb near Mirbat, evidence of the historical connection between Dhofar and Yemen.

CHRIS MELLOR

CHRIS MELLOR

DAVID PETHERBRIDGE

DAVID PETHERBRIDGE

From subterranean splendour to tranquil fjords and majestic mountain landscapes, the Musandam peninsula is the jewel in Oman's crown.

inland and north of Bukha Fort. Around the other side of the hill there are more recent ruins of a large house or castle. The town's residential and commercial centre is another kilometre further down the road. The town's administrative buildings, such as the post office, and its petrol station are 2km south of the town centre on the road towards Tibat. Being only 27km from Khasab by road, it makes an easy and scenic day trip.

Bukha Fort has towers at three of its corners. It is photogenic but not usually open to the public. The ruined fort is really little more than a single large tower inside a walled enclosure. More fortifications can be seen 3km north of Bukha in the village of Al-Jadi which has one restored watchtower dominating the southern edge of its beach and another overlooking the settlement from a hilltop to the north.

South of Bukha, on the way to Tibat border checkpoint, there is a great (unofficial) *camping spot* on the beach, with shelters and drinking water. Many spots along this road are suitable for swimming (but remember to cover up).

KUMZAR

For the truly adventurous, few Arabian excursions can top a trip to Kumzar. Set on an isolated cove at the northern edge of the Musandam peninsula, Kumzar is accessible only by boat. The village's residents do not speak much Arabic. Their language, known as Kumzari, is a mishmash of Farsi, Hindi, English, Portuguese and Arabic (for the record, Arabic is widely understood in Kumzar. English, however, is an entirely different matter).

The village's only 'sight' is a **well** about 500m up the wadi that serves as Kumzar's main street. The well was Kumzar's sole source of water until the government built a small desalination plant next to the harbour in the 1970s. Today most of the town's water is delivered through communal taps – note the incredibly long hoses running from the taps into houses – and the well is filled with fresh water each week. The old **stone houses** are also interesting to look at, quite unlike anything you will see in the rest of

Oman. The houses appear to get older as you move further up the wadi.

The main attraction of a visit to Kumzar is the spectacular scenery on the boat trip there and back. Visits by foreigners are still not an everyday occurrence in Kumzar – don't take photos of people without asking their permission first, and dress conservatively. Children follow you around and love to have their photo taken, but ask permission first.

Getting There & Away

Water-taxis travel between Khasab and Kumzar, charging OR3 per head. This can be a pretty harrowing trip. Most of the speedboats used as water-taxis have no seats and maybe 15cm clearance between the deck and gunwale. There's really nothing to hold onto once the boat heads out into the open ocean which can get pretty choppy, nor is there any safety gear. The water-taxis won't leave until they have crammed 15 or so people into the boat, which tends to make the two-hour trip to Kumzar an extremely nerve-racking experience. Also, there is no guarantee that you will be able to get back the same day. If you do get trapped you can probably camp on the beach at the edge of the village.

Alternatively, you could hire the entire boat. The captains on the dock in Khasab may start by asking OR30 for a one-way trip, but with a little tenacity you should be able to get someone to take you over to Kumzar, wait for a couple of hours and then bring you back for OR35. If you can split this cost among four or five people you will have a faster (it takes about 1½ hours each way with three to five people on the boat instead of 15 to 17) and probably safer trip, not to mention a more comfortable ride and a guaranteed lift back. It's not cheap, but it does have its advantages. If money is no concern, Khasab Travels & Tours will take you to Kumzar and back on a more comfortable boat for OR60 a head for two to three people or OR40 for four plus.

KHOR ASH SHAM

Khor Ash Sham, also referred to as the Sham fjords, cuts across Musandam between

OMAN

Khasab and Kumzar, almost to the other side. It is home to a few Musandam families who, like the Kumzaris, lead a very isolated existence. As you pull into the *khor* (inlet) from the rather rough waters of the Arabian Sea, the peace and quiet hits you like a sledgehammer. It's quite spooky. There are a few 'villages' dotted around the khor where the mountains offer a small stretch of flat, habitable beach before sliding under the water. A village usually consists of one family whose only contact with the outside world is by boat. There is no electricity, telephones or running water. The government now delivers water each week but apart from that there are no creature comforts for these people caught in a time warp.

A trip here can be easily combined with a trip to Kumzar if you get an early start. If you just want to explore the khor then you should be able to get a local fisherman to take you there for a couple of hours for OR10 or you can arrange a tour with Khasab Travel & Tours – see Organised Tours in the Khasab section for more details. It really is worth making a trip around the fjords of Musandam, as reader Andy Hurst found:

We spent a fantastic three hours skirting the coast in a boat – the driver knew the area well and was able to take us to fjords/villages/beaches that are totally inaccessible by anything other than a boat. Our three hour trip cost Dh300 (UK£50) and for the view and sights alone was worth every penny (dirham) – thoroughly recommended.

KHOR NAJD

Khor Najd (Khor A'Najd) is the only one of Musandam's fjords that can be reached from Khasab in an ordinary car, although it needs to be a car in a fairly decent state of repair considering how steep (both climbing and descending) the last portion of the drive is. It is 24.5km by road from Khasab's centre, about a 30-minute drive. The best view of the area is your first view of it – from the point where the road from Khasab finally cuts through the mountains. The small beach below is better suited to camping than swimming, and is a popular weekend

Telegraph Island

This island in Khor Ash Sham was a strategic base for the British telegraph lines to India late last century. You'll see only a few crumbling remains of the building that housed the base. A large number of British workers who were assigned to duties on the island apparently went quite mad from the isolation and eerie quiet here. Telegraph Island was located at one of the most remote bends in one of the most remote peninsulas of the world. When someone was touched by this isolation madness it was known as 'going round the bend', a saying that has stuck to this day.

spot with both Omani and Emirati families, particularly since it has a concrete ramp for launching boats. There are a few shelters and drinking water is available.

To reach Khor Najd go south from the new souq roundabout. After a few km you will come to a T-junction with a sign pointing right to the airport and left to Dibba. Turn left here. After 8.5km you will see a green sign pointing to, among other places, 'Khor A'Najd 10km'. Turn left, follow this road for another 5.6km and then turn left again. After another 1.5km you will come to a three-way fork in the road, take the road that winds up the mountain. After 2.3km you will reach the outlook, and your first view of Khor Najd. Another, even steeper, 2.8km descent brings you to the water's edge.

RAWDAH BOWL

If you have a 4WD, a trip to Rawdah Bowl is highly recommended for the spectacular mountain scenery and for a glimpse of traditional mountain life. Rawdah Bowl is a wide valley scattered with acacia trees and pre-Islamic tombs and is suitable for camping.

A steep but well-maintained road takes you up to and then across the Sayh plateau where vegetables are cultivated by a small agricultural community. It then climbs Jebel Harim, the highest point in Musandam at around 1980m. You will pass a telecommu nications tower; the descent over the other side of the mountain gives you the best views in Musandam, if not all Oman. Agricultural terraces are cut out of mountain sides and stone houses built into the steep slopes. Sometimes caves in the mountain sides are also inhabited. These dwellings have neat stone walls built up at cave entrances.

The road then extends along a rather narrow ridge before coming down into Wadi Bih and Rawdah Bowl. If you continue for another 10km on the main road you will come to an Omani military checkpoint and won't be able to go any further.

The drive takes about 1½ hours but add on at least half an hour for photo stops.

Facts about the United Arab Emirates

The United Arab Emirates (UAE) is a union of seven sovereign sheikhdoms, formed in 1971 when the British withdrew from the Gulf. The UAE is a land of contrasts: mountains, beaches, deserts and oases, camel racing, Bedouin markets and Dubai's legendary duty-free shopping. It's also small and compact, with good hotels and no-fuss visas. At Buraimi oasis you can even visit Oman for a few hours, without needing a visa.

The capital, Abu Dhabi, is one of the most modern cities on earth, where few buildings are more than 30 years old. Dubai is the most vibrant city in the Gulf, sporting the region's best nightlife as well as its most diverse economy. In the emirates north of Dubai – Sharjah, Ajman, Umm al-Qaiwain and Ras al-Khaimah – life moves at a slower pace. The Hajar mountains provide a dramatic backdrop for both Ras al-Khaimah, the northernmost of the Gulf coast emirates, and Fujairah, which overlooks the Gulf of Oman on the country's east coast.

Although the UAE is a popular tour destination, it is also one of the best places in the Gulf for independent travellers – make sure you see it soon before mass tourism really hits its stride.

HISTORY

As Oman and the UAE share much of their early history up to the Islamic era (7th century AD), this is covered in the Facts about the Region chapter earlier in this book.

Caravan Route

During the Middle Ages most of what is now the UAE was part of the kingdom of Hormuz, which was based on the island of Hormuz (in the strait of the same name) and controlled the entrance to, and most of the trade in, the Gulf. The first known reference to the area by a European is a manuscript written in AD 1498 by the Portuguese explorer Vasco da Gama that records his rather sketchy observations of Khor Fakkan, Dibba and Ras al-Khaimah. By 1515, the Portuguese had occupied Julfar (near the city of Ras al-Khaimah in present-day UAE) and built a customs house where they taxed the Gulf's flourishing trade with India and the Far East. Later, they also built a fort. In 1633 the Portuguese lost control of Hormuz and were forced to abandon the area in the face of attacks on two fronts – from hostile tribes by land and the British and Dutch by sea.

After the departure of the Portuguese, the Gulf was taken over by the Al-Ya'ruba imams of Oman before passing into Persia's sphere of influence in the mid-18th century.

The Qawasim

The rise of British naval power in the Gulf in the mid-18th century coincided with the rise of two important tribal confederations along the coast of what is now the UAE – the Qawasim and the Bani Yas.

The Qawasim, whose descendants now rule Sharjah and Ras al-Khaimah, was a seafaring clan based in Ras al-Khaimah and its influence extended to the Persian side of the Gulf. Its main rivals for local power were the Al-Busaids (who are now the ruling family of Oman). In 1798, the Al-Busaids signed a treaty with the British, which enabled the British to keep the French out of Oman and away from India. The Qawasim felt that the British had allied themselves with their enemies, which justified their attacks on British ships. The Qawasim's hostility towards the British was exacerbated by the influence of the strict and somewhat xenophobic doctrines of Wahhabi Islam (for more details on this doctrine, see Religion in the Facts about the Region chapter). The British East India Company, which owned most of the ships in question, and the British government looked on the Qawasim's activities as simple piracy.

UNITED ARAB EMIRATES

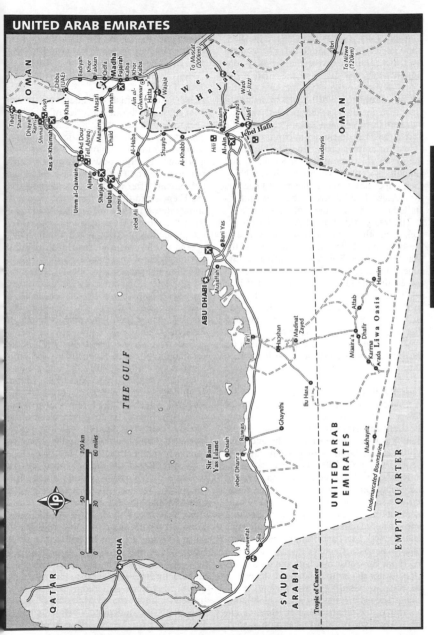

The British dubbed the west coast of present-day UAE the 'Pirate Coast'. In 1805, 1809 and 1811, they launched raids against the Qawasim but between raids, piracy continued unabated. In 1819 the British decided to resolve the situation once and for all by mounting a full-scale invasion of Qawasim territory. A large fleet was dispatched from Mumbai (Bombay) in India and, in 1820, it destroyed or captured every Qawasim ship it could find and occupied the Qawasim forts at Ras al-Khaimah and Linagh (in Persia). The British Royal Navy then imposed a General Treaty of Peace on nine Arab sheikhdoms in the area and installed a garrison in the region.

The treaty still allowed the sheikhs to attack each other – much to the annoyance of the British. In 1835, the British imposed the Maritime Truce. This was modified several times (notably in 1839 when the British forced the sheikhs to ban slavery) until, in 1853, the truce became the Treaty of Peace in Perpetuity. Under this latest treaty, the British assumed responsibility for arbitrating disputes among the sheikhs. What is now the UAE became known as the Trucial Coast (to the Europeans at least), a name it retained until 1971.

The Bani Yas

While the Qawasim held the balance of power on the coast, the main power among the Bedouin tribes of the interior was the Bani Yas tribal confederation, the ancestors of the ruling families of present-day Abu Dhabi and Dubai. The Bani Yas was originally based in Liwa, an oasis on the edge of the Empty Quarter in the south of the UAE, but moved to Abu Dhabi island in 1793. Its members engaged in the traditional Bedouin activities of camel herding, small-scale agriculture in the Liwa and Buraimi oases, tribal raiding and extracting protection money from merchant caravans passing through their territory. After the British outlawed slavery on the coast, the Bani Yas also took over the slave trade. The Buraimi oasis, which today consists of the Omani town of Buraimi and the UAE town of Al-Ain, became eastern

Arabia's main slave market, a position it retained until the 1950s. The Bani Yas divided into two main branches in the early 19th century when Dubai split from Abu Dhabi.

The Trucial Coast

In 1892, the British extended their power over the coast through a series of exclusive agreements under which the sheikhs accepted formal British protection and, in exchange, promised to have no dealings with any other foreign power without British permission. The British had insisted on the agreements after rival powers, particularly the French and the Russians, had begun to show interest in the Gulf region. London regarded control of the area as essential for the protection of Britain's empire in India.

Apart from this concern the British did not much care what happened in the Gulf, and the area became a backwater. Throughout the late 19th and early 20th centuries, the sheikhdoms were all tiny enclaves of fishermen, pearl divers and Bedouin. The area's few merchants were mostly Indian or Persian.

For most of this period, Sharjah was the most populous and powerful of the emirates. As the 19th century drew to a close, Sharjah lost influence to Abu Dhabi which, from 1855 until 1909, was ruled by the forceful Sheikh Zayed bin Mohammed, usually referred to today as Zayed the Great. Following Sheikh Zayed's death, however, Abu Dhabi fell into decline as his family fought a succession battle.

During Zayed the Great's rule, Sharjah was the area's main trading centre. But Sharjah's rulers in the early years were weak and xenophobic and Persian traders from Linagh chose to settle in Dubai. In 1903 they arranged for the main Indian-based British steamship line to drop Linagh in favour of Dubai as its main port of call in the Gulf. The opening of regular sea links with India and the northern Gulf marked the beginning of Dubai's growth as a trading power, under the leadership of the Al-Maktoum family.

In the years immediately before and after WWI, the British connection kept Abdul

Aziz bin Abdul Rahman al-Saud, the future king of Saudi Arabia, from conquering the sheikhdoms of the Trucial Coast. Even so, the British presence during this time remained very low-key. In fact there were no permanent British facilities in what is now the UAE until 1932, when Imperial Airways (the predecessor of British Airways) built a hostel in Sharjah for passengers and crew on its flights to India. (Footage of the first landing can be seen at Al-Hisn Fort in Sharjah.) A permanent British Political Agent was not appointed anywhere on the Trucial Coast until WWII.

It was the prospect of oil that changed the way the British ran their affairs on the Trucial Coast. Before oil concessions could be granted (ie, the right to drill in the UAE in exchange for payment to the UAE of a proportion of the profits), there was an immediate need to determine the boundaries between the sheikhdoms. Each of the local rulers claimed enormous swaths of territory and was willing to concede nothing to his neighbours. Eventually, the borders of the seven emirates that now make up the UAE were drawn up by the British. This, incredibly, involved a British diplomat spending months riding a camel around in the mountains and across the desert asking village heads, tribal leaders and groups of Bedouin which sheikh they swore allegiance to. Even that failed to settle all of the competing claims. As part of an ongoing and only partially successful attempt to modernise the governments of the Trucial Coast, and in the hope of settling the rival territorial claims amicably, the British set up the Trucial States Council in 1951. This was a cabinet consisting of the rulers of the sheikhdoms and was the direct predecessor of today's UAE Supreme Council.

The Oil Era

There is a certain irony in Abu Dhabi's present status as the UAE's richest member: in the decades prior to the discovery of oil, Abu Dhabi was the poorest of the Trucial Coast sheikhdoms. The early years of the 20th century, particularly the two decades following the death of Zayed the Great, had also been among the most violent. With the ascension of Sheikh Shakhbut bin Sultan in 1928, some stability returned to the emirate but the decline of the pearl industry a few years later left the emirate destitute.

In 1939, hoping to break the cycle of poverty, Sheikh Shakhbut granted a concession to the British-owned Iraq Petroleum Company. In 1953, still desperate for oil, Sheikh Shakhbut gave another concession, this time for offshore exploration, to an Anglo-French consortium. Five years later, this group of prospectors made the first oil strike on the Trucial Coast. It soon became apparent that Abu Dhabi's reserves were enormous. Exports began in 1962 and, with a population at the time of only 15,000, the emirate was obviously on its way to becoming very wealthy. Later, under the leadership of Sheikh Zayed, the emirate set up the Abu Dhabi National Oil Company (Adnoc) through which it nationalised the concession agreements during the 1970s.

Oil revenue firmly established Abu Dhabi as the leader among the Trucial Coast sheikhdoms. Meanwhile, Dubai was cementing its reputation as the region's trading hub. In 1939, Sheikh Rashid bin Saeed al-Maktoum became the regent for his ailing father, Sheikh Saeed. (Rashid formally succeeded Saeed when his father died in 1958.) He quickly moved to bolster the emirate's position as the Gulf's main entrepot. At about the same time, the rulers of Sharjah made the costly mistake of allowing their harbour to silt up. Unfortunately for them, in nearby Dubai Rashid was improving facilities along Dubai's waterfront, the Creek.

In 1966, Dubai struck oil of its own. The other sheikhs, however, were not so lucky, and all of them inevitably began to look to Abu Dhabi for subsidies.

The problem was that Sheikh Shakhbut, having waited so long for oil money, proved to be completely incapable of handling his newly found wealth. In the early and mid-1960s his rule became increasingly erratic. Shakhbut had little understanding of modern banks and did not trust them. He also became increasingly suspicious of all foreigners and

The Buraimi Dispute

In October 1949, Saudi Arabia formally laid claim to the Buraimi oasis (on the border between Oman and the UAE) on the grounds that it had been part of the Saudi empire in the late 18th century. The Saudis ignored the fact that for over a century the oasis had been divided between Abu Dhabi emirate and Oman. In fact, the dispute was about oil which geologists from Aramco (the oil concessionaire in Saudi Arabia) suspected lay beneath the sand.

In 1952, the Saudis occupied part of Buraimi, allegedly after offering Sheikh Zayed bin Sultan (now the ruler of Abu Dhabi but then the governor of the oasis) a large bribe to recognise the Saudi claim. Three years and several arbitration attempts later, Zayed and the Trucial Oman Scouts (who were commanded by British officers) drove the Saudis out of the oasis. The current UAE-Oman border running through the oasis was settled in 1966 though Saudi Arabia did not drop its claim to Buraimi until 1974, and then only in exchange for a percentage of the oil revenues from Abu Dhabi's portion of the oasis.

is once said to have told oil company representatives that he was the one with the upper hand because they needed the money more than he did! In 1966, the British engineered Shakhbut's deposition by his brother, Sheikh Zayed, the long-time governor of Al Ain, Abu Dhabi's portion of the Buraimi oasis. After spending several years abroad, Shakhbut eventually retired to Al-Ain.

The Federation

Britain's announcement in 1968 that it would leave the Gulf three years later came as a shock to most of the ruling sheikhs. Within a few weeks, the British began work on forming a single state consisting of Bahrain, Qatar and the Trucial Coast. Plans for such a grouping, which was to be known as the Federation of Arab Emirates, were announced in February 1968. The federa-

tion came into existence on 30 March of that year but it collapsed almost immediately, largely because of the area's numerous boundary disputes.

The British decided to try again and negotiations dragged on for the next three years. Bahrain eventually pulled out of the talks, claiming that the proposed formulas did not give it enough standing within the federation. Qatar followed suit, on the theory that if Bahrain was going to be an independent state, so would Qatar. Finally, in July 1971, a provisional constitution for a new federation, to be known as the United Arab Emirates, was announced. The emirs agreed to a formula under which Abu Dhabi and Dubai (in that order) would carry the most weight in the federation but each emir would remain largely autonomous. The new country came into existence on 2 December 1971.

At the time many outsiders dismissed the UAE as a loosely assembled, artificial and largely British creation. While there was some truth in this charge, it was also true that the emirs of the smaller and poorer sheikhdoms knew that their territories had no hope of surviving as independent states. The provisional constitution was supposed to be in place for only five years but it was formally extended in 1976 and has remained in force ever since.

Post Federation

Since independence, the UAE has been one of the most stable and untroubled countries in the Arab world. Although the Trucial Oman Scouts suppressed an attempted coup in Sharjah a few weeks after independence, the country has remained remarkably calm since then.

This does not mean that political life in the UAE has been devoid of controversy. Border disputes among the emirates continued throughout the 1970s and '80s, and the degree to which 'integration' among the seven sheikhdoms should be pursued has been a subject of constant debate.

When his first five-year term as president of the UAE expired in 1976, Sheikh Zayed threatened to resign if the other six emirs did not settle their outstanding border disputes and give up their private armies. Nobody dared to call his bluff. In 1979, Sheikh Zayed and Sheikh Rashid of Dubai sealed a formal compromise under which each gave a little ground on his respective vision of the country. The result was a much stronger federation in which Dubai remained a bastion of free trade while Abu Dhabi imposed a tighter federal structure on the other emirates. In practice, this meant the federalising of the welfare-state system, the police, the legal system and also the telecommunications network. Rashid, who was already vice president, also agreed to take the title of prime minister as a symbol of his commitment to the federation.

The collapse of oil prices in the mid- to late 1980s, and more recently in 1998, hit the country unevenly. Abu Dhabi remained very rich but was forced to scale back its subsidies to the smaller emirates. Dubai weathered the financial storm fairly well but Sharjah, which had only recently begun oil production and was in the midst of a building boom, ended up deeply in debt. In 1987, the brother of Sharjah's ruler used this debt as an excuse to attempt a palace coup. The ruler, Sheikh Sultan bin Mohammed al-Qasimi, was in the UK at the time but returned to Dubai where he enlisted the help of the ruling Al-Maktoum family. The Al-Maktoums threatened to use force if necessary to restore Sheikh Sultan to power. The coup leader, Sheikh Abdul Aziz bin Mohammed, eventually backed down under pressure from the Supreme Council. At the council's suggestion, Sultan appointed Abdul Aziz as crown prince as a gesture of reconciliation. In February 1990, apparently feeling that enough face-saving time had elapsed, Sheikh Sultan sacked Abdul Aziz. Sultan's son, Ahmed, was named as the new crown prince a few months later.

In 1990–91, the UAE contributed troops to the allied coalition against Iraq and foreign soldiers and sailors were based there during the months prior to the liberation of Kuwait. The result was a strengthening of the country's already strong ties with the West, though this has not prevented the

The BCCI Affair

In the summer of 1991, Abu Dhabi found itself on the receiving end of a lot of unwelcome publicity when Western financial regulators, led by the Bank of England, closed down the scandal-ridden Bank of Credit & Commerce International (BCCI), of which Abu Dhabi was the major shareholder. BCCI was a bank regulator's nightmare. It had over 430 branches in 73 countries, was registered in Luxembourg through holding companies in the Cayman Islands (funded mostly by Abu Dhabi) and managed from London by Pakistanis.

In the UAE, where BCCI's retail operations had made it one of the largest local banks, the collapse posed a delicate political problem. While negotiating over BCCI's future with the Bank of England and other Western regulatory and legal authorities, Abu Dhabi moved to protect the bank's local customers by buying up all of its branches in the UAE and reconstituting them as the Union National Bank. The government also arrested and prosecuted a dozen of the bank's senior officials, most of whom were eventually sentenced to between three and five years in prison.

UAE in general, and Dubai in particular, from maintaining good relations with Iran.

The UAE Today

The desire to maintain and improve its already friendly ties with the West, while remaining fiercely loyal to the rest of the Arab world, is high on the UAE's current political agenda. The UAE is rapidly becoming an important world-class centre of business and commerce, and the country's rulers see good international relations as vital to the UAE's ongoing development and wealth. A territorial dispute with Iran over three small islands in the Gulf has dragged on for years and periodically bubbles to the surface. That aside, when the rest of the world reads about events in the UAE these days it is usually on the sports pages of the morning newspapers.

Dubai now plays host to several important world sports events in golf, horse racing, tennis and motorboat racing, and Sharjah is an equally important venue for the world's cricket fans. People will also be familiar with Dubai's reputation as a shopper's paradise with its variety of goods to buy and duty free status.

GEOGRAPHY

The UAE is about 83,600 sq km in area. The emirate of Abu Dhabi represents over 85% of this total. The coastal areas, particularly along the Gulf, are marked by salt flats. Much of the inland area in the south of the UAE is a nearly featureless desert running to the edges of the Empty Quarter. The only features are a few oases such as Liwa and Buraimi.

The coastal lands immediately north-east of Abu Dhabi are much the same as the desert to the south and west of the city, but further north along the coast the land slowly becomes greener until, when you reach Ras al-Khaimah, the landscape is relatively lush.

The western end of the Hajar mountains, which run across the north of Oman, extend northwards through the UAE, ending in the Omani enclave of the Musandam peninsula on the southern side of the Strait of Hormuz. These northern and eastern sections of the UAE – the inland areas around Ras al-Khaimah and the east coast of the country from Fujairah to Dibba and inland to Hatta – are green and inviting, with striking mountain scenery.

The sands of the UAE change colour as you move from emirate to emirate, ranging from grey in Fujairah to cream in Dubai to a deep reddish-brown in Abu Dhabi. The high iron oxide content gives the sands around Al-Ain a deep red colour.

CLIMATE

The further south you travel in the UAE, the hotter and more humid the summer weather becomes. From May to September, daytime temperatures are in the low to mid 40s in Abu Dhabi and Dubai. During most of July and August temperatures tend to sit on 46° to

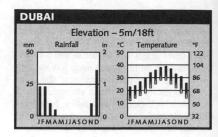

48°C. On the east coast and in the mountainous north you're more likely to feel a breeze. The inland desert areas are sometimes a few degrees hotter, but are much less humid than the coast, making the heat more bearable. Many sheikhs have their summer palaces inland, in and around Al-Ain.

In the winter months the average temperature is about 22°C, although it can get very windy in Abu Dhabi, Dubai and Sharjah. In the desert areas it can get chilly at night, with temperatures sometimes dropping to single figures. It does not rain much in the UAE but if it does (usually in December or January) getting around can suddenly become difficult, with wadis filling and streets turning into rivers and, occasionally, washing out entirely.

ECOLOGY & ENVIRONMENT

Afforestation is a major part of the government's fight against desertification. Outside the mountain areas much of the vegetation you are likely to see is part of the local government's 'greenery' program. There are over 100 sq km of parks and oases in and around Al-Ain and Abu Dhabi. Areas such as Liwa oasis have been turned into productive agricultural land. Massive irrigation networks disperse water over the country. Some areas of the desert have been fenced off to protect the delicate vegetation from overgrazing by camels and goats.

Unfortunately, there are still vast amounts of rubbish left on beaches, in wadis and thrown out of car windows, despite the effort by government agencies to educate the community about protecting the environment and its resources. Nevertheless, clean-up days are common. Dubai generates one of the highest per capita volumes of waste in the world, and it has recently opened a number of recycling centres around the city. Unfortunately, there are no such centres in the rest of the emirates yet.

The Breeding Centre for Endangered Species in Sharjah has had some success in increasing the numbers of indigenous Arabian species such as the Arabian oryx. Sir Bani Yas Island, off the western coast of Abu Dhabi emirate, is a breeding ground for gazelles and oryx, as well as other rare species.

The mangrove swamps at Khor Kalba on the east coast are a protected reserve for rare and endemic bird species and the artificial coral reefs (constructed to encourage natural reef formation) off the coast of Fujairah have been declared as marine parks. In Dubai, thousands of flamingos inhabit an area of swampy land along Oud Metha Rd which has been set aside as a waterbird and wildlife sanctuary.

It is possible to visit all of these places, however trips to the Dubai Waterbird and Wildlife Sanctuary can only be organised through the Emirates Bird Records Committee (call Colin Richardson on ☎ 04-472 277 or mobile 050-650 3398). Trips to Sir Bani Yas Island can generally be arranged only through special invitation by Sheikh Zayed himself and sometimes through special interest groups. You could try contacting the Emirates Natural History Group on ☎ 02-665 3094 for more information.

As you can imagine, there is a high risk of oil spills off the coast of the UAE. Over the years the devastation caused by these environmental disasters has prompted a concerted effort by government agencies to monitor and control marine pollution. The major oil companies are required to spend money on research and protection of the coast and the adjacent desert.

The UAE joined the Convention on International Trade in Endangered Species in 1990 and it is an active member of the Regional Organization for the Protection of the Marine Environment.

Environmental Organisations

In addition to the Federal Environment Agency and the Environmental Research and Wildlife Development Agency, there are many nongovernmental organisations concerned with the environment. The Arabian Leopard Trust in Sharjah (☎ 06-311 411, PO Box 24444) and Dubai (☎ 04-444 871) is concerned with protecting all endangered species. Its main goal is to set up four nature reserves around the UAE by the year 2000. Emirates Environmental Group (☎ 04-318 100, PO Box 7013, Dubai) promotes its cause in schools and businesses. It has a Web site at www.eeg.uae.com. Environment Friends Society (☎ 04-668 854, PO Box 4940, Dubai) is a community group that receives an annual budget from the Ministry of Labour & Social Affairs.

GOVERNMENT & POLITICS

The UAE consists of seven emirates: Abu Dhabi, Dubai, Sharjah, Ajman, Umm al-Qaiwain, Ras al-Khaimah and Fujairah. Though there is a federal government over which one of the emirs presides (in practice this is always Sheikh Zayed of Abu Dhabi), each of the rulers is completely sovereign within his own emirate. Each emirate is named after its principal town.

The degree of power which the seven emirs should cede to the federal government has been one of the hottest topics of debate in government circles since the founding of the UAE in 1971. Over the years, Abu Dhabi has been the strongest advocate of closer integration while Dubai has fought hardest to preserve as much of its independence as possible.

Politics in the Gulf tends to be rather opaque but in the UAE the relative interests of the various emirs are fairly clear. Abu Dhabi is the largest and wealthiest emirate and has the biggest population. It is, therefore, the dominant member of the federation and is likely to remain so for some time. Further integration of the seven emirates is obviously in Abu Dhabi's interest. Dubai is a reasonably wealthy emirate with an equally obvious interest in upholding its free trade market. Sharjah and Ras al-Khaimah both have relatively small oil revenues but they, and the other emirates, are dependent on subsidies from Abu Dhabi, although the extent of this dependence varies widely. The smaller emirates wish to strike a balance be-, tween integration (which reduces the prerogatives of the individual emirs) and independence (which leaves them in a potentially precarious financial position).

The forum where these issues are discussed is the Supreme Council, the highest body in the country. The Council comprises the seven emirs and tends to meet informally. On an official level, its main duty is to elect one of the emirs to a five-year term as the country's president. In 1991, Sheikh Zayed bin Sultan al-Nayan of Abu Dhabi was elected to his fifth term as president, a position he seems likely to hold for life. Sheikh Maktoum, the ruler of Dubai, is the country's vice president and prime minister.

There is also a cabinet and the posts are distributed among the emirates. Most of the federal government's money comes from Abu Dhabi and Dubai. They each contribute a portion of their oil revenues and so get to hold most of the important cabinet posts.

The cabinet and Supreme Council are advised, but cannot be overruled, by the Federation Council of Ministers. This is a 40-member consultative body whose members are appointed by the respective emirs. Abu Dhabi and Dubai hold nearly half of the council's seats. All the council's members come from leading merchant families.

The UAE is committed to Arab unity in the region. It is a member of the Arab League and its foreign policy aim is to push for greater cooperation among Arab states while forging closer defence ties with the major Western powers. The UAE sees the West as its only guarantee of security. It must strike a balance, therefore, between support for Western military presence in the region and its loyalty to Arab states.

ECONOMY

The seven emirates are quite diverse economically. Abu Dhabi is the third-largest oil producer in the Gulf, after Saudi Arabia and Kuwait. Like the other big oil producers in the region it has diversified into petrochemicals and other oil-related industries. Abu Dhabi is also a generous donor of development aid. Most of this is channelled to poor Arab countries through the Abu Dhabi Fund for Arab Economic Development which was established in 1971.

Dubai is the second-richest emirate. Its income from oil is now about a quarter of that received by Abu Dhabi but in the decades before Abu Dhabi became oil-rich, Dubai had already established itself as the main trading (and smuggling) port in the region. The discovery of oil in the mid-1960s boosted the economic modernisation program implemented by Dubai's ruler, Sheikh Rashid bin Saeed al-Maktoum. In addition to its oil production and position as one of the Gulf's main business centres, Dubai is also the home of a huge dock complex, one of the Middle East's busiest airports and a large free-trade zone at Jebel Ali.

Sharjah, once the most prosperous of all the emirates, has spent most of this century living in the shadow of Dubai. It has received a modest income from oil since the early 1970s but found itself deeply in debt after the oil price collapse of the mid-1980s. Both the airport and seaport facilities in Sharjah derive much of their income from cargo, although in recent years Sharjah airport has also become a port of entry for tourists visiting the UAE.

Ras al-Khaimah, the northernmost emirate on the country's Gulf coast, derives its income from oil and tourism. Fujairah, the only emirate without a coastline on the Gulf (it is bordered instead by the Arabian Sea), has also entered the tourist market although it remains primarily a cargo port. Fujairah, Ajman and Umm al-Qaiwain all receive substantial subsidies from the federal government and all three have concentrated efforts to attract the tourist industry that is so profitable in other emirates.

The UAE nationals are highly dependent upon expat labour. The government has made some attempt to 'Emiratise' the economy by placing nationals in the workforce. A lack of work ethic among young people who have never had to work to gain an income and unrealistic salary demands are proving to be the biggest obstacles to this process.

POPULATION & PEOPLE

There are an estimated 2.4 million people living in the UAE, of whom about 27% (650,000) are UAE citizens (referred to as 'nationals' in the local media). The expat community makes up the rest of the population, the majority of whom (about 75%) are from India, Pakistan and the Philippines, supplying the country with cheap labour. There is also a substantial number of Arab expatriates, mainly from Lebanon, Syria, Egypt and Iran.

The Emiratis themselves come from a number of different backgrounds. All of the northern emirates have substantial communities of people of Persian, Indian or Baluchi ancestry (Baluchistan is part of present-day Afghanistan and Pakistan). Abu Dhabi is probably the most purely 'Arab' of the emirates, because until the discovery of oil its main population centres were in the isolated oases of Al-Ain and Liwa, deep in the desert. The most populated areas are the cities, especially along the west coast.

EDUCATION

As in all the Gulf States, universal education is a relatively new concept but great strides have been made towards it in the last 20 to 30 years. As recently as 1952, there were no schools in any of the emirates except for a handful of traditional Islamic schools (kuttab) where boys and some girls learnt the Quran by rote and were taught to read and write. The first modern school was opened in 1953 in Sharjah. By 1962 there were 20 schools and 4000 students and by federation in 1971 there were 28,000 students, mostly in towns and cities.

Primary education is now compulsory in the UAE and secondary education is nearly universal. It is estimated that there are around 300,000 children at government schools. There are also a number of schools specifically catering to different groups of expats. A great variety of curriculums and language teaching are offered.

At one time Emiratis had to go abroad, usually to Pakistan or the UK, with the help of government grants to seek a tertiary education. This changed in 1977 with the establishment of the United Arab Emirates University in Al-Ain. There are now three government universities and several private universities and colleges in the UAE. In 1998 there were approximately 38,000 tertiary students. As a way of encouraging nationals to contribute to the workforce, those who do go on to tertiary studies are given a very generous monthly salary simply for attending their course. The government is also willing to pay the cost of overseas study for UAE citizens. This includes a monthly salary and the cost of moving a spouse and children overseas as well.

ARTS

Traditional music and dance are an important part of the cultural heritage of the UAE and are covered in detail in Arts in the Facts about the Region chapter. For information about traditional handicrafts, see the special section 'Shopping' at the end of the Regional Facts for the Visitor chapter.

Painting

Although painting in the Western sense is not an artistic tradition in most of the Arab world, it is becoming popular in the UAE and exhibitions by local artists are common. Many of the themes of these works centre on family life and traditional pastimes but there are also some very modern works from the younger artists.

The encouragement of artists is still a relatively new thing in the UAE although gallery owners in Dubai, Sharjah and Abu Dhabi agree that there has been an increase in patronage over the last five years. This generally takes the form of commissions from government offices and hotels as well as from sheikhs and other wealthy nationals.

A few Emirati artists have demanded well-deserved attention from the international art

UNITED ARAB EMIRATES

community. Sheikha Hessah, the eldest child of Sheikh Maktoum bin Rashid al-Maktoum (Dubai's ruler), was trained by renowned Bangladeshi artist, Tina Ahmed. Abdul Qader al-Rais is considered a torchbearer of the artistic movement in the Emirates. Abdul Rahim Salem, chairman of the Emirates Fine Arts Society, is a well-known and successful artist. Other Emirati artists include Azza al-Qasimi, Sawsan al-Qasimi (of the ruling family of Ras al-Khaimah), Safia Mohammed Khalfan and Khulood Mohammed Ali.

Much of the art you will see in the galleries and shops, though, is by resident expatriates. This is due to the simple fact that they make up such a large percentage of the population. Many of the themes adopted by these artists represent the history and tradition of the UAE: family life, traditional pastimes, souq life, Bedouin heritage and seafaring.

Small exhibitions by local artists and by school children are held almost every week in galleries, hotel lobbies, community centres, shopping centres or schools. You'll find details of these exhibitions in *Gulf News* or *What's On* magazine. The Sharjah Art Museum (see the Sharjah section in the Northern Emirates chapter for more details) exhibits much of this work and conducts art classes. There is also a government-run art gallery and workshop at the Cultural Foundation in Abu Dhabi (see that chapter for more details). In Dubai, the Dubai International Arts Centre (☎ 04-444 398, off Jumeira Rd, Jumeira) and the Orient Gallery (☎ 04-558 832, Bur Juman Centre, Bur Dubai) both exhibit the work of local artists.

SOCIETY & CONDUCT

As the traditional cultures of the UAE and Oman are similar in most aspects, this topic is covered in detail in Society & Conduct in the Facts about the Region chapter at the beginning of this book.

Traditional Dress

Most nationals wear traditional dress. Men wear the 'I-don't-know-how-they-keep-it-so-clean' ankle-length, white *dishdasha*.

The *ghutra* is the white cloth worn on the head and held in place by a black material coil called an *agal*. Sometimes men wear a red- or gold-checked ghutra. Underneath the ghutra men wear a lace skull cap called a *taqia*. Sometimes men just wear the taqia on its own. On special occasions, sheikhs and other important men will wear a black or gold cloak, called an *abba*, over their dishdasha. If you look in any local newspaper, you'll usually see a picture of Sheikh Zayed or one of the other rulers wearing their abbas for important diplomatic meetings.

Women wear a long, black cloak called an *abaya* which covers everything from the head to the feet. In addition a black headcloth called the *shayla* is usually worn over the top. Many women, especially those in the more conservative rural areas, also wear a

Falconry

Falconry is a traditional hunting method still practised in rural areas of the UAE (and Oman), although now not so much out of necessity but as a social pastime, and as a way of reaffirming a cultural identity. Traditionally, falcons were caught and trained in time for the migration season of the houbara bustard, a desert bird similar to a chicken. The houbara (now protected) was the preferred prey of the falconer because it was small enough to be caught by the falcon yet big enough to feed a small family. At the end of the migration season in spring, the falcon was released and another would be caught in autumn to repeat the process. Now most people buy their falcons already trained from an animal souq.

The Bedouin had many ways of catching falcons. One method was for a man to be buried in the sand with just his head and arm above the surface. His arm was then hidden within a bush which had a live pigeon tied to it. The fluttering pigeon would attract the falcon and, when the unsuspecting falcon was close enough, the buried man would throw a cloth over its head and catch it.

burqa. This is a stiff mask made of gold-coloured material that covers the eyebrows, nose and mouth. Underneath their abayas women wear whatever they want. Traditionally, they often wear a simply designed floral dress called a *kandoura*. Men, too, wear a kandoura which ressembles a short-sleeved kaftan. Women often have henna decorations on their hands and feet, especially in more traditional, rural areas. See the boxed text 'Henna Patterns' in the Dubai chapter for more details on this traditional practice.

MODERN ARCHITECTURE

One of the most striking features of the Dubai and Abu Dhabi skylines is the blend of traditional Arabian-style buildings with ultramodern architectural creations. The building boom in these cities, the richest in the UAE, has lured architects from the world over, and there is enough wealth to fund the most ambitious of projects. The result is that a tour around the city centre can make you feel like you've wandered onto the set of a science-fiction movie.

These modern constructions sit a little awkwardly with the relatively few examples of traditional architecture left in the two cities – an illustration of the conflict between traditional and modern, Western and Islamic that is at the heart of modern Emirati society. In Abu Dhabi all new architecture must incorporate Islamic features (such as archways), but there are no such restrictions on architects in Dubai, although some effort has been made to incorporate traditional features into contemporary designs.

The intense heat and humidity reduces the lifespan of buildings by up to 25%, although this is only just being recognised by municipal councils. About 90% of Dubai's architecture can be described as 'cosmopolitan' or 'international', and is made of concrete, steel and glass. These materials, more than any others, absorb the heat and transfer it to all parts of the construction, causing damage over a period of time. Recently, lightweight thermal blocks have been introduced as an alternative to concrete and steel. Although they are expensive, and therefore not widely used, they have great heat resistance. In addition, the final coating on modern buildings is usually light and contains reflective paint.

TONY WHEELER

TONY WHEELER

Top: The clubhouse of the Dubai Golf & Yacht Club mirrors the sails of a traditional dhow. (Photo by Lou Callan)

Bottom Left: The Burj al Arab (Arabian Tower) at the Jumeira Beach Hotel has become Dubai's most recognisable feature.

Bottom Right: Space-age building on the Corniche in Abu Dhabi, one of the most modern cities in the world.

Most of the large-scale building projects in the cities of the UAE are carried out by foreign architecture firms, usually from Europe. Fortunately, these companies tend to take into account the heat and humidity and design and build accordingly.

A boat ride along the Creek in Dubai is one of the best ways to see the city's contrasting architectural treasures. From the wind-tower houses in the Bastakia Quarter of Bur Dubai to the shimmering curve of the National Bank of Dubai building and the pointed dhow-like roof of the Dubai Creek Golf & Yacht Club, it's hard to believe they are all part of the same city. Outside the city centre, the Burj al-Arab tower at the Jumeira Beach Hotel, completed in 1999, has become a major landmark of the city. Built on an artificially constructed island about 300m from the shore, the 60-floor, sail-shaped tower is 321m high, including the spire on top. Combined with the older, S-shaped original hotel building, the two structures represent a sail hovering above a breaking wave, symbolising Dubai's maritime heritage.

A walk along the Corniche in Abu Dhabi provides a good view of the city's glittering forest of high-rises. There are very few old buildings left in Abu Dhabi, which makes the contrast between the traditional, whitewashed form of the Al-Husn Palace and the surrounding, ultramodern high-rises all the more striking.

Right: The Cultural Foundation in Abu Dhabi, with Etisalat tower in background. Etisalat buildings throughout the UAE are crowned by a giant, sparkling golf ball. Designed by Canadian firm Cansult Ltd, the ball represents the world encompassed by the power of global communications.

CHRIS MELLOR

Facts for the Visitor

SUGGESTED ITINERARIES

One Day

If you are in Dubai, visit the Creek for an *abra* (motorboat) ride and wander around the dhow wharfage. Take a stroll through the Gold Souq and the Spice Souq for a feel of traditional Dubai and be sure to make time for a visit to the Dubai Museum.

If you are in Abu Dhabi, visit the Al-Hosn Palace and the Cultural Foundation. A dhow cruise from the Al-Dhafra wharf to the Corniche will give you a great view of the city and, at night, a meal under the stars at the Breakwater Local Cafe followed by a *sheesha* (traditional pipe) are a must.

Two Days

Follow the one-day itinerary on the first day then take a 4WD safari to the desert or one of the wadis on the second day.

One Week

You should have enough time to see the main sights in Dubai and Sharjah or Abu Dhabi, take an overnight desert safari and camel ride, plus an overnight excursion to the east coast, staying at Fujairah or Khor Fakkan. You might even be able to throw in a day trip to Hatta.

Two Weeks

We highly recommend extending your trip from the cities out to the east coast, incorporating a visit to Fujairah, Khor Fakkan and Dibba over two or three days, followed by an overnight visit to Al-Ain, a day trip to Hatta, plus a two-day jaunt to the north coast.

Three Weeks

All of the two-week with an extra day in Al-Ain and the northern emirates, plus a visit to Liwa in the south of the country.

One Month

This is enough time to see everything mentioned in this book without having to rush

Highlights

- The Creek, soul of Dubai; as with all great trading ports, the city is best seen from the water.
- Deira souqs in Dubai, the most traditional part of the city and a fascinating area to stroll around.
- The east coast from Fujairah to Dibba, for some of the most striking scenery in the country.
- Hatta, an easy drive from Dubai, popular for its refreshingly cooler climate and stunning mountain scenery.
- The desert around Al-Ain, best experienced with a camel safari into the dunes and an overnight stay.
- Sharjah's Central Market, an excellent place for a shopping expedition and some hard bargaining, especially if you are in the market for Persian and Turkish carpets.

too much. Your best bet is to hire a car and see the country at your leisure.

MAPS

There are not many good maps of the whole country. They're either missing scales or north points or they're just plain wrong. Geoprojects publishes a map of the entire country which is probably the best of the road maps. It's widely available for Dh50. See the individual chapters for the best local maps.

TOURIST OFFICES

There is no official government tourist office that covers all of the emirates but the Dubai Department of Tourism & Commerce Marketing has a helpful Welcome Bureau (☎ 04-224 5252 or 228 5000), as well as three visitor centres. Another good place for tourist information is at the big hotels and tour operators (See Organised Tours in the

UAE Getting Around chapter for contact details of tour operators).

There are also quasi-official travel brokers in each emirate who have a monopoly on travel services at the wholesale level. They include the Dubai National Travel & Tourist Authority (DNATA or 'danata' as it is known) in Dubai, SNTTA in Sharjah and RNTTA in Ras al-Khaimah.

VISAS & DOCUMENTS
Passport
To visit the UAE you must have at least two months' validity left on your passport from the date of arrival.

Visas
Everyone needs a visa to enter the UAE except citizens of GCC countries and British nationals with the right of abode in the UK. A transit or visit visa must be arranged through a sponsor.

If your passport shows any evidence of travel to Israel you will be denied entry to the UAE. A few readers have informed us, however, that there is no longer a problem with Israeli stamps in passports although the embassy has not officially declared this.

The original of visit and transit visas are almost always deposited at the airport for you to pick up on arrival. If you are picking up your original visa from the airport, make sure you have a faxed copy of your visa before your flight to the UAE or you may find that the airline will not allow you to board. You can also pick up visas at the port in Sharjah if you are arriving by boat from Iran.

It is possible, in theory, to arrange a UAE visa that doesn't need to be picked up from an airport, ie, to have one stamped in your passport before you leave home. This is not very common, but it does give you the option of entering the UAE by land. You must make it clear when you apply for your visa that you want to enter by land. You will still need a sponsor. They just need to return a faxed letter of sponsorship (a standard letter produced by UAE embassies) to the

STOP PRESS: Visas for the UAE

After the first print-run of this title went to press, the UAE government relaxed tourist visa regulations. Visitor visas valid for 60 days are now available on arrival in the UAE at approved ports of entry (namely all the airports and ports) for citizens of most developed countries. These include all western European countries (except for Malta and Cyprus), the USA, Canada, Australia, New Zealand, Japan, Brunei, Singapore, Malaysia, South Korea and Hong Kong. Visas can be extended for another 30 days for Dh500, but only at the Department of Immigration and Naturalisation in the emirate in which you first arrived.

Citizens of other Gulf Cooperation Council (GCC) countries do not need visas to enter the UAE, and can stay pretty much as long as they want.

For citizens of other countries, a transit or tourist visa must be arranged through a sponsor. This can be a hotel, a company or a resident of the UAE. Most hotels charge a fee of around Dh100 for arranging a visa.

The above information overrides references to tourist visas in the Visas section of this chapter. For completely up to date information about visas and border crossings, check with the UAE embassy before you leave home.

UAE embassy you are arranging your visa through.

Transit & Single-Entry Visas The most common way to enter the UAE is on a 14-day transit visa which costs Dh150 (US$40). This must be organised through a sponsor in the UAE (usually a hotel if you are a tourist – see Hotel-Sponsored Visas later in this section for more details).

If you are flying Gulf Air or Emirates Airlines from Europe to Asia or Africa (or vice versa) they can arrange an on-arrival 96-hour transit visa at a cost of US$65 per day. This includes accommodation at a four-star hotel for the duration of your stopover. You pay more, obviously, if you want five-star accommodation.

A standard, single-entry visit visa is valid for two months, costs Dh110 (US$30) and must be used within three months of the date of issue. If you are flying on Emirates Airlines or Gulf Air they can arrange a single-entry visa for a total cost of Dh150 (US$40).

Multi-entry Visas Multi-entry visas are available, in theory, to anyone from the UAE embassy in their home country. If you can get one, these visas cost Dh400 (US$100) for GCC residents or around Dh1200 (US$320) for others. They are valid for two years.

Hotel-Sponsored Visas Phone or fax one of the big hotels and ask them to sponsor you. Most hotels charge about Dh180 (US$50), and in some cases Dh300 (US$80) or more, for arranging it. The hotel will usually require you to stay between one and three nights. Once you receive the visa, you are free to go anywhere in the country or to move to a cheaper hotel. You will need to get the hotel to fax you a copy of the visa when it is ready or the airline may not let you travel.

Processing the visa can take anything from two days to three weeks. Generally, the biggest and most expensive hotels in Dubai are the fastest while smaller hotels anywhere, and big hotels in out-of-the-way places (like Fujairah) take the longest. If you are planning to get your visa through a hotel, try to enter the country through the airports of Abu Dhabi, Dubai or Sharjah. All of this can be expensive and difficult. If you are planning to stay a few days only you are better off having Emirates Airlines arrange your visa and hotel booking (see Transit & Single-Entry Visas earlier in this section).

Visa Extensions Transit visas cannot be extended, although people have been known to stay in the UAE simply by flying out to Bahrain, Doha (Qatar) or Kish (off the Iran-

ian coast) every other weekend and picking up a new visa on their return for about Dh450 (US$120). Visit visas can be extended for one month through the sponsor but it is expensive at Dh500 (US$140), not to mention complicated. You'll probably get a better deal in a visa run to Bahrain.

Driving Licence
Most foreign driving licences are accepted in the UAE so long as you are either a citizen or a resident of the country which issued the licence. If you live in the UAE, you will need to get a permanent UAE licence. For most nationalities this means just swapping your own driving licence for a UAE one. For other nationalities, including Indians, Pakistanis and most South-East Asians, it is necessary to sit a test.

EMBASSIES & CONSULATES
UAE Embassies
Contact details for UAE embassies in some key countries include the following:

Australia (☎ 02-6286 8802, fax 6286 8804) 36 Culgoa Circuit, O'Malley ACT 2606

Bahrain (☎ 723 737, fax 727 343) House No 221, Road 4007 – Complex 340, Manama

Egypt (☎ 02-360 9722, fax 570 0844) 4 Ibn Seena Street, Giza, Cairo

France (☎ 01-45 53 94 04, fax 01-47 55 61 04) 3 rue de Lota, 75116 Paris

Germany (☎ 0228-26 70 70, fax 267 07 14) Erste Fahrgasse, D-54113, Bonn

India (☎ 011-687 2822, fax 687 3272) E.P. 12 Chandra Gupta Marg, Chanakyapuri, New Delhi 11002

Iran (☎ 295 027, fax 878 9084) Wali Asr Street, Shaheed Waheed Dastakaardi St No. 355, Tehran

Kuwait (☎ 252 1427, fax 252 6382) Al-Istiqlal Street, Embassy Area, Qaseema 7, Al-Assaffa, PO Box 1828, Kuwait 13019

Oman (☎ 600302, fax 602584) Jameat ad-Duwal al-Arabiyya St, Al-Khuwair, Muscat

Qatar (☎ 885 111, fax 822 837) 22 Al Markhiyah Street, Khalifa Northern Town, PO Box 3099, Doha

Saudi Arabia (☎ 01-482 6803, fax 482 7504) Diplomatic Area, Abu Bakr al-Karkhi Zone, Amr bin Omayad Street, PO Box 94385, Riyadh 11693

UK (☎ 020-7581 1281/4113) 30 Princes Gate, London SW1

USA (☎ 202-338 6500, fax 337 7029) 3000 K Street NW, Suite 600, Washington DC 20007

Yemen (☎ 248 780, fax 248 779) Circular Lane, behind Central Security Bldg, PO Box 2250, San'a

Embassies in the UAE

All the embassies in the following list are in Abu Dhabi. The telephone area code for Abu Dhabi is ☎ 02.

Australia (☎ 789 946, fax 779 909) Diplomatic Area, Airport Rd (behind the Pepsi Cola plant), about 10km south of the centre. Open 8 am to 5 pm Saturday to Wednesday. The Australian embassy opened in 1999 but, at the time of writing they were not yet issuing visas. For this you have to go to the consulate in Dubai (☎ 331 3444, fax 331 4812) Dubai World Trade Centre, 6th floor. Open 8 am to 3.30 pm Sunday to Wednesday, 8 am to 2.45 pm on Thursday.

Bahrain (☎ 312 200, fax 311 202) Al-Najda St, behind Abu Dhabi Islamic Bank. Open 8 am to 2 pm Saturday to Thursday.

Canada (☎ 456 969, fax 458 787) Al-Nahayan St (near the Batin Palace). Open 8 am to 4 pm Saturday to Wednesday.

France (☎ 435 100, fax 434 158) Al-Nahayan St (near the Batin Palace). Open 9 am to 12 pm Saturday to Wednesday.

Germany (☎ 435 630, fax 455 712) Al-Nahayan St (near the Batin Palace). Open 9 am to 12 pm Saturday to Thursday.

Kuwait (☎ 446 888, fax 444 990) Diplomatic Area, Airport Rd (behind the Pepsi Cola plant), about 10km south of the centre. Open 8 am to 2.30 pm Saturday to Wednesday.

Oman (☎ 463 333, fax 464 633) Saeed bin Tahnoon St (next to Immigration Department), about 8km south of the centre. Open 8 am to 1.30 pm Saturday to Wednesday.

Qatar (☎ 493 300, fax 493 311) Diplomatic Area, Airport Rd (behind the Pepsi Cola plant), about 10km south of the centre. Open 8 am to 2.30 pm Saturday to Wednesday.

Saudi Arabia (☎ 445 700, fax 446 747) Diplomatic Area, Airport Rd (behind the Pepsi Cola plant), about 10km south of the centre. Open 8 am to 1 pm Saturday to Wednesday.

UK (☎ 326 600, fax 342 676) Khaled bin al-Walid St, just south of the Corniche. Open 8 am to 1 pm Saturday to Wednesday

USA (☎ 436 691, fax 435 441) Sudan St (between Al-Karamah St and the intersection where King Khalid bin Abdul Aziz St becomes Al-Nahayan St). Open 8.30 am to 1 pm Saturday to Wednesday.

Yemen (☎ 448 457, fax 447 978) Diplomatic Area, Airport Rd (behind the Pepsi Cola plant). Open 9 am to 1.30 pm Saturday to Wednesday.

CUSTOMS

Arriving in the UAE is a treat. Dubai, in particular, has a reputation for its fast processing of arrivals: making it from the aircraft to the street in under 20 minutes is possible.

The duty-free allowances for tobacco are huge: 2000 cigarettes, 400 cigars or 2kg of loose tobacco (this is not a country cracking down on smoking). Non-Muslims are allowed to import 2L of wine and 2L of spirits, unless they are arriving in Sharjah, where alcohol is prohibited throughout the emirate. You are generally not allowed to bring in alcohol if you cross into the country by land. No customs duties are applied to personal belongings.

MONEY
Currency

The UAE dirham (Dh) is divided into 100 fils. Notes come in denominations of Dh5, 10, 20, 50, 100, 200, 500 and 1000. Coins are Dh1, 50 fils, 25 fils, 10 fils and 5 fils, although these last two coins are rarely used now. A few years ago the government issued new coins which are smaller than the old ones. Both types remain legal tender, but check your change as the new Dh1 coins are only slightly smaller than the old 50 fils coins.

You may hear the currency occasionally referred to as rupees, especially by elderly people. When Britain controlled India, the rupee was the official currency in what is now the UAE and from 1948 until independence in 1971, a currency known as the 'Gulf rupee' was legal tender throughout the area.

Exchange Rates

The dirham is fully convertible and is pegged to the US dollar. At the time of writing, exchange rates were as follows:

country	unit		dirham
Australia	A$1	=	Dh2.360
Canada	C$1	=	Dh2.450
euro	€1	=	Dh4.070
France	FF10	=	Dh6.20
Germany	DM1	=	Dh2.080
Japan	¥100	=	Dh3.00
New Zealand	NZ$1	=	Dh1.98
UK	UK£1	=	Dh6.03
USA	US$1	=	Dh3.68

Exchanging Money

General information on exchanging cash and travellers cheques is covered in the Regional Facts for the Visitor chapter at the beginning of this book.

Costs

Fairly decent hotels can be found for Dh100 to Dh150 in Dubai, but they tend to be more expensive elsewhere. Eating for Dh10 to Dh15 is rarely a problem, though if you have a penchant for alcohol the bill is going to be a lot dearer. For example, a pint of beer costs around Dh16 plus tax; a bottle of house wine is going to cost at least Dh80 plus tax. Getting around is cheap in shared long-distance taxis and minibuses and admission to most museums and sites is free.

Plan on spending Dh150/200 per day for budget/mid-range travel. In Dubai, Fujairah and Sharjah, where there are youth hostels, you might be able to keep your budget down to half that.

Taxes

In Dubai, most hotels and restaurants add a 10% service charge and a 10% municipality tax. In Abu Dhabi, hotels and restaurants have a 16% service charge added to their bills and in Sharjah it's 15%. If a price is quoted 'net', this means that it includes all taxes and service charges.

POST & COMMUNICATIONS
Postal Rates

Letters up to 20g cost Dh3 for Europe; Dh3.50 to USA, Australia and the Far East; Dh2.50 to the subcontinent; Dh1.50 to Arab countries; and Dh1 to GCC countries. These rates double for letters weighing 20g to 50g. Postcard rates are Dh2 to Europe, the USA, Australia and Asia, Dh1 to Arab countries and 75 fils to GCC countries.

Sending a 1kg-package to Australia, the USA and the Far East costs Dh130; to Europe and South Africa it costs Dh85; to the subcontinent Dh68; to Arab countries outside the GCC Dh64; and within GCC countries it costs Dh45.

Sending Mail

Mumtaz Speed Post is available from main post offices in each emirate but is very expensive. For example, a letter to Australia costs Dh100. If you need to send something in a hurry, it costs half as much to use a courier company.

Receiving Mail

Poste restante facilities are not available in the UAE. The American Express (AmEx) offices in Abu Dhabi and Dubai will hold mail for clients, ie, card holders and people with AmEx travellers cheques. If you are checking into a five-star hotel, the reception desk will usually hold letters and small packages for two or three days prior to your arrival. Be sure to mark these 'Guest in Hotel' and, if necessary, 'Hold for Arrival'.

We don't recommend you have anything of value sent to you in the UAE by mail. Incoming packages have a habit of disappearing in the UAE and there does not seem to be any way of tracing them.

Telephone

The UAE has a splendid telecommunications system and you can connect with just about anywhere in the world from even the remotest areas. The state telecom monopoly is Etisalat, recognisable in each city by the giant golf ball on top of its office buildings.

Coin phones have almost completely been taken over by cardphones. Phone cards are available from street vendors around Etisalat offices and from grocery stores and petrol stations.

The UAE country code is ☎ 971. To dial out from the UAE dial '00', followed by the

Telephone Troubles?

At the time of writing, telephone numbers around the UAE were changing from six to seven digits. Most numbers will have changed by July 2000, but you should still be able to call the old number for some months and receive a recorded message telling you the new number. There are no set rules for how the numbers are changing, but many numbers repeat the first digit at the beginning, eg, 200 000 becomes 220 0000; also numbers beginning with 08 (ie, Hatta and Liwa) will drop the 0. For Dubai, it seems you just have to add a 6 to the beginning of the old number. If you need information on these changes, you can call the Etisalat helpline on ☎ 04-222 0444 – if the number doesn't change!

international country code. Mobile numbers begin with 050 in the UAE. Often people will give their seven-digit mobile number without mentioning this prefix. There are area codes in the UAE; these are given in the individual town and city sections throughout the UAE chapters.

If you are dialling a UAE number from outside the UAE, drop the '0' of the area code. There are Home Country Direct services to 43 countries. Dialling these codes connects you directly to an operator in the country being called. A list of access codes to these countries is in the Etisalat Services section of the phonebook.

Call Charges The peak/off-peak direct-dial rates from the UAE to the following destinations are Dh4.62/2.54 to Australia and Canada, Dh4.62/3 to the USA (excluding Alaska and Hawaii), Dh4.62/3.21 to UK, France and Italy, Dh5.45/4.50 to Germany and Switzerland, Dh6.43/4.50 to India, Dh5.81/5.29 to Hong Kong, Dh6.21/5.45 to Japan. There is a complete list of rates at the back of the phonebooks for the major cities.

The off-peak rates apply 9 pm to 7 am every day and all day on Fridays and public holidays.

Fax, Telex & Telegraph

Most Etisalat offices are also equipped to send and receive fax, telex and telegraph messages. They may ask for your local address and contact number before they'll send a fax. The service is fairly good but it is expensive at Dh10 per page to most international destinations.

In all the cities of the UAE you'll find small shops advertising typing and photocopying services. Many of these can also send faxes for about half the cost of Etisalat.

Email & Internet Access

Private Internet access is available through the national phone company, Etisalat, and there are Internet cafes in the main cities. Most top-end hotels have Internet access for guests, although the rate is usually much higher than at an Internet cafe. See the individual city entries for contact details of Internet cafes.

INTERNET RESOURCES

For general information on travel within the UAE go to www.emirates.org.ae. This site has information on what there is to see and do, news and media, arts and crafts. Or check out www.uaeforever.com, which breaks up information by emirates. It has comprehensive lists of travel agents in each city as well as things to see and do. It also includes lists of government departments and embassies.

A relatively new site is www.godubai .com. This is a large site with lists of travel agencies, airlines, libraries and links to other sites. It also has information on the Emirates Environmental Group, as well as promotions and giveaways.

BOOKS

This section lists books specific to the UAE. See the Regional Facts for the Visitor chapter for a list of more general books on the Gulf and the Middle East.

Guidebooks

Dubai Explorer and *Abu Dhabi Explorer* from Explorer Publishing include heaps of information on just about everything there is to see and do in these cities, from paragliding to Mexican restaurants, and lists of all kinds of clubs and societies. They're particularly useful for expats.

UAE – a MEED Practical Guide is geared mainly towards resident expats (where to find a school for your child, a vet for your pet etc) and business travellers.

For those who have 4WDs, *Off Road in the Emirates I* and *II* by Dariush Zandi are a must, although directions given to sites can be vague and confusing. They are published by the UAE-based Motivate Publishing and are widely available for Dh55.

The Green Guide to the Emirates by Marycke Jongbloed (who founded the Arabian Leopard Trust and now heads the Breeding Centre for Endangered Species in Sharjah), touts itself as 'an environmentally friendly guide to little-known places of beauty and interest in the United Arab Emirates'. The same author has also written *Wild About Cats* which looks at the endangered felines of Arabia.

History & Society
Father of Dubai: Shaikh Rashid Bin Saeed al Maktoum by Graeme Wilson is a tribute to the acknowledged founder of modern Dubai. Mohammed al-Fahim's *From Rags to Riches* traces the 30-year transformation of the UAE from a Bedouin society into one of the richest countries in the world. *The Merchants* by Michael Field sketches the rise of Dubai as a trading centre.

For a personal account of the development of the UAE read *The Wells of Memory*. It's the autobiography of Easa Saleh al-Gurg who was the director of the Board of the Trucial States Development Office and the most senior Arab staff member of the British Bank of the Middle East and, later, the UAE's ambassador to London.

For an Emirati view of local history and Britain's role in the Gulf see *The Myth of Arab Piracy in the Gulf* by Sultan Muhammad al-Qasimi, the emir of Sharjah. The book, which is widely available in Sharjah for Dh150 (the profits go to charity), is es-

sentially a reworking of the emir's doctoral thesis from the University of Exeter in the UK.

Mother Without a Mask by Patricia Holton is a very enlightening account of a British woman's involvement with a family from Al-Ain. It takes you inside the closed doors of the women's world in the UAE.

NEWSPAPERS & MAGAZINES
Gulf News and *Khaleej Times*, both based in Dubai, are the UAE's two English-language newspapers. Both cost Dh2 and carry pretty much the same international news, although *Gulf News* is the better of the two. Local news in both papers consists largely of 'business' stories which are little more than advertisements masquerading as news. Like most countries in the Gulf, you're rarely told what decisions have been made by political bodies in the country. They also tend to have fairly comprehensive coverage of the Indian and Pakistani political and entertainment scenes.

The Arabic major dailies are *Al-Bayan*, *Al-Khaleej* and *Al-Ittihad*. Foreign newspapers are available in larger bookshops in Dubai and Abu Dhabi, larger hotels and some Western supermarkets.

What's On is a monthly magazine catering mostly to the expat community. It's a pretty good source of information about what's new at the UAE's hotels, bars, clubs and discos. The magazine costs Dh12, though you will often find it is free in five-star hotels.

RADIO & TV
Emirates FM at 99.3 is the only UAE-wide radio station. The Dubai radio station, Dubai FM, is at 92 FM and Channel 4 FM is on 104.8. All are English-language and all feature hyped-up DJs playing mainstream chart music along with the occasional speciality music programs such as classical or country-and-western music. QBS in Dubai, at 97.5 FM and 102.6 FM, features radio plays in English, jazz specials and world music shows. Abu Dhabi's Capital Radio, at 100.5 FM, has similar music.

Abu Dhabi and Dubai each have an English-language TV channel in addition to their Arabic broadcasts, although outside the two main cities the quality of reception is decidedly mixed. Channel 33 in Dubai has an English-language movie and one or two programs from the US or Australia most nights of the week. Abu Dhabi Channel 2 has a mixture of English-language programs, movies and documentaries. Abu Dhabi and Dubai also have a sports channel each that broadcast soccer matches from around the Middle East. Dubai Business channel broadcasts from 6 pm to 2 am and features news and business news (in Arabic and English) from around the world with a particular focus on the Middle East and Asia. You can watch Omani TV (mostly Arabic but with a daily newscast in English at 8 pm, as well as occasional English-language movies) in Al-Ain. Qatar TV's English channel's reception is OK in Abu Dhabi when the weather is good.

PHOTOGRAPHY & VIDEO

Apart from the usual provisos (see Photography & Video in the Regional Facts for the Visitor chapter), there is no problem with taking photographs in the UAE.

Getting colour prints developed is never a problem – 20-minute services are advertised by photo developers on nearly every street in the country. These places will also do four passport photos for Dh10. A 36-print roll of film will cost you about Dh39 to develop. You'll also get another film and a photo album thrown in. The best place to get slides and black-and-white film developed is Prolab (π 04-669 766) on Abu Baker al-Siddiq Rd in Dubai. They also sell a wide range of photographic accessories.

HEALTH

The standard of health care is reasonably good throughout the UAE. Western medicines are widely available at pharmacies. If you need to find a doctor, try your hotel (if you are in an upmarket hotel) or your embassy for recommendations for a local doctor. If this is not possible, you can go to any

hospital. Some major hospitals are listed under Information in the relevant city sections throughout this book.

There are no compulsory vaccinations for travel in the UAE, but some vaccinations might be a good idea as a general precaution before you travel. See Health in the Regional Facts for the Visitor chapter for more general travel health information.

The tap water in Abu Dhabi, Dubai and Al-Ain is OK to drink, but it often tastes horrible and is heavily chlorinated. Most residents stick to bottled water throughout the UAE.

Emergency care in the UAE is free at government hospitals. Nonurgent health care in the UAE is neither free nor very cheap. Travel insurance would be very much in order. Expats are usually covered by a health card entitling them to receive free care at government hospitals and clinics.

BUSINESS HOURS

Government offices start work at 7.30 am and finish at 1 or 1.30 pm Saturday to Wednesday. Some are also open on Thursday mornings but this will gradually be phased out with the reduction of the working week from 5½ days to five days. Shops and companies open from 8 or 9 am until 1 or 1.30 pm and reopen in the afternoon from 4 to 7 or 8 pm Saturday to Wednesday. Some businesses, especially those where the majority of staff are Western, are open straight days, which means 8 am to 5 pm. Banks are generally only open in the morning. Most shops and souqs are also open on Friday evenings until about 10 pm.

This is all subject to some local variation. In Ras al-Khaimah, for example, all shops are required to close for about half an hour at prayer time.

PUBLIC HOLIDAYS & SPECIAL EVENTS

In addition to the main Islamic holidays (see Public Holidays & Special Events in the Regional Facts for the Visitor chapter for details), the UAE observes the secular holidays of New Year's Day (1 January) and National

Day (2 December). Each emirate also observes its own holidays. In Abu Dhabi, for example, 6 August is a public holiday marking the accession of Sheikh Zayed.

The death of a minister, a member of the royal family, or the head of state of another Arab country is usually marked by a three-day holiday. Note that if public holidays fall on a weekend, the holiday is taken at the beginning of the next working week.

Festivals

Dubai plays host to a number of tourist-oriented events each year. These are the Dubai ('Do Buy') Shopping Festival in March/April and the Dubai Summer Surprises in July/August. Both are designed to attract tourist dollars, mainly from other GCC countries. Apart from raffles, discounts and cash giveaways, the shopping centres and hotels play host to traditional culture displays such as dancing and henna painting. There are also events for children, though you have to wonder at the intelligence behind such events as burger-eating competitions.

ACTIVITIES

There are lots of clubs and societies in the UAE offering all kinds of activities from ballet to martial arts – far too many to list here. The Explorer guides (see Books earlier in this chapter) include detailed listings.

Have Kids, Will Travel

The UAE offers plenty of options when it comes to entertaining the kids. Almost every park in the UAE has a kids' playground and there are plenty of grassy stretches where they can expend energy. Most shopping centres have nurseries or play areas for little kids though, most of the time, you won't be able to leave them unattended. A sand-skiing excursion into the dunes is another activity kids might enjoy (see Activities for more details).

If you're planning to visit Dubai, the best time to take kids is during the Dubai Shopping Festival. Every day there is some activity for children at one shopping centre or another such as face painting or competitions.

In Dubai, Magic Planet at the City Centre shopping mall has rides and minigolf as well as numerous video games and is aimed primarily at kids under 12. It's open 10 am to 11 pm Saturday to Thursday and 1 to 11 pm on Friday. Individual rides cost Dh2.50 or Dh40 for unlimited rides with six video game tokens thrown in.

Also in Dubai, Encounter Zone at Wafi Shopping Centre is a kind of techno-adventure playground for kids. It is divided into Galactica, which has amusements and rides for teenagers and adults, and Lunarland, which is a play area for kids under 10. It's open from 10 am to midnight every day. Individual rides cost Dh4.50 or you can pay Dh40 for free access to everything. Younger children can be left under the supervision of employees at Lunarland for Dh40 for half a day.

Wonderland in Dubai, next to the Al-Boom Tourist Village, has a number of space age and watery rides for Dh10 entrance fee.

By far the most appealing place for older kids in Dubai is the Wild Wadi waterpark. The entry fee will put a dent in your budget at Dh120/95 for adults/children but the rides are some of the most exciting in the world – see the boxed text in the Activities section of the Dubai chapter for more details.

Outside Dubai, there are a few good options. The Sharjah Science Museum in Sharjah is guaranteed to keep children and adults fascinated for a couple of hours. Dreamland Aquapark on the Dubai–Ras al-Khaimah road claims to be the largest waterpark in the Middle East. There is also Hili Fun City & Ice Rink in Al-Ain. For more details on all these places, see the relevant chapters.

Running

If you have the stamina of a mountain goat you can join in the annual Dubai Desert Endurance Marathon. This is a five-day test of fitness where teams cycle, run and walk across 220km of dunes, coastline and rugged gravel plains. The fifth day involves an abseiling finale.

There are a number of clubs in the UAE whose members regularly go on desert runs (or walks or strolls) to keep fit and meet people. They are called the Hash House Harriers and there are lots of them around the Emirates. Contact them in Dubai (☎ 050-625 4605), Abu Dhabi (☎ 02-742 882) or Al-Ain (☎ 03-620 611).

Diving

The best diving in the UAE is on the east coast around Fujairah. The waters off the Gulf coast are murky and visibility is usually poor. There are several dive centres, most of which are attached to the larger hotels. If you're interested, you could try some of the following dive companies, based in Dubai:

Al-Boom Marine Diving Unlimited (☎ 04-394 1267) behind the Eppco petrol station on Al-Jumeira Rd, 1.4km south of Jumeira Beach Park. Offers dives off the east coast and charges Dh130 for one dive or Dh200 for two dives with full equipment hire.
Inner Space Diving Centre (☎ 04-331 0203) at the Diving Village in Shindagha will arrange a dive off the Dubai coast if you really want, for Dh125 to Dh215 (with equipment). Inner Space can also take you up to the east coast and into the waters off the Musandam peninsula; dives range from Dh200 to Dh500 (with equipment), depending on how far up the coast you go.
Scuba International (☎ 04-420 553) on Al-Wasl Rd, just south of the Iranian Mosque, and **Scubatec** (☎ 348 9888) in the Sana building, on the corner of Trade Centre and Al-Adhid Rds in Karama, both arrange dives off the east coast for around Dh220 to Dh250, including equipment hire.

Outside Dubai, you could try the Fujairah Hilton, the Oceanic Hotel in Khor Fakkan, the Sandy Beach Diving Centre in Badiyah or the Holiday Beach Hotel just south of Dibba. Contact details and costs are in the relevant city sections.

Open-water diving courses are available from Al-Boom Marine in Dubai for Dh1200. Advanced courses cost Dh800. PADI courses can be done through Inner Space Diving Centre in Dubai for Dh1400 for beginners or Dh900 for advanced. The diving centre at the Oceanic Hotel in Khor Fakkan also offers PADI courses. *Dubai Explorer* has a full listing of diving courses on offer around the UAE.

Golf

In the Gulf, golf courses are either grass (rare) or sand/gravel (common). The UAE is home to most of the Arabian peninsula's real grass golf courses. The cost of maintaining such courses is reflected in the exorbitant green fees. At sand courses players carry a small square of astroturf around a series of grassless, gravelly fairways in order to be able to hit the ball. There are three grass courses in Dubai, one in Abu Dhabi and a pitch-and-putt course in Al-Ain. If you want to play at these courses, you'll have to pay handsomely for the privilege. There are also a number of sand (well, more like gravel) courses that are larger and cheaper but definitely not as attractive.

Off-Road Safaris

If you plan to head off the beaten track into the sands and mountains you need a copy of *Off-Road in the Emirates* and/or *Off-Road in the Emirates II*. Another handy book which gives useful tips on driving in the desert is Jim Stabler's *Desert Driver's Manual*. See Activities in the Regional Facts for the Visitor chapter for more information on this favourite pastime.

If you don't want to drive yourself, there are plenty of tour companies offering desert and wadi tours. In general, a desert safari or wadi drive with lunch and/or dinner will cost between Dh125 and Dh185 per person. Overnight desert trips cost about Dh350 (see Organised Tours in the UAE Getting Around chapter for contact details of tour companies).

Gulf News sponsors the Overnighter Fun Drive each year, usually in early February, which involves a scenic drive through the desert over two days. In 1999 there were over 2000 participating vehicles. You must have your own 4WD and apply for tickets well in advance.

Sand-skiing

Something has to be done with all those dunes. This sport involves a monoski and an arduous climb up the highest dune you can find. Arabian Adventures charges Dh195 for a half-day of sand-skiing and camel riding. Orient Tours charges Dh180/25 for adults/ children for sand-skiing and camel riding.

LANGUAGE COURSES

Language courses are available in Dubai and Abu Dhabi. Polyglot Language Institute (☎ 04-223 429) in Al-Maktoum Rd, Deira, offers beginner courses and conversation classes in Arabic, French, German and English, as well as computer courses. The Dubai World Trade Centre (DWTC; ☎ 04-308 6036) offers courses in Arabic from beginner to advanced levels. The British Council in Abu Dhabi (☎ 02-659 300) and Dubai (☎ 04-337 1540) has courses in Arabic for beginners. Berlitz Language School (☎ 02-672 287, Bin Haiyat Bldg, Zayed the First St, Abu Dhabi) offers courses in a number of languages including Arabic and Urdu (useful as this is the language of many of the Pakistani expats in the UAE).

ACCOMMODATION
Camping

There are no official camp sites in the UAE but camping in the desert and on beaches is quite common. The best time to camp is November to March when it's not too hot. For practical tips on camping in the region see Accommodation in the Regional Facts for the Visitor chapter.

Hostels

There are three youth hostels in the UAE – in Dubai, Sharjah and Fujairah. The Dubai and Sharjah hostels offer beds for Dh35.

Beds in the Fujairah hostel are Dh15 per night. In all cases, a Hostelling International card is required and a working knowledge of Arabic would be useful. If you don't have an HI card you can always pay for a year's membership (Dh75) at one of these hostels.

Hotels

Dubai has the widest range of hotels, to suit most tastes and budgets. Elsewhere, the choice is more limited, with a preponderance of four- and five-star places. Most of the country's cheap hotels are in and around the Deira souq area in Dubai. These bottom out at around Dh70 to Dh80 for a single and Dh100 to Dh120 for a double, but we would not recommend the really cheap places to single women travellers. The cheapest places that provide reliable visa service cost from Dh250/350 for singles/doubles.

In Dubai, the five-star hotels cost anything upwards of Dh600/750. Top hotels in Abu Dhabi are a bit cheaper, starting from around Dh450/525. You can get discounted hotel rates during Ramadan, summer and the Dubai Shopping Festival in March/April.

FOOD

Eating cheap in the UAE generally means eating in the small Indian/Pakistani restaurants that are found everywhere. Meals in one of these places will cost you around Dh6 and snacks about Dh2.50. Cheap Lebanese food is easy to find. In most cities Chinese and Filipino food is also fairly easy to come by, and as you would expect, American fast food chains have arrived throughout the emirates. At the top end of the market almost any kind of food can be found in Abu Dhabi and Dubai. In the smaller emirates, 'top-end' food means eating at the big hotels – although this is no guarantee of quality.

For more information on the types of food available in the UAE, see Food in the Regional Facts for the Visitor chapter.

DRINKS

Nonalcoholic drinks, such as soft drinks, fruit juices and mineral water, are available throughout the country. Alcohol is banned in the emirate of Sharjah but is available in the other emirates. Alcohol can only be sold in restaurants and bars attached to hotels (in practice, three-star hotels or better). The selection is what you would expect to find in any well-stocked bar. The prices are pretty outrageous – expect to pay around Dh18 for a pint of beer or a glass of wine.

There are 'holes in the wall' around the country where alcohol is sold illegally to those without licences, ie, nationals and Muslim expats. The police tend to turn a blind eye and these places do a roaring trade.

ENTERTAINMENT
Cinema
You can catch relatively recent Western flicks at a number of cinemas in the main cities. The films shown are all Hollywood mainstreamers, action being the name of the game. You won't find anything even remotely arthouse or foreign, unless you have a passion for the dozens of blockbuster Hindi films that seem to come out each week.

Films are subject to censorship and, as sex and romance are the main ingredients of most Hollywood flicks, films are usually cut to shreds. The films are subtitled in Arabic and French. Cinemas are comfortable and clean and ticket prices range from Dh18 to Dh25, depending on the cinema.

Pubs & Bars
Considering that Muslims are prohibited by Islamic law from drinking alcohol, there are a surprising number of drinking holes in the UAE. Every emirate, except Sharjah (where alcohol is banned), has pubs attached to hotels. Don't be surprised if you see locals enjoying a pint just as much as non-Muslims.

Pubs and bars are usually open until about 11 pm or midnight. In Dubai they stay open until 1 or 2 am. Expect to pay about Dh16 to Dh18 for a pint of beer or a glass of wine, more at the five-star hotels. Most bars and pubs have a happy hour, when all drinks are about 30% cheaper.

At most places, Tuesdays and Sundays are 'Ladies' Night' which means those of the right sex get one or two free drinks. Not

surprisingly, it tends to attract more men than women. The biggest problem with many of the bars in Dubai and Abu Dhabi is that the managers all seem to feel that a bad, loud lounge singer is an essential part of any drinking establishment. This usually means that your quiet conversation over a pint of beer will be completely drowned out by a loud rendition of a Whitney Houston song.

Nightclubs
If you want to dance the night away, Dubai is the place to be. While there are nightclubs in most of the larger hotels in Abu Dhabi, Fujairah, Al-Ain and Ras al-Khaimah, Dubai is the unrivalled star of the UAE's nightlife. Nightclubs are always attached to the four- or five-star hotels and they often tend to be segregated into Arabic, Western, Filipino and Indian clubs – nationality is not an entry requirement, it's just the way people socialise. All nightclubs have DJs and some have live bands as well. Wednesday, Thursday and Friday nights are the biggies and closing time is about 3 am.

Concerts & Theatre
UAE residents just can't get enough 1970s and '80s music. If it's not enough that the English-language radio stations are stuck in the past, every couple of months there is a visit from a band that has long since departed the scene in other parts of the world. At the time of writing, for instance, there were concerts by Boney M, James Brown, Ian Dury and the Blockheads, Human League and, who could forget, Kajagoogoo. You can see an international act of this type just about every month in Dubai. The other emirates don't offer this kind of entertainment.

Western theatre companies (usually from the UK) regularly visit the UAE, usually under the sponsorship of some international company. These performances almost always take place in one of the five-star hotels. Once or twice a year you can be treated to a classical music concert, usually from a European orchestra and/or choir. There is always plenty of advance publicity for these sorts of events so watch the newspapers.

SPECTATOR SPORTS
Golf

The Dubai Desert Classic is one of the richest golf tournaments in the world with prize money of US$1 million, and it attracts some of the best players. Held at the Dubai Creek Golf & Yacht Club or at Emirates Golf Club each February, it runs for four days and costs Dh75 for the day. Throughout the year there are small amateur tournaments at the golf clubs in Dubai. See the daily newspapers for details.

Horse Racing

Many wealthy sheikhs have taken a liking to horse racing and some of the finest horses in the world are owned by Emiratis. The Dubai World Cup is well known as the world's richest horse race with prize money of US$12 million. It is held at Nad al-Sheba racecourse, 5km south-east of Dubai (signposted from Shaikh Zayed Rd). The newspapers have details of exact dates of race meetings but they are usually held in March. General admission to the races is free.

Camel Racing

This is the main spectator sport in the UAE (and Oman). Camel racing takes place in various spots around the country during the winter. Ras al-Khaimah is one of the best places to see camel races, partly because the racing schedule there is relatively predictable and partly because the track is well laid out for viewing. Races around the country usually take place on Fridays during the winter and sometimes also on Tuesdays or Wednesdays. Admission is free but get there early. The races usually start around 6 am and continue until about 9 am. If you miss out on a race meeting you can usually catch training every morning at about the same time.

While camel racing sounds like fun, it is not for the faint-hearted. Since the races begin on a 4km straight, the moment the gun sounds, dozens of Emiratis go tearing down the side of the track in their 4WDs, paying far more attention to the camels than to where they are going.

The jockeys themselves are also at risk from these unwieldy ships of the desert. Due to allegations of child abuse, a decree was issued in 1993 prohibiting children from racing camels. In keeping with the international standards set for horse jockeys, the decree stated that all jockeys must weigh at least 45kg. However, despite efforts to enforce this ruling, the practice does not appear to have been completely wiped out in all areas.

LOU CALLAN

Camels prepare for a race at Nad al-Sheba Racetrack in Dubai.

Tennis & Cricket

The Dubai Duty Free Tennis Open, held annually in February, is a part of the ATP world series tour and total prize money is just over US$1 million. It is held at the Dubai Tennis Stadium at the Aviation Club in Al-Garhoud. Tickets get more expensive as the tournament progresses. It's about Dh100 for the first few matches and goes up to Dh250 for the finals. Tickets for the tournament, with food and beverage service, cost Dh2000 per person. Call ☎ 04-206 2425 for more information.

Sharjah is home to a couple of international cricket events each year. In April you can see the Sharjah Cup and in October the Coca-Cola Trophy. Participating teams change every year but there are three competing nations each time. Matches are played at the Sharjah Cricket Stadium on Al-Qasimia Rd and daily admission prices range from Dh20 to Dh300.

Marine Events

If fast boats give you a thrill you should visit Dubai or Abu Dhabi during autumn and spring when they play host to the Class One World Championship Power Boat races. In Dubai, heats are held at the Dubai International Marine Club in Mina al-Seyahi, about 35km along the coast south of the centre, on Dubai Creek. In Abu Dhabi, they are held just off the coast. Heats are held in October, November, March, April and May.

It's hard to imagine it but they do race those big dhows. Up to 50 of them take part in a race. When they're all lined up with their sails hoisted, ready to begin, it's a spectacular sight. Races take place every weekend from late September to May at the Dubai International Marine Club.

Every year in March is the President's Cup Dubai-Muscat Sailing Regatta, beginning in Dubai at the Dubai International Marine Club and finishing in Muscat at the Marina Bandar al-Rowdha.

You can call the Race Department of the Dubai International Marine Club on ☎ 04-399 4111 for more information and exact dates of any of the above events.

SHOPPING

For many visitors, shopping is the main reason for travelling to the UAE. Dubai's reputation as a shopper's paradise stems from the lack of duty and taxes as well as relatively cheap shipping costs. This means that travelling to Dubai purely for a shopping expedition is worthwhile. The Dubai Shopping Festival held every March/April is promoted aggressively and brings in thousands of tourists, especially from other Arab countries and the CIS states. Abu Dhabi has tried to attract tourists with its own shopping festival and airport duty free centre but it has yet to rival Dubai.

The UAE is a good place to buy gold – prices are reasonable and there's a large selection. Although Dubai has the largest and best-known gold souq (see the boxed text 'All That Glitters ...' in the Dubai chapter), you'll also find a good selection in Abu Dhabi, Sharjah and Al-Ain. Most of the silver (Bedouin) jewellery on sale in the UAE comes from Oman. Dubai has the best selection but you'll also find a limited range in shops in Al-Ain and Abu Dhabi.

If you're looking for Arabian souvenirs such as coffeepots and decorated metal food platters, the best places are Al-Arsah Souq in Sharjah and shopping centres in Dubai.

The UAE is renowned as the cheapest place in the Middle East to buy electrical goods. Other good buys include carpets (Dubai and Sharjar are some of the best places to buy Persian carpets outside Iran) and Iranian caviar (Dubai is the cheapest place outside Iran to buy Iranian caviar), as well as a huge range of souvenirs from India, Thailand and Africa. These include carved or leather stuffed camels (Dh30 for a small one up to Dh350 for a big one), wooden Quran holders (Dh30 to Dh50), brass candleholders (up to Dh20) and a huge selection of scarves and textiles. These are widely available in shopping centres in Abu Dhabi and Dubai but the best place for them is probably Sharjah's Central Market.

For a guide to the region's best buys, see the special section 'Shopping' at the end of Regional Facts for the Visitor chapter.

Getting There & Away

AIR

Dubai and Abu Dhabi are the country's main international airports, although an increasing number of airlines serve Sharjah as well. International flights also operate from Ras al-Khaimah, Al-Ain and Fujairah, although services are limited, usually to flights between the UAE and Pakistan, India and Egypt.

The national airline is Emirates Airlines. Gulf Air is a regionally based airline, partly owned by the UAE. To date, both airlines have faultless safety records. Emirates Airlines has services to Dubai, Abu Dhabi and Sharjah. Gulf Air has services to these three as well as to the smaller airports at Ras al-Khaimah, Al-Ain and Fujairah.

Emirates Airlines flies to around 50 destinations in the Middle East, Europe, Australia, Africa and the subcontinent. Dubai is the main hub. The only direct services from Abu Dhabi with Emirates Airlines are to/from Amman (Jordan), Beirut (Lebanon), Karachi (Pakistan) and London (UK); all other services involve a stop at Dubai. Gulf Air services all the main cities of the Middle East and has flights to many of the same long-haul destinations as Emirates Airlines.

All the major European, Asian and Middle Eastern airlines serve Dubai and some also serve Abu Dhabi. For more details of international flights to/from the UAE, see the regional Getting There & Away chapter earlier in this book.

To Oman, Gulf Air, Emirates Airlines and Oman Air each have a few services per week to Muscat. The one-way/return fare from Dubai to Muscat is Dh540/700, and fares don't vary much from airline to airline. The only time you can get a direct flight from the UAE to Salalah in southern Oman is during the Khareef Festival in July and August. Flights at this time from Dubai to Salalah cost OR99/185 with Oman Air.

There is no departure fee if you fly out of the UAE.

LAND

The UAE has land borders with Saudi Arabia and Oman. There is a bus service between Dammam in Saudi Arabia and Abu Dhabi, continuing on to Dubai. There are dozens of bus companies with services from the UAE to Syria, Jordan, Lebanon and Egypt via Saudi Arabia. A ticket costs around Dh500 return, including the cost of the Saudi transit visa. For more details of these services, see Land in the regional Getting There & Away chapter earlier in this book.

There are a number of border crossings between the UAE and Oman. Into Oman's Musandam peninsula, the main crossing is at Tibat on the west coast, just north of Sham. (This crossing is often called the Sham crossing point, although the border is at Tibat.) You can also cross into the Musandam peninsula at Dibba on the east coast, although at the time of research it was no longer possible to get to Khasab from Dibba.

Into the main part of Oman, the principal crossing point is the Wajaja crossing near Hatta, on the road to Shinas on the northern coast of Oman. You can cross freely between Al-Ain and the Omani town of Buraimi without any border formalities. The border crossings are at Wadi al-Jizzi, 53km into Oman on the road to Sohar, and at Hafit, just south-east of Al-Ain, on the road south to Ibri. There is a border crossing at Khor Kalba but it is in the mountains, reachable by 4WD only and manned by an old man who speaks no English.

Oman National Transport Company (ONTC) has daily bus services linking Muscat with Dubai and Abu Dhabi; there are no UAE-based services to/from Muscat. See Getting There & Away in the Muscat chapter for more details of these services.

Note that there is a departure tax of Dh20 payable if you leave by land. However, if you leave the UAE through Hatta or Al-Ain where there is no Emirati border post (although there is an Omani post), you do not pay the tax for the simple reason that there is nobody there to collect it.

SEA

There are passenger services between the UAE and both Iran and Iraq, as well as cruises that take in ports in Oman and Iran. See the regional Getting There & Away chapter earlier in this book for details of services to Iran and Iraq, and see Boat in the UAE Getting Around chapter following for details of cruises from the UAE.

A departure tax of Dh20 is payable if you leave the UAE by sea.

ORGANISED TOURS

Several international tour companies offer package holidays to the UAE. These packages are generally to Dubai, which is more of a tourist attraction than Abu Dhabi. The programs are either 'sea and sun' holidays or a combination of sea, sun, desert safari and sightseeing outside the city. These companies tend to accommodate clients at the beach hotels on the outskirts of Dubai or at the larger, resort-style hotels near Abu Dhabi (the facilities are wonderful, but you may end up wishing that you were closer to town). If you can face the thought of the UAE in high summer, the discounts offered are very

good. At the time of research, Flightbookers .com was offering a great summer deal which included a return flight from London and five nights in a five-star hotel for UK£359. Also at the time of research, the London office of the Dubai National Travel & Tourist Authority (☎ 020-7932 9900), was offering a return flight and three nights' accommodation in Dubai for the Shopping Festival in March/April for UK£299.

In the UK, other companies arranging tours and packages to the UAE include Abercrombie & Kent (☎ 020-7730 9600), British Airways Holidays (☎ 012393-722 628), Arabian Odyssey (☎ 01242-224482, fax 253078) and Kuoni (☎ 020-7499 8636).

In the USA, African Travel (☎ 1-800-421 8907, ✉ ati@africantravelinc.com) offers five-day packages to Dubai from New York during the Shopping Festival (March/April) each year for around US$2600. Global Destinations (☎ 757-490 3466, fax 490 3468, ✉ global@visi.net) offers a 10-day trip to Dubai from New York for around US$2725 per person, including the airfare.

In Australia, contact Abercrombie & Kent (☎ 03-9699 9766) or Destination Dubai (☎ 03-9576 0952). Both these companies offer upmarket packages tailored to your requirements.

Getting Around

AIR

At the time of writing there were no air services between the emirates, although there were plans for a charter service between Dubai and Al-Ain. Check with Gulf Air for further developments (☎ 04-271 3222).

MINIBUS

Dubai Transport has had a minibus service to the other emirates since mid-1998 but at the time of writing there was still no return service. Yes, that's right: the buses go back to Dubai empty, unable to take passengers until the necessary paperwork is done to operate the service in the other direction!

The minibuses are a great way to get around and are the same price or cheaper than the long-distance taxis. They are also more comfortable, and are the best way for single women travellers to get around – travelling alone in long-distance taxis can be problematic (see the boxed text on this page for more details). If it's hot, try to sit near the front of the minibus as the air-conditioning sometimes doesn't make it to the back rows.

The following table lists sample minibus fares between Dubai and some key destinations in the UAE.

destination	fare (Dh)
Abu Dhabi	30
Ajman	7
Al-Ain	30
Fujairah	25
Ras al-Khaimah	20
Sharjah	5
Umm al-Qaiwain	10

To get to Khor Fakkan and Dibba on the east coat you will need to get a minibus to Fujairah, then a shared taxi from there.

LONG-DISTANCE TAXI

Long-distance taxis are the only other way to travel between the emirates. They usually

---

Women Travellers – Warning

If you can, it is probably best to avoid travelling alone in long-distance taxis as there have been some instances of Western women being harassed in this situation. This can involve pulling up beside your taxi and staring, making kissy faces, pulling in behind your taxi and flashing lights or even pulling in front and putting on the brakes to try to get the driver to stop. Although it can seem dangerous, it's usually not an attempt to frighten you, or even a precursor to more sinister actions, it is simply a way of trying to attract your attention. If you find yourself in a situation like this, let them know in no uncertain terms that you are not interested. I've heard of one women who asked her taxi driver to pull up, beckoned the driver of the offending vehicle over, then punched him right on the nose! He got the message. You should also make sure you get the number plate and report any such incidences of harassment to the police – punishment for the offender can be a fine or even jail.

Lou Callan

---

carry seven passengers (although there are a few five- and nine-passenger taxis) and they leave when they are full. In Abu Dhabi and Dubai the local governments operate large taxi depots. Everywhere else the long-distance taxi station is usually little more than a vacant patch of ground in town or on the outskirts where the drivers wait for their cars to fill up.

Shared taxis can be a bit cramped but they are cheap. The main problem is that, apart from the busy Abu Dhabi–Dubai route, they don't fill up very quickly. The alternative is to take the taxi engaged (ie, privately) if you are willing to pay for all of the seats in it. This still works out relatively cheap and it's quicker, more reliable and definitely more comfortable than sharing a taxi.

The following table lists some shared and engaged taxi fares. Note that some shared fares are not available as it's unlikely you will be able to find enough people going to that destination. If you do find a shared taxi to one of these places you should pay about 20% of the engaged fare.

from	to	shared (Dh)	engaged (Dh)
Abu Dhabi	Al-Ain	30	150
Abu Dhabi	Dubai	30	150
Ajman	Umm al-Qaiwain	N/A	35
Al-Ain	Fujairah	40	200
Dubai	Sharjah	5	30
Dubai	Ajman	N/A	30
Dubai	Al-Ain	30	150
Dubai	Fujairah	30	150
Dubai	Hatta	25	100
Dubai	Ras al-Khaimah	20	100
Fujairah	Dibba	N/A	40
Fujairah	Khor Fakkan	N/A	20
Ras al-Khaimah	Ajman	10	50
Ras al-Khaimah	Dubai	15	70
Ras al-Khaimah	Fujairah	25	125
Sharjah	Ajman	N/A	10

CAR

The UAE is one of those countries where having your own car can mean the difference between a good holiday and a great one. Being able to explore some of the smaller villages and camp or drive a little off the beaten track is the real joy of coming to the UAE. Of course, hiring a 4WD will take you to the most remote spots, but many interesting places in this book can be reached without 4WD. Major roads around the UAE are very good. However, bad driving is endemic in the UAE and accidents are common – see Dangers & Annoyances in the Regional Facts for the Visitor chapter for more details. In Dubai and Sharjah traffic congestion can be a real problem at peak times.

Road Rules

See the Getting Around the Region chapter for road rules that are common to both the UAE and Oman. Remember that there are speed cameras on major highways around the UAE. The speed limit is 100km/h on these roads, with a maximum of 120km/h.

In Abu Dhabi it is illegal for trucks and larger vehicles (such as buses and minibuses) to overtake any smaller vehicle. This rule, designed to lower the number of accidents involving reckless truck drivers, means that you could find yourself in a minibus travelling from Dubai or Abu Dhabi to Al-Ain, for example, stuck behind a car in the right-hand lane travelling at 60km/h. Unless your driver does something illegal (which they tend to do), you could have a very long journey ahead. This ridiculous rule also means that impatient truck and bus drivers, not wanting to break the law, will force slow drivers into the fast lane so that they can pass them on the outside lane. Not a safe scenario at all.

All accidents, no matter how small, must be reported to the police. And do not move your car until the traffic police get there, even if it is causing a traffic jam. For insurance claim reasons you must have a police report and if you move your car, the police are not able to provide one. Over time, however, the police in Dubai have realised what a silly rule this is, and that traffic jams could be avoided if cars were moved out of the way and drivers sorted out their own insurance and reports. So, in Dubai, move your car out of the way if it is causing a traffic jam or risk being fined Dh100. Outside Dubai, however, you should leave your car exactly where it is, no matter what, and call the police.

Petrol

As you can imagine, the UAE is not short of petrol stations. Petrol is sold by the imperial gallon (an imperial gallon is just over 4.5L). Regular petrol costs Dh3.65 per gallon and premium is Dh3.95.

Rental

At the bigger agencies, such as Budget and Avis, small cars start at about Dh120 per day with another Dh20 for insurance. At the smaller agencies you should be able to negotiate a net rate of around Dh100 per day, including insurance. At the larger agencies you won't have any liability if you take out collision damage waiver (CDW) insurance. With the smaller agencies you may still be liable for the first Dh1000 of damage in the event of an accident, even if you've paid CDW insurance. Ask questions and check the fine print.

The first 100km to 150km per day are usually free with a charge of 40 fils to 50 fils for each additional km over this. If you rent a car for more than three days you will usually be given unlimited mileage. Although smaller agencies are generally cheaper than the larger chain companies, it's worth considering the convenience of being able to contact the local office of a bigger company wherever you are in the country in case something goes wrong. It's also worth making sure you have complete insurance cover (zero liability).

As seems to be the case with most things in the UAE, you must have a credit card to be able to hire a car. There are few exceptions to this. If you do find a car rental com-pany that will take a cash deposit instead, you will probably have to leave your passport with them as security, which can be tricky as most hotels require you to leave your passport with them for the duration of your stay. Some agencies insist on a credit card deposit as well as your passport. Find another agency if this is the case, or see if they will accept a photocopy of your passport.

BOAT

Arabian Adventures (☎ 04-343 9966) in Dubai offers an eight-day cruise on a 56-passenger boat from Dubai to the other emirates and on to Oman, Bahrain and Iran. Two different cruises are available – the east cruise takes you to Khasab in the Musandam peninsula, Muscat (with a day tour to Nizwa), Fujairah, Ras al-Khaimah, Sharjah and a coach tour to Hatta; the west cruise takes you to Bandar Abbas in Iran, Bahrain, Doha (Qatar), Sir Bani Yas Island (off the coast of Abu Dhabi) and Abu Dhabi city. At each port of call you have a city tour and/or a 4WD tour of the area. Accommodation is on the boat. The cost for each tour is US$1400 which is inclusive of everything – tours, meals, snacks and port taxes.

Arabian Sail Charters (☎ 04-332 9567) operates a three-night cruise on board a 58-foot catamaran from the UAE to Oman's Musandam peninsula. The cruise leaves Dubai on Saturday and returns on Tuesday. The cost of Dh2000 per person includes food, bedding, fishing and snorkelling equipment, and a buffet dinner at the Khasab Hotel on the Monday night.

LOCAL TRANSPORT
Bus

Only Abu Dhabi, Al-Ain and Dubai have municipal bus services and these are of varying usefulness. Unfortunately, Abu Dhabi's bus service is nearly useless for the traveller, as it is basically designed to transport labourers to and from the industrial areas on the edge of the city. The bus services in Dubai and Al-Ain are much more comprehensive and can get you to most of these cities' points of interest fairly easily.

Are You Covered?

If you're planning on driving around the emirates, note that unless you make other arrangements the insurance on your rental car will only be good inside the UAE. This means that if you make a shopping trip from Al-Ain to the Buraimi souq or want to take a look at the Omani portion of Dibba or drive to Hatta from Dubai through a section of Oman – all of which can be done without an Omani visa – you had better not have even a minor accident while you are on the Omani side of the border. It is possible to add Oman to a rented car's insurance (if, say, you want to rent a car in Dubai and drive to Muscat), but the insurance will go up by Dh10 or Dh20 per day and the cost of renting the car itself may double. Renting a car in Oman is expensive but it's not that expensive.

Finding Your Way Around

If you are out and about in the UAE's cities and towns, you will probably discover that most people living here haven't the faintest idea what the streets are called – officially or unofficially. And this goes triple for the taxi drivers! Directions still tend to come in the form of: 'It's the blue building on the left after you pass the such-and-such supermarket near whatever and across from...' Landmarks, such as roundabouts or buildings, are used as orientatation points, and directions are given from there.

Taxi

All taxis in Abu Dhabi and Al-Ain have meters, as do the Dubai Transport taxis, but those in the other emirates, and other taxis in Dubai, do not. See the boxed text 'Fare's Fair' in the Getting Around the Region chapter for a strategy for dealing with unmetered taxis.

ORGANISED TOURS

There are many companies in Abu Dhabi, Dubai, Sharjah and Ras al-Khaimah offering half-day, full-day and overnight tours of the various emirates as well as camel safaris, 4WD trips and dhow cruises. Many tour companies leave their brochures in hotels.

In this section we've listed a couple of the larger companies offering tours. See also Organised Tours in the individual city Information sections later in this book for details of city tours on offer. Alternatively, for a complete list of tour companies in each of the emirates, look up the Tourist Guide section at the front of the local phonebook. There is also a smaller listing in the direc-

tory pages of the widely available *What's On* magazine.

One of the largest companies is Arabian Adventures (☎ 04-343 9966) in Dubai which is run by Emirates Airlines. Their Grand Canyons tour (Dh340 per person) goes from Dubai to Masafi market and Dibba, then off-road through wadis in the Hajar mountains and back to Ras al-Khaimah via a camel farm. One of their 4WD tours (Dh425 per person) takes you to a camel race, then through sand dunes to a camp site in the desert and back to Dubai the next day across the Hajar mountains.

Orient Tours has offices in Dubai (☎ 04-828 238) and Sharjah (☎ 06-549 333). They offer an east coast tour which is a bit cheaper than Arabian Adventures, taking in Masafi market, Dibba, Badiyah mosque, Khor Fakkan souq and Fujairah for Dh175/85 for adults/children. They also have a trip (Dh395) to the sand dunes of Liwa oasis with a picnic lunch.

With Desert Rangers (☎ 04-453 091) in Dubai you can take a tour to the archaeological sites in Ras al-Khaimah then across to Dibba, Khor Fakkan and Fujairah for Dh190. They also have a trip to the Hatta rock pools with some dune-bashing on the way for Dh200. For Dh300, including lunch, you can take a canoe trip around the mangrove swamps at Khor Kalba.

When you book a tour with one of these companies you will usually be picked up from your hotel. Some of them require a deposit which is nonrefundable if there is less than 24 hours' notice of cancellation. Bear in mind that for what you pay for a day's tour with one of these companies, you could hire a car for up to three days and take yourself to lots more places in your own time.

UNITED ARAB EMIRATES

Abu Dhabi Emirate

Abu Dhabi is the richest and the largest emirate in the UAE, occupying about 85% of the country's total area. It borders Saudi Arabia to the south and west, and Oman to the east. In the south lies part of the Empty Quarter, the vast sea of dunes that covers much of eastern Saudi Arabia and western Oman. Sheikh Zayed bin Sultan al-Nayan, the ruler of Abu Dhabi, is also the supreme ruler of the UAE. Abu Dhabi city is the capital of the emirate.

Abu Dhabi

☎ 02

In the 1950s, visitors to Abu Dhabi remarked on how remote it was and how bleak it looked. What was then a small fishing village is now a sprawling city covering virtually all of Abu Dhabi island. Everything is modern, sleek and shiny. Some say it's soulless, but that's probably going too far. The UAE's capital may not have the attractions Dubai has, especially when it comes to nightlife, but it has its own feel and pace. The Corniche has been beautified over the last couple of years, providing a much-needed boost to the city's attractions.

HISTORY

Abu Dhabi is by far the richest and the most politically important of the seven emirates. It was founded in 1761, but the ruling Al-Nayan family did not move to the coast from their inland base at Liwa, near the Saudi border, until 1793, when a freshwater well was discovered. Al-Hosn Palace was built over this well when the ruler moved up from the desert.

The town expanded rapidly during the heyday of the pearl trade in the late 19th century. Abu Dhabi was never a major pearling or trading centre like Bahrain, but it was prosperous by the rather limited standards of the time. Under Zayed the Great,

who ruled the emirate from 1855 to 1909, Abu Dhabi became the most powerful of the Trucial Coast sheikhdoms.

The collapse of the pearling industry in the 1930s caused Abu Dhabi to go into a decline. In a desperate attempt to salvage the emirate, Sheikh Shakhbut (reigned 1928 to 1966) granted oil concessions in the late 1930s, but until the oil money began coming in some 30 years later, the town remained little more than a fishing village.

It is difficult today to imagine what Abu Dhabi looked like only 40 years ago. When Geoffrey Bibby, the archaeologist, first arrived in early 1958 he saw from the window of his airplane only the fort and a few huts along a stretch of white sand. The airport at which he landed consisted of 'two rows of black-painted oil-drums marking the approach to a stretch of salt flat'. Al-Ain, in the eastern region of the emirate, was a five-day journey across the desert by camel.

It is sadly ironic that after waiting two decades for oil to rescue his impoverished emirate, Sheikh Shakhbut was unable to manage the flood of money that came his way in the 1960s. In 1966, the British eased him out in favour of his brother, Sheikh Zayed, who has ruled ever since and has been the president of the UAE federation since independence in 1971.

ORIENTATION

The city of Abu Dhabi sits at the head of a T-shaped island. It is very spread out, making it impossible to cover on foot. The airport is on the mainland about 30km from the centre. To get to the centre of Abu Dhabi from the airport you cross the Al-Maqta Bridge. If you are approaching Abu Dhabi island from south or west of the emirate, you cross the Al-Ain Bridge.

The main business district is the area bounded by Sheikh Khalifa bin Zayed and Istiglal Sts to the north, Zayed the Second St to the south, Khalid bin al-Walid St to the

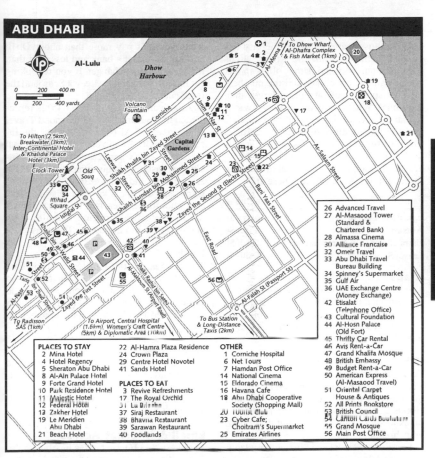

ABU DHABI

26	Advanced Travel
27	Al-Masaood Tower (Standard & Chartered Bank)
28	Almassa Cinema
30	Alliance Francaise
32	Omeir Travel
33	Abu Dhabi Travel Bureau Building
34	Spinney's Supermarket
35	Gulf Air
36	UAE Exchange Centre (Money Exchange)
42	Etisalat (Telephone Office)
43	Cultural Foundation
44	Al-Hosn Palace (Old Fort)
45	Thrifty Car Rental
46	Avis Rent-a-Car
47	Grand Khalifa Mosque
48	British Embassy
49	Budget Rent-a-Car
50	American Express (Al-Masaood Travel)
51	Oriental Carpet House & Antiques
52	All Prints Bookstore
53	British Council
54	Carlton Cards Bookstore
55	Grand Mosque
56	Main Post Office

PLACES TO STAY
2 Mina Hotel
4 Hotel Regency
5 Sheraton Abu Dhabi
8 Al-Ain Palace Hotel
9 Forte Grand Hotel
10 Park Residence Hotel
11 Majestic Hotel
12 Federal Hotel
13 Zakher Hotel
19 Le Meridien Abu Dhabi
21 Beach Hotel

22 Al-Hamra Plaza Residence
24 Crown Plaza
29 Centre Hotel Novotel
41 Sands Hotel

PLACES TO EAT
3 Revive Refreshments
17 The Royal Orchid
31 La Brioche
37 Siraj Restaurant
38 Bhavna Restaurant
39 Sarawan Restaurant
40 Foodlands

OTHER
1 Corniche Hospital
6 Net Tours
7 Hamdan Post Office
14 National Cinema
15 Eldorado Cinema
16 Havana Cafe
18 Abu Dhabi Cooperative Society (Shopping Mall)
20 Tourist Club
23 Cyber Cafe; Choitram's Supermarket
25 Emirates Airlines

west, and As-Salam St to the east. The inland side of the Corniche is dominated by modern office buildings. The main residential areas are all south of the centre, although there are many upmarket apartment blocks lining the Corniche.

Street Names
Just be aware that some of the streets in Abu Dhabi centre are better known by their old or common names. For example, Bani Yaas St generally extends all the way to the Corniche, well past the point where it offi-

cially becomes Umm al-Nar St. Other common names include the following:

official name	common name
Al-Falah St	Passport St
East Rd	Muroor Rd
Hazaa bin Zayed St	Defence St
Shaikh Hamdan bin Mohammed St	Hamdan St
Shaikh Rashid bin Saeed al-Maktoum St	Airport Rd or Old Airport Rd
Zayed the Second St	Electra St

The word Sheikh is often abbreviated to SH or SHK on street signs.

To confuse matters further, the city has taken to numbering all the streets. Signs with both numbers and names often appear on the same street corner and the numbers (always spelled out) are often larger than the names. What is not immediately obvious is that the city is also divided into districts and the streets are numbered by district. Thus, there are 20 or so 'Twentieth' streets in the city. The numbers you need to know are the ones applied to a handful of the main thoroughfares in the centre. These are:

name	number
East Rd & Lulu St	Fourth St
Al-Nasr St	Fifth St
Umm al-Nar St & Bani Yaas St	Sixth St
Leewa St	Tenth St

Maps

The best map of Abu Dhabi is produced by Geoprojects. It costs Dh45 and is available from All Prints Bookstore (see Bookshops later in this section) and from the larger hotel bookshops.

INFORMATION
Tourist Offices

There is no tourist office in Abu Dhabi, but the emirate-owned Abu Dhabi National Hotels Company (ADNHC) apparently has plans to set one up 'soon' – but don't hold your breath.

Some of the Dubai and Sharjah-based tour companies have offices in Abu Dhabi and they can provide some information on the city. Alternatively, you could call ADNHC on ☎ 449 914.

Money

In the centre, and especially along Shaikh Hamdan bin Mohammed and Shaikh Khalifa bin Zayed Sts, it often seems like every third building is a bank. Despite all of the competition for business, the rates for changing money are pretty standard. Shopping around is probably not worth the time unless you are changing US$500 or more, though you might want to ask what the commission is before signing on the dotted line. You shouldn't pay more than about Dh10 per transaction at a bank and less than that, if any, at a moneychanger. If you're looking for moneychangers, try Leewa St around the intersection with Hamdan.

American Express (☎ 213 045) is represented in Abu Dhabi by Al-Masaood Travel & Services on Al-Nasr St, west of the intersection with Khalid bin al-Waleed St. All the usual AmEx services are provided, including cashing cheques and holding mail. Any mail should be addressed c/o American Express, PO Box 806, Abu Dhabi, UAE, and should be clearly marked 'Client's Mail'. The office is open 8.30 am to 1 pm and 4 to 6.30 pm Sunday to Thursday.

Post

The main post office (☎ 215 415) is on East Rd between Al-Falah and Zayed the Second Sts. It's open 8 am to 8 pm Saturday to Wednesday, 8 am to 6 pm Thursday and 8 to 11 am Friday. There is a philatelic bureau on the 1st floor.

Telephone

The Etisalat office, on the corner of Zayed the Second and Shaikh Rashid bin Saeed al-Maktoum Sts, is open 24 hours a day. Fax, telex and telegram services are also available here.

Email & Internet Access

There are two Internet cafes in Abu Dhabi. The Cyber Cafe is above Choitram's supermarket on the corner of Shaikh Zayed the Second and Bani Yaas Sts. There is a coffee shop here and a separate computer room for women. Havana Cafe is on the corner of Hamdan and As-Salam Sts. Rates at both places are Dh20 per hour.

Travel Agencies

Travel agencies appear to be the only businesses that outnumber banks in Abu Dhabi. Of the larger operations, handling all major airlines and routes, the following agencies are recommended:

Advanced Travel (☎ 347 900) in the tiled red and black building on East Rd near the corner of Shaikh Hamdan bin Mohammed St

Al-Masaood Travel & Services (☎ 212 100) Al-Nasr St, west of Khalid bin al-Waleed St

Omeir Travel (☎ 223 500) corner of Shaikh Khalifa bin Zayed and Leewa Sts

Bookshops

All Prints Bookstore on Al-Nasr St has an excellent selection of English-language books. It also has a selection of French books and magazines, and maps of Abu Dhabi. Carlton Cards has a good selection of English-language books and a large travel section but it doesn't sell maps. It has two stores, one on Zayed the First St, west of Khalid bin al-Waleed St, and another at the Hamdan Centre on East Rd, near the corner of Shaikh Hamdan bin Mohammed St.

Cultural Centres

The British Council (☎ 659 300) on Al-Nasr St, off Tariq ibn Ziyad St, is open 9 am to 1 pm and 4.30 to 7 pm Monday to Wednesday. It doesn't operate a library, concentrating instead on English courses and other educational programs.

The US Information Service (USIS; ☎ 443 6567) is at the US embassy on Sudan St. It offers information on educational opportunities in the US but no library.

The Alliance Francaise (☎ 260 404) has a library and offers French courses and other cultural activities. The office is above the Jameela supermarket, behind the Lulu Centre, on the north side of Shaikh Hamdan bin Mohammed St between Leewa and Lulu Sts.

Left Luggage

There is no left luggage facility at Abu Dhabi airport but most hotels should be able to hold luggage for residents for up to a day.

Medical Services

Most hospitals will take walk-in patients for consultations and treatment. Your embassy can probably provide you with a list of doctors who speak your language. In an emergency try the following hospitals:

Abu Dhabi Central Hospital (☎ 214 666 for the general switchboard or ☎ 344 663 for the emergency unit) Al-Manhal St; the emergency entrance is on the corner of Al-Manhal and Karamah Sts

Corniche Hospital (☎ 724 900 for the general switchboard or ☎ 202 4221 for emergencies) next to the Sheraton at the eastern end of the Corniche

Emergency

For the police, dial ☎ 999, ambulance ☎ 998, fire ☎ 997.

CULTURAL FOUNDATION

This large, faceless building on Zayed the First St is more interesting than its outward appearance suggests. It is an impressive piece of architecture, designed by an American architect and incorporating Arabic elements of design. It houses the National Archives, the National Library and the Institute of Culture and Art. There is a large auditorium where lectures are given on everything from Arab culture to computer technology. The Foundation also offers a variety of language courses, but not Arabic. Literary and art exhibitions, as well as films, theatre performances and musical concerts, are hosted here regularly. You'll find details of what's on in the newspapers.

Behind the Foundation is an art workshop where courses are given in photography, painting, ceramics and sculpture. The hallways and lobby of the Foundation are dotted with interesting examples of Arabian art and artefacts. Even if there is no exhibition on, it's worth having a look around the building.

The Foundation is open 7.30 am to 1.30 pm and 4 to 10 pm Saturday to Wednesday, 7.30 am to noon and 4 to 9 pm Thursday, closed Friday. Admission is free.

AL-HOSN PALACE

Al-Hosn Palace is commonly known as the Old Fort or the White Fort. It is one of the oldest buildings in Abu Dhabi and its whitewashed walls are just as eye-catching amid today's skyscrapers as they would have been against a backdrop of reed and mudbrick huts 50 or 100 years ago.

UNITED ARAB EMIRATES

The first fort on the site was built over the city's freshwater well at the beginning of the 19th century by Shakhbut bin Dhiyab, the first ruler of the Al-Nayan dynasty. The present fort was built in the late 19th century by Sheikh Zayed the Great. It has been completely modernised and is now used by the Cultural Foundation as a documents and research centre.

You can enter the fort and wander around its gardens and courtyards. If the gate on Khalid bin al-Waleed St is closed, try the main entrance on Shaikh Hamdan bin Mohammed St. As you enter the fort, look at the tilework over the main (north) gate. The fort is open 7.30 am to 1.30 pm Saturday to Wednesday and 7.30 am to noon Thursday. Admission is free.

CAPITAL GARDENS
Abu Dhabi's central park occupies most of the area south of Shaikh Khalifa bin Zayed St between Umm al-Nar and Lulu Sts. It's a relaxing place to get away from the traffic for a few minutes, and there is a playground for children, as well as a kiosk and restaurant. The main entrance is near the

corner of Shaikh Khalifa bin Zayed and Umm al-Nar Sts, and there is another entrance on the south side, just back from Shaikh Hamdan bin Mohammed St.

DHOW WHARF & FISH MARKET
At the far eastern end of the Corniche, near the port, lies Abu Dhabi's small dhow wharf, also called Al-Dhafra. Although it can't compete with Dubai's waterfront, it does offer good local colour and an excellent view back towards the city. The fish market on the wharf is good but get here early – the smell becomes overpowering by the middle of the day.

To get there take Al-Meena St east until you reach the crossroads at the port's entrance gate. Turn left and follow the signs for Al-Dhafra Restaurant. The market and wharf are on the opposite side of the road.

IRANIAN SOUQ & VEGETABLE SOUQ
On your way to the fish market you will pass these two souqs on the right-hand side of the road. The Iranian souq really just offers endless piles of plastic wares and

Women's Craft Centre

This is a government-run operation where traditional crafts are made, displayed and sold. Although most of the items in the exhibition hall are for sale, some are just for display. You'll find woven bags, cushion covers, shawls and small rugs. There are also some coffeepots, trays and baskets. It's possible to visit the little round workshops in the courtyard where many of the items are made. Most of the women at work here are fully veiled and may be uncomfortable with male visitors so it's best to ask permission before entering the workshops.

Prices are fixed. The small baskets at Dh15 to Dh20 make nice, easily transportable gifts. The quality of the artisanship on display is very high, and prices reflect this. Mats and rugs are quite expensive, and many are made with artificial fibres instead of the traditional goat or camel hair or sheep's wool.

The centre (☎ 476 645) is open 9 am to noon Saturday to Wednesday, 9 to 11 am Thursday, closed Friday. Admission to the exhibition hall is Dh2.

To reach the craft centre take Shaikh Rashid bin Saeed al-Maktoum St south from the centre and exit at the small black and white sign pointing right, just after the overpass which traverses Shaikh Saeed bin Tahnoon St (it is easy to overshoot this turn-off so keep your wits about you). It is in a compound marked 'Handicraft Industrial Centre'. A number of buses go along Shaikh Rashid bin Saeed al-Maktoum St. Just check with any of the drivers at the bus station. A taxi should cost about Dh10.

kitchen goods, but it's a bustling, colourful area. The vegetable market is very extensive and worth a visit, and there is also a small meat souq at one end.

OLD SOUQ

If you're looking for a break from the world of banks and boutiques that is modern Abu Dhabi take a walk through what remains of the old souq in the small area east of Al-Ittihad Square, near the clock tower, and north of Shaikh Khalifa bin Zayed St. There are numerous moneychangers, a small gold market, shoe shops galore and lots of household goods on offer. You will also find one or two shops with Indian, Omani and Iranian antiques and souvenirs. Unfortunately there are plans for the souq to be replaced with multistorey shopping malls by 2002 but knowing how slowly things get done in the UAE, let's hope that the souq will be around for a while longer.

BEACHES

Most five-star hotels have private beaches as well as access to jet-ski and boat hire. If you are not a guest of a hotel with a beach club it will cost you about Dh60 on weekdays and Dh100 on weekends for a day visit. There is an area of public beach out on the Breakwater. To get there just continue past the restaurants for about 200m.

There is a government-managed **Women's Beach** is on the headland at the western end of the Corniche. To get there take the Corniche west to the final roundabout by the Khalidia Palace Hotel and turn right onto the road that has a gate across it (the gate should be up). After 1.25km, at the point where the road turns right, you'll see the entrance to the beach straight ahead. The beach is open 1 to 6 pm Saturday to Wednesday, noon to 6 pm Thursday and 10 am to 6 pm Friday. The entrance fee is Dh5.

The Tourist Club, at the eastern end of Shaikh Hamdan bin Mohammed St, is a cheaper alternative to the five-star hotels. For Dh10 Saturday to Wednesday or Dh20 Thursday to Friday you can use the gym and beach and hire paddle boats. If you

want to use the tennis courts or do an aerobics class you will have to pay extra. The club is open 8 am to midnight daily.

GOLF

Abu Dhabi Golf Club (☎ 445 9600) is about 5km from the town centre next to the racecourse off Saeed bin Tahnoon St. To play the grass course will cost you dearly. Nine holes is Dh140, 18 is Dh230.

CRUISES

Blue Dolphin (☎ 669 392) runs 45-minute cruises from Al-Sofon Restaurant on the Breakwater at the far western end of the Corniche to Al-Dhafra wharf. This costs a very reasonable Dh10 each way and boats leave every hour on the hour from 9 am to about 5 pm in winter, later in summer.

The Forte Grand Hotel runs two evening cruises. One is a sunset cocktail cruise leaving from the dhow wharf at about 6 pm. It lasts for one hour and costs Dh35 per person. The second is a dinner cruise, leaving at 9 pm for about two hours and a buffet dinner is served. This costs Dh150 per person. Bookings are essential through the Forte Grand on ☎ 742 020.

The Al-Dhafra complex (see Places to Eat later in this section) offers a dinner cruise every night at 8.30 pm for Dh85. Phone ☎ 732 266/88 for information on cruises. Net Tours (see Organised Tours, following) has a dhow dinner cruise, leaving at 10 pm, for Dh135/80 for adults/children.

ORGANISED TOURS

Most of the UAE's tour companies are based in either Dubai or Sharjah, but nearly all of them offer tours of Abu Dhabi. Net Tours (☎ 794 656) is a Dubai-based company but it has an office in Abu Dhabi next to Merrylands Travel Agency, opposite the Sheraton hotel. It offers a city tour for Dh75 (Dh50 for children) that takes in Al-Hosn Palace, the Women's Craft Centre, the Oriental Carpet House, the Breakwater and Corniche, and the dhow wharf.

Sunshine Tours (☎ 449 914) is run by ADNHC. It has a desk (usually abandoned) in the lobby of the Sheraton hotel and details of its tours and prices are displayed in the lobbies of some hotels. For Dh80 you can take a city tour or a sunset dhow cruise with light refreshments.

Cyclone Tours (☎ 313 515) is represented by Al-Toofan Travel & Tours and its city tour costs Dh80. Al-Toofan doesn't have an office as such, but everything is arranged over the phone.

PLACES TO STAY

At the time of writing there was no youth hostel in Abu Dhabi but indications are that one will be opened sometime in the future. There are no cheap hotels in Abu Dhabi. The prices quoted in this section include service charges. They are the rack rates so bear in mind that hotels will usually offer discounts if you ask.

PLACES TO STAY – BUDGET

Zakher Hotel (☎ 275 300, fax 272 270, Umm al-Nar St) is the only place in Abu Dhabi where you can get a room for under Dh200 per night. Singles/doubles start at Dh150/200.

Federal Hotel (☎ 789 000, fax 794 728, Shaikh Khalifa bin Zayed St) charges Dh200/225. The hotel is in a good central location, across from the Forte Grand, but is not as good value as hotels nearby with similar rates.

Majestic Hotel (☎ 710 000, fax 741 221) is next to the Federal Hotel near the corner of Shaikh Khalifa bin Zayed and Umm al-Nar Sts. Single rooms at Dh300 have two beds; double rooms for Dh250 have the two beds pushed together. The rooms are large and clean and the hotel also has 24-hour room service.

Park Residence (☎ 742 000, fax 785 656, Shaikh Khalifa bin Zayed St) is across from the Forte Grand in the same block as the Federal Hotel. It has comfortable rooms for Dh200/225.

Hotel Regency (☎ 765 000, fax 777 446) is an excellent hotel with five-star amenities. It is behind the Mina Hotel on the corner of Al-Meena and As-Salam Sts. Rooms

cost Dh250/350 and all have kitchenettes. Guests can use the beach and health club at the Sheraton nearby.

Mina Hotel (☎ 781 000, fax 791 000), at the intersection of As-Salam and Al-Meena Sts, is under the same management as Hotel Regency and the rates are the same at Dh250/350. Rooms here are large and comfortable but not quite as good as those at Hotel Regency as they don't offer sea views.

PLACES TO STAY – MID-RANGE

Khalidia Palace Hotel (☎ 662 470, fax 660 411) at the far western end of the Corniche is expensive at Dh450/550, considering it is a fair way from the city centre. It has a number of restaurants and a private beach club.

Centre Hotel Novotel (☎ 333 555, fax 343 633, Shaikh Hamdan bin Mohammed St) is better value at Dh400/500 and is right in the heart of the commercial and shopping district.

Al-Ain Palace Hotel (☎ 794 777, fax 795 713) near the eastern end of the Corniche has rooms, many with a sea view, for a rather pricey Dh460/575. There are also some good restaurants, a bar and a large pool.

Al-Hamra Plaza Residence (☎ 725 000, fax 766 228, Zayed the Second St) near Bani Yaas St has rooms for Dh350/450.

Sands Hotel (☎ 335 335, fax 335 766) at the junction of Shaikh Rashid bin Saeed al-Maktoum and Zayed the Second Sts has rooms for Dh402.50/437.

PLACES TO STAY – TOP END

The following hotels all have private beach clubs and health facilities as well as numerous restaurants and bars.

Abu Dhabi Hilton (☎ 681 1900, fax 669 696) is at the western end of the Corniche. Singles/doubles cost Dh975/1090.

Abu Dhabi Inter-Continental (☎ 666 888, fax 669 153) is just south of the western end of the Corniche, off Bainunah St. Rooms start at Dh986/1102.

Le Meridien Abu Dhabi (☎ 776 666, fax 644 9315, Zayed the Second St) is a luxurious hotel with the best health club and restaurants in town. Rooms are Dh840/928.

Beach Hotel (☎ 644 3000, fax 644 2111, Zayed the Second St) is on the same road as Le Meridien about 500m to the south-east. It was thoroughly renovated in 1998 and has rooms for Dh580/750.

Forte Grand Hotel (☎ 644 2020, fax 644 2552, Umm al-Nar St) has large rooms starting at Dh997/1114.

Sheraton Abu Dhabi (☎ 773 333, fax 725 149) is at the eastern end of the Corniche. Rooms cost Dh870/986, which is overpriced considering the hotel has slipped into a state of shabbiness over the years and is due for renovation.

Crown Plaza (☎ 210 000, fax 217 444, Shaikh Hamdan bin Mohammed St) has rooms for Dh783/870 and a late checkout of 2 pm.

Radisson SAS (☎ 666 220, fax 666 291, Zayed the First St) is designed for long-term guests and offers large suites for Dh1276 as well as standard singles/doubles for Dh638 (one price). All rooms have cooking facilities, and the rooftop pool has great views of Abu Dhabi from 18 floors up. The hotel doesn't have its own beach club but guests can use the one at the Khalidia Palace Hotel.

PLACES TO EAT
Budget Dining
You'll find plenty of shwarma places in the centre of town; a shwarma or felafel sandwich is usually about Dh2.50.

Revive Refreshments on Al-Meena St near the Mina Hotel, with the red bench seats inside, has the best omelette sandwiches (Dh250) in the country.

Siraj Restaurant on Zayed the Second St is another good place for cheap snacks, including biryani and kima for about Dh6, omelette sandwiches for Dh2.50 and samosas and pakoras for 50 fils each.

Bhavna Restaurant on Zayed the Second St has vegetarian Indian food. Samosas are Dh2.50 each and the *masala dosa* (curried vegetables in a pancake) is good for Dh3. It also sells a selection of Indian sweets.

Sarawan Restaurant, also on Zayed the Second St, has excellent biryanis. The portions are large and, at Dh8, excellent value.

La Brioche on Shaikh Khalifa bin Zayed St, between Lulu and Leewa Sts, is a good bet at any time of day. It offers good coffee, including cappuccino, which at Dh7 to Dh10 is worth the extra dirham or two. For breakfast, croissants and various other pastries are available for Dh3 to Dh6, and there is a set breakfast menu for about Dh10 to Dh15. Excellent and generous baguette sandwiches go for Dh10 to Dh12, while hot plates such as beef stew with tagliatelle are more expensive at Dh30 to Dh35.

Restaurants
If you want alcohol with your meal you will need to go to the hotel restaurants but be prepared to pay for the privilege. We've listed a selection of recommended restaurants in this section; for a complete listing of all Abu Dhabi's restaurants, pick up a copy of the widely available *What's On* magazine or the *Abu Dhabi Explorer*.

Foodlands (☎ 330 099, Zayed the Second St) is a popular Chinese/Indian restaurant. The food is varied (beef stroganoff alongside carrot halva on the menu) and the servings are generous. Main dishes cost Dh10 to Dh25.

Bukharah is in the Hotel Regency (see Places to Stay – Budget earlier). It bills itself as a Central Asian restaurant which, in practice, means the menu features both Indian and Iranian dishes with the emphasis on subtle combinations of spices rather than sheer heat. The dining room is a treat – the tables are laid with beautiful Iranian tablecloths from Isfahan – and the service is fairly good. Main dishes cost from Dh15 to Dh30.

Al-Sofon (☎ 655 135) and *Al-Sufina (☎ 662 085)* are Arabic-style fish restaurants on the Breakwater at the western end of the Corniche. They both specialise in catering for large groups and are worth visiting at night for the spectacular views of Abu Dhabi. To get to the Breakwater turn right at the Hilton roundabout on the Corniche.

The Royal Orchid (☎ 744 400) is a Thai/Chinese restaurant on As-Salam St near Shaikh Hamdan bin Mohammed St. It has a great atmosphere (notice the goldfish

UNITED ARAB EMIRATES

under your feet as you enter), and interesting dishes. Mains are Dh20 to Dh25, which is good value for this quality of food, and it also offers a Mongolian barbecue.

Al-Dhafra at the dhow wharf near the fish market is a complex built around a series of traditional *barasti* (palm-leaf) houses, which includes two restaurants. *Al-Mina Coffee Shop* specialises in local dishes including three different types of bread. A few metres away is *Al-Arish* (☎ 732 266), a fancier place offering a huge buffet for Dh45 or Dh95 for a choice of fresh fish. There is a playground for children and private booths (for families) overlooking the waterfront.

Pizzeria Italiana in the Federal Hotel (see Places to Stay – Budget earlier) has basic but good pizzas and pastas for Dh12 to Dh18. It makes a welcome change from biryanis and shwarma and you can enjoy a glass of house wine with your meal.

Chi-Chis at the Le Meridien (see Places to Stay – Top End) is a nicely decorated and friendly place serving huge helpings of Mexican food, with main dishes for about Dh35.

Self-Catering

For fresh fruit and vegetables try the *markets* out by the port area. The produce here is better and cheaper than in the supermarkets. If you don't want enough fruit and vegetables to feed an extended family, just hand over a dirham or two and point to what you want. There are meat souqs too but you may prefer to buy packaged and refrigerated meat from the supermarket where hungry flies don't hover around.

Al-Khaleej bakery on As-Salam St, just up from The Royal Orchid restaurant, is one of a number of bakeries around town where you can get Arabic bread and sweets.

For European-style bread head for *La Brioche* on Shaikh Khalifa bin Zayed St. It offers a large selection of white and brown loaves, baked daily.

ENTERTAINMENT
Bars & Clubs

Most four- and five-star hotels have bars, pubs and nightclubs. Many venues have happy hours with reduced-price drinks, live entertainment and theme nights throughout the week – '70s, karaoke, sport etc. Most have 'ladies' nights' where women get their first drink free. Listed in this section are some recommended pubs and clubs. For a complete listing of bars, pubs and clubs see *What's On*, which also has information on performers and musicians in town.

The Tavern, a British-style pub at the Sheraton hotel, is a good place for a drink. On Saturday nights it has a 'lad's night out' with plenty of sport on the TV, curry and chips – don't say we didn't warn you!

Cheers at the Al-Ain Palace Hotel is an American bar and *Finnegans* at the Forte Grand is an Irish pub with two outside terraces, which are nice in winter.

Illusions is a slick disco at the Forte Grand Hotel with lots of over-the-top lighting. It's open until late.

Cinemas

The *Eldorado Cinema* on Zayed the Second St, *Almassa Cinema* on Shaikh Hamdan bin Mohammed St, and *National Cinema* off Bani Yaas St all show Western films. See the Tabloid section of *Gulf News* for listings.

Coffeehouses

You will find a few small coffeehouses with *sheesha* (traditional pipes) along the backstreets in the city centre. The best place is the *Breakwater Local Café*, at the Breakwater. It has a lovely setting overlooking the water and city and there are private barasti booths, candlelit and decked out with rugs and cushions. A late-night visit here is a must.

SPECTATOR SPORTS

Abu Dhabi's camel racecourse lies about 40km from the city centre off the road to Al-Ain. Follow the signs for Al-Wathba out of the city.

SHOPPING

The best place for locally made crafts is the government-run Women's Craft Centre – see the boxed text earlier in the Abu Dhabi section.

Al-Nasr St, especially around the AmEx office, has several shops with a good selection of handicrafts, many made in Egypt, Syria, Iran, India or Pakistan. Oriental Carpet House & Antiques on Al-Nasr St has carpets, antiques, jewellery, souvenirs from India and pottery from Oman. The large complex behind the Abu Dhabi Cooperative, near Le Meridien has similar items for sale.

You also might want to poke around the old souq (see Old Souq earlier in this chapter) for local items such as mosque clocks and coffeepots, household goods and shoes.

For nontourist-oriented shopping, there are several shopping centres with large department stores. If you're after designer clothes you'll love the shopping in Abu Dhabi. The main areas for these shops are along the Corniche at its western end and along Tariq ibn Ziyad St.

GETTING THERE & AWAY
Air

Abu Dhabi international airport is on the mainland, about 30km from the centre. Phone ☎ 575 7611 for airport information. The airport's self-promotion efforts rival those of Dubai (raffles for Dh500,000 cash are Abu Dhabi's staple promotion, much as the car raffles are a fixture at Dubai). Like Dubai, Abu Dhabi airport has a duty-free shop for arriving passengers and, unlike Dubai, it has alcohol for sale on arrival.

There are no airport taxes as such but there is a 'fuel surcharge' from Abu Dhabi. To Europe, Australasia and South-East Asia the surcharge is Dh40 one way and Dh80 return; to the rest of Asia and the Middle East the surcharge is Dh30 one way and Dh60 return, included in the ticket price.

Following is a list of office addresses for some of the airlines flying to Abu Dhabi:

Air India (☎ 322 300) Abu Dhabi Travel Bureau Bldg, Al-Ittihad Square
British Airways (☎ 224 540) in Omeir Travel, corner of Shaikh Khalifa bin Zayed and Leewa Sts
Emirates Airlines (☎ 315 888) Shaikh Hamdan bin Mohammed St, between East Rd and Bani Yaas St

Gulf Air (☎ 331700 or, 24 hours a day at the airport, ☎ 575 7083) corner of Shaikh Rashid bin Saeed al-Maktoum and Shaikh Hamdan bin Mohammed Sts
KLM (☎ 323 280) Abu Dhabi Travel Bureau Bldg, Al-Ittihad Square
Oman Air (☎ 311 144) Shaikh Hamdan bin Mohammed St, between Lulu and Shaikh Rashid bin Saeed al-Maktoum Sts
Royal Jordanian (☎ 220 398) in Omeir Travel, corner of Shaikh Khalifa bin Zayed and Leewa Sts
Singapore Airlines (☎ 221 110) in Omeir Travel, corner of Shaikh Khalifa bin Zayed and Leewa Sts

Bus

There is a daily international bus service between Muscat and Abu Dhabi via Al-Ain, departing Abu Dhabi at 3 pm from the Madinat Zayed Shopping Centre which is on East Road near the corner of Zayed the Second St (one way/return Dh67/133, 6½ hours). Children get 50% off the adult fare and there is a family fare of Dh300 return for two adults and two children. There are also bus services to Egypt, Jordan, Lebanon and Syria, across Saudi Arabia. See Land in the regional Getting There & Away chapter for more details.

Intercity service on buses is only available within the Abu Dhabi emirate. To get to Dubai and the other emirates you have to take a shared taxi or a minibus.

The main bus station is on East Rd, south of the centre. Although the buses are really designed to carry workers around the emirate – it's assumed that tourists will drive or catch shared taxis – they are a great way to get around. They are clean, air-conditioned, punctual, and much more comfortable than squishing into a shared taxi with dodgy air-conditioning.

Buses run to Al-Ain every half-hour from 6 am to 10 pm every day (2½ hours, Dh10), and to Ruwais (three hours, Dh12) at 10.30 am, 1 pm and 6 pm. Buses for Madinat Zayed (Badr Zayed) leave every hour from 6 am to 8 pm daily (2½ hours, Dh10). To Liwa oasis there are two buses per day at 11.30 am and 9 pm (five hours, Dh15). To Sila (five hours, Dh15), near the UAE's far western border, there are daily buses at 7.30 am and 1.30 pm.

Minibus

These are found adjacent to the main bus station on East Rd. They take 14 passengers and charge Dh20 per person to Dubai or Al-Ain and Dh25 to Sharjah. It costs Dh33 to get from Dubai to Abu Dhabi with a Dubai Transport minibus. If there are enough passengers, depending on the mood of the driver, you may be able to catch a minibus further north to Umm al-Qaiwain and Ajman, but don't rely on this. Minibuses also go to the same places within Abu Dhabi emirate as the large buses for the same price, but only if they have a full load.

Long-Distance Taxi

These leave from the same place as the minibuses, adjacent to the main bus station on East Rd. To take an engaged taxi (ie, one to yourself) to Dubai, Sharjah or Al-Ain costs about Dh150. A shared taxi with five to seven people costs Dh30 per person. If you have luggage you will have to pay Dh30 for that too.

Car

If you are planning to travel widely around the UAE by rented car it is probably best to stick to one of the larger agencies. The main ones are:

Avis (☎ 323 760, fax 330 734) corner of Al-Nasr St and Khalid bin al-Waleed St. There are also branches at the airport and at the Inter-Continental, Le Meridien, Sheraton, Hilton and Al-Ain Palace hotels.

Budget (☎ 334 200, fax 331 498) Al-Nasr St, on the other side of Khalid bin al-Waleed St from Avis. There is also an office at the airport (☎ 575 7188, fax 575 7178).

Thrifty (☎ 345 663, fax 340 234) Al-Nasr St, east of the Avis office. There are also offices at the Radisson SAS and the airport.

GETTING AROUND
To/From the Airport

Bus No 901 runs from the main bus station to the airport around the clock, departing every 20 minutes (every 30 minutes between midnight and 6 am). The fare is Dh3. If you are taking this bus from the airport into the city, get off at whatever location in

the old souq looks good, see if you can convince the driver to take you to a specific location in the centre, or wait until he takes you to the bus station on East Rd.

Airport limos and Al-Ghazal taxis (Abu Dhabi's only private taxi service) charge Dh65 from the airport to the city. A regular taxi should cost around Dh40 from the city centre. The regular taxis from the airport are orange and white and have no meters as opposed to other Abu Dhabi taxis which are gold and white.

Bus

You will notice municipal buses running throughout Abu Dhabi. These are cheap – fares are only Dh2 or Dh3 depending on the distance travelled – but they are of limited use to travellers because they follow no fixed routes. Most buses originate at the main bus station on East Rd and there is also a major bus stop at the Tourist Club. Most bus routes around Abu Dhabi take in the three main roads (East Rd, Sheikh Rashid bin Saeed al-Maktoum Rd and the western Corniche). The buses end up in various industrial zones and labourers' camps on the mainland. They usually leave every 30 minutes or so but there appear to be no fixed timetables.

It is much easier and costs very little more to take a taxi but if you simply must catch a bus just hail one where you see it, jump on, tell the driver where you want to go and hope for the best.

Taxi

Taxis are equipped with meters. The flag fall is Dh2 and the meters turn over at 50 fils a kilometre. The fares add up slowly, making taxis a very affordable way to get around. There are always plenty of taxis around so you shouldn't have any trouble hailing one when you need it. An average fare from one end of the centre to the other is about Dh3.50. Most of the drivers know all the hotels, shopping centres and major roads (by the colloquial name usually, not the official name – see the Street Names section earlier in this chapter).

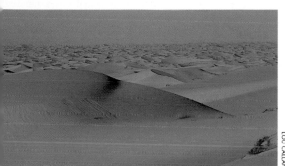

Underground water makes Liwa oasis (top), on the edge of the Empty Quarter, a striking vision of greenery in the midst of a sea of sand (middle left). Date plantations (middle right and bottom) stay deliciously cool, even in the heat of the day, allowing people to live in the hostile desert environment.

One of the most intriguing aspects of the UAE is the juxtaposition between modern and traditional – Dubai's Jumeirah Mosque (top right) vies for space with the latest architectural follies (middle); abras in Dubai (top left) and dhows (Abu Dhabi, bottom) dock in the shade of glittering high-rises.

Western Abu Dhabi

Only if you have the time, the curiosity and you really feel you want to touch down at each corner of the country should you venture out this way. The only real attraction of this region is the desert around Liwa in the south. Romping in these dunes and gazing out over a seemingly endless orange sea is an interesting experience. Most of the rest of the region, however, is characterised by featureless salt flats and gravel plains that extend as far as the eye can see. One thing's for sure if you decide to travel out west, you will learn the true meaning of 'desolate'.

RUWAIS
☎ 081

There's no real reason to visit this gigantic industrial complex, 250km west of Abu Dhabi, unless business takes you here. The industrial complex and the oil terminal at nearby **Jebel Dhanna** are only accessible to those with proper passes. Without a pass you are limited to the bus stop, which is by the turn-off for the main non-Adnoc (Abu Dhabi National Oil Company) workers' camp, and the Ruwais Housing Complex, where Adnoc and its associated companies' employees hang their hard hats.

The only available accommodation is at the **Dhafra Beach Hotel** (☎ 71600, fax 71002), an obscenely overpriced place near the main gate for the Jebel Dhanna oil terminal. The hotel caters mainly to people visiting the companies in Ruwais and to those down from Saudi Arabia for a drink or three (the hotel's brochure helpfully notes that the Aramco camp at Dhahran in Saudi is only 6½ hours away by car). Singles/doubles cost Dh388/545 and discounts are not usually given.

Food at the hotel's **restaurant** is also expensive. Those on a budget might consider self-catering from the **supermarket** behind the East Mosque in the Ruwais Housing Complex or having a biryani at one of the small **Indian places** by the oil terminal gate or on the main road.

The **Falcon Bar** at the hotel offers the area's only nightlife. Those staying long enough to make use of it should purchase a book of beer chits from the bartender. Each chit is good for one pint and they wind up costing a few dirhams less per pint than paying over the bar. The hotel's saving grace is that it does have decent sports facilities, including tennis, squash and one of those all-sand golf courses that seem to be unique to Arabia.

The UAE's Garden of Eden

About 10km offshore, just west of Ruwais, is Sir Bani Yas Island. Since the 1970s, this island has been developed as a nature reserve and breeding sanctuary for rare species. There are over 22 species of mammals on the island including 30,000 gazelles and 120 Arabian oryx. Other animals include llamas, water bucks, ostriches, emus, giraffes and spotted deer. They roam within vast fenced areas designed to give them as much freedom as possible.

There are also an estimated 86 bird species on the island along with citrus fruit trees, pineapples, apple trees, pear trees, fig trees, grapevines and olive groves. The idea is that the 15,000 olive trees will be marketed some time in the future.

Animal and plant life are not the only attractions of the island. Archaeological excavations have revealed ruins from the 5th to 8th centuries AD. The ancient settlement includes what is believed to be a pre-Islamic Christian monastery.

Although there are plans to develop the island as a tourist destination for organised tour groups, there is no way on to the island now unless you are invited by Sheikh Zayed himself or you are a member of a special interest group. The only guests so far have been diplomats, natural history groups and the occasional private guest of Sheikh Zayed.

There are three buses a day to Ruwais from Abu Dhabi at 10.30 am, and 1 and 6 pm. The fare is Dh12 one way.

SILA
☎ 081

If you thought the trip out to Ruwais was bleak wait until you see the road to Sila. The 100km of desert separating the UAE's main oil port from this border town is some of the most monotonous desert we've ever seen and has absolutely nothing to recommend it.

Sila itself is little more that a way-station on the road to Saudi Arabia and Qatar. The UAE border post at Gheweifat is another 18km to the west. The only accommodation is a government-run *resthouse* (☎ 21009) with bare but adequate rooms for Dh60 per night, single or double. Gluttons for punishment can ride the bus out here from Abu Dhabi for only Dh15. If you do arrive or leave by bus, you should hang out at the police post on the eastern edge of town.

A right turn at Sila's one roundabout and another 5km of driving brings you to the small town of **Baya Sila**, which has an impressive copper-domed mosque and long stretches of quiet, eerie coastline.

MADINAT ZAYED
☎ 088

Madinat Zayed, also called Badr Zayed, is the administrative centre for the huge desert region that includes the Liwa oasis. It lies some 40km south of the coast road along a stretch of tarmac that takes you through one of Abu Dhabi's main onshore oil production areas where gas pipelines crisscross the landscape on either side of the road. About 10km from Madinat Zayed you will notice fenced-in treed areas on either side of the road. These are Sheikh Zayed's private breeding grounds for deer and gazelles and if you look hard enough you might spot some. Watch out for the unsigned speed humps as you approach Madinat Zayed.

There is nothing to see in Madinat Zayed itself but it makes a useful base for exploring the Liwa area which is only 60km from here. Even though the dunes further south in

the oasis are the attraction of this area, there is more activity and more restaurants in Madinat Zayed and you may want to consider staying here rather than in Liwa. The main cross street is the one by the Ruler's Representative's Court (which is signposted). The taxi stand and bus station are both just south of this building and across the road from it.

Places to Stay & Eat
The only place to stay is the *resthouse* (☎ 46281) run by ADNHC. Rooms are Dh165, single or double, including breakfast. There's a restaurant offering decent but dull food at very good prices. The turn-off is on the left about 50m past the Adnoc Fod petrol station. There are a number of *biryani joints* in town and a *Pizza Inn* which provides welcome relief from biryani and kima.

Getting There & Away
There are 15 buses per day from Abu Dhabi to Madinat Zayed (2½ hours, Dh10). There are also nine buses daily from Madinat Zayed to Liwa (one hour, Dh4). These run roughly every two hours from 7 am until 9.30 pm. Shared taxis cluster at a lay-by near the bus station and run to Abu Dhabi (Dh150) and Liwa (Dh50). They fill up quickly.

LIWA OASIS
☎ 088

Liwa oasis is the ancestral home of Abu Dhabi's ruling Al-Nayan family. With the extension of the blacktop roads deep into the desert it has now become possible to see some of Liwa's wondrous desert scenery without a 4WD, and some tour companies offer trips to this remote area.

Lying on the edge of the Empty Quarter, Liwa's main attractions are its dunes. Liwa's secret is that while the surface environment is arid, water lies just below the surface, often at depths of only a few metres. As a result, the oasis has become one of the most agriculturally productive areas in the country. The kilometres of green plots stretching from the roadside to the base of the mountains of sand make a striking and bizarre sight.

Liwa is not a single stand of greenery, like the huge Al-Hasa oasis in eastern Saudi Arabia; instead it is a collection of small villages spread out over a 150km arc of land.

Orientation

About 60km from Madinat Zayed you reach **Mizaira'a** roundabout where the road turns sharply to the left. The Liwa bus station is on the right. Opposite it, on the east side of the roundabout, are a number of small shops and a few restaurants. You will notice Sheikh Zayed's huge palace on the right at the first roundabout you come to in Mizaira'a.

Things to See & Do

There's not a whole lot to see here apart from the sand dunes. The road from Liwa bus station east to the village of **Hamim** offers a spectacular trip through some truly dramatic desert scenery. Going west from Liwa takes you to **Karima**, 40km from Liwa, although the scenery is less striking. There is not much else to see in the area except a couple of three-towered **forts**. One is on the road to Karima and Arada (west of Mizaira'a) and the other is off the road to Hamim at Attab (east of Mizaira'a). Both forts are ruled by pigeons and covered in graffiti. If you have your own car you can continue past Hamim to where the blacktop road ends. Here the dunes come right up to the roadside. Just wander into them and enjoy a good romp.

Tour operators based in Dubai and Abu Dhabi offer overnight trips to Liwa, with accommodation at the resthouse.

Places to Stay & Eat

Unless you plan to camp, the only place to stay in Liwa until the new hotel opens is the *resthouse* (☎ 22075, fax 29311). Book ahead if you plan a weekend visit. It's about 7km west of the bus station along the Arada road. Rooms cost Dh165 for single or double, including breakfast. Bring your own supplies if you are planning to visit during Ramadan as the resthouse restaurant is closed at this time and you can't get food served in your room.

The huge new hotel on the hill off the Arada road before you reach the resthouse was completed at the time of writing, but the Liwa Municipality was looking for a management group to run it.

The *Metieb Mohd restaurant* across the roundabout from the bus station has excellent biryanis for Dh8.

Getting There & Away

There are nine buses per day to Madinat Zayed (one hour, Dh4) from Liwa bus station. Two local routes serve the oasis communities: one goes 64km east to Hamim (Dh3) and the other goes 40km west to Karima (Dh2). Each of the local buses makes three trips per day and takes about two to 2½ hours. A taxi (engaged) to Liwa from Abu Dhabi costs Dh160, from Madinat Zayed it costs Dh50.

Al-Ain & Buraimi

Al-Ain ☎ 03, Buraimi ☎ 00968

The Buraimi oasis straddles the border between Abu Dhabi emirate and Oman. There are a number of settlements in both parts of the oasis but in the UAE the entire area is referred to by the name of the main town, Al-Ain (pronounced so that it rhymes with 'main'). Buraimi technically refers to the entire oasis but is also used to refer to the Omani section alone.

In the days before the oil boom, the oasis was a five-day journey by camel from Abu Dhabi. Today, the trip takes about two hours (160km) on a tree-lined freeway. Once in the oasis, you can cross freely between the UAE and Oman – the Omani customs post is about 50km from Buraimi, on the road to Muscat – and it is this fact that makes the oasis so appealing.

Al-Ain is the birthplace of Sheikh Zayed, the ruler of Abu Dhabi emirate (and the UAE), and he has lavished money on it. The Omani side of the oasis has not undergone the same treatment. Buraimi is comfortable but still very much a provincial town. The resulting contrasts make Al-Ain/Buraimi one of the most interesting places in the country to visit.

UNITED ARAB EMIRATES

There is a lot to see in both Al-Ain and Buraimi and the area is a popular weekend destination from both Abu Dhabi and Dubai. In the summer, one of Al-Ain's main attractions is the dry air, which is a welcome change from the humidity of the coast.

HISTORY

The Buraimi oasis has probably been inhabited for longer than any other part of present-day UAE. The country's oldest known artefacts are potsherds from the 4th millennium BC which were found in the Jebel Hafit area, near the oasis. Archaeological digs near Al-Ain have also turned up a Bronze Age (3rd millennium BC) culture which may have had ties to the Umm al-Nar civilisation that then existed on the coast near the modern city of Abu Dhabi.

As Arabia's climate became warmer, oases such as Buraimi became increasingly important. The population of Buraimi is known to have increased significantly during the 2nd and 3rd centuries AD, apparently as a result of migration to the oasis by

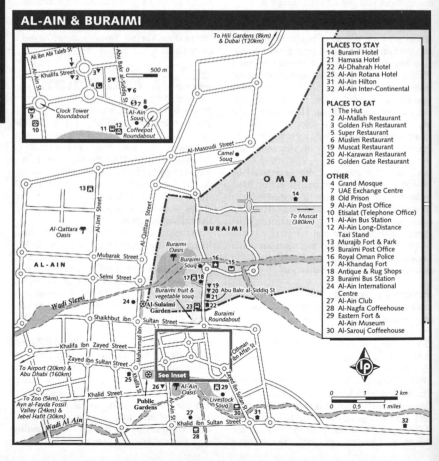

AL-AIN & BURAIMI

To Hili Gardens (8km) & Dubai (120km)

Ali ibn Abi Taleb St
Khalifa Street
Abu Bakr al-Siddiq St
Al-Ain St
Clock Tower Roundabout
Al-Ain Souq
Coffeepot Roundabout

0   500 m

Al-Masoudi Street
Camel Souq

O M A N

To Muscat (380km)

BURAIMI

Al-Qattara Oasis
Al-Jimi Street
Al-Qattara Street

Buraimi Oasis
Buraimi Souq

AL-AIN
Mubarak Street
Selmi Street

Buraimi fruit & vegetable souq
Al-Sulaimi Garden
Buraimi Roundabout
Abu Bakr al-Siddiq St

Wadi Slemi

Shaikhbut ibn Sultan Street

Khalifa ibn Zayed Street
Zayed ibn Sultan Street

To Airport (20km) & Abu Dhabi (160km)

Othman ibn Affan St
Mohammad ibn

See Inset

To Zoo (5km), Ayn al-Fayda Fossil Valley (24km) & Jebel Hafit (30km)

Khalid Street
Al-Ain Oasis
Public Gardens
Livestock Souq

Al-Ain Oasis

Zayed ibn Sultan St

Khalid ibn Sultan Street

Wadi Al Ain

0   1   2 km
0   0.5   1 miles

PLACES TO STAY
14 Buraimi Hotel
21 Hamasa Hotel
22 Al-Dhahrah Hotel
25 Al-Ain Rotana Hotel
31 Al-Ain Hilton
32 Al-Ain Inter-Continental

PLACES TO EAT
1 The Hut
2 Al-Mallah Restaurant
3 Golden Fish Restaurant
5 Super Restaurant
6 Muslim Restaurant
19 Muscat Restaurant
20 Al-Karawan Restaurant
26 Golden Gate Restaurant

OTHER
4 Grand Mosque
7 UAE Exchange Centre
8 Old Prison
9 Al-Ain Post Office
10 Etisalat (Telephone Office)
11 Al-Ain Bus Station
12 Al-Ain Long-Distance Taxi Stand
13 Murajib Fort & Park
15 Buraimi Post Office
16 Royal Oman Police
17 Al-Khandaq Fort
18 Antique & Rug Shops
23 Buraimi Bus Station
24 Al-Ain International Centre
27 Al-Ain Club
28 Al-Nagfa Coffeehouse
29 Eastern Fort & Al-Ain Museum
30 Al-Sarouj Coffeehouse

tribes from the surrounding desert. By the 10th century, Al-Ain, which was then called Tawwan, was a trading centre along one of Arabia's many caravan routes.

In the 18th century, the ancestors of the present-day Saudi Arabian royal family incorporated the oempire. The legacy of this period was Wahhabism, the puritanical strain of Islam practised in Saudi Arabia which, in a somewhat milder form, remains a strong influence in the Al-Ain/Buraimi area to this day.

Abu Dhabi's ruling Al-Nayan family first moved to the oasis sometime in the 19th century, well after the founding of Abu Dhabi. Since the early years of the 20th century, the family has ruled the oasis jointly with the Omanis. The 18th-century Saudi presence in Buraimi, however, led the Saudi government to claim the entire oasis for its kingdom in 1949. The Saudi claim was prompted by Aramco, the Saudi-based oil company, who wanted to drill for oil in the oasis.

In 1952 the Saudis occupied part of Buraimi. The question of sovereignty eventually went to an international arbitration panel in Geneva. When the talks collapsed in 1955, the British and the Al-Nayan family took matters into their own hands. A Bedouin force led by Sheikh Zayed, who was then the governor of Abu Dhabi's portion of the oasis, along with the Trucial Oman Scouts, who were commanded by British officers, drove the Saudis out of Buraimi. However, the dispute continued on a lesser level for several more years. The current Abu Dhabi–Oman border was demarcated in 1966. Saudi Arabia formally dropped its claim to the area in 1974.

ORIENTATION

The Al-Ain/Buraimi area can be very confusing, at least at first. All the streets in Al-Ain look pretty much the same and people tend to navigate their way around by the numerous roundabouts and not by street names. As in Abu Dhabi, there are very few residents or taxi drivers who know the street names out of the town centre. The streets in Buraimi don't have names but this doesn't make navigation any more difficult than in Al-Ain. The three landmarks you need to know for navigational purposes are the clock tower and coffeepot roundabouts in Al-Ain, and the Buraimi roundabout which is the main thoroughfare between the two towns.

Basically, Al-Ain wraps around an arm of Omani territory with most of Al-Ain's business district lying just south of Buraimi. To get to Dubai or to some of Al-Ain's suburbs from the centre you drive through Oman for about 4km before emerging back into the UAE. Most of the area's services are in Al-Ain's town centre. The main streets in Al-Ain are Khalifa ibn Zayed St (referred to as Khalifa St) and Zayed ibn Sultan St (referred to as Main St) which run east-west. The main north-south cross streets are Abu Bakr al-Siddiq St, which extends into Buraimi, and Al-Ain St.

Distances in both towns are large. You could, in theory, walk from the bus or taxi station in Al-Ain to the semi-cheap hotels just over the Omani border, but with luggage you'd probably prefer not to, especially when it's hot.

INFORMATION

There is no tourist office in either city but it's fairly easy to find most of the things worth seeing in Al-Ain by following the big purple road signs. The Hilton and Inter-Continental in Al-Ain are also good sources for local tourist information.

Money

There are lots of banks in Al-Ain near the clock tower roundabout and the main post office. The area around the Grand Mosque also has several moneychangers and a Thomas Cook office. The UAE Exchange Centre is on Abu Bakr al-Siddiq St.

In Buraimi you'll find several banks along the main road. UAE currency is accepted in Buraimi at a standard rate of approximately OR1 = Dh10. With the exception of taxi drivers, Omani currency is rarely accepted in Al-Ain.

Post

Al-Ain's main post office is near the clock tower roundabout. It's open 8 am to 1 pm and 4 to 7 pm Saturday to Wednesday, 8 am to 4.30 pm Thursday and 8 to 11 am Friday.

To get to Buraimi's post office turn right at the first roundabout as you enter Buraimi from Al-Ain. Continue for 500m and it is on your left. The sign for the post office is in Arabic only. It is open 8 am to 2 pm Saturday to Wednesday, 8 to 11 am Thursday, closed Friday.

Telephone

The Etisalat office is next to the main post office in Al-Ain. Opening hours are 7 am to 3 pm Saturday to Wednesday and 8 am to 1 pm Thursday.

There is a phone line connecting the two cities so that a call from Al-Ain to Buraimi is not charged at international rates.

In Buraimi, the telephone office is about 500m west of the mosque roundabout.

Email & Internet Access

There is an Internet cafe (☎ 628 686) at the Al-Ain International Centre on Al-Qattarah St, opposite Al-Sulaimi Garden. It costs Dh15 per hour or Dh120 for 10 hours.

Emergency

In Al-Ain, the phone number for the police is ☎ 999, ambulance ☎ 998 and the fire department ☎ 997. In Oman dial ☎ 999 for the police, an ambulance or to report a fire.

AL-AIN
Eastern Fort & the
Al-Ain Museum

The museum and fort are in the same compound, south-east of the overpass near the coffeepot roundabout. The museum is open 8 am to 1 pm and 3.30 to 5.30 pm Sunday to Wednesday (4.30 to 6.30 pm from May to October), 8 am to noon Thursday and 9 to 11.30 am Friday. It's closed all day Saturday. Museum admission is 50 fils.

As you enter the museum, take a look at the *majlis* (meeting room) set up to the left of the manager's office. It's a display of what the reception area of a traditional Bedouin tent or home looks like. This particular room is also used to welcome visiting VIPs (which may be why it always looks like it only lacks hot coals for the coffee to be served).

The first gallery (to the right of the entrance) has an interesting display of photographs of Al-Ain, Abu Dhabi and Liwa taken in the 1960s. It's striking to see how much the area has developed since then. The gallery also includes exhibits on traditional education and a small but good selection of Bedouin jewellery.

The next gallery has reconstructions of everyday life in the pre-oil days. Note how most of the figures are dressed more like Omanis than like Gulf Arabs (ie, wearing turbans instead of the *ghutra* or headcloth). The opposite wall has a large display of weapons.

The third gallery has more weapons, musical instruments and some stuffed examples of the local desert fauna. There are also displays of some of the decorations Sheikh Zayed has received over the years. The collection is rather eclectic, including both the Order of Isabel the Catholic, bestowed on the sheikh by King Juan Carlos I of Spain, and a bullet 'from the Palestinian Commando Lyla Khalid' (a leader of the Popular Front for the Liberation of Palestine's guerilla squad that hijacked three aircraft to Jordan in September 1970 and, in so doing, touched off a bloody civil war in that country).

The other two galleries house a chronological display on the region's archaeology.

The Eastern Fort, next to the museum, is open to the public, but there's not a lot to see beyond the old cannon in the courtyard. The fort was built in 1910 by Sheikh Sultan bin Zayed al-Nayan and was the birthplace of his son, Sheikh Zayed.

Livestock Souq

You can see the entrance to the livestock market from the museum/fort parking lot. It's an interesting place to wander around and an excellent spot to go shopping for sheep and goats (a live sheep costs about Dh120). There are all kinds of animals, from

Brahmin cows to Persian cats. The souq attracts people from all over the southern UAE and northern Oman. Don't be surprised if you see people loading goats they've just bought into the back seat of a brand-new Mercedes. Those who can't bear to see animals caged up into small spaces should avoid this place.

Old Prison

The prison is the fort-like building on Zayed ibn Sultan St near the coffeepot roundabout. It is open rather erratic hours. Sometimes the courtyard is used for community displays (such as Traffic Safety Week). If you get into the courtyard, it may be possible to climb to the roof of the prison tower for a view out over the oasis (one reader, however, has warned of unofficial 'guides' accompanying people up the tower and then demanding tips). Other than that, there is not a lot to see here.

Murajib Fort & Park

This small fort is on Al-Jimi St, several kilometres north-west of Al-Ain's centre. The restored remains of the fortifications are scattered within a beautifully landscaped garden. The garden is open 4 to 10 pm Saturday to Thursday, 10 am to 10 pm Friday and holidays. Admission is Dh1 but this is not always strictly enforced. In theory the park is only open to women and small children (ie, no men, even as part of family groups) but this, too, is not always enforced.

Murajib can be reached by bus No 80 from the Al-Ain bus station to Hili Jimi. The fare is Dh1.

BURAIMI
Souqs

Buraimi's main souq is bigger than it looks from the road and is worth a visit for the atmosphere. It's the large brown building at the horse roundabout and sells fruit, vegetables, meat and household goods. The enclosed (concrete) part of the souq includes a few shops that sell Omani silver jewellery and *khanjars*, the ornate daggers worn by many Omani men. Although things have im-

proved over the last few years, the selection in these souvenir shops is still not very good. If you are heading for Oman, it's probably best to wait and do your shopping in Muscat.

The other main souq is just fruit and vegetables, but what a collection! It is open every morning and evening and is on the left just after the Buraimi roundabout as you enter Buraimi from Al-Ain.

Al-Hilla Fort

The Al-Hilla Fort, immediately behind the souq in Buraimi, is not open to the public but if you ask the workers they may let you wander around. If you do manage to get inside, look for the mud-walled path leading out of the back of the fort into the oasis. This is a good place to start an oasis walk. Be careful not to get lost and be sure the workers are not getting ready to leave for the day or you could find yourself locked inside the fort and left with trespassing through someone's yard as your only route out!

Al-Khandaq Fort

This fort is much larger than Al-Hilla and is said to be about 400 years old. If you're coming from the centre of Al-Ain you'll see it to your left 200m or so from the road, about 750m past the border. It was recently restored and is now open 8 am to 6 pm Saturday to Wednesday and 8 am to 1 pm and 4 to 6 pm Thursday and Friday. Admission is free.

The fort's restoration (which took several years) has been impressively thorough. Even the dry moat around the structure has been restored to its former glory. Stroll through the courtyards and climb one of the battlements for a view of the surrounding oasis. There are no displays inside, but it is a fun place to prowl around. The design, though approximately square, includes only three corner towers and, unusually for an Omani fort, there are both inner and outer defence walls. Once you get into the courtyard head directly across it and slightly to the left to reach a large, well-restored room. This was the majlis, or meeting room, where the fort's commander would have conducted his official business.

Camel Souq

The Al-Ain and Buraimi camel souq is (just) in Buraimi on a large vacant block off Al-Masoudi St. It's a great spectacle and a fascinating place to visit. The merchants here really do seem to think that that they can convince tourists to buy a camel, and you'll probably be approached by a number of people all trying to explain to you why their camels are the best.

The souq is open from early morning until about noon every day, then from about 4 pm until dusk. To get there go 4km up the main street of Buraimi from the Buraimi roundabout. Then turn right onto a paved road just after a red-and-white transmitter tower. Go for 1.5km and the camels will be on your left. There is no public transport but a taxi from Al-Ain shouldn't cost more than Dh15.

The large enclosed yard just east of the fort is Buraimi's Eid prayer ground, where people gather to pray during the holidays marking the end of Ramadan and the end of the pilgrimage season.

OASES & PARKS

Al-Ain and Buraimi are replete with shady oases – great for when it is hot. You'll stumble across them with a little exploration of the area. One of the nicest places is **Al-Qattarah oasis** just off Al-Jimi St in Al-Ain. Don't be fooled by the ruins here. Even though they look impressive, they're only about 30 to 40 years old. **Al-Ain oasis**, south-west of the museum and livestock souq, is a labyrinth of narrow tracks and has dozens of mosques spread throughout the oasis for the workers to use during the day. There are a number of entrances on the north side of the oasis. **Buraimi oasis** lies just west of Al-Khandaq Fort.

Some of Al-Ain's sculptured gardens and parks are for women and children only. If this is the case men will be stopped at the gate. Most parks have an entry fee of Dh1. The main park is on Zayed ibn Sultan St in

the block just west of the clock tower and the other, Al-Sulaimi Garden, is on Al-Qattarah St, opposite the Al-Ain International Centre.

ACTIVITIES

Visitors can use the sports facilities at the Hilton, Inter-Continental and Rotana hotels for Dh45 per day (free if you're staying in the hotel). For this you get access to the pool, sauna, fitness centre and game room.

The Hilton golf course is a nine-hole, par three course. The shortest hole is 45 yards and the longest a mere 107 yards. Greens fees are Dh50 for the first nine holes and Dh25 to play a second nine. You can rent clubs for Dh20. There is also a sand (well gravel, really) course just out of Al-Ain, 3km past the Inter-Continental Hotel along the same road. It costs Dh40 for 18 holes.

You will find a number of snooker and billiards halls in town, and there are bowling alleys at Ayn al-Fayda, just out of town, and at the Al-Ain International Centre on Al-Qattarah St.

ORGANISED TOURS

Al-Ain Camel Safaris (☎ 768 8006 or on mobile 050-447 7268) in the lobby of the Hilton hotel offers a variety of desert trips ranging from short one-hour rides (Dh100) to overnight trips with a barbecue dinner and breakfast (Dh450). The best part about this company's offerings is that they do not require a group of four to six people. They will even do the desert camping trip for just one or two people.

Most of the tour companies operating out of Dubai, Abu Dhabi and Sharjah offer city tours of Al-Ain.

PLACES TO STAY

Al-Ain and Buraimi do not have a huge selection of accommodation. There are six hotels altogether and only two of them remotely qualify as cheap.

Al-Ain

In the UAE, your choice is limited to five-star hotels but you can often get discounts on the rates quoted here. All three hotels have bars and restaurants as well as health clubs and pools.

Al-Ain Hilton (☎ *768 6666, fax 686 888)* charges Dh535/585 for singles/doubles. It's at the falcon roundabout on Khalid ibn Sultan St, south-east of the town centre.

Al-Ain Inter-Continental (☎ *768 6686, fax 686 766)* charges Dh464/580. It's on Khalid ibn Sultan St, about 3km east of the Al-Ain Hilton.

Al-Ain Rotana Hotel (☎ *515 111, fax 515 444)* which opened in 1999, is the only hotel to have opened in Al-Ain for 15 years. It's on Zayed ibn Sultan St, 1km west of the clock tower roundabout. Rooms cost Dh638/696. Round the side of the hotel and down a ramp is a 'hole in the wall' where alcohol is sold to anyone who desires it.

All three hotels can arrange visas for travellers to the UAE. Note, however, that if you have them send the visa to Dubai or Abu Dhabi airport they will also charge you several hundred dirhams for a limo ride to Al-Ain, whether you use the limo or not (the rationale for this is that the car and driver have to go to the airport to drop off the visa).

Around Al-Ain

About 10km to the south of Al-Ain there is one more hotel, the *Rest House* (☎ *838 333, fax 838 900)* at the Ayn al Fayda resort complex. It is rather remote and alcohol is not served, but the rooms are remarkably good and fairly cheap. Singles/doubles cost Dh110/165, including breakfast and service charge. There are also one and two-bedroom chalets near the boat lake for Dh330/440 which are very popular at weekends for parties or gatherings – and clandestine alcohol consumption.

At the time of writing a colossal hotel was under construction on Jebel Hafit, the mountain above Al-Ain. No doubt it will be very expensive and exclusive but the setting is spectacular.

Buraimi

The two cheapest hotels are in Buraimi. Both are only a 10-minute walk from the centre of Al-Ain, closer to town than the Al-Ain Inter-Continental or Hilton. None of the hotels on the Omani side of the border can sponsor a UAE visa for you, nor do they serve alcohol.

Al-Dhahrah Hotel (☎ *650492, fax 650881)* just over the border in Buraimi, on your right if you enter Oman from the centre of Al-Ain, has singles/doubles for Dh130/160 and a small restaurant.

Hamasa Hotel (☎ *651200; in the UAE call* ☎ *050-619 4248, fax 651 210)* is a few doors down from the Al-Dhahrah Hotel towards Buraimi and is the better of the two cheap hotels. Clean, bright rooms are Dh150/200.

Buraimi Hotel (☎ *652010, fax 652011; in the UAE call* ☎ *050-474 954)* can be found easily enough by following the blue-and-white signs strategically positioned throughout the Omani part of the oasis. Rooms are Dh351/427 and they sometimes offer summer specials, with discounts of up to 50%.

PLACES TO EAT
Al-Ain

You won't have any trouble finding cheap eats in the centre of Al-Ain. For alcohol and more expensive and exotic fare, you have to head for the hotels.

Muslim Restaurant, just north of the overpass on Abu Bakr al-Siddiq St, is recommended. Offering the usual fare of rice with mutton, chicken or fish for Dh7, it also makes very good *hadas* (a spicy lentil paste) for Dh3 and bakes its own bread on the premises.

Golden Fish at the eastern end of Khalifa St is a good place for (yes, you guessed) fish.

Golden Gate Restaurant on Al-Ain St is more upmarket and serves very good Chinese and Filipino food for Dh15 to Dh25. The Western-style meals are nothing to write home about, though.

The Hut is a Western-style coffee shop on Khalifa St. It offers good coffee, including cappuccino and latte, as well as a wide selection of cakes, pastries and sandwiches. At Dh5 for a cappuccino the prices are a bit high, but the comfortable surroundings make up for it.

UNITED ARAB EMIRATES

Super Restaurant, just west of Abu Bakr al-Siddiq St, between Khalifa St and Zayed St, is a very popular Indian restaurant with expats, both Western and Indian. It has a large menu and meals are around Dh10 to Dh12.

Al-Mallah, on Khalifa St, has very good Lebanese food. Portions are huge and with each meal you get a giant salad, pickles and piles of Arabic bread. A serving of humous costs Dh7, and mixed grills and other main meat dishes cost Dh18 to Dh20.

Buraimi

Buraimi has fewer eating places than Al-Ain. You will probably find your options limited to the standard cheap fare of a helping of biryani rice with fish, chicken or mutton for about Dh10/OR1. Try the *Al-Karawan Restaurant* and the *Muscat Restaurant*, both opposite the turn-off to the Al-Khandaq Fort. There are also a few Chinese and Filipino restaurants on the main street.

ENTERTAINMENT

Paco's at the Hilton hotel is a south-of-the-border-style pub and the *Horse & Jockey* at the Inter-Continental is a British pub through and through (complete with a darts board and pork pies). Both hotels also have nightclubs.

Al-Ain is not short on coffeehouses. The best one is *Al-Sarouj Coffeehouse* about 50m north of the falcon roundabout near the Hilton. It has a huge grassed outdoor area, two big screens usually blaring out soccer matches, and a snooker centre. A coffee and sheesha here will cost you less than Dh10 and it's open just about all night. *Al-Nagfa*, on top of a rocky ridge across from the Al-Ain Club, serves sheesha and snacks for nearly three times the price as the Al-Sarouj.

There is only one English-language *cinema* in the area. It's at the Al-Ain Club (enter from Al-Ain St). It shows one English-language movie each day.

SHOPPING

There are shops in the lobbies of the Hilton and the Inter-Continental hotels selling Omani jewellery and other souvenirs. The shop in the Inter-Con has particularly nice antiques and is run by an expat who really knows his stuff. You can also buy some jewellery and souvenirs in the Buraimi souq where they will definitely cost less but are also likely to be in much worse condition. Next to Al-Khandaq Fort there are two shops in an octagonal-shaped building. Fort Antiques specialises in souvenirs and some antiques and Al-Majan sells machine-made rugs and tacky homewares.

For nontourist-oriented shopping, try any of the malls in the centre. There are a number of department stores along the two main streets. To buy Omani honey go to Ali ibn Abi Taleb St, just north of Khalifa St.

GETTING THERE & AWAY

For details on how to visit Buraimi from Muscat see the Buraimi entry in the North-West Oman chapter earlier in this book.

Air

Al-Ain international airport is approximately 20km west of the centre. To get there take the Abu Dhabi road out of the centre until you see signs for the airport. For airport information call ☎ 785 5555 ext 2211.

Gulf Air offers direct services from Al-Ain to Bahrain, Doha (Qatar) and Muscat. EgyptAir flies twice a week from Al-Ain to Cairo and there is also a twice-weekly service to Amman (Jordan) on Royal Jordanian. Pakistan International Airlines has one flight each week to Karachi and Lahore (Pakistan).

Bus

Buses run from Al-Ain to Abu Dhabi (2½ hours, Dh10) about once an hour starting around 6 am with the last trip at about 9.30 pm. The bus station is behind the Al-Ain souq.

Oman's national bus company, ONTC, has three buses a day to and from the Ruwi station in Muscat via Sohar. The buses leave from a parking lot across from the Al-Dhahrah Hotel in Buraimi at 7 am, and 1 and 3 pm. The 7 am and 3 pm trips take about six hours. The 1 pm bus is an express service which reaches Muscat in just over 4½ hours. The trip to Muscat costs OR3.600. Tickets can be purchased from the driver. To take this bus you will need an Omani visa which allows you to enter the country by land. Expatriates resident in the UAE can pick up a visa at the border. The Omani customs post is 53km from Buraimi.

Minibus

You can get to Al-Ain by minibus (but not *from* Al-Ain – see Getting There & Away in the Dubai chapter for more details). Fourteen-passenger minibuses leave Dubai every 15 to 20 minutes and cost Dh30.

Long-Distance Taxi

Al-Ain's taxi station is next to the bus station, between the souq and the Al-Ain oasis. Taxis can take four or seven passengers to Dubai (Dh30) and Abu Dhabi (Dh20). An engaged taxi to either city will cost you Dh130 to Dh150 and takes about two hours. You can also occasionally find cabs from Al-Ain to Fujairah (Dh40 shared) but don't count on it. Long distance taxis leave when they are full.

Car Rental

If you want to rent a car, head for the rental desks at the Hilton (Avis, ☎ 687 262), Inter-Continental (Europcar, ☎ 650 150) or Rotana hotels. There are also several rental agencies just north of the coffeepot roundabout on the way to the Al-Ain Hilton, along Khalifa St and near the clock tower roundabout.

GETTING AROUND
To/From the Airport

Bus No 500 is an express service that runs every 30 minutes, 24 hours a day, between the bus station and the airport. The fare is Dh3 and the trip takes about 40 minutes. Bus No 130 also goes to the airport for Dh3 but it is a regular service and takes about an hour. Airport limos charge Dh40 for the trip into Al-Ain (Dh50 to Ayn al-Fayda). A taxi to or from Al-Ain running on the meter should cost about Dh25.

Bus

Al-Ain has a fairly reasonable bus system once you figure it out. The trick is to know the right route. The route numbers given here may change, but the routes themselves are less likely to do so. All buses run roughly half-hourly from 6 am to midnight. All fares are Dh1 except to Ayn al-Fayda and the airport, both of which are Dh3.

You cannot get to the Inter-Continental hotel by bus, but bus Nos 10 to Defence (Difa'a), No 70 to Mezaid, and No 120 to Umm Ghafa will take you to the Hilton. Bus No 110 goes to Ayn al-Fayda. The Ayn al-Fayda bus also goes to the zoo, as does bus No 60 to Zakhe. Hili Gardens and Hili Fun City can be reached via bus Nos 80 (Hili Jimi), 100 (Hili Garden) and 203 (Shueib Fakat). Bus No 80 also goes to Murajib.

There are no local buses in Buraimi.

Taxi

The Al-Ain taxis have meters; use them to avoid arguments over the fare with the Omani taxi drivers whose vehicles are not equipped with meters. Al-Ain's taxis charge Dh2 for the flag fall and 50 fils for each additional kilometre. If you want to go somewhere like Jebel Hafit, however, you'll have to arrange a price with the driver.

AROUND AL-AIN
Jebel Hafit

The views from the top of this mountain are well worth the effort to get there. The summit is about 30km by road from the centre of Al-Ain. To get there head south from the clock tower roundabout on Al-Ain St and turn right at Khalid ibn Sultan St. From there follow the purple tourist signs.

There are no buses to Jebel Hafit, though the Ayn al-Fayda bus (No 110) will take you as far as the turn-off from the highway to the mountain. This will leave you stranded on the outskirts, however, and you are better off taking a taxi all the way from the centre. A taxi should make the round trip for Dh50.

If you have a 4WD you can get to the hundreds of stone **tombs** at the base of the eastern side of Hafit. Take the road to Mezyad from the falcon roundabout near the Hilton hotel. Drive for about 22km, then turn right onto a dirt track, about 500m before you hit the Omani border post. This track will lead you past a few houses and yards to the base of the mountain from where you are free to explore – there's no set route. As you get closer to the jebel, you will notice hundreds of stone piles which are the remnants of cairn tombs dating from 3200 to 2800 BC. Items found here include pots which are on display in the Al-Ain Museum. It is believed the tombs were constructed as a burial ground for the villages which grew up in the Buraimi oasis.

Ayn al-Fayda

Ayn al-Fayda is a resort south of the oasis 1.5km beyond the Jebel Hafit turn-off. It's favoured mostly by expatriate Arab families. The decrepit-looking *ayn* (spring) itself is a sulphur pool which is not suitable for

Fossil Valley

Fossil Valley is actually in Oman but no visa is required to get there. The valley is proof that the Hajar mountains were formed from the sea bed when tectonic movement caused them to rise up above the water surface. Marine fossils are abundant in the valley, just at the base of the hills. The valley has long been known to the local expat community. Needless to say, there are not as many spectacular fossils here now as there once were!

To get there take the road to Madha from Buraimi. You need to drive past the Buraimi Hotel and turn left at the next roundabout. Continue along this road for exactly 8.3km then turn off the road to the right where you see a camel crossing sign. There will be a few faint tracks leading into large open basin. Pick any one and drive for about 1km, keeping close to the hill on your right, until you see a large monolithic rock sticking straight up out of the ground. Park near here and explore the area on this hillside.

swimming. There is a swimming pool, a resthouse (see Places to Stay in the Al-Ain & Buraimi section), bowling alley, game room, restaurants, park and a lake where you can hire paddle boats. There are also a lot of children running around everywhere making lots of noise, especially on Fridays.

Ayn al-Fayda is the terminus for Bus No 110. The fare from the bus station is Dh3. An engaged taxi should take you there for Dh20.

Hili Archaeological Gardens

This combination public park and archaeological site is about 8km north of the centre of Al-Ain, off the Dubai road. The site is open 4 to 11 pm daily (10 am to 10 pm public holidays). Admission is Dh1.

The main attraction is the round structure which is a 3rd millennium BC **tomb**, possibly connected with the Umm al-Nar culture. It was discovered by a group of Danish archaeologists in 1962, excavated during the late 60s and restored to its present form in 1973. The tomb has two porthole entrances and is decorated with relief carvings of animals and people. Even though this structure is referred to as a tomb, it may not have been a tomb at all. No bones were ever found here, just remnants of pottery, indicating that it may have been a temple.

At the time of writing there were further excavations taking place on another tomb which dates back to somewhere between 2300 and 200 BC. This tomb is 8m long and adjoins the older circular tomb. More than 250 skeletons have been found here. The great variety of local and imported objects found with the skeletons differentiates it from most other tombs from the Umm al-Nar period.

There is also a playground for children inside the park. To reach Hili from the centre, take the Dubai road (through Oman) and follow the signs for Hili and Dubai until the purple 'tourist' signs appear. Look for signs directing you to 'Hili Archaeological Site'. The park can be reached via bus No 80 to Hili Jimi, bus No 203 to Shueib Fakat or bus No 100 to Hili Gardens. The fare is Dh1.

Hili Fun City & Ice Rink

The amusement park (☎ 03-845 542) and skating rink are a few kilometres down the road from Hili Archaeological Gardens. They are open 4 to 10 pm Sunday to Wednesday, 4 to 11 pm Thursday and 9 am to 10 pm Friday and holidays. Both places are closed Saturday. Tuesday and Wednesday are for women and small children only. Admission is Dh10 and everyone over the age of three has to have a ticket.

Admission to the ice rink (☎ 03-845 542, ext 224), including skate rental, is Dh10 on weekdays and Dh15 on Friday and holidays. Admission is only Dh3 if you bring your own skates. The same buses that run to Hili Archaeological Gardens go here too. The fare is Dh1.

Zoo

Al-Ain's zoo has not always had a good reputation with many animals becoming sick and dying from neglect and inappropriate feeding regimens. The zoo has apparently been upgraded and animals are better cared for but you can judge that for yourself.

The indigenous species here include Arabian oryx and gazelle, Saluki dogs and bustards. There are also kangaroos, pygmy hippos and vultures, among other animals. The zoo is large and somewhat confusing in its layout. If you want to see something in particular take a moment to study the map by the entrance.

The zoo lies about 5km south-west of the centre and is open 7 am to 5.30 pm daily except Saturday. Admission is Dh2. It can be reached via bus No 110 to Ayn al-Fayda or bus No 60 to Zakhe.

If you are driving follow the purple tourist signs. You'll know you're there when you see the enormous animal roundabout near the zoo entrance.

Dubai Emirate

The emirate of Dubai includes the city of Dubai and its environs on the Gulf coast and the enclave of Hatta in the Hajar mountains, about 100km east of Dubai. Although not as wealthy or as large as Abu Dhabi emirate, Dubai has an enviable status as the Gulf's leading entrepot. Dubai is also the main centre of tourism in the UAE. Many people travelling between Europe and Asia use the city as a shopping stopover. Those staying longer use the city as a base and take day or overnight trips from here.

Of all the emirates, Dubai has fought the hardest to preserve its independence and to minimise the power of the country's federal institutions. The ruler of Dubai is Sheikh Maktoum, who is also the UAE's vice president and prime minister.

Dubai

☎ 04

In less than a century, Dubai has been transformed from a backwater into a metropolis, the commercial hub of the region and an internationally renowned shoppers paradise. It is one of the last bastions of all-out capitalism: a sort of Middle Eastern Hong Kong. What opium was to the growth of Hong Kong in the late 19th century, gold was to Dubai in the 1960s. Dubai's wealth is founded on trade, not oil. Oil, when it was discovered in 1966, merely contributed to trade profits and encouraged modernisation.

The city remains first and foremost a trading port and most of the local government's activity is directed towards promoting Dubai as a business centre and protecting the city's status as the Gulf's leading trade centre.

There is plenty to see and do in Dubai. The older parts of the city (around Deira's souqs and near the *abra*, or motorboat, dock in Bur Dubai), provide a startling contrast to the slick, shiny, modern Dubai of Jumeira or Shaikh Zayed Rd. This dichotomy of char-

acter makes for an interesting experience. You won't find a more easy-going place anywhere in the Gulf – or a place with a more vibrant nightlife.

HISTORY

Dubai's modern history really begins in the 1830s when the city broke away from Abu Dhabi. At that time, neighbouring Sharjah was the main trading centre on the Trucial Coast, and for the rest of the 19th century Dubai was simply another sleepy pearling village with a small merchant community.

Things began to change around the turn of the century. In 1894 Dubai's ruler, Sheikh Maktoum bin Hasher al-Maktoum, exempted foreign traders from taxes. Around the same time Linagh, in what is now Iran, lost its status as a free port. The Al-Maktoum family made a concerted effort to lure Linagh's disillusioned traders to Dubai and also managed to convince some of Sharjah's merchants to relocate. Next, the Al-Maktoums, probably with the assistance of the newly arrived Persian traders, prevailed on a British steamship line to switch its main port of call in the lower Gulf from Linagh to Dubai, which it did in 1903. This gave Dubai regular links with both British India and the ports of the central and northern Gulf (Bahrain, Kuwait, Bushire in Iran and Basra in Iraq). The town's prosperity quickly grew. By 1908 there were 350 shops based in Deira and 50 in Bur Dubai.

The next key event in Dubai's growth occurred in 1939 when Sheikh Rashid bin Saeed al-Maktoum took over as regent for his father, Sheikh Saeed. Sharjah's leadership had, by then, been relatively weak and xenophobic for some years. The entire region was also suffering from the collapse of the pearling industry which, Rashid concluded, was probably never going to revive. With that in mind, Rashid set out to transform Dubai into the region's main trading centre. As Sharjah's harbour silted up,

Rashid improved the facilities along the Creek, Dubai's waterfront.

The emirate came to specialise in the 're-export trade' – its merchants imported goods which they then sold to other ports rather than peddling them at home. In practice, this usually meant smuggling in general, and smuggling gold to India in particular. During the 1950s, Sheikh Rashid became one of the earliest beneficiaries of Kuwait's Fund for Arab Economic Development which loaned him money to dredge the Creek and build a new breakwater near its mouth. The project was completed in 1963, and gold smuggling took off like a rocket.

A building boom had begun along the Creek before the discovery of oil near Dubai in 1966 but, even after oil revenues began coming in, trade remained the foundation of the city's wealth. Gold smuggling peaked in 1970, when 259 tons of gold flowed through the emirate.

In the early 1970s, the Indian government began to crack down on gold smugglers, but Dubai's merchants had already laid the foundations of today's enormous 're-export trade' in consumer goods bound for the rest of the Arabian peninsula and the subcontinent. This is not to say that Dubai's days as a smuggler's paradise are over. The trade now supposedly focuses on Iran: the dhows take VCRs and Levis jeans to Iranian ports and return laden with caviar and carpets. As was the case with gold, all of these goods leave Dubai perfectly legally; it's the countries at the *other* end of the trade that look on it as smuggling.

Dubai's trade and oil-fuelled building boom eventually provided it with one of the busiest airports in the Middle East, a large dock complex and, at Jebel Ali, a huge free-trade zone and what is said to be the largest artificial port in the world. At the time it was built, the port was one of only two artificial structures in the world that was visible from space (the other being the Great Wall of China). In 1988 Dubai opened the first golf course in the Gulf with real grass. By the mid-'90s, the Dubai Desert Classic had become a well-established stop on the annual PGA tour and the city's golf courses had tripled in number.

The man who was the driving force behind all of this, Sheikh Rashid, died in 1990 after a long illness and was succeeded as emir by his son, Sheikh Maktoum. For several years prior to Rashid's death, Maktoum had been regent for his father in all but name, and the new emir has continued his father's policies.

The core of these policies is to promote Dubai whenever and wherever possible. The golf courses were built, in part, so that big-name tournaments played there could place Dubai on the international sporting calendar. The same logic is behind the world-class tennis tournaments, boat and horse racing and desert rallies hosted by the city, its air show (one of the four largest in the world) and its high profile events, such as the Dubai Shopping Festival.

ORIENTATION

Dubai is really two towns: Deira to the east, and Dubai to the west, separated by the Creek (al-Khor in Arabic), an inlet of the Gulf. The Dubai side is sometimes referred to as Bur Dubai, and includes the area around the bus station and abra dock and stretches away from the Creek for a couple of kilometres. Deira, however, is the city centre. Although Deira and Bur Dubai are actually small districts on either side of the Creek, people often use these terms to refer to the entire areas either side of the Creek.

Activity in Deira focuses on Beniyas Rd, which runs along the Creek, Beniyas Square (which used to be called Al-Nasr Square and is still generally known by that name), Al-Maktoum Rd, Al-Maktoum Hospital Rd, and Naif Rd. The Deira Souq, around which most of the cheap hotels are located, occupies most of the area west of Beniyas Square and south of Naif Rd.

On the Dubai side, the older souq area runs from Al-Ghubaiba Rd (where the bus station is) to the Ruler's Office and inland as far as Khalid bin al-Waleed Rd. Shaikh Zayed Rd is one of the main business areas on the Bur Dubai side.

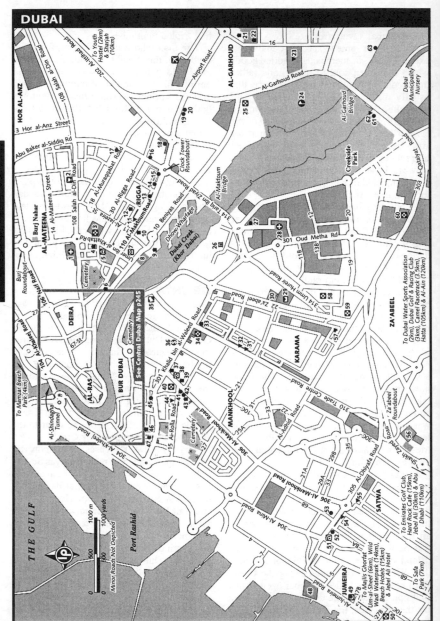

DUBAI

PLACES TO STAY		OTHER			
4	Tourist Hotel	1	Al-Maktoum	35	British Consulate-
6	Dubai Inter-		Hospital		General
	Continental Hotel	2	Harry's Place	36	Banks
9	Sheraton Dubai	3	Al-Ghurair Centre	38	Etisalat
10	Al-Khaleej Palace	5	Deira Taxi Stand	40	Al-Khaleej Shopping
12	Vendome Plaza	7	Etisalat		Centre; La Brioche
	Hotel; Caves des Rois	8	Docks for Tour Boats	41	24 hour
21	Le Meridien Dubai	13	Al Ghaith & Al Moosa		Convenience Store
22	Al-Bustan Rotana		Travel Agency	42	Al-Rais Travel
33	Regent Palace Hotel	14	Avis	45	Al-Warda al-Ahmar
37	Heritage	15	White Falcon		Laundry
	International Hotel		(Car Rental)	47	Meraj Typing Centre
39	Ramada Hotel	16	Patriot Rent-A-Car	48	Ruler's Guesthouse
43	Panorama Hotel	17	The Travel Market	49	Jumeira Mosque
46	Swiss Plaza Hotel	18	Dubai Airline Centre	50	Magrudy's Shopping
		19	Hertz		Centre & Bookshop
PLACES TO EAT		20	Budget	51	Internet Cafe
11	Sadaf Restaurant	24	Dubai Creek Golf	52	Book Corner
23	The Irish Village		& Yacht Club	53	Adnan Ali Laundry
31	All Spice Fast Food	25	Deira City Centre	56	World Trade Centre
32	Thai Terrace		(Shopping Mall)		(Dubai Hilton; Australian,
44	Kowloon	26	Palace		Italian, Swiss, Turkish &
54	Istanbouli Restaurant	27	British Council		US Consulates)
55	Ravi Restaurant	28	Rashid Hospital	58	Al-Nasr Plaza
57	Fiesta Filipino	29	Main Post Office	59	Lamcy Plaza
62	Fishmarket Floating	30	AmEx (Kanoo Travel)	60	Wafi Centre
	Restaurant	34	Bur Juman Centre	61	Al-Boom Tourist Village
				63	Jet-ski Hire

There are four ways of getting from one side of the Creek to the other. The Shindagha Tunnel runs under the Creek at the northern end, near its mouth. The Al-Maktoum Bridge, on the southern edge of the centre, is the main traffic artery across the waterway. Further south, the Al-Garhoud Bridge is used mostly by traffic trying to bypass the centre. The final method of crossing the Creek is by abra, the small, open water-taxis that criss-cross the waterway throughout the day and into the evening.

Street Names
Many main streets in Dubai are known by more familiar names. You should be aware of the following:

official name	common name
Al-Jumeira Rd	Jumeira Rd, Jumeira Beach Rd or Beach Rd
Al-Wasl Rd	Iranian Hospital Rd
Beniyas Square	Al-Nasr Square
Khalid bin al-Waleed Rd (between Za'abeel Rd to Trade Centre Rd)	Bank St
Shaikh Zayed Rd	Abu Dhabi Rd

Maps
Geoprojects publishes a fold-out map of Dubai which is good but it doesn't include the names of all the minor streets. It has a bluey cover and is available from most bookshops and hotels for Dh50. The maps in *Dubai Tourist and Business Guide* are also by Geoprojects. They are very detailed and are probably the best maps available if you are negotiating your way around Dubai by car. The guide costs Dh50 from bookshops and hotels.

INFORMATION
Tourist Offices
The Department of Tourism & Commerce Marketing has a Welcome Bureau. Call ☎ 224 5252 or 228 5000 for information on

what to do in Dubai or help in booking hotels and tours. There are also three visitor centres in and around the city: one at the airport arrivals area, another in Beniyas Square in Deira and one about 40km out of town on the road to Abu Dhabi. They offer a few glossy pamphlets with fairly useless maps, but they will give you an idea of what to see while in Dubai and they can book hotels for you. The one at the airport is open 24 hours and the other two are open 7 am to 11 pm daily. Tour operators and some of the larger travel agencies and hotels are also good sources of information.

Dubai National Travel & Tourist Authority (DNATA or 'Danata', as it's known) is the quasi-official travel agency in Dubai. Basically, this means that it has a monopoly on travel services at wholesale level. The head office (☎ 295 1111) is at the Airline Centre on Al-Maktoum Rd, Deira.

Lonely Planet's *Dubai City Guide* maps out two walking tours of the city – one on either side of the Creek. *Dubai Town Walk* is a locally produced brochure, available from the Majlis Gallery in the Bastakia Quarter for Dh5. It has two walking tours of the city, although it is more than five years old and in need of an update to include some of the newer tourist attractions.

Money

Unless it's unavoidable, don't change money at the airport – the rates on offer are terrible. There is no shortage of banks and exchange houses in the city. In central Deira, especially along Sikkat al-Khail St and around Beniyas Square, every other building seems to contain a bank or a moneychanger. In Bur Dubai, there are a lot of moneychangers (although most only take cash, no travellers cheques) around the abra dock. In either case, shopping around is worthwhile if you are changing more than a few hundred US dollars.

The highest concentration of international banks is along Khalid bin al-Waleed Rd in Bur Dubai, east of Al-Mankhool Rd. If you need an ATM in central Deira look for Emirates Bank International. Its ATMs

are tied into the Electron, Cirrus, Switch and Global Access systems. There's a branch on Beniyas Rd near the Al-Khaleej Hotel and another on Al-Maktoum Rd. In Bur Dubai there is a branch on Al-Souq St. ATMs at British Bank branches are linked with the Global Access system. You'll find one on Beniyas Square and another in Bur Dubai, opposite Al-Falah St.

AmEx (☎ 336 5000, fax 336 6006) is represented in Dubai by Kanoo Travel. The office is on the 1st floor of the Hermitage Building, next to the main post office on Za'abeel Rd. It's open 8.30 am to 1 pm and 3 to 6.30 pm daily, except Friday. They don't cash travellers cheques but they will hold mail for AmEx clients. Address mail to: c/o American Express, Client's Mail, PO Box 290, Dubai, UAE.

Post

The main post office is on the Bur Dubai side, on Za'abeel Rd. It is open 8 am to 11.30 pm Saturday to Wednesday, 8 am to 10 pm Thursday and 8 am to noon Friday. It has a philatelic bureau.

The Deira post office, on Al-Sabkha Rd near the intersection with Beniyas Rd, is much smaller. It is open 8 am to midnight Saturday to Wednesday, 8 am to 1 pm and 4 to 8 pm Thursday and closed Friday.

There are also a number of fax and postal agencies dotted along the small streets around the Deira and Dubai souq areas.

Telephone

The Etisalat office on the corner of Beniyas and Umer ibn al-Khattab Rds is open 24 hours a day. In addition to telephones, the office has fax, telex and telegram facilities. Note that it's the building with the thing that looks like a golf ball on top, not the older, white building across the street. There is another Etisalat office on Mankhool Rd in Bur Dubai, next to the Heritage International Hotel.

If you need to make a call from the airport, there are telephones in the baggage claim area beyond the arrivals duty-free shop, from which local calls (within Dubai) can be made free. Some of the lounges at the gates in the departures area also have phones from which you can make free local calls.

Email & Internet Access

The Internet Cafe (☎ 453 390) on Al-Dhiyafa Rd in Jumeira charges Dh15 per hour and is open 10 am to 3 am Saturday to Thursday and 2 pm to 3 am on Friday. For the same cost you can use the Internet at the British Council Library 10 am to 1 pm and from 5 to 8 pm Saturday to Wednesday. Meraj Typing Centre, opposite the Swiss Plaza Hotel in Bur Dubai, offers Internet access for Dh10 per hour. There are plans for public libraries to have public Internet access in the near future.

Travel Agencies

The highest concentration of travel agencies is along Al-Maktoum Rd in Deira (between the clock tower and Omar ibn al-Khattab St). The following agencies are recommended, and offer some of the best air fares available.

Al Chaith & Al-Moosa Travel Agency (☎ 221 1164, fax 223 3054) on Al-Maktoum Rd, just west of the clock tower roundabout, Deira
Al-Rais Travels (☎ 557 700, fax 532 411) Al-Rais Centre, Al-Mankhool Rd, Mankhool
The Travel Market (☎ 664 455, fax 685 168) corner of Al-Murraqqabat and Abu Baker al-Siddiq Rds, Deira
MMI Travel Centre (☎ 209 5000, fax 229 1928) Al-Khor St, Al-Ras, Deira

Bookshops

Dubai's best bookshop, Magrudy Books, is in the shopping centre of the same name on Al-Jumeira Rd. It also sells books through its Web site (www.magrudy.com). Note that it is open all day (8.30 am to 8 pm) on Wednesday and Thursday.

Other options include Book Corner at the Dune Centre, Al-Dhiyafa Rd, Satwa and the Hyatt Galleria. There is also Books Gallery at the Al-Ghurair Centre on the corner of Omar ibn al-Khattab and Al-Rigga Rds. Most of the larger hotels have small selections in their bookshops. The House of Prose is an excellent second-hand bookshop in the

Jumeira Plaza on Al-Jumeira Rd, about 500m south of Magrudy's Shopping Centre.

Laundry

In Deira, try Tide Drycleaners & Laundry on the north side of Beniyas Square or Golden Laundry on Naif Rd. In Bur Dubai, there's Al-Warda al-Ahmar Laundry on Al-Esbij St near the corner with Khalid bin al-Waleed St. In Satwa, try Adnan Ali Laundry on 6b St just off Al-Dhiyafa Rd.

Medical Services

For nonurgent care ask your embassy/consulate for the latest list of recommended doctors. For emergency care you can try one of the following government hospitals:

Al-Maktoum Hospital (☎ 221 211) Al-Maktoum Hospital Rd, near the corner of Omar ibn al-Khattab St
Rashid Hospital (☎ 337 4000) off Oud Metha Rd, near Al-Maktoum Bridge, Bur Dubai

Emergency

For an ambulance and police call ☎ 999. For fire emergencies call ☎ 997.

SOUQS

Compared with how it would have been only 20 or 30 years ago, not much of the old covered souqs remain but they still operate in the early morning and in the evening from around 5 to 8 pm. The **Deira Covered Souq** off Al-Sabkha Rd sells just about anything. Here you will find textiles, spices, kitchen wares, walking sticks, sheeshas, clothes and a lifetime supply of henna.

The **Deira Old Souq**, or **Spice Souq** as it is also known, is a wonderful place to wander around and take in the smells of a myriad spices, nuts and dried fruits. The spices are mainly found at the souq's eastern end, closest to the Creek. Sacks brim with frankincense, dried lemons, ginger root, chilli and cardamom among others. Other shops in this souq sell tacky trinkets, kitchen wares, shoes, rugs, glassware and textiles.

Deira's **Gold Souq** is on and around Sikkat al-Khail St between Suq Deira and Old Baladiya Sts. If you don't spot the glittering gold

Henna Patterns

Marking the hands and feet with henna, a powder derived from the leaves of the henna tree, is a traditional form of decoration used by women in the Middle East (and the subcontinent). You'll see mounds of the greenish henna powder for sale in souqs throughout the UAE and Oman. The powder is mixed with water to form a reddish-brown paste, which is then applied to the skin. Traditionally, the incredibly intricate patterns are painted free-hand, using a paper cone to squeeze the henna paste onto the skin. The paste has to stay on for 12 hours or so, then can be washed off, leaving a reddish dye on the skin. The patterns lasts for about four to six weeks. These days patterns are often applied using a plastic stencil, sold in the souq. Nails and the soles of the feet are also dyed.

Henna painting is often done for a special event such as a wedding, and stays on for about six weeks. In the more conservative and traditional areas of the UAE, such as Al-Ain, most of the Emirati women have some form of henna decoration on their hands and feet.

There are many beauty salons in Dubai and elsewhere in the UAE that do henna decorations – just look for the signs with painted hands on them.

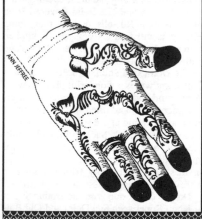

in the windows you'll recognise the souq by the wooden lattice archways at the entrances. The Gold Souq is probably the largest such market in Arabia and attracts customers from all over the Middle East and subcontinent. For more details see the boxed text 'All That Glitters…' later in this chapter.

At the eastern end of the Gold Souq along Sikkat al-Khail St is the **Perfume Souq**. A number of shops along here sell a staggering range of Arabic and European perfumes.

The **Dubai Souq** in Bur Dubai has been beautifully reconstructed in order to be more appealing to tourists, but it still seems to be frequented almost exclusively by the local Indian population. It sells mostly materials and shoes. There is very little in the way of Arabic antiques or souvenirs.

DUBAI MUSEUM

Dubai's museum (☎ 353 1862) is well worth visiting. It occupies the Al-Fahidi Fort on the Dubai side of the Creek, next to the Ruler's Office. Al-Fahidi Fort was built in the early 19th century and is thought to be the oldest building in Dubai. For many years it was both the residence of Dubai's rulers and the seat of government. It was converted into a museum in 1971.

At the entrance is a display of aerial photographs showing the growth of Dubai over the years. In the courtyard, you'll see a tank for carrying fresh water on pearling boats, as well as several small boats and a barasti house with a wind tower. (See 'Traditional Architecture' in the Facts about the Region chapter for more information on wind towers.) The hall along the right-hand side of the courtyard has a display on the fort itself and another display featuring *khanjars* (daggers) and other traditional weapons. The hall to the left of the courtyard has a video of traditional Emirati dances, a display of musical instruments and more weapons.

The tower at the far corner of the courtyard leads down to a large underground area where the rest of the museum's exhibits are housed. These begin with a slick multimedia presentation of the city's development. Then you come to very detailed re-creations of a

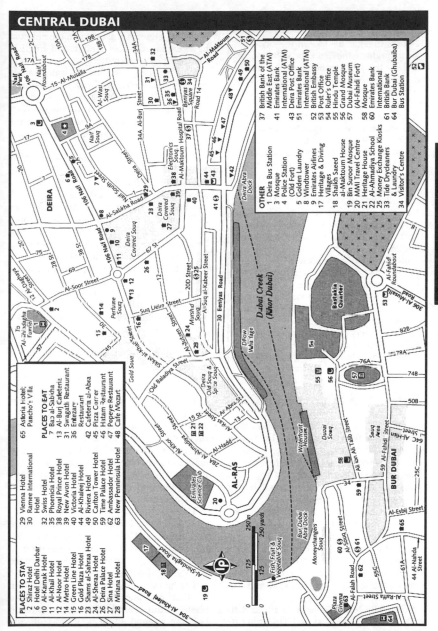

CENTRAL DUBAI

PLACES TO STAY
2 Shiraz Hotel
5 Hotel Delhi Darbar
10 Al-Karnak Hotel
11 Al-Khail Hotel
12 Al-Noor Hotel
14 Metro Hotel
15 Green Line Hotel
16 Gold Plaza Hotel
23 Shams al-Sahraa Hotel
24 Al-Sheraa Hotel
26 Deira Palace Hotel
27 Sina Hotel
28 Miriana Hotel
29 Vienna Hotel
30 Ramee International Hotel
32 Swiss Hotel
35 Phoenicia Hotel
38 Royal Prince Hotel
39 New Avon Hotel
40 Victoria Hotel
44 Al-Khaleej Hotel
49 Riviera Hotel
50 Carlton Tower Hotel
59 Time Palace Hotel
62 Ambassador Hotel
63 New Penninsula Hotel
65 Astoria Hotel; Pancho's Vila

PLACES TO EAT
7 Baz al-Sakiha
13 Al-Burj Cafeteria
31 Swagath Restaurant
36 Entezar Restaurant
42 Cafeteria al-Abra
45 Pizza Corner
46 Hatam Restaurant
47 Popeye Restaurant
48 Cafe Mozart

OTHER
1 Deira Bus Station
3 Mosque
4 Police Station (Old Fort)
5 Golden Laundry
8 Windtower
9 Emirates Airlines
17 Heritage & Diving Villages
18 Shaikh Saeed al-Maktoum House
19 Bin Suroor Mosque
20 MMI Travel Centre
21 Heritage House
22 Al-Ahmadiya School
25 Money Exchange Kiosks
33 Tide Drycleaners & Laundry
34 Visitor's Centre
37 British Bank of the Middle East (ATM)
41 Emirates Bank International (ATM)
43 Deira Post Office
51 Emirates Bank International (ATM)
52 British Embassy
53 Post Office
54 Ruler's Temple
55 Hindu Temple
56 Grand Mosque
57 Dubai Museum (Al-Fahidi Fort)
58 Mosque
60 Emirates Bank International
61 British Bank
64 Bur Dubai (Ghubaiba) Bus Station

The Creek

Dubai's Creek is the soul of the city. Take an abra ride on the Creek for an hour or so and see this great trading port as it should be seen – from the water. If you do only one 'touristy' thing in Dubai this is it.

If you go to the Heritage and Diving Villages (see this section later in this chapter), you will notice signs along the waterfront offering boat cruises for Dh100 per hour. If you want to take a boat ride it's better to make a deal with one of the many boatmen who cruise up and down the Creekside and you should only pay Dh30 to Dh35 for half an hour or Dh40 to Dh45 for one hour (for the whole boat, not per person). The shorter trip should take you up to the Al-Maktoum Bridge and back. For Dh40 the boatman should extend that route to include a trip down to the mouth of the Creek and back. These prices take a bit of bargaining to achieve.

It's also fascinating to walk along the dhow wharfage on the Deira side of the Creek to the west of the abra dock. Dhows bound for every port from Kuwait to Mumbai (Bombay) dock here to load and unload all sorts of interesting cargo. You'll see tyres, jeans, kitchen sinks, cars and probably just about anything you can imagine.

typical souq, a home and school as they would have looked in the 1950s. These come complete with disturbingly lifelike dummies of people – you always have the feeling that someone is standing right next to you. This is followed by a display on water and how it was conserved in the desert.

There is also a interactive display on the flora and fauna of the UAE, a display of seafaring life and the area's archaeology, including a complete grave from the Al-Qusais archaeological site (950–550 BC). Another room features finds from the digs at both Al-Qusais and Jumeira (5th and 8th centuries AD respectively).

Dubai Museum is open 8.30 am to 8.30 pm Saturday to Thursday and 3 to 9 pm Friday. Admission is Dh7, or Dh3 for children up to age eight. All displays in the museum have explanations in Arabic and English. Photography is permitted.

Bus No 19 goes past the museum. If you've come across the Creek from Deira by abra, turn left and go through the entrance to the Bur Dubai souq. Turn right into any of the small lanes that lead inland from the souq, and you will be on the road that leads directly to the museum. If you are catching a taxi, the word for museum is 'mathaf'.

SHAIKH SAEED AL-MAKTOUM HOUSE

The house of Sheikh Saeed, the grandfather of Dubai's present ruler, has been restored as a museum of pre-oil times. It's by the Creek on the Dubai side. The 30-room house was built in the late 19th century and, for many years, it served as a communal residence for the Al-Maktoum family. This is in keeping with the Arabian tradition of having several generations living in separate apartments within the same house. Sheikh Saeed lived here until his death in 1958.

The house was reopened as a museum in 1986 and houses a fascinating exhibition of photographs, mainly from the 1940s and '50s, documenting the history and development of Dubai. It is amazing to see how different the city looked only a few decades ago. Some of the photos go back to the late 20th century and there are some fascinating shots of traditional life in Dubai.

There are models of the different sorts of dhows used in Dubai – not quite as good as the one at the Dubai Museum but interesting all the same. There is also a model of Bur Dubai from the 1950s.

There's a display of coins used in the region, including Indian rupees, which were the currency in Dubai during British control of India. From 1948 until federation in 1971, a currency known as the Gulf rupee was the legal tender.

The house is built of coral quarried from the Gulf and then covered with lime and plaster. Until recently this was a common building method along both the Gulf and

Red Sea coasts of Arabia. The entrance on Al-Shindagha Rd, the one used by visitors today, was the back door to the house. The main entrance, opening onto the large, central courtyard, faced the sea. (The Port Rashid complex, which now occupies almost 1.5km between the house and the open sea, is mostly on reclaimed land.)

Shaikh Saeed House is next to the Heritage and Diving Villages on Al-Shindagha Rd in Bur Dubai. It is open 7.30 am to 9.30 pm Saturday to Thursday and 3 to 9.30 pm on Friday. Admission is Dh2.

HERITAGE & DIVING VILLAGES

These villages, next to Shaikh Saeed al-Maktoum House on Al-Shindagha Rd, were under construction at the time of writing but were open to visitors for free.

The Heritage Village (☎ 393 7151) recreates traditional Bedouin and coastal village life, complete with barasti homes, a traditional coffeehouse and a small souq where you can buy freshly made *dosa* (a flat, grilled bread made from flour and water) for Dh1 from Emirati women. The other shops in the souq sell some rather nice traditional handicrafts, Bedouin jewellery and pottery as well as some tacky and overpriced souvenirs from India and Africa. The Ramesh Art Gallery sells some lovely paintings and photographs of Dubai but they are expensive.

When finished, the Diving Village (☎ 393 9390) will have displays of pearl diving, once the livelihood of the city, and models of various types of dhows and pearling boats. There are a few shops selling (modern) diving equipment (available for hire). A large outdoor restaurant and *sheesha* (traditional pipe) bar affords a nice view of the Creek and Dubai.

There is a small museum displaying artefacts and diagrams from archaeological sites found at Al-Qusais and Jumeira in Dubai, and at Al-Sufouf near Hatta.

MAJLIS GHORFAT UM-AL-SHEEF

It is unusual to find a traditional building still standing so far from the Creek but this one, located just south-east of Jumeira Beach Park, has been well restored and is worth a visit. The two-storey Majlis Ghorfat Um-al-Sheef, built in 1955, was where Sheikh Rashid bin Saeed al-Maktoum would come in the evenings to listen to his people's complaints, grievances and ideas. It was a place of open discussion and exchange. Donald Hawley, a former British political resident of Dubai, saw the majlis as 'an Arabian Camelot' and Sheikh Rashid as King Arthur.

The majlis also provided a cool retreat from the heat of the day. It is made of gypsum and coral rock – traditional building materials of the Gulf – and the roof is made of palm fronds *(areesh)*. The columns, windows and doors are all made of teak from India.

A falaj and garden of date palms and fig trees has been constructed around the majlis, and a traditional barasti cafe sits in one corner of the enclosure.

The majlis is located on 17 St which runs off Al-Jumeira Rd, on the inland side, just past the Jumeira Beach Park. It is open 8.30 am to 1.30 pm and 3.30 to 8.30 pm Saturday to Thursday, 3.30 to 8.30 pm Friday. Admission is free. You can catch bus No 8 and get off just south of Jumeira Beach Park.

> ### The Majlis
>
> *Majlis* translates as 'meeting place' or 'reception area'. In terms of government, the Majlis was a forum or council where citizens could come and speak to their leaders and make requests, complaints or raise issues that were troubling them. This system is still in place today around the region.
>
> A majlis, in its domestic sense as a reception area, is found in every fort in the region, and in many private homes. Its Western cousin is probably the lounge room. It is still an important room in an Arab household and is usually the domain of the male members of the family. It's a place where they can get together and talk without disturbing the women of the house. Some traditional houses had a separate majlis for women.

BASTAKIA QUARTER

This district, on the waterfront east of the Dubai Souq and the Ruler's Office (also called the Diwan, the main administrative body of the emirate), features a number of traditional old wind-tower houses. Built at the turn of the 20th century, these houses were once the homes of wealthy Persian merchants who were lured to Dubai by its relaxed trade tariffs. Most came from the Bastak district in what is now southern Iran, hence the name Bastakia. Wind towers were a traditional form of air-conditioning – see the special section 'Traditional Architecture' in the Facts about the Region chapter for an explanation of how they work.

The quarter has been declared a conservation area and restoration work is under way on a few of the houses. If you pass one of the houses under restoration ask the workmen if you can have a look around. The Majlis Gallery is housed in one of the restored wind towers and is well worth visiting to see some local artwork. Bus No 19, the same bus as for Dubai Museum, goes to the quarter.

AL-AHMADIYA DISTRICT

The Al-Ahmadiya School and the Heritage House on Al-Ahmadiya St in the souq area of Deira, were not officially open at the time of writing but it was still possible to wander through and have a look. The school will eventually be turned into a museum detailing early education in Dubai.

The Heritage House, next to the Al-Ahmadiya School, was once home to a wealthy Iranian merchant and was built in 1890. It differs to the old houses in the Bastakia Quarter on the other side of the Creek as it is has no wind towers. The house is characterised by many wooden shutters at street level and a balcony railing along the roof. Once inside you find yourself in a large courtyard surrounded by rooms and a verandah at one end.

The small area around the school is home to a number of traditional houses which have been recently restored.

You can catch any of the buses that go along Beniyas Rd and around the Al-Ras

district to get here. You'll need to get off at the Public Library and walk from here.

WORLD TRADE CENTRE

The World Trade Centre tower was once Dubai's tallest building. Even though it has been overshadowed by taller and more modern looking skyscrapers, it is still a very important and recognisable landmark in the city. There is a viewing gallery on the 37th floor for those who want a bird's-eye view of the city but can't afford to hire a helicopter. You can only visit the gallery as part of a tour. These leave from the information desk in the tower lobby at 9.30 am and 4.30 pm. Admission is Dh5. For more information call ☎ 331 4200.

You can catch buses No 6, 61, 90 or 98 to get there.

JUMEIRA ARCHAEOLOGICAL SITE

This site is considered to be one of the largest and most significant sites in the UAE. Remains found here date to the 6th century AD and can be seen in the small museum at the Heritage Village in Shindagha. The settlement is particularly interesting in that it spans the pre-Islamic and Islamic eras. Now surrounded by modern villas and shopping centres, the settlement was once a caravan station on a route linking Ctesiphon (in what is now Iraq) to northern Oman.

Remains at the site link it with the Persian Sassanid empire, the dominant culture in the region from the 3rd to the 6th century. Other Sassanid settlements have been found at Kush and Julfar in what is now the emirate of Ras al-Khaimah (see the Northern Emirates chapter for more information on these sites.) The Sassanids were wiped out with the coming of Islam in the 7th century by Arab tribes, notably the Umayyad dynasty. The Umayyads extended and restored many of the original buildings and the site continued to exist until at least the 10th century.

There is no access to the site for the public as archaeologists are still working to uncover the area. If someone is there you may be able to have a look inside, otherwise you'll just have to make out parts of the site through the fence.

To get there head south down Al-Jumeira Rd and do a U-turn when you get to the Jumeira Beach Park, just past the Hilton Beach Club. Take the first street on the right which is 27 St and go straight to the end. Turn right and you will see a large fenced in area about 50m along on your left. You can catch bus No 8 bus as far as the Jumeira Beach Park from where the site only a five-minute walk.

AL-BOOM TOURIST VILLAGE

This is really just a nice place to go for a coffee in traditional barasti surrounds or to have a meal on the Fishmarket Floating Restaurant (see Places to Eat later in this chapter). The rest of the 'village' is just made up of function rooms, Arabic restaurants and a gallery which seems to be closed most of the time. There is also a sheesha cafe which gets going in the evenings. It is next to the Al-Garhoud bridge on the Bur Dubai side of the Creek.

PARKS

Dubai has a number of large, established parks. **Creekside Park** is the largest of these and runs 2.6km on the Bur Dubai side of the Creek from Al-Garhoud Bridge towards Al-Maktoum Bridge. It has children's play areas, dhow cruises, kiosks, restaurants, an amphitheatre and beaches (although it's not advisable to swim in the Creek). At the time of writing a cable car was under construction which will run along the creek edge of the park. It is open 8 am to 11 pm Saturday to Wednesday, until 11.30 pm Thursday, Friday and public holidays. Wednesday is for ladies and children only.

Jumeira Beach Park on Al-Jumeira Rd is a lovely park and a walk on the grass here is a real treat. There is a children's play area, barbeques, picnic tables, walkways and kiosks. The long stretch of beach is clean and lined with date palms for shade and there are lifeguards on duty. The park is open 8 am to 10.30 pm Saturday to Wednesday, to 11.30 pm on Thursday and Friday. Saturday and Monday are for women and children only.

Admission is Dh5 or Dh20 per car. You can catch bus No 8 or 20, which run along Al-Jumeira Rd to the park.

Al-Mamzar Beach Park, on the border of Dubai and Sharjah at the mouth of Mamzar Creek is open 8 am to 9.30 pm Saturday to Wednesday and 8 am to 10.30 pm Thursday, Friday and public holidays. Admission is Dh3. There are beaches, a swimming pool, children's play areas, and free transport around the park and kiosks.

Al-Safa Park, on Al-Wasl Rd in Jumeira, is one of the most impressively verdant parks in the city. It has a reconstruction of a city on a small scale, complete with buildings, roads and traffic lights, as well as famous landmarks from around the world. There is a boat lake and an artificial waterfall. It is open 6.30 am to 9.30 pm Saturday to Wednesday and 7.30 am to 10.30 pm Thursday, Friday and public holidays. Admission is Dh3.

BEACHES

If you want to spend a day on the beach, there are a few nice stretches of public beach around Dubai or you can go to one of the beach parks listed in the Parks section earlier. Most beaches along the Dubai coast are the private domains of the five-star beach hotels and, unless you are a guest, you will pay dearly for the use of their facilities. The average cost for a day visit is Dh100 with Dh50 redeemable on food and drinks. Some are only open to hotel guests and members. For single women, however, the male attention can sometimes be more of a hassle than the private beach club fees.

Next to the Marine Beach Resort just off Al-Jumeira Rd, more or less opposite the Jumeira Mosque, there is a stretch of public beach with facilities – showers, shelters, toilets and plenty of newly planted date palms (although it will be some years until these are big enough to provide shade). A little further from town, on either side of Jumeira Beach Hotel, there are public beaches. The beach further south has shelters and showers and the beach to the north has jet skis for hire.

On the Deira side of the Creek there is a public stretch of beach running along the bank of the Khor al-Mamzar, which looks out over Sharjah. Follow the signs for Al-Mamzar Beach Park and you'll see the beach about 50m past the entrance to the park. There are no sun shelters or lifeguards here, only rubbish bins.

ACTIVITIES

There are far too many activities and clubs in Dubai to list here. The best source for this sort of information is the *Dubai Explorer*. It has an alphabetical listing of all the activities you can do in Dubai, where to do them and how much it will cost you. *What's On* also has information on clubs and leisure activities in Dubai.

Golf

The Emirates Golf Club (☎ 473 222), on the road to Jebel Ali, is the site of the Dubai Desert Classic, part of the European PGA Tour. Greens fees are Dh330 for 18 holes plus Dh45 for cart rental. The Dubai Creek Golf & Yacht Club (☎ 295 6000), near the Deira side of the Al-Garhoud Bridge, has the same green fees. It also has a floodlit nine-hole par-three course, which costs only Dh30 per round.

The newest grass course in Dubai is the Dubai Golf & Racing Club (☎ 336 3666), beyond the inland edge of the Creek. Green fees are Dh220 and you need to book five days in advance. The Club is off Oud Metha Rd.

With all of these courses there is a discount of about 10% if you have UAE Golf Association membership. To play you must be wearing a shirt with sleeves and a collar, and trousers. Jeans and 'beach wear' are not allowed. They will probably ask you for a handicap certificate but it's not compulsory.

Water Sports

Water sports are popular in Dubai although most facilities are tied either to a big hotel with huge fees or a private club, and are therefore not generally accessible to budget travellers. If your life depends on a spot of jet-skiing you can pay for the use of a five-star hotel beach club for the day and then pay

Wild Wadi

Attached to the Jumeira Beach Hotel, this 12-acre waterpark opened to much fanfare in 1999. Two million gallons of water are pumped through the park's various tunnels, tubes, slides, caves and pools every day. The 24 rides are all interconnected so you can get off one and jump straight onto another. Some of the hairier rides reach speeds of 80km/h while the 'Jumeira Sceirah' is the highest and fastest free-fall water slide outside North America (gulp!). There are wave pools for swimmers and surfers as well as more sedate rides for younger kids and nervous adults.

The park is an expensive day out at Dh120/95 for adults/children. Bus No 8 along Al-Jumeira Rd will get you there.

Dh100 per half-hour on top of that, or you can go to the Creek bank just south of Al-Garhoud Bridge on the Deira side. They have a number of jet-skis for hire at Dh50 for half an hour Saturday to Thursday, Dh100 on Friday mornings and Dh75 on Friday afternoons. You'll find the jet-skis here everyday from about 10 am until it begins to get dark. There is another jet-ski area next to the Jumeira Beach Hotel on its northern side. Here they charge Dh100 per half hour.

The only place to water-ski apart from the five-star hotel beach clubs is at the Dubai Water Sports Association (☎ 334 2031). It's located at an off-the-track part of the Creek bank on the Dubai side. There is an entry fee of Dh15 on weekdays and Dh25 on weekends. Water-skiing costs Dh45 for a 13-minute tow.

The club is open 9 am to dusk every day although there is no water-skiing on Sunday. To get there from the Dubai side of the Creek head along Al-Qataiyat Rd towards Al-Garhoud Bridge. Take the first exit to the right after the Dubai Police Headquarters. Go past the nursery and turn right just before the Dubai Docking Yard. The tarmac road ends but continue on a sand track for 1.4km as it skirts around a large fenced-in compound. At this point you'll see the lonely looking club ahead and to your right. You can get bus No 14 as far as the fenced-in compound but you will have about a 10-minute walk from here.

If you want to go diving, you're better off going to the east coast, as visibility in the water is not very good around Dubai. See Diving in Activities in the UAE Facts for the Visitor chapter for contact details of Dubai-based dive companies offering east coast trips.

ORGANISED TOURS

Arabian Adventures (☎ 331 7373, fax 331 4696) is a Dubai-based company run in tandem with Emirates Airlines. It offers a half-day tour of Dubai daily for Dh110 per person, which includes a visit to Jumeira Mosque, the Bastakia Quarter and Dubai Museum, as well as an abra ride across the Creek and a visit to the Gold Souq and Deira Covered Souq. Considering how cheap taxis are, it is hard to understand why anyone would want to pay this sort of money.

Net Tours (☎ 666 655, fax 668 662) offers a similar day tour plus a visit to one or two shopping malls for Dh90 per person.

You can also take a 45-minute Fly By Dubai tour with Desert Air Tours (☎ 299 4411) on a Cessna 207 for Dh250 per person.

Coastline Leisure (☎ 398 4867, fax 398 5497) offers one-hour, guided tours of the Creek by dhow daily at 11.30 am, 3.30 and 5.30 pm for Dh35 per person. The boats depart from the docks next to the Sheraton Hotel. It also offers dinner cruises on Tuesday and Sunday for Dh240, and the charter of larger, fancier boats.

Danat Dubai is a 34m catamaran that cruises the Creek every day of the week for lunches and dinners for Dh180 (half-price for children under 12). A one-hour cruise without a meal costs Dh50. Call ☎ 223 5755 to book.

For something different you might want to take a ride on Seascope to see some of the marine life around Dubai. This semi-submersible submarine lives at the Diving Village in Shindagha and can take up to 24

people for a 45-minute cruise of the Dubai coast. The cost is Dh55 per person; call Sam Tours on ☎ 592 930 for bookings.

PLACES TO STAY

With around 250 hotels and more on the way, Dubai is definitely not short of accommodation options. The only really busy time is during the Dubai Airshow in November, when you'll need to book well ahead.

Dubai has a good range of hotels to suit most budgets. The highest concentration of cheap hotels is in Deira Souq, particularly along Al-Sabkha Rd and in the side streets off Suq Deira St. Four- and five-star hotels line the Creek, dot the outskirts of the souq area and are everywhere on the Bur Dubai side of the Creek and around Rigga Rd on the Deira side.

The Deira Souq is a great place to stay because of its central location. If your budget can manage it, something on or around Beniyas Square will put you right in the heart of the city. Bur Dubai is also quite close to the action but has fewer really cheap hotels. Staying in the youth hostel is cheap but puts you some distance from the centre. The luxury beach hotels down past Umm Suqeim are great if you are just after a beach holiday but they are a long way from the centre, and you'll find yourself notching up a Dh40 taxi fare each time you want to go into town.

The rates quoted in this section are inclusive of the 20% tax and service charge. With the exception of the youth hostel you can almost always negotiate some kind of discount. At the mid- and top-end range you'll most likely get 20–30% off if you ask, and in summer you can expect to get 50–70% off the rates. All mid-range and top-end hotels require you to leave your passport in their safe for the duration of your stay. They also require you to leave a credit card authorisation of Dh500 per night. If you don't have a credit card you will have to leave a cash deposit.

PLACES TO STAY – BUDGET
Hostel

Dubai's one and only *Youth Hostel* (☎ 625 578, *Qusais Rd*) is on the eastern outskirts of the city, near the Jamiat al-Islah relief agency. To get there from central Deira take the main road for Sharjah (Al-Ittihad Rd) and turn right onto Qusais Rd. The Al-Ahli Club is the place on the left with a stadium; the hostel is another 100m along on the same side of the road. Beds are Dh35 per night in clean, comfortable two- and three-bed dormitory rooms. Meals are available at Dh10 for breakfast and another Dh15 for lunch and dinner. Women and men are welcome and there are separate rooms for families, although the manager reserves the right to turn away unaccompanied women if the hostel is full of rowdy young males (which, he says, is rare). The doors do not have locks but each bed has a locker with a key which you can take with you when you go out for the day.

Bus No 13 runs from the Deira bus station to the hostel every 10 minutes between 6.00 am and 11.45 pm. The fare is Dh1. A taxi from central Deira will cost about Dh14.

Hotels

Few of Dubai's cheapest hotels still arrange visas, which is probably just as well considering the chequered record of some of these places. In any event, our experience has been that you're far better off coming in via a more upmarket place and sleeping cheap later on. All the hotels listed here have fridges and TVs, only some of which work.

Deira is simply laden with Russians on shopping trips. Some hotels will not accept Russian guests because, we were told, 'they bring in a criminal element'. One of these elements is, no doubt, prostitutes from the CIS who have their 'offices' in Deira hotels. Single women travellers staying in these hotels also run the risk of being mistaken for a prostitute, but that's as far as the problem goes. It is very unlikely that you will suffer any kind of harassment beyond a whispered, misguided request. Aim to stay at places that advertise themselves as 'family hotels'. This means that they will not accept single men but will usually accept single women. Again, if you are a non-Russian man, you may be accepted at these places, as long as you do not bring home company.

Deira The *Tourist Hotel* (☎ 229 388, fax 224 8992) next to the Deira taxi stand is very good value, although it is a bit of a walk from the souqs. The staff are friendly and helpful and the rooms are standard for a mid-range hotel (Dh150/180).

Al-Karnak Hotel (☎ 226 8799, fax 225 2793, Naif Rd) is probably the best value hotel in Deira with large, clean rooms at Dh120 for singles and doubles.

Al-Noor Hotel (☎ 225 5455, fax 229 1682) is your second best bet in Deira. The hotel, just off Sikkat al-Khail St, had almost finished refurbishment at the time of writing. Rooms are large and cost Dh120/165.

Al-Khail Hotel (☎ 226 9171, fax 226 9226, Naif Rd) next to Al-Karnak Hotel is a cheaper option in Deira at Dh100 for singles/doubles, but rooms are only just OK.

Swiss Hotel (☎ 221 2181, fax 221 1779, Al-Mussalla Rd) is a very friendly place and is better value than most of the hotels closer to the souq area of Deira. Singles/doubles cost Dh120/150. In spite of its name, the hotel caters mainly to Indian clientele – its bars are even separated into south and north Indian sections.

Deira Palace Hotel (☎ 229 0120, fax 225 5889, 67 St) advertises itself as a 'family hotel' and has decent rooms for Dh150 for singles and doubles. The hotel reception is always bustling with activity and there is a good restaurant on the 1st floor.

Al-Sheraa Hotel (☎ 226 5213, fax 225 4866, Al-Buteen St) credibly claims to be able to arrange visas, but at Dh80/120 for singles/doubles (without bath) it is definitely a step down from many of the other Deira hotels.

Shams al-Sahraa Hotel (☎ 225 3666, fax 225 3647) on the corner of Al-Buteen and Old Baladiya Sts, has cheap rooms at Dh80/120. The pink walls and red carpets give the place a strange but pleasant feel, if you can put up with the smell.

Gold Plaza Hotel (☎ 225 0240, fax 225 0259) at the entrance to the Gold Souq has singles/doubles for Dh120/150. It is a family hotel and does not accept Russian guests. Be warned, however, the rooms are cramped.

Metro Hotel (☎ 226 0040, fax 226 2098) is in an alley between Sikkat al-Khalil St and Al-Soor St. It has singles/doubles at Dh80/100, but accepts only families.

Shiraz Hotel (☎ 225 4800, fax 225 4867) opposite the bus station on Al-Khor St has relatively good rooms at Dh120/150.

New Avon Hotel (☎ 225 8877, fax 225 2061, Al-Sabkha Rd) near Al-Soor St charges Dh140/180 – a little overpriced for what you get.

Sina Hotel (☎ 225 2323, fax 225 2606) is behind the Al-Sabkha Rd bus stop in an alley inside the Deira Covered Souq. The rooms are small and not very clean and cost Dh120/150, although this rate is probably negotiable. The hotel seems to cater mainly to single men who appear to be long-term residents; it's not recommended to single women travellers.

Royal Prince Hotel (☎ 223 9991, fax 221 9757, Al-Sabkha Rd) has rooms for Dh130/160. The single rooms are a bit pokey but the doubles are very good value.

Vienna Hotel (☎ 221 8855, fax 221 2928, Al-Sabkha Rd) can arrange visas and has good, clean rooms for Dh130 (singles and doubles).

Mariana Hotel (☎ 225 9333, fax 225 9185) across the street has rooms at Dh150/160. Both this hotel and the Vienna Hotel cater mostly to Russians and other travellers from the CIS.

Green Line Hotel (☎ 226 8661), opposite the Metro Hotel, between Al-Soor and Sikkat al-Khalil Sts is very cheap at Dh80/100. The rooms are absolutely crammed with furniture and have a rather crowded feel about them.

Bur Dubai The *Swiss Plaza Hotel* (☎ 393 9373, fax 393 9370) is one of the very few real budget hotels on this side of the Creek. It is basic but clean and comfortable and well located near the bus station on Al-Ghubaiba St. Rooms cost Dh150/180.

Time Palace Hotel (☎ 532 111, fax 539 948) is the only other cheapie in Bur Dubai and has a good location on the edge of the souq. Rooms cost Dh150/240 and they are pretty shabby, although the management has done a good job of jazzing up the hallways.

PLACES TO STAY – MID-RANGE

Even in this price category many hotels either won't arrange visas or seem very reluctant when asked. Sometimes it's just up to how the management feels when you book the hotel so it's worth asking. Most hotels in this price range offer courtesy buses to and from the airport.

Deira

Ramee International Hotel (☎ 224 0222, fax 224 0221) just off Beniyas Square is very good value for the standard of rooms. Singles/doubles cost Dh262.50/367.50.

Victoria Hotel (☎ 226 9626, fax 226 9575) in an alley near the intersection of Al-Sabkha and Al-Maktoum Hospital Rds is a decent, if dull, place with rooms for Dh200/250.

Hotel Delhi Darbar (☎ 733 555, fax 733 737, Naif Rd) is, as its name implies, an Indian-oriented establishment. It is a little overpriced at Dh201/287.50 but rooms are large and spotless. It sponsors transit visas but only at the management's discretion which implies that if you are Russian you probably won't be able to get a visa through this hotel.

Riviera Hotel (☎ 222 2131, fax 221 1820) on Beniyas Rd is well located with views over the creek. It does not serve alcohol but is better value than the Carlton Tower next door at Dh300/375 for a souq view and Dh350/425 for a Creek view.

Bur Dubai

Regent Palace Hotel (☎ 396 3888, fax 335 3080, Trade Centre Rd) is an excellent and reasonably priced four-star hotel. It's just across from the Bur Juman Centre. Rooms are Dh375/437.50.

Panorama Hotel (☎ 518 518, fax 518 028, Al-Mankhool Rd) is one of the better value hotels in Bur Dubai with rooms for Dh220/275.

Ambassador Hotel (☎ 531 000, fax 534 751, Al-Falah Rd) is the oldest hotel in

Dubai, established in 1968, and has singles/doubles for Dh312.50/475.

Astoria Hotel (☎ 534 300, fax 535 665; Al-Nahdha St) is a large, ugly place, charging Dh345/517.50.

PLACES TO STAY – TOP END

Unless otherwise noted, all the hotels in this category will arrange visas.

Deira

Al-Khaleej Hotel (☎ 221 1144, fax 223 7140), between Beniyas Square and Al-Sabkha Rd, is one of the better value places in this category, with singles/doubles for Dh625/750.

Phoenicia Hotel (☎ 222 7191, fax 222 1629) has a prime location on Beniyas Square. It charges Dh345/460 for its rather ostentatious rooms.

Carlton Tower Hotel (☎ 227 111, fax 228 249, Beniyas Rd) has a great location on the Creek with nice rooms starting at Dh460/575.

Al-Khaleej Palace (☎ 223 1000, fax 221 1293, Al-Maktoum Rd) offers singles/doubles at Dh468/556.

Dubai Inter-Continental Hotel (☎ 222 7171, fax 228 4777, Beniyas Rd) overlooks the Creek and has rooms for an overblown Dh1360/1486.

Le Meridien Dubai (☎ 824 040, fax 825 540) is one of the newer hotels and is near the airport. Rooms cost Dh1200/1300.

Al-Bustan Rotana (☎ 820 000, fax 828 100) is next door to Le Meridien and rooms cost Dh1125/1375.

Hyatt Regency Dubai (☎ 209 1234, fax 209 1235) is the hideous construction off Al-Khaleej Rd overlooking the Gulf. Rooms are Dh925/1350.

Sheraton Dubai (☎ 228 1111, fax 221 3468, Beniyas Rd) is right on the Creek and rooms are Dh930/1030.

Bur Dubai

Ramada Hotel (☎ 521 010, fax 527 589, Al-Mankhool Rd) has luxurious rooms for a massive Dh875/1000 but discounts can be negotiated.

New Penninsula Hotel (☎ 393 9111, fax 393 7070), next to the Dubai bus station and close to the abra crossing, charges Dh437.50/562.50.

Heritage International Hotel (☎ 590 111, fax 590 181) on the corner of Al-Mankhool and Khalid bin al-Waleed Rds is one of the newer hotels in Bur Dubai and has rooms for Dh660/780.

Dubai Hilton (☎ 331 4000, fax 331 3383) is in the World Trade Centre complex on the outskirts of Bur Dubai. Singles/doubles cost Dh787.50/937.50.

Bur Dubai is also riddled with places offering 'suites' and 'residences', which means you get slightly larger rooms than normal and a kitchen for around Dh500 per night. You will find these places along Al-Rolla Rd and behind the Ramada Hotel.

Elsewhere

If you come to Dubai on a package tour you will probably stay at either the *Jebel Ali Hotel (☎ 836 000, fax 835 543)*, an opulent five-star hotel 40km west of the centre near Jebel Ali Port, or one of the five-star hotels at Umm Suqeim, about midway between the centre and Jebel Ali. The Jebel Ali asks a mind-blowing Dh984/1104, but it does provide a free shopping shuttle to Deira (although the shuttle does not go to the airport and will not let you take luggage).

Jumeira Beach Hotel (☎ 480 000, fax 482 273) is easily recognised by the spectacular Burj al-Arab (Arabian Tower) that rises up out of the water and has become a landmark of the city. Rooms are very expensive at Dh1375/1500. Suites at the Burj al-Arab are in a different league altogether – from Dh6000 per night to Dh55,000 for the Royal Suites. It's well worth visiting the hotel for a view of Dubai from one of the top floors.

Oasis Beach Hotel (☎ 846 222, fax 846 200), with its Gilligan's Island feel, is also out this way and has rooms for Dh687.50/812.50. It seems to be *the* place for German package tourists.

The more upmarket *Le Meridien Beach Hotel (☎ 399 3333, fax 399 3111)* costs

Dh1062.50/1187.50, and the **Radisson SAS** (☎ 845 533, fax 845 577) has rooms for Dh750/875. All these hotels have beach clubs, pools and water sports facilities.

For something very different (and very exclusive) there is an ecotourism resort about 20km from Dubai off the Dubai–Al-Ain highway. **Al-Maha Resort** (☎ 303 4224, fax 343 9696) was receiving its final touches at the time of writing and exact prices were not yet available but it will cost around US$900 per night including meals and activities such as dune driving, camel trekking and falconry. It is set in 16 sq km of sculptured oasis among the sand dunes. Each guest room is a luxurious, tent-style suite complete with Bedouin antiques and a private plunge pool. The idea is that the area will also be home to endangered species such as the Arabian oryx and gazelle, Arabian foxes and caracals. The resort uses recycled paper and packaging, biodegradable products and solar energy. There are also permanent exhibitions of paintings, sculptures and handicrafts by UAE artists. Children under 12 are not allowed at the resort.

PLACES TO EAT
Budget Dining
Deira For a good, quick and cheap meal while watching the activity on the Creek, try **Cafeteria al-Abra**. It has good shwarma and samosas along with fruit juice and soda. The coconut juice is even served fresh in the shell. It is at the intersection of Al-Sabkha and Beniyas Rds, next to the abra dock.

Popeye, a bit further up Beniyas Rd, has shwarma, burgers and other snacks. They have a pretty good offer of two shwarmas and one drink for Dh5.

Al-Burj Cafeteria is a stand-up affair near the main entrance to the Gold Souq offering excellent shwarma, fresh fruit juices, soda and popcorn.

Just down the street from the Ramee International Hotel (off Beniyas Square), is **Swagath Restaurant**, a north Indian vegetarian restaurant with mains for Dh6 to Dh8.

Pizza Corner, on Beniyas Rd not far from the abra dock, is a good medium-priced place with pizzas and burgers. Their sandwiches go for Dh9 to Dh16.

Bab al-Sabkha on Naif South St has good, cheap Pakistani food as does **Gulf Restaurant & Cafeteria** at the intersection of Al-Sabkha Rd and Deira St. Chicken, lamb or fried fish on a pile of rice costs Dh12.

Entezary Restaurant, just off Beniyas Square, offers good-value food. A dinner of kebab, rice, soup, salad, humous, bread and tea costs only Dh15.

Hatam Restaurant, just off Beniyas Rd, is highly recommended, with excellent Persian food at very reasonable prices. A traditional chelo kebab (kebab served on rice; it appears on the Hatam's menu as a 'sultan kebab') costs Dh17, including soup and salad. Other full dinners cost Dh14 to Dh25 with most under Dh20.

Bur Dubai The place to go for Indian snacks and sandwiches is **All Spice Fast Food** on Trade Centre Rd in Karama. Most snacks cost Dh2 to Dh4 each.

Ravi is a Pakistani restaurant just off Al-Dhiyafa Rd in Satwa and comes highly recommended by readers. A meal consisting of a curry or biryani with bread, salad and a drink comes to about Dh15.

Emirates Restaurant (Al-Esbij St, Bur Dubai) specialises in south Indian vegetarian dishes. It's clean and comfortable and dishes range from Dh2.50 to Dh5.

Bhavna Deluxe Restaurant (☎ 530 707, 25C St, Bur Dubai) is a well known vegetarian establishment where vegans are also catered for. No egg or dairy products are used in the cooking.

Restaurants
There are literally hundreds of restaurants in Dubai – much more choice than in the capital. For a complete listing by cuisine, see *What's On* or *Dubai Explorer*. Most of the restaurants we've listed in this section are attached to Dubai's big hotels and they are usually expensive. They also serve alcohol.

Deira For a real slice of Britain, try **The Irish Village** (☎ 824 750, Al-Garhoud Rd)

UNITED ARAB EMIRATES

behind the Aviation Club (opposite Dubai Creek Golf & Yacht Club), which is popular with the Western expats. The pub and large outdoor area is very traditional as is the food (stew, bangers and mash, baked potatoes, fish and chips). Mains cost Dh20 to Dh30.

Little Italy (☎ *223 1000*) in the Al-Khaleej Palace Hotel has excellent and simple Italian meals for Dh25 to Dh30. This place is easy to come back to again and again.

Hana (☎ *222 2131*) at the Riviera Hotel is an enormous place offering three different menus: Japanese, Thai and Korean. Food is good and reasonable at about Dh30 for mains but alcohol is not served.

The Pub (☎ *222 7171*) in the Dubai Inter-Continental Hotel is about as good an imitation of the real thing as you'll find in the Gulf. It serves a varied menu of sandwiches and 'traditional pub grub' (shepherd's pie, roast beef etc). The sandwiches cost Dh20 to Dh30 and other main dishes go for Dh30 to Dh50.

Sadaf Restaurant (☎ *223 7049, Al-Maktoum Rd*), a Persian restaurant, has excellent food, although it does not serve alcohol. Large chelo kebab meals cost Dh25 to Dh30 and appetisers cost Dh7 to Dh12. It also offers an enormous buffet at both lunch and dinner for Dh54 and there is a separate room for families and women.

The Blue Elephant (☎ *820 000*) at the Al-Bustan Rotana hotel serves the best Thai food in the city. The restaurant is decked out like a Thai village, complete with a pond and the service and food are impeccable. Mains will set you back about Dh40 to Dh50.

Bur Dubai The service is friendly and the food is good value at *Fiesta Filipino* (☎ *334 4121, 45B St*). Main meals are Dh12 (Dh15 for seafood). Try *kare-kare* (oxtail curry) which is a very popular dish or *lapa-lapa* which is a baked fish dish, usually served with *sinigang*, a kind of tamarind soup.

Istanbouli (☎ *450 123, Al-Dhiyafa Rd*), just west of the Satwa roundabout, is an excellent Lebanese restaurant. Mezze costs Dh7 to Dh15 apiece and main dishes are Dh15 to Dh25.

Kowloon on Al-Rolla Rd next to the Rolla Residence has excellent Chinese food at about Dh18 for mains. Their buffet lunch on Friday and buffet dinner on Sunday is very good value at Dh30 per person but the quality of the food is not as good as the a la carte menu. The place has a nice atmosphere and the staff are friendly. Alcohol is not served.

Pancho Villa's (☎ *532 146*), a Tex-Mex restaurant in the Astoria Hotel, is one of the Gulf's best known restaurants (its bumper stickers can be seen far and wide). Appetisers and main dishes cost Dh20 to Dh50. The restaurant is a bit cheaper at lunch, when it offers a variety of specials.

Thai Terrace (☎ *336 7356, Trade Centre Rd*) in Karama is a favourite for connoisseurs of authentic and interesting Thai food. The food is on the expensive side at Dh28 to Dh34 for mains but the servings are generous and the food is excellent. Especially good is the crispy fish salad – try it. As it is not part of a hotel, alcohol is not served.

At the *Fishmarket Floating Restaurant* (☎ *324 3438*) in the Al-Boom Tourist Village you choose the fish you want from a display and the chef will cook it any way you like. Be prepared to spend about Dh150 per person for three courses. There is also a dinner cruise (Dh110) along the Creek every night from 8.30 to 10.30 pm. Phone ☎ 341 444 to make a booking.

Cafes

When it comes to coffee, our highest recommendation goes to *Cafe Mozart*, which recreates the atmosphere, food, coffee and service of a Viennese coffee shop, right down to the change purse carried by the waitress. The pastries and croissants cost about Dh3 each and are good. The coffee is excellent.

Gérard (☎ *443 327*) is *the* place to see and be seen. This French-style patisserie and coffee shop, in the Magrudy's Shopping Centre on Al-Jumeira Rd, is the haunt of 'Jumeira Janes' (the nonworking wives of well-to-do expats).

La Brioche (☎ *553 726*) in the Al-Khaleej Shopping Centre on Al-Mankhool

If you get tired of waiting for UAE's first snowfall, you can always try sand-skiing instead.

The Dubai World Cup is one of the most lucrative horse races in the world.

Urban Eden: The Dubai Creek Golf Club is home to the Dubai Creek Open on the Asian PGA Tour.

With their cultural heritage under siege from the influx of money and the rapidity of social change, Emiratis see the preservation of traditional life, and the wearing of traditional dress, as vital to their identity as a nation.

Rd is a Western-style cafe, with good coffee and a selection of bakery items.

Self-Catering
You'll find plenty of small grocery stores and supermarkets around Deira, Bur Dubai and Rigga. You can get fresh fruit at stalls around the bus stop on Al-Sabkha Rd and from Shindagha Market in Bur Dubai. We don't recommend you buy meat from the market in Shindagha, however. It hangs in the open air for too long. It's probably best to buy wrapped and refrigerated meat from the supermarket. You can get Arabic breads and sweets at bakeries around town.

ENTERTAINMENT
There is plenty of nightlife in Dubai at the bars and discos in the big hotels.

Bars
Duke's Bar on the top floor at the Al-Khaleej Hotel, between Beniyas Square and Al-Sabkha Rd, has pool tables. Prices here are not as grotesque as at some of the five-star hotels and the view over the Creek at sunset really is worth a beer or two (if you can see through the filthy windows).

The Irish Village (see Restaurants/Deira in Places to Eat) is the best of the Irish pubs. It's very popular with the Brits in Dubai and is a good, casual watering hole. It is expensive though – Dh18 for a pint and Dh9 for a soft drink. The pub has a large outdoor area with wooden tables and chairs and serves good, honest pub grub.

Harry's Place at the Renaissance Hotel is a bit of a legend in Dubai. It's a shrine to Hollywood in a most unusual way – the walls are covered in framed mug shots and arrest reports of many Hollywood celebrities. From Jane Fonda to Robert Downey Jr, no one is spared exposure. This is a sophisticated place with experienced and friendly bar staff plus a great menu. Tucked away in a little room off to the side is the 'Cigar Room', adorned with leather couches and Arab men enjoying the good life.

The Old Vic at the Ramada Hotel is another good place for a drink. The bar has nicely subdued lighting and the walls are decorated with theatre posters from London's West End. The atmosphere is very relaxed but prices here are pretty extreme.

Bordertown opposite Rolla Residence on Al-Rolla Rd in Bur Dubai is a Mexican pub known for its margaritas and any kind of tequila cocktail you can think up. There is a band most nights from about 9.30 pm until 1 am.

Planet Hollywood, next to the Wafi Pyramids off Al-Qataiyat Rd, is the ultimate in American kitsch. There is a band most nights, drinks are hideously expensive and you are encouraged to spend as much money as possible on gimmicky Planet Hollywood souvenirs.

Cinemas
Most of Dubai's cinemas specialise in Indian and Pakistani films but you can catch relatively recent Western flicks at the Galleria, the shopping complex attached to the Hyatt Regency Hotel, at the cinemas at Lamcy Plaza on the Bur Dubai side of the Creek and at the Almassa complex next to the Metropolitan Hotel on Shaikh Zayed Rd. Details of movies showing are listed in the *Gulf News*. Tickets cost Dh20.

Nightclubs
Pancho Villa's at the Astoria Hotel on the edge of the Bur Dubai Souq has long been one of Dubai's most popular nightspots. There's a dance floor as well as a bar and restaurant and live music is featured several nights a week, often with bands from the UK playing 1980s covers.

Atlantis is attached to the Hard Rock Cafe off Shaikh Zayed Rd past Interchange No 4 – a long way from the centre. If you're staying at the beach hotels it's only a two-minute taxi ride. Atlantis was the newest and slickest nightclub at the time of the writing but this probably won't be the case for long. It holds about 1000 people and, although it's so far from everything else, there are still long queues on Thursday and Friday nights.

Cave des Rois at the Vendome Plaza Hotel, behind Al-Maktoum Rd in Rigga has a belly-dancing dinner show each evening. It's not cheap at Dh125 per person. Call ☎ 222 2333 to make a booking.

SPECTATOR SPORTS

If there is one sport to watch specifically in Dubai, it has to be camel racing. Races take place early on Friday mornings during winter and spring at the track in Nad al-Sheba. Head down Oud Metha Rd until you get to the main roundabout that leads out of town and then follow the signs. Admission is free but try to get there by 8 am. (See the boxed text 'Camel Racing' in the UAE Facts for the Visitor chapter for more general information on this sport.)

SHOPPING

All kinds of shops filled with the latest of everything can be found in Dubai's many shopping malls. These open at the rate of about one per year with each one being bigger and flashier than the last. Among the main shopping centres are the Al-Ghurair Centre near the Deira service-taxi station, the Bur Juman Centre on the corner of Khalid bin al-Waleed and Trade Centre Rds, the massive City Centre off Tariq ibn Ziyad Rd (adjacent to the Dubai Creek Golf & Yacht Club) and the upmarket Wafi Centre on the Bur Dubai side near Al-Garhoud Bridge. If you're really serious about hitting the shops get the *Dubai Shopping Centres Directory*, available in bookshops and most four- and five-star hotel rooms.

If you are looking for cheap electronics try the area at the Al-Sabkha Rd end of Beniyas Square.

Even seasoned veterans of Middle East gold markets are likely to be impressed by the scale of Dubai's Gold Souq. As gold goes, the prices are fairly good. Small items, such as simple earings or a pendant, can be purchased for under Dh100 for lower grades of gold (such as 14 carat). You don't have to buy anything; it's a great place just to window shop – and to see what everyone else is buying.

Persian carpets are cheaper at the Sharjah Souq where you'll find a far greater range.

All That Glitters...

Even if you have no plans to buy anything, the Gold Souq in Dubai is worth a visit simply to take in the atmosphere and to goggle at the size of some of the jewellery on offer. Many Westerners find the bright yellow quality of the gold here too gaudy for their tastes. Most of the gold on sale here is 22 carat.

About 40% of the gold jewellery on sale in the souq is made in Dubai. The rest comes from India, Saudi Arabia, Bahrain, Kuwait, Turkey and Singapore. A large amount also comes from Italy and you will find that some stores deal exclusively in Italian-made gold.

People come to Dubai to buy gold for three reasons: the low import duty (meaning low prices), the massive competition between retailers (also keeping prices down) and the large array of gold to choose from.

Dubai's Gold Souq is patronised mainly by Indian and Arabic families. In India, the father of a bride is expected to give her about 400g of gold for the dowry. Other family members usually contribute to this gift too. In Gulf countries a bride is expected to be laden with gold jewellery on her wedding day. Antique or second-hand gold passed down from previous generations is not considered good enough as a gift. Gold presented to a bride must be new, so this keeps a constant flow of customers coming to the Gold Souq. This also means that a lot of the gold bought eventually comes back as scrap to be re-used.

Another reason why gold is popular with buyers from the subcontinent and the Middle East is the investment opportunity it offers. Although the price of gold has fallen dramatically on the international market over the years, there is still a belief in this part of the world that gold is a sensible investment that will provide a family with security for many generations.

Carpet shoppers in Dubai should try Deira Tower on Beniyas Square and Deira City

Centre, both of which have lots of small carpet boutiques.

If you are looking for Middle Eastern-looking souvenirs go to the Galleria Shopping Centre and Deira City Centre. These are the places to look for small coffeepots, little carved camels and similar kitsch. Most of these shops also have a limited selection of silver Bedouin jewellery. For similar merchandise try the shops in the Heritage Village on Al-Shindagha Rd. As this is a very touristy place prices tend to be a little high and bargaining doesn't bring them down by much. The Ramesh Art Gallery here sells some lovely old photographs by the owner who was once the Royal Photographer. The photographs with frames are about Dh600 but they really are stunning.

Although most five-star hotels have shops selling good quality souvenirs, jewellery and carpets, remember that you are paying about 50% more than you would elsewhere.

Duty-Free Shopping

Outside the Middle East, the words most often associated with Dubai are probably 'duty free'. For around 15 years, Dubai international airport has been known as one of the best duty-free zones in the world, and has picked up awards for it from various travel magazines. This is predominantly to do with the sheer volume of items for sale, as well as very competitive prices compared to other airport duty-free complexes, such as Singapore.

Arriving, departing and transit passengers are all welcome to shop in the duty-free complex. Most shops are open 24-hours as flights tend to arrive or depart in the small hours of the morning.

GETTING THERE & AWAY
Air

You can fly to almost anywhere from Dubai international airport. The emirate's long-standing reputation as the travel hub of the Gulf was built on a combination of easy landing rights for transiting aircraft and a very large and cheap duty-free shop at the airport. At the time of writing the airport

was undergoing a massive expansion of facilities. For general airport information call ☎ 224 5555.

Following is a far from complete list of the carriers, large and small, that fly to and from Dubai. Some of the carriers with offices listed in town also have desks at the Airline Centre, a type of shopping mall for air travel, on Al-Maktoum Rd in Deira.

Air India (☎ 227 6787, fax 227 1293) Al-Maktoum Rd, Deira, just west of the clock tower roundabout

British Airways (☎ 307 5555, fax 347 403) Airline Centre, Al-Maktoum Rd, Deira

Cathay Pacific (☎ 228 3126, fax 227 9954) Pearl Bldg, 11th floor, 18 St, Deira (near Beniyas Square)

Emirates Airlines (☎ 295 3333, fax 295 1410) Airline Centre, Al-Maktoum Rd, Deira (main reservations office); other offices are on Naif Rd near the Al-Karnak Hotel in the Deira Souq and on Shaikh Zayed Rd, near Interchange No 2

Gulf Air (☎ 713 111, fax 736 465) Salah al-Din Rd, Rigga

KLM (☎ 224 4747, fax 224 4452) Dubai airport, above Emirates Airlines departures

Malaysia Airlines (☎ 520 250, fax 527 286) 1st floor, National Bank of Umm al-Qaiwain Bldg, Khalid bin al-Waleed Rd, Bur Dubai

Qatar Airways (☎ 221 4448, fax 221 5561) Doha Centre, Al-Maktoum Rd, Deira (opposite Al-Khaleej Palace Hotel)

Singapore Airlines (☎ 223 2300, fax 221 8357) Pearl Bldg, 3rd floor, St 18, Deira (near Beniyas Square)

Yemenia (☎ 295 8883, fax 295 8877) Al-Rais Travel, clock tower roundabout, Deira

Bus

Intercity buses only operate within the Dubai emirate. To go to another emirate, you have to take a Dubai Transport minibus.

The only intercity route that really matters is the one to Hatta (route No 16, Dh10, about 1¼ hours,). This passes several small villages along the way. It leaves from the Deira bus station, near the Gold Souq and also stops at the Dubai bus station and a number of other places on the way out of town. Buses depart every hour from 6.10 am to 9 pm. From Hatta they begin at 6 am and finish at 9 pm.

There are two buses per day to Muscat, Oman. These depart at 7.30 am and 5.30 pm from the parking lot of the Airline Centre on Al-Maktoum Rd, Deira. The trip takes five to six hours and costs Dh75 one way, Dh140 return (Dh48/96 for children). For information, call ☎ 203 3799. Tickets are available at the Airline Centre or from the bus driver.

Long-Distance Taxis
If you're taking one of these engaged (ie, privately) you'll need to haggle over a price but it should be roughly five times as much as the fare for sharing a taxi. Long-distance taxis are found at the bus and minibus stations. For a list of shared/engaged long-distance taxi fares from Dubai to the other emirates see the UAE Getting Around chapter.

Minibus
Dubai Transport has replaced the privately owned long-distance taxis that used to be the only means of transport between the emirates. The private taxis still operate within greater Dubai but they rarely take passengers out of the emirate.

The minibuses carry 14 passengers and run every 15 or 20 minutes depending on when they fill up. They are very clean and efficient and fixed prices save you the hassle of bargaining for a seat. Minibuses leave Deira from the bus and taxi station near the intersection of Umer Ibn al-Khattab and Al-Rigga Rds. Minibuses for Abu Dhabi and Al-Ain leave from the Dubai bus station on Al-Ghubaiba Rd, on the Bur Dubai side of the Creek. Get your tickets from the ticket windows at each station. See the UAE Getting Around chapter for a list of minibus fares.

Car Rental
The highest concentrations of smaller, local car rental companies are on Abu Baker al-Siddiq Rd just north of the clock tower roundabout, and on Umar ibn al-Khattab St, just north of the Claridge Hotel. They are also found opposite the taxi and minibus station on Omar ibn al-Khattab St in Deira and on the Dubai side of the Creek on Trade Centre Rd just north of Al-Adhid Rd.

Avis (☎ 295 7121, fax 295 6807) Al-Maktoum Rd, Deira (main office); (☎ 224 5219, fax 224 4150), Dubai international airport (24-hour service); (☎ 331 3731, fax 331 7394) World Trade Centre

Europcar (☎ 520 033) at the Hilton, Inter-Continental, Al-Bustan Rotana and Hyatt Regency hotels

Hertz (☎ 824 422) Al-Maktoum Rd, just before Cargo Village

Patriot Rent-A-Car (☎ 221 4440, fax 227 3386) Abu Baker al-Siddiq Rd, Deira; (☎ 224 4244) Dubai international airport

White Falcon (☎ 295 8000, fax 295 8008) Al-Maktoum Rd at the clock tower roundabout

GETTING AROUND
To/From the Airport
From the Deira bus station, bus Nos 4 and 11 go to the airport about every half-hour for Dh1. Only the beige-coloured Dubai Transport taxis are allowed to pick up passengers outside the arrivals area. These have a flag fall of Dh16. A ride from the Deira Souq area to the airport with a (metered) Dubai Transport taxi costs Dh10 to Dh12. Keep that in mind if you opt for a bargaining session with the driver of an unmetered taxi.

Bus
Local buses operate out of the main stations in both Deira and Bur Dubai. The main bus station is the Bur Dubai bus station on Al-Ghubaiba Rd. The Deira bus station is off Al-Khor St, near the Gold Souq. Note that in the official timetables the two stations appear as 'Ghubaiba Bus Stn' and 'Gold Souq Bus Stn', respectively. Numbers and routes are posted on the buses in English as well as Arabic. Fares are Dh1 to Dh3.50 depending on the distance travelled. Various types of bus passes (*taufeer* in Arabic) are available. For Dh20 you can buy a Smart Card that gives you Dh22 worth of travel. Each time you use the card the fare is automatically deducted from the credit. Monthly bus passes are available too. There are two versions: The Dh75 pass gets you unlimited travel for a month on one side of the Creek and the Dh120 pass unlimited travel within the city.

Neither pass can be used on the intercity buses within the Dubai emirate, ie, for trips to Jebel Ali, Hatta etc. Taufeer can be purchased at both the Deira and Dubai bus stations. You'll need two passport photos to purchase the monthly passes.

The best way to get to where you're going is just to say where you want to go and someone will point you to the right bus. If you tell the bus driver where you're going he will tell you when to get off. Note that most buses both start and finish their days a bit later on Friday. All buses stop for prayers at noon on Friday, and you can count on there being no Friday service from about 11.30 am until about 1.30 pm.

Taxi

The minimum fare in Dubai Transport taxis is Dh3. Most of Dubai's orange-and-white taxis have no meters. As in many other Middle Eastern cities this presents you with a choice: negotiate the fare in advance (and pay too much) or get in, tell the driver your destination, pay him what you think is appropriate once you get there and hope that there is no argument. Should you go for the latter option, expect to pay Dh4 or Dh5 for trips within the centre that do not involve crossing the Creek. Crossing the Creek immediately runs the standard fare up to Dh7. Drivers will expect a 50% premium after midnight.

You can also call Dubai Transport (☎ 208 0808) to send a taxi to pick you up. These cars are very comfortable and clean, the drivers are helpful and friendly, the fares are reasonably cheap and you won't have to haggle over fares or risk being ripped off. You'll find the beige-coloured Dubai Transport taxis around the souqs, shopping centres, hotels and the airport.

Expensive fixed-price cabs also operate from some of the bigger hotels. If you ask someone to call a taxi for you be sure you know which taxi firm they are calling. One cab service in Dubai uses Jaguars – and charges accordingly.

Shared local taxis run from the Dubai bus station on Al-Ghubaiba Rd to Jumeira, Al-Quoz, Al-Bada, Karama and Satwa for Dh1 to Dh2 per person or Dh7 to Jebel Ali. These are mostly seven-passenger cars and are really only a good bet if you are at the bus station anyway, one going in your direction is nearly full and you can't wait for the next regular bus to your destination.

Car

If you decide to drive in Dubai, remember that traffic congestion is a real problem at peak hours – 7 to 9 am, 1 to 2 pm and most of the evening from 6pm onwards. The traffic situation in Dubai has improved immensely since the government started forcing people to pay for the privilege of parking in the centre. For years the flow of traffic through the city had been clogged, in no small part because of all the triple-parked cars in Beniyas Square. On the square, and in other parts of the centre, there is now a strictly enforced four-hour limit on parking. Once you find a space, get a ticket from one of the many machines around the centre. Rates are Dh2 for the first hour, Dh5 for up to two hours, Dh8 for up to three hours and Dh11 for up to four hours. Place the ticket on top of your dashboard – or else. Parking rates apply from 8 am to 1 pm and 4 to 9 pm Saturday to Thursday. Parking in the centre is free on Fridays and holidays.

Abra

Scores of abras (small motorboats) cross the Creek constantly from early morning until about midnight. On the Deira side of the Creek the main dock is at the intersection of Al-Sabkha and Beniyas Rds. On the Bur Dubai side, the main dock is at the western end of the souq, just west of the waterfront houses. There is a secondary dock on the Deira side, at the intersection of Beniyas Rd with Al-Baladiya St, and a secondary dock on the Bur Dubai side about 500m or so west of the main abra dock. Abras, like shared taxis, leave when full but it never takes more than five minutes for one to fill up. The fare is 50 fils which is collected once you are out on the water.

Hatta

☎ 85

Hatta, an enclave of the Dubai emirate nestled in the Hajar mountains, is a popular weekend getaway spot. It is 105km from Dubai by road, about 20km of which runs through Omani territory. There is no customs check along this road but remember that if you are driving a rental car your insurance does not cover accidents in Oman.

There is not much to see in Hatta itself, although it's an interesting place to walk around if you want to get a sense of what rural life is like. And look for the modern architecture in the hills around town – quite unlike the white villas and concrete boxes that are the norm in much of the country. However, Hatta's main attractions are the relatively cool, dry climate (compared with the coast) and the mountain scenery. It is also a good jumping-off point for off-road trips through the mountains. The creek running through Hatta often flows all year round.

For tourist information go to the Dubai Municipality – Hatta Centre at the fort roundabout, opposite the Hatta Fort Hotel. The hotel also has information on Hatta and sells a colourful 3D map of the town, which is the only good map available.

Market

A large rug and pottery market begins about 12km west of Hatta along the main highway and stretches for a couple of kilometres. This is the only other large country market besides the one at Masafi (see the Around Fujairah section in the East Coast chapter for more information on Masafi). If you are looking for rugs, it's worth a stop as you can pick up a great bargain. Most of the rugs on display are machine-made acrylic floor rugs but they also have a few good-quality woollen rugs from Iran, Afghanistan and Turkey, so just ask to see them.

Heritage Village

At the time of writing, the government had almost finished building a Heritage Village in Hatta, a re-creation of a traditional mountain village from the pre-oil era. If the village is not officially open when you visit it is still possible to walk through the site. From the top of the watchtower there are some great views over the valley. There is a functioning falaj system which irrigates small but lush agricultural plots just below the Heritage Village. To get to the village turn right at the fort roundabout on the edge of town and head into the centre of Hatta. The turn-off for the Heritage Village is signposted to the left, 2.7km from the fort roundabout.

Hatta Pools

Most people bypass the town altogether and head instead for these magnificent rock pools, about 20km south of Hatta. Although the pools are actually a couple of kilometres over the border in Oman, there are no border formalities up to that point. There is usually water year round in the pools, which have been hollowed out in the rock, deep in the wadi floor. You can swim in the pools and there are a couple of small waterfalls to play in. Unfortunately the pools are becoming more litter-strewn as time goes by. At weekends they are very popular with local youths.

You don't need a 4WD to get to the rock pools from Hatta but if you want to continue past the pools and on to the town of Al-Ain you may need one. To get to the rock pools from Hatta, follow the directions for the Heritage Village. Go past the entrance to the Heritage Village for a couple of hundred metres and turn left when you get to the T-junction at the mosque. Follow this road, as it bends around to the left, for 1.4km. At this point take the turn-off onto the blacktop road to the right. There should be a blue-and-white sign in Arabic here pointing in the direction you want to go. Continue along this road for 7.2km until the blacktop road ends. At the stop sign, turn right onto a graded track. The pools are in a large wadi, 7.5km from this turn-off.

Places to Stay & Eat

The only place to stay in Hatta is the *Hatta Fort Hotel* (☎ 23211, fax 23561). Singles/

doubles cost Dh400 on weekdays, Dh450 on weekends, plus 10% tax and the service charge. The hotel has extensive sports facilities, including a golf course with grass greens but all-sand fairways, an archery range and clay-pigeon shooting, in addition to the usual swimming pool and tennis courts. The hotel also offers outrageously priced 4WD safaris to the water pools out of Hatta or into the Hajar mountains and out to the desert. These cost Dh600 for three hours for up to four people. An eight-hour trip costs Dh1400 for up to four people and includes a picnic lunch.

Getting There & Away

There are six buses per day between Dubai and Hatta (just under 1½ hours, Dh7). In Dubai they leave from the Deira bus station. In Hatta, the buses depart from the red bus shelter near the Hatta Palace grocery store. You can get bus tickets from the driver. Buses leave Hatta for Dubai daily at 6.20, 8.50 and 11.20 am and at 1.50, 4.20 and 6.50 pm. Many tour operators in Dubai offer full- and half-day tours of Hatta and/or the surrounding wadis. See Organised Tours in the UAE Getting Around chapter for contact details of some companies.

The Northern Emirates

This chapter covers the emirates on the north-west coast of the UAE – Sharjah, Ajman, Umm al-Qaiwain and Ras al-Khaimah. The attractions of the north-west coast are a wealth of archaeological sites as well as the stunning mountain scenery. These emirates do not have the wealth and associated glamour of Dubai and Abu Dhabi, and, with the exception of Sharjah, services and facilities for tourists are much more limited. Being so close to Dubai, Sharjah shares much of the tourist trade with its richer neighbour and as a result has a wide range of hotels and attractions on offer. However, the northern emirates are more traditional than their wealthier counterparts and the laid-back pace of life makes a pleasant contrast to the hustle and bustle of Dubai.

Sharjah is the only emirate in the UAE to ban alcohol completely.

Sharjah Emirate

The third-largest of the seven emirates, Sharjah (Ash-Sharqa in Arabic) has long been seen as Dubai's poor cousin, although Dubai's ascendancy in terms of wealth and political power is relatively recent. During the first half of the 19th century, Sharjah was the most important port on the Arabian side of the Gulf, and during the latter half of the century its rulers vied with those of Abu Dhabi for the area's leading political role.

Even after Dubai began to take off as a trading centre, Sharjah remained the more developed of the two in terms of infrastructure. It was in Sharjah that the British chose to set up their main military base in this part of the Gulf and it was here that Imperial Airways developed the Trucial Coast's first international airport.

Sharjah emirate consists of the city of Sharjah and its environs, as well as territory on the east coast, including Kalba and Khor Kalba, Khor Fakkan and part of Dibba.

Sharjah's east coast enclaves are covered in the East Coast chapter later in this book. The ruler of the emirate is Sheikh Sultan Saqr al-Qasimi.

SHARJAH
☎ 06

The city of Sharjah is a place that many visitors to the UAE either miss entirely or pass through too quickly. It promotes itself as the cultural capital of the UAE and, with the proliferation of museums, galleries and theatres in the last couple of years, it's easy to see why. Sharjah has some of the most interesting architecture in the country. Its main souq, the Central Market, offers shopping to rival that of Dubai and the recently restored old souq provides a rare window onto an older way of life that has now all but disappeared in the UAE. Although metropolitan Dubai and metropolitan Sharjah almost join up, Sharjah remains distinctly different from Dubai, not only because it bans alcohol and smoking *sheesha* (traditional pipe).

Orientation

Sharjah's main business district is the area bounded by Corniche Rd, Al-Zahra Rd, the Central market and Shaikh Mohammed bin Saqr al-Qasimi Rd (also known as Mohammed Saqr St). Sharjah's main street is Al-Arouba Rd. The centre is a dreadful place for driving because the streets are so crowded. Corniche Rd skirts around Khor Khalid which has a very impressive water fountain.

There is a secondary business district stretching back towards Dubai along King Faisal Rd.

Note that on some street signs Al-Soor Rd is labelled as Al-Mina St; it's also known as Port or Harbour Rd or, further inland, as Ibrahim Mohamed al-Madfa'a St.

Maps The best map is the *Sharjah Tourist City Map*, available free at most of the big-

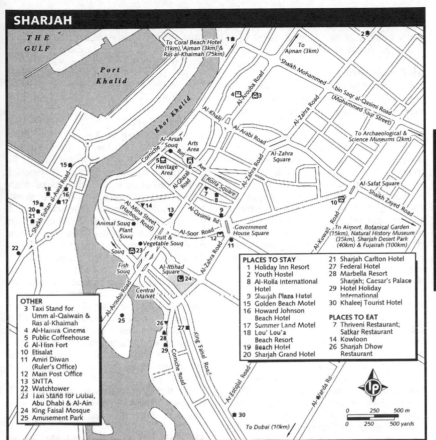

SHARJAH

THE GULF

Port Khalid

To Coral Beach Hotel (1km), Ajman (3km) & Ras al-Khaimah (75km)

To Ajman (3km)

Shaikh Mohammed...

bin Saqr al-Qasimi Road (Mohammed Saqr Street)

Khor Khalid

Al-Arouba Road

Al-Khalij

Al-Arabi Road

Al-Zahra Road

To Archaeological & Science Museums (2km)

Al-Arsah Souq

Arts Area

Corniche

Al-Zahra Square

Heritage Area

Burj Ave

Al-Zahra Road

Al-Ghubaiba Road

Rolla Square

Al-Safat Square

Shaikh Zayed Road

Al-Mina Street (Harbour Road)

Al-Qasimia Rd

Al-Soor Road

Government House Square

Animal Souq

Plant Souq

Fruit & Vegetable Souq

Al-Kuwait Road

To Airport, Botanical Garden (15km), Natural History Museum (35km), Sharjah Desert Park (40km) & Fujairah (100km)

Souq

Fish Souq

Al-Ittihad Square

Al-Zahra Road

Central Market

Al-Arouba Road

King Faisal Road

Corniche Road

Al-Esqlali Rd

Al-Wanda Rd

To Dubai (10km)

PLACES TO STAY	
1	Holiday Inn Resort
2	Youth Hostel
8	Al-Rolla International Hotel
9	Sharjah Plaza Hotel
15	Golden Beach Motel
16	Howard Johnson Beach Hotel
17	Summer Land Motel
18	Lou' Lou'a Beach Resort
19	Beach Hotel
20	Sharjah Grand Hotel
21	Sharjah Carlton Hotel
27	Federal Hotel
28	Marbella Resort Sharjah; Caesar's Palace
29	Hotel Holiday International
30	Khaleej Tourist Hotel

PLACES TO EAT	
7	Thriveni Restaurant; Satkar Restaurant
14	Kowloon
26	Sharjah Dhow Restaurant

OTHER	
3	Taxi Stand for Umm al-Qaiwain & Ras al-Khaimah
4	Al-Hamra Cinema
5	Public Coffeehouse
6	Al-Hisn Fort
10	Etisalat
11	Amiri Diwan (Ruler's Office)
12	Main Post Office
13	SNTTA
22	Watchtower
23	Taxi Stand for Dubai, Abu Dhabi & Al-Ain
24	King Faisal Mosque
25	Amusement Park

0   250   500 m
0   250   500 yards

ger hotels and at some of the larger travel agencies. A few of the hotels also give away a 3-D *Sharjah Tourist Map* which has little drawings of all the sights on it. It shows you where just about everything is in Sharjah but don't rely on its street layout too much.

Information

Money On Burj Ave (also called Bank St, for obvious reasons) just about every building houses a bank. Moneychangers can be found on the small streets immediately to the east and west of it.

Post The main post office is on Government House Square. It is open 8 am to 8 pm Saturday to Wednesday and 8 am to 6 pm on Thursday.

Telephone & Fax The Etisalat office is on Al-Soor Rd, on the corner of Al-Safat Square (formerly Kuwait Square). It is open 24 hours a day, and telex and fax services are also available.

Travel Agencies The Sharjah National Tourist and Transport Authority (SNTTA,

☎ 351 411) handles all travel-related matters. Its office is on Al-Arouba Rd. There are also a number of independent travel agencies on Al-Arouba Rd near Rolla Square.

Al-Arsah Souq

Just in from Corniche Rd on the south side of Burj Ave is Al-Arsah Souq which was restored by the government after large sections of it fell to pieces during the 1970s and '80s. The *areesh* (palm leaf) roof and wooden pillars give it a traditional feel and it's a lovely place to wander around. The government seems to have managed to strike that most delicate of balances between setting up something that will appeal to tourists and something authentic that will actually be used by Sharjah's citizens. You can get Arabic and Bedouin souvenirs here. Despite the efforts to re-create a traditional atmosphere you can buy all kinds of non-Arabic souvenirs here too, including Princess Di telephone cards and old Coca Cola bottles. There is also a traditional coffeehouse and restaurant.

Central Market

From certain angles Sharjah's new souq, the Central Market (also called the Blue Souq or the Sharjah Souq), looks like a set of oversized oil barrels that have tipped over and had wind towers glued to their sides. Once inside, however, the design works, and it stays cool even when it's crowded.

Inside there are hundreds of shops and stalls selling just about everything imaginable, including lots of souvenirs and antiques from India, Thailand and Iran, but it is probably best known to tourists as having the biggest selection of oriental rugs in the UAE. Prices are pretty good for souvenirs and, in many cases, a bit cheaper than in Dubai but you do have to bargain. See Shopping later in this section for tips on how to get a good bargain.

Other Souqs

At the **Animal Souq**, just off Al-Mina St, you'll find all kinds of animals for sale, but most people are here to buy goats and sheep.

There are a few shops that sell falcons and falcon accessories. There is a large **Plant Souq** along Corniche Rd near the taxi stand. Prices here are very reasonable but be prepared to bargain. On the other side of road is the **Fish Souq** which is one of the best in the country – get there early before the before the heat of the day makes the smell unbearable.

Al-Hisn Fort

This fort, originally built in 1822, was almost completely demolished in 1969 but was saved and rebuilt by the present ruler of the emirate, Sheikh Sultan bin Saqr al-Qasimi. It now houses a fascinating collection of photographs and documents, mainly from the 1930s, showing various members of the ruling family and the British Trucial Oman Scouts. As you enter the fort there is a room on your left showing footage of Sharjah in the 1930s when the first Imperial Airways flights from London landed here on the way to India. The contrast between Sharjah then and now is striking. Back then the area was flat and sandy, and boasted just a few barasti and mud huts. Locals would carry their fish and other supplies around by donkey. It's definitely worth taking time to see this film.

There is also a section documenting the restoration of the fort in the early 1970s after its near demolition.

The fort is in the middle of Burj Ave. It is open 4.30 to 8.30 pm Tuesday to Sunday, closed Monday. Admission is free.

Sharjah Archaeological Museum

The central entrance hall has a wide-ranging display on archaeological methods and techniques. The first hall you come to includes exhibits on Sharjah's geography, traditional *falaj*-based irrigation systems and on the emirate's history during the Iron Age (1200 to 400 BC).

At the back of the central hall there is a display of old coins, both Islamic and pre-Islamic, a small display on the region's trade routes and a funerary slab dated between 250 and 150 BC with an inscription in the ancient language of South Arabian. The slab was found in Saudi Arabia's Al-Hasa oasis.

The second hall features extensive displays on the French excavations at Meleiha, an inland site in the Sharjah emirate, focusing particularly on the period between about

Heritage Area

The Heritage Area, a block just inland from the Corniche Rd between Burj Ave and Al-Qasimia Rd, includes a number of museums, a library, a theatre and the Al-Arsah Souq. All the buildings have been faithfully reconstructed using traditional materials where possible, which unfortunately includes sea coral.

Coming from the Al-Hisn Fort the first place you will come across is **Literature Square**. It was under construction at the time of writing but when completed it will house a library specialising in Arabic poetry and it is intended that it will become a gathering place for writers and poets. Across from here is **Bait Shaikh Sultan bin Saqr al-Qasimi**, a house set around a courtyard, displaying traditional costumes, jewellery, ceramics, cooking utensils and furniture. The **Heritage Museum** displays much the same thing but includes a children's room featuring traditional kids' toys and games.

Next door is the **Islamic Museum** which definitely should not be missed. There is an interesting display on the covering of the holy Qaaba stone at Mecca which includes a copy of the embroidered cloth. There is a large collection of coins from all over the Islamic world and a number of handwritten Qurans and writing implements. There are ceramics from Iran, Turkey, Syria and Afghanistan as well as artefacts, jewellery, and elaborate tea and coffeepots. Don't miss the display on the astrolabe, an extraordinary instrument that was an early type of sextant developed in the Arab world.

All the museums are open 8 am to 1 pm and 5 to 8 pm Tuesday to Sunday, closed Monday. Wednesdays are for women only at most museums. Admission is free but it seems compulsory to sign each and every visitor's book.

150 BC and AD 100. Other displays follow the site's history into the Islamic period.

Upstairs is the museum's collection of Islamic antiquities.

The museum (☎ 06-366 466) is on Shaikh Rashid bin Saqr al-Qasimi Rd near Cultural Square. It is open 8.30 am to 12.30 pm and 5 to 8 pm daily. On Friday it is open only in the afternoon. Admission is free. All exhibits are labelled in English, French and Arabic.

The Arts Area

Tucked away on the other side of Burj Ave from the Heritage Area (see the boxed text) is the Arts Area. There is a large **Art Museum** featuring modern art from local as well as foreign artists. On the upper level is a library with a great collection of art books and periodicals. It is open 9 am to 1 pm and 5 to 8 pm Saturday to Thursday, closed Friday. The **Bait Obeid al-Shamsi** next to it is a restored house that is now used as artists' studios. It is a lovely building featuring intricate plasterwork and pillars on the upper level. The Arts Cafe on the main square serves traditional snacks and drinks such as hot milk with ginger (delicious) for about Dh1.

Sharjah Science Museum & Planetarium

Although designed to educate and entertain children, this museum (☎ 514 777) is just as much fun for adults. The displays are all interactive and you can easily spend more than a couple of hours trying everything out. The Shadow Tunnel is especially spooky. There are demonstrations throughout the day in English and Arabic on cryogenics, static electricity and other physics matters. These manage to produce lots of gasps from utterly enthralled children.

The museum is next to the Archaeological Museum on Shaikh Rashid bin Saqr al-Qasimi Rd, just off Cultural Square. It is open 3.30 to 8.30 pm Monday to Saturday, closed Sunday.

King Faisal Mosque

Sharjah's central mosque is the largest mosque in the UAE, and is said to be able to accommodate 3000 worshippers. The mosque dominates Al-Ittihad Square next to the Central Market.

Parks

Sharjah's **Botanical Garden** is 15km out of the centre on the road to Dhaid, near the airport. The grounds are large and well kept and there are plenty of shady and grassed areas for picnics. The park has native trees and plants from the Far East, Africa and the Americas which are watered by a traditional falaj (irrigation) system. It's very popular with local families at the weekend.

A pocket-sized **amusement park** sits on an island in Khor Khalid. The park is open 3.30 to 10.30 pm Sunday to Thursday and 9.30 am to 10.30 pm Friday, closed Saturday. Mondays are reserved for women and children only. Admission is Dh2/5 for children/adults.

Beaches

There is a long stretch of public beach near the Coral Beach Hotel, about 4km northeast of the Holiday Inn Resort on the road to Ajman.

Organised Tours

The main tour operators based in Sharjah are SNTTA (☎ 351 411), Emirates Tours (☎ 548 296) and Orient Tours (☎ 549 333). SNTTA offers half-day tours of Dubai, Sharjah or Ajman for Dh100. Typically a tour of Sharjah will include the fort and museums, King Faisal Mosque, the Central Market and

Covering Up

If you are planning to go for a dip, it's important to note is that it is illegal for women to wear swimsuits on public beaches in Sharjah. You can wear what you want on private hotel beaches but elsewhere shoulders, stomachs, thighs and knees must be covered. This law was brought into effect in 1998 and, while you could technically be arrested for flaunting your flesh, it's more likely that you will just be told to cover up.

maybe one or two of the other souqs. Orient Tours' city tours cost Dh110 per person.

The SNTTA office on Al-Arouba Rd in central Sharjah is open 8 am to 1 pm and 2 to 7 pm Saturday to Thursday. SNTTA also has a dinner cruise aboard a dhow (Dh220) and a '1001 Nights Evening' (a Lebanese dinner and a belly dancing show) for Dh250. Both require a minimum of six people.

Brochures for these agencies can be found in the lobbies of most of Sharjah's (and a few of Dubai's) larger hotels.

Places to Stay

The room rates quoted in this section include a 15% service charge where applicable.

Places to Stay – Budget

There's a youth hostel a kilometre or so out of town, as well as three semi-cheap hotels in town.

The *Youth Hostel* (☎ 522 5070, Al-Zahra Rd) is 1.2km north-east of Al-Zahra Square, next to the Children's Hospital. Beds cost Dh35 per night and you'll need a Hostelling International card. The hostel has about 30 beds in four-bed dorms; however, you are likely to have a room to yourself. Residents in the hostel can generally use the club's swimming pool and bowling alley. In theory the hostel is open to women and to families. In practice, it's probably best avoided by unaccompanied women travellers, and the management seems reluctant to accept couples. There is no way of reaching the hostel by public transport.

Khaleej Tourist Hotel (☎ 597 888, fax 598 999, King Faisal Rd) charges Dh90/120 for singles/doubles. It is simple but clean and has unbelievably small bathrooms (some with squat toilets). Look out for the brightly painted hallways and patches of mismatched wallpaper.

Sharjah Plaza Hotel (☎ 377 555, fax 373 311, Al-Qasimia Rd) on Government House Square is very basic and rooms are small but clean. Rooms cost Dh120/150 but this is negotiable. The hotel can sponsor visas.

Federal Hotel (☎ 572 4106, fax 572 4394, King Faisal Rd) doesn't look much from the outside but rooms are large, clean and comfortable, for Dh176/200. The hotel has two restaurants, Lebanese and Italian, which are quite good value.

Places to Stay – Mid-Range

Al-Rolla International Hotel (☎ 512 000, fax 512 111) on the southern edge of Rolla Square is a fairly new hotel with comfortable but small rooms for Dh295/375 but you should be able to negotiate a substantial discount. The hotel sponsors visas.

The following hotels are all on Shaikh Sultan al-Awal Rd, south-west of the centre on the other side of Khor Khalid.

Golden Beach Motel (☎ 528 1331, fax 528 1151) is highly recommended. It has large rooms with kitchens and cooking facilities (but no utensils) and balconies overlooking the beach. The 1970s decor suits this place down to the ground and rooms are very good value at Dh200.

Beach Hotel (☎ 528 1311, fax 528 5422) charges Dh200/250 for singles/doubles, including breakfast, and is just as good as the top-end hotels along this road.

Summer Land Motel (☎ 528 1321, fax 528 0745) has rooms with sitting area for Dh200. Guests can use the Beach Hotel's private beach. Neither the Summer Land nor the Beach Hotel can arrange visas for tourists. Both cater to a largely Russian clientele.

Places to Stay – Top End

Unless otherwise noted, all of the following hotels can arrange visas.

Holiday Inn Resort (☎ 371 111, fax 524 090, Corniche Rd), at the end of Shaikh Mohammed bin Saqr al-Qasimi, is Sharjah's top hotel. Rooms are Dh690/805 but the weekend rate drops to Dh300 for a double, including tax and breakfast. This is incredibly good value for the standard of hotel but you'll need to book ahead.

Marbella Resort Sharjah (☎ 741 111, fax 572 6050, Corniche Rd) has Spanish-style villas set among trees and gardens. Junior suites (bedroom, bathroom and lounge) are Dh517.50 and master suites (bedroom, bathroom, lounge, dining area and kitchenette) are Dh805. This is a popular place and many of the villas seem to be permanently booked by the local government for diplomatic and business guests. Book ahead if you want to stay here.

Hotel Holiday International (☎ 573 6666, fax 572 5060), next door to the Marbella Resort, has been recently refurbished. Rooms are tasteful (but not as good as the hallways might suggest) and cost Dh460/575. It is difficult to get a discount on these prices.

Coral Beach Hotel (☎ 522 1011, fax 527 4101, Corniche Rd), on the outskirts of Sharjah, on the road to Ajman, is the one upmarket hotel that doesn't sponsor visas. Rooms are Dh300/375. The Coral Beach has become the main Russian hang-out in Sharjah.

The following top-end places are all outside the city centre along Shaikh Sultan al Awal Rd.

Sharjah Grand Hotel (☎ 528 5557, fax 528 2861) charges Dh460/575. Many of its customers are Germans on package tours.

Sharjah Carlton Hotel (☎ 528 3711, fax 528 4962) asks Dh345/460, more if you want a sea view from your room. It will only sponsor visas for Americans and Western Europeans.

Howard Johnson Beach Hotel (☎ 528 5444, fax 528 3728) is the newest place along this stretch. The lobby area is pleasant but the rooms are Dh345/431 are rather bland. The hotel is not on the beach side of the road but guests can use the beach club at Sharjah Grand Hotel.

Lou Lou'a Beach Resort (☎ 528 5000, fax 528 5222) charges Dh402.50/467.50 for pretty ordinary rooms, more if you want a sea view.

Places to Eat

The *Public Coffeehouse* in Al-Arsah Souq is not to be missed. For Dh10 you not only get a fairly large biryani but also salad and a bowl of fresh dates for dessert. The restaurant is a traditional-style coffeehouse with walls decorated with palm matting and seating on high wooden benches. Backgammon sets are available and sweet tea is served out of a huge urn. Unusually, both the staff and the customers are almost exclusively Emirati.

Thriveni Restaurant on Rolla Square or the slightly fancier *Satkar Restaurant* above it in the same building are also worth visiting. The Thriveni provides a pretty good meal for under Dh5. The Satkar offers good *thalis* (set meals, usually a selection of vegetables with bread and rice) from as little as Dh6. The surroundings are better than at the Thriveni and the view out over the square is worth the extra dirham or two.

Sharjah Dhow Restaurant (☎ 730 222 or 730 330, Corniche Rd) is next to the Marbella Resort. Prices are quite reasonable although the menu is pretty uninspired.

Kowloon (☎ 523 739 or 527 984, Al-Mina St) is the place to go if you are looking for something a bit more upmarket, or simply something not Indian. The Chinese food is very good by UAE standards. Soups cost Dh10 to Dh12 and most main dishes are in the Dh20 to Dh30 range.

Caesar's Palace (☎ 741 111) is an up-market place at the Marbella Resort. It has good basic Italian food for Dh25 to Dh28 and luxurious surroundings, although when we were there it was spoilt somewhat by the noisy lounge act during dinner.

Entertainment

Sharjah's emir banned alcohol in 1985 and all of the emirate's discos were closed. Smoking sheesha in public places has also been banned so the number of coffeehouses has been drastically reduced. Apart from the amusement park, the main form of entertainment is the cinema. The fare is mostly subcontinental although the Al-Hamra Cinema on Al-Arouba Rd sometimes shows (old and low-budget) English-language films.

Shopping

Sharjah is one of the best places in the Gulf to buy Persian carpets. Most of the carpet shops are in the Central Market. Shops here can arrange shipping and there are no export taxes. Prices vary wildly depending on your bargaining skills and the size and quality of

The Art of Buying Carpets

Buying carpets can be a serious business but if you know a little bit about the subject, you are less likely to regret your purchase later. Here are some basic facts to bear in mind before you head for the souq.

Carpets from Iran are generally more valuable than those from Kashmir or Turkey. What the carpets are made of is important. Silk rugs are more valuable than wool ones. Some Iranian rugs have a cotton base and silk pile, others are silk on silk. Some carpets are wool on wool, some are wool on cotton. Some piles are a mixture of wool and silk. They can be handmade or machine made, antique or new.

The more knots there are per square inch, the more valuable the rug (have a look at the back of the rug). A high-quality Iranian silk rug may have 950 knots per square inch, a less valuable woollen Afghan rug may have only 250 knots.

Often the value of a carpet is increased depending upon the family or tribe who made it. Some carpet weavers have better reputations than others. Look closely at the detail in the design of the carpet and compare it with others. This will give you an idea of the quality of workmanship.

Natural dyes are more desirable – and more expensive – than artificial dyes. Antique rugs are always naturally dyed. Some typical natural colours are rusty reds and browns, indigo blue and saffron yellow. A naturally dyed rug will appear to be slightly faded but this is not considered a flaw. The settling down of the natural dyes creates a carpet that is well balanced in colour and tone. Artificial dyes are used widely now and can be just as attractive as natural dyes. If you are buying an artificially coloured carpet, check that the colours have not bled. Unless you are a real purist (and have buckets of money) it really doesn't matter.

For more information on Persian carpets, including how they are made and what to look for when buying one, see *Oriental Carpets: A Buyer's Guide* by Essie Sakhai.

the carpet – see the boxed text for more advice on this. Another tip is to seek out the shops that sell rugs wholesale to other shops in the souq. They will usually give much better discounts than the retail-only stores. There is no way of telling the retail shops from the wholesale shops, though, so just ask.

There are some good antique shops in the Al-Arsah Souq selling Arabic and Bedouin items, including jewellery from Oman. A couple of antique dealers have also set up in the Central Market but most of their wares are from India, Thailand and Africa. The Central Market is also good for non-tourist-oriented shopping.

Getting There & Away

Air Sharjah international airport (☎ 581 111) is 15km from the centre. Although it lives in the shadow of Dubai, Sharjah airport is putting up a good fight. The idea of raffling off expensive cars to departing and transit passengers with only 1000 tickets sold per car and free delivery anywhere in the world for the winner, now a standard feature at Abu Dhabi, Dubai, Bahrain and Muscat airports, originated here.

The following lists the offices of some of the scheduled carriers serving Sharjah:

EgyptAir (☎ 352 163) Al-Mina St, next to the cinema
Gulf Air (☎ 371 366) Al-Arouba Rd, near the overpass and intersection with Al-Soor Rd
Indian Airlines (☎ 374 789) Government House Square, behind the courthouse

Minibus The only bus service to Sharjah is the Dubai Transport minibus, for Dh6 one way. The minibuses drop passengers at the taxi stand next to the Plant Souq. There is no bus service away from Sharjah, however, so if you don't have a car you'll have to get a taxi.

Long-Distance Taxi Sharjah has two taxi stands. Taxis for Umm al-Qaiwain (Dh28 engaged, Dh7 shared) and Ras al-Khaimah (Dh50 engaged, Dh15 shared) leave from the stand on Al-Arouba Rd across from the Al-Hamra Cinema. Taxis for Dubai (Dh30 en-

gaged, Dh5 shared), Abu Dhabi and Al-Ain (Dh150 to Dh175 engaged, Dh30 shared) leave from a stand next to the Plant Souq. It's worth noting that shared taxis to Abu Dhabi and, especially, Al-Ain rarely fill up – the stand seems mostly to be overflow space for the Dubai taxi stand. You are far better off taking a taxi to Dubai and travelling on to Abu Dhabi or Al-Ain from there.

Ajman, for travel purposes, is regarded as an extension of Sharjah so there are no shared taxis going there.

Car Rental In addition to the international car rental companies in the big hotels, there are a number of small firms along Al-Mina St, near the overpass, and along Al-Wahda Rd near King Faisal Rd.

Getting Around

Only special airport taxis can pick up passengers at Sharjah airport. These charge fixed rates depending on your destination. The trip to central Sharjah costs Dh40. If you need to go to Dubai the fare is Dh60 to Deira and Dh70 to central Bur Dubai (ie, not including Chicago Beach or Jebel Ali).

Since Sharjah has no bus service, getting around without your own car means either taking taxis or walking. The taxis don't have meters but trips around the centre should cost Dh5 to Dh10 (agree on the fare before you get in). If you hire a taxi by the hour expect to pay around Dh25 per hour, although you might be able to bargain that down a little. When the heat is not too debilitating Sharjah's centre can be covered on foot quite easily.

AROUND SHARJAH
Sharjah Natural History Museum & Desert Park

This is possibly the slickest, most modern museum in the Gulf. Unfortunately, it also happens to be out in the desert, 35km east of Sharjah's centre on the road to Fujairah.

Many of the museum's exhibits are aimed at children (most can be touched and there are a large number of interactive displays) but adults will probably find it fascinating as well. Everything is labelled in both English and Arabic.

After a fairly ordinary opening section on the origins of the earth, photosynthesis and the formation of Arabia's deserts, you come to a 35m model of the emirate's landscape. Opposite this are displays of the different plants and animals in each of the emirates.

The next gallery examines human settlement in Arabia, agriculture, and the domestication of various animals. It includes a bizarre full-size mock-up of a camel in which common household items illustrate the various parts of the animal's body (a fly swatter for the tail, for example).

The third hall focuses on geology and evolution. It includes a wraparound theatre with a short, dramatic film on the origins of the universe. There are also several casts of dinosaur skeletons on display (these can be touched – the real ones are safely in storage).

On the upper level is the requisite 'benefits of oil' portion of the museum, including another film. A lift takes you back down to a botanical gallery and an exhibit on ecology that includes a number of computer games designed to teach children about ecology and the environment.

The final gallery deals with the sea. All the fish and other sea creatures displayed in the hall are found in local waters. In fact, all the fish from which the displays were cast were purchased in the Sharjah and Ajman fish souqs – including the huge whale shark.

A desert park and breeding centre are adjacent to the museum complex. This area is gradually being developed into a small safari park featuring endangered species native to Arabia. Initially the breeding centre was supplied with a pair of Arabian wolves, a pair of rare Arabian leopards and several gazelles. There is not a lot to see and most of the area is not open to the public but if you walk through the garden under the walkway at the back of the museum you may be lucky enough to see Arabian gazelles in the field off to your right. To the left there are some fenced yards where, at the time of writing, a couple of Arabian oryx were being accommodated.

The museum (☎ 06-311 411) is open 9 am to 7 pm Saturday and Monday to Thursday, 2 to 8 pm Friday and public holidays, closed Sunday. Admission is Dh5. Photography is not allowed inside and cameras will be kept at the entrance.

Ajman Emirate

The smallest of the seven emirates, Ajman is hardly the mere extension of Sharjah that some people imagine. The emirate occupies a small stretch of coast between Sharjah and Umm al-Qaiwain and also has two inland enclaves. One is Masfut, at the western edge of the Hajar mountains, and the other is Manama, in the interior on the road from Sharjah to Fujairah. The ruler of Ajman is Sheikh Humaid bin Rashid al-Nuaimi.

Ajman has attempted to increase tourism in the emirate with the construction in its main city of a five-star resort and shopping centre in 1998. The resort attracts mainly package tourists from Europe and the shopping centre brings in local money from the surrounding emirates. As is the case with all the less wealthy emirates, Ajman is keen to lessen its financial reliance upon Abu Dhabi and to generate more of its own wealth.

AJMAN
☎ 06

Ajman's central square (in the middle of a large roundabout) is within walking distance of pretty much everything, including the museum, hotels, small restaurants and the coastline. Leewara St on the coast is where you'll find most of the city's few sites other than the museum. The main post office is on Masfut St, and the local government offices and the telephone office are on Shaikh Khalifa St. Banks are along Humaid bin Abdul Aziz St. The gift shop at the museum sometimes has an excellent map of the city for Dh10. Otherwise, there is a slightly blurred map on the back of the free museum brochure.

There is no tourist office. The place marked on maps as 'Ajman Tourist Centre' is a combination video arcade and cafe.

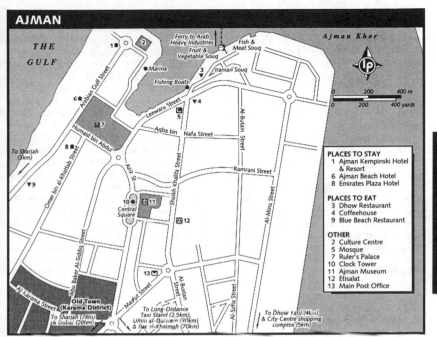

AJMAN

THE
GULF

Ajman Khor

Ferry to Arab
Heavy Industries
Fruit &
Vegetable Souq

Fish &
Meat Souq

Marina

Iranian Souq

Fishing Boats

Leewara Street

Araban Gulf Street

Humaid bin Abdul

To Sharjah
(3km)

Omer bin al-Khattab Street

Aqba bin   Nafa Street

Al-Butain Street

Ramrani Street

Aziz St

Sheikh Khalifa Street

Central
Square

Al-Mina Street

Abu Baker Al-Siddiq Street

Al Karama Street

Old Town
(Karama District)

To Sharjah (3km)
& Dubai (20km)

Madjut Street

Al-Bustan Street

To Long-Distance
Taxi Stand (2.5km),
Umm al-Quiwain (30km)
& Ras al-Khaimah (70km)

Al-Sofia Street

To Dhow Yard (4km)
& City Centre shopping
complex (5km)

0   200   400 m
0   200   400 yards

PLACES TO STAY
1 Ajman Kempinski Hotel & Resort
6 Ajman Beach Hotel
8 Emirates Plaza Hotel

PLACES TO EAT
3 Dhow Restaurant
4 Coffeehouse
9 Blue Beach Restaurant

OTHER
2 Culture Centre
5 Mosque
7 Ruler's Palace
10 Clock Tower
11 Ajman Museum
12 Etisalat
13 Main Post Office

UNITED ARAB EMIRATES

Ajman Museum

Ajman's museum occupies an old fort on the emirate's central square. It is one of the best museums in the UAE and is well worth the drive from Dubai.

The fort was built in the late 18th century and served as the ruler's palace and office until 1970. From 1970 to 1978, the fort was used as Ajman's main police station. Items on display in the museum include a collection of manuscripts, weapons, archaeological finds and reconstructions of traditional rooms and activities. Also on display are gifts and decorations that the emir has received over the years. Everything in the museum is labelled in Arabic and English, except for parts of the police exhibit. Bear in mind that dates of manuscripts, archaeological finds etc are given according to the Islamic calender.

Until fairly recently, Ajman issued its own passports. Some of these are on display in the museum, including Ajman Passport No 1 that belonged to the present emir's father, Sheikh Rashid.

There's also a reconstruction of a traditional street in a souq. It's at the far edge of the main courtyard, opposite the museum entrance.

Immediately to your right as you come through the gate is a reconstructed tomb from the Umm al-Nar civilisation. The tomb was excavated in the Mowaihat area and moved to the museum after suffering water damage.

The museum is open 9 am to 1 pm and 4 to 7 pm (5 to 8 pm from May to August) Sunday to Wednesday, 9 to noon Thursday, 4 to 7 pm Friday, closed Saturday. Admission is Dh4 (Dh2 for children under six). Photography is not permitted. The museum shop is worth a look for its small collection of local handicrafts. A guide to the museum is available for Dh5.

Souqs

Fruit, vegetables, meat and fish are sold in two purpose-built souq areas along the coast, off Leewara St. The best time to come is early in the morning, around 7 or 8 am, when the fishermen are back in port with the day's catch and the fish souq is at its busiest.

Around the parking lot in front of these markets an area known as the Iranian souq has grown up in the last few years. It's a fascinating place to prowl around. You are unlikely to find much in the way of souvenirs (unless your idea of a souvenir is a plastic washing bucket), though you can sometimes find interesting pottery. Cheap household goods are the market's main stock in trade. Many of the first merchants to set up stalls here were Iranians, hence the name, although there's nothing particularly Iranian about what's on offer here.

Dhow Yard

There is a traditional dhow building yard on the north side of the Ajman Khor, just a few kilometres from the centre. Follow Al-Mina St right around the *khor* (inlet) and keep veering left. Morning is the best time to see people working on the enormous dhow hulls.

Beaches

The public beach stretches from Sharjah to the Ajman Beach Hotel. It is wide and clean and one of the best spots on the Gulf to swim. There is not a lot of shelter, however, so bring a hat and plenty of sunscreen lotion.

Places to Stay

Emirates Plaza Hotel (☎ 744 5777, fax 744 6642, Omer bin al-Khattab St) has basic but clean singles/doubles for Dh130/150. It's the best value hotel in Ajman and the staff are helpful and friendly. Rooms facing the sea offer a stunning view of the Gulf, and the beach is just across the road.

Al-Waha Hotel (☎ 742 4333, fax 742 6272, Abu Baker al-Siddiq St) is probably best avoided – old and grotty rooms are Dh130/150, the furniture is grimy, the bathrooms are smelly and you get the impression that the management really doesn't care for

your patronage. There is a restaurant inside the hotel which seems to be open only some of the time, but there is a good coffeehouse serving sheesha outside the hotel.

Ajman Beach Hotel (☎ 742 3333, fax 742 3363, Arabian Gulf St). Once the only good place to stay in Ajman, this hotel has been completely overshadowed by the luxurious Kempinski Resort further up the road. The rooms were refurbished in 1998 so they are clean and comfortable for Dh200/250. The hotel has a bar and a restaurant but there are no plans to rebuild the swimming pool. It will also arrange visas for travellers arriving through Dubai airport.

Ajman Kempinski Hotel & Resort (☎ 745 1555, fax 745 1222, Arabian Gulf St), opened in September 1998 and is one of the most impressive hotels in the country. It offers utter luxury, with all the usual five-star facilities as well as a six-lane bowling alley. It is predictably more expensive than five-star hotels in Dubai as there is no competition. The hotel seems to attract mainly German package tourists. Rooms start at Dh862.50/977.50 and go right up to Dh5000 for the royal suite.

Places to Eat

If you are just after a quick snack or simple Indian or Pakistani meal, there are many cafes and restaurants around the old town (Karama district).

Dhow Restaurant along the waterfront is actually a coffeehouse in a traditional barasti shelter. It's a nice place for a cup of coffee or tea late in the afternoon. Look for the blue-and-white sign with two coffeepots and a rosewater urn on it.

Blue Beach Restaurant is a Chinese restaurant on Arabian Gulf St. It is rather expensive at Dh10 to Dh15 for entrees and Dh20 to Dh30 for mains but the food is excellent and the service relaxed and friendly.

Falcon Restaurant at the marina has snacks and main meals, with a mixture of Arabic and Western food. It has a good view over the marina and the prices are reasonable. Sometimes it is hired out for functions. There is also a bar, open to all visitors, next to the restaurant with a good view over the little harbour.

There is a basic *coffeehouse* on the corner of Leewara and Shaikh Khalifa Sts where you can get a coffee and sheesha for around Dh8 but it's pretty much a men-only hangout and women, especially those travelling alone, may feel a little uncomfortable here.

Shopping

There is not much to buy in the way of oriental rugs or antiques. The Iranian souq sells some tacky souvenirs but that's the extent of it. For other shopping there are a few department stores along Humaid bin Abdul Aziz St and a City Centre shopping complex opened in late 1998 just outside Ajman city to the north of the khor.

Getting There & Away

Ajman has no bus service. There is an unofficial taxi stand on Omer bin al-Khattab St just down from the Emirates Plaza Hotel but you can hail a taxi anywhere to take you to Sharjah for Dh10 to Dh15 or Dubai for Dh25. If you want to go further north along the coast, you'll have to go to the taxi stand at the main roundabout on the highway just out of town. It will cost you Dh50 to go to Ras al-Khaimah and Dh35 to go to Umm al-Qaiwain.

AROUND AJMAN
Manama

Manama is an inland enclave of Ajman, lying approximately halfway between Ajman and Fujairah, on the east-west road linking Dubai and Sharjah with the east coast. It is an oasis town in the midst of an agricultural area. The town consists of a few small Indo-Arab restaurants and grocery stores, a couple of garages and a petrol station. In the centre is a roundabout with a miniature Eiffel Tower (yes, you read that correctly).

The only thing to see is the **fort** near the main roundabout. It is quite well preserved, probably because the police still use it. It is not open to the public. It is best to steer well clear of the red fort on the edge of town. Do not photograph it – it is part of an army base.

Umm al-Qaiwain Emirate

With a population of around 35,000, Umm al-Qaiwain (Umm al-Quwain or Umm al-Qawain) is the least populous of the seven emirates. The ruler of the emirate is Sheikh Saqr bin Mohammed al-Qasimi.

Like Ajman, Umm al-Qaiwain is seeking to bring in money from the wealthier emirates through domestic tourism. A multimillion dirham waterpark attracts thousands of visitors to this little emirate every day and has added a new facet to the economy of the emirate whose main industries were fishing and agriculture.

The largest area of mangrove swamp on the west coast of the UAE, home to many bird species, is found off the Umm al-Qaiwain peninsula.

UMM AL-QAIWAIN
☎ 06

More than any other place in the UAE, Umm al-Qaiwain provides a glimpse of what life throughout the UAE was like not so long ago. There are no high-rise buildings in the town centre and the pace of life is still unhurried. The recently built waterpark is 10km north of the capital, and has its own hotel, so there hasn't been any obvious effect on the town itself yet. It's not necessarily worth the drive from Dubai on its own, but as a short diversion off the main road from Dubai to Ras al-Khaimah it is definitely worth an hour of your time.

Orientation & Information

Umm al-Qaiwain lies on a narrow peninsula of sand jutting north from the main road linking Dubai and Sharjah with Ras al-Khaimah. It stretches east as far as the Falaj al-Mu'alla, an important agricultural area. It is about 20 minutes drive from Ajman – a very bleak and uninteresting drive littered with faded road sign after faded road sign. Notice the large expanse of swampy inlets along the way, home to many wading birds.

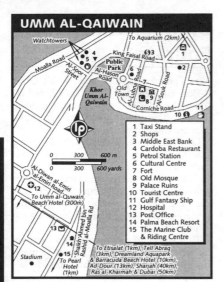

UMM AL-QAIWAIN

Watchtowers
To Aquarium (2km)
King Faisal Road
Moalla Road
Al-Soor Street
Al-Hason Road
Public Park
Old Town
Khor Umm Al-Qaiwain
Al-Lubna Road
Al-Souk Road
Corniche Road
Al-Diwan al-Emiri al-Emir Road
To Umm al-Quwain Beach Hotel (300m)
Shaikh Ahmed bin Rashid al-Moalla Rd
Stadium
To Pearl Hotel (1km)
To Etisalat (1km), Tell Abraq (3km), Dreamland Aquapark & Barracuda Beach Hotel (10km), Ad-Dour (13km), Sharjah (40km), Ras al-Khaimah & Dubai (50km)

0 300 600 m
0 300 600 yards

1 Taxi Stand
2 Shops
3 Middle East Bank
4 Cardoba Restaurant
5 Petrol Station
6 Cultural Centre
7 Fort
8 Old Mosque
9 Palace Ruins
10 Tourist Centre
11 Gulf Fantasy Ship
12 Hospital
13 Post Office
14 Palma Beach Resort
15 The Marine Club & Riding Centre

The old town and the emirate's small business district are at the northern tip of the peninsula, particularly along King Faisal Rd. Khor Umm al-Qaiwain lies to the north of the peninsula and is popular with swimmers and fishermen alike. If you are driving, watch out for cows on the road – they tend to congregate in the shade on roundabouts.

The best road signs in the country can be found in Umm al-Qaiwain which is ironic considering it is the hardest place in which to get lost! A number of banks and supermarkets line King Faisal Rd and the post office is south of the centre on Shaikh Rashid bin Saeed al-Maktoum Rd, not far from the sports stadium. The Etisalat office is on King Faisal Rd near the intersection with Al-Diwan al-Emiri Rd.

Old Town

The old town covers a very small area around the intersection of Al-Hason Rd and Al-Lubna Rd. A small **fort** was under construction at the time of writing. The word is that when it's completed it will house Umm al-Qaiwain's first museum, which among other things will display many treasures from the archaeological excavations in the emirate.

The **mosque** next to the fort has an interesting open design. An inscription over the doorway dates its construction to June, 1962 (Moharram, 1382 AH). Along the coast near the fort and mosque you can see a few dhows and fishing boats but there is not a lot left of the old harbour atmosphere. A few old **watchtowers** are scattered around town.

Aquarium

This is in the Marine Research Centre at the Ministry of Agriculture and Fisheries which is at the very end of the peninsula. There are large tanks of live fish (including stingrays, reef sharks and green turtles) as well as preserved specimens. The aquarium is open 8 am to 1 pm Saturday to Wednesday, 8 to 11am Thursday and closed Fridays. To get there just go along Moalla Rd to its end.

Umm al-Qaiwain Tourist Centre

The centre has all kinds of sea-going vessels for hire. The motorised varieties are rather expensive at about Dh140 per hour. There are boat trips from here to Sinaiyyah Island, a nature reserve just off the peninsula in the swampy khor. Only a chosen few are allowed to disembark; the island also serves as a private retreat for the ruler's family. Occasionally environmental and history groups are permitted to visit for field trips.

There is a swimming pool, private beach, a jacuzzi, a bar and a cafe. At the time of research, a hotel, restaurant and another bar were being built here. The admission fee for the day is Dh20. On Fridays the Tourist Centre offers free one-hour boat trips around the khor.

The Tourist Centre is at the top of the Corniche Rd where it bends around to the left. Look for the large, white cruise ship, the Gulf Fantasy Ship, which has been docked here for some years, in need of repair.

Marine Club & Riding Centre

This peaceful and clean centre (☎ 665 446) has a small private beach and hires out yachts, motorboats and jet-skis. A large dhow is docked here but this is only used for functions. This beach club seems quieter than others in the UAE; there was no incessant Arabic pop music screaming from stereos when we visited. There is a kiosk selling drinks, sandwiches and ice creams. Admission is free.

Next door are some well-kept stables housing some very well-kept horses. The stables are run by an English woman who gives riding lessons and will take experienced riders for a beach ride. For bookings phone ☎ 665 446. The complex is on Shaikh Ahmed bin Rashid al-Moalla Rd between the Palma Beach Resort and the Pearl Hotel.

Dreamland Aquapark

The pride of the emirate, this inevitably grotesque waterpark claims to be the largest in the Middle East. There are many rides, slides and pools, as well as an open-air theatre, restaurants and kiosks. There's a hotel next to the park. The park appears to attract an enormous number of young male Emiratis with lots of time on their hands.

Admission is Dh30 for adults, Dh20 for five- to 12-year-olds and free for children under five. It's open 10 am to 7 pm but usually closes later in summer. Fridays are for pre-booked groups and members only. The park is 10km north of the town on the road to Ras al-Khaimah.

Places to Stay

None of Umm al-Qaiwain's hotels are cheap and none sponsors visas. They all have swimming pools, a bar and a restaurant.

Pearl Hotel (☎ 666 678, fax 666 679, Shaikh Ahmed bin Rashid al-Moalla Rd) is about 5km south of the town centre and has singles and doubles for Dh250. The rooms are large and good value compared with the other hotels. Just be warned, though, that the place appears to be a popular 'naughty weekend' getaway for locals.

Palma Beach Resort (☎ 667 090, fax 667 388), about 2.5km north of the Pearl Hotel, is Umm al-Qaiwain's newest hotel. A small prefab cabin on the beach will cost you Dh220, slightly larger ones cost Dh250. The hotel also has newer, motel-style rooms surrounding a swimming pool for Dh260 to Dh400 for larger rooms. They have a kitchen area but no cooking facilities.

Umm al-Quwain Beach Hotel (☎ 666 647, fax 667 273, Moalla Rd) is another kilometre back towards the centre on the western side of the peninsula. It is a slightly musty place which rents one-bedroom aluminium cabins on the beach for Dh400. Behind these it has roomier brick bungalows that start at Dh700 for one bedroom and go up to Dh2000 for three bedrooms. This hotel seems to be very popular with groups of young Emiratis and Filipinos. The turn-off for the hotel is about 50m past KFC on the left as you enter Umm al-Qaiwain.

Barracuda Beach Hotel (☎ 681 555, fax 681 556) is next to Dreamland Aquapark on the Dubai–Ras al-Khaimah road. It has very ordinary chalets on the beach for Dh300 but newer, more luxurious accommodation was being built at the time of writing. In case you're wondering why there is so much traffic in and out of the hotel but very few guests, it's because of the 'hole in the wall' next to reception where alcohol is sold.

Places to Eat

All the hotel restaurants serve up similar Western and Arabic meals (Dh20 to Dh30) and snacks (Dh10 to Dh12).

Umm al-Quwain Beach Hotel Restaurant has the advantage of being on the beach but its layout is reminiscent of a school camp dining hall. The restaurant at the *Pearl Hotel* has similar meals at similar prices but a better atmosphere. The centre of town also has a collection of *biryani and Indian restaurants*. They can be found around the top of King Faisal Rd.

KFC, looking very out of place here, is on King Faisal Rd, about 1.5km from the centre. Next to the Pearl Hotel there is a barasti structure which is the *UAQ Public Kitchen and Tea Stall*, a traditional coffeehouse. If you want to cook your own food, there is a fish, fruit and vegetable *market* next to the coffeehouse.

Getting There & Away

Without your own car the only way in or. out of Umm al-Qaiwain is by taxi, either shared or engaged. The taxi stand is on King Faisal Rd, across from Al-Salamia restaurant. Taxi fares – both shared and engaged – from Umm al-Qaiwain have now been fixed by the local government. Shared/engaged taxis cost Dh5/20 to Ajman, Dh10/40 to Dubai, Dh10/50 to Ras al-Khaimah, Dh25/100 to Fujairah, Dh40/150 to Al-Ain and Dh50/200 to Abu Dhabi.

You could, in theory, get from Dubai to Umm al-Qaiwain and back the same day by shared long-distance taxi (with your own car you could do it in under two hours), but it may be necessary to take a taxi engaged. There does not seem to be a lot of action at the taxi stand in Umm al-Qaiwain, and in Dubai taxis bound for Umm al-Qaiwain do not fill up quickly either.

AROUND UMM AL-QAIWAIN

There are two archaeological sites in Umm al-Qaiwain emirate: Tell Abraq and Ad-Dour. The latter is of major significance because it is to date the only Hellenistic site discovered in the UAE. You don't need a 4WD to reach these sites and you can walk freely around them.

Tell Abraq

This site dates back to the 3rd millennium BC and was first excavated in 1973. In 1991, due to a dispute between the emirates of Sharjah and Umm al-Qaiwain about who the site belongs to, work was stopped indefinitely. It's now just an abandoned site, no doubt breaking the hearts of many archaeologists. Revealed so far are foundations of three defence towers, a well and a fireplace. The rectangular walls on top of the mound date from the Iron Age occupation of the site in the late 2nd millennium. If you look down into the trenches you will see several post holes, revealing evidence of barasti houses built here. Also found here was a tomb containing 20 skeletons.

Artefacts from the site come from as far away as Afghanistan and can be seen at the Sharjah Museum. Much of the stone used at Tell Abraq has been cut from reef rock – look for shells in the walls of the ruins.

To get to Tell Abraq from Ajman, turn right at the Umm al-Qaiwain roundabout on the main Ajman–Ras al-Khaimah highway, following the sign for Falaj al-Mualla. About 500m up the road on the right you'll see a mound of ruins. Driving up to the mound from the road is not recommended – there are reports of cars being found at the bottom of the site's deep trenches.

Ad-Dour

Inhabited from 200 BC to sometime in the 3rd century AD, this Hellenistic site is 4km long and 1km wide. It is believed that the settlement ended when the khor that joined the settlement to its lifeblood, the sea, silted up and became impassable.

The many artefacts found here will eventually be on display at the planned Umm al-Qaiwain museum (see Old Town earlier in this section), when it is opened. These include glazed pottery, coins, beads, cooking implements and a lamp. There are foundations of a large house with three fortification towers. Artefacts found here include two statues of eagles, a symbol of worship in pre-Islamic Arabia, that guarded the entrance to the house.

Further inland the area is scattered with dozens of tombs. In one of these a skeleton was found buried with a camel that would have been slaughtered for the burial.

To get to the site, drive for approximately 10km north along the main highway from the Umm al-Qaiwain roundabout. Turn right at the sand track about 200m before the Emirates petrol station and double back parallel to the road for about 50m until you come to some stone foundations. This is believed to be the house of a ruler or dignitary in the town because of its large size overlooking the sea. The ruins reveal foundations of three round towers.

Continue through the gate and along the track for about 500m to two trees standing very close to each other. All around this area are remains of ancient **tombs**. Head along the track veering off to the left and after 100m there are remains of a 4th-century **fort** with a watchtower at each corner. The fort is surrounded by the remains of the village's houses which date from the same time.

Back at the two trees, continue straight along the track for about 300m and you will come to the remains of a **temple** on the left next to a sandy mound. The walls of the temple have remained remarkably intact since the 1st century AD. The stone walls are covered in gypsum plasterwork which was once decorated with reliefs of grapevines. The large stone block in the middle of the temple is believed to have been a basin for sacrificial purposes. There are **tombs** all around this area too.

Ras al-Khaimah Emirate

Ras al-Khaimah is one of UAE's more interesting emirates. The sudden appearance of the hazy Hajar mountains as you approach the city is very dramatic after the bleak drive from Dubai. It is the country's northernmost emirate, stretching 64km up to the mountainous border with Oman's Musandam peninsula. It is also the most fertile of the emirates as it catches the water running down from the Hajar mountains. The result is an area of abundant greenery bordered by sea, mountains and desert. The emirate also includes the islands of Greater Tunub and Lesser Tunub in the Gulf. Ras al-Khaimah is a favourite weekend getaway for people from Dubai and is also becoming increasingly popular with package tourists from northern Europe.

Ras al-Khaimah is said to have the proportionately greatest number of indigenous Arabs of any of the emirates. It has no long-established Indian or Persian merchant communities like Dubai or Sharjah. It is also the only place in the UAE where, as in Saudi Arabia, all shops are required to close at prayer time.

History

Flints and potsherds found near the Khatt Hot Springs indicate that Ras al-Khaimah has been inhabited since the 3rd millennium BC. For much of its history the region's main town was Julfar, a few kilometres to the north of the present-day city of Ras al-Khaimah.

By the 7th century AD, Julfar was an important port of the Sassanian empire. This empire was one of the major powers in the 7th century. It was based in Iran and its colonies were established on the coasts of Arabia in order to control the region's resources of copper, land for cultivation and frankincense. Excavations in Ras al-Khaimah since 1995 have revealed a fortification wall believed to belong to the Sassanians whose colonies were destroyed by Arab tribes of the interior when they united under Islam in the early 7th century. Pottery and other finds from this era indicate that Julfar had significant trade links with both China and India. In the 15th century Julfar was the birthplace of Ahmed bin Majid, the great Arab sailor whose books on navigation are still studied and who was hired by Vasco da Gama to guide him to India in 1498.

In the early 16th century, the Portuguese occupied Julfar where they built a customs house and, in 1631, a fort. No trace of either remains today and their exact location is uncertain. The Portuguese abandoned the fort in 1633 after a series of attacks by both the local tribes and the British and Dutch navies. By the time they left, Julfar was in ruins and its Arab inhabitants moved further south to Ras al-Khaimah.

Different branches of the Al-Qasimi family rule both Ras al-Khaimah and Sharjah emirates. Throughout the 18th century the Qawasim, as the ruling clan was known, were the most powerful rulers in this part of the Gulf, and by the beginning of the 19th century they had a large fleet. The early 19th-century British raids on the Qawasim-controlled coast were partly in retaliation for attacks on British shipping, but they were also prompted by a belief that the Qawasim posed a threat to Oman's independence.

Britain had a treaty with the Omanis and regarded Oman's independence as crucial to the protection of its own supply lines to India.

In 1809 and 1819, the British raided Ras al-Khaimah and briefly occupied it. The British withdrew after imposing a General Treaty of Peace on the sheikhs of the coast in 1820 and the Qawasim never quite recovered their previous power and status.

It was because of this background that Ras al-Khaimah initially chose to stay out of the UAE when the federation was formed in December 1971. Three months later the ruler changed his mind, apparently after concluding that the emirate couldn't survive as an independent state. Small quantities of oil were discovered in Ras al-Khaimah in 1976 but the revenues from this never amounted to much. In 1997 oil was again discovered and it is hoped this will lead to the enrichment of the emirate and lessen its financial dependence on the wealthier emirates. The emirate's economy is still based mainly on agriculture (particularly vegetables and citrus fruits), and it is sometimes referred to as the breadbasket of the UAE. There are also cement and petrochemical plants and an increasingly important tourism industry.

RAS AL-KHAIMAH
☎ 07

Ras al-Khaimah's capital is relaxing, has its share of interesting sites and is a good base for exploring the countryside.

Orientation

Ras al-Khaimah is really two cities. Ras al-Khaimah proper, which is the old town on a sandy peninsula along the Gulf coast, and Al-Nakheel, the newer business district on the other side of Khor Ras al-Khaimah. There is a bridge across the khor and another road to the south which joins the two parts of town by skirting the water's edge. Only a few of the streets in either town have names and there are no street signs.

Apart from the museum and the old town's souq, there isn't very much to Ras al-Khaimah proper. Most of the hotels and services, and even the city's lone traditional coffeehouse, are in Al-Nakheel.

Most of Al-Nakheel's shops and offices are on Oman St, between the Hospital and

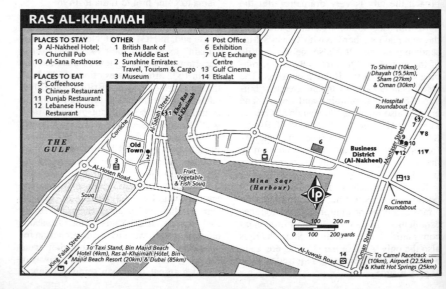

RAS AL-KHAIMAH

PLACES TO STAY	OTHER	4	Post Office
9 Al-Nakheel Hotel;	1 British Bank of	6	Exhibition
Churchill Pub	the Middle East	7	UAE Exchange
10 Al-Sana Resthouse	2 Sunshine Emirates:		Centre
	Travel, Tourism & Cargo	13	Gulf Cinema
PLACES TO EAT	3 Museum	14	Etisalat
5 Coffeehouse			
8 Chinese Restaurant			
11 Punjab Restaurant			
12 Lebanese House			
Restaurant			

THE GULF

Old Town

Al-Hosen Road

Souq

Corniche

Al-Sabah Street

Khor Ras al-Khaimah

Fruit, Vegetable & Fish Souq

Mina Saqr (Harbour)

To Shimal (10km), Dhayah (15.5km), Sham (27km) & Oman (30km)

Hospital Roundabout

Business District (Al-Nakheel)

Muntasar Street

Oman Street

Cinema Roundabout

King Faisal Street

To Taxi Stand, Bin Majid Beach Hotel (4km), Ras al-Khaimah Hotel, Bin Majid Beach Resort (20km) & Dubai (85km)

Al-Juwais Road

To Camel Racetrack (10km), Airport (22.5km) & Khatt Hot Springs (25km)

0   100   200 m
0   100   200 yards

Cinema roundabouts (both of which, despite the names, are intersections, not roundabouts). This area also includes the city's two cheap hotels and several small restaurants.

Information

You can change money at any of the banks along Al-Sabah St in Ras al-Khaimah or Oman St in Al-Nakheel.

The main post office is a red-brick building on King Faisal St, about 4km north of the Bin Majid Beach Hotel. The Etisalat (telephone) office is on Al-Juwais Rd in Al-Nakheel. It is open 7 am to 3 pm and 4.30 to 8 pm Saturday to Thursday. It is closed on Friday except for bill payments.

Ras al-Khaimah Museum

The museum is in the old fort on Al-Hosen Rd, next to the police headquarters. The fort was built in the mid-18th century. Until the early 1960s it was the residence of the ruling Al-Qasimi sheikhs. The courtyard of the fort is paved with stones from the fossil bearing strata of Wadi Haqil, further inland.

One room on the ground floor has a particularly good display of Arabian silver jewellery and another room features a collection of sea shells from all over the UAE. The lower floor also includes exhibits on Ras al-Khaimah's archaeology and ethnography and the region's natural history. The highlight of the upper floor is the working wind tower, beneath which you can sit and cool down. A few of the other rooms upstairs have displays of traditional dress, concentrating mainly on women's clothing, and a display on the ruling family.

All the signs are in both Arabic and English and a detailed guide to the museum is on sale at the gate for Dh10. The museum is open 8 am to noon and 4 to 7 pm Wednesday to Monday, closed Tuesday. Thursday is women only. Admission is Dh2 for adults and Dh1 for children. Cameras require an additional ticket costing Dh5.

Old Town

Ras al-Khaimah's old town is a wonderful place to stroll around. The souq area, south of the museum, has a few small tailors' shops but the main attraction is the unspoiled atmosphere. Ras al-Khaimah welcomes tourists without bending itself out of shape to cater to them. The other part of the old town worth seeing is the kilometre or so of coast immediately north of the bridge where the fishing port is. Here there is a thriving souq where you can buy fruit, vegetables, fish, poultry, plants, pottery and household wares.

Saqr Public Park

There are amusement rides and a large grassed area here. The park is open 8 am to 10 pm Saturday to Thursday, 4 to 11 pm Friday. Admission is Dh2. Take the airport road turn-off from the main Dubai–Ras al-Khaimah road near the KFC. After 5km turn right at a large roundabout and the park is about 700m along on the left.

Camel Racing

Ras al-Khaimah's camel racecourse is one of the best in the country. It is in Digdagga, about 10km south of town. Races usually take place on Fridays during the winter and sometimes also on Tuesday or Wednesday. The schedule is irregular, so ask locally or check with the tour operators at the hotels. Admission is free but come early.

To reach the racecourse, take the airport road south from Al-Nakheel and turn right at the Ras al-Khaimah Poultry & Feeding Company (there's a yellow sign on the building). Look for a large, free-standing minaret at the turn-off. Keep following the road from there until you reach the track.

Water Sports

Water sports are promoted by the Bin Majid Beach Hotel, Bin Majid Beach Resort just out of town and the Ras al-Khaimah Hotel. If you are staying in one of these places they can provide you with information on windsurfing, water-skiing, diving etc. Next to the Ras al-Khaimah Hotel is the Waterski Club (☎ 354 444, fax 354 545) which was closed for renovation at the time of writing.

UNITED ARAB EMIRATES

Organised Tours

While Ras al-Khaimah figures on many tourists' itineraries there is little you can do to book a tour once you are there. A number of places around town advertise tour services, but they seem suspiciously unable to produce lists of their offerings or prices. Sunshine Emirates: Travel, Tourism and Cargo (☎ 324 939, fax 324 936/106) advertises its tours in the Bin Majid Beach Hotel. Alternatives to local agencies are the large operators in Dubai who will be able to arrange tours to and around the emirate (see Organised Tours in the Dubai chapter).

Places to Stay

There are four places to stay in Ras al Khaimah and one out of town. At the time of writing a new five-star hotel was being built just outside the town. All prices quoted here are inclusive of service charges. These hotels can all arrange visas for tourists; if you're arriving at Dubai or Sharjah, it would be a good idea to arrange this at least two weeks in advance.

Al-Sana Resthouse (☎ 229 004, fax 223 722, Oman St) has poky, dusty rooms but it is the cheapest place to stay in town. Singles/doubles cost Dh70/120, including breakfast. All rooms have TV and a fridge and a few rooms have attached baths and kitchenettes. Be warned, the shared bathrooms are very small. Bring your own towel and toilet paper.

Al-Nakheel Hotel (☎ 222 822, fax 222 922, Muntaser St) has the cheapest bar in town but not much else to recommend it. There is a pool table and a seriously overpriced restaurant offering very average Indian, Arabic and Western meals. Rooms are Dh140/190 and the hotel offers room service.

Bin Majid Beach Hotel (☎ 352 233, fax 353 225, King Faisal Rd) is the favoured haunt of Russian tour groups. Rooms are Dh250/350, including breakfast. There is a beach club and pool area where nonguests are welcome for Dh30 per day.

Bin Majid Beach Resort (☎ 446 644, fax 446 633), not to be confused with the hotel of the same name, is 20km south of Ras al-Khaimah on the road to Dubai. Also popular with Russian tourists, the resort charges Dh450/650 for rooms. Without a car it's too far out of town to be practical.

Ras al-Khaimah Hotel (☎ 362 999, fax 362 990, Khuzam Rd) has rooms for Dh330/440. Discounted weekend specials are sometimes available. The Ras al-Khaimah Hotel does not serve alcohol. There is apparently an Internet cafe in a small room in the lobby, but it didn't appear to have any computers at the time of research.

Places to Eat

Punjab Restaurant is a Pakistani and northern Indian restaurant in the souq area of Al-Nakheel. Generous helpings of exotic curries are heated in big pans at the front of the restaurant. A chicken curry costs Dh6, *dahl* (lentils) costs Dh3 and all meals include bread and salad.

Al-Sana Restaurant, next to the Al-Sana Resthouse, is highly recommended. It has Western, Chinese, Indian and Filipino food. Meals should not run to more than Dh15 or Dh20.

Lebanese House Restaurant on Muntaser St, next door to the Al-Nakheel Hotel, is another very good place to eat. It serves great Lebanese mezze for Dh5 to Dh7. Most main dishes and grills cost from Dh10 to Dh12.

Chinese Restaurant on Oman St, a few hundred metres north of the Al-Sana, has been recommended by several readers. Main dishes cost from Dh15 to Dh25.

Entertainment

If you're looking for a drink try the *Churchill Pub* at the Al-Nakheel Hotel. It is cheap although the restaurant attached to it is not. There's also a tiny *bar* in the Bin Majid Beach Hotel.

There's a *disco* at the Bin Majid Beach Hotel, and lounge acts will assault your ears both there and at the Al-Nakheel. Gulf Cinema on Oman St shows English and Hindi movies.

The last of Ras al-Khaimah's old-style *coffeehouses* is well worth a visit. It is in an unmarked barasti structure near Mina Saqr overlooking the creek. Very sweet tea costs 50 fils a cup (Dh1 with milk) and there are snacks. It is one of the few places serving sheesha as a new law in the emirate states that only cafes on the Corniche or by the creek are allowed to serve it. Note that you have to be over 18 to be served sheesha in Ras al-Khaimah. There are a number of small coffeehouses on the Corniche in the old town.

Getting There & Away
Air Ras al-Khaimah's small airport (☎ 448 111) is 22.5km south of Al-Nakheel. Three airlines operate international services from here. Gulf Air flies twice a week to Muscat and on to Karachi (Pakistan), and once a week to Doha (Qatar) and Bahrain. Indian Airlines flies once a week to Kozhikode (Calicut, in southern India) and EgyptAir has a weekly flight to Cairo. Contact details of airline offices in Ras al-Khaimah are:

EgyptAir (☎ 335 000) Al-Sabah St, above Nasa Trading Est, Ras al-Khaimah Old Town
Gulf Air (☎ 210 033) Oman St, Al-Nakheel, between Al-Juwais Rd and the cinema
Indian Airlines (☎ 221 789) cinema roundabout, Al-Nakheel

Long-Distance Taxi Ras al-Khaimah's taxi stand is on King Faisal St, just south of the Bin Majid Beach Hotel, across the road from KFC. Taxis to Dubai and Sharjah charge Dh70 (shared). Fares to Ajman or Umm al-Qaiwain are Dh40 to Dh50 (shared). If you want to get to Abu Dhabi or the east coast by taxi your best bet is to go to Dubai and change there. Long-distance taxis (engaged) to Abu Dhabi charge Dh250, and to Fujairah it's around Dh125.

If you are trying to get to Oman's Musandam peninsula the Ras al-Khaimah taxi drivers will take you to Khasab, the main town in Musandam, for Dh200 one way. For Dh40 they will dump you at the border in Sham from where you'll just have to try your luck. If you do engage a taxi to Khasab make absolutely sure that your driver is an Emirati (ie that he does not need a visa to enter Oman), that he owns the car and has the papers to prove it in his possession be-

fore you start out. You have to pay a Dh20 departure tax at the UAE side of the border.

Shared taxi destinations north of Ras al-Khaimah include Rams (Dh6), Khor Khwair (Dh8) and Sham (Dh8).

Car Rental cars are available in the top-end hotels or from one of the small agencies along Oman St in Al-Nakheel.

Getting Around
Taxis in Ras Al Khaimah have no meters. Fares within Ras al-Khaimah old town or within Al-Nakheel are about Dh5. Between Ras al-Khaimah and Al-Nakheel, expect to pay Dh10 engaged and Dh3 shared.

AROUND RAS AL-KHAIMAH
The northern tip of the UAE has the largest concentration of archaeological sites in the country, as well as Khatt Hot Springs. It would not be too hard to cover everything listed here in one long day from Ras al-Khaimah, provided you make an early start and have your own transport. With the exception of Kush, none of the archaeological sites listed here are fenced in so you can explore them to your heart's content.

Shimal
The village of Shimal, 10km north of Ras al-Khaimah, is the site of some of the most important archaeological finds in the UAE. The area has been inhabited since the late 3rd millennium BC. Excavations have revealed hundreds of tombs at the base of the hills, indicating that it was one of the largest settlements in this part of Arabia. The site contains the largest Umm al-Nar tomb in the UAE, containing over 700 skeletons.

The main attraction is the **Queen of Sheba's Palace**, a set of ruined buildings and fortifications spread over two small plateaus overlooking the village. On a clear day the view is great. Despite its name, the palace was not built by the Queen of Sheba who is generally thought to have come from what is now Yemen. It may, however, have been visited by Queen Zenobia who ruled a sizeable chunk of the Middle East in the 4th century AD from Palmyra in modern Syria. The fortifications are known to have been in use as recently as the 16th century. What is visible today sits on top of a much older structure. Pottery found here dates from the 16th and 17th centuries. There is a large well and walls around the ruins.

Getting There & Away To get to the site from Ras al-Khaimah, head north for 4.3km from the hospital roundabout in Al-Nakheel and turn right onto a blacktop road where there are a number of signs. (One has a red arrow, another has red Arabic script on a white background, for those who read Arabic, the sign points to the Shimal Health Centre, and another has the falcon crest on it.) Follow this road for about 1.5km until you reach a roundabout. Turn right and follow the road for another 2.3km through a village until you come to the People Heritage Revival Association, a new building made to look like a fort. Turn left. After about 400m the blacktop ends. Continue on a dirt track through the village. You'll pass a small green and white mosque on the left. Keep going straight, heading for the base of the hills and get onto the blacktop road to your left. Continue along this road for about 1km until you see a track leading to a large green water tank. At this point you will see a gap in the fence on your right. Walk through the gap in the fence and follow a faint track to the base of the closest hill. At the top of this hill (which will be on your right) you should see the remains of a stone wall. Begin the 15-minute climb up the hill, which starts at a ruined cistern which looks like a stone box. The climb is fairly steep in parts and the stones underfoot are loose.

A taxi (engaged) from Ras al-Khaimah to Shimal costs Dh15, but this only gets you there. Going to Shimal, waiting while you climb the hill, and then taking you back will cost more. Decide on a fare before you set out and don't pay the driver until you return.

Kush

Kush is the old site of the ancient city of Julfar before it had to move further west to the coast just north of Ras al-Khaimah as the coastline changed. The trading city of Julfar was very important from the 7th to the 17th centuries – see History at the beginning of the Ras al-Khaimah section for more details. The site at Kush consists mainly of a thick mud-brick wall which runs around the top of a mound. This mound (called a *tell*, pronounced 'tull') was formed by the constant rebuilding of mud-brick dwellings on top of the collapsed remains of others. The site was inhabited by the Sassanians from the 4th century. Thin layers of ash discovered here are evidence of the defeat of the Sassanians at Julfar by Arab tribes in the 7th century.

Other findings at the site include pottery, animal bones, a gold dinar dating back to the era of Umar Yusuf who ruled Oman in the mid-10th century and the oldest preserved coffee bean in the world which dates back to the 12th century.

Getting There & Away Kush lies just off the blacktop road on the way to Shimal. Follow the directions to Shimal given in the previous section as far as the turn-off from the main road. Take this turn-off. After about 300m, you will pass the Shimal Folks Arts & Theatre Society. Immediately after this building there is a dirt track off to the right. Follow this track as it bends around in a semicircle for about 300m and you will come to a fenced-in mound. There is a black sign written which forbids entry to the site.

Rams

A quiet village 12km north of Ras al-Khaimah, Rams has a scenic coastline and a few old **watchtowers**. Rams has played an important role in Ras al-Khaimah's history. It was one of the sites at which the British fleet landed in 1819 during the invasion of the Gulf which led, the following year, to the area coming under de facto British rule.

Coming from Ras al-Khaimah, the easiest way to reach the town is by taking the second Rams turn-off.

Long-distance taxis between Rams and Ras al-Khaimah cost Dh6 per person shared and Dh30 engaged.

Dhayah

Another 3.5km beyond Rams is Dhayah, a small village beneath a ruined fort. It was here that the people of Rams retreated in the face of the advancing British in 1819 and surrendered after a four-day siege. The site has recently been partly restored.

The **fort** sits atop a sharp, cone-shaped hill behind the village. It takes 15 to 20 minutes to climb the hill, longer if you stop to collect some of the numerous sea shells which blanket the slopes. The rock is very loose and it is easy to slip. The easiest approach is from the west side of the hill (the side facing the sea), moving towards the south side as you ascend. At the top the only easy way into the fort is through the south wall.

There are some more ruined fortifications just south of the hill.

Getting There & Away To reach the hill, turn right off the road from Ras al-Khaimah immediately after you pass Dhayah's new white mosque and the grocery store on the right (the turn is 14.5km north of the hospital roundabout). If you pass a sign saying 'Sha'm 15km', you've gone too far. The dirt track swings around to the right behind the village. After about 500m you'll see the Al-Adal grocery. Keep to the left of this. The road forks just past the grocery. Take the track to the right (the one that runs along the fence). There is an old watchtower on the left. From there the track twists and turns for another 450m. When you get to a white wall turn right and head towards the hill. You'll only be able to drive for about 80m. The easiest way is to climb up the west side of the hill.

Sham

This place, where the mountains really begin to close in, is the last town before the border with Oman. At 40km from Ras al-Khaimah it's a long way to go considering there is no particular attraction but if you have a car and feel like a drive, head for this rather lively village. There is a geriatric home (no tooting of horns we are told), a small beach and a sports club, as well as numerous shops selling all kinds of plastic goods and car parts.

From Ras al-Khaimah a taxi should cost Dh50 engaged.

Khatt Hot Springs

These popular springs are naturally hot mineral water baths and the temperature is about 50° to 55°C – too hot to enjoy in summer. There are separate areas for men and women. Not surprisingly, the pool in the men's section is much larger and you are able to dive and swim quite comfortably. The women's pool gets too crowded to enjoy and is really only big enough to sit in and have a little paddle. The women there are likely to be completely covered, which makes you feel that you should be too. You might want to wear something on your feet if you go in – the rocks inside the pool are quite sharp!

The springs are open 5 am to 11 pm daily. Admission is Dh3.

Near the spring, the *Khatt Guest House for Families* (☎ 448 181) offers simple but roomy accommodation with attached bathroom and kitchen.

The springs are about 25km from Ras al-Khaimah. To reach Khatt, head south out of Al-Nakheel following the signs for the airport; you'll see signs for Khatt further along the road. When you reach the roundabout in the village of Khatt, turn left. The springs are another 800m down the road. Taxis in Ras al-Khaimah charge Dh20 to Dh25 to go to Khatt.

The East Coast

The east coast is the most beautiful part of the UAE. The Hajar mountains provide a stunning backdrop to the beaches and the incredible blue waters of the Arabian Sea. The mountains are in perpetual haze, which gives them a surreal, almost one-dimensional, appearance. There is a lot of greenery here as the run-off from the mountains provides natural irrigation throughout most of the year. Farming and fishing are the main industries on the east coast, not oil.

The network of wadis and the many camping spots in the mountains attract people from other emirates on the weekends. Artificial coral reefs have been constructed along the east coast in an attempt to encourage natural reef formations, and to attract rare species of fish. As a result, the area has become well known for the diving and snorkelling it offers.

Khor Kalba, the southernmost town on the east coast (near the border with Oman), has the oldest mangrove forest in Arabia and is home to dozens of species of birds.

Fujairah, the only emirate without any territory on the Gulf, dominates the east coast. Until 1952 it was part of Sharjah, making it the youngest of the seven emirates.

Several of the east coast towns, including Khor Fakkan, are part of the Sharjah emirate. There is also a small enclave of Omani territory between Fujairah and Khor Fakkan which is entirely surrounded by the UAE.

FUJAIRAH
☎ 09

The capital of Fujairah emirate has a stunning location overlooking the Gulf of Oman. It may not be cheap as far as accommodation is concerned but it is a good base for exploring the east coast. The busy port attracts commercial traffic, with ships preferring to unload their cargo here instead of Dubai or Sharjah. The international airport brings in shoppers from the CIS and subcontinent and the Fujairah Tourism

Board promotes the area as a weekend getaway to residents of the other emirates.

If you visit the beaches here, especially around the Hilton Hotel, you will notice the famous black sand of Fujairah. It's actually more charcoal grey and, unfortunately, it gives the beaches a deceptive appearance of grubbiness.

Orientation

Fujairah is quite spread out, but most of the services that travellers will require are in a fairly compact area. The main business area is along Hamad bin Abdullah Rd, between the Fujairah Trade Centre and the coast. Along this stretch of road you will find the main post office, several banks and, at the intersection with the coast road, the central market. There is a concentration of good, cheap restaurants near the Hilton Hotel.

The coastal road changes its name three times, which can be confusing. Passing through the city from south to north it is called Regalath Rd, Gurfah Rd and Al-Faseel Rd, in that order.

Maps The best map is the free promotional *Northern Emirates Tourist Map*. You can pick this up at the Ritz Plaza Hotel and from the Fujairah Tourism Board.

Information

Tourist Offices The Fujairah Tourism Board (☎ 223 1554, fax 223 1006) publishes a few brochures on the area, including one with a very obviously touched-up photo of the city centre. It also has information on wadi tours. This information doesn't seem to be available anywhere except the office itself. It is on Hamad bin Abdullah Rd in the Fujairah Trade Centre building.

Money There are a number of banks on or near the roundabout at the intersection of Shaikh Zayed bin Sultan and Hamad bin Abdullah Rds.

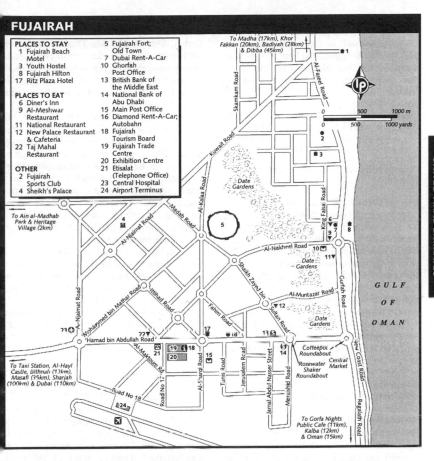

FUJAIRAH

PLACES TO STAY
1 Fujairah Beach Motel
3 Youth Hostel
8 Fujairah Hilton
17 Ritz Plaza Hotel

PLACES TO EAT
6 Diner's Inn
9 Al-Meshwar Restaurant
11 National Restaurant
12 New Palace Restaurant & Cafeteria
22 Taj Mahal Restaurant

OTHER
2 Fujairah Sports Club
4 Sheikh's Palace
5 Fujairah Fort; Old Town
7 Dubai Rent-A-Car
10 Ghorfah Post Office
13 British Bank of the Middle East
14 National Bank of Abu Dhabi
15 Main Post Office
16 Diamond Rent-A-Car; Autobahn
18 Fujairah Tourism Board
19 Fujairah Trade Centre
20 Exhibition Centre
21 Etisalat (Telephone Office)
23 Central Hospital
24 Airport Terminus

To Madha (17km), Khor Fakkan (20km), Badiyah (28km) & Dibba (45km)

Skamkam Road

Al-Fasel Road

Kuwait Road

Al-Kalaa Road

Macab Road

Date Gardens

King Faisal Road

Gurfah Road

0   500   1000 m
0   500   1000 yards

To Ain al-Madhab Park & Heritage Village (2km)

Al-Njimat Road

Al-Njimat Road

Mohammed bin Mathar Road

Ittehad Road

Sheikh Zayed bin Sultan Road

Fahim Road

Al-Nakheel Road

Al-Muntazar Road

Date Gardens

Date Gardens

GULF OF OMAN

'Hamad bin Abdullah Road

Al-Maktoum Road

Al-Sharqi Road

Tunis Road

Jerusalem Road

Jamal Abdul Nasser Street

Mersashid Road

Coffeepot Roundabout
Rosewater Shaker Roundabout
Central Market

New Coast Road

Regalath Road

To Taxi Station, Al-Hayl Castle, Bithnah (13km), Masafi (35km), Sharjah (100km) & Dubai (110km)

Road No 17

Road No 18

To Gorfa Nights Public Cafe (11km), Kalba (12km) & Oman (15km)

UNITED ARAB EMIRATES

Post & Communications The main post office is on Al-Sharqi Rd just off Hamad bin Abdullah Rd. It is open 8 am to 2 pm and 3 to 9 pm Saturday to Wednesday, 8 am to 1 pm and 2 to 7 pm Thursday and 8 to 11 am Friday. The Etisalat office is on the corner of Hamad bin Abdullah Rd and Road No 17. It's open 7 am to 9 pm daily.

Fujairah Museum

At the time of writing the museum had been closed for six months. It will re-open inside the fort in the old town when restoration

work is completed, which may well take until late 2000.

Old Town

Spooky might be the best word to describe the old town, which consists of a cemetery and a fort (at least 300 years old) overlooking the ruins of old Fujairah. Relics found at the fort date back to the 15th and 16th centuries. At the time of writing the fort was being restored but little else here seems to have been touched since the inhabitants left the crumbling site a generation or so ago.

When finished the fort will house the new museum. The date gardens behind the old town are in a sad state of neglect. There are a few people living around here so if you are poking around the old town be sure to re-spect their privacy. Andy Hurst wrote in with this warning:

Some of the old 'deserted' parts of Fujairah's Old Town are actually inhabited and I was made very unwelcome. It is interesting to look around the di-lapidated buildings/old fort but I was virtually chased away by one of the locals – there are also a few dogs around, so be very careful if visiting this area.

Ain al-Madhab Garden
On the western edge of town, this park-cum-hotel is a pretty sorry sight. None of the kid-die rides dotted around the place look as if they have been used in a very long time. The swimming pools, however, are clean, cool and segregated (the men's and women's sec-tions are as far away from each other as pos-sible). The garden is open 10 am to 10 pm and the pools are open 10 am to 7 pm daily.

Admission to the park is Dh2; Dh5 if you want to use the pools. It also rents out rooms at Dh100/200 for singles/doubles in very or-dinary and slightly musty mobile homes.

To get there follow the signs for 'Mineral Water and Tourism' or 'Park'. It's about 2km from Al-Njaimat Rd.

Heritage Village
This was almost finished at the time of writ-ing. It features half a dozen barasti shelters, a *majlis* (traditional reception area), wells, traditional barasti boats, a kiosk and a real cow. It is next to Ain al-Madhab Garden and is open 9 am to 6 pm daily. Admission is free.

Places to Stay
The *Youth Hostel* (☎ 222 2347) is just off Al-Faseel Rd near the sports club. The staff is friendly and the rooms are very basic but clean. They have three beds each and lock-ers for your luggage. Lockout is 11 pm. Beds are Dh15 each but you'll need to have a Hostelling International membership card. If you don't have one, membership will cost

you Dh75 for one year. It may not be worth it unless you plan to use the other hostels in Dubai, Sharjah and Abu Dhabi. The hostel will only accommodate women if it is empty enough to segregate them from men. Considering how small the hostel is, there is a fairly high chance of a single woman being turned away.

Fujairah Beach Motel (☎ 228 111, fax 228 054) is several kilometres north of the centre. The rooms are good, if slightly musty. The Emirati teenagers who used to terrorise the bar have been replaced by large numbers of Russians, which may or may not be an improvement depending on your point of view. The hotel has a pool, restau-rant and a nightclub with live entertainment on weekends. Single/double rooms cost Dh262.50, including tax and service.

Fujairah Hilton (☎ 222 2411, fax 222 6541, Al-Faseel Rd) is closer to the centre. The US Navy uses Fujairah airport to re-supply its ships in the Indian Ocean and has a long-term lease on about half the Hilton's rooms, so expect to see some American military personnel. Rooms are Dh570/635 plus 5% municipality tax. Cheap weekend packages are sometimes offered on Thurs-days and Fridays. Both the Hilton and the Beach hotels sponsor visas for tourists with 15 days notice.

Ritz Plaza Hotel (☎ 222 2202, fax 222 2203, Hamad bin Adbullah Rd) opened in July 1998 and was the newest hotel in Fu-jairah at the time of writing. This place is popular with German tour groups. It has comfortable but small rooms for Dh460/575. There are cheaper deals for weekend visits.

At the time of writing a new five-star hotel was under construction on the corner of Al-Sharqi and Hamad bin Abdullah Rds, just across from the Ritz Plaza Hotel.

Places to Eat
Taj Mahal (☎ 225 225) serves excellent In-dian and Chinese food and is cheap at Dh10 to Dh12 for mains. The place is clean, cool and comfortable and the service is good. It is at the back of the building opposite Eti-salat on Shaikh Hamad bin Abdullah Rd.

Diner's Inn (☎ 226 351) on Al-Faseel Rd, across from the Hilton, has good cheap Indian and Chinese food served in reasonably large helpings. Meals can cost as little as Dh8.

National Restaurant, also on Al-Faseel Rd but on the other side of the intersection with Al-Nakheel Rd, has cheap chicken, rice and biryani dishes for about Dh10.

Al-Meshwar is a medium-priced, more upmarket Lebanese restaurant with mezze from Dh7 to Dh12 and main dishes from Dh12 to Dh25. It's on King Faisal Rd in the block behind Diner's Inn.

New Palace Restaurant & Cafeteria on the corner of Shaikh Zayed bin Sultan and Al-Muntazar Rds (specialising in dishes from Kerala) and biryani dishes for Dh6 to Dh8. Arabic meals are Dh10 to Dh15 and Chinese meals (which aren't very authentic) cost Dh8 to Dh12. It has separate rooms for families. Just avoid the Arabic coffee – it's terrible.

Entertainment

On the way to Kalba there are two traditional barasti coffeehouses. One (unnamed) is between the coast road and the inland road, 2.3km from the coffeepot roundabout in Fujairah. The other is called *Gorfa Nights Public Cafe*, and is on the right just before the big roundabout that leads from Fujairah to Kalba. *Sheesha* (traditional pipe) and coffee here will set you back about Dh10.

Getting There & Away

Air Fujairah international airport, on the southern edge of town, is served by Gulf Air (one flight a week to Bahrain and Doha, Qatar; two to Muscat) and Indian Airlines (one flight a week to Kozhikode in southern India). For information call ☎ 222 6222.

Gulf Air's office (☎ 222 6969) is in the Fujairah Trade Centre on Hamad bin Abdullah Rd. Indian Airlines (☎ 223 1989) is on Hamad bin Abdullah Rd between Jerusalem Rd and Jamal Abdul Nasser St. EgyptAir (☎ 02-277 511) also flies to Cairo on an irregular schedule during June and July.

Long-Distance Taxi The taxi stand is on the edge of town on the road to Dubai. The fare to Dubai, Sharjah or Ras al-Khaimah is Dh175 engaged or Dh25 per person in a shared taxi (don't hold your breath waiting for taxis to Ras al-Khaimah to fill up). A taxi to Abu Dhabi or Al-Ain will cost you Dh250, less if you're prepared to bargain hard or Dh50 in a shared taxi. Engaged taxis to Dibba cost Dh40, Dhaid Dh40, Masafi and Khor Fakkan Dh20. The only places to which taxis seem to travel with any regularity are Dubai, Sharjah, Khor Fakkan and Dibba.

There are no intercity buses to or from Fujairah.

Getting Around

To/From the Airport Fujairah's international airport is close to the city centre. There are no public buses but a few taxis loiter around the front and a trip to, say, the Ritz Plaza Hotel will only cost a few dirhams. To the Hilton you will pay around Dh5.

Car Rental Dubai Rent-A-Car/Europcar (☎ 222 1318) has an office opposite the Hilton hotel. Diamond Rent-A-Car (☎ 241 321) has branches around the UAE as does Autobahn (☎ 223 2226). They are both in the block of shops next to the Ritz Plaza Hotel. There are a few other smaller agencies on Shaikh Hamad bin Abdullah Rd further towards the Etisalat building

Taxi There are no local buses in Fujairah, so if you don't have a car you are at the mercy of the taxis (which have no meters). Fares around town should not be more than Dh5. Hiring a taxi by the hour should cost about Dh20.

AROUND FUJAIRAH
Al-Hayl Castle

You need a 4WD to get to these ruins set among the mountain peaks in Wadi Hayl, 13km north-west of Fujairah. Once the summer palace of the ruling sheikhs of Fujairah, the castle looks stunning against the green mountains, with its free-standing pillars and watchtowers. Take the time to explore the place and you'll notice that much of the decorative plasterwork still remains. There are ladders leading up to the tops of the watchtowers, but they don't look very stable. Nor do the floors of the watchtowers.

The signposted turn-off for Al-Hayl Castle is on the left about 2km past the main roundabout at the edge of Fujairah as you head towards Dubai. The tarmac road continues for 7km to a village. Drive straight through it and into a wadi which goes off to the left. From here it's a 2.1km rough road to the castle. The track rises up and runs along the left bank of the wadi. After almost 2km it joins up with a graded track that goes up a hill to the castle. Allow half a day for a trip from Fujairah.

Kalba & Khor Kalba

The largely residential town of Kalba, just south of Fujairah, is part of the Sharjah emirate. Its **beach** is more inviting than Fujairah's as it has barasti shelters, a grassed esplanade and swings. The whitewashed building on the right at the main roundabout into town is supposedly a museum, but at the time of writing it was well and truly closed. The similar building opposite is the **Shaikh Qasimi House** which was undergoing some renovations. There is a **fish market** on the corniche every morning but you'll need to get there early.

Keep driving south along the corniche and you'll come to Khor Kalba, a lovely old **fishing village**. It's very quiet and traditional and you can see fishermen on the beach pulling in nets each morning and evening. There are some old, crumbling houses along the coast road, just before you get to the Breeze Motel, which really give the place atmosphere. Most of the villagers have moved a little further inland to the large, new villas that were built by the government when money came into the emirate during the late 1970s and 1980s.

The oldest **mangrove forest** in Arabia is in Khor Kalba. This conservation reserve has abundant birdlife and is the only home in the world to the Khor Kalba white-collared kingfisher. It's possible to hire canoes and paddle up the inlets into the mangroves. Make a deal with the fishermen on the beach. To get there continue south along the coast, past the Breeze Motel; turn left at the roundabout and go over the bridge. You can also go straight at the roundabout and drive down a dirt track to go further into the forest but it would be better to have a 4WD for this just in case the road is muddy. There is a children's play area here and note that fishing in the swamps is not allowed.

Breeze Motel (☎ 778 877, fax 776 769) on the coast in Khor Kalba is the only place to stay. Rooms are Dh250/300 but those rates can drop by up to Dh100. Try to bargain because the run-down prefab cabins are not worth the asking price. Note that Kalba is part of the Sharjah emirate so the hotel does not serve alcohol.

Ain al-Ghamour

About 15km south-west of Kalba is the hot spring of Ain al-Ghamour where the water temperature is a searing 55° to 60°C. The spring is just a small concrete pool (about 4m long, 3m wide and 1m deep) that sits at the bottom of a hill. It is filled with spring water by a narrow canal that runs down the hill from a natural spring. At the time of writing, however, there were plans to upgrade the spring to make it more tourist-friendly. The spring can be reached without a 4WD.

Getting There & Away To get to Ain al-Ghamour, take the inland road from Kalba that runs south-west towards the Omani border. After 4km you'll pass through a roundabout. After another 1.2km you will reach an Adnoc petrol station on your right. Just past here is a turn-off to the right onto an unsealed road. There should be a sign for Ain al-Ghamour but you can never be sure. After 2.5km the track diverges. Take the track that swings around to the right. Another 3.6km from here there is a turn-off to the right. Turn here and the springs are another 1.1km along. The first thing you'll come to is an area with shelters and an abandoned office. Park the car and continue walking along a track, past the shelters to the spring.

Masafi

This small town, 35km inland from Fujairah, is at the junction where the road from Dubai to the east coast splits into two, heading north to Dibba and south to Fujairah. Known as the location of the Masafi water-bottling factory, the town is most famous for its **Friday market**, confirmed by the number of tour buses that have recently begun to stop here on their way to the east coast. The market is actually open every day of the week and has an enormous number of carpets, plants and souvenirs for sale. You are sure to get a bargain here but you have to work at it – aim to pay 50% of the asking price for any rug.

BITHNAH

The village of Bithnah is an easy trip from Fujairah or a quick diversion off the road from Dubai to Fujairah. Nestled by the roadside in the foothills of the mountains, the village has a number of interesting archaeological sites.

The T-shaped site or **Long Chambered Tomb** was excavated in 1988 and is thought to have been a communal burial place. Its main period of use appears to have been between 1350 and 300 BC but the tomb itself may date from an earlier period. About 10 skeletons were found during the excavations, and there was evidence that the tomb had been re-used several times.

The other site in Bithnah is the **fort** which was important until fairly recently because it controlled the main pass through which the highway now cuts into Fujairah. Unfortunately it has fallen into a very sad state of neglect over the years. It is now more of a rubbish dump than anything else and is inhabited by a man who looks as if he could even outdate the fort! He will be only too glad to open up and show you around but give him a bit of time to answer the door.

Getting There & Away

To get to the tomb, take the main road from Fujairah towards Dubai for about 12km. Turn right at the exit marked 'Bithnah' and turn right again almost immediately at the T-junction. Follow this road for 500m to the radio tower. At this point turn onto a dirt road on your left. After 100m it will fork; keep right and look for the metal sunshade that covers the site on your right.

To get to the fort, exit the main road and turn right at the T-junction, as for the tomb. Go 250m and turn left onto a dirt track straight through the village and over two inclines (keep left) down into the wadi. The fort is behind some trees about 500m up the wadi. The wadi is passable in a regular car, but only just.

MADHA

Madha is the main village of the small Omani enclave just off the main coastal road heading north from Fujairah to Dibba. Even if a trip to Oman is not on your itinerary, it is worth a quick sojourn to Madha. The architectural differences are striking. Even the style of the road signs changes. Madha isn't poor, but it is significantly less affluent-looking than similar villages a kilometre or two away that simply happen to be on the other side of the border. You may also notice that, unlike small villages in the UAE, most of the people you see on the street are Arabs, not Pakistanis or Indians since Oman imports much less foreign labour than the UAE does.

The village centre is noteworthy mainly for the odd Victorian-style lampposts on the main street. There is a small hilltop **fort**, but this is still used by the Omani military and is not open to the public. There are also a few **watchtowers** which, unlike their Emirati counterparts, are whitewashed.

The road continues into the enclave and winds through a number of tiny villages which are much more attractive than Madha itself. Remember, however, to respect the privacy of the villagers. Mid- to late afternoon is a good time to drive through as everyone is usually inside their houses at this time.

If you are driving a rental car remember that your UAE car insurance will not be valid should you have an accident in Madha. Also remember that, despite appearances to the contrary, you are in another country. You'll sometimes see the Royal

UNITED ARAB EMIRATES

Oman Police hanging around just off the main Fujairah–Khor Fakkan road and they have every right to stop and question you as you pull off the highway and onto the Madha road. The turn-off for the Omani enclave is 4.5km south of Khor Fakkan.

KHOR FAKKAN
☎ 09

One of Sharjah's enclaves and the largest town on the east coast after Fujairah, Khor Fakkan is the most beautiful spot in the UAE. It's also a trendy weekend resort but while the port has proved to be a roaring success, the development of tourism has been somewhat held back by Sharjah's ban on alcohol.

The sweeping corniche is bound by the port at the southern end and the luxury Oceanic Hotel to the north, with a nice stretch of beach and parkland in-between. Occasional tyre tracks in the sand are a dead giveaway about the favourite pastime of the local male teenagers in their 4WDs. Other activities, such as sailing, water-skiing and diving are concentrated at the Oceanic which has a fence around its stretch of beach largely, the manager told me, to keep away the 4WD brigade. There is not much to see but Khor Fakkan is such a beautiful spot it's worth a bit of your time. The fort that once dominated the coast is long gone.

Souq

The fish, fruit and vegetable market is at the southern end of the corniche. A colourful, busy spot, it's nice just to sip a cup of sweet tea, watch the hive of activity and admire the view of the town against the mountains. There is a newer souq on the corniche close to the roundabout but the small number of shops open here indicates that it hasn't really taken off.

Al-Wurrayah Falls

About 4.5km north of the Oceanic Hotel there is a signposted turn-off for Al-Wurrayah Falls. To drive through the wadi to the falls you need a 4WD although a saloon car can take you along a tarmac road above the

---

Rifaisa Dam

This dam, in the mountains behind Khor Fakkan, resembles a Swiss mountain lake without the greenery and is worth a visit. The story goes that the dam was built over a village and, when the water is very still, you can see the tops of the old houses.

To get to the dam, turn inland (a right if you are coming from the corniche, a left if you are entering Khor Fakkan from Fujairah) at the Select N Save store on the main street of Khor Fakkan, just near the mosque. The road swings round to the right and over a bridge. Turn left immediately after the bridge onto a dirt road. Follow this road for 4.7km as it bends around the mountains to the dam. There are some great views back over Khor Fakkan on the way. Notice the remains of a hilltop watchtower on your left at the last bend before the dam.

---

wadi from where you get a nice view. The tarmac road ends before the falls, but it's a nice drive towards the mountains and along the road as it dips in and out of the wadi. If you have a 4WD, the turn-off into the wadi is 8km from the highway at the point where the sealed road dips right down. Take your swimming trunks and a towel.

Places to Stay

Oceanic Hotel (☎ 238 5111, fax 238 7716) at the northern end of the corniche is expensive with singles/doubles for Dh460/575. Special deals are sometimes available on weekends. The hotel has a small private beach and offers free camel rides each morning along the beachfront between 10 and 11 am. The decor is unashamedly 1970s and quite appealing. The staff are very friendly and they will arrange visas with five days notice. The hotel also offers a number of activities such as snorkelling trips, boat rides and joy flights.

Al-Khaleej Hotel (☎ 238 7336) is about 3.5km inland on the road to Fujairah. Coming from Fujairah it is one of the first buildings you will see on the right upon entering Khor Fakkan. It's the only other place to stay in Khor Fakkan and is overpriced for what you get. The entrance is on the left side of the building. It consists of a four-bedroomed flat with a small kitchen and a bathroom. One of the rooms has its own bathroom. The sparsely furnished and rather dingy rooms sleep two people and cost Dh150.

Places to Eat

There are lots of small restaurants and cafes on the road from Fujairah between the Al-Khaleej Hotel and the corniche. On the corniche there are two restaurants worth trying. The *Lebanon Restaurant* is the better of the two, with both Lebanese mezze and the usual cheap Indian fare of biryanis and tikka dishes. The mezze cost Dh5 to Dh15 and main dishes cost around Dh20 apiece.

Further north along the corniche the *Green Beach Cafeteria & Restaurant* has similar fare. You can't miss *Golden Fork* which has been plonked very intrusively in the middle of the corniche. It has Arabic, Filipino and Western food for Dh10 to Dh25.

Avoid the appealing looking *Iranl Pars* restaurant at the roundabout on the Corniche near the souq. It is overpriced at Dh20 to Dh25 for mains, and the food is average at best. The restaurant on the top floor of the *Oceanic Hotel* is expensive but try to drop in for a cup of coffee and a chance to admire the view over the bay.

Getting There & Away

If you don't have your own car, taxis are your only public transport option. From Fujairah, an engaged taxi is Dh20.

BADIYAH

☎ 09

Badiyah, 8km north of Khor Fakkan and part of the Fujairah emirate, is one of the oldest towns in the Gulf. Archaeological digs have shown that the site of the town has been settled more or less continuously since the 3rd millennium BC. There is evidence that the 3rd-millennium BC tombs that have been found here were re-used up

until Hellenistic times, ie, as recently as the 1st century BC, although no inhabited Hellenistic sites have been discovered in the Fujairah area so far.

Today, Badiyah is known mainly for its **mosque**, a small whitewashed structure of stone, mud-brick and gypsum. Built in about 640 AD, it's the oldest mosque in the UAE and is still in use. It is built into the hillside just north of the village on the main road and is surrounded by a barasti fence. A small heritage display is next to the mosque but you could question what they mean by 'heritage' when you see the odd Coca Cola can or plastic water bottle placed next to traditional coffeepots as part of the display. On the hillside above and behind the mosque are several ruined **watchtowers**. You may be asked for money here by the Indian keepers but you don't have to pay anything.

The **market** in Badiyah village is open everyday (although Thursday is the main day) and has locally grown fruit and vegetables for sale. You can walk or drive through the farm plots behind the market towards the beach where, among other things, bananas and coconuts are grown.

There's a small **graveyard** on the right-hand side of the road as you head north out of Badiyah.

Diving

There is a Diving Centre (☎ 445 050, fax 445 900) at the Sandy Beach Motel, 6km north of Badiyah. It charges Dh190 per person for one dive with full equipment hire. If you have all your own equipment it costs Dh50 for the boat ride. Night dives, diving lessons and underwater photography trips are also offered. You can hire snorkelling gear for Dh30 per day.

Places to Stay & Eat

There is no place to stay in Badiyah but 6km to the north, near the village of Al-Aqqa, there's the *Sandy Beach Motel* (☎ 445 555, fax 445 200). Very ordinary hotel rooms with smelly bathrooms cost Dh267.50, shabby one-bedroom chalets cost Dh399 and two-bedroom chalets cost Dh577.50. The

East Coast Diving

A snorkelling or diving trip is one of the highlights of a trip to the east coast. Snoopy Island (you'll see why it got this moniker when you get there) is a short swim from the beach at the Sandy Beach Motel near Badiyah. The island is surrounded by a coral reef and a paddle around here will reveal all kinds of colourful fish, eels, starfish, black-tip reef sharks and the occasional turtle. Dolphins have been spotted off the coast on a number of occasions.

Nick Hewitt wrote to us, extolling the virtues of the waters further north at Dibba:

I have visited Dibba many times specifically to go snorkelling over the fantastic coral reef here. The reef comes right into the beach at the southern corner of Dibba Bay and has a great variety of hard and soft coral and fish (including stone fish). You are also likely to get good close up views of turtles.

Most of the coastline from Snoopy Island to Dibba is suitable for snorkelling and diving but you will need your own equipment if you plan to do it away from the Sandy Beach Motel in Badiyah or the Holiday Beach Motel in Dibba. Alternatively, you can arrange a trip with Al-Boom Marine Diving Unlimited (☎ 04-394 1267) or Scuba International (☎ 04-420 553), both in Dubai. Khasab Travel & Tours (☎ 968-836 233) is an Oman-based operation, but they have an office in Dibba and can arrange diving trips further up the coast in the waters off Oman's Musandam peninsula. Prices vary, depending on where you want to go, and how many dives you want to make.

prices here are exorbitant, the food is terrible and the service leaves a lot to be desired. There is a bar which is very popular with the locals as it is the only place for miles around serving alcohol. The hotel is popular with package tourists from the CIS during summer and autumn. The beach is open to nonguests for Dh25.

It's also possible to *camp* at Al-Aqqa beach next to the motel but you will need to bring everything as there are no amenities or shelters.

Getting There & Away

Taxis are the only public transport option as there are no bus services. There are car rental agencies in Fujairah.

DIBBA
☎ 09

Dibba's name lives in Islamic history as the site of one of the great battles of the Ridda Wars, the reconquest of Arabia by Muslim armies in the generation after the death of the Prophet. The Muslims were fighting against a number of tribes and towns which had sworn allegiance to Mohammed during his lifetime but did not feel themselves bound to the new religion following his death. The victory at Dibba in 633 AD, a year after the Prophet's death, traditionally marks the end of the Muslim reconquest of Arabia. The **graveyard** on the vast flat area before the mountains plunge directly into the sea is the only evidence of these battles. Up to 10,000 rock headstones protrude from the flat ground. It is an amazing sight.

Today, Dibba is a quiet set of seaside villages. Since Dibba is only 145km from Dubai, a popular weekend excursion is to make a loop from Dubai via Masafi, Fujairah, Khor Fakkan and Badiyah.

In fact, there are three Dibbas, each belonging to a different ruler: Dibba Muhallab (Fujairah), Dibba Hisn (Sharjah) and Dibba Bayah (Oman). As in Al-Ain, you can walk or drive freely across the Omani border and explore some of the Omani villages on the southern edge of the spectacular Musandam peninsula. However, this does not seem to be formalised and accepted to the extent that it is at Buraimi, and the Omani police may turn you back if they spot you. If driving, remember that once you are across the border your UAE car insurance is invalid.

Dibba is a really nice spot. It has been compared to an Italian fishing village, and it is true that the main street of Dibba Hisn does resemble a small European coastal town. The architecture is very different to other villages in the country as buildings tend to be two- and three-storeys and attached to each other. Note the colourfully painted gates in the Omani portion of Dibba.

There is nothing much to see except the **fort** in Dibba Hisn, which is still used by the police. There is a fish market, harbour and a lovely **beach**. Women planning to swim here should cover up as much as possible as the residents are very traditional and not used to visitors.

Oman-based Khasab Travel & Tours (☎/fax 968-836233) offers a dhow trip from Dibba to Lima along the dramatic coast of the Musandam peninsula. If there is no answer at this office you can call the head office in Khasab (☎ 968-830464, fax 830364). Although these trips are very expensive (less if there is a group of you), the scenery is absolutely stunning. An alternative is to make a deal with one of the local fishermen.

Places to Stay & Eat
Don't be fooled by the large yellow-and-red sign on the main coast road in Dibba Hisn which says 'Hotel' – there are no hotels in the centre of Dibba. *Holiday Beach Motel (☎ 445 540, fax 445 580)* is on the main highway about 5km south of Dibba. It is a popular place with locals on the weekends but it is expensive at Dh370 for a studio chalet and Dh475 for a chalet with a living room. The hotel has a dive centre, charging Dh130 for one dive or Dh200 for two with full equipment.

The hotel has an enormous restaurant which indicates that it probably caters for large functions occasionally. The menu is rather ordinary but the prices are reasonable.

Getting There & Away
If you don't have a car, you can get here by taxi from Fujairah. An engaged taxi from Fujairah is Dh40.

AROUND DIBBA
There is an unsealed road through the Musandam peninsula from Dibba to Khasab in the Omani enclave but you won't be able to pass through the Omani military checkpoint after about 50km. Some years ago this was possible but it was definitely not possible when we were there.

It is possible to get through to Ras al-Khaimah on the west coast of the UAE from Dibba, through part of the Musandam peninsula. This road will take you through steep gorges and around mountains into the peninsula for about 40km then out again towards the west coast for about 25km. You do not need any visas or road permits for this, but you will need a 4WD. The roads get very steep and they can be quite rough. Avoid taking this trip if there has been rain or if rain is forecast. The steep mountain roads can easily get washed out and you could be stranded up there. If you want a little taste of Omani mountain life you can take a saloon car along this road for about 8.5km before it starts to get too rough. You'll pass a number of (occupied) stone houses built into the hillsides.

Language

English is widely spoken throughout Oman and the UAE, but a few words of Arabic can do a lot to ease your passage through the region.

There are several different varieties of Arabic. Classical Arabic, the language of the Quran, is the root of all of today's dialects of spoken and written Arabic. A modernised and somewhat simplified form of classical Arabic is the common language of the educated classes in the Middle East. This language, usually known as Modern Standard Arabic (MSA), is used in newspapers and by TV and radio newsreaders. It's also used as a medium of conversation by well-educated Arabs from different parts of the region. Such a written language is necessary because the dialects of spoken colloquial Arabic differ to the point where a few of them are mutually unintelligible. Mercifully, the words and phrases a traveller is most likely to use are fairly standard throughout Oman and the UAE. The words and phrases in this chapter should be understood anywhere in the region.

Transliteration

It's worth noting here that transliterating from Arabic script into English is at best an approximate science. The presence of sounds unknown in European languages, and the fact that the script is 'incomplete' (most vowels are not written), combine to make it nearly impossible to settle on one method of transliteration. A wide variety of spellings is therefore possible for words when they appear in roman script – and that goes for places and people's names as well.

The matter is further complicated by the wide variety of dialects and the imaginative ideas Arabs themselves often have on appropriate spelling in, say, English. Words spelt one way in a Gulf country may look very different in Syria, heavily influenced by French (not even the most venerable of western Arabists have been able to come up with an ideal solution).

Pronunciation

Pronunciation of Arabic can be tongue-tying for someone unfamiliar with the intonation and combination of sounds. Pronounce the transliterated words slowly and clearly.

This language guide should help, but bear in mind that the myriad rules governing pronunciation and vowel use are too extensive to be covered here.

Vowels

a	as in 'had'
e	as in 'bet'
i	as in 'hit'
o	as in 'hot'
u	as in 'put'

A macron over a vowel indicates that the vowel has a long sound:

ā	as the 'a' in 'father'
ē	as in 'ten', but lengthened
ī	as the 'e' in 'ear', only softer
ō	as in 'for'
ū	as the 'oo' in 'food'

You may also see long vowels transliterated as double vowels, eg, 'aa' (ā), 'ee' (ī) and 'oo' (ū).

The Transliteration Dilemma

TE Lawrence, when asked by his publishers to clarify 'inconsistencies in the spelling of proper names' in *Seven Pillars of Wisdom* – his account of the Arab Revolt in WWI – wrote back:

Arabic names won't go into English. There are some 'scientific systems' of transliteration, helpful to people who know enough Arabic not to need helping, but a washout for the world. I spell my names anyhow, to show what rot the systems are.

The Arabic Alphabet

Final	Medial	Initial	Alone	Transliteration	Pronunciation
ﺎ			ﺍ	ā	as the 'a' in 'father'
ﺐ	ﺒ	ﺑ	ﺏ	b	as in 'bet'
ﺖ	ﺘ	ﺗ	ﺕ	t	as in 'ten'
ﺚ	ﺜ	ﺛ	ﺙ	th	as in 'thin'
ﺞ	ﺠ	ﺟ	ﺝ	g	as in 'go'
ﺢ	ﺤ	ﺣ	ﺡ	H	a strongly whispered 'h', almost like a sigh of relief
ﺦ	ﺨ	ﺧ	ﺥ	kh	as the 'ch' in Scottish *loch*
ﺪ			ﺩ	d	as in 'dim'
ﺬ			ﺫ	dh	as the 'th' in 'this'
ﺮ			ﺭ	r	a rolled 'r', as in the Spanish word *caro*
ﺰ			ﺯ	z	as in 'zip'
ﺲ	ﺴ	ﺳ	ﺱ	s	as in 'so', never as in 'wisdom'
ﺶ	ﺸ	ﺷ	ﺵ	sh	as in 'ship'
ﺺ	ﺼ	ﺻ	ﺹ	ş	emphatic 's'
ﺾ	ﻀ	ﺿ	ﺽ	ḍ	emphatic 'd'
ﻂ	ﻄ	ﻃ	ﻁ	ţ	emphatic 't'
ﻆ	ﻈ	ﻇ	ﻅ	ẓ	emphatic 'z'
ﻊ	ﻌ	ﻋ	ﻉ	'	the Arabic letter 'ayn; pronounce as a glottal stop – like the closing of the throat before saying 'Oh oh!' (see Other Sounds on p.298)
ﻎ	ﻐ	ﻏ	ﻍ	gh	a guttural sound like Parisian 'r'
ﻒ	ﻔ	ﻓ	ﻑ	f	as in 'far'
ﻖ	ﻘ	ﻗ	ﻕ	q	a strongly guttural 'k' sound; in Egyptian Arabic often pronounced as a glottal stop
ﻚ	ﻜ	ﻛ	ﻙ	k	as in 'king'
ﻞ	ﻠ	ﻟ	ﻝ	l	as in 'lamb'
ﻢ	ﻤ	ﻣ	ﻡ	m	as in 'me'
ﻦ	ﻨ	ﻧ	ﻥ	n	as in 'name'
ﻪ	ﻬ	ﻫ	ﻩ	h	as in 'ham'
ﻮ			ﻭ	w	as in 'wet'; or
				ū	long, as the 'oo' on 'food'; or
				aw	as the 'ow' in 'how'
ﻲ	ﻴ	ﻳ	ﻯ	y	as in 'yes'; or
				ī	as the 'e' in 'ear', only softer; or
				ay	as the 'y' in 'by' or as the 'ay' in 'way'

Vowels Not all Arabic vowel sounds are represented in the alphabet. See Pronunciation on p.296 for a list of all the Arabic vowel sounds.

Emphatic Consonants To simplify the transliteration system used in this book, the emphatic consonants have not been included.

Consonants

Pronunciation for all Arabic consonants is covered in the alphabet table on the preceding page. Note that when double consonants occur in transliterations, both are pronounced. For example, *al-Hammam* (toilet/bath), is pronounced 'al-ham-mam'.

Other Sounds

Arabic has two sounds that are very tricky for non-Arabs to produce: the 'ayn and the glottal stop. The letter 'ayn represents a sound with no English equivalent that comes even close. It is similar to the glottal stop (which is not actually represented in the alphabet) but the muscles at the back of the throat are gagged more forcefully – it has been described as the sound of someone being strangled. In many transliteration systems, 'ayn is represented by an opening quotation mark, and the glottal stop by a closing quotation mark. To make the transliterations in this language guide (and throughout the rest of the book) easier to use, we have not distinguished between the glottal stop and the 'ayn, using the closing quotation mark to represent both sounds. You'll find that Arabic speakers will still understand you.

Pronouns

I	*ānē*
you (sg)	*inta/inti* (m/f)
he	*huwa*
she	*hiya*
we	*nahnu*
you (pl)	*untum/inti* (m/f)
they	*uhum*

Greetings & Civilities

Hello.	*as-salāma alaykum*
Hello. (response)	*wa alaykum e-salām*
Goodbye. (person leaving)	*ma'al salāma*
Goodbye. (person staying)	*alla ysalmak* (to a man)
	alla ysalmich (to a woman)
	alla ysallimkum (to a group)

Goodbye.	*Hayyākallah* (to a man)
	Hayyachallah (to a woman)
	Hayyakumallah (to a group)
Goodbye. (response)	*fi aman ullah* or *alla yHai'īk* (to a man)
	alla yHai'īch (to a woman)
	alla yHai'īkum (to a group)
Good morning.	*sabaH al-kheir*
Good morning. (response)	*sabaH an-nur*
Good afternoon/ evening.	*masa' al-kheir*
Good afternoon/ evening. (response)	*masa' an-nur*
Good night.	*tisbaH ala-kheir* (to a man)
	tisbiHin ala-kheir (to a woman)
	tisbuHun ala-kheir (to a group)
Good night. (response)	*wa inta min ahlil-kheir* (to a man)
	wa inti min ahlil-kheir (to a woman)
	wa intu min ahlil-kheir (to a group)
Welcome.	*ahlan wa sahlan* or *marHaba*
Welcome to you.	*ahlan fik* (to a man)
	ahlan fich (to a woman)
	ahlan fikum (to a group)
Pleased to meet you. (also said on leaving)	*fursa sa'ida*
Pleased to meet you. (response)	*wa ana as'ad* (by an individual)
	wa iHna as'ad (by a group)

Basics

Yes.	*aiwa/na'am*
No.	*lā*

Maybe.	*mumkin*
Please.	*min fadhlik* or
	lō tsimaH
	(to a man)
	min fadhlich or
	lō tsimiHīn
	(to a woman)
	min fadhelkum or
	lō tsimiHūn
	(to a group)
Thank you.	*shukran* or
	mashkur
	(to a man)
	mashkura
	(to a woman)
	mashkurin
	(to a group)
You're welcome.	*afwan/al afu*
Excuse me.	*lō tsimaH*
	(to a man)
	lō tsimiHīn
	(to a woman)
	lō tsimiHūn
	(to a group)
I'm sorry/	*ānē āsef*
Forgive me.	
After you.	*atfaddal* or
	min badik
	(to a man)
	min badak
	(to a woman)
OK.	*zein/kwayyis/tayib*
No problem.	*mafī mushkila*
Impossible.	*mish mumkin*
It doesn't matter/	*ma'alish*
I don't mind.	

Small Talk

How are you?	*kef Halak?*
	(to a man)
	kef Halik?
	(to a woman)
	kef Halkum?
	(to a group)
Fine, thanks.	*(zein) al-Hamdulillah*
	(by a man)
	(zeina) al-Hamdulillah
	(by a woman)
	(zeinin) al-Hamdulillah
	(by a group)

What's your name?	*shismak?*
	(to a man)
	shismich?
	(to a woman)
	shisimkum?
	(to a group)
My name is ...	*ismi ...*
Do you like ...?	*tahabi ...?*
I like ...	*ahib ...*
I don't like ...	*la ahib ...*
God willing.	*inshallah*
I'm from ...	*ana min ...*
Australia	*usturālyē*
Canada	*kanadē*
Egypt	*masur*
Ethiopia	*ithyūbyē*
Europe	*ōrobba*
France	*faransa*
Germany	*almania*
Jordan	*elerdon*
Netherlands	*holanda*
New Zealand	*nyūzilande*
South Africa	*jinūb afrīqye*
Switzerland	*swissra*
Syria	*sūriye*
Tunisia	*tūnis*
UK	*britania*
USA	*amrika*

Language Difficulties

I understand.	*ana fahim*
	(by a man)
	ana fahma
	(by a woman)
We understand.	*iHna fahmīn*
I don't understand.	*ana afHām*
We don't understand.	*iHna nafHām*
Please repeat that.	*lō simaHt ti'id hādtha*
I speak ...	*ana atkallam ...*
Do you speak ...?	*titkallam ...?*
English	*inglīzi*
French	*fransawi*
German	*almāni*
I don't speak Arabic.	*ma-atkallam arabi*
I speak a little Arabic.	*atkallam arabi shwayē*

What does this mean?	*shu ya'ani?*
How do you say ... in Arabic?	*kef igūl ... bila'arabi?*
I want an interpreter.	*urīd mutarjem*

Getting Around

I want to go to ...	*abga arouH li ...*
When does the ... leave?	*mata yamshi il ...?*
When does the ... arrive?	*mata tosal il ...?*
What is the fare to ...?	*cham il tadhkara li ...?*
Which bus/taxi goes to ...?	*ai bas/tax yrouH il ...?*
Does this bus/taxi go to ...?	*Hadhal bas yrouH il ...?*
How many buses go to ...?	*cham bas yrouH li ...?*
Please tell me when we arrive at ...	*lau samaHtit goul li mata nosal li ...*
May I sit here?	*mumkin ag'id hina?*
May we sit here?	*mumkin nag'id hina?*
Stop here, please.	*'ogaf hina, law samaHt*
Please wait for me.	*law samaHt, intidherni*

Where is the ...?	*wein al ...?*
How far is the ...?	*cham yibe'id ...?*
airport	*al-matār*
bus stop	*mokaf al-bas*
bus station	*maHattat al-bas*
taxi stand	*maHattat tax/ maHattat ajara*
train station	*maHattat al-qatar*

boat	*markab*
bus	*bas*
camel	*jamal*
car	*sayyara*
donkey	*Hmār*
horse	*Hsan*
taxi	*tax/ajara*

daily	*kil yōm*
ticket office	*maktab al-tadhāker*
ticket	*tadhkara/bitāq*
first class	*daraje ūlā*

second class	*daraje thānye*
crowded	*zaHme/matrūs*

Where can I rent a ...?	*min wein agdar asta'ajir ...?*
bicycle	*saikel*
motorcycle	*motorsaikel*

Directions

Where is the ...?	*wein al ...?*
Is it near?	*uhwe girīb?*
Is it far?	*uhwe bi'īb?*
How many kilometres?	*kam kilometer?*
Can you show me the way to ...?	*mumkin tdallini mukān ...?*

address	*onwān*
street	*shāri'*
number	*raqam*
city	*madina*
village	*qaria*

here	*hnī*
there	*hnāk*
next to	*yam*
opposite	*gbāl/mgābel*
behind	*warā/khaif*
to	*min*
from	*ile*
left	*yasār*
right	*yimīn*
straight	*sīda*

Signs

ENTRY *dukhūl*		مدخل
EXIT *khurūj*		خروج
TOILETS (Men) *Hammam lirrijal*		حمام للرجال
TOILETS (Women) *Hammam linnisa'a*		حمام للنساء
HOSPITAL *mustashfa*		مستشفى
POLICE *shurta*		الشرطة
PROHIBITED *mamnu'u*		ممنوع

north	shimāl
south	jinūb
east	sharug
west	gharub

Around Town

I'm looking for the ...	ga'ed adawwēr ala ...
Where is the ...?	wein al ...?
bank	al-bank
barber	al-Hallaq
beach	il-shatt/il-shāt'i
city centre	wasat al-balād
customs	aljamarek
embassy	al-safara
mosque	al-masjid
museum	al-matHaf
old city	al-madina il-qadima
palace	al-qasr
passport & immigration office	markaz aljawazat welhijrā
police station	al-makhfar
post office	maktab al-barīd
telephone	al-telefon/ul-hataf
telephone centre	maqsam al-hatef
toilet	al-Hammam
tourist office	isti'ilāmāt al-suyyaH
university	il-jam'a
zoo	Hadiqat il-Haywan

What time does it open?	mita tiftaH?
What time does it close?	mita tsaker?
I'd like to make a telephone call.	abgyi attisel telefōn/ abi akhuber
I want to change money.	abga asrif flūs
I want to change travellers cheques.	abga asrif sheikat syaHīa

Accommodation

Where is the hotel?	wein al-funduq/el-ōtel?

I'd like to book a ...	abgyi aHjiz ...
bed	sarīr/frāsh
cheap room	ghurfa rikhīsa
single room	ghurfa mifred
double room	ghurfa mijwīz

room with a bathroom	ghurfa ma'Hammam
room with air-con	ghurfa mukhayyafa

for one night	la leila wiHdē
for two nights	la leiltein thintein
May I see the room?	mumkin ashuf al-ghurfah?
May I see other rooms?	mumkin ashuf ghuraf dhānia?
How much is this room per night?	cham ujrat hādhil ghurfah fīl-leila?
How much is it per person?	shtiswa ala eshshakhs al-āhed?
Do you have any cheaper rooms?	fih ghuraf arkhas?
This is fine.	hadha zein.

This is very ...	hādhi wāhed ...
noisy	muzi'ije
dirty	waskha
expensive	ghalye

address	al-unw
blanket	buttaniyye
camp site	emakan al-mukhayyam
electricity	kahruba
hotel	funduq/ōtel
hot water	māi Hār
key	miftaH
manager	al-mudīr
shower	al-dūsh
soap	sābun
toilet	Hammām

Food

I'm hungry.	āne jūda'ān
I'm thirsty.	āne atshān
I'd like ...	aHib/abghi ...
Is service included in the bill?	al-fatūra fihā qīmat al-khidma?
What is this?	shinū hādhe?
Another one, please.	ba'ad wiHde min fadhlik

breakfast	riyūg/ftūr
lunch	al-ghade
dinner	al-ashe
restaurant	mata'ām
set menu	qa'imat al-akel muHaddada

LANGUAGE

Emergencies

Call the pŏlice!	khaber eshurta!
Call a doctor!	khaber ettabīb!
Help me please!	sa'idnī lō simaHt!
Where is the toilet?	wein al-Hammam?
Go away!	rūh wallī!/isref!
Go/Get lost!	imshi!
Thief!	Harāmi!/bawwāg!
They robbed me!	bagonī!
Shame on you!	yā eibak!/yal mā
(woman to man)	tistiHi!

bread	khubz
chicken	dajaj
coffee	qahwa
fish	samak
meat	laHma
milk	laban/halīb
pepper	felfel
potatoes	batatas
rice	roz
salt	sel/melaH
sugar	suker
tea	chai
water	mayya

Shopping

I want ...	abga ...
Do you have ...?	indik ...? (to a man)
	indich ...? (to a woman)
Where can I buy ...?	wein agdar ashtiri ...?
How much is this?	kam hadha?
How much is that?	kam hadhak?
How much are those?	kam hadhol?
How much ...?	kam ...?
It costs too much.	ghalia wai'd

bookshop	al-maktaba
chemist/pharmacy	saydaliyya
laundry	masbagha
market	souq
newsagents/ stationers	maktabet-al-qurtāsiyye

big	chibīr
bigger	akbar

Numbers

Arabic numerals are simple to learn and, unlike the written language, run from left to right. Note the order of the words in numbers from 21 to 99.

0	٠	sifir
1	١	waHid
2	٢	idhnīn
3	٣	dhaladha
4	٤	arba'a
5	٥	khamsa
6	٦	sitta
7	٧	sab'a
8	٨	dhimania
9	٩	tis'a
10	١٠	ashra
11	١١	Hda'ash
12	١٢	dhna'ash
13	١٣	dhaladhta'ash
14	١٤	arba'ata'ash
15	١٥	khamista'ash
16	١٦	sitta'ash
17	١٧	sabi'ta'ashr
18	١٨	dhimanta'ash
19	١٩	tisi'ta'ash
20	٢٠	'ishrīn
21	٢١	waHid wa 'ishrīn
22	٢٢	idhnīn wa 'ishrīn
30	٣٠	dhaladhīn
40	٤٠	arbi'īn
50	٥٠	khamsīn
60	٦٠	sittīn
70	٧٠	saba'īn
80	٨٠	dhimanīn
90	٩٠	tis'īn
100	١٠٠	imia
101	١٠١	imia wa-waHid
200	٢٠٠	imiatayn
300	٣٠٠	dhaladha imia
1000	١٠٠٠	alf
2000	٢٠٠٠	alfayn
3000	٣٠٠٠	dhaladha-alaf

Ordinal Numbers

first	awwal
second	dhānī
third	dhālidh
fourth	rābi'
fifth	khāmis

small	*sighīr*
smaller	*asghar*
cheap	*rikhīs*
cheaper	*arkhas*
expensive	*ghāli*
open	*āmaftūH*
closed	*msakkar/mughlaq*
money	*flūs*

Health

I need a doctor.	*abi tabīb*
My friend is ill.	*sidiji marīd/ayyān*
headache	*wija' rās*
hospital	*mustashfa*
pharmacy	*saydaliyye*
prescription	*wasfa tibbiyā*
stomachache	*wija' batun*
tampons	*fuwat siHiyya lalHarīm*

Time & Dates

What time is it?	*as-sa'a kam?*
It is ...	*as-sa'a ...*
one o'clock	*waHda*
1.15	*wuIIda wa rob'*
1.20	*waHda wa tilt*
1.30	*waHda wa nus*
1.45	*idhnīn illa rob'* (lit: 'quarter to two')

When?	*mita?*
now	*alHīn*
after	*ba'ad*
daily	*kil yom*
today	*al-yom*
yesterday	*ams*
tomorrow	*bukra*
morning	*es-subāH*
afternoon	*ba'ad ezzuhur/edhuhur*

evening	*al-masa*
day	*nahār*
night	*leil*
week	*esbū'u*
month	*shahar*
year	*sine*
early	*mbach'ir/badri*
late	*mit'akhir*
on time	*alwaqit*

Monday	*yom al-idhnīn*
Tuesday	*yom al-dhaladh*
Wednesday	*yom al-arbā'*
Thursday	*yom al-khamis*
Friday	*yom al-jama'a*
Saturday	*yom as-sabt*
Sunday	*yom al-Had*

In Oman and UAE the names of the months are virtually the same as their European counterparts and easily recognisable.

January	*yanāyır*
February	*fibrāyir*
March	*māris*
April	*abrīl*
May	*māyu*
June	*yunyu*
July	*yulyu*
August	*aghustus*
September	*sibtimbir*
October	*'uktūbir*
November	*nufimbir*
December	*disimbir*

Glossary

Here, with definitions, are some unfamiliar words and abbreviations you might meet in this book or while you are in Oman and the UAE.

abaya – woman's full-length black robe
abba – *sheikh's* black or gold cloak worn over the *dishdasha* on formal occasions
abra – small, flat-decked motorboat; used as water taxis in Dubai
abu – father; saint
ADNHC – Abu Dhabi National Hotels Company
Adnoc – Abu Dhabi National Oil Company
agal – (also *'iqal*) black coiled rope used to hold a *ghutra* in place
ahwa – see *qahwa*
ain – spring
Al-Busaid – the ruling dynasty in Oman
Allah – God
areesh – palm leaf
attar – Arabic oil-based perfume
Ayyalah – traditional *Bedouin* dance
azzan – call to prayer

bahoor – generic term for incense
Baluchistan – mountainous region in Pakistan and Afghanistan from where many migrants in the UAE and Oman originate
barasti – traditional method of building using palm leaf, also the name of the house
barjeel – Arabic for *wind tower*
Bedouin – often shortened to Bedu; desert dweller of Arabia
beit – also written 'bait' or sometimes 'bayt'; house
birnah – ceramic pot used to store milk
biryani – very common Indo-Pakistani dish consisting of spiced meat or fish with rice
biryani cafe – used in this book to mean a small Indo-Pakistani restaurant, usually serving biryani, tea, soft drinks and snacks
blacktop road – used in this book as a general term for a sealed, paved or tarmac road; see also *graded road*

burj – tower
burqa – stiff material face mask worn by women in the UAE to cover eyebrows, nose and mouth

caliph – Islamic ruler
chai – tea

dalla – traditional copper coffeepot
dhow – traditional sailing vessel of the Gulf
dishdasha – man's shirt-dress
diwan – ruler's office; highest administrative body of an emirate in the UAE
DNATA – Dubai National Travel & Tourist Authority, the quasi-official government tourist authority

Eid al-Adha – Feast of Sacrifice marking the pilgrimage to Mecca
Eid al-Fitr – Festival of Breaking the Fast; celebrated at the end of *Ramadan*
emir Islamic ruler, military commander or governor; literally, prince
engaged – when used of a taxi this means taking it by yourself (as opposed to shared); you pay for the whole vehicle, usually at a rate of the shared fare by the number of seats
Etisalat – the national telephone company of the UAE

falaj – traditional irrigation system used in Oman and the UAE
Farsi – official language of Iran
felafel – deep-fried balls of chickpea paste with spices served in a piece of flat bread with tomatoes or pickled vegetables
fuul – dish made from stewed broad beans, usually eaten for breakfast

GCC – Gulf Cooperation Council; members are Saudi Arabia, Kuwait, Bahrain, Qatar, Oman and the UAE
ghutra – white or checked headcloth worn by men in the UAE and other Gulf States
graded road – used in this guide to mean any road that is not a blacktop road

habban – Arabic goatskin bagpipes

hadith – a saying by the Prophet Mohammed, or a story about his life

haj – annual pilgrimage by Muslims to Mecca

halal – religiously acceptable or permitted

hamour – common species of fish found in Gulf waters

Hanbali – the strictest of the Islamic schools of thought

haram – forbidden by Islam; religiously unacceptable

hareem – the women of the household or family

Hejira – literally, migration; also the name of the Islamic calendar

hibb – ceramic pot used to keep water cold

Ibadi – Islamic sect to which most Omanis belong, which is practised nowhere else in the world; a fundamental Ibadi belief is that the leader of the community must be elected rather than hereditary

imam – prayer leader, Muslim cleric

inshallah – commonly used phrase, meaning 'God willing'

'iqal – see *agal*

iwan – vaulted hall, opening into a central court in the *madrassa* of a mosque

jebel – hill, mountain

jefeer – shopping basket woven from palm leaves

jihad – literally: striving in the way of the faith; holy war

kandoura – casual shirt-dress worn by men and women

khanjar – also written 'khanja'; Omani dagger with a traditional curved sheath

khareef – the monsoon season in southern Oman

khir – ceramic pot used to store dates

khor – creek or inlet

kuttab – school where children were taught to recite the *Quran* by rote

Liwa – traditional Emirati dance with its roots in East Africa; also an oasis region in the south of the UAE

luban – frankincense

madrassa – Muslim theological seminary; also modern Arabic word for school

mafraj – room with a view; top room of a tower house

majlis – formal meeting room or reception area; also parliament

Maliki – one of the Islamic schools of thought

manzar – attic; room on top of a tower house

mashrabiyyah – ornately carved wooden panel or screen; a feature of traditional Islamic architecture

mehaffa – hand fan woven from palm leaves

mezze – a selection of dishes, usually served in Lebanese restaurants

mihrab – niche in a mosque indicating the direction of Mecca

mimzar – traditional wind instrument like a small oboe

mina – port or harbour

minaret – the spire or tower of a mosque; there can be one or several

minbar – pulpit used for sermons in a mosque

mosque – the Muslim place of worship

muezzin – person who sings the *azzan* (call to prayer) from the minaret

Muslim – follower of Islam; literally, one who submits to God's will

Omantel – Oman's national telecommunications company

ONTC – Oman National Transport Company

Qaaba – also written 'Kaaba'; the rectangular structure at the centre of the Grand Mosque in Mecca (containing the Black Stone) around which pilgrims circumnambulate during the *haj*

qahwa – (also *ahwa*) coffee

Quran – also written 'Koran'; the holy book of Islam

rakats – cycles of prayer during which the *Quran* is read and bows and prostrations are performed in different series

Ramadan – the Muslim month of fasting
ras – cape or headland; also head

salat – prayer
Sassanian empire – based in Persia (Iran) from around AD 200 to 600; occupied the UAE for a time
sawm – fasting
semma – woven palm mat on which food is placed
shahadah – a Muslim's profession of their faith
shaikh – see *sheikh*
shared taxi – common means of transport, you pay for one seat in the taxi; sometimes also referred to as 'service taxi'
Sharia'a – Islamic law
shayla – woman's headscarf
sheesha – tall, glass-bottomed smoking implement
sheikh – also written 'shaikh'; title used in the UAE for members of the ruling family (sheikha is the female term); also used to refer to a venerated religious scholar
Shi'ite – sect of the Islamic religion which believes that the line of *caliphs* should descend through the Prophet Mohammed's son-in-law, Ali.
shwarma – grilled meat sliced from a spit and served in a pita (flat) bread with salad
sirwal – women's trousers, worn under the *kandoura*
souq – market or shopping centre
SNTTA – Sharjah National Travel & Tourist Authority
sultan – absolute ruler of a Muslim state
Sunnah – works recording the sayings and doings of the Prophet and his family

Sunni – follower of the faction of Islam that holds that any Muslim who rules with justice and according to the *Sharia'a* (Islamic law) can become a *caliph*
surood – cone-shaped, woven palm mat used to cover food

talli – different coloured cotton, silver and gold threads interwoven to make decorative ankle, wrist and neck bands
tamboura – traditional harp-like stringed instrument
taqia – men's lace skullcap worn under the *ghutra*
tell – an ancient mound created by centuries of urban rebuilding
tolah – a measurement of weight (12g or 12ml) used in the UAE
Trucial Coast – old name for the UAE

Umayyads – also written 'Omayyad'; first great dynasty of Arab Muslim rulers, based in Damascus (AD 661–750)
umm – mother
Umm al-Nar – an ancient culture dating from about 3000 BC that arose near present-day Abu Dhabi

wadi – dried-up river bed, seasonal river; often used for off-roading
wilayat – administrative region in Oman
wind tower – *barjeel* in Arabic; a traditional architectural feature that helps keep houses cool
wusta – influence high up

zakat – alms or charity
zatar – Arabic herbal tea

ON THE ROAD

Travel Guides explore cities, regions and countries, and supply information on transport, restaurants and accommodation, covering all budgets. They come with reliable, easy-to-use maps, practical advice, cultural and historical facts and a rundown on attractions both on and off the beaten track. There are over 200 titles in this classic series, covering nearly every country in the world.

 Lonely Planet Upgrades extend the shelf life of existing travel guides by detailing any changes that may affect travel in a region since a book has been published. Upgrades can be downloaded for free from **www.lonelyplanet.com/upgrades**

For travellers with more time than money, **Shoestring** guides offer dependable, first-hand information with hundreds of detailed maps, plus insider tips for stretching money as far as possible. Covering entire continents in most cases, the six-volume shoestring guides are known around the world as 'backpackers bibles'.

For the discerning short-term visitor, **Condensed** guides highlight the best a destination has to offer in a full-colour, pocket-sized format designed for quick access. They include everything from top sights and walking tours to opinionated reviews of where to eat, stay, shop and have fun.

CitySync lets travellers use their Palm™ or Visor™ hand-held computers to guide them through a city with handy tips on transport, history, cultural life, major sights, and shopping and entertainment options. It can also quickly search and sort hundreds of reviews of hotels, restaurants and attractions, and pinpoint their location on scrollable street maps. CitySync can be downloaded from **www.citysync.com**

MAPS & ATLASES

Lonely Planet's **City Maps** feature downtown and metropolitan maps, as well as transit routes and walking tours. The maps come complete with an index of streets, a listing of sights and a plastic coat for extra durability.

Road Atlases are an essential navigation tool for serious travellers. Cross-referenced with the guidebooks, they also feature distance and climate charts and a complete site index.

LONELY PLANET

ESSENTIALS

Read This First books help new travellers to hit the road with confidence. These invaluable predeparture guides give step-by-step advice on preparing for a trip, budgeting, arranging a visa, planning an itinerary and staying safe while still getting off the beaten track.

Healthy Travel pocket guides offer a regional rundown on disease hot spots and practical advice on predeparture health measures, staying well on the road and what to do in emergencies. The guides come with a user-friendly design and helpful diagrams and tables.

Lonely Planet's **Phrasebooks** cover the essential words and phrases travellers need when they're strangers in a strange land. They come in a pocket-sized format with colour tabs for quick reference, extensive vocabulary lists, easy-to-follow pronunciation keys and two-way dictionaries.

Miffed by blurry photos of the Taj Mahal? Tired of the classic 'top of the head cut off' shot? **Travel Photography: A Guide to Taking Better Pictures** will help you turn ordinary holiday snaps into striking images and give you the know-how to capture every scene, from frenetic festivals to peaceful beach sunrises.

Lonely Planet's **Travel Journal** is a lightweight but sturdy travel diary for jotting down all those on-the-road observations and significant travel moments. It comes with a handy time-zone wheel, a world map and useful travel information.

Lonely Planet's eKno is an all-in-one communication service developed especially for travellers. It offers low-cost international calls and free email and voicemail so that you can keep in touch while on the road. Check it out on **www.ekno.lonelyplanet.com**

FOOD & RESTAURANT GUIDES

Lonely Planet's **Out to Eat** guides recommend the brightest and best places to eat and drink in top international cities. These gourmet companions are arranged by neighbourhood, packed with dependable maps, garnished with scene-setting photos and served with quirky features.

For people who live to eat, drink and travel, **World Food** guides explore the culinary culture of each country. Entertaining and adventurous, each guide is packed with detail on staples and specialities, regional cuisine and local markets, as well as sumptuous recipes, comprehensive culinary dictionaries and lavish photos good enough to eat.

LONELY PLANET

OUTDOOR GUIDES

For those who believe the best way to see the world is on foot, Lonely Planet's **Walking Guides** detail everything from family strolls to difficult treks, with 'when to go and how to do it' advice supplemented by reliable maps and essential travel information.

Cycling Guides map a destination's best bike tours, long and short, in day-by-day detail. They contain all the information a cyclist needs, including advice on bike maintenance, places to eat and stay, innovative maps with detailed cues to the rides, and elevation charts.

The **Watching Wildlife** series is perfect for travellers who want authoritative information but don't want to tote a heavy field guide. Packed with advice on where, when and how to view a region's wildlife, each title features photos of over 300 species and contains engaging comments on the local flora and fauna.

With underwater colour photos throughout, **Pisces Books** explore the world's best diving and snorkelling areas. Each book contains listings of diving services and dive resorts, detailed information on depth, visibility and difficulty of dives, and a roundup of the marine life you're likely to see through your mask.

LONELY PLANET

OFF THE ROAD

Journeys, the travel literature series written by renowned travel authors, capture the spirit of a place or illuminate a culture with a journalist's attention to detail and a novelist's flair for words. These are tales to soak up while you're actually on the road or dip into as an at-home armchair indulgence.

The range of lavishly illustrated **Pictorial** books is just the ticket for both travellers and dreamers. Off-beat tales and vivid photographs bring the adventure of travel to your doorstep long before the journey begins and long after it is over.

Lonely Planet **Videos** encourage the same independent, tough-minded approach as the guidebooks. Currently airing throughout the world, this award-winning series features innovative footage and an original soundtrack.

Yes, we know, work is tough, so do a little bit of deskside dreaming with the spiral-bound Lonely Planet **Diary** or a Lonely Planet **Wall Calendar**, filled with great photos from around the world.

TRAVELLERS NETWORK

Lonely Planet Online. Lonely Planet's award-winning Web site has insider information on hundreds of destinations, from Amsterdam to Zimbabwe, complete with interactive maps and relevant links. The site also offers the latest travel news, recent reports from travellers on the road, guidebook upgrades, a travel links site, an online book-buying option and a lively travellers bulletin board. It can be viewed at **www.lonelyplanet.com** or AOL keyword: lp.

Planet Talk is a quarterly print newsletter, full of gossip, advice, anecdotes and author articles. It provides an antidote to the being-at-home blues and lets you plan and dream for the next trip. Contact the nearest Lonely Planet office for your free copy.

Comet, the free Lonely Planet newsletter, comes via email once a month. It's loaded with travel news, advice, dispatches from authors, travel competitions and letters from readers. To subscribe, click on the Comet subscription link on the front page of the Web site.

Lonely Planet Guides by Region

Lonely Planet is known worldwide for publishing practical, reliable and no-nonsense travel information in our guides and on our Web site. The Lonely Planet list covers just about every accessible part of the world. Currently there are 16 series: Travel guides, Shoestring guides, Condensed guides, Phrasebooks, Read This First, Healthy Travel, Walking guides, Cycling guides, Watching Wildlife guides, Pisces Diving & Snorkeling guides, City Maps, Road Atlases, Out to Eat, World Food, Journeys travel literature and Pictorials.

AFRICA Africa on a shoestring • Botswana • Cairo • Cairo City Map • Cape Town • Cape Town City Map • East Africa • Egypt • Egyptian Arabic phrasebook • Ethiopia, Eritrea & Djibouti • Ethiopian Amharic phrasebook • The Gambia & Senegal • Healthy Travel Africa • Kenya • Malawi • Morocco • Moroccan Arabic phrasebook • Mozambique • Namibia • Read This First: Africa • South Africa, Lesotho & Swaziland • Southern Africa • Southern Africa Road Atlas • Swahili phrasebook • Tanzania, Zanzibar & Pemba • Trekking in East Africa • Tunisia • Watching Wildlife East Africa • Watching Wildlife Southern Africa • West Africa • World Food Morocco • Zambia • Zimbabwe, Botswana & Namibia
Travel Literature: Mali Blues: Traveling to an African Beat • The Rainbird: A Central African Journey • Songs to an African Sunset: A Zimbabwean Story

AUSTRALIA & THE PACIFIC Aboriginal Australia & the Torres Strait Islands •Auckland • Australia • Australian phrasebook • Australia Road Atlas • Cycling Australia • Cycling New Zealand • Fiji • Fijian phrasebook • Healthy Travel Australia, NZ & the Pacific • Islands of Australia's Great Barrier Reef • Melbourne • Melbourne City Map • Micronesia • New Caledonia • New South Wales • New Zealand • Northern Territory • Outback Australia • Out to Eat – Melbourne • Out to Eat – Sydney • Papua New Guinea • Pidgin phrasebook • Queensland • Rarotonga & the Cook Islands • Samoa • Solomon Islands • South Australia • South Pacific • South Pacific phrasebook • Sydney • Sydney City Map • Sydney Condensed • Tahiti & French Polynesia • Tasmania • Tonga • Tramping in New Zealand • Vanuatu • Victoria • Walking in Australia • Watching Wildlife Australia • Western Australia
Travel Literature: Islands in the Clouds: Travels in the Highlands of New Guinea • Kiwi Tracks: A New Zealand Journey • Sean & David's Long Drive

CENTRAL AMERICA & THE CARIBBEAN Bahamas, Turks & Caicos • Baja California • Belize, Guatemala & Yucatán • Bermuda • Central America on a shoestring • Costa Rica • Costa Rica Spanish phrasebook • Cuba • Cycling Cuba • Dominican Republic & Haiti • Eastern Caribbean • Guatemala • Havana • Healthy Travel Central & South America • Jamaica • Mexico • Mexico City • Panama • Puerto Rico • Read This First: Central & South America • Virgin Islands • World Food Caribbean • World Food Mexico • Yucatán
Travel Literature: Green Dreams: Travels in Central America

EUROPE Amsterdam • Amsterdam City Map • Amsterdam Condensed • Andalucía • Athens • Austria • Baltic States phrasebook • Barcelona • Barcelona City Map • Belgium & Luxembourg • Berlin • Berlin City Map • Britain • British phrasebook • Brussels, Bruges & Antwerp • Brussels City Map • Budapest • Budapest City Map • Canary Islands • Catalunya & the Costa Brava • Central Europe • Central Europe phrasebook • Copenhagen • Corfu & the Ionians • Corsica • Crete • Crete Condensed • Croatia • Cycling Britain • Cycling France • Cyprus • Czech & Slovak Republics • Czech phrasebook • Denmark • Dublin • Dublin City Map • Dublin Condensed • Eastern Europe • Eastern Europe phrasebook • Edinburgh • Edinburgh City Map • England • Estonia, Latvia & Lithuania • Europe on a shoestring • Europe phrasebook • Finland • Florence • Florence City Map • France • Frankfurt City Map • Frankfurt Condensed • French phrasebook • Georgia, Armenia & Azerbaijan • Germany • German phrasebook • Greece • Greek Islands • Greek phrasebook • Hungary • Iceland, Greenland & the Faroe Islands • Ireland • Italian phrasebook • Italy • Kraków • Lisbon • The Loire • London • London City Map • London Condensed • Madrid • Madrid City Map • Malta • Mediterranean Europe • Milan, Turin & Genoa • Moscow • Munich • Netherlands • Normandy • Norway • Out to Eat – London • Out to Eat – Paris • Paris • Paris City Map • Paris Condensed • Poland • Polish phrasebook • Portugal • Portuguese phrasebook • Prague • Prague City Map • Provence & the Côte d'Azur • Read This First: Europe • Rhodes & the Dodecanese • Romania & Moldova • Rome • Rome City Map • Rome Condensed • Russia, Ukraine & Belarus • Russian phrasebook • Scandinavian & Baltic Europe • Scandinavian phrasebook • Scotland • Sicily • Slovenia • South-West France • Spain • Spanish phrasebook • Stockholm • St Petersburg • St Petersburg City Map • Sweden • Switzerland • Tuscany • Ukrainian phrasebook • Venice • Vienna • Wales • Walking in Britain • Walking in France • Walking in Ireland • Walking in Italy • Walking in Scotland • Walking in Spain • Walking in Switzerland • Western Europe • World Food France • World Food Greece • World Food Ireland • World Food Italy • World Food Spain **Travel Literature:** After Yugoslavia • Love and War in the Apennines • The Olive Grove: Travels in Greece • On the Shores of the Mediterranean • Round Ireland in Low Gear • A Small Place in Italy

Lonely Planet Mail Order

Lonely Planet products are distributed worldwide. They are also available by mail order from Lonely Planet, so if you have difficulty finding a title please write to us. North and South American residents should write to 150 Linden St, Oakland, CA 94607, USA; European and African residents should write to 10a Spring Place, London NW5 3BH, UK; and residents of other countries to Locked Bag 1, Footscray, Victoria 3011, Australia.

INDIAN SUBCONTINENT & THE INDIAN OCEAN Bangladesh • Bengali phrasebook • Bhutan • Delhi • Goa • Healthy Travel Asia & India • Hindi & Urdu phrasebook • India • India & Bangladesh City Map • Indian Himalaya • Karakoram Highway • Kathmandu City Map • Kerala • Madagascar • Maldives • Mauritius, Réunion & Seychelles • Mumbai (Bombay) • Nepal • Nepali phrasebook • North India • Pakistan • Rajasthan • Read This First: Asia & India • South India • Sri Lanka • Sri Lanka phrasebook • Tibet • Tibetan phrasebook • Trekking in the Indian Himalaya • Trekking in the Karakoram & Hindukush • Trekking in the Nepal Himalaya • World Food India **Travel Literature:** The Age of Kali: Indian Travels and Encounters • Hello Goodnight: A Life of Goa • In Rajasthan • Maverick in Madagascar • A Season in Heaven: True Tales from the Road to Kathmandu • Shopping for Buddhas • A Short Walk in the Hindu Kush • Slowly Down the Ganges

MIDDLE EAST & CENTRAL ASIA Bahrain, Kuwait & Qatar • Central Asia • Central Asia phrasebook • Dubai • Farsi (Persian) phrasebook • Hebrew phrasebook • Iran • Israel & the Palestinian Territories • Istanbul • Istanbul City Map • Istanbul to Cairo • Istanbul to Kathmandu • Jerusalem • Jerusalem City Map • Jordan • Lebanon • Middle East • Oman & the United Arab Emirates • Syria • Turkey • Turkish phrasebook • World Food Turkey • Yemen **Travel Literature:** Black on Black: Iran Revisited • Breaking Ranks: Turbulent Travels in the Promised Land • The Gates of Damascus • Kingdom of the Film Stars: Journey into Jordan

NORTH AMERICA Alaska • Boston • Boston City Map • Boston Condensed • British Columbia • California & Nevada • California Condensed • Canada • Chicago • Chicago City Map • Chicago Condensed • Florida • Georgia & the Carolinas • Great Lakes • Hawaii • Hiking in Alaska • Hiking in the USA • Honolulu & Oahu City Map • Las Vegas • Los Angeles • Los Angeles City Map • Louisiana & the Deep South • Miami • Miami City Map • Montreal • New England • New Orleans • New Orleans City Map • New York City • New York City City Map • New York City Condensed • New York, New Jersey & Pennsylvania • Oahu • Out to Eat – San Francisco • Pacific Northwest • Rocky Mountains • San Diego & Tijuana • San Francisco • San Francisco City Map • Seattle • Seattle City Map • Southwest • Texas • Toronto • USA • USA phrasebook • Vancouver • Vancouver City Map • Virginia & the Capital Region • Washington, DC • Washington, DC City Map • World Food New Orleans **Travel Literature**: Caught Inside: A Surfer's Year on the California Coast • Drive Thru America

NORTH-EAST ASIA Beijing • Beijing City Map • Cantonese phrasebook • China • Hiking in Japan • Hong Kong & Macau • Hong Kong City Map • Hong Kong Condensed • Japan • Japanese phrasebook • Korea • Korean phrasebook • Kyoto • Mandarin phrasebook • Mongolia • Mongolian phrasebook • Seoul • Shanghai • South-West China • Taiwan • Tokyo • Tokyo Condensed • World Food Hong Kong • World Food Japan **Travel Literature:** In Xanadu: A Quest • Lost Japan

SOUTH AMERICA Argentina, Uruguay & Paraguay • Bolivia • Brazil • Brazilian phrasebook • Buenos Aires • Buenos Aires City Map • Chile & Easter Island • Colombia • Ecuador & the Galapagos Islands • Healthy Travel Central & South America • Latin American Spanish phrasebook • Peru • Quechua phrasebook • Read This First: Central & South America • Rio de Janeiro • Rio de Janeiro City Map • Santiago de Chile • South America on a shoestring • Trekking in the Patagonian Andes • Venezuela **Travel Literature**: Full Circle: A South American Journey

SOUTH-EAST ASIA Bali & Lombok • Bangkok • Bangkok City Map • Burmese phrasebook • Cambodia • Cycling Vietnam, Laos & Cambodia • East Timor phrasebook • Hanoi • Healthy Travel Asia & India • Hill Tribes phrasebook • Ho Chi Minh City (Saigon) • Indonesia • Indonesian phrasebook • Indonesia's Eastern Islands • Java • Lao phrasebook • Laos • Malay phrasebook • Malaysia, Singapore & Brunei • Myanmar (Burma) • Philippines • Pilipino (Tagalog) phrasebook • Read This First: Asia & India • Singapore • Singapore City Map • South-East Asia on a shoestring • South-East Asia phrasebook • Thailand • Thailand's Islands & Beaches • Thailand, Vietnam, Laos & Cambodia Road Atlas • Thai phrasebook • Vietnam • Vietnamese phrasebook • World Food Indonesia • World Food Thailand • World Food Vietnam

ALSO AVAILABLE: Antarctica • The Arctic • The Blue Man: Tales of Travel, Love and Coffee • Brief Encounters: Stories of Love, Sex & Travel • Buddhist Stupas in Asia: The Shape of Perfection • Chasing Rickshaws • The Last Grain Race • Lonely Planet ... On the Edge: Adventurous Escapades from Around the World • Lonely Planet Unpacked • Lonely Planet Unpacked Again • Not the Only Planet: Science Fiction Travel Stories • Ports of Call: A Journey by Sea • Sacred India • Travel Photography: A Guide to Taking Better Pictures • Travel with Children • Tuvalu: Portrait of an Island Nation

LONELY PLANET

You already know that Lonely Planet produces more than this one guidebook, but you might not be aware of the other products we have on this region. Here is a selection of titles that you may want to check out as well:

Africa on a shoestring
ISBN 0 86442 663 1
US$29.99 • UK£17.99

French phrasebook
ISBN 0 86442 450 7
US$5.95 • UK£3.99

Read this First: Africa
ISBN 1 86450 066 2
US$14.95 • UK£8.99

Healthy Travel Africa
ISBN 1 86450.050 6
US$5.95 • UK£3.99

Mediterranean Europe
ISBN 1 86450 154 5
US$27.99 • UK£15.99

Egypt
ISBN 0 86442 677 1
US$19.95 • UK£12.99

Egyptian Arabic phrasebook
ISBN 0 86442 070 6
US$3.95 • UK£2.50

Morocco
ISBN 0 86442 762 X
US$19.99 • UK£12.99

Middle East
ISBN 0 86442 701 8
US$24.95 • UK£14.99

Cairo
ISBN 0 86442 548 1
US$14.95 • UK£8.99

Available wherever books are sold

Index

Abbreviations

O – Oman

U – United Arab Emirates

Text

Bold indicates maps.

Boxed Text

MAP LEGEND

CITY ROUTES

Freeway .... Freeway
Highway .... Primary Road
Road .... Secondary Road
Street .... Street
Lane .... Lane

===== ..... Unsealed Road
====→ ..... One Way Street
===== ..... Pedestrian Street
⊃=== ..... Tunnel
===== ..... Footbridge

REGIONAL ROUTES

===== .... Tollway, Freeway
===== .... Primary Road
===== .... Secondary Road
==== Unsealed Sec Road

BOUNDARIES

—·—·— ..... International
— — — ..... Disputed
▬▬■▬ ..... Fortified Wall

HYDROGRAPHY

~·~·~ .... Wadi

TRANSPORT ROUTES & STATIONS

⊢——o— .... Train
-----□ .... Ferry
------- ..... Walking Trail

AREA FEATURES

.... Building
.... Market
.... Desert
⊕ ..... Park, Gardens
.... Sports Ground
.... Cemetery

POPULATION SYMBOLS

✪ CAPITAL .... National Capital
● CITY .... City
● Town .... Town
• Village .... Village
.... Urban Area

MAP SYMBOLS

■ .... Place to Stay
▼ .... Place to Eat
● .... Point of Interest

🖾 .... Airport
⊖ .... Bank
ℷ .... Beach
⊕ .... Border Crossing
🚌 .... Bus Stop
🚏 .... Bus Terminal
⌂ .... Cave
🕆 .... Church
🎬 .... Cinema

▯ .... Embassy
🏰 .... Fort
⚓ .... Fountain
⛳ .... Golf Course
🛕 .... Hindu Temple
✚ .... Hospital
🖵 .... Internet Cafe
※ .... Lookout
▲ .... Monument

☪ .... Mosque
🏛 .... Museum
🌴 .... Oasis
🏛 .... Palace
🅿 .... Parking
⛽ .... Petrol Station
✚ .... Police Station
✉ .... Post Office
🍺 .... Pub or Bar

🏯 .... Ruins
🛍 .... Shopping Centre
🏊 ..... Swimming Pool
🚕 .... Taxi Rank
☎ .... Telephone
🚻 .... Toilet
▣ .... Tomb
❶ .... Tourist Information

Note: not all symbols displayed above appear in this book

LONELY PLANET OFFICES

Australia
PO Box 617, Hawthorn, Victoria 3122
☎ 03 9819 1877 fax 03 9819 6459
email: talk2us@lonelyplanet.com.au

USA
150 Linden St, Oakland, CA 94607
☎ 510 893 8555 TOLL FREE: 800 275 8555
fax 510 893 8572
email: info@lonelyplanet.com

UK
10a Spring Place, London NW5 3BH
☎ 020 7428 4800 fax 020 7428 4828
email: go@lonelyplanet.co.uk

France
1 rue du Dahomey, 75011 Paris
☎ 01 55 25 33 00 fax 01 55 25 33 01
email: bip@lonelyplanet.fr
www.lonelyplanet.fr

World Wide Web: www.lonelyplanet.com *or* AOL keyword: lp
Lonely Planet Images: www.lonelyplanetimages.com